EARLY AMERICAN LITERATURE

THE OXFORD HANDBOOK OF

··

EARLY AMERICAN LITERATURE

··

Edited by

KEVIN J. HAYES

OXFORD

UNIVERSITY PRESS

2008

OXFORD
UNIVERSITY PRESS

Oxford University Press, Inc., publishes works that further
Oxford University's objective of excellence
in research, scholarship, and education.

Oxford   New York
Auckland   Bangkok   Bogotá   Buenos Aires   Cape Town   Chennai
Dar es Salaam   Delhi   Hong Kong   Istanbul   Karachi   Kolkata
Kuala Lumpur   Madrid   Melbourne   Mexico City   Mumbai   Nairobi
São Paulo   Shanghai   Singapore   Taipei   Tokyo   Toronto

Copyright © 2008 by Oxford University Press, Inc.

Published by Oxford University Press, Inc.
198 Madison Avenue, New York, New York, 10016
www.oup.com

Oxford is a registered trademark of Oxford University Press

Library of Congress Cataloging-in-Publication Data
The Oxford handbook of early American literature / edited by Kevin J. Hayes.
p. cm.
Includes bibliographical references.
ISBN 978-0-19-518727-4
1. American literature—Colonial period, ca. 1600–1775—History and criticism.
2. American literature—Revolutionary period, 1775–1783—History and criticism.
3. United States—Intellectual life—18th century. I. Hayes, Kevin J.
PS185.O94 2008
810.9'001—dc22   2007020587

9 8 7 6 5 4 3 2 1

Printed in the United States of America
on acid-free paper

In memoriam
A. Owen Aldridge

Contents

Part III: The Augustan Age in America

Part IV: Contexts of Reading

Part V: Expressions of Individuality

Part VI: The Revolutionary Era

Part VII: Late Eighteenth-Century Prose

CONTRIBUTORS

JOSHUA DAVID BELLIN, Associate Professor of English at La Roche College in Pittsburgh, is the author of *The Demon of the Continent: Indians and the Shaping of American Literature* (2001) and *Framing Monsters: Fantasy Film and Social Alienation* (2005). He has also published several articles, including "Taking the Indian Cure: Thoreau, Indian Medicine, and the Performance of American Culture," which received the 2005 Herbert Ross Brown Prize from *New England Quarterly*. He is currently working on a study of Indian sacred performance and American literature.

KEVIN J. BERLAND, Associate Professor of English at Penn State Shenango, has co-edited *The Commonplace Book of William Byrd II of Westover* (2001) and *William Beckford and the New Millennium* (2004). His essays have appeared in *Dalhousie Review, Journal of the History of Ideas,* and *Philological Quarterly,* among many other scholarly journals.

CHRIS BEYERS, Associate Professor of English at Assumption College in Worcester, Massachusetts, is currently working on a project studying the nexus of culture, economics, and poetics in the colonial Chesapeake area, tentatively entitled *Ebenezer Cooke's World: White Men Wanting Money in British America*. His essays have appeared in *College Literature, Early American Literature,* and *Southern Literary Journal*.

RONALD A. BOSCO is Distinguished Professor of English and American Literature at the University at Albany, State University of New York, and General Editor for *The Collected Works of Ralph Waldo Emerson*. He is author or editor of many books, including *Nature's Panorama: Thoreau on the Seasons* (2005), *The Emerson Brothers: A Fraternal Biography in Letters* (Oxford University Press, 2006, with Joel Myerson), *Emerson Bicentennial Essays* (2006, with Joel Myerson), and *Hawthorne in His Own Time: A Biographical Chronicle of His Life, Drawn from Recollections, Interviews, and Memoirs by Family, Friends, and Associates* (2007, with Jillmarie Murphy).

DAVID J. CARLSON is Associate Professor of English at California State University, San Bernardino, where he specializes in early American and Native American literature. He is the author of *Sovereign Selves: American Indian Autobiography and the*

Law (2006). His essays have appeared in *American Indian Quarterly, Early American Literature,* and *Studies in Puritan American Spirituality.*

LORRAYNE CARROLL, Associate Professor of English at the University of Southern Maine, is the author of *Rhetorical Drag: Gender Impersonation, Captivity, and the Writing of History* (2006).

SARAH FATHERLY is Associate Professor of History and Director of Women's Studies at Otterbein College. Her areas of expertise are eighteenth-century British American social history and early American women's history. She has recently completed a book-length manuscript focusing on women's involvement in elite class formation in colonial Philadelphia and is now working on a project centered around a woman's diary from the Seven Years' War.

KEVIN J. HAYES, Professor of English at the University of Central Oklahoma, is the author of *A Colonial Woman's Bookshelf* (1996), *Folklore and Book Culture* (1997), *The Library of William Byrd of Westover* (1997), *The Library of John Montgomerie, Colonial Governor of New York and New Jersey* (2000), *An American Cycling Odyssey, 1887* (2002), *The Library of Benjamin Franklin* (2006, with Edwin Wolf 2nd), and *A Peep into Korea* (2007), among other books. He has received the Virginia Library History Award, presented by the Library of Virginia, and the Virginia Center for the Book and the Distinguished Service Award, presented by the Association for Documentary Editing.

MELISSA J. HOMESTEAD is Associate Professor of English and Women's and Gender Studies at the University of Nebraska–Lincoln. The author of *American Women Authors and Literary Property, 1822–1869* (2005), she is currently working on a study of Catharine Sedgwick's engagements with antebellum print culture and a coauthored study (with Anne L. Kaufman) of the creative partnership of Willa Cather and Edith Lewis.

SUSAN CLAIR IMBARRATO, Associate Professor of English at Minnesota State University, Moorhead, is the author of *Declarations of Independency in Eighteenth-Century American Autobiography* (1998) and *Traveling Women: Narrative Visions of Early America* (2006).

THOMAS S. KIDD is Assistant Professor of History at Baylor University. He is the author of *The Protestant Interest: New England after Puritanism* (2004) and the forthcoming *Awakenings: The First Generation of American Evangelical Christianity,* for which he received a 2006–2007 NEH fellowship. He is also writing a book on American Christians' views of Islam from the colonial period to the present.

APRIL LANGLEY is Assistant Professor of English at the University of Missouri. She specializes in eighteenth- and nineteenth-century Africana and American literature. She has published essays in scholarly journals ranging from *A/B: Auto/Biography Studies* to *Western Journal of Black Studies*. She is currently completing a book-length work to be called *The Black Aesthetic Unbound: Theorizing the Dilemma of an Eighteenth-Century African-American Literature.*

CHRISTINE A. MODEY is a Lecturer at the Sweetland Writing Center and the Department of English Language and Literature at the University of Michigan, Ann Arbor.

CARLA MULFORD is Associate Professor of English at Pennsylvania State University, where she teaches early American studies, comparative colonial studies, and Native American studies. Besides serving as one of the founding editors of the groundbreaking *Heath Anthology of American Literature,* she has edited several other books, including *Only for the Eye of a Friend: The Poems of Annis Boudinot Stockton* (1995), *Teaching the Literatures of Early America* (1999), *Finding Colonial Americas: Essays Honoring J. A. Leo Lemay* (2001, with David Shields), and *Early American Writings* (2002, with Angela Vietto and Amy E. Winans). She is the recipient of the Richard P. McCormick Prize in History presented by the New Jersey Historical Commission.

JILLMARIE MURPHY teaches literature and writing at Schenectady County Community College. She has recently completed *Hawthorne in His Own Time: A Biographical Chronicle of His Life, Drawn from Recollections, Interviews, and Memoirs by Family, Friends, and Associates* (2007, with Ronald A. Bosco). She is currently writing a critical study of adult obsession and childhood trauma in the novel.

STEVEN OLSEN-SMITH is Associate Professor of English at Boise State University, where he teaches courses on early and antebellum American literature. He is also General Editor of Melville's Marginalia Online. His essays have appeared in *ESQ, Leviathan, Nineteenth-Century Literature,* and *Walt Whitman Quarterly Review.*

NAOKI ONISHI is the Chair of the Division of Humanities at International Christian University, where he teaches courses in early American literature and culture. His work in Japanese includes critical studies of New England Puritan literature and translations of works treating classic American literature and American humor. His essays have appeared in *Early American Literature, Humanities,* and *Japanese Journal of American Studies.*

SUSAN SCOTT PARRISH is Associate Professor in the Department of English Language and Literature and the Program in the Environment at the University of Michigan. Her book, *American Curiosity: Cultures of Natural History in the Colonial British*

Atlantic World (2006), won the annual Jamestown Prize. Her current projects include work on slavery and portraiture in the eighteenth-century Atlantic world and a new edition of Robert Beverley's *History and Present State of Virginia* (1705).

DANIEL ROYOT, Emeritus Professor of American Literature and Civilization at the Sorbonne, Paris, has often taught as a visiting professor in the United States. He was a fellow at the Robert H. Smith International Center for Jefferson Studies, Monticello, in 1998. He has written extensively on American literature, ethnicity, cultural studies, and humor. He is past president of the American Humor Studies Association. His publications include articles in English on Benjamin Franklin, Edgar Allan Poe, James Russell Lowell, Benjamin Shillaber, and Thomas Berger. His book *Go West: Histoire de l'Ouest américain, d'hier à aujourd-hui* (2004) belongs to the classical Champs collection, Flammarion. Several of his works have been translated into Swedish, Chinese, Turkish, and Korean. He is the editor of a standard anthology of American literature (Presses universitaires de France). His book *Divided Loyalties in a Doomed Empire: The French in the West from New France to the Lewis and Clark Expedition* (2007) bears on colonial culture set in a comparative perspective.

KAREN SCHRAMM is Associate Professor of English at Delaware Valley College, where she teaches courses in literature, communication, semantics, and writing. She has published essays on American literature, history, biography, pedagogy, and environmental studies.

JASON SHAFFER teaches in the Department of English at the United States Naval Academy. He is the author of the forthcoming *Performing Patriotism: National Identity in the Colonial and Revolutionary American Theatre.* His essays have appeared in *Comparative Drama, Early American Literature,* and *Theatre Survey.*

E. THOMSON SHIELDS JR. teaches early American literature at East Carolina University. He is also director of the Roanoke Colonies Research Office, for which he edits the *Roanoke Colonies Research Newsletter.* He has published essays and reviews on Spanish and English literature and culture of colonial North America, on early North Carolina literature, and on Latin and Hispanic American writers.

FRANK SHUFFELTON teaches English and American literature at the University of Rochester. He has written widely on early American literature. His works include *Thomas Hooker, 1586–1647* (1977), critically annotated bibliographies on writing about Thomas Jefferson from 1826 to the present, and numerous essays in various journals and edited collections. He has edited *A Mixed Race* (1993), a collection of essays about ethnicity in early America; *The American Enlightenment* (1993), another collection of essays; Thomas Jefferson's *Notes on the State of Virginia* (1999); and *The Letters of John and Abigail Adams* (2004).

COLIN WELLS is Associate Professor of English at St. Olaf College in Northfield, Minnesota. He is the author of *The Devil and Doctor Dwight: Satire and Theology in the Early American Republic* (2002) and is currently at work on a study of poetry and politics in America from 1765 to 1815.

ED WHITE teaches at the University of Florida. He is the author of *The Backcountry and the City: Colonization and Conflict in Early America* (2005). He is currently writing about Charles Brockden Brown's utopian historical sketches and the formation of Crèvecoeur's English and French letters.

THE OXFORD HANDBOOK OF

EARLY AMERICAN LITERATURE

INTRODUCTION

KEVIN J. HAYES

In 1713, White Kennett, bishop of Peterborough, published *Bibliothecae Americanae*, the first systematic attempt to define a body of writings that constitute American literature. Bishop Kennett issued this work upon presenting his personal library of Americana to the Society for the Propagation of the Gospel in Foreign Parts. Hoping the library would aid the society's mission, he was open-minded enough to recognize that many others could benefit from its holdings: colonial administrators, historians, mariners, members of trading companies, merchants, and ministers of state. Kennett advocated broad accessibility, suggesting that the library could provide for "the Information of Strangers, and the Entertainment of all Persons" (Kennett 1713, iv).

Mentioning the collection's entertainment value, Kennett suggested that these books not only were instructive but also contained much to delight readers. To delight and instruct: this Horatian paradigm succinctly articulates the dual purpose of literature in Bishop Kennett's time and, indeed, through the remainder of the eighteenth century. His bibliography implicitly defines American literature in terms of both language and geography. Though it lists a few titles in Spanish and a few others in Latin, otherwise it consists of works in English. In terms of geography, Kennett included works pertaining to both North and South America. From his perspective, early American literature consists of writings in English pertaining to the Americas that both delight and instruct. This definition would change as the study of American literature developed in the coming years.

THE RECOGNITION OF EARLY AMERICAN LITERATURE

Many readers recognized the value of Kennett's bibliography. Both Benjamin Franklin and Thomas Jefferson owned copies of the work. Jefferson found his especially useful when he and John Adams were discussing early American literature in their correspondence. Adams introduced the subject. He was motivated by a pamphlet volume John Quincy Adams had found in Germany, which contained three seventeenth-century works, all now recognized as classics of the period: Edward Johnson's *Wonder-Working Providence,* Thomas Morton's *New English Canaan,* and William Wood's *New Englands Prospect.* Adams asked Jefferson what he knew about *New English Canaan.* Jefferson consulted Kennett's *Bibliothecae Americanae* and other pertinent works. The most useful volume he had at Monticello for Adams's purpose was Nathaniel Morton's *New-England's Memorial,* a work detailing Thomas Morton's exploits in New England. Responding to Adams, Jefferson took the time to transcribe several pages from *New-England's Memorial.*

This exchange, which occurred nearly a hundred years after Kennett published *Bibliothecae Americanae,* reveals a burgeoning interest in early American literature. Actually, American readers had become curious about their unique literary past decades earlier. A new edition of Mary Rowlandson's *Sovereignty and Goodness of God* in 1770, for example, sparked a revival of interest in her work. Originally published in 1682, Rowlandson's captivity narrative had not been republished since 1720. Retitled *The Narrative of the Captivity,* this new edition reflects an interest in uniquely American books among American readers in the run-up to the Revolution. Rowlandson's *Narrative* went through several more editions in the early 1770s. After the Revolutionary War, it was revived again. The work became so well known that her name became part of a proverbial comparison: "as many removes as Mrs. Rowlandson" (Hayes 1997, 10). Jeremy Belknap, the New Hampshire author whose historical and biographical writings contribute significantly to early national literature, used the phrase in a letter to Ebenezer Hazard, another important historian: "I remember, when you removed your family to New York, you complained of the inconvenience. I now can, more fully than I could then, adopt the same language and entertain the same feelings. Once I could be at home anywhere. From the time I went to college till my settlement at Dover I had near as many removals as Mother Rowlanderson (this is a New England comparison, and will make Mrs. Hazard laugh)" (Belknap 1877).

The references to Thomas Morton in the Adams-Jefferson correspondence and to Mary Rowlandson in Belknap's provide instances of early American literature referring to itself. These letters establish continuity with their literary past even as they form contributions to American literature in themselves. Similar examples abound. Benjamin Franklin's reference to Cotton Mather in his *Autobiography* may be the most well-known instance of early American literature referring to itself. Franklin not only mentions the *Magnalia Christi Americana,* Mather's epic history of New England but also refers to Mather's *Essays to Do Good.*

Franklin mentioned the titles of many books in his autobiography, partly to give readers a program of self-education they could follow. In Mather's case, Franklin's scheme worked brilliantly. The autobiography prompted a revival of Mather's *Essays to Do Good.* After its publication, a flurry of reprints of Mather's work followed. In the early nineteenth century, American editions of *Essays to Do Good* were published in Delaware, Kentucky, Massachusetts, New Hampshire, New York, Pennsylvania, and Vermont. British editions appeared in Glasgow and London. Influenced by Franklin's reference to the work, Thomas Jefferson ordered a copy of *Essays to Do Good* for the University of Virginia library (Jefferson 1950, 30).

Despite the numerous reprints, Cotton Mather was not known primarily for *Essays to Do Good* in the early nineteenth century. Nor was he known primarily for the *Magnalia Christi Americana,* though that work was reprinted in 1820. In the popular imagination, Mather was best remembered for his belief in witchcraft. In "The Legend of Sleepy Hollow," which appeared around the same time as the new edition of the *Magnalia,* Washington Irving has Ichabod Crane read Mather's "History of New England Witchcraft" (Irving 1983, 1063). The work Irving had in mind was *Wonders of the Invisible World,* in which Mather documented many supposed instances of witchcraft. During the nineteenth century, Cotton Mather came to represent all the prejudice and parochialism of colonial New England, yet he came to represent early American literature, too. For years to some, references to Mather in the popular culture would continue to function as a barometer of national attitudes toward early American literature.

In *Grandfather's Chair* (1841), Nathaniel Hawthorne asserted that Cotton Mather saw "evil spirits all about the world. Doubtless he imagined that they were hidden in the corners and crevices of his library, and that they peeped out from among the leaves of many of his books, as he turned them over, at midnight" (Hawthorne 1883, 513). Reading another book by Mather, the narrator of Herman Melville's short story "The Apple-Tree Table" (1856) observes, "His style had all the plainness and unpoetic boldness of truth. In the most straightforward way, he laid before me detailed accounts of New England witchcraft." The more the narrator reads, the more he frets: "I began to think that much midnight reading of Cotton Mather was not good for man; that it had a morbid influence upon the nerves, and gave rise to hallucinations. I resolved to put Cotton Mather permanently aside" (Melville 1987, 382, 385).

The study of early American literature came of age in 1829. This year William Hazlitt used a recent publication by William Ellery Channing, then considered an important American author, to reconsider American literature as a whole. In

Hazlitt's opinion, three American authors before Charles Brockden Brown deserved recognition: Benjamin Franklin, Jonathan Edwards, and J. Hector St. John de Crèvecoeur. Franklin was, in Hazlitt's words, "a great experimental philosopher, a consummate politician, and a paragon of common sense." Edwards was "one of the acutest, most powerful, and, of all reasoners, the most conscientious and sincere." And Crèvecoeur's great work, *Letters from an American Farmer,* offered "a tolerable idea how American scenery and manners may be treated with a lively poetic interest. The pictures are sometimes highly-coloured, but they are vivid and strikingly characteristic. He gives not only the objects, but the feelings, of a new country" (Hazlitt 1829, 130–131).

Unbeknownst to Hazlitt, American scholars were simultaneously taking stock of their national literary heritage. Samuel Knapp's *Lectures on American Literature,* the first history of American literature, appeared this same year. So did Samuel Kettell's three-volume *Specimens of American Poetry,* the fullest anthology of American literature published to that time. Not since White Kennett's *Bibliothecae Americanae* had there been such significant contributions to the study of early American literature.

Not all readers were pleased with these two works. Hugh Swinton Legaré may have been their most vocal critic. Discussing both in the *Southern Review,* Legaré recognized Kettell's New England bias. Instead of insisting on more southern authors, he questioned the entire project of distinguishing a uniquely American literature. Both Knapp and Kettell clamored for an autochthonous literature, that is, a literature freed from external influence, the influence of Europe in general and of England in particular. Legaré disagreed. He saw no reason that American readers should reject English literature in favor of a less accomplished indigenous literature: "Whatever be the wonders that Cotton Mather and his heroical successors have effected, we not only think that the English literature is good enough for us at present, but that it may actually continue good enough for perhaps a century to come. We have certainly produced bards and philosophers many a one—but neither Miltons, Shakespeares, nor Bacons as yet" (Legaré 1831, 438).

In her review of Kettell's *Specimens of American Poetry,* a contributor to the *Ladies' Magazine* offered a different perspective: "Here the curious student may find the remains of our elder poets in the quaint phraseology, enriched and embued with the scriptural learning, of that primitive and peculiar people." According to this viewpoint, the poems Kettell collected were curiosities, examples of how people used to write, artifacts useful for understanding the past but scarcely what can be called great literature. This reviewer also felt that Kettell should have included more work by female poets: "We must be watchful that our own sex suffer no injustice at the literary tribunal" (Anon. 1829). In the waning decades of the twentieth century, many academics would critique the male-dominated canon of early American literature. Such criticism was nothing new. As this review verifies, gender-based critiques of the canon occurred as early as 1829.

How Edgar Allan Poe Read Early
American Literature

Edgar Allan Poe questioned the literary value of the poetry Kettell included in his anthology, too. Poe observed, "The 'specimens' of Kettell were specimens of nothing but the ignorance and ill taste of the compiler. A large proportion of what he gave to the world as American poetry, to the exclusion of much that was really so, was the doggerel composition of individuals unheard of and undreamed of, except by Mr. Kettell himself" (Poe 1984, 550). Poe considered writing a history of American literature but ultimately abandoned the project in favor of a description of current American letters. Poe's lack of resources was one reason he abandoned his history of American literature, but not the primary reason. He simply cared little for early American literature (Hayes 2000, 106). His short story "The Business Man" satirizes one of the most revered works of the period, Benjamin Franklin's *Autobiography* (Lemay 1982). Of Joel Barlow's epic poem, Poe admitted, "We cannot stand being told . . . that 'Barlow's *Columbiad* is a poem of considerable merit'" (Poe 1842). Poe felt comfortable restricting his literary study to contemporary authors because, like Legaré, he did not see American literature beginning much before the nineteenth century.

Poe's dislike of early American literature partly stems from the break he made with traditional ways of thinking about literature. Eschewing the long-standing requirement that art both delight and instruct, Poe established the idea of art for art's sake (Hayes 2004, 225). While this phrase has been attributed to both Algernon Charles Swinburne and Walter Pater, Poe anticipated it in an 1844 book review, in which he insisted "that under the sun there exists no work more intrinsically noble, than this very poem *written solely for the poem's sake*" (Poe 1984, 295). The fact-filled, often didactic, and frequently admonitory literature of colonial America had no place in Poe's aesthetic.

Poe did appreciate some early American authors, even if he refused them a place on his American Parnassus. When his friend William Gowans published a scholarly edition of Daniel Denton's *Brief Description of New York* in 1845 as the first title in his Bibliotheca Americana series, Poe appreciated Denton's promotional tract as a work "of exceeding interest—to say nothing of its value in an historical point of view" (Poe 1845, 168). Though interesting and historically valuable, Denton's tract does not measure up as literature when considered from Poe's aesthetic.

Gowans's Bibliotheca Americana series represents an important step in the literary recognition of early American prose, but Gowans was more interested in issuing quality editions than rushing works through the press. The fifth title in the series, George Alsop's *Character of the Province of Maryland*, did not appear until 1869, nearly a quarter century after the first title. Alsop's delightful tract had been almost completely forgotten in the two centuries since it first appeared. Gowans's edition helped American readers recognize its literary qualities. As one reviewer observed, "Our old author writes in a sharp and pungent style, and his ardent loyalty as a cavalier, and his sufferings whet his sarcasms to a keen edge and give piquancy to his contrasts of civilized and barbarous life" (Anon. 1869, 385).

Rufus Wilmot Griswold, Poe's literary executor, did much to make early American literature more accessible. He established his editorial reputation with *The Poets and Poetry of America* (1842), *The Prose Writers of America* (1846), and *The Female Poets of America* (1848). He subsequently prepared new editions of all three, revising and expanding their contents to suit public demand and to compete in the marketplace. Though Griswold largely plagiarized *The Poets and Poetry of America* from Kettell's *Specimens of American Poetry,* his work succeeded commercially whereas Kettell's had failed (Cutting 1975, 227). Dependent on Kettell for most of the seventeenth- and eighteenth-century verse he used, Griswold abbreviated Kettell's selections considerably and improved their pace. He also added a handful of poems not in Kettell, including "New England's Annoyances," which is now recognized as the earliest known American folksong (Lemay 1985). *The Prose Writers of America,* though more original than *The Poets and Poetry of America,* is less expansive in its scope. Without an anthology of prose comparable to Kettell's verse anthology, Griswold ignored the seventeenth century altogether. *Prose Writers of America* begins with Jonathan Edwards.

THE CYCLOPAEDIA OF AMERICAN LITERATURE

Part encyclopedia and part anthology, Evert and George Duyckinck's *Cyclopaedia of American Literature* (1855) excelled any previous work on the subject. In their preface the Duyckinck brothers cautioned against reading the selections for their aesthetic qualities. Early American literature "is not so much an exhibition of art and invention, of literature in its immediate and philosophical sense, as a record of mental progress and cultivation, of facts and opinions, which derives its main interest from its historical rather than its critical value." Still, they encouraged readers to keep an open mind: "The many noble sentiments, just thoughts, the eloquent orations, the tasteful poems, the various refinements of literary expression, drawn together in these volumes, are indeed the noblest appeal and best apology for the work. The voice of two centuries of American literature may well be worth listening to" (Duyckinck and Duyckinck 1855, 1: v, viii).

The general purpose of the *Cyclopaedia* was "to exhibit and illustrate the products of the pen on American soil." These words express an important truth: there is an inextricable relationship between land and literature. Works produced by authors who have spent time in North America reflect the physical influence of the American environment. Whereas previous anthologies were biased toward the literature of New England, the Duyckincks made a conscious effort to include representative selections from southern writers, too. Regardless whether from the North or South, all American authors display the influence of the land on their writings.

The work's chronological organization follows "as nearly as practicable the date of birth of each individual" (Duyckinck and Duyckinck 1855, 1: vi). The Duyckincks violate this stated organizational scheme within their first ten pages. George Sandys, the subject of the first entry, was born in 1578. Thomas Hariot, the subject of the seventh entry, was born in 1560. Starting their *Cyclopaedia* with Sandys gave the Duyckincks a distinct advantage. Traditionally, it had been assumed that the colonists were so busy carving their communities from the wilderness and guarding against Indian attack they had neither the time nor the inclination for belles lettres. The example of Sandys proves the opposite. Appointed treasurer of the Virginia colony and a member of its governing council, Sandys reached Virginia in 1621. Present for the great Indian uprising that occurred on March 22, 1622, he personally led the first counterattack against the Indians. He remained in Virginia to 1625. During his stay he completed *Ovids Metamorphosis Englished* (1626), a translation that profoundly affected Milton, Dryden, and Pope. As the Duyckincks tell the story, the premier author of American literature influenced some of the foremost authors of English literature.

MOSES COIT TYLER

Though indebted to the work of the Duyckincks, Moses Coit Tyler elevated the study of early American literature to a professional, scholarly level. Tyler combed public and private libraries seeking out original manuscripts and rare first editions (Vanderbilt 1986, 82–83). When he published his *History of American Literature* (1878), which took the story to 1765, he could boast, "Upon no topic of literary estimation have I formed an opinion at second hand. In every instance, I have examined for myself the work under consideration" (Tyler 1878, vii). Tyler could make a similar boast two decades later when he published his follow-up study, *The Literary History of the American Revolution, 1763–1783* (1897). Tyler brought to the field a seriousness and dedication the finest literary scholars have since emulated.

Like the Duyckincks, Tyler recognized the connection between land and literature. He defined American literature in terms of both language and geography. For him, American literature begins with the establishment of the first permanent English colony in America. Unlike Poe, Tyler did not see literature as being constrained to belles lettres. But by the time his literary history appeared in 1878, the phrase "art for art's sake" had become so firmly entrenched in the critical discourse that he found it necessary to allude to it, if only to recognize it as an anachronism when applied to early American literature. Speaking of early colonial days, Tyler observed, "Undoubtedly literature for its own sake was not much thought of, or lived for, in those days" (Tyler 1878, 1: 7).

Tyler devoted his second chapter to the individual he identified as the first author of American literature, Captain John Smith. Like other early settlers of both Virginia and New England, Smith was born in England, but his writings are American through and through. Taking other seventeenth-century works for example in subsequent chapters, Tyler emphasized the influence of the American environment on its literature. After quoting from John Hammond's promotional tract, *Leah and Rachel: or, The Two Fruitful Sisters Virginia, and Maryland* (1656), for example, Tyler characterized what Hammond had to say: "Here, certainly, in these brusque sentences, do we find a literature smacking of American soil and smelling of American air. Here, thus early in our studies, do we catch in American writings that new note of hope and of help for humanity in distress, and of a rugged personal independence, which, almost from the hour of our first settlements in this land, America began to send back, with unveiled exultation, to Europe" (Tyler 1878, 64). Tyler is convincing: the American strand has had a deep and abiding impact on the literary imagination.

EARLY AMERICAN LITERATURE IN THE CLASSROOM

When Tyler's literary history first appeared in 1878, there were really no college classes devoted to the study of American literature, but courses on American literature proliferated in colleges and high schools toward the end of the century. The textbook industry recognized the trend, and the brief literary history emerged as the preferred pedagogical tool. Around the turn of the century, a dozen or so different works were available. Take *American Literature: An Elementary Text-book for Use in High Schools and Academies* (1891), for example. Written by Julian Hawthorne (Nathaniel's son) and Leonard Lemmon, a Texas school superintendent, this work was published by D. C. Heath, a major textbook publisher. Though Hawthorne and Lemmon referred to Tyler's history to write theirs, they did not share his appreciation of early American literature. They observed: "The productions of our colonial period can be called literature by courtesy only. They consist of historical and geographical memoranda, and of theological essays and arguments. The Revolutionary era is rich in speeches, protocols and declarations, often elevated in sentiment and massive in thought, but dyed in the passionate hues of patriotism and partisanship, and necessarily lacking the repose and balance that belong to pure literature" (Hawthorne and Lemmon 1891, x–xi). Their first chapter, "Colonial Literature," shows little understanding of the period, as its opening sentence indicates: "As the physical analysis of the Universe begins with protoplasm, so must intelligent study of a literature begin with examination of the inchoate material upon which the literature is based." Protoplasm? Inchoate material? These are harsh terms to describe early American literature. Hawthorne and Lemmon mention Captain John Smith's *True Relation of Virginia* and his *Map of Virginia* but assure students that they need not read them. They also mention George Alsop and Daniel Denton, an indication that William Gowans's Bibliotheca Americana series had done its work. Ultimately, they suggest that Samuel Sewall's diary may be "the only book of the Colonial period that can be read through with pleasure" (Hawthorne and Lemmon 1891, 1, 6).

In a note to teachers, Hawthorne and Lemmon explain, "Standard writers are now obtainable at so cheap a rate, that any one may afford the material for a year's reading in connection with this manual" (Hawthorne and Lemmon 1891, viii). While there were numerous cheap editions of prominent nineteenth-century authors available, there were no comparable collections for earlier centuries. Ten years would pass before a convenient, reasonably priced, relatively thorough anthology of early American literature would become available. When William P. Trent and Benjamin W. Wells published *Colonial Prose and Poetry* in late 1901, it was warmly received. Trent and Wells took great pains to include representative works from throughout the American colonies in their three-volume anthology. Authors represented include George Alsop, Robert Beverley, William Byrd, Daniel Denton, Philip Vickers Fithian, Sarah Kemble Knight, Mary Rowlandson, Patrick Tailfer, and John Woolman. "Outwardly delightful and intellectually stimulating," one reviewer called it. "To those who are doubtful of the intellectual stimulus to be got from Cotton Mather and Michael Wigglesworth, we can say only that our colonial writers have abundant interest for those who are willing to look for it. Viewed from the narrow standpoint of aesthetics, they have little to offer; but seen in the wider vision that broadens before the student of social history and the spiritual life, they occupy a large place in our annals." This reviewer also emphasized the book's convenience and originality: "Nothing of the sort has heretofore been accessible to the general reader, unless, perchance, he happened to own a Duyckinck," but the reader "can put these books in his pocket" (Anon. 1902, 91). *Colonial Prose and Poetry* was reissued in 1903 as part of the series Handy Volume Classics. It was also republished in a convenient one-volume edition specifically designed for college classroom use, which went through numerous reprintings through 1929. Rachael Childrey, for example, read one of the later printings of this work while a student at Cornell in 1926.

Another classroom anthology appeared in 1909 and went through multiple reprintings through the 1920s. In his preface to *Selections from Early American Writers, 1607–1800*, William B. Cairns observed, "Teachers of American literary history are coming pretty generally to recognize that some knowledge of the temper and the manner of Colonial and Revolutionary writers is necessary to the full understanding of their successors" (Cairns 1909, v). This anthology begins with five selections from Captain John Smith, followed by a description of a storm and a shipwreck by William Strachey, included because of its supposed influence on *The Tempest.* The next several selections come from New England. In fact, the collection as a whole is decidedly biased toward New England. One selection from early Maryland literature, Ebenezer Cook's *The Sot-weed Factor,* is included because, in Cairns's words, it forms "one of the more curious bits of early Americana" (Cairns 1909, 252).

Hildegarde Hawthorne (Julian's daughter) reviewed the work and noticed the New England slant. Though she generally enjoyed it, she disagreed with what Cairns said in his preface. In fact, she saw no "link between this beginning and the immense superstructure of our present output." In contrast to the numerous Puritan selections, she found the selections from the Revolutionary period quite refreshing: "The latter part of the book contains excerpts from the writings of Jefferson, Paine, and Hamilton, sonorous and immortal pages where a new spirit is already to be observed spreading pinions far beyond the confines of the Puritan prison" (Hawthorne 1909, 475).

The Cambridge History of American Literature

William P. Trent was the prime mover behind *The Cambridge History of American Literature,* which he edited with John Erskine, Stuart P. Sherman, and Carl Van Doren. Together they, too, recognized that the modern emphasis on belles lettres was inappropriate to the study of early American literature. As one contemporary reviewer summarized their approach: "The editors believe that to write the intellectual history of America from the modern aesthetic standpoint would be to miss precisely what makes it significant among modern literatures. A people that devoted its main energies to exploration, settlement, labor for sustenance, religion, and statecraft had no time and no disposition to pursue art for art's sake" (Anon. 1917, 646).

Book 1 of *The Cambridge History of American Literature,* "Colonial and Revolutionary Literature," includes nine chapters. Book 2, "Early National Literature," contains two chapters that treat other genres belonging to the previous period, specifically travel writing from the middle to late eighteenth century and early American drama. Each chapter is written by a different contributor. Two are devoted to major authors (Benjamin Franklin and Jonathan Edwards). Others are devoted to different types of writing such as poetry and political writing, and others to different types of writers: divines, historians, philosophers, travelers. One is devoted to print culture. This multifaceted approach makes good sense. The only problem, Walter Bronson (1918) noticed, was that each chapter took its subject back to its beginnings and thus hindered the historical continuity of the work as a whole.

The Cambridge History of American Literature was the first comprehensive, collaborative history of American literature. In Perry Miller's words, the work "was as much a battle-cry as a work of scholarship. It was a manifesto of the Americanists that American literature was no longer to be merely a subsection of the English, but was henceforth to be coequal in dignity and repute" (Miller 1948, 4). Subsequent generations of literary scholars have produced their own comprehensive, collaborative histories: Robert Spiller's Literary History of the United States (1948), Emory Elliot's Columbia Literary History of the United States (1988), and Sacvan Bercovitch's eight-volume Cambridge History of American Literature (1994–2005). All of these works have been devoted to American literature as a whole. There has never been a comprehensive, collaborative literary history of early American literature— until now.

A New England State of Mind

Without a collaborative history specifically devoted to early American literature, the field of study was left to individual scholars. Tyler's History of American Literature had been reprinted numerous times through the late nineteenth century, but it went out of print after 1909. The fullest work on the subject to emerge in the middle third of the twentieth century was Perry Miller's two-volume opus, The New England Mind (1939–1953). More a history of ideas than a literary history, Miller's work makes for difficult reading. To be sure, more people bought The New England Mind than actually read it. Regardless whether they read it, many people bought into Miller's argument. He struck a chord that reverberated across the nation. For decades, elementary school history lessons and annual Thanksgiving Day rituals had reminded Americans of the importance of the Puritans to the development of American culture. While publicly acknowledging their cultural significance, many were privately embarrassed by the Puritans' stern ways and narrow thinking. The great value of The New England Mind was to show that the Puritans were deep and serious thinkers, that they devoted enormous amounts of time pondering their condition, that they did not simply accept their prejudices but worked hard to reconcile reality and faith. Miller gave Americans of the mid–twentieth century great comfort: he let them know that they could be proud of their Puritan ancestors maugre their apparent narrow-mindedness.

There had been a New England bias to the study of early American literature ever since the days of Messrs. Knapp and Kettell; Miller's work reinforced the New England bias all the more. Though important works devoted to the intellectual, literary, and cultural history of the South also appeared in the middle third of the twentieth century—W. J. Cash's *The Mind of the South* (1941), Jay Hubbell's *The South in American Literature, 1607–1900* (1954), and much of Richard Beale Davis's impressive body of work—none captured the popular mind-set the way *The New England Mind* did. Furthermore, none really changed the general way early American literature was taught.

When Davis's three-volume opus, *Intellectual Life in the Colonial South, 1585–1763,* appeared in 1978, the Miller-inspired New England bias was so fully ingrained in the study of early American literature that it seemed impossible to change. Writing this same year, James M. Cox observed, "The Puritan ascension could be attributed to three causes: Harvard, Yale, and Perry Miller" (Cox 1978, 635). Professor Cox was being facetious, but he is not far wrong. The appearance of the second volume of *The New England Mind* in 1953 coincided with the rise of the anthology as the dominant pedagogical tool for teaching American literature. The anthologies further institutionalized the New England bias. As recently as 1989, the third edition of the *Norton Anthology of American Literature* titled its first section, "Early American Literature, 1620–1820." In other words, the editors dated the start of the period from the arrival of the Puritans in New England, not from the establishment of Jamestown in 1607. Eleven of the first twelve authors represented in this edition of the *Norton Anthology* are from New England.

Expanding the Canon

In the history of literary scholarship, certain times and places form wellsprings to nourish and accelerate the development of the field of study. In the history of Melville scholarship, for example, the seminars conducted by Stanley T. Williams at Yale in the 1940s were a watershed. Many prominent Melville scholars of the following generation took Williams's seminar, wrote their doctoral dissertations under him, and went on to publish important Melville editions and critical studies. When it comes to the study of early American literature, the same can be said of the seminars conducted by J. A. Leo Lemay at the University of Delaware in the late twentieth century.

Following the lead of Richard Beale Davis, much of Lemay's own scholarship has involved expanding the canon of early American writings to include works from the colonial South. Upon its publication in 1972, *Men of Letters in Colonial*

Maryland broadened the canon of early American literature to include many delightful yet little known authors. Lemay's *Robert Bolling Woos Anne Miller: Love and Courtship in Colonial Virginia, 1760,* and his separate publication of "Neanthe" established Robert Bolling as an important early American author. And Lemay's *Calendar of American Poetry in the Colonial Newspapers and Magazines* (1972) forms a useful research tool that anyone studying the period can use to broaden the canon of early American verse on their own. As significant as they are, Lemay's writings may not be his greatest contribution to the study of early American literature. The classes he has taught—Colonial American Literature, Southern Colonial Literature, Complicity in American Literature—may ultimately prove to be his greatest legacy to the field.

In Colonial American Literature, for example, Professor Lemay's instructions the first week of the semester were intimidating in their simplicity: come back next week with an original essay on *any* work of early American literature. He did provide his students with a list of suggested topics—a single-spaced, ten-page list—but otherwise he left it up to them to choose which authors and what works to study. Suddenly, early American literature no longer meant William Bradford, Cotton Mather, and John Winthrop; it also involved Robert Beverley, William Byrd, Dr. Alexander Hamilton, and Richard Lewis. No longer was early American literature just Puritan histories and sermons; it now included promotion literature, picaresque travel narratives, and bawdy Hudibrastic verse.

Carla Mulford, one of Lemay's students, became a founding editor of *The Heath Anthology of American Literature* (1990). Published by D. C. Heath ninety-nine years after the firm had published the Hawthorne and Lemmon textbook, this anthology begins with traditional Native American stories, includes excerpts of numerous European voyages from Christopher Columbus through Samuel de Champlain, presents a liberal sampling of literature from the English colonies on the mainland, and includes a selection entitled "Emerging Voices of a National Literature: African, Native American, Spanish, Mexican." No longer can early American literature be called protoplasm, but the *Heath Anthology* still makes the field seem somewhat inchoate. Suddenly, inclusivity had become more valuable criterion than literary quality. Diversity had become more valuable than continuity.

In the decade and a half since the first edition of the *Heath Anthology* appeared, the canon of early American literature has continued to expand. Essentially, two new approaches to the field have emerged. Whereas early American literature had been defined in the past in terms of language *and* geography, now it is being defined in terms of language *or* geography. Some prefer to take a hemispherical approach and look at early American literature as involving all literature written in the Americas during colonial times in any language. Others take a linguistic approach and see early American literature as literature in English about America. This approach, which encompasses North America, Great Britain, and the West Indies, can be called the transatlantic approach.

Though well intended, both the hemispherical approach and the transatlantic approach ignore a central fact about American culture that Tyler and the Duyckincks understood intuitively. Both approaches ignore how important the American soil has been to the development of American literature. New England, the Middle Colonies, and the South all shared a similar geography. Settled along the East Coast, the colonies were separated from the rest of the continent by the Appalachians. Beyond that was a vast and sparsely populated land that stretched westward for thousands of miles. This unique geographic situation contributed immeasurably to make American literature what it would become. "Nota: man is the intelligence of his soil," Wallace Stevens wrote in "The Comedian as the Letter C." Before this long poem is through, its speaker revises the phrase to "Nota: his soil is man's intelligence." Either way, Stevens identified an inextricable link between the land and the intellectual activity that occurs there, a link that is essential for understanding early American literature.

THE STRUCTURE OF THIS VOLUME

The canon of early American literature has expanded so rapidly in recent decades that advances in the field made twenty or thirty years ago have been forgotten in the face of more recent discoveries. In other words, the South is being neglected yet again. Ignored in favor of early New England literature through much of the twentieth century, the literature of the colonial South is now ignored in favor of Spanish voyages, Native American legends, and the poetry of the West Indies. While taking advantage of efforts to expand the canon of early American literature, *The Oxford Handbook of Early American Literature* seeks to consolidate recent gains and impose some order on the field of study. While acknowledging the importance of the hemispherical and transatlantic approaches as important contexts for understanding colonial America, the *Oxford Handbook* sees early American literature as something that can be defined in terms of *both* language and geography. As defined here, early American literature is literature written in English in the region contemporary writers referred to as the "colonies of the main," that is, the British colonies on the American mainland and, after 1776, in the United States. The present work takes the story of early American literature through the period of the Revolutionary War to the mid-1790s. An *Oxford Handbook* devoted to the next period of study will begin with Charles Brockden Brown.

The Oxford Handbook of Early American Literature is subdivided into seven parts, each part containing from three to five chapters. Five chapters are devoted to major authors: Crèvecoeur, Edwards, Franklin, Hamilton, and Smith. Other chapters are devoted to different literary genres: autobiography, captivity narratives, diaries, novels, plays, political writings, promotion literature, and slave narratives. Some genres receive more than one chapter. Travel writing receives two, one on early voyages and another on picaresque travel narratives. Natural history is treated in a chapter devoted to scientific discourse, as well as in another chapter that examines two of the masterworks of early American literature, Thomas Jefferson's *Notes on the State of Virginia* and William Bartram's *Travels*. History writing receives two chapters, and poetry receives three. Part 4 contains three chapters treating different aspects of print culture in early America. And one chapter takes Native American voices as its subject.

The contributors to this volume take advantage of many emerging approaches to literature. Both Melissa Homestead and David Carlson display the usefulness of understanding the transatlantic contexts. In her study, Homestead, for example, shows that the early American novel evolved within the cultural dynamic of ocean crossing. Recent developments in the field of cultural studies are also useful to the study of literature, as several of the contributors demonstrate. The history of the book has become a lively field of study in its own right. The section devoted to contexts of reading makes an effort to integrate the history of the book within the study of literature, but other chapters incorporate advances made by those who study the history of the book, including the profound importance of understanding the interrelationship between manuscript and print culture. Performance studies is another growing field with vast implications for literary study. In his study of Augustan American poetry, Chris Beyers, for example, suggests that the composition of a poem functions as a cultural performance. Intended to explore many different aspects of early American literature, the chapters that follow are arranged in a rough chronological order and, therefore, form, a literary history, the fullest history of early American literature since the days of Moses Coit Tyler. *The Oxford Handbook of Early American Literature* is not just a history of the subject; it is also a celebration of American culture.

REFERENCES

Anon. 1829. Literary Notices. *Ladies' Magazine* 2: 292–293.

Anon. 1869. Review of George Alsop, *A Character of the Province of Maryland. American Literary Gazette and Publishers' Circular* 13 (October 15): 385.

Anon. 1902. The Beginnings of American Literature. *Dial*, February 1, 91.

Anon. 1917. Review of *The Cambridge History of American Literature*, edited by William P. Trent, et al. *Dial*, December 20, 646.

Belknap, Jeremy. 1877. *The Belknap Papers*. Boston: Massachusetts Historical Society.

Bronson, Walter C. 1918. Review of *The Cambridge History of American Literature*, edited by William P. Trent et al. *American Historical Review* 24: 100–102.

Cairns, William B., ed. *Selections from Early American Writers, 1607–1800.* New York: Macmillan, 1909.

Cox, James M. 1978. Jefferson's *Autobiography:* Recovering Literature's Lost Ground. *Southern Review* 14: 633–652.

Cutting, Rose Marie. 1975. America Discovers Its Literary Past: Early American Literature in Nineteenth-Century Anthologies. *Early American Literature* 9: 226–251.

Duyckinck, Evert A., and George L. Duyckinck. 1855. *Cyclopaedia of American Literature: Embracing Personal and Critical Notices of Authors, and Selections from Their Writings.* 2 vols. New York: Scribner.

Hawthorne, Hildegarde. 1909. Our Literature in By-Gone Days. *New York Times Saturday Review of Books,* August 7, 475.

Hawthorne, Julian, and Leonard Lemmon. 1891. *American Literature: An Elementary Textbook for Use in High Schools and Academies.* Boston: Heath.

Hawthorne, Nathaniel. 1883. *A Wonder-Book, Tanglewood Tales, and Grandfather's Chair,* edited by George Parsons Lathrop. Boston: Houghton, Mifflin.

Hayes, Kevin J. 1997. *Folklore and Book Culture.* Knoxville: University of Tennessee Press.

———. 2000. *Poe and the Printed Word.* New York: Cambridge University Press.

———. [2002] 2004. One-Man Modernist. In *The Cambridge Companion to Edgar Allan Poe,* edited by Kevin J. Hayes, 225–240. Reprint. Shanghai: Shanghai Foreign Language Education Press.

[Hazlitt, William.] 1829. American Literature; Dr Channing. *Edinburgh Review* 50: 125–144.

Irving, Washington. 1983. *History, Tales, and Sketches,* edited by James W. Tuttleton. New York: Library of America.

Jefferson, Thomas. 1950. *Jefferson's Ideas on a University Library: Letters from the Founder of the University of Virginia to a Boston Bookseller,* edited by Elizabeth Cometti. Charlottesville: Tracy W. McGregor Library, University of Virginia.

Kennett, White. 1713. *Bibliothecae Americanae Primordia: An Attempt towards Laying the Foundation of an American Library.* London: for J. Churchill.

Kettell, Samuel, ed. 1829. *Specimens of American Poetry, with Critical and Biographical Notices.* 3 vols. Boston: S. G. Goodrich.

Knapp, Samuel L. 1829. *Lectures on American Literature with Remarks on Some Passages of American History.* New York: Elam Bliss.

[Legaré, Hugh Swinton.] 1831. American Literature. *Southern Review* 14: 436–459.

Lemay, J. A. Leo. 1982. Poe's "The Business Man": Its Contexts and Satire of Franklin's *Autobiography. Poe Studies* 15: 29–37.

———. 1985. *"New England's Annoyances": America's First Folk Song.* Newark: University of Delaware Press.

Melville, Herman. 1987. *The Piazza Tales and Other Prose Pieces, 1839–1860,* edited by Harrison Hayford, Alma A. MacDougall, and G. Thomas Tanselle. Evanston and Chicago: Northwestern University Press and the Newberry Library.

Miller, Perry. 1948. A Scholarly Summing Up of American Literature. *New York Times Book Review,* December 5, 4, 47.

Poe, Edgar Allan. 1842. Review of Roswell Park, *Pantology; or A Systematic Survey of Human Knowledge. Graham's Lady's and Gentleman's Magazine* 20: 191.

———. 1845. Critical Notices. *Broadway Journal* 2 (September 20): 167–168.

———. 1984. *Essays and Reviews,* edited by G. R. Thompson. New York: Library of America.

Trent, William P., and Benjamin W. Wells, ed. 1901. *Colonial Prose and Poetry.* New York: Thomas Y. Crowell. (The Rachael Childrey–James Rupp–Kevin Hayes copy.)
Tyler, Moses Coit. 1878. *A History of American Literature.* 2 vols. New York: Putnam's Sons.
Vanderbilt, Kermit. 1986. *American Literature and the Academy: The Roots, Growth, and Maturity of a Profession.* Philadelphia: University of Pennsylvania Press.

PART I

EXPLORATION AND PROMOTION

CHAPTER 1

THE LITERATURE OF EXPLORATION

E. THOMSON SHIELDS JR.

"He did also see in that country, both elephants and onces [pumas]," goes one of the most frequently cited lines from the September 1582 deposition of English sailor David Ingram (Hakluyt 1589, 560). The line strikes modern readers because Ingram was being deposed about experiences in North America. In October 1568, Ingram had volunteered with a hundred others to be left along the largely unexplored Gulf of Mexico somewhere along the coast of the present-day northeastern Mexican state of Tamaulipas. The men agreed to be set ashore to lighten the load of an over-burdened and floundering ship in John Hawkins's fleet. After being trounced by the Spanish, these men decided to risk their fate in territories ruled by the Spanish or by unknown Indians rather than risk drowning or starvation at sea. Ingram's de-position, taken thirteen years after his return to England, is one of only three docu-ments from the men left ashore. Two others—by Miles Philips and Job Hortop—tell of capture by the Spanish, the death of almost all the others, and ultimate escape. Ingram's story is different. He tells of traveling with surviving companions from the Gulf of Mexico to Cape Breton Island along the Canadian coast, where they were picked up by a French captain eleven months and 3,000 miles later. Ingram's deposi-tion tells about the indigenous people he encountered as well as the flora and fauna seen along his trip, including the elephant.

THE EXAMPLE OF DAVID INGRAM'S DEPOSITION

Beyond the elephants and onces, David Ingram also relates to his inquisitors that he saw "another strange beast bigger than a bear. He had neither head nor neck. His eyes and mouth were in his breast. This beast is very ugly to behold, and cowardly of kind. It beareth a very fine skin like a rat, full of silver hairs" (Hakluyt 1589, 560). Ingram's deposition is in many ways illustrative of American exploration literature in its first years. It has both factual and fantastic elements; it crosses national lines; it relates first-person experiences and yet is mediated by the interests of others; and it has a form not traditionally studied as literature.

Most, though not all, works dealing with the European exploration of early America were not belles lettres. Most were what today fall under the heading of technical and professional communications—commercial reports, military reports, scientific reports, legal depositions. What defines exploration literature is not its form but its purpose. Exploration literature is a rhetorical genre, a group of writings that share a rhetorical purpose, in this case, the desire to convey experiences of a new place to people who have not shared that experience. As Carolyn Miller notes, a rhetorical approach to genre is "centered not on the substance or the form of discourse but on the action it is used to accomplish" (Miller 1984, 151). What action these works of early American exploration wish to accomplish is to explain the New World to people in Europe who have not been there, who did not conceive of such a place until after Christopher Columbus's return from his 1492–1493 voyage to the Caribbean. While such works share a purpose, they have significant differences from one another. Thinking in terms of the basic elements of written rhetoric—writer, audience, subject, and form—the variations in the ways that similar stories will be told are endless. How these elements fit together is what shapes the text (Shields 2005).

The makeup of Ingram's deposition illustrates the wonderfully complex relationship between the various rhetorical elements in a work of exploration literature. To begin with, it is impossible to pinpoint a single author for the text. As a deposition, the text purports to give only the information that Ingram provided under questioning. Though Ingram is generally treated as the work's author, he does not record his own answers. They are recorded by a scribe in response to questions developed by Sir Humphrey Gilbert, who was planning an expedition to Newfoundland, and Sir Francis Walsingham, the secretary of state and a backer of Gilbert's ventures. In other words, the voice is an anonymous third-person voice, and the form of the report is cast by the desires of those who have required Ingram to retell his experiences thirteen years after they happened. In this manner, the audience partly become the author. This can be seen by comparing the fullest known version of Ingram's deposition, which appears in Richard Hakluyt's *The Principall Navigations, Voiages and Discoveries of the English Nation* (1589), with a shorter, manuscript version of the deposition (Quinn 1979, 3: 212–213).

The longer version excludes the questions Ingram was asked, giving the sense that he provided the information spontaneously. The shorter, manuscript version gives each question followed by Ingram's answer. The first questions appear objective—how long he traveled, whether the country is fruitful, what kind of people are there. But by the end, the questions lead the answers in some specific directions: "whether there is any quantitye of gold, silver and pearle, and of other jewelles in that country" and "whether he sawe a beaste farre exceydinge an ox in bignes." In this context, we are unsurprised to read that Ingram "has confessed that there is great aboundaunce of gold sylver and pearle," telling his interrogators as much what they want to hear as he may be (or may not be) telling what he actually encountered. However, in the print version, without the questions, this information comes out in a seemingly natural manner. Ingram comes across as making observations rather than fulfilling European readers' desires. The deposition presents what the interrogators would like it to say, but it does so in a manner that does not make it appear as if the inclusion of this information had been influenced by leading questions. Even the title of the printed piece, "The Relation of David Ingram," gives the impression of storytelling, using the term *relation* rather than *deposition*.

Ingram's answer about the exceedingly large beast in the manuscript version illustrates another way the audience affects the answers given. Ingram fulfills the interrogators' desire to hear of fantastic creatures: "He hath confessed that there be in that country great aboundaunce of a kinde of beaste almost as bigge agayne as an oxe, in shape of body not much differing from an oxe, sayinge that he hath eares of a great bignes, that are in fashion much like unto the eares of a bloodhound having there on very longe heare, and lykewyse on his breast, and other orates of his bodye long heare" (Quinn 1979, 3: 213). To describe this fantastic creature to people who have not encountered it before—a creature we recognize as a bison—Ingram compares it with things familiar to Europeans, like oxen and bloodhounds. The printed version moves along these same lines, including the comparison of the beast's ears to those of bloodhounds, but now saying that these creatures are "as big as two Oxen, in length almost twentie foot." The "Relation" goes on to report that "their hornes be crooked like Rams hornes, their eyes blacke, their haires long, blacke, rough, and shagged as a Goat" (Hakluyt 1589, 560). The comparisons allow the creature to move from being like a long-haired, long-eared ox, to becoming a more fantastic animal, combining features of rams and goats with those of an ox, only twice as big. As we look at this description, having some idea that what is being portrayed is the American bison, and knowing that the description is built from four influences—(1) the question "whether he sawe a beaste farre exceydinge an ox in bignes," (2) Ingram's answer, (3) the scribe's record of his answer, and (4) an apparent rewriting of that answer into a larger "Relation"—it is possible to see the coming together of various author and audience desires and experiences as well as the effects of the textual forms being used. If we accept that Ingram did see the American bison, but also recognize that he describes a creature he would have encountered some thirteen years earlier under stressful circumstances; if we recognize that those experiences are being filtered through a language that would not have had a term that specifically described the American bison; if we recognize that the interrogators (and perhaps Ingram, too) had been exposed to works telling of fantastic creatures in the Americas; and if we recognize that the material was transformed from oral presentation to handwritten scribal record to published relation—if we recognize that all of these elements come together to create the story of David Ingram in North America, we also recognize the complex nature of the rhetorical genre of exploration literature. The elephant in the "Relation" should be seen as a complex creation of several rhetorical elements, not necessarily as a bald-faced lie on Ingram's part.

In this complexity, too, is it any wonder that exploration literature also addresses the line between what is real and what is imagined, between what is fact and what is fiction? The manuscript version ends with an interesting line about Ingram's answers: "Divers other matters of great importaunce he hath confessed (yf they be true) which he sayeth that upon his lyfe, which he offereth to goe to the place, to approve the same true" (Quinn 1979, 3: 213). Coming on the heels of the description of the bison—added to which is the claim that there are other wild animals whose hides are valuable and that there are interesting plants as well, such as a poison apple–like fruit and a tree whose bark tastes like pepper—it seems that Ingram's descriptions of flora and fauna are in question. It is unclear whether his statements about the presence of gold and other precious commodities are brought under this same suspicion. However, by the time this material is rewritten and published in Hakluyt's *Principall Navigations* (1589), the question of the truth of Ingram's information has been dropped. The published "Relation" is presented without the editorial questioning that ends the manuscript. Yet one more step occurs in the story of the Ingram "Relation": Hakluyt left it out of his expanded revision, *The Principal Navigations* (1598–1600). What had changed by 1600 to have Hakluyt drop the "Relation" from his work as he was expanding it? Exploration literature depends not only on when experiences occur and when they are recorded, but also on when they are read about. For all of the complexities of this rhetorical genre, there are patterns that can be seen in exploration literature of the sixteenth century. Most of these patterns can be found in all three of the major periods of English exploration of the Americas from the 1490s until the first decade of the 1600s.

PERIODS OF EXPLORATION AND MODES OF EXPLORATION LITERATURE

The first of these periods follows Christopher Columbus's 1492–1493 voyage. On his return to Spain, a letter about the voyage was published—one of the first

European-wide publishing successes, being published in Barcelona, Rome, Basel, Paris, and Antwerp all by the end of 1493. Soon after, the Italian navigator and merchant John Cabot (Giovanni Caboto) sailed on behalf of England in 1497, explored the coast of Newfoundland, returned to England, and sailed again in 1498. Cabot never returned from this second voyage. In 1508, John Cabot's son Sebastian led an expedition for England that found the entrance to Hudson's Bay. From then until the 1570s, a few English expeditions to the Americas were attempted to explore further and to set up colonies, but without success. And English fishermen began to visit the coast of Newfoundland to catch and salt cod from the time of John Cabot's voyage on, but did not set up any permanent colony.

The second period of English exploration began in the 1570s with Martin Frobisher's 1576, 1577, and 1578 explorations along Baffin Island in search of a northwest passage to China and the East Indies. In 1578, Humphrey Gilbert, who had written *A Discourse of a Discoverie for a New Passage to Cataia* (1576), gained the right to explore and colonize parts of America not already settled by Christians. After a failed voyage in 1578, Gilbert took a second expedition to America in 1583, which claimed Newfoundland in the name of England; however, Gilbert died on his return voyage to England. In 1584, Walter Raleigh, Gilbert's half brother, was granted Gilbert's patent, beginning the era of the 1584 to 1590 Roanoke colonization voyages, including the 1587 "Lost Colony." The end of the Roanoke voyages in 1590 begins the third period of English exploration before the 1607 settlement of Jamestown. During this period, miscellaneous English voyages took place—including Bartholomew Gosnold's 1602 and George Waymouth's 1605 voyages to New England and, most famously, Walter Raleigh's 1595–1596 expedition to Guiana—none resulting in the establishment of permanent English settlements in the New World.

The core of exploration literature consists of works written by the actors in the explorations. Not many of these first-person accounts exist for English explorations during the first period of English involvement of the Americas, from the time of John Cabot's 1497 expedition until Martin Frobisher's voyages in search of the Northwest Passage to the East Indies of the 1570s. The writings that exist about these early explorations are primarily secondhand accounts. But with the Frobisher expedition of 1577–1578 and the Humphrey Gilbert expedition of 1583 to explore and colonize Newfoundland, a number of first-person accounts began to appear, sometimes by the leaders of the expeditions, sometimes by expedition members; sometimes as stand-alone publications, sometimes as parts of collections of voyages, and sometimes as both. As with any work of exploration literature, all of these shared the rhetorical feature of explaining the New World to people who had not traveled there. However, as the context for this explanation differed from writer to writer, so did the form that the explanation took.

No English exploration led to the successful establishment of a permanent English colony in the Americas during all three periods. The lack of success helped set up several different modes within the genre of exploration literature. In these modes can be seen the aesthetic or formal element of the works: while we may group works by emphasizing their rhetorical context (rhetorical genres) or by emphasizing their aesthetic forms (aesthetic or formal genre), all works have both elements. Depending on the rhetorical situation of the writer, especially in relationship to the reader, works use different rhetorical strategies, which lead writers to use different forms. If the writer were the leader of an expedition writing to the backers of that expedition, an apologia might be typical. However, if the writer were only a member of the expedition but not its leader, one typical strategy would be to portray an unsuccessful expedition in tragic terms, often presenting the leader as a tragic hero or protagonist. However, if a member of an expedition is a central member of a financial backer's circle, he may write a piece that is less narrative and more descriptive to highlight the commodities of the newly explored land. All these modes must fulfill their rhetorical purposes while describing places and peoples that readers had never encountered before.

One work often contains two different modes to convey what the writer feels needs to be expressed about the New World for readers. For example, an apologia, the mode used by leaders of expeditions that did not pan out as well as hoped, may also use the descriptive mode to highlight the value, particularly the economic value, of the New World. With two other modes—tragedy, usually written by a member of the expedition to explain the expedition's failure, and promotional narration, usually written during an expedition or at the end of the first voyage of a multivoyage exploration—these form the four main modes that first-person writers of exploration literature used during the sixteenth century. All four—apologia, promotion narrative, descriptive mode, and the mode of tragedy—deserve further elaboration, but first it is important to understand the single most important literary figure in the history of English exploration literature, Richard Hakluyt, whose collections chronicled all three periods of exploration and especially encouraged the third period.

Richard Hakluyt's *Principal Navigations*

Collections of voyages illustrate the point that English exploration literature about the Americas did not occur in isolation. The most famous of these collections is one in English, Richard Hakluyt's *Principal Navigations*. While Hakluyt emphasizes English explorations—including, in the third section, English explorations to the Americas—both the format of his work and its subject matter connect Hakluyt's collection to works by writers from other countries in other languages. The form of Hakluyt's collection has its roots in at least two earlier collections. The first is Peter Martyr d'Anghiera's *Decades,* a collection of narratives written in Latin about Spain's discovery and settlement of the Americas from Columbus's first voyage in 1492 through the 1520s. Martyr, an Italian historian working in the Spanish court, began his *Decades* in 1501, publishing the first installment in 1511. In 1530, all eight of the *Decades* were gathered together and published under the title *De Orbe Novo* (*Of the New World*). The work had widespread circulation, being translated into French, Italian, German, and in 1555, into English by Richard Eden, under the title *The Decades of the Newe Worlde or West India.* And in 1587, while in Paris, Hakluyt brought out a new Latin edition of the work. Martyr's *Decades* influenced Hakluyt not only by providing a model of how one might gather accounts from actors in the expeditions but also by giving prominence to Spain's conquests in America. Hakluyt's work would be a response to that Spanish prominence. The second major collection of voyages is Giovanni Battista Ramusio's three-volume *Delle Navigationi et Viaggi* (*Of the Navigations and Voyages*), published between 1550 and 1559. As would Hakluyt in *Principall Navigations,* Ramusio published accounts of European voyages made around the world, with his third volume being about voyages to the Americas. Ramusio, like Martyr, was Italian, but unlike Martyr, he worked from Italy, in particular Venice. Because of his subject matter, Ramusio's third volume on the Americas highlights accounts of the Spanish in the New World but is not exclusively about Spain in America.

In fact, Hakluyt's first forays into publishing rely a good deal on Ramusio's *Delle Navigationi et Viaggi.* In 1580, Hakluyt persuaded John Florio to translate Jacques Cartier's collected narratives about his explorations in Canada during the 1530s as *A Shorte and Briefe Narration of the Two Navigations and Discoveries to the Northweast Partes Called Newe Fraunce* (1580). Then, in 1582, Hakluyt published *Divers Voyages,* his first collection of travel narratives. Like Ramusio, whose *Delle Navigationi et Viaggi* provided sources for several pieces included in *Divers Voyages,* and like Martyr, whose *Decades* Hakluyt would soon publish in a new Latin edition, Hakluyt created his work using firsthand accounts though he had never seen the worlds being described firsthand.

While all three collections are edited by people who had not been to the places described, Hakluyt's differs from the other two because Hakluyt has a different rhetorical purpose for his work than do Martyr or Ramusio. Martyr records the ventures of the Spanish as the appointed chronicler for the Spanish court. Ramusio published his collection of travels from the vantage point of Italy, which had engaged several people in American exploration, but always seeming to be working for other countries—Christopher Columbus for Spain, Amerigo Vespucci for Spain and Portugal, John Cabot for England, or Giovanni da Verrazano for France. Hakluyt, on the other hand, assembled his *Divers Voyages*—as well as his expanded *Principal Navigations* (1598–1600) and most of the other works he helped publish—in order to encourage English exploration and colonization of the New World. Therefore, Hakluyt emphasizes the primacy of the English in American exploration, something few historians of the day would imagine doing. These are, for Hakluyt, the relations "Touching the Discoverie of America" that were "Made First of All by Our Englishmen, and Afterward by the Frenchmen and Britons." What these discoveries are, however, defines English exploration in a geographically limited manner.

For Hakluyt, English explorations—and the colonies that ought to follow from those explorations—are to be found in the northern parts of America. In the dedicatory epistle to Philip Sidney in *Divers Voyages,* Hakluyt "the Portingales time to be out of date, and that the nakedness of the Spaniards, and their long hidden secretes are nowe at length espied," so "we of England may share and part stakes (if wee will our selves) both with the Spaniarde and the Portingale in part of America, and other regions as yet undiscovered" (Hakluyt 1582, sig. ¶r). England can still take part in the exploration and settlement of America, if it has the will to do so. Hakluyt explains that he met a Portuguese geographer, "most privie to all the discoveries of his nation, who wondered that those blessed countries, from the point of Florida Northward, were all this while unplanted by Christians" (Hakluyt 1582, sig. ¶v). In other words, the Spanish and Portuguese, to that time the main players in American exploration and colonization, had left the lands north of Spanish Florida free for the English to take. Hakluyt then goes on to lay out the history of exploration in this region through documents, beginning with the 1496 letters patent from King Henry VII to John Cabot (Quinn 1974, 2: 338–340). Through his collection of documents, his introduction to those documents, and even their arrangement in *Divers Voyages,* Hakluyt explains the New World to his readers with the intent of inspiring English exploration and colonization of the northern parts of America.

Hakluyt's magnum opus, the two editions of *Principal Navigations,* follows a similar pattern but is much more complex in conception and context. First, *Principal Navigations* tells not only about America but also about British expeditions—as well as some by people of other European nations—throughout the newly expanded and circumnavigated world. But in both editions, Hakluyt uses the same general layout—first voyages to the south and southeast, that is, to Africa, Asia, including the Middle East; then voyages to the north and northeast, that is, to the polar regions and to Russia; and finally to the west, southwest, and northwest, that is, to the Americas. In the 1598–1600 edition, the voyages to the south and southeast are reversed with those to the north and northeast, but the overall effect is the same, building from attempts to span the globe, especially to find a practical route for the English to China and the East Indies, to the more promising possibilities of reaching East Asia via the Americas. And if the Americas provide their own riches that England can exploit, all the better. Hakluyt expands his history of British exploration in America not only by including materials from expeditions that occurred after the 1582 publication of *Divers Voyages* but also by extending British primacy in the discoveries of these lands. He begins the third section of the 1589 edition and the third volume of the 1598–1600 edition with the story written by David Powell of Prince Madoc, a Welsh prince who traveled in 1170 to a previously unknown land to the west, across the ocean, where he plants a colony of Welsh who have grown tired of the fighting at home. This legend Hakluyt accepts as truth, especially because it gives the English, who have control over the Welsh, the right to claim American discovery before the Spanish. As Powell writes and Hakluyt excerpts: "This land must needs be some part of that Countrey of which the Spanyards affirme themselves to be the first finders since Hannos time. For by reason, and order of Cosmographie, this land to which Madoc came, must needs be some part of Nova Hispania or Florida. Whereupon it is manifest that that country was long before by Britaines discovered, afore either Columbus or Americus Vesputius led any Spanyards thither" (Hakluyt 1589, 506). At the time Hakluyt published *Principall Navigations* (1589), there was an ongoing attempt to establish a British colony in North America, on Roanoke Island along the coast of what is today North Carolina, and definitely in territory that Spain would have seen as part of Spanish Florida. The rhetorical need for expanded and more complex content in *Principal Navigations* (1598–1600) was, at least in part, a response to a more complex context.

Hakluyt also expands beyond North America in *Principal Navigations*. In the third volume of the 1598–1600 edition, he includes voyages to the northern reaches of North America, in the area of Newfoundland, unquestionably outside the range of Spanish Florida, and to the North Carolina coast, unsettled by the Spanish but explored and claimed by them. But he also includes voyages to Spanish Florida, along the Spanish-controlled Gulf of Mexico, along the California coast, to central and South America, and throughout the Caribbean. While many of the relations of these voyages into Spanish claims are about Spanish expeditions and are written by Spanish writers, many others are about British expeditions, including Walter Raleigh's voyage to Guiana in 1595 and Drake's 1579 landing along the California coast during his circumnavigation of the globe. Hakluyt's expanded vision of British connections to the Americas begins in the 1589 edition of *Principal Navigations*. The rhetorical context for this literary foray into Spanish America must be, at least in part, the open hostility of the 1588 Spanish Armada, a failed start at Roman Catholic Spain's invading Protestant England. Until this point, Hakluyt suggested that there were sufficient and rich enough areas not under Spanish claim in North America. Such a view was outlined most fully in Hakluyt's one extant work completely in his own voice, the manuscript written for Queen Elizabeth and her court, "A Particuler Discourse Concerninge the Greate Necessitie and Manifolde Comodyties that are Like to Growe to the Realme of Englande by the Westerne Discoveries Lately Attempted, Written in the Yere 1584." This "Discourse of Western Planting" is most often cited to show that many English of Hakluyt's time believed their country was dangerously overcrowded. But the "Discourse of Western Planting" acts as a transition between the picture in *Divers Voyages* of a northern part of the Americas beyond Spanish Florida available for English colonization and the invasion, at least the textual invasion, of Spanish America by the English in *The Principal Navigations*. In the "Discourse of Western Planting," Hakluyt describes much of the Spanish Caribbean as being lightly populated at best (Quinn 1979, 3: 82, 92). If the English move into North America, the Spanish, which look strong in the Caribbean, are in fact so weak that the English can take whatever part the Spanish do not already posess without fearing reprisal from them. Having already moved in this direction in "Discourse of Western Planting," Hakluyt can suggest in the post-Armada world that England may want to look farther afield than just those lands north of Spain's Florida. Hakluyt's exploration of America grows rhetorically as the historical context surrounding the publication of his collections of voyages changes.

Promotional Narrative

The most positive in outlook, writings using the mode of promotional narration are often the ones that become almost mythic for later readers. The most famous of these among early English accounts might be Arthur Barlowe's description of the expedition led by himself and Philip Amadas to Roanoke Island on behalf of Walter Raleigh, the first of the Roanoke colonization voyages that occurred between 1584 and 1590. Written some months after the expedition's return in the fall of 1584, the report did not appear in print until it was included in Hakluyt's *Principall Navigations* (1589) as "The First Voyage Made to the Coastes of America, with Two Barkes, Wherein were Captaines Master Philip Amadas, and Master Arthur Barlowe, Who Discovered Part of the Countrey, Now Called Virginia, Anno 1584." It tells of nothing but goodness found along the Outer Banks of present-day North Carolina, including on Roanoke Island. For example, on first coming along the Outer Banks, Barlowe writes, "we found shole water, which smelt so sweetely, and was so strong a smell, as if we had been in the midst of some delicate garden." Or, having tried some experiments in planting, Barlowe writes, "the soile is the most plentifull, sweete, fruitfull, and wholesome of the world." The people encountered, too, are portrayed as being almost prelapsarian—as if they were still in the Garden of Eden before the fall of humankind. "Wee found the people most gentle, loving, and faithfull," writes Barlowe, "void of all guile, and treason, and such as lived after the manner of the golden age. The earth bringeth foorth all things in aboundance, as in the first creation, without toil or labour" (Hakluyt 1589, 728, 731). As one of the leaders of the expedition, sent to scout this part of the New World as a precursor to further colonization efforts, Barlow has little need for the apologia. He has found what he came for, and can report it in glowing terms.

However, the rhetorical situation gives Barlowe reason to use the narrative mode. Portraying a world moving through time, rather than the static or eternal world of the descriptive mode, allows Barlowe to show this as just the start of a colonization effort. Even so, the narrative form has built into it the underpinnings of how the view of this place as Edenic might not be completely true. One such point in the narrative that mixes the Edenic and the non-Edenic comes immediately after Barlowe's description of the people and land of Roanoke Island as part of the golden age. As the king's wife serves the English explorers a meal, two or three men come in from hunting with their bows and arrows. The Englishmen look at each other and reach for their weapons, but the king's wife chases the hunters away, breaking their arrows. Then, as evening approaches, the king's wife is disappointed because the English head back to their boats to sleep and will not stay in the village:

> She, perceiving our jealousie, was much grieved, and sent divers men, and thirtie women, to sitte all night on the bankes side by us, and sent us into our boates fine mattes to cover us from the rayne, using very many wordes to intreat us to rest in their houses: but because wee were fewe men, and if wee had miscarried, the voyage had beene in very great daunger, we durst not adventure any thing, although there was no cause of doubt: for a more kinde and loving people, there can not be found in the world, as farre as we have hitherto had triall. (Hakluyt 1589, 731)

By laying out the story in narrative form, Barlowe has to give the good with the bad: even though he wants to portray these people as the finest ever met, he and the rest of the crew still could not trust them completely. The future portrayed is one in which life will probably go on wonderfully between the English and the Native Americans, but the possibility of trouble quietly underlies.

This mythically Edenic New World of Barlowe's is reinforced by Ralph Lane, one of the leaders of the next Roanoke expedition in 1585. In a September 3, 1585, letter to Richard Hakluyt from Roanoke Island, Lane writes what has become one of the most repeated lines in North Carolina culture: "We have discovered the maine [land] to bee the goodliest soile under the cope of heaven" (Hakluyt 1589, 793). This line has had such mythic power that it recurs frequently in modern attempts to promote North Carolina. Like Barlowe, Lane writes about an ongoing venture, and, as such, he conjoins sections in the descriptive mode with ones in the narrative mode in his promotional narrative. Most of this element has been edited out by Hakluyt, but one part that remains is the narrative of a wished-for future for Virginia, the name given to all of the English claims by the expeditions under Walter Raleigh's patent. Lane writes that "if Virginia had but Horses and Kine in some reasonable proportion, I dare assure my selfe being inhabited with English, no realme in Christendome were comparable to it" (Hakluyt 1589, 793). This imagined future allows the current leader of the Virginia expedition to portray the New World in glowing terms to his backers in England (Shields 2003).

Apologia

As the context of Ralph Lane's writing changed, so did the mode of his writing. In June 1586, Ralph Lane returned to England with his remaining colonists, having left Roanoke Island with Francis Drake because of a lack of supplies—supplies that showed up, according to Hakluyt, some two weeks later (Hakluyt 1589, 748). Now in writing about the 1585–1586 colony, Lane does so in an atmosphere in which many people saw the expedition, under Lane's leadership, as a failure. In response to the new context, Lane changes his mode of writing exploration literature from using promotional narrative to explain the Virginia colony to those who were not there to using apology (Moran 2003). A more complex context creates a more complex rhetorical strategy than in the September 1585 letter. Lane must continue to show Raleigh's Virginia as worth pursuing in order to meet the desires of his employer, but he must also show that there was good reason for abandoning "the goodliest and most pleasing territorie of the world" (Hakluyt 1589, 793). To do so, Lane uses a narrative mode similar to that in the September letter, an imagined successful enterprise, but this time the conditional element of the imagined enterprise is not some future date but the past of the actual enterprise under different circumstances, circumstances that were outside of Lane's control.

In "An Account of the Particularities of the Imployments of the English Men Left in Virginia by Sir Richard Greenevill Under the Charge of Master Ralfe Lane Generall of the Same, from the 17. of August, 1585, Vntill the 18. of June 1586," Lane tells what he would have liked to have done in order to connect the Roanoke Island colony with the Chesapeake Bay:

> My meaning was further at the head of the River in the place of my descent where I would have left my boates to have raysed a sconse with a small trench, and a pallisado upon the top of it, in the which, and in the garde of my boates I would have left five and twentie, or thirtie men, with the rest would I have marched with as much victuall as every man could have carried, with their mattocks, spades, and axes, two dayes journey. In the ende of my marche upon some convenient plot would I have raised another sconse according to the former, where I would have left 15. or 20. And if it would have fallen out conveniently, in the way I woulde have raised my sayd sconse upon some corne fielde, that my companie might have lived upon it.

> And so I would have holden this course of insconsing every two dayes march, until I had bene arrived at the Bay or Porte he [Menatonon, a Native American king] spake of: which finding to be worth the possession, I would there have raised a mayne forte, both for the defence of the harboroughs, and our shipping also. (Hakluyt 1589, 793)

However, as Lane notes to Raleigh, the successful imagined enterprise could have happened only "if your supplie had come before the end of April" (Hakluyt 1589, 793). Lane would never have abandoned the goodness of Virginia, and would have been able to increase Raleigh's control over a larger area of the region only if there had been access to more supplies than Lane had. But to ensure that Lane does not lay the blame at the feet of his employer, Raleigh, he ends by reminding his readers that it is God who chooses whether such success is to be achieved or not:

> Thus sir, I have though simply, yet truely set downe unto you, what my labour with the rest of the gentlemen, and poore men of our company, (not without both payne, and peril which the lorde in his mercy many wayes delivered us from) could

yeelde unto you, which might have bene performed in some more perfection, if the lorde had bene pleased that onely that which you had provided for us had at the first bene left with us, or that he had not in his eternall providence now at the last set some other course in these things. (Hakluyt 1589, 742)

Lane allows for future colonization of Virginia by Raleigh because the riches that can be found there—including the pearls and copper (and, by implication through copper, silver)—are within reach, but only if God allows it to be so.

The Descriptive Mode

Another work coming out of the 1585–1586 Roanoke colonization attempt illustrates the coming together of different modes in order to explain the New World to readers in England. *A Briefe and True Report of the New Found Land of Virginia,* written by the Elizabethan scientist and mathematician Thomas Hariot, who accompanied Lane on the 1585–1586 Roanoke Island expedition, was first published in 1588 and was then reprinted as part of Hakluyt's 1589 edition of the *Principall Navigations.* A description of the commodities, flora, fauna, and Native Americans of the region around Roanoke Island, *A Briefe and True Report* begins with a note from Lane followed by Hariot's impassioned defense of both the lands explored and the people doing the exploration. Before he begins any of his observations about Roanoke Island's riches, Hariot writes:

> There have bene divers and variable reportes, with some slaunderous and shamefull speaches bruited abroad by many that returned from thence [i.e., Roanoke Island]. Especially of that discoverie which was made by the Colonie transported by Sir Richard Greenvill in the yeere 1585, being of all the others the most principall and as yet of most effect, the time of their abode in the countrey being a whole yeere, when as in the other voiage before they staied but six weekes, and the others after were onely for supplie and transportation, nothing more being discovered then had bene before. Which reports have not done a litle wrong to many that otherwise would have also favoured and adventured in the action, to the honour and benefite of our nation, besides the particular profite and credite which would redound to themselves the dealers therein; as I by the sequell of events to the shame of those that have avouched the contrary shall be manifest. (Hakluyt 1589, 749)

Hariot then goes on to speak about members of the 1585–1586 expedition who have spoken out against the lands of Virginia: "Of our companie that returned some for their misdemeanour and ill dealing in the countrey, have bene there worthily punished, who by reason of their bad natures, have maliciously not onely spoken ill of their Gouernours, but for their sakes slaundered the countrey it selfe" (Hakluyt 1589, 749). Through this introduction, Hariot makes certain that his readers understand that his work is a defense of the land of Virginia. At the same time, the work is also an apology for Ralph Lane. By placing the slanders against the land on a par with the slanders against the leaders of the expedition—that is, against Lane—any argument in favor of the land's goodness is an implied statement of the expedition's good leadership as well. Hariot's *Briefe and True Report* serves as a tacit apologia for Lane's leadership of the 1585–1586 expedition.

While the prefatory material is an act of apologetics, the main body of Hariot's text uses the third mode found in exploration literature, the descriptive mode. In the descriptive mode, some of the problems in meeting the central goal of exploration literature can be most easily seen. Hariot begins his description of what was found in Virginia by describing "Marchantable commodities." Included in this list of items a colony might sell profitably back to England are silk, flax, hemp, alum, *wapei*, pitch, tar, rosin, turpentine, sassafras, cedar, wine, oil, furs, deer skins, civet cats, iron, copper, pearls, sweet gums, dyes of various kinds, and woad (Hakluyt 1589, 750–752). It is interesting that almost all these commodities are items found in Europe or those that Europeans had found in other parts of the world. The riches of the New World are found in its ability to replicate profitable commodities found in the Old World, including items less familiar to us today such as the musk of the civet cat used in perfumes, sweet gums used medicinally, and the indigo-like dye of woad. It is assumed that readers in England would understand America only as it matched up to Europe, not as a place special unto itself, with its own special commodities. The one exception on Hariot's list seems to be *wapeih*, "a kind of earth so called by the naturall inhabitants, very like to Terra sigillata, and having bene refined, it hath bene found by some of our Phisitions and Chirurgions to bee of the same kind of virtue, and more effectuall. The inhabitants use it very much for the cure of sores and wounds: there is in divers places great plentie, and in some places of a blew sort" (Hakluyt 1589, 751). While wapeih is identified as special to that part of America where the Virginia colony has been settled, its value comes from being refined into a medicine similar to one found on the Greek island of Lemnos, terra sigillata.

Even in his description of everyday items in "The Second Part of Such Commodities as Virginia Is Knowen to Yeeld, for Victuall and Sustenance of Mans Life, Usually Fed Upon by the Naturall Inhabitants: as Also by Us, During the Time of our Aboad," Hariot finds it necessary to equate Native American crops with English crops. For some items, the identity is fairly straightforward: "*Macocquer*, according to theyr severall formes, called by us *Pompions, Mellions*, and *Gourds*, because they are of the like formes as those kindes in England." For others, there is now an English term for a formerly exotic plant: "*Pagatowr*, a kinde of graine so called by the inhabitants: the same in the West Indies is called *Mayze*: English men call it *Guinney wheat*, or *Turkie wheat*, according to the names of the countries from whence the like hath beene brought." But for some items, the identification with a European counterpart seems to be a stretch in order to convey the experience of this food to those who had not shared it: "*Okindgier*, called by us Beanes, because in greatnesse and partly in shape they are like to be the beanes in England, saving that they are flatter, of more divers colours, and some pide [pied]. The leafe also of the stemme is much different. In taste they are altogether as good as our English peaze" (Hakluyt 1589, 753). These beans do not taste like beans, more like dried peas, and they come in a variety of different colors and growing on a plant that isn't much like the European bean plant. The simile of okindgier with the English broad beans is a necessary way to explain this American food (most likely the *Phaseolus vulgaris,* or common bean, indigenous to the Americas) to an audience unfamiliar with it. Exploration literature, particularly when using the descriptive mode, linguistically turns the exotic into the familiar.

One addition to exploration literature using the descriptive mode is the use of illustrations. In 1590, the Flemish engraver Theodor de Bry published an illustrated edition of Hariot's *Briefe and True Report* in Frankfurt. De Bry used as the basis of his engravings the watercolors that John White had made during the 1585–1586 expedition. What we see in De Bry's engravings is the visual equivalent of Hariot's explaining the North Carolina Algonquian Indian culture of the Roanoke Island vicinity in English terms. White's watercolors probably did a good job of capturing the look of the Algonquians, their villages, and their culture. However, to turn these watercolors into engravings, De Bry had to work within the limitations of the technology. The multicolored palette of White's paintings become black and white in the engravings. More significantly, the rounded, soft edges of White's paintings become the harder edges of De Bry's engravings. The effect is best seen in the engravings of individual Algonquians, in which muscles become much more defined, faces become much more European, tattoos are played down, and blank backgrounds are filled in with some details provided by White's other drawings but also with standard European ideas of such things as trees and forests. De Bry interprets America for his audience using the technology and conventions available to him as a European.

The Mode of Tragedy

A fourth mode used within first-person exploration literature during the sixteenth century is the tragedy. Writers who were members of expeditions but not the expeditions' leaders most often use this mode. It allowed them to illustrate the failures of the expedition, placing the blame on human shortcomings, in particular those of the expedition leader. No major work from the Roanoke expeditions uses this mode as a central feature. As Ralph Lane's use of apologia and Thomas Hariot's opening to *Briefe and True Report* show, this was not because people were not blaming the failure of the 1585–1586 expedition on Lane. But the literature about the Roanoke colonies seems to have been tightly controlled by Raleigh, Hakluyt, and their circle. However, there is a good example of the use of tragedy in the writings about the 1583 expedition to Newfoundland led by Raleigh's half brother, Humphrey Gilbert. Gilbert received the patent to explore and settle North America in 1578 and at the end of that year made an unsuccessful voyage in an attempt to use his patent, a voyage about which little is known. Gilbert was unable to try to sail to America again until 1583. With a fleet of four ships, he sailed to Newfoundland, where he claimed a settlement at St. John's Bay, a settlement that turned out to be temporary, but at which Gilbert made his claim on the land. After taking possession, Gilbert led his fleet on a reconnaissance trip southward along the coast, heading back to England at the insistence of the sailors who were afraid the expedition was running out of provisions. On the return voyage home, in a storm off the Azores, Gilbert and his ship went down.

One source about Gilbert's voyage is the narrative by Edward Hayes (or Haies) first published in Hakluyt's *Principall Navigations* of 1589, "A Report of the Voyage and Success thereof, Attempted in the Yeere of our Lord, 1583. by Sir Humfrey Gilbert, Knight, with Other Gentlemen Assisting Him in that Action, Intended to Discover and to Plant Christian Inhabitants in place Convenient, upon Those Large and Ample Countries Extended Northward from the Cape of Florida, Lying Under Very Temperate Climes, Esteemed Fertile and Rich in Minerals, Yet Not in the Actual Possession of Any Christian Prince." As the title Hakluyt gives this piece indicates, the voyage is to be seen as a success. And much of what Hayes writes does give promise for future expeditions. Hayes writes that the land, while it may suffer from a bit of cold weather, provides "incredible quantitie, and no lesse varietie of kindes of fish in the sea and fresh waters." It also provides the riches of naval stores, good soil for agriculture, and "the grasse and hearbe doth fat sheepe in very short space, proved by English merchants which have caried sheepe thither for fresh vitaile, and had them raised exceeding fat in lesse then 3. weekes." The most important commodity to make the colonization of the area economically feasible was metal—iron, copper, silver, or gold. It is on this point that the break between Hayes, the survivor of the voyage, and Gilbert, its lost leader, occurs. According to Hayes, "the General was most curious in the search of mettals," and while Hayes says that iron, lead, and copper definitely were found, he holds back about silver. Gilbert is pleased when the expedition's mineralogist, who found "some sorts of oare, seeming rather to be yron then other mettall. The next time he found oare, which with no small shew of contentment he delivered unto the General, using protestation, that if silver were the thing which might satisfie the General and his followers, there it was, advising him to seek no further" (Hakluyt 1589, 689–690). Hayes and Gilbert do not reject the possibility that they have found silver, but they reserve judgment until it can be tried aboard ship away from the prying eyes of the Portuguese, Spanish, and French fishermen working out of St. Johns along the Grand Banks.

But it is at this point that the story turns. The ship with the mineral samples onboard sinks, and the men aboard the remaining ships insist on returning to England. Gilbert agrees, and the ships turn toward home. Then Hayes plays off his growing belief that the ore found—then lost at sea—was valuable against what he labels the tragic end of his story. "Leaving the issue of this good hope unto God, who knoweth the trueth only, and can at his good pleasure bring the same to light," writes Hayes in reference to the possibility of mineral wealth in Newfoundland, "I will hasten to the end of this tragedie, which must be knit up in the person of our Generall." The tragedy is that Gilbert refused the good advice to stay aboard Hayes's own ship during the storms they were experiencing. Instead, Gilbert insisted on returning to the smaller frigate he had been traveling on, which, as Hayes describes, "was overcharged upon their deckes, with fights, nettings, and small artillerie, too cumbersome for so small a boate, that was to passe through the Ocean sea at that season of the yeere, when by course we might expect much storme and foule weather." At this point, Hayes reveals Gilbert's tragic flaw: "And in very trueth, hee was urged to be so over hard, by hard reports given of him, that he was afraid of the sea, albeit this was rather rashness, then advised resolution, to preferre the winde of a vaine report to the weight of his owne life" (Hakluyt 1589, 695). Gilbert, who as commander of the expedition has the responsibility to keep himself safe to lead the expedition home, puts himself in harm's way because he has heard rumors that people think he is scared of the sea. As Hayes and others predict, Gilbert loses his life in a storm while on the least seaworthy of the expedition's remaining ships.

Such a tragedy would not be a useful rhetorical mode if it did not in some way address the exploratory element of the writing. Therefore, Hayes finishes his narrative by explaining fully the problems that the tragic figure of Gilbert brought on. Hayes gives Gilbert his due, stating that Gilbert "remain[ed] firme and resolute in a purpose by all pretence honest and godly, as was this, to discover, possesse, and to reduce unto the service of God, and Christian pietie, those remote and heathen countries of America." "Even so," continues Hayes, "he may justly be taxed of temerity, and presumption." The presumption Hayes points out is that when there was neither a permanent settlement made nor a proven certainty of commodities, Gilbert was still willing to gamble his own and his fellow investor's money on an "imagined good" (Hakluyt 1589, 696). The temerity for Hayes is shown in Gilbert's fear of losing of face, not only as in the example given here but in not being willing to face his fellow investors with the possibility of a second less than successful voyage. What the tragedy allows for Hayes—and for Hakluyt, who publishes Hayes's account, and for Raleigh who acquired the patents to explore and settle North America following the death of his half brother—is the ability to see the potential in North America, albeit unproven, despite Gilbert's failed expedition. The failure rests on the tragic flaws of the now dead expedition leader, not on the land itself.

It is worth noting that while English exploration writing of the sixteenth century did not depend much on the tragic mode, it had great play in writings about Spanish exploration of North America during the same period. Tragedy defines the first half of Alvar Núñez Cabeza de Vaca's *Relación* (1542), in which the leader of the expedition, Pánfilo de Narváez, dies because of his own arrogance, leaving what remained of the expedition shipwrecked along the Texas coast. It defines the Gentleman of Elvas's portrayal of Hernando de Soto leading his expedition farther and farther into the interior of North America and into more and more danger, published in 1551 as *Relación Verdadera…de la Florida.* It defines how Pedro de Castañeda characterizes Francisco Vázquez de Coronado during the 1540s expedition in his manuscript narrative of the expedition written around twenty years later (Castañeda 1964). All three works were written by members of the expeditions they wrote about, but none of the authors were the leaders of the expeditions. Both Narváez and de Soto died during their expeditions, as in a classic, Aristotelian tragedy, but Coronado did not; however, Castañeda portrays Coronado as having lost his reputation, never being given the chance to engage in exploration the rest of his days. And it is interesting to note that in 1609, as the Jamestown colony was just getting established, Hakluyt chose to publish his own translation of the Gentleman of Elvas's tragedy of Hernando de Soto as *Virginia Richly Valued.* Using the rhetorical strategy of the tragedy—to blame the expedition leader while retaining the reputation of the land—and renaming the land explored as Virginia, in which "are truly observed the riches and fertilitie of those parts," Hakluyt is able to use this story to his own ends to promote English exploration and colonization.

The Third Period of English Exploration

These modes carry on into the third period of English exploration, and exploration writing, in the era before the 1607 permanent settlement of Jamestown. In addition to the regular voyages of Newfoundland fishermen, English venturers sent out several expeditions, none with long-term success in terms of establishing permanent colonies. Among these were two expeditions that both explored along the New England coast and that produced pamphlet accounts of their ventures, one led by Bartholomew Gosnold and Bartholomew Gilbert in 1602 and one led by George Waymouth in 1605. The pamphlet about the Gosnold and Gilbert expedition, *A Briefe and True Relation of the Discoverie of the North Part of Virginia,* is a fascinating mix of works. In its title is hidden the context of the work. The expedition went to New England, which at that time went under the name "the North Part of Virginia," and which continued to be under Walter Raleigh's patent for exploration and settlement going back to the 1580s. Despite the title, the expedition went without Raleigh's permission. Raleigh sanctioned the explorers after the fact, having discovered them upon their return and having confiscated the sassafras they had brought back. Addressing *A Briefe and True Relation of the Discoverie of the North Part of Virginia* to Raleigh is an appeasement in response to having been caught making a voyage without the explicit approval needed under his patent. At the same time, the work helps promote Raleigh's continued claim by illustrating that venturers are going to the lands under his patent seemingly on his behalf.

The mixed nature of *A Briefe and True Relation* adds to the sense that Raleigh has been and remains active in his New World lands. The relation of the title is by John Brereton (under whose name it is cataloged), but the work contains much more than just Brereton's narrative. Following the initial narrative of the voyage is a list of commodities the expedition members saw in the New World. Next comes the one-page "A Briefe Note of the Sending Another Barke this Present Yeere 1602. by the Honourable Knight, Sir Walter Ralegh, For the Searching Out of His Colonie in Virginia," about an expedition led by Samuel Mace to search for the "Lost Colony" of 1586. The first edition of the pamphlet finished with a two-part piece on the commodities of the northern reaches of Raleigh's Virginia and on the possibility of a passage to the Pacific, written by Edward Hayes, the same Edward Hayes who had accompanied Humphrey Gilbert in 1583 and written the report on that expedition. In this form, *A Briefe and True Relation of the Discoverie of the North Part of Virginia* combines the promotional narratives of the Gosnold and Gilbert expedition on the northern Virginia territories and of the Mace expedition to the southern Virginia territories (both telling about bringing back sassafras, "a tree of high price and profit") with the eternally fixed value of these New World lands given in the descriptive mode of the other two sections (Brereton 1602, 7).

It appears, though, that *A Briefe and True Relation* was making a stir. A second edition soon appeared, with the exact same material as in the first edition, but added to it several more pieces, making it more like a miniature anthology by Richard Hakluyt, who may have had a hand in *A Briefe and True Relation's* publication. The first added piece is by Richard Hakluyt, the elder, cousin to the editor, called "Inducements to the Liking of the Voyage Intended Towards Virginia in 40. and 42. Degrees of Latitude, Written in 1585," a list of reasons—both spiritual and commercial—why England should engage in colonization of the Americas, in the descriptive mode. Next is added "A Briefe Note of the Corne, Fowles, Fruits and Beasts of the Inland of Florida on the Backside of Virginia," taken from the Gentleman of Elvas's *Relación Verdadera*. Continuing on in the same vein, "A Note of Such Commodities as Are Found in Florida, Next Adjoining unto the South Part of Virginia" is given next, taken from the writings of Rene Laudonnière's accounts of the French voyages to North America in the 1560s, and then an extract from the section "Merchantable Commodities Found in the South Part of Virginia" of Thomas Hariot's *A Briefe and True Report*. The material added to the second edition of *A Briefe and True Relation of the Discoverie of the North Part of Virginia* is rounded out with several brief notes on commodities found in Spanish and French Florida and in English Virginia, all "gathered out of the works...of such as were personall travellers in those countries" (Brereton 1602, 46). In all, the descriptive mode has been expanded in *A Briefe and True Relation*. The works in the second edition range from pieces connected with Spanish and French explorations in the 1540s and 1560s, to one by a member of the 1583 Gilbert expedition, to items from the original Raleigh ventures of the 1580s, to the ventures of the present day of the pamphlet in 1602. Together, the pieces of description concerning the commodities found in North America give added value to Raleigh's claims, building on the promotional narratives that highlight how the work of exploration, settlement, and commercial exploitation of Raleigh's Virginia, from what is today Georgia and the Carolinas to the coast of Canada, is ongoing and not a lost piece of the past.

In these last years before permanent settlement finally came about, it is impossible to tell whether the writing about it expresses what readers of the day (and what writers) would have seen as believable assertions of control over English claims in the New World or simply claims of control in writing—perhaps flailing claims—in hopes that to say it might make it true. Whichever way, James Rosier's pamphlet *A True Relation of the Most Prosperous Voyage Made... in the Discovery of the Land of Virginia* (1605) about an expedition sponsored by merchants from Plymouth interested cod fishing and by Sir Thomas Arundell, looking to found a colony for English Catholics in America. With his imprisonment in the Tower of London in 1603, Raleigh was in no position to defend his letters patent, opening the field for expeditions such as Waymouth's.

Rosier's promotional narrative fulfills the main rhetorical requirement of exploration literature—explaining the new experience to those who had not shared in it. For example, Rosier writes about some of the New World foods introduced to them by Native Americans, foods that were not part of his world—or familiar to his palate—back in England:

> They shewed uus great cups made very wittily of barke, in forme almost square, full of a red berry about the bignesse of a bullis, which they did eat, and gave us by handfuls; of which (though I liked not the taste) yet I kept some, because I would by no meanes but accept their kindnesse. They shewed me likewise a great piece of fish, whereof I tasted, and it was fat like Porpoise; and another kinde of great scaly fish, broiled on the coales, much like white Salmon, which the Frenchmen call Aloza. (Rosier 1605, sig. C3r-v)

Like earlier writers, Rosier uses the familiar to describe the unfamiliar, coming close but never quite being able to explain exactly what he had experienced—the red berries, the different kinds of fish. But unlike earlier writers, Rosier is willing to admit that not everything the New World has to offer is wonderful. The berries are not tasty, and the fish is not described as being either tasty or unpleasant.

Rosier's text also reveals that the years of exploration have had their effect on European culture. Some things that were once unfamiliar now no longer need explanation. The canoe is an American craft, first encountered by Columbus on his 1492–1493 voyage. It was in his letter from the first expedition that the word "canoe" came to Europe, the word coming from the Arawak language. The word appears in print in English for the first time in Richard Eden's 1555 translation of Peter Martyr's *Decades*. By 1605, Rosier writes about canoes: "Their Canoas are made without any iron, of the bark of a birch tree, strengthened within with ribs and hoops of wood, in so good fashion, with such excellent ingenious art, as they are able to beare seven or eight persons, far exceeding any in the Indies" (Rosier 1605, sig. B3v). Though he explains what is special about the canoes of what is now the Maine coast to people who have not seen them before, he does not have to explain what a canoe is. Even without the canoe itself having become part of English culture, Rosier assumes that the idea of a canoe has become part of his readers' psyches.

Rosier's text also uses the mode of promotional narrative in order to assert English control both over the commodities available in what still was called the north part of Virginia and over its native peoples. As Rosier notes in his introductory section "To the Reader," he had not written anything of the expedition before it left, and even now he excludes specifics such as the latitude of the expedition's discoveries, "because some forrein Nation (being fully assured of the fruitfulness of the countrie) have hoped hereby to gaine some knowledge of the place, seeing they could not allure our Captaine or any speciall man of our Company to combine with them for their direction, nor obtaine their purpose, in conveying away our Salvages, which was busily in practice" (Rosier 1605, sig. A2v). Rosier withholds information because other European nations might misuse it to find and settle this fruitful land and, most worrisomely, to take away the Native Americans, the savages of the English. One of the more interesting features of Rosier's narrative is his discussion of how, without qualm, the expedition lures aboard ship several Indians to take back to England, whether they want to go or not. The very last part of the text, following a list of what goods the country explored can yield, is a list of the names of the Indians who were brought back to England (Rosier 1605, sig. C4r).

Rosier, in explaining the New World to his English readers, shows a place that can be settled and controlled, up to and including its native inhabitants.

But looking at exploration literature as a rhetorical genre allows us to remember that while most people in England writing about the New World did so from a perspective that promoted its exploration, settlement, and commercial exploitation, not everyone in England held this view of the Americas. Most pieces of exploration literature from the second and third phases of English exploration before the founding of Jamestown were written and published within a relatively small, if sometimes loosely confederated, circle of explorers and promoters. How far the hand of someone like Richard Hakluyt extended can be seen not only in his direct involvement in publications beginning with the 1580 Florio translation of Cartier's *A Shorte and Briefe Narration of the Two Navigations and Discoveries to the Northweast Partes Called Newe Fraunce* and going to the 1611 second edition of Hakluyt's translation of the Gentleman of Elvas's narrative (now titled *The Worthye and Famous History, of the Travailes, Discovery, and Conquest, of that Great Continent of Terra Florida Being Lively Paraleld, with that of Our Now Inhabited Virginia*), but also in such things as the fact that the Brereton and Rosier pamphlets were published by one of the same persons who published both editions of Hakluyt's *Principal Navigations,* George Bishop. Thomas Hariot, Walter Raleigh, and even Edward Hayes appear again and again in primary or secondary roles from the 1580s until the early 1600s.

From its beginnings in the late fifteenth century to the days just before the Jamestown settlement of the early seventeenth century, English exploration of the New World is described to readers back in England through the rhetorical genre of exploration literature. It has no single vision of the New World, and no single form that it takes. But as the context of these explorations changed over the first century-plus of English involvement in the Americas, so too did the literature written to explain to readers what this place was like, explanations meant to persuade readers of the goodness—or lack thereof—of the lands and peoples involved in the explorations.

REFERENCES

Brereton, John. 1602. *A Briefe and True Relation of the Discoverie of the North Part of Virginia*. London: George Bishop.

Cabeza de Vaca, Alvar Núñez 1542. *La relacion que dio Aluar nuñez cabeça de vaca de lo acaescido enlas Jndias enla armada donde yua por gouernador Pãphilo de narbaez, desde el año de veynte y siete hasta el año d'treynta y seys que boluio a Seuilla con tres de su compañia*. Zamora: por Augustin de paz y Juan Picardo.

———. 2003. *The Narrative of Cabeza de Vaca*, translated and edited by Rolena Adorno and Patrick Charles Pautz. Lincoln: University of Nebraska Press.

Cartier, Jacques. 1580. *A Shorte and Briefe Narration of the Two Navigations and Discoveries to the Northweast Partes Called Newe Fraunce*, translated by John Florio. London: H. Bynneman.

Castañeda de Naçera, Pedro de. [1896] 1964. Relacion de la Jornada de Cibola. In *The CoronadoExpedition, 1540–1542*, edited by George Parker Winship, 108–185. Reprint. Chicago: Rio Grande Press.

Gentleman from Elvas. 1609. *Virginia Richly Valued, by the Description of the Maine Land of Florida, Her Next Neighbour Out of the Foure Yeeres Continuall Travell and Discoverie, for Above One Thousand Miles East and West, of Don Ferdinando de Soto, and Sixe Hundred Able Men in his Companie. Wherin Are Truly Observed the Riches and Fertilitie of Those Parts, Abounding with Things Necessarie, Pleasant, and Profitable for the Life of Man: With the Natures and Dispositions of the Inhabitants*, translated by Richard Hakluyt. London: Felix Kyngston for Matthew Lownes.

———. 1611. *The Worthye and Famous History, of the Travailes, Discovery, and Conquest, of that Great Continent of Terra Florida Being Lively Paraleld, with that of Our Now Inhabited Virginia. As Also the Comodities of the Said Country, with Divers Excellent and rich Mynes, of Golde, Silver, and other Mettals, &c. Which Cannot but Give Us a Great and Exceeding Hope of Our Virginia, Being so Neere of One Continent. Accomplished and Effected, by that Worthy Generall and Captaine, Don Ferdinaudo de Soto, and Six Hundred of Spaniards His Followers*, translated by Richard Hakluyt. London: Mathew Lownes.

Hakluyt, Richard, ed. 1582. *Divers Voyages Touching the Discoverie of America, and the Ilands Adjacent unto the Same Made First of All by Our Englishmen, and Afterward by the Frenchmen and Britons: and Certaine Notes of Advertisements for Observations, Necessarie for Such as Shall Heereafter Make the Like Attempt, With Two Mappes Annexed Heereunto for the Plainer Understanding of the Whole Matter.* London: Thomas Woodcocke.

———, ed. 1589. *The Principall Navigations, Voiages and Discoveries of the English Nation, Made by Sea or over Land, to the Most Remote and Farthest Distant Quarters of the Earth at any Time within the Compasse of these 1500. Yeeres.* London: George Bishop and Ralph Newberie.

———. 1598–1600. *The Principal Navigations, Voyages, Traffiques and Discoveries of the English Nation.* 3 vols. London: George Bishop, Ralph Newberie and Robert Baker.

Miller, Carolyn R. 1984. Genre as Social Action. *Quarterly Journal of Speech* 70: 151–167.

Moran, Michael G. 2003. Ralph Lane's 1586 Discourse on the First Colony: The Renaissance Commercial Report as Apologia. *Technical Communication Quarterly* 12: 125–154.

Quinn, David B., ed. 1974. *The Hakluyt Handbook.* 2 vols. London: Hakluyt Society.

———, ed. 1979. *New American World: A Documentary History of North America to 1612.* 5 vols. New York: Arno.

Rosier, James. 1605. *A True Relation of the Most Prosperous Voyage Made This Present Yeere 1605, by Captaine George Waymouth, in the Discovery of the Land of Virginia Where he Discovered 60 Miles up a Most Excellent River; Together with a Most Fertile Land.* London: George Bishop.

Shields, E. Thomson, Jr. 2003. Ralph Lane and the Rhetoric of Identity Creation. In *Searching for the Roanoke Colonies: An Interdisciplinary Collection,* edited by E. Thomson Shields Jr., and Charles R. Ewen, 25–31. Raleigh: Office of Archives and History, North Carolina Department of Cultural Resources.

———. 2005. The Genre of Exploration and Conquest Narratives. In *A Companion to the Literatures of Colonial America,* edited by Susan Castillo and Ivy Schweitzer, 353–368. Malden, MA: Blackwell.

CHAPTER 2

CAPTAIN JOHN SMITH

STEVEN OLSEN-SMITH

Decisive leader, prolific writer, astute American visionary, Captain John Smith was the crucial founder of the 1607 Jamestown colony in Virginia and an inspired promoter of English colonization in North America. Controversial in his own day, Smith's posthumous reputation has fluctuated considerably owing partly to his unabashed self-promotion and his role in America's violent colonial history. Yet Smith's prominence as an American literary and historical figure has increased steadily over the decades and promises to keep growing. Notwithstanding his national and ideological affiliations as an Englishman, and their connection to Old World conceptions of class hierarchy and social order, Smith was first among early colonial writers to recognize the opportunities presented by North America for post-Renaissance social reform. Besides helping to establish the first successful European colony here, Smith was first to project the secular vision of human rights and political liberty that would shape American identity and sustain this vision's ongoing struggle for human progress.

Smith's prominence as a historical and literary figure has traditionally rested upon his significance as the key preserver of the 1607 Jamestown settlement, and afterward as an outspoken and influential champion of English colonization of North America. Compromised by supply shortages, bad weather, and diseases, and harried militarily by the Powhatan Indians and confederate tribes of the Chesapeake Bay region, Jamestown in its first two years of existence struggled daily to avoid destruction. Its vulnerability to external hazards was further aggravated by incompetent planning and the poor character of the colony's initial leadership. Smith, alone among the governing council, had earned his position by experience (Smith 1988, 222). He effectively responded to crises with courageous action and impromptu resourcefulness—often in direct violation of impractical instructions laid out before settlement by the colony's distant London financiers.

After departing Jamestown in 1609 because of a debilitating gunpowder wound, Smith continued to promote colonization from afar in the form of robust prose, publishing *A Map of Virginia* and *The Proceedings of the English Colonie* in 1612— collaborative works preceded by *A True Relation of Such Occurrences and Accidents of Noate as Hath Hapned in Virginia* (1608), which he had written at Jamestown. He went on to explore the coasts of the region he named New England, and promoted the idea of northern settlement in *A Description of New England* (1616) and *New Englands Trials* (1620), which were influential to English colonists who would settle at Plymouth and Massachusetts Bay. Smith's literary and promotional efforts culminated in the publication of his extensive *Generall Historie of Virginia, New-England, and the Summer Isles* (1624), followed by *An Accidence or the Pathway to Experience* (1626), enlarged for republication as *A Sea-Grammar* (1627). In 1630 Smith published his autobiography, *The True Travels, Adventures, and Observations of Captaine John Smith*, and in 1631—the year of his death—appeared *Advertisements for the Unexperienced Planters of New England, or Any Where*. Historians have emphasized Smith's personal and written contributions to English colonization in North America, but it is his compelling vision of America and its opportunities for human advancement that have proved most prescient to posterity, and which identify Smith as an important forerunner of pervasive concepts and ideals in American literature.

EARLY LIFE AND ADVENTURES

Born in early January 1580 (baptized January 9), John Smith was the eldest son of Alice Rickard and George Smith, whose yeoman status positioned the family above the peasantry yet beneath the gentry. As a freeholder, George Smith farmed his own land but paid tribute to Peregrine Willoughby of Eresby, lord of the manor of Willoughby by Alford, Lincolnshire—John Smith's birthplace. There is considerable disagreement about the implications of these middle origins for Smith's life and character, with some historians stressing their formative influence on the defiant class consciousness that pervades his writing, and others maintaining that the Smith family enjoyed considerable respectability in Lincolnshire. In any case, Smith's first successful effort to surmount his lot occurred in late 1596 or early 1597, when in an act of self-determination he abandoned a merchant apprenticeship arranged by his late father and joined an army regiment bound for France and Holland, where England had joined the Dutch in their war of independence against Spain. There in the Low Countries Smith spent three or four years learning the life of a soldier and finally accompanied Robert and Peregrine Bertie, sons of his late father's benefactor, Lord Willoughby, on a tour of France. Following a brief sojourn in Scotland, Smith returned to the region of his boyhood and isolated himself to pursue a study of military science and character facilitated by Machiavelli's *The Art of War* and Marcus Aurelius's *Dial of Princes.* In this application he was mentored for a time (with phenomenal results for Smith's subsequent military career) by an Italian expatriate named Theodore Paleologue, horse master to a local earl, who helped Smith improve his skills of riding and jousting. This episode receives little historiographical attention owing to the scant record of biographical evidence. But the discernible sequence of ground-level military enlistment followed by concerted and prolonged, patient study exemplifies habits and values of self-visualization, preparation, and reinvention that would characterize Smith's future endeavors and inform his writings.

With enhanced military knowledge and combative skills, Smith returned to the Low Countries in 1600 sometime after July 22, when an uneasy détente among the warring nations compelled him to look elsewhere for the opportunity to distinguish himself in arms. According to *True Travels,* Smith determined to "trie his fortune against the Turkes," who for the past century had menaced central Europe from footholds in the Balkans and Hungary. However, Smith's journey east took nearly twelve months owing to a sequence of misadventures and deliberate sidetracks. He was robbed of his belongings by a group of men who had taken up with him under the pretext of accompanying him to Austria, one of whom he subsequently encountered again in Brittany and bested in a duel. En route to Italy on the Mediterranean, he was thrown overboard by Catholic pilgrims to Rome who were convinced that bad sailing weather had been caused by the English Protestant in their midst. Picked up on an island by a French merchant, Smith accompanied the trader to ports on the coasts of Tunisia, Cyrenaica (now Libya), Egypt, the Levant, and Greece. He returned to France with a portion of the spoils won in a sea fight with a Venetian trader that had fired upon the ship. These mixed experiences contributed, *Candide*-like, to notions of the fickleness of fortune and of the vanity of human experience that garnish Smith's writings.

Smith next toured Italy and in mid-1601 reached Vienna, where he joined a regiment of the Holy Roman imperial army assembled for the purpose of beating back Turkish troops that had overrun western Hungary and invaded Austria. He was awarded the rank of captain after helping to liberate the besieged Austrian border town of Limbach by means of signal flames he had learned about from a section on pyrotechnices in Machiavelli's *Art of War.* As an officer in command of 250 horsemen he entered Hungary at the height of the age of trisection—the bloodiest period of its history, with the eastern European nation divided among Austrian, Transylvanian, and Ottoman forces. In the siege of Alba Regalis, or Székesfehérvár, he again distinguished himself in arms and as an expert of incendiary warfare, devising explosive earthenware pots ("fiery Dragons," he called them), which his men lobbed over the walls of the city with devastating effect (Smith 1986, 3: 166). But it was in the war-ravaged principality of Transylvania where Smith displayed his military prowess to greatest renown. There, during the siege of an unknown fortification near the capital Alba Iulia (or perhaps of the city itself), Smith defeated three Ottoman challengers in separate single combats—a feat for which he received a coat of arms representing the three heads of the vanquished Turkish champions.

Smith's service in the imperial army effectively ended in late 1602 when his regiment was overwhelmed by a Crimean army that had entered Transylvania to reinforce the Turks. Wounded, captured, and enslaved, Smith was brought south through the Balkans to Istanbul. He passed through a succession of owners and wound up in the possession of an Ottoman official stationed at the outer reaches of the empire, northeast of the Sea of Asov, in southern Russia. Shaven, manacled, and subjected to frequent beatings, he there experienced the miseries of human bondage, "for the best was so bad, a dog could hardly have lived to endure," as he would recall in *True Travels* (Smith 1986, 3: 189). Eventually Smith struck back and killed his owner, escaping by horse across uninhabited lands now consisting of the border area between Russia and the Ukraine. He found assistance at a Muscovite outpost and crossed the Ukraine into Transylvania (Gregorovich 2002, 21). Before the close of 1603 he was back in central Europe to receive a discharge and compensation for his military service from the exiled Transylvanian prince Zsigmond Báthory, who also presented him with a document affirming his captaincy and coat of arms. Smith toured Germany and crossed the Spanish peninsula to Gibraltar, and from there journeyed to Morocco—all apparently with straightforward goals of achieving travel and experience. In late 1604 he spent time aboard a French man-of-war off the coast of Africa, participating in a skirmish with Spanish warships, and returned to England in 1605. At twenty-four, Smith arrived there (and would remain) the most experienced and widely traveled soldier of the newly inaugurated Jacobean age, which had begun in Smith's absence with the 1603 ascension of King James I.

VIRGINIA EXPLORATIONS AND WRITINGS

England under Queen Elizabeth I had made only one serious effort to plant and sustain a settlement in North America, Sir Walter Raleigh's colony of Roanoke, in the Outer Banks of present-day North Carolina, which failed sometime in 1588–1589. Now in 1605 a new effort was under way to establish a permanent colony in Virginia, the stretch of North American coastland named by Ralegh in honor of Elizabeth and extending north of present-day Florida to New England. The colony would be financed by the London Company (also called the Virginia Company) as a joint-stock venture, with preparations coordinated in large part by Bartholomew Gosnold, who was related by marriage to Lord Willoughby. Presumably Smith renewed his ties with the Willoughby family soon after he returned to England, and it was perhaps through Robert and Peregrine Bertie that Smith met Gosnold around spring 1605.

Winning the confidence of Gosnold and the merchants who constituted the London Company, Smith set about promoting the venture and preparing himself for colonization with the same seriousness of purpose he had applied to soldiering and to the study of armaments before his earlier adventures. That military experience is what likely interested the colonial backers in Smith's potential services to the enterprise. But their extraordinary decision to make him a member of the new colony's governing council (a decision that would not be disclosed until the colonists arrived on the shores of Virginia and sealed orders were opened and read) can only be explained by the degree of practical expertise he achieved while still under the company's observation in England. This consisted, first, in Smith's mastery of cartography. Before his continental adventures, he had no logical impetus to learn mapmaking, and his military experiences in the Low Countries and eastern Europe afforded slight opportunity to take up the practice. Yet the superb quality of his 1612 map of Virginia shows that he had developed considerable skill before exploring the rivers and inlets of the Chesapeake Bay region. Only during the predeparture preparations of 1605–1606 would the opportunity for gaining such skills have presented itself.

Smith's other acquired skill is indicated by his considerable ability upon arrival in Virginia to comprehend and communicate with the Powhattan Indians and other Chesapeake Bay groups who used varieties of the Algonquian language spoken by the Indians of Roanoke. As Smith's biographer surmised, in fulfillment of this objective he may have sought out Thomas Hariot, author of *A Briefe and True Report of the New Found Land of Virginia* (1588), who had himself learned Algonquian directly from Roanoke Indians and had spent a year in the Outer Banks interacting with coastal groups and recording his observations of their culture (Barbour 1964, 98–99; Quinn 1985, 246). In fact, Algonquian-speaking Indians recently brought to England by Captain George Waymouth were in London when Virginia preparations peaked in mid-1606. If Smith gained access to these Indians and to Harriot, the contact may explain why he was able to display, in Barbour's words, "more insight into what the Indians said and meant, and what their intentions were, than any of his associates during his whole stay in Virginia" (Barbour 1964, 99). In addition to the *Brief and True Report,* Harriot had compiled a dictionary of Algonquian, now lost but presumably still in his possession when Smith may have consulted with him.

Smith's experiences and writings show that he studied Hariot's work closely. For instance, in *Briefe and True Report* Hariot lays no greater stress on any single factor of Anglo-Indian interaction than on the amazement the Roanoke Indians experienced when confronting European technology. Hariot emphasized their reaction to underscore its promise for the colonial agenda to control and assimilate the natives: "Most things they sawe with us, as Mathematicall instruments, sea compasses, the vertue of the loadstone in drawing yron, a perspective glasse whereby was shewed manie strange sightes . . . were so straunge unto them, and so farre exceeded their capacities to comprehend the reason and meanes how they should be made and done, that they thought they were rather the works of gods then of men, or at the leastwise they had bin given and taught us of the gods" (Quinn 1991, 1: 376). In *A True Relation* and later works Smith indicates he was not only aware of this strategem but had means to employ it through language. He uses it to win the respect of the Powhatan war chief Opechancanough, whose men had abducted Smith on an exploring expedition after slaying his companions: "I presented him with a compasse diall, describing by my best meanes the use therof, whereat he so amazedly admired, as he suffered me to proceed in a discourse of the roundnes of the earth, the course of the sunne, moone, starres and plannets. With kind speeches and bread he requited me" (Smith 1986, 1: 47).

Smith himself would compile a list of Algonquian terms for inclusion in *A Map of Virginia* and *A Generall Historie,* marking the first appearance in print of the words "Mockasins" and "Tomahacks," among others. But most revealing is the extraordinary respect granted Smith by the Indians, a respect surpassing their impression of any other original colonist at Jamestown, and inconceivable without a considerable degree of mutual linguistic comprehension. The esteem was such that when Pocahontas visited London in 1616 (seven years after Smith had left Virginia), a member of her retinue, Uttamatomakkin, had been charged by her father Powhatan to seek Smith out and to confirm whether or not reports of his death were true.

Smith gained the respect of the Indians in Virginia more easily than the acceptance of the rest of the governing council and other members of the ruling gentry at Jamestown. To the Indians, Smith's capabilities as a negotiator and fighter made him immediately recognizable as a "weroance," an accomplished warrior and effective leader of men. But Smith was a soldier, *merely,* to the other leaders of the colony, whose post-Renaissance conception of social order was still recognizably feudal in its rigid conception of class distinctions, and in its equation of respectability with wealth and family lineage. With the exception of Gosnold (who would die shortly after the arrival of the colonists) and Christopher Newport (who would return even sooner to England), the Jamestown aristocrats lacked effective leadership and survival skills, but they nonetheless insisted on privileges customary to their rank as gentleman, and the deference owed by commoners to their "betters." That Smith refused to conform to these assumptions is indicated by events that occurred even before the colonists reached their destination, while the three ships *Susan Constant* (the largest, and carrying Smith), *God Speed*, and *Discovery* were navigating the Atlantic in early 1607.

Evidence of what happened is unclear, but according to Smith's testimony he was "restrained as a prisoner" while the ships were anchored for water at the Canary Islands, and he remained under arrest for the duration of the ocean voyage (Smith 1986, 2: 206). At the Caribbean island of Nevis, in fact, a gallows was erected for the purpose of hanging Smith, but the planned execution came to nothing. The charges against him involved mutiny, and their main instigator appears to have been Edward Maria Wingfield, also a passenger aboard the *Susan Constant*, and a ranking gentleman among the colonists. The aborted hanging and Smith's liberation following arrival at Virginia suggest the charges were unsustainable and ultimately baseless—fabricated by Wingfield and others in retaliation against some insult (real or perceived) to their sense of superiority. Smith himself treats the affair with deadpan humor that unveils Wingfield's impotence when he recollects in *True Travels* that "a paire of gallowes was made, but Captaine Smith, for whom they were intended, could not be perswaded to use them" (Smith 1986, 3: 236). But the symbolic import of Smith's arrival at Virginia in chains, and his subsequent rise to power, has proved significant beyond measure to American literary history. As with the writings of a number of prominent figures who succeed him in the American literary canon, such as Benjamin Franklin, Ralph Waldo Emerson, and Frederick Douglass, the rhetorical trademark of Smith's account of the Virginia colonists consists in the exposure of unjustified authority and its displacement by genuine merit and integrity, however unlikely in appearance, and however humble in origin.

Smith's first literary work was also the first English book written in America, and the first American book in English (Emerson 1993, 34, 42). It emerged from Smith's mind and experiences in the form of a letter describing events of the first year of settlement, completed hastily by June 2, 1608, and sent by him to a friend in London. The identity of the recipient is unknown, but the letter quickly made the rounds of interested parties and was soon published in the form of a highly expurgated pamphlet entitled *A True Relation of Such Occurrences and Accidents of Noate as Hath Hapned in Virginia* (1608). By the time it appeared in London bookstalls, negative rumors were already circulating there about how poor planning for the colony had made it a hotbed of competing political factions and a locus for disease epidemics and Indian attacks. At the time of writing, Smith had not been aware of the negative publicity, and he made no effort to propagandize in *A True Relation*, which was published without his authorization and supervision. Yet the author's fierce commitment to colonization and strong optimism helped to dispel anxieties among the London Company and potential investors. News of its publication and subsequent success may have been transformative for Smith, for whom no evidence exists to suggest he had ambitions of authorship up to this point.

A True Relation briefly recounts the departure of the colonists from England, their Atlantic voyage, and their erection of James Fort (later named Jamestown), then reports in detail Smith's experiences as supply officer of the fort and explorer of the Chesapeake Bay region. Presumably out of a concern not to reinforce bad publicity in London, most of what Smith reported about altercations among the colonists (primarily, one assumes, between himself and other members of the governing council) were expurgated when his letter was edited for publication. In result, A True Relation centers overwhelmingly on Smith's penetration of the surrounding wilderness and his interactions with the Indians. Smith's narrative voice and controlling consciousness gain prominence as A True Relation proceeds (Spengemann 1994, 70–75). Rhetorically, the development of self through experience of the natural environment imbues the colonial experience with mythic overtones in A True Relation, exemplifying literary conventions considered by many critics to be uniquely American. Yet as Frederic W. Gleach observes, the phenomenon worked in both directions, for the Indians as well as for Smith: "We can forget too easily that the Other being observed by Europeans was another group of people who were engaged in precisely parallel attempts at understanding Others, and that both sides were living, acting co-creators of the events recorded in those accounts" (Gleach 2003, 39). This observation calls attention to the value of Smith's Virginia writings for illuminating the cultural traits and social practices of the Powhatan Indians, and for inferring the group's sense of their own interests and challenges in relation to colonization.

Certainly the best-known episode of Smith's experiences with the Indians is his alleged rescue by Pocahontas when Smith was brought for execution in front of her father, Chief Powhatan. In A Generall Historie Pocahontas is said to have "got his head in her armes, and laid her owne upon his to save him from death" when the executioner's club was raised (Smith 1986, 2: 151). The event is absent from A True Relation, although the earlier narrative does describe the experience of capture in which Smith, his companions slain, is cornered by braves who subsequently bind and convey him deep into Powhatan territory. Smith's truthfulness was first seriously challenged in 1867 by Henry Adams, who privately confessed that his critique of Smith was an attack on the Virginia aristocracy (Hayes 1991, 201). Since then the omission of the episode in A True Relation has been cited numerous times as grounds for dismissing Smith's account in A Generall Historie as a romantic fabrication created for his own self-aggrandizement. Yet the fullest scholarly treatment of the subject provides persuasive evidence that the event occurred as Smith describes it, with Pocahontas's involvement (Lemay 1992). The most important lingering question involves whether Smith was indeed on the verge of being put to death or was experiencing an elaborate ceremony, perhaps intended to adopt him within the tribe. In supporting the latter possibility, Gleach goes further to suggest the entire English colony may have been ceremoniously adopted in the event, with gifts of land and tribal allegiance (Gleach 2003, 29–40). Such an act, if properly understood by the English, might have substantially altered and ameliorated the course of Anglo-Indian relations in early settlement.

As a source of data on daily Indian social and cultural activities, Smith's importance has never been disputed. Despite the early rapprochement sanctified by Smith's adoption (if such it was), colonial relations with the Powhatans remained uncertain at best, and Smith occupied the vexed center of these relations throughout his sojourn at Jamestown. As supply officer, he had the responsibility of procuring food for the settlement through trade with the Indians. Consequently, he interacted with them more than any other colonist and became, in J. A. Leo Lemay's words, "the most careful observer of Indian customs, manners, language, religion, and individuals of his day" (Lemay 1991, 142–143). Observations on Indian activities occur throughout the text accompanying *A Map of Virginia,* and Smith included a detailed section entitled "Of the naturall Inhabitants of Virginia," containing unique information on such varied topics as the Chesapeake Bay Indians' lodgings and agriculture, tools and weapons, hunting and battle practices, and religious beliefs. The text concludes with a section on "the manner of the Virginians government" (Smith 1986, 1: 160, 173). The map itself (reprinted along with the text in *A Generall Historie*) remains the fullest record of Virginia tribal locations as they existed at the time of English settlement.

Lemay's claim for Smith as a careful observer of Indian individuals deserves particular attention. An incipient quality of *A True Relation,* Smith's attention to the various personalities, attributes, strengths, and weaknesses of Indians as human beings would become more and more refined and developed as his writings on Jamestown accumulated. The keen interest in character is present in his earliest description of Powhatan's daughter Pocahontas as "a child of tenne yeares old, which not only for feature, countenance, and proportion, much exceedeth the rest of his people, but for wit, and spirit, the only Nonpariel of his Country" (Smith 1986, 1: 93). Aspects of Powhatan's own character, in particular, magnify and expand as Smith continued to write about Jamestown and reflect upon his experiences there. In *A True Relation* Powhatan is almost wholly objectified, but in the *Generall Historie* he springs to life on account of Smith's expanded treatment of colonial efforts to trade and negotiate with the chief—episodes that shine a spotlight on his intelligence and subtlety in dealing with the English colonists. Smith's portrait of Powhatan includes transcriptions of his speeches, which are recollected and approximate rather than verbatim, but nonetheless coincide with Smith's descriptions of the chief's opinions and behavior, and augment our sense of his character as a formidable physical and psychological antagonist of Jamestown.

In addition to strengthening his written portraiture, Smith's responsiveness to the individuality of Indians governed the policies by which he interacted with them in Virginia. In the altercations and conflicts that marred early Anglo-Indian relations, his method was normally to respond in kind to the Indians involved, rather than to treat individual actions as a pretext for dealing with groups. Methods had been less enlightened at the colony of Roanoke, where the English under their military commander, Ralph Lane, had performed preemptive strikes against entire villages to discourage hostilities (Quinn 1985, 127). These tactics achieved little genuine security, and the colony failed.

The lessons of Roanoke were not lost on merchants of the Virginia Company, who before colonization had issued instructions "not to Offend the naturals" (Barbour 1969, 1: 51). Yet this blanket dictum to avoid conflict proved just as unsuitable for a colony interacting with diverse communities and varied indigenous personalities. The complexities of the situation can be inferred from Smith's account of how the Indians' theft of tools spiraled out of control at Jamestown, and how he corrected the situation through force of action:

> At last by ambuscadoes at our very Ports they would take them perforce, surprise us at worke, or any way; which was so long permitted, they became so insolent there was no rule; the command from England was so strait not to offend them, as our authoritie-bearers (keeping their houses) would rather be any thing then peace-breakers. This charitable humor prevailed, till well it chanced they medled with Captaine Smith, who without farther deliberation gave them such an incounter, as some he so hunted up and downe the Isle, some he so terrified with whipping, beating, and imprisonment, as for revenge they surprised two of our forraging disorderly souldiers, and having assembled their forces, boldly threatned at our Ports to force Smith to redeliver seven Salvages, which for their villanies he detained prisoners, or we were all but dead men. But to try their furies he sallied out amongst them, and in lesse then an houre, he so hampred their insolencies, they brought them his two men, desireing peace without any further composition for their prisoners. (Smith 1986, 2: 159)

Smith's references to corporal punishment imposed upon the Indians are disturbing to modern sensibilities, for they invoke our knowledge of the catastrophic native mortality, territorial loss, and cultural disinheritance that would result from English colonization of North America. But if we judge Smith's behavior by the standards of his times, we find him to be an equitable and temperate figure of authority. It is important, for instance, to acknowledge that his methods of dealing with the thievery of individual Indians in the preceding passage would have been no more severe than routine treatment of Englishmen guilty of the same actions. By contrast, the Indians themselves inflicted torture upon captured enemies, and when after Smith's 1609 departure control was assumed by other colonists, they employed draconian means of punishment upon the Indians, put prisoners to death, and devastated whole villages. For years after his departure from Virginia, Smith was remembered by Indians as an honest negotiator and valuable ally among the colonists, and at worst as an honorable enemy.

Mutual respect notwithstanding, Smith's allegiance was quite naturally to colonization rather than to the Indians. His opinions of Indian policy at Jamestown would become less diplomatic after hostilities culminated, more than a decade after his departure, with an Indian uprising that left more than 300 colonists dead. The 1622 massacre incensed popular British opinion and radically altered colonial Indian relations in Virginia, replacing efforts to assimilate the Indians with a policy of retribution. Smith joined the punitive climate of opinion, and in a proposal to the London Company he offered to lead a force of 100 soldiers to "inforce the Salvages to leave their Country, or bring them in that feare and subjection that every man should follow their businesse securely." His efforts would be maintained in part, he added, by "the proper labour of the Salvages" (Smith 1986, 2: 306–307). Smith did not call for the extermination of the Indians. He proposed instead to disperse them and drive them away from the colonies (Barbour 1964, 353). His plan to exploit the Indians' labor probably involved not outright enslavement but enforced tribute, to be supplied from the Indians' "proper," or customary, practices of hunting, gathering, and agriculture. The policy had been used by Smith against hostile groups during his original sojourn at Virginia, where for centuries rival tribes had exacted tribute from one another.

Smith's hardened position on Anglo-Indian relations can likewise be seen in the ways he altered some of his earlier accounts of native interaction for publication in *A Generall Historie*. For instance, in *A True Relation* Smith had described the scornful treatment he received while attempting to trade with the Indians of Kecoughtan at the mouth of the Powhattan River. The Indians deemed the English famished and weak, and openly ridiculed them by offering only "small handfulls" of food for their hatchets and copper. Describing the event in *A True Relation,* Smith reacted to the Indians' insults with the talents of a shrewd and patient negotiator: "In the like maner I entertained their kindnes, and in like scorne offered them like commodities, but the Children, or any that shewed extraordinary kindenes, I liberally contented with free gifte, such trifles as wel contented them." By the next day, when the English offered to trade again, the free gifts had achieved their purpose, for even the scornful individuals of the day before had become, in Smith's words, "no lesse desirous of our commodities then we of their Corne" (Smith 1986, 1: 35–36). The account in *A True Relation* aptly illustrates the subtlety and discernment that made Smith such a successful provider throughout his sojourn at Jamestown.

Smith's revised account of the Kecoughtan trading expedition for the *Generall Historie* appears remarkably altered. In the punitive atmosphere following the 1622 massacre, he recast himself and his role as that of a relentless military commander, willing and able to bring haughty Indians into submission. According to his 1624 account: "Being but six or seauen in company he went downe the river to Kecoughtan, where at first they scorned him, as a famished man, and would in derision offer him a handfull of Corne, a peece of bread, for their swords and muskets, and such like proportions also for their apparell. But seeing by trade and courtesie there was nothing to be had, he made bold to try such conclusions as necessitie inforced, though contrary to his Commission: Let fly his muskets, ran his boat on shore, whereat they all fled into the woods" (Smith 1986, 2: 144). In Smith's continued rendition in the *Generall Historie,* a skirmish ensues in which the English capture the Kecoughtans' idol and the Indians sue for peace. There is here no mention of the dispersal of gifts to Indian children or of the group's gradual change of attitude. The same group of individuals he had charmed and persuaded in *A True Relation* is here compelled to trade in just retribution through force of arms.

Smith's increasing emphasis on military force seems directly calculated, in the early 1620s, to promote his goal of returning to America in a position of authority, in this case as a military leader who would protect the colonists from further native aggression. Karen Ordahl Kupperman speaks for numerous contemporary historians when she observes of Smith that "after 1622 all the subtlety and sensitivity in his understanding of the Indian side of the equation are gone" (Smith 1988, 12). Yet Smith continued to distinguish between positive and negative qualities of Indian character and behavior in the *Generall Historie,* where he remained as critical of reckless and indiscriminate colonial violence as he was of native hostility. The 1622 massacre, he seems to have felt, had destroyed any immediate prospect for Anglo-Indian harmony, and his hardened attitude toward the Indians seems to have reflected both a realistic sense of this change and his commitment to the spread of Western civilization. As Lemay has demonstrated, Smith's fundamental attitude toward Indians reflects his belief in the comparative method and stage theory of civilization, which held that human progress involved rising from a primitive state to civilized culture, and that it was the destiny of all humanity to advance along these lines (Lemay 1979, 187–223; 1991, 116–119).

A commitment to civilized behavior and order lies at the heart of Smith's writings, where he was quick to condemn English atrocities. Attacking colonial policies toward Indians in *A Generall Historie,* Smith observed: "Ever since the beginning of these Plantations, it hath been supposed the King of Spaine would invade them, or our English Papists endevour to dissolve them. But neither all the Counsels of Spaine, nor Papists in the world could have devised a better course to bring them all to ruine, then thus to abuse their friends." Virginia, he charged, was by such means "made a stage where nothing but murder and indiscretion contends for victory" (Smith 1986, 2: 314). Here Smith's condemnation of bad judgment as a crime comparable with murder reveals how thoroughly he absorbed the profound lessons of a career punctuated by life-and-death situations. Discretion—that rare quality by which he believed character was born and developed—made him the only competent governing representative for the colony in its original relationships with neighboring tribes.

Smith's background, training, and character were profoundly different from those of other individuals in authority at Jamestown. With the exceptions of Smith and Christopher Newport (captain of the voyage), the original 1607 council consisted entirely of aristocrats who were averse to physical labor, accustomed to sensual pleasures, and contemptuous of those beneath them in the Jacobean social hierarchy. In privilege and temperament they embodied the corrupt class system of western Europe, and their appointments to the governing council reflect the intentions of the London Company to erect in Virginia an English manorial system of fiefdoms controlled by lords and maintained by laboring classes. Moreover, the council members and other gentry among the colonists were motivated by impractical expectations of easy wealth in Virginia, such as the discovery of gold, and of a water route through North America to the Pacific Ocean that would allow for lucrative trade with the East Indies—the fabled but nonexistent "Northwest Passage." They were disillusioned, sullen, and primarily useless during the colony's early periods of struggle and hardship.

Instead of rising to challenges and adapting to adversity, the Jamestown aristocrats monopolized resources and exploited their social inferiors. As Smith would observe sardonically in the *Generall Historie* of Wingfield's hoarding of resources:

> Had we beene as free from all sinnes as gluttony, and drunkennesse, we might have beene canonized for Saints; But our President would never have beene admitted, for ingrossing to his private, Oatmeale, Sacke, Oyle, Aquavitae, Beefe, Egges, or what not, but the Kettell; that indeed he allowed equally to be distributed, and that was halfe a pint of wheat, and as much barley boyled with water for a man a day, and this having fryed some 26. weekes in the ships hold, contained as many wormes as graines. (Smith 1986, 2: 143)

George Percy, made president after Smith's departure in 1609, also reserved inordinate privileges for himself and his retinue, and did so as much for his aristocratic image as for his sensual enjoyment: "it standing upon my reputation (being Governour of James Towne) to keep a continuall and dayly Table for Gentlemen of fashioun aboute me" (quoted in Shirley 1949, 239). When stores diminished, indeed, Wingfield attempted to abandon his charge and the colony by absconding for England with its only remaining ship. He was prevented by Smith and deposed from the council.

According to one of the colonists who contributed to Smith's *Proceedings*, "had we beene in Paradice it selfe (with those governours) it would not have beene much better with us" (Smith 1986, 1: 276). To the rank and file of Jamestown, who were used to scornful treatment by gentlemen, Smith must have seemed an outright anomaly (though a welcome one) among the councillors. Accustomed as a soldier to psychological and physical duress, and especially inured to coarse fare, he was prepared for colonization and impatient with the arrogance and failings of nominal superiors. With a soldier's deliberateness, he had trained himself for the experience in body and mind. Moreover, he recognized in the colonization of Virginia a major event in world history, and he was more interested in winning renown than wealth. In the earliest satirical treatment of gold lust in American literature, Smith ridiculed the "durtie skill" of a fellow councillor who put colonists to work excavating mud and sand on the James River. In similar fashion he condemned the dietary niceties and flight risks presented by the gentry, pointing out that a temporary period of plenty brought "fish, fowle, and diverse sort of wild beasts as fa[s]t as we could eat them, so that none of our tuftaffaty humorists desired to go for England" (Smith 1986, 2: 158, 145–146). To Smith it was both farcical and tragic that Jamestown was led by men of weak dispositions, men of "fashioun," who had entered the wilderness wearing lace.

Smith responded to the situation, first in person, and subsequently in prose, by positing a new model of identity and leadership that would assume archetypal proportions in American cultural consciousness. Distinguishing himself from the Jamestown aristocrats, who were "of weake judgement in dangers, and lesse industrie in peace," he recounts in *A Generall Historie* how he endeavored to set a standard of discretion and hard work on his own. In Smith's Virginia writings such emphases on resourceful industry are bolstered by his unflattering treatment of "Gentlemen, whose breeding never knew what a daies labour meant," and were "ten times more fit to spoyle a Common-wealth, then either begin one, or but helpe to maintaine one" (Smith 1986, 2: 235–236, 225). Honoring labor and condemning sloth, Smith preceded the Puritan work ethic in America by more than a decade, for the Plymouth pilgrims would not establish their colony until 1620. As he would proclaim as president of Jamestown in 1609 (all other original councilmen either having died or fled the colony): "he that will not worke shall not eate (except by sicknesse he be disabled) for the labours of 30 or 40 honest and industrious men shall not bee consumed to maintaine 150 idle varlets" (Smith 1986, 1: 259). With this new heroic paradigm in place, Smith secured Jamestown and instituted a process of advancement whereby fellow colonists were promoted according to merit rather than privilege.

When we consider the intentions of the London Company to create a social order in America that would mirror England's, it is especially significant to observe with Lemay that Smith was the only democratically elected president of colonial Virginia. He assumed his presidency at the "request of the company" as a whole—laborers, artisans, and council members—rather than being appointed by London financiers or installed by the king of England, as subsequent governors would be (Smith 1986, 1: 233; Lemay 1991, 201–203). When he was forced to depart Virginia after being severely burned in an accident with his powder bag, the colony was bereft of its most effective and promising leader. In the words of fellow colonists Richard Pots and William Phettiplace:

> Thus we lost him, that in all his proceedings, made Justice his first guid, and experience his second; ever hating baseness, sloth, pride, and indignitie, more than any dangers; that never allowed more for himselfe, then his souldiers with him; that upon no danger would send them where he would not lead them himselfe; that would never see us want what he either had, or could by any meanes get us; that would rather want then borrow, or starve then not pay; that loved actions more then wordes, and hated falsehood and cousnage worse then death: whose adventures were our lives, and whose losse our deathes. (Smith 1986, 1: 273)

This tribute by Pots and Phettiplace appears near the end of *The Proceedings of the English Colonie,* in which a number of Smith's fellow colonists joined ranks in vindicating Smith and protecting the Jamestown project as a whole from ill repute being generated in London by disaffected former colonists. The *Proceedings* was published along with Smith's *Map of Virginia* (1612). Smith never returned to Virginia, but he vigorously applied the lessons of the colony and the example he set there in his future writings. His paradigm for heroic action, and its potential role in American colonization, would be developed more fully in his literary treatment of New England.

NEW ENGLAND EXPLORATIONS AND WRITINGS

In England, Smith's publication of *A Map of Virginia* and its accompanying prose documents served to establish his contemporary reputation as an explorer and colonial leader. The work was modeled after Hariot's *Briefe and True Report of the New Found Land of Virginia,* with extensive (for the time period) geographic, ethnological, and anthropological observations. It was the first major work of its kind since Harriot's, and it made Smith an instant authority and likely candidate for leadership in future efforts to plant a profitable colony in America. Sometime in 1613 Smith accepted the invitation of Marmaduke Rowden, a prominent English merchant, to command a reconnaisance of the northern parts of Virginia, to learn what resources this region might offer. Smith departed England in March 1614 in command of two ships and arrived at the coast of modern-day Maine late in April.

Though charged to search for gold, Smith directed his crew to exploit more reliable resources of fish and fur, and he devoted himself to exploring the coastline of northeastern America and mapping its terrain. In these efforts he interacted and traded fairly extensively with northeastern Indian groups. Although he would not go on to publish substantial ethnological observations of the sort printed in *A Map of Virginia,* he records visiting various villages, and his efforts to communicate with native groups are attested by the large number of Indian place-names he notes, including "Massachusets," "Kinebeck," and "Pennobscot" (Smith 1986, 1: 319). Despite several skirmishes, Smith's own interactions with the coastal groups were by and large peaceful. But the voyage was marred when his second in command, Thomas Hunt, absconded with his ship and crew after kidnapping twenty-four Indians whom he subsequently sold into slavery at Spain. In northern Virginia, too, Smith's vision of new standards for character in a new land was dogged and compromised by Old World corruption.

Smith returned to England with the intention of establishing a colony in northern Virginia. He won the confidence of backers and gave the region its modern name of New England, but his efforts to return there were from 1615 to 1619 plagued by unseaworthy vessels, bad weather, and, eventually, unresponsive investors. In 1615, on his second attempted embarkation, his ship was boarded by French privateers, and Smith wound up a captive on their ship when the vessels were separated. He remained onboard for several months a hapless victim of circumstance, and there began writing about New England "to keepe my perplexed thoughts from too much meditation of my miserable estate" (Smith 1986, 1: 357). The result was *A Description of New England* (1616), which he completed in England after returning there before the end of 1615.

Smith's *Description* and later New England writings would prove influential to colonization and prophetic for American cultural life. Although Smith himself would never return to New England, his map of New England and written account of the region made possible the Plymouth and Massachusetts Bay settlements of the following decade. The pilgrims, particularly, are known to have obtained a copy of Smith's *Description,* though they declined his offer to command their armed contingent, opting instead for the services of Myles Standish (Smith 1986, 3: 221). The pilgrims had originally intended to settle in what is now New York, but their decision to land instead at Cape Cod was probably clinched by their knowledge of Smith's map and writings. Smith's *Description* revealed that northern Virginia was habitable by Europeans, a fact that had been unconfirmed before he assessed the landscape himself in preparation for planting a colony there. Smith's influence on the Massachusetts Bay Colony can be seen in the decision of the organizers to transfer their charter from England to the location of settlement, where, persuaded by Smith's arguments against colonial control from afar, they made their own colony the seat of decision making (Lemay 1991, 210–211).

The significance of *A Description of New England* in Smith's colonial vision can be seen in its coalescence of the writer's promotional purposes with the extraordinary moral and social positions we see taking shape in his earlier writings. In his accounts of Virginia colonization, Smith's antiaristocratic conceptions of meritocracy and the dignity of labor informed his evaluations of events but remained ultimately subordinate to narrative organization and historical reportage. They were, as Everett Emerson observes, "sporadically apparent" in the earlier writings (Emerson 1993, 63). By contrast, Smith devoted large portions of his *Description* to the transformative qualities of colonization. His approach consisted in litanizing widespread corruptions in the debt-ridden lives of Englishmen, such as the idle consumption of expensive food and drink, the prevalence of gambling, and the indignity of relying for one's welfare on siblings and elders. Why, Smith asks, would anyone

> live at home idly (or thinke in himselfe any worth to live) onely to eate, drink, and
> sleepe, and so die? . . . toil out thy heart, soule, and time, basely, by shifts, tricks,
> cards, and dice? . . . deceive thy friends, by faire promises, and dissimulation,
> in borrowing where thou never intendest to pay; offend the lawes, surfeit with
> excess, burden thy Country, abuse thy selfe, despaire in want, and then couzen thy
> kindred, yea even thine owne brother, and wish thy parents death (I will not say
> damnation) to have their estates? though thou seest what honours, and rewards,
> the world yet hath for them will seeke them and worthily deserve them. (Smith
> 1986, 1: 344)

What is extraordinary about this passage is Smith's conception of colonization as an opportunity not just to obtain wealth but also to improve moral character.

Smith understood fully the powerful colonial motive of economic gain, explaining, "I am not so simple, to thinke, that ever any other motive then wealth, will ever erect there a Commonweale" (Smith 1986, 1: 346). Yet wealth without virtue, he argued, had brought about the ruin of all the world's great cities and empires, such as Constantinople and Rome, and he believed fate would be no more tolerant of English sloth and corruption. The antidote to England's malaise was "imployment" in America, where planters, fisherman, carpenters, masons, tailors and smiths would all find their labor rewarded not just by financial gain but by the honor of determining their own worth and destinies. Smith's emphasis on the transformative qualities of colonization led him to project both a new kind of individual and a new social order. In an inspired pronouncement marking the earliest invocation of political and social freedom in American literature, Smith observed, "Heer nature and liberty affords us that freely, which in England we want, or it costeth us dearely" (Smith 1986, 1: 346–347).

Smith recognized in America a combination of political liberty and abundant natural resources that was unique in the history of opportunities available to human progress. His conception of the possibilities provided by New England, in particular, display this dual-themed promotional vision. In *New Englands Trials* Smith laid out thirteen statistically backed "proofes" that the region could support a fishing industry and could supply all necessary commodities to sustain a commonwealth. But unlike earlier promoters, Smith stressed carefully the importance of patience and hard work to the colonial enterprise, and the importance of good character among the founders, who "requireth all the best parts of art, judgement, courage, honestie, constancie, diligence and experience." Conversely, the greatest obstacle to colonization was not the severity of the natural environment or the hostility of Indians (probably the two most popularly viewed deterrents) but the danger of greed among the colonists themselves. In Virginia, he observed, "the desire of present gain (in many) is so violent, and the endevors of many undertakers so negligent, every one so regarding their private gaine, that it is hard to effect any publick good." An honest fishing industry, he assured the readers of *New Englands Trials*, would supply "as good gold as the mines of Guiana" without the hardship, disappointment, and conflict that normally attend efforts to get rich quickly (Smith 1986, 437, 441).

In his final book, *Advertisements for the Unexperienced Planters of New England*, Smith extended his most eloquent, nuanced, and far-reaching projection of how liberty and nature in the New World could reward colonists if they resisted greed and embraced the honor of hard work. He argued that trade would be best cultivated if colonists refrained from such policies as charging customs fees to incoming vessels, and that the colonists would do well to rely on their own resources rather than depend on the backing of wealthy investors who were far removed from the scene of action. As in his earlier New England writings, the reward would be good character as well as material prosperity. Most important, Smith urged that colonists be allowed to reap the benefits of their own industry regardless of their social and economic positions. This could be accomplished by extending "freedome" and "true dealing" to colonists escaping servitude, for in New England "a servant that will labour, within foure or five yeares may live as well there as his master did" in old England. The "very name of servitude," on the other hand, "will breed much ill blood, and become odious to God and man." Equitable policies, moreover, would honorably benefit "the common good" rather than hungry merchant monopolies, which sought "the commons goods" (Smith 1986, 3: 287, 285). Distilling the lessons of his own private experience for the benefit of colonial posterity, Smith declared: "It is a happy thing to be borne to strength, wealth, and honours, but that which is got by prowesse and magnanimity is the truest lustre; and those can the best distinguish content, that have escaped most honourable dangers, as if out of every extremity he found him-selfe now borne to a new life to learne how to amend and maintaine his age" (Smith 1983, 3: 299). While similar pronouncements of self-actualization and rebirth would echo throughout succeeding generations of American writers, the priority of Smith's vision places him solidly at the origins of American literature.

NAUTICAL, POETIC, AND AUTOBIOGRAPHICAL WRITINGS

In *A Description of New England,* Smith assured potential sponsors and all would-be colonists of his willingness "not to perswade them to go onely; but goe with them; Not leave them there; but live with them there" (Smith 1986, 1: 346). Here as else-where, Smith's pledge of personal involvement and direct experience set him apart from most other promoters of his day. Yet he would never return to America, despite several attempts, nor ever leave England again. In addition to *Advertisements,* which appeared in the year of his death, Smith in his final years published two works on seamanship, at least three poems, and his autobiography, *The True Travels, Adventures, and Observations of Captaine John Smith,* which recounts Smith's youth and adventures in Europe and the Mediterranean and continues his historical treatment of American colonization from where *A Generall Historie* had left off. With mixed results, scholarship of the past half century has endeavored to sort the narrative's historically verifiable facts from its inaccuracies, of which the latter can be shown to stem both from Smith's imperfect memory of distant events and from the sensation-alistic spirit in which he wrote the book. Frustrated and resentful about his abortive role in American colonization, Smith sought in his autobiography—one of the earli-est specimens of the genre in English—to revive his reputation and regain influence in colonial affairs, urging emigration in the autobiography's final paragraph.

Whereas Smith's remaining writings do not constitute the work of his fame, they can still be seen to display the values of self-actualization and direct experience that distinguished his vision of American colonization. Smith's *An Accidence or the Path-Way to Experience,* a glossary of nautical terms published in 1626, is addressed to "all young seamen, or those desirous to go to sea" (Smith 1986, 3: 9). The book was modeled on a work by Gervase Markham published the previous year entitled *Souldier's Accidence or An Introduction to Military Discipline,* with both authors employing the term *accidence* to denote the rudiments or first principles of a subject. Both works were prompted by English preparations then under way for a war against Spain. As implied by the work's secondary title, Smith had conceived of *An Accidence* as an aid to experience in the abstract, with competent seamanship leading to a life of various forms of action and proficiency. He expanded the book for publication in 1627 as *A Sea Grammar* (newly modeled on Markham's enlarged *Soldiers Grammar,* 1627).

As works intended to assist preparedness for a life of action, with indirect benefit to England's colonial progress, Smith doubtless took considerable satisfaction in *An Accidence* and the revised *Sea Grammar.* The expanded version benefited from Smith's access during composition to an early manuscript of Henry Mainwaring's *Sea-man's Dictionary,* which would not be printed until 1644 (Smith 1986). *A Sea Grammar* contains chapters on shipbuilding; ships' parts, timbers, and riggings; duties of ship personnel; and methods of sailing, fighting, and ship repair, among other subjects. Smith filled a niche with these works, which sold well as the earliest nautical glossaries written in English. The appeal of *A Sea Grammar,* in particular, consisted in the vividness of its descriptions and the sense of immediacy Smith brought to the subject of seamanship.

The nautical theme governs Smith's poem, "Master John Taylor, and his Armado," which appeared in commendatory fashion among other poems in the front matter of Taylor's *An Armado, or Navye of 103 Ships and other Vessels,* published (1627). In commending Taylor's book (a rhetorical tour de force on the subjects of friendship, courtship, etc.), Smith effectively matched the author's humorous spirit while indirectly indulging his personal faith in civilized humanity's potential to master nature and the unknown. The poem opens, "Arme, Arme, Arme, Arme, great *Neptune* rowze, awake/And muster up, thy monsters speedily," averring (accurately enough) that the natural world has never encountered such a force as Taylor's "navy" (Smith 1986, 3: 369). Smith's tribute pits the fleet against "Rockes, shoales, Lee-shores . . . waters, ayre and skies," and finally against the "Devill, Hell, vice and all," with clear implications that the forces of nature will prove unfit for the task of stemming human ingenuity. The poem's great achievement consists in its amicable balance between Smith's deft and humorous performance of the commendatory task at hand and his expression of a mind-set that penetrates to the very core of his writings.

In 1628 Smith again contributed verse to commend the publication of a fellow author's work. In *The Gunner, Shewing the Whole Practise of Artillerie,* Robert Norton pronounced "Experience the Mistris of all Arts, Action being the best Tutor."

Norton had contributed verse of his own to commend Smith's *Generall Historie*, and for the publication of Norton's 1628 *Gunner* Smith reciprocated with a poem acknowledging the author's perfection of a work based on "Study and Experience." The poem, headed "In the due Honor of the Author Master Robert Norton, and his Work," draws a clear line between individuals of action who discern and meet life's perils, and England's pampered but unprepared sensualists:

> Let sweeter Studies lull a sleepe and please
> Men, who presume security, but these
> Thy Labors practizd, shall more safely guard
> Those that foresee the Danger, th' other bar'd
> This benefite . . .
> (Smith 1986, 3: 370)

The alliterative evolution in these enjambed lines from soft aspirant sounds to hard labeals contributes rhetorically to their rejection of unwary hedonism in favor of toil and vigilance. Their high quality suggests that by the late 1620s Smith had written more poetry than what is contained in the collected record of his verse.

The best known of Smith's three collected poems is his latest, "The Sea Marke," which appeared opposite his opening note "To the Reader" in *Advertisements for the Unexperienced Planters of New England*. That work constituted Smith's final promotional effort for the cause of colonization, and "The Sea Marke" (its only accompanying poem) records his poignant reflection upon the diminished role he had come to assume in the enterprise. The poem's title refers to its dominant image of a wrecked ship incapacitated but still partly visible above the surface of the sea, warning that all vessels coming after it should "not forget to sound." That the ship broke against rocks when the "Seas were calme" and the "wind was faire" again bespeaks Smith's keen sense of the perils encircling even a pampered existence, and the need for vigilance in human life. The poem's dominant tone of despair is rejected in the final three lines and replaced by a resolute faith in future deliverance:

> The Winters cold, the Summers heat,
> alternatively beat
> Upon my bruised sides, that rue
> because too true
> That no releefe can ever come.
> But why should I despaire
> being promised so faire
> That there shall be a day of Dome.
> (Smith 1986, 3: 265)

Smith died on or shortly after June 21, 1631, probably in the London home of his friend Samuel Saltonstall, who had financed the publication of Smith's *A Sea Grammar*. An Englishman from birth to death, Smith's ultimate allegiance was to the vision of opportunity he associated with North America. Although he was preceded by other European colonial authors, he should be considered the first American writer of note because he was the first American visionary, and because his vision of America comes closer than the projections of any previous writer to the cultural consciousness that attended its rise to power and influence, and its promise for continued progress. As its original prophet of nature and liberty, Captain John Smith ranks among the most important figures in American literary history.

REFERENCES

Barbour, Philip. 1964. *The Three Worlds of Captain John Smith.* Boston: Houghton Mifflin.
———, ed. 1969. *The Jamestown Voyages under the First Charter: 1606–1609.* 3 vols. New York: Cambridge University Press.
Emerson, Everett. 1993. *Captain John Smith.* Rev. ed. New York: Twayne.
Gleach, Frederic W. 2003. Controlled Speculation and Constructed Myths: The Saga of Pocahontas and Captain John Smith. In *Reading beyond Words: Contexts for Native History,* edited by Jennifer S. H. Brown and Elizabeth Vibert, 39–74. 2nd ed. Peterborough, Ontario: Broadview Press.
Gregorovich, Andrew. 2002. Captain John Smith in Ukraine. *Forum* 106: 19–23.
Hayes, Kevin J. 1991. *Captain John Smith: A Reference Guide.* Boston: Hall.
Kupperman, Karen Ordahl. 1999. Smith, John. In *American National Biography,* edited by John A. Garraty and Mark C. Carnes, vol. 20, pp. 222–224. New York: Oxford University Press.
Lemay, J. A. Leo. 1979. The Frontiersman from Lout to Hero: Notes on the Significance of the Comparative Method and Stage Theory in Early American Literature and Culture. *Proceedings of the American Antiquarian Society* 88: 187–223.
———. 1991. *The American Dream of Captain John Smith.* Charlottesville: University Press of Virginia.
———. 1992. *Did Pocahontas Save Captain John Smith?* Athens: University of Georgia Press.
Quinn, David Beers, ed. 1985. *Set Fair for Roanoke: Voyages and Colonies, 1584–1606.* Chapel Hill: University of North Carolina Press.
———, ed. [1955] 1991. *The Roanoke Voyages 1584–1590.* 2 vols. Reprint. New York: Dover.
Shirley, John. W. 1949. George Percy at Jamestown, 1607–1612. *Virginia Magazine of History and Biography* 57: 227–243.
Smith, John. 1986. *The Complete Works of Captain John Smith (1580–1631),* edited by Philip L. Barbour. 3 vols. Chapel Hill: University of North Carolina Press.
———. 1988. *Captain John Smith: A Select Edition of His Writings,* edited by Karen Ordahl Kupperman. Chapel Hill: University of North Carolina Press.
Spengemann, William. 1994. *A New World of Words: Redefining Early American Literature.* New Haven, CT: Yale University Press.

CHAPTER 3

PROMOTION LITERATURE

KAREN SCHRAMM

Imagine a land possessing "for certain the best ground and sweetest climate," where strawberries grow "in abundance, very large ones, some being two inches about," and birds course by in flocks "seeing neither beginning nor ending, length or breadth of these millions of millions." It is an alluring locale where "every two families have a spring of sweet waters betwixt them" filled with "more variety of fish winter and summer" than anywhere else—a marvelous region where women frequently give "double births" and enjoy "a more speedy recovery" than usual, no one knows sickness, the very mountains contain "the Spaniard's bliss," gold, and the land provides "creatures . . . affording not only meat for the belly but clothing for the back," and "a good store of woods" to supply every "commodity" one could possibly desire. Find such a land, and you have found America. These enticing words from William Wood's *New Englands Prospect* beautifully embody the genre that Howard Mumford Jones terms "promotion literature" (Jones 1952, 179). Such writings offered glowing accounts of plenitude, designed expressly to promote the colonization of America.

THE FEATURES OF PROMOTION LITERATURE

Howard Mumford Jones formally distinguishes eight types of such literature: (1) the "formal treatise on colonization"; (2) the "general prefaces or other introductory matter in collections of voyages or reports on colonial enterprises"; (3) the "official request to government for a patent, or the request plus the patent, published to persuade 'adventurers' to invest and settlers to migrate"; (4) the "reports of exploratory voyages"; (5) "the circulation of material having both official sanction and a personal tang"; (6) the "official laws and . . . regulations concerning the acquirement of land"; (7) "that cleverest form of company-inspired propaganda, the official sermon on such an occasion as the departure of an important person for the colony"; and (8) "the personal report by an interested observer" (Jones 1952, 179–181). Clearly, the tract, both as land and as literature, is vital to our understanding of colonial culture.

Scores of promotional tracts poured forth in the seventeenth century, aimed at an eager and appreciative audience. Some examples include Captain John Smith's *Description of New England* (1616), the anonymous *Mourt's Relation* (1622), Edward Winslow's *Good Newes from New England* (1624), William Wood's *New Englands Prospect* (1634), George Alsop's *Character of the Province of Mary-Land* (1666), Daniel Denton's *Brief Description of New York* (1670), and John Josselyn's *New England's Rarities Discovered* (1672). The promotional trend continued into the eighteenth century, with such works as Benjamin Franklin's *Information For Those Who Would Remove to America* (1784), and the spirit persisted with the publication of lavish descriptive accounts of various regions of America, such as William Bartram's *Travels* (1791), and the popular and voluminous travel literature of the nineteenth century. This time-honored tradition thrives today, in current real estate rhetoric spangled with superlatives, touting the very best place in America in which to dwell.

Rationales or "Inducements" for "planting" colonies in America varied. They included solving the perceived problem of England's overpopulation; reforming lazy, idle, or corrupt people; converting the Indians to Christianity; escaping religious persecution; and enhancing the glory and economic well-being of England through travel and trade. What Jones labels a "rivalry for space" was an economic, geopolitical gambit somehow explicitly sanctioned by God. As Richard Hakluyt observes, "through the speciall assistance, and blessing of God," the English "have excelled all the nations and people of the Earth" in exploration (quoted in Jones 1952, 183–184). Thus, so the argument logically proceeded, they might as well take the "faire" land that so invitingly awaited.

Detailing the generous land's wonderful "commodities," promotion literature proves both entertaining and informative, though admittedly not always reliable. Not merely factual, promotion literature "must make readers dream in order to persuade them to act. . . . The literature of colonial description, insisting on strict realism, conceals the distinction between fancy and fact, fuses the ideal and the real." While the "generic conventions of the promotional tract include a utilitarian tone," we should not allow the undeniable focus on economic benefit to stop us from discerning also the pleasing tonal expressions of joy, wonder, whimsy, and wit likewise present in such texts. For writing "true relations" about the fertile and "delicious" land must have been pleasant work, especially to those like Wood, who had "the pen of experience" with which to describe America and to encourage colonization (Jehlen 1994, 33; Sweet 2002, 178; Wood 1977, 69).

The English were keenly interested in settling the vast region that they termed "Virginia," an expanse that from 1580 to 1620 encompassed "the entire mid-Atlantic coast between Florida and Acadia." Two plantations were to be established, a patent dividing Virginia into "the Northern" and "the Southern" colonies. The northern part did not receive the designation "New England" until Captain John Smith so named it, a moniker that J. A. Leo Lemay terms Smith's most brilliant neologism (Taylor 2001, 113; Hayes 2001, 375; Lemay 1991, 47).

Typically, features of promotion literature include a discussion of air and climate; the soil; the potential for valuable mineral extraction; the plants and trees and crops that grow naturally or could be introduced; the water; animals; people's improved health; the prospect of profitable trade; the spaciousness of the land; its inviting "emptiness"; and information about the Indians' appearance and customs, plus their urgent need for religious conversion and true purpose. Indeed, of particular interest is the belief expressed by Edward Williams in *Virginia . . . Richly and Truly Valued* (1650) that as long as "spyes" watched over them, the Indians could be made to tend to silkworms for the benefit of England. Occasionally, too, the literature contains a sort of advice column on what supplies should accompany the voyagers and what attitudes to convey as well. Entwined throughout are themes of environmental one-upmanship and benediction. All told, as the title of Edward Winslow's promotional chronicle indicates, there is "Good Newes" emanating from America. The tracts frequently make references to events in history and legend, designed not only to demonstrate the writer's learning but also to set the English enterprise into a glorious context and establish its propriety. The tone of self-righteousness manifests itself in works like *A True Declaration of the Estate of the Colonie in Virginia* (1610). With "divine, humane, externall, and domesticall examples" before them, God's approbation of English colonization is certain (Force 2002, 38, 4).

THE LANGUAGE OF PROMOTION LITERATURE

The power of promotion literature lies in its distinctive language, the sense of agency that inheres within the rhetoric of discovery, exploration, and colonization. In essence, promotion literature whets the appetite by focusing on the environment (although without being what we today would call "green"). It provides reportage, commonly characterized as "relations," "descriptions," or "accounts" of the land and its contents.

Accurate vision is key, with writers eager to, as Thomas Morton often says in *New English Canaan* (1637), "shew you" the "natural indowements" of the area.

A splendid "picture-book" or travel brochure quality pervades all, a sweetly aesthetic gloss. Thus, like a docent, William Wood guides the reader through a warehouse of "the most desirable, useful, and beneficial creatures" and then prompts, "Let me lead you from the land to the sea, to view what commodities may come from there" (Wood 1977, 48, 53). A "happy Countrey," America offers everything: It is one giant zoo, arboretum, and parterre, direct from God. Here is a region full of a wondrous variety of plants and animals, some known and many novel—of huge trees and innumerable flowers, of opossums and hummingbirds and who knows what else. It is a rapturous vision indeed, with writers such as Captain John Smith and John Josselyn practically breathless in their enumeration of the resources. Anticipating skeptical responses to their ecstatic outlook, the authors of promotion narratives are at pains to assert their truthfulness.

The insistence on visual veracity in accounts of the "faire" land is neatly underscored by writers' declarations that they "have been an eye-witness," have truly seen this choice expanse (Denton 1973, 31). Delineation is good, certainly valuable to anyone interested in the flora and fauna, geology, climatology, and the like, present in the New World. It is all there, all nicely cataloged for your consideration.

But wait: this is promotion literature—propaganda for peopling paradise. As such, it cannot simply rest on identifying laurels and larks. Indeed, a salient feature of such literature is hyperbole, with writers relying on a small stock of expansive words emphatic about perfection. Everything is "most excellent," as Smith pronounces, or as Christopher Columbus said, "marvelous"—utterly superlative: today's lavish real estate ads in the making. In the quantifying imperative, the keynote is clearly plenitude, for the fabulous New World land and sea offer "plentie" to feast the eyes on: "incredible abundance," "great store," with "abundant hills," "countless valleys," and "numerous rivers," the waters being "very well furnished," "full of fish of all sorts," the lands filled with "numberless kinds" of fruits, and "immense woods" replete with "much variety" of trees, "infinite flocks" of birds, and "innumerable multitudes" of other creatures (Mulford 2002, 556). Such a dazzling display is practically inconceivable.

In this nature-as-pantry vision, everything in the woods and water and wild blue yonder is prime, naturally of the "goodliest and best" sort possible. The grandly effusive diction represents a far-reaching cliché, appearing everywhere in writings, from Amerigo Vespucci describing what is now Patagonia and Brazil in "Mondo Novus" (1503) to William Penn, promoting Pennsylvania, in his work *A Further Account of the Province of Pennsylvania* (1685). Perhaps such remarkable bounty genuinely existed, yet one cannot help but wonder about the sheer biomass: how did all this abundance manage to fit?

The answer, according to promotional writers, was that the New World constituted a very expansive space. As Daniel Denton confidently observes in *A Brief*

Description of New York, there is land "enough to entertain Hundreds of Families."
Best of all, it exists with the express purpose to please; "here is hundreds, nay thousands of Acres, that would invite inhabitants" (Denton 1973, 67, 71). Throughout the
pages of promotion literature, we find the land positively beckoning the amazed
traveler to come hither and settle. It is a clever rhetorical strategy, this promise of
"entertainment," "pleasure," and "satisfaction," so prominent in these "Relations."
They are intimate relations indeed.

The land allures, a veritable fertility goddess. Strategically America is envisioned in promotion literature as a lovely lady. For instance, Alsop assures us, in *A
Character of the Province of Mary-Land,* that Mary-Land is charming, "being within
her own imbraces extraordinary pleasant and fertile." Her "armes" are "her green,
spreading, and delightful Woods," and her "natural womb (by her plenty) maintains
and preserves the several diversities of Animals that rangingly inhabit her Woods."
She is "drest in her green and fragrant mantle of Spring," and "within her doth dwell
so much of variety, so much of natural plenty, that there is not any thing that is or
may be so rare, but it inhabits within this plenteous soyle" (Mulford 2002, 555–556).
Merging the sensuous woman image with an arcadian vision, Thomas Morton cher-
ishingly details the land's "goodly groves of trees, dainty fine round rising hillocks,
delicate fair large plains, sweet crystal fountains, and clear running streams that
twine in fine meanders through the meads, making so sweet a murmuring noise to
hear as would even lull the senses with delight asleep." He notes that "millions of
turtledoves on the green boughs . . . sat pecking of the full ripe pleasant grapes that
were supported by the lusty trees" (Mulford 2002, 251–252). The land awaits, willingly "yielding" everything, so that, as Captain John Smith habitually tells us, the
whole experience is a "pleasure." "If you please," you may load your boat, for "a man
may take . . . what he will" of the land and waters; "at your pleasure," abundance
awaits. This is heady rhetoric. Such is the potency of promotion literature that it
will "satisfie the desires" of those craving connection to the wonderful environment
(Denton 1973, 87).

Often America is characterized as Edenic, the "land flowing with milk and
honey." Yet if it be Eden, it is Eden on steroids. The ground is so "fat" that it can grow
anything, and to utterly prodigious extents. Given an environment that avowedly
produces forty- or fifty-pound turkeys and deer giving birth to three fawns at a
time, what else could one expect, but hemp that "shewteth up to be tenne foote
high"?

As this representative image reveals, measurement proves vital in promotional
discourse. One quickly realizes, though, that it is not only a physical but also a spiritual metrics, a yardstick of health, profit, and benediction operant in the New World.
Whether native or transplanted, everything thrives. As Wood expresses, "Whatsoever
grows well in England grows as well there [in New England], many things better and
larger" (Wood 1977, 36). Hence promotional authors' constant comparative or superlative diction, with color, climate, contents, and contours reminiscent of Europe,

and attestations that natural resources are "as good as" those found in England or elsewhere, or more often of "a better sort." The New World "could be understood, perhaps, by discovering likeness with the Old" (Gray 2004, 2). Parity established a comforting connection to the familiar Old World, taming the strangeness of New World phenomena, while superiority promised fulfillment of financial fantasies, that is, economic self-sufficiency. Intriguingly, these compositions include a fine mathematical gloss on the New World's commodities, with everything customarily characterized as "twice as good" as or "three times larger" than the natural resources of other countries. Ultimately, though, America is a land without parallel. In a tract from 1562, French Huguenot sailor Jean Ribaut gushes, the land "is the fairest, frutefullest and pleasantest of all the worlde. . . . It is a thinge inspeakable, the commodities that be sene there and shal be founde more and more in this incomparable land" (Ribaut 1927, 72–73).

Keen to portray America as "superabundant," the authors of promotion literature proclaim that the soil will produce multiple harvests each year, without the need for manure or any agricultural effort. Arthur Barlowe excitedly declares that "the earth bringeth forth all things in aboundance, as in the first creation, without toile or labor" (Franklin 1979, 106), a statement regularly repeated in promotional passages regardless of geography.

ATTITUDES TOWARD THE ENVIRONMENT

Promotion literature may be divided into three categories: discovery, exploration, and settlement. Whereas discovery accounts convey wonder at the divine plenitude and include a "simple timeless stare" at such perfection, exploration narratives feature action, use of the land, introducing "an edge of calculation and containment" (Franklin 1979, 22, 69). Wood and others routinely remark that the land is "fit for the plow" (Wood 1977, 65). If not put into cultivation, it is "wasted," serving "no use" but to feed and shelter wild animals. (This reductive attitude is why we cannot call the bulk of promotion literature "green," or ecocritically sensitive. Deep ecology it is not.)

From the outset, the English (and the Dutch, French, and Spaniards, too) had designs on the land, a horticultural and architectonic imperative of exploitation and development. Accordingly, one major feature of early American writing is the eager anticipation of enactment, of what can "be done with" America. In Puritan ideology, this preoccupation famously fostered an environmental double vision, whereby the teeming land was somehow seen as an empty, barren "desert" needing taming and civilizing. Yet even from a more secure perspective, America was a moralized landscape. If the land was there for the taking, all its contents were fair game.

Despite the natural-historical bent of some promotion literature, the settlers seem not so much merely appreciative of the land's bounty in environmental fact as desirous of using it all up. How else are we to react to the record of rapacity gleefully provided by promotional writers? Wood proclaims, if one wants to go hunting with hawks, "any . . . may have his desires. . . . If I should tell you how some here have killed a hundred geese in a week, fifty ducks at a shot, forty teals at another, it may be counted impossible, though nothing more certain" (Wood 1977, 52). The concept is hardly original with him: an investor in the Company of Adventurers for New Plymouth, Emmanuel Altham, makes a similar comment in a 1623 letter, stating that "one man at six shots hath killed 400" fowl (Mulford 2002, 288). Likewise, William Penn observes that people enjoy nature's "produce" and "almost shovel . . . up in their tub" the copious fish (quoted in Franklin 1979, 102). Granted, the settlers must eat and have goods to trade. Yet the very diction of promotion literature details the degree to which the getting is good. After all, of everything from oaks to codfish, there is "great store."

A basic tenet of promotional writings is the healthfulness of the environment. A splendid spa and pharmacopeia, America is fabulously curative, abounding in floral and faunal physic "sovereign" for health. As Jones points out, "The theory of a special vis naturae curatrix in the New World lingered long" (Jones 1952, 38). Wood states it well: "For the common diseases of England, they be strangers to the English now in that strange land. . . . Some that were long troubled with lingering diseases, as coughs of the lungs, consumptions, etc., have been restored by that medicineable climate to their former strength and health." Offering testimonial, Wood proclaims that he, having been sickly, now "being planted in that new soil and healthful air . . . scarce did I know what belonged to a day's sickness" (Wood 1977, 32–33). The English cattle likewise prosper; in fact, attests Wood, they grow bigger in America than in England.

THE RHETORIC OF ERASURE

For its vivid portrayal of plenitude and perfect health, promotion literature is remarkable. Yet it is equally notable for its diction of denial, of what it purposefully removes from the picture. To accomplish this goal, the writers cleverly weave bits of what we today would call "magic rhetoric" with a rhetoric of erasure. Magic rhetoric refers to the language of agency, the phrasing of fiat. The rhetoric of erasure concerns strategic omission of unsavory realities. The elements of this formula of facilitation may be itemized as follows:

1. The voyage to America is portrayed as quick and easy, or it is not described at all, thus effectively projecting the traveler immediately into the scene without travail and weariness.
2. Victuals and drink shall await the instant traveler's pleasure.
3. The traveler need not worry about vicious animals, insects, or Indians.
4. The land provides limitless wood for shelter and settlement, and there is no need for toil, since America is a garden of delight.
5. There is no sickness; health reigns supreme.
6. The persons there "planted" shall be self-sufficient, vitiating the struggle of international trade competition.
7. The planters will experience joy, being planted so propitiously in the best spot on Earth.

Clearly, all potential problems vanish. How could it be otherwise when, as seemingly everyone agrees, America is "the pleasantest and most commodious dwelling of all the world"?

Promotion literature presents an exuberant fantasy of paradise, found on the shores of America. Still, in the preceding list, the third item deserves special comment. Not only are animals generally "defanged" in the literature, but noisome insects are usually nonexistent. In like manner, the native inhabitants, the Indians, perform a neat disappearing act. Although promotional discourse is replete with references to their existence, their languages and customs, their agricultural ideas and occasional assistance, look away for a moment and you may miss them. Despite their presence in America, it miraculously remains "empty," awaiting the settlement of "good honest Christians." Peter Hulme observes that the English characterized the Indians as nomads, not settlers, and thus, they "left the land empty and virgin." To the English mind-set, the Indians did not "use" the land, so they evidently were not part of God's plan. Although early promotional writers envisioned English and Indian coexistence, later authors often finessed the issue. The English would "civilize" the natives, or those "wild" ones would perish. Because the "savages" did not possess writing, they were "virtually excluded by definition from the human community" (Hulme 1986, 194; Greenblatt 1991, 10). It is eerily as if the Indians are an anomaly, a flaw in the picture of perfection. Harnessing the outrageous ethnocentricity of the era, Daniel Denton declares, "It hath been generally observed, that where the English come to setle, a Divine Hand makes way for them, by removing or cutting off the Indians" (Denton 1973, 49). Apparently, God practices biological warfare in this otherwise pristine environment, for in *Mourt's Relation,* a bubonic plague outbreak that wiped out much of the native American population is tacitly attributed to Providence. Now the land, suitably cleared, welcomes the worthy and "industrious" English plantation.

How many writers truly subscribed to the arrogant assumptions articulated in promotion propaganda or actually witnessed all that they wrote of remains uncertain, given the authors' strong tendency to credentialize their tracts by liberal cross-referencing. Some writers make reference to others' work, some to their own earlier efforts, and several simply lift passages wholesale from each other. In accordance with the name-dropping habits of the times, Thomas Morton cites Wood's *New Englands Prospect* in *New English Canaan*. In turn, Wood mentions the "thrice-memorable Captain John Smith" in his *Prospect*. Smith incorporates information from his own *Description of New England* and his *New England's Trials* (1622), plus material from the anonymous *Mourt's Relation* and Edward Winslow's *Good Newes From New-England,* into his *Generall Historie of Virginia, New-England, and the Summer Isles* (1624). Passages of *Mourt's Relation* likewise appear in William Bradford's *Of Plymouth Plantation* (written 1630–1646). Thus, in promotion literature there exists a fair degree of redundancy in diction and idea.

Captain John Smith's Description of New England

Despite the formulaic quality of promotion literature, individual tracts possess distinctive attributes. A brief discussion of particular writings demonstrates their diversity. The narratives of the entrepreneurial Captain John Smith are a case in point. His *Description of New England* (1616) offers both depiction and economic analysis. Smith "underplayed his picture, because he well knew that inflated expectations led to disappointment and withdrawal" (Smith 1988, 207). Nevertheless, his work includes breathless catalogs of natural abundance and a keen tabulation of economic benefits to be gained in America. Every item of flora and fauna, minerals and metals, carries a price tag identifying profit. Smith follows his torrents of nouns with commentary confirming plenitude and pleasure. His descriptive specificity is significant because he had already been to France, Germany, Italy, Greece, Austria, Poland, the Balkans, and North Africa. In rendering his analysis, therefore, he had much data for comparison. Interestingly, he engages in self-promotion as well as land promotion, grandly announcing that he was "a real Actor" in the English enterprise.

The themes of promotion literature are well represented in Smith's influential tracts. As he says in *Description of New England,* "Who can but approve this a most excellent place, both for health and fertilitie? . . . I would rather live here then any where" (Smith 1988, 226). His encomia on interacting with the land and sea—hunting, fishing, planting crops and people—are exuberant. Smith relates, "If a man worke but three days in seaven, he may get more then hee can spend, unless he will be excessive" (Mulford 2002, 176). Gleefully obliterating the threat of trade competition, he asks, "Why should wee more doubt, then Holland, Portugale, Spaniard, French, or other, but to doe much better then they, where there is victual to feede us, wood of all sorts, to build Boats, Ships, or Barks; the fish at our doors, pitch, masts, yards, and most other necessaries onely for making?" Thanks to the ample resources of America, England can "equalize any of these famous Kingdomes, in all commodities, pleasures, and conditions" (Mulford 2002, 172–173).

Still, Smith underscores the need for industrious participants. He wishes to eradicate the laziness and foolishness of those settlers who envision a life of "Idlenesse and carelessnesse." "Intemperate idleness" proves a frequent target in promotion literature. Yet who could be blamed for expecting instant gratification, when the purpose of promotional writing is to accentuate the dazzling prospect of America? Nourished on the nectar of New World promise, who would want to work? With tales and treatises endlessly celebrating America's glory, it must have seemed that simply arriving there would end all troubles forever. Without a doubt, colonists like Smith who attractively promoted America contributed mightily to the problem: one could surely be forgiven for dreaming of an idyllic dwelling in this enchanted area when, by all accounts, America was so wonderful.

For Smith, colonization is an adventure and imperative. Weighing the options, he muses, "Then, who would live at home idly (or thinke in himself any worth to live), onely to eate, drink, and sleepe, and so die?" Highlighting action, he identifies the types of workers necessary for success: "Carpenters, Masons, Fishers, Fowlers, Gardiners, Husbandmen, Sawyers, Smiths, Spinsters, Taylors, Weavers, and such like" (Mulford 2002, 175–176). He undercuts the America-as-Eden notion that so readily generated "slothfulness": yes, America awaits, a place of plenty, but people must put forth some effort to realize their dreams. Invoking the special partnership of Providence and the populace, he notes that "by Gods blessing and his own industrie," the individual advances. For its vigorous narrative detail and style, *Description of New England* is considered the finest work of seventeenth-century promotion literature.

MOURT'S RELATION

For another historical account, we turn to *Mourt's Relation,* the short title for *A Relation or Journal . . . of the English Plantation Setled at Plimoth*. Until recently, *Mourt's Relation* was attributed either to Bradford or to Edward Winslow; currently, its authorship is uncertain. The short title possibly derives from George Morton, who ensured the journal's publication. Whatever the case, the *Relation* contains five unsigned "Relations" that present details from the colony's life during the period from September 1620 to March 1621, including the creation of the Mayflower Compact. Although set up as a history, *Mourt's Relation* is a promotional piece encouraging settlement. A fairly straightforward account of experiences, the work is of historical interest due to its variance from Bradford's ideologically flavored descriptions in *Of Plymouth Plantation*. For example, it mentions sea travel as comprising "many difficulties in boisterous storms" but does not dwell on them, instead concentrating on the safe arrival in America; thus, it minimizes the arduous voyage of "long beating at sea" that Bradford details. Second, whereas Bradford famously calls attention to a threatening landscape, with "wild and savage hue," the *Relation* renders the environs in typical promotional style. The travelers view "so goodly a land, and wooded to the brink of the sea." We find catalogs of useful trees, fruits, and herbs, and praise for the fertile earth, and (naturally) the "greatest store" of commodities (Anon. 1963, 15–16).

Mourt's Relation makes the expected comparison to other lands, with the rhetoric promising parity and soon set on superiority: As the stock phrasing goes, New England is "one of the most pleasant, most healthful, and most fruitful parts of the land." Seeing sand hills, the author of one section notes that they are "much like the downs in Holland, but much better." He also mentions discovering "excellent clay, no better in the world." As for the water, "our first New England water" is consumed "with as much delight as ever we drunk drink in all our lives," for it is "the best water that ever we drank." However sweetly satisfying her bounty, the settlers view the land always with an eye to economic opportunity. For instance, seeing whales, they calculate that had they "instruments and means to take them," they could have "made three or four thousand pounds' worth of oil." At Cape Cod, they "saw daily great whales of the best kind for oil and bone." Likewise, surveying the land, they label it "excellent black mould, and fat," perfectly "fit for the plow" (Anon. 1963, 3, 16, 18, 20–21, 30, 39).

Mourt's Relation does include elements of honesty about inclement weather: the settlers frequently endured rain, sleet, and snow. Given the necessity of walking in frigid waters and foul weather, many people sickened and died. Yet, overall, this day-by-day account of adventure promotes the positive. It contains the usual rationalization for Christians to plant themselves on such superior land: so much of the region is "open" and "waste," seemingly inviting "industrious" Christians to "use" it. Of historical note, the text contains the earliest description of the first Thanksgiving with the natives, the basis for that grand American feel-good vision of cornucopia and coexistence. *Mourt's Relation* provides greater detail about Indian culture than some other promotional pieces do. According to the narrative, the settlers do have to be watchful for such Indians as remain. Naturally, though, the text states, "If we have once but kine, horses, and sheep, I make no question but men might live as contented here as in any part of the world." Given farm animals and willing workers,

New England can be comfortable and commercially viable. There follow the typical summations of promotional discourse: here is a land of opportunity, anticipating occupants. Of course, when settlers plan to come, they should bring practical items such as clothes, paper, butter, and weapons. One of the final thoughts in the text is the conveniently environmental announcement that the Indians do not "have art, science, skill or faculty to use either the land or the commodities of it, but all spoils, rots, and is marred for want of manuring, gathering, ordering, etc." Obviously, those agricultural heroes, the English, should "take a land which none useth, and make use of it" (Anon. 1963, 43, 51, 63, 83–85, 91–92).

EDWARD WINSLOW'S GOOD NEWES FROM NEW-ENGLAND

Another promotional tract dealing with the Plymouth Plantation is Edward Winslow's *Good Newes from New-England*. Winslow's work continues the plantation's "Very Remarkable" narrative from the end of *Mourt's Relation*. The author uses an "advice column" technique, informing the reader that "three things are the overthrow and bane . . . of Plantations. 1. The vain expectation of present profit . . . 2. Ambition in their governors and commanders . . . 3. The carelessness of those that send over supplies of men unto them, not caring how they be qualified." It is a point to which he returns, creatively arguing that people must not entertain foolish notions of paradise awaiting them: "And can any be so simple as to conceive that the fountains should stream forth wine or beer, or the woods and rivers be like butchers' shops, or fishmongers' stalls, where they might have things taken to their hands? If thou canst not live without such things, and hast no means to procure the one, and wilt not take pains for the other, nor hast ability to employ others for thee, rest where thou art" (Winslow 1996, 4, 71).

In addition to chastising idle dreamers, Winslow offers evidence that God approves of the colonizing endeavor. Although he acknowledges the Indians' presence, they patently have no rightful claim on the land. Confidently he announces, "So that when I seriously consider of things, I cannot but think that God hath a purpose to give that land as an inheritance to our nation." What a propitious place: After all, "In my best observation, comparing our owne condition with the Relations of other parts of America, I cannot conceive of any to agree better with the constitution of the English" (Winslow 1996, 57, 68). Despite the frequent mention of God's providence, however, the narrative reveals that the Indians represent a real peril. One look at the lengthy full title of the work raises more questions than it answers: given the "many apparent deaths and dangers" and "troubles" that Winslow and company encounter, one wonders how promising an enterprise colonization actually is!

WILLIAM WOOD'S *NEW ENGLANDS PROSPECT*

For a "true, lively, and experimental description" offering more obviously bright prospects, we turn to William Wood. His engaging *New Englands Prospect* is aimed, as his title page announces, at both "the mind-travelling reader" and "the future voyager." Well regarded by fellow writers, Wood is frequently quoted in their texts, an honor extending into the nineteenth century, with Thoreau's own literary nods. Having spent four years in Massachusetts, from 1629 to 1633, Wood provides a wealth of accurate detail and occasional poetry celebrating New England's commodities, such as the "luscious lobster" and "sky-towering pines." Never merely a catalog of moneymaking goods, his verse lists reflect appreciation for the natural bounty and variety of New England. Wood's aesthetically rich text is the earliest comprehensive account of the climate, geography, soil, minerals, plants, and animals present in the area. Indeed, unlike Winslow's chronicle of the colonists' experience, *Prospect* focuses on natural history. It is therefore refreshingly free of theological moralizing.

Accentuating ease, Wood downplays the fury of the ocean and threat of disaster en route to America. Whereas William Bradford highlights the danger of ocean passage, Wood encourages the potential traveler to perceive the ship as a "cradle rocked by a careful mother's hand." Travelers will arrive, safe and sound. Once disembarked, they will experience good health in America, "that strange land" where, though "death [is] certain to all," it will be a long time a-coming, so salubrious is the locale (Wood 1977, 70, 32).

New Englands Prospect proves interesting for its admission that pernicious creatures exist in America. Rather than participating in the traditional rhetoric of omission, Wood identifies rattlesnakes, wolves, mosquitoes, biting flies, wasps, and spiders as "Things as are Hurtful in the Plantation" (Wood 1977, 65–67). Yet it is telling that he for the most part places them toward the middle of his tract, thereby effectively denying them agency as real threats. They clearly will not deter the colonization process. Right on cue, the next chapter concerns the appropriate supplies to bring to America: homey little details like salad oil and lemon juice (which *Mourt's Relation* also recommends), candles and frying pans. He sketches, too, the proper character of travelers. This last item, a legitimate concern of propagandists, is in common with Smith's advice: bring industrious, skilled people. Promoting a particular portion of paradise, Wood recommends that passengers come to New England, not Virginia, for the climate is better for English bodies. Having depicted the biology and geography of New England in part I and offered practical advice, Wood shifts in part II to a focus on Indians. Unlike in Winslow's work, however, the Indians in *Prospect* receive their due. Wood presents a valuable ethnographic treatment of them, rather than portraying them as incongruous and inimical creatures.

JOHN JOSSELYN'S *NEW ENGLAND'S RARITIES DISCOVERED*

A reader of Wood's *Prospect,* Smith's *Description,* and Morton's *New English Canaan* was John Josselyn, whose *New England's Rarities Discovered* celebrates the environment's flora and fauna. Curiously, Josselyn asserts that there are lions in the land (which *Mourt's Relation* suggests as well), and frogs "as big as a Child of a year old." Appreciative of New England's "rarities," Josselyn proclaims that here are "absolutely the best Trees in the World." Like Wood, Josselyn occasionally offers verses, such as lines rejoicing in New England's springtime. His focus is on the types and uses of plants and animals. Despite—or perhaps due to—its dubious medical claims, *Rarities* makes for engaging reading, as Josselyn combines bits of folklore and natural history. His work includes catalogs of species, plus lively descriptions, such as of hummingbirds ("of variable glittering Colours"), and fascinating analyses of plants' and creatures' benefits: loons supposedly cure aches, watermelons quench fevers, and pulverized codfish bones stop a woman's "overflowing courses notably." Examining Josselyn's book, one senses that people were forever getting burned, suffering "fluxes," "stabs," and "plague of the Back," but that, thankfully, New England contained the necessary cure-alls (Josselyn 1992, 6, 32, 38, 63).

Not only is *Rarities* absorbing as a record of people's medical complaints and the available curatives, it also offers intriguing information about plants inadvertently transported from England. According to Alan Taylor, "Today botanists estimate that 258 of the approximately 500 weed species in the United States originated in the Old World" (Taylor 2001, 48). Significantly, Josselyn's *Rarities* expresses early concern about species reduction, including the substantial decline of turkeys, a loss that he imputes to both "the English and the Indian." It is a valuable text, for as Thomas Lyon states, in it "we see . . . many of the materials of the American nature essay assembling loosely, in effect, ahead of their time" (Lyon 2001, 42).

DANIEL DENTON'S *BRIEF DESCRIPTION* OF *NEW-YORK*

To be sure, New England did not have an exclusive corner on the market for colonists. New places such as New York and Maryland piqued the English fancy, too. A fine promoter of New York, a "known unknown part of America," is Daniel Denton. One of the first settlers of Jamaica, New York, Denton wrote the first printed account in English of the area. In *A Brief Description of New-York,* he labels the land ideal for settlement: spacious, inviting, full of "great store" of all necessities, a land flowing "with milk and honey" (Denton 1973, 85). To the usual promotional fare he adds the insistence that the land is actively seeking "use"; it actually does not want to be "wasted" by lying "empty." Denton's aggressively imperialistic viewpoint prefigures people of today who commonly look at a flourishing ecosystem and claim that the land lies "empty" or "vacant," just yearning to be "developed."

However empty of English inhabitants New York was, of one resource it proved blissfully full: strawberries. Denton presents a delightful mock-chivalric vignette of raiding the Long Island strawberry patch (Denton 1973, 40). Here he participates in a mini-tradition of literature, the encomium upon these luscious berries. One finds similar praise for such delicacies in *Virginia . . . Richly and Truly Valued,* for instance: "In its season your foot can hardly direct itself where it will not be died in the bloud of large and delicious Strawberries," and in Wood's *Prospect,* where he exults that berries grow "two inches about" (Force 2002, 11; Wood 1977, 36).

As Denton's vigorous image of strawberry raiding reflects, the people in New York are able-bodied, for the land promotes health and self-sufficiency: "There is no disease common to the Countrey, but may be cured without Materials from other Nations." Besides, "many people in twenty years time never know what sickness is." Everything thrives in this goodly region, for there exists "no place in the North of America better." To Denton, the English absolutely belong there. Though he spends several pages describing the Indians' habits, he then dismisses them and proclaims that the land "is capable of entertaining more inhabitants": food abounds, "enough to entertain Hundreds of Families," and plentiful space, since "here is hundreds, nay thousands of Acres, that would invite inhabitants." Miraculously, the vision steadily expands, culminating in the assertion that the country is "capable of entertaining many thousand" (Denton 1973, 42, 45, 66–67, 71, 75, 84). Why should anyone live in New England or Virginia, asks Denton, when New York is so obviously the best?

Enumerating the advantages of the area, Denton offers a sweet benediction upon the colonizing enterprise. In closing, he declares that "with Gods blessing, and their own industry," people there may "live as happily as any people in the world," and, one strongly suspects, even more so (Denton 1973, 85, 87). Still, having been transplanted into American soil, will they retain their Englishness? Herein lies a key concern of the early colonial era: how to reap the benefits of the New World without losing one's English nature.

George Alsop's *Character of the Province of Mary-Land*

George Alsop addresses this issue in his lively, bawdy *Character of the Province of Mary-Land,* the "jewel in the genre of the promotion tract" (Lemay 1972b, 70). An indentured servant in Maryland for four years, Alsop can offer details about the province based on observation. Yet he is not interested in providing a simple recitation of facts, nor in presenting a typical promotional tract. In fact, he mocks the herbal catalog approach, if not the whole promotional genre. After asserting that no place "can parallel this fertile and pleasant piece of ground in its multiplicity"—thus rendering any detail unnecessary—he then proceeds to extol Maryland's character as perfection incarnate. Nature could not "in convenienter terms have told man, Dwell here, live plentifully, and be rich" (Mulford 2002, 555–556).

As for the "rarities" found in parts of America, forget even trying to make comparison, for Maryland is glorious; she "flourishly abounds in" glory. The turkeys Alsop has "seen in whole hundreds," and waterfowl "arrive in millionous multitudes." Fish are plentiful and easily caught. Although Alsop identifies some creatures, he recognizes that to tally them all would be to render them finite and thus perhaps unimpressive for being a known quantity. Therefore, he archly insists that "it is impossible to give you an exact description of them all, considering the multiplicity as well as the diversity of so numerous an extent of Creatures," his bombastic syntax expressive of infinity. Naturally, crops thrive in Maryland without the need for manure. Combining the promotional conventions of inexhaustible fertility and the perfection of a particular place, Alsop breaks into verse, his paean declaring that "there is a Land now found,/That all Earth's Globe can't parallel its Ground" (Mulford 2002, 557).

Decrying their hesitation, the author encourages the English to emigrate. What would stop such a noble enterprise? He cleverly reduces people's fears to absurdity and states that his "Relation" will cure people's "low and base Cowardize" (Mulford 2002, 560). Travel to America represents not a voyage to the frightening unknown but a satisfying rendezvous with a lovely and eager maiden. That comely lady would welcome the English presence, a point important to colonists concerned with maintaining their English identity. Would transplantation to a new terrain somehow dilute the Englishness of the travelers? This concern had a long duration, showing up throughout the decades in various writings as admonitions against "Criolian degeneracy": the transplanted English "Vine" would be corrupted, and God's English garden would wither and die (Canup 1989).

Instead, Alsop boldly argues that staying in America somehow enhances one's Englishness—indeed, is vital to the well-being of England. *Character* is a colossal, witty put-down of ignorance, a brilliantly scatological vision that simultaneously asserts the propriety of the English presence in America and insists on American superiority to boot. Never mind the efficacy of individual herbs and airs. Maryland herself will restore the corrupted English body. Who needs Spanish gold, when the very dirt of Maryland effects a salubrious transformation? Playful and proud, *Character* is a promotional tract par excellence. A delicious "Pye," it embodies the goodness of America, nourishing all who partake of the tract.

A major irony of promotion literature is that its glorious premise did not come to fruition quite as readily as planned. The colonizing ventures "failed during the seventeenth century to yield many of the benefits predicted by Richard Hakluyt in the 1580s" (Greene 1993, 61). England's deep-rooted problems persisted, and indeed, many of its fond schemes simply did not work: moose and elk were not successfully trained as beasts of burden, for instance, and as for silk production, America's indigenous mulberries were of the wrong sort to feed silkworms.

Yet, individuals in America could thrive; personal ambitions could blossom and set spectacular fruit. In the eighteenth century, the colonies substantially developed. Their success was a source of fascination for all. In *The Wealth of Nations* (1776), Adam Smith accounts for colonial growth, identifying six main causes. The secret lay in the land—its availability, healthfulness, and general excellence—its inhabitants, and their actions. Provided that they were "industrious," they could experience a happy, healthy, secure life in the wondrous realm. Naturally, of course, the people populating each region of America conceived of their surroundings as superior to others'. Every colony had its ardent supporters, offering testimonials to the certainty of success (Greene 1993, 68–78). Due to the generous expanse of exceptional land, coupled with honest effort, people could reap substantial benefits, far exceeding those possible in crowded and careworn England.

Constant was the theme of a recipe or formula for success in these fair and fertile fields. Echoing the discourse of promotion, for example, a representative writer observes, immigrants could establish "such Farms as afford[ed] them . . . all the Necessaries of Life in plenty" (quoted in Greene 1993, 102). The outlook proved bright, especially in comparison to the dismal prospects of an unstable and sickly Europe. Promoting the interior of the land in *A New Voyage to Carolina* (1709), John Lawson boasts of its beauty, fertility, and potential for "Productions" of "profitable Commodities," and then makes a pointed comparison to other countries. Unlike European lands, which endure earthquakes (nicely representing their overall instability), "pestilential fevers," "consumptions and catarrhs," Carolina is "very agreeable to European Bodies and makes them healthy" (Mulford 2002, 493). Relocation appeared essential, for who would be so foolish as to not take advantage of this invitation to improve the very standard of living by landing in America?

BENJAMIN FRANKLIN'S *INFORMATION FOR THOSE WHO WOULD REMOVE TO AMERICA*

In much literature of the era, America is portrayed as the cynosure of civilization; progress and possibilities form a vital motif. It seemed that everyone wanted to know "what this new nation represented, and what the character and best hopes of the American might be" (Gray 2004, 73). Therefore, scores of writers explored the issue. The key to success is brilliantly represented in Benjamin Franklin's *Information for Those Who Would Remove to America,* considered the finest work of eighteenth-century promotion literature. Lemay states, "America was already, because of the influence of promotion literature, regarded as a country where a man could become whatever he desired." It is fitting that in his writings, Franklin incorporates the conventions and conceits common to the promotional genre. For instance, in a piece from 1765, he spoofs the English concerns about American wool production by playing up the promise of plenitude, noting waggishly, "The very Tails of the American Sheep are so laden with Wool, that each has a Car or Waggon on four little Wheels to support and keep it from trailing on the Ground" (Lemay 1972a, 240, 227).

In *Information,* the promotional outlines are familiar: the environment is genial, "the salubrity of the air, the healthiness of the Climate, the plenty of good provisions" a given. Metaphorically planted in goodly soil, people thrive, for "the increase of inhabitants by natural generation is very rapid in America." The natural conditions are propitious, but Franklin is emphatic on the effort necessary for economic success. Skilled, industrious people are welcome and vital in America. Echoing previous cautions against visions of ease, he chides those who imagine that "the fowls fly about ready roasted, crying come eat me!" Assuring the reader of veracity, he states that his tract provides "clearer and truer notions" of America than others'. With his careful analytical approach, he aims to squelch individuals' "wild imaginations" about paid passage, free land and servants, tools, and cattle awaiting travelers. Forget about stupendous "commodities." Instead of being rich, "it is rather a general happy mediocrity that prevails," with "very few rich enough to live idly." He catalogs the cultural benefits and occupational outlook of America: educational opportunities abound, for several colleges and universities flourish, but a paucity of "civil offices, or employments" await. Franklin advises would-be

Greenblatt, Stephen. 1991. *Marvelous Possessions: The Wonder of the New World.* Chicago: University of Chicago Press.

Greene, Jack P. 1993. *The Intellectual Construction of America: Exceptionalism and Identity from 1492 to 1800.* Chapel Hill: University of North Carolina Press.

Hayes, Kevin J. 2001. How Thomas Prince Read Captain John Smith. In *Finding Colonial Americas: Essays Honoring J. A. Leo Lemay,* edited by Carla Mulford and David S. Shields, 367–378. Newark: University of Delaware Press.

Hulme, Peter. 1986. *Colonial Encounters: Europe and the Native Caribbean, 1492–1797.* London: Methuen.

Jefferson, Thomas. 1953. Letter to John Banister, Jr., October 15, 1785. In *The Papers of Thomas Jefferson,* edited by Julian P. Boyd et al., Vol. 8, pp. 635–637. Princeton, NJ: Princeton University Press.

Jehlen, Myra. 1994. The Literature of Colonization. In *The Cambridge History of American Literature.* Vol. 1, 1590–1820, edited by Sacvan Bercovitch, 11–168. New York: Cambridge University Press.

Jones, Howard Mumford. 1952. *O Strange New World: American Culture, The Formative Years.* New York: Viking.

Josselyn, John. 1992. *New-England's Rarities Discovered.* Bedford, MA: Applewood Books.

Lemay, J. A. Leo. 1972a. Benjamin Franklin. In *Major Writers of Early American Literature,* edited by Everett Emerson, 205–243. Madison: University of Wisconsin Press.

———. 1972b. *Men of Letters in Colonial Maryland.* Knoxville: University of Tennessee Press.

———. 1991. *The American Dream of Captain John Smith.* Charlottesville: University Press of Virginia.

Lyon, Thomas J. 2001. *This Incomparable Land: A Guide to American Nature Writing.* Minneapolis, MN: Milkweed Editions.

Mulford, Carla, ed. 2002. *Early American Writings.* New York: Oxford University Press.

Ribaut, Jean. 1927. *The Whole and True Discovery of Terra Florida.* Deland: Florida State Historical Society.

Smith, Adam. 1776. *An Inquiry into the Nature and Causes of the Wealth of Nations.* London: W. Strahan and T. Cadell. 2 vols.

Smith, John. 1988. *Captain John Smith: A Select Edition of His Writings,* edited by Karen Ordahl Kupperman. Chapel Hill: University of North Carolina Press.

Sweet, Timothy. 2002. *American Georgics: Economy and Environment in Early American Literature.* Philadelphia: University of Pennsylvania Press.

Taylor, Alan. 2001. *American Colonies: The Settling of North America.* New York: Penguin.

Winslow, Edward. 1996. *Good Newes from New England.* Bedford, MA: Applewood Books.

Wood, William. 1977. *New Englands Prospect,* edited by Alden T. Vaughan. Amherst: University of Massachusetts Press.

PART II

DEVOTIONAL LITERATURE

CHAPTER 4

PURITAN HISTORIANS AND HISTORIOGRAPHY

NAOKI ONISHI

"There is special Providence in the fall of a sparrow," Hamlet murmurs to himself in act 5, scene 2, just before his duel with Leartes. William Shakespeare composed *Hamlet* in 1600 in England during the reign of Queen Elizabeth I. Seven years later, a small group of Separatists left England for Holland, and thirteen years after that, in 1620, they continued to the New World to maintain their religious freedom. Originally aiming for the outlet of the Hudson River, at that time part of Virginia, they ended up at Cape Cod and chose to land on the shores of Plymouth. Governor William Bradford left a memoir of their audacious but dangerous voyage and their settlement, which he titled *Of Plymouth Plantation* and in which he repeatedly used the word "Providence" to interpret the significant events that happened aboard the *Mayflower* and then later in Plymouth Plantation.

During their second expedition on the shores of Cape Cod, for instance, a group of some thirty men found two Indian houses containing various implements and different kinds of corn and bean. Bradford wrote: "And here is to be noted a special Providence of God, and a great mercy to this poor people, that here they got seed to plant them corn the next year, or else they might have starved, for they had none nor any likelihood to get any till the season had been past, as the sequel did manifest" (Bradford 1970, 66). Without finding this corn, those Separatists, later called the Pilgrim Fathers, could not have survived their first New England winter. But the corn had been preserved for the survival of other people, the Wanpanoags. What

Bradford interpreted as a special Providence was thievery from the Indian point of view. The Puritans, however, interpreted what was happening from their own perspective and assumed that their interpretation was sanctioned by God.

Generally, the New England Puritans considered whatever happened to them as manifestations of divine will. Anxious to understand the hidden significance of daily events, they eagerly recorded what was happening to them. Thus, not only the histories they wrote but all kinds of writing—autobiographies, biographies, church histories, diaries, memoirs, poetry—reflect their quest to comprehend the meaning of whatever they encountered. It is no wonder that they left numerous personal and public records. They were keenly conscious that the daily event, whether trifling or dramatic, would give them a clearer idea why certain things happened at certain times. Divine will, they thought, directed everything that was happening and would continue to lead them to the promised land. The reason the New England Puritans left so many historical documents, especially compared with the English colonists elsewhere in America, stems from their never-ending quest to understand Providence.

In order to verify the efforts of their community, the Puritans needed to interpret events, thereby justifying their endeavor to create a new commonwealth based upon their understanding of the Bible. Simultaneously, this interpretive process let them understand their salvation, which was realized by God's Providence. They considered the settlement of a biblical commonwealth as a mission conducted under contract with God. Their historical writings illustrate the peculiar historical sense necessary to construct the ethos of this new land.

CHARACTERISTICS OF PURITAN HISTORIOGRAPHY

In their quest to understand God's ways, seventeenth-century New England Puritans tried to see Providence in virtually everything, including natural phenomena both ordinary and extraordinary: birth defects, comets, earthquakes, eclipses, famine, hurricanes, or pestilence. They felt responsible to these phenomena, and often held days of thanksgiving to express their gratitude for their delivery from them. Nathaniel Hawthorne's depiction in *The Scarlet Letter* of an object the Reverend Arthur Dimmesdale sees in the sky shaped as an "A" provides a convenient example of this way of thinking. Describing the Puritan impulse to interpret natural phenomena, Hawthorne observed:

> Nothing was more common, in those days, than to interpret all meteoric appearances, and other natural phenomena, that occurred with less regularity than the rise and set of sun and moon, as so many revelations from a supernatural source.

Thus, a blazing spear, a sword of flame, a bow, or a sheaf of arrows, seen in the midnight sky, prefigured Indian warfare. Pestilence was known to have been forboded by a shower of crimson light. We doubt whether any marked event, for good or evil, ever befell New England, from its settlement down to Revolutionary times, of which the inhabitants had not been previously warned by some spectacle of this nature. (Hawthorne 2006, 196)

The same mind-set can be more vividly and widely found in the writings of seventeenth-century New England Puritans. David Hall (1989) has shown how the extraordinary natural phenomena were interpreted by the common people and the contemporary historians at that time. The Puritan tendency toward the interpretation of natural phenomena helped to fashion popular religious belief and create a collective imagination.

The Puritans were prone to scrutinize, investigate, and interpret the significance of their surroundings. By keeping detailed records of events they may not have understood at the time, they allowed the possibility of recognizing the significance of those events later. Almost every pastor in seventeenth-century New England kept a diary, out of which he constructed historical writings of his own. Conscious that they stood on the starting point of a new history, the Puritans' obsession with history was keen.

New England Puritans had a deep awareness of both the past and the present, which they used to understand their religious and cultural endeavors. In their historical writings, they structured their interpretation into in a temporal scheme. Instead of interpreting distinct events to understand God's meaning as Hamlet does, the Puritan historian often situated multiple events within a process originating in a specific approach to biblical exegesis: typology. Furthermore, Puritan historical writings often suggest that the completion of history is near. This eschatological understanding takes the form of millennialism, which pervades their historical writings.

Typology and Millennialism

Typology is an exegetical method of interpreting the Bible used by the church fathers in the Middle Ages: Augustine, Origen, and many others. It presumes a rigid structural relationship between the Old and the New Testament. Events and figures described in the Old Testament, which are called "types," are taken as prophecies to be realized and fulfilled in the events and the figure of Christ in the New Testament, which are called "antitypes." The significance of this typological way of understanding to the New England Puritans lies in the fact that the relationship between the Old and the New Testament can be applied to the historical relationship between the Old and the New World. Just as the prophecy embedded in the Old Testament is to be realized in the New Testament, things unrealized in the Old World should be realized in the New. With the analogical extension of that relationship between Old and New Testaments to Old and New Worlds, America has been considered as a unique place where prophecy is to be fulfilled. Sacvan Bercovitch and others have convinced us that the Puritan writings in the seventeenth century were saturated with this biblical framework of typology (Bercovitch 1972). To put it simply, the biblical framework used in interpreting history offers a precursor for the American Dream. The often-repeated phrase "the dream come true" can be considered as a secular version of typological thinking.

Essential to the typological understanding of American history is the idea of millennialism. Whereas typology merely indicates that the realization of prophecies will be brought forth in antitype, millennialism provides a temporal condition and offers a frame for historical understanding. It prophesies the timing of the Second Coming, sometimes very ambiguously and at other times quite precisely. At any rate, it makes the completion of history imminent. Thus, millennialism could function as a cultural power to enhance certain social movements by a time-set program agenda, especially in the case of social upheaval like revolutions. Puritan millenialism anticipates the American preoccupation with time. Except for the studies of Ira V. Brown (1952) and David E. Smith (1965), millennialism received little scholarly attention before the late 1960s. Such neglect may indicate that the close ties of millennialism with fundamentalist denominations had baffled previous mainstream religious historians. Following up Brown's interests and concerns, J. F. Maclear (1975) produced an informative article, which stimulated the eschatological study of American culture in the 1970s.

American millennialism, which was initiated with the Puritans' dire image of the end of the world, can be divided into two categories: pre- and postmillennialism. According to premillennialism, the imminent Calvinistic Second Coming was a selective and onetime event. The Second Coming would bring forth a violent judgmental intervention followed by a thousand years of glory. Seventeenth-century Puritans were preoccupied with this idea. Around the time of the Second Great Awakening in the late nineteenth century, however, promoted mainly by New Divinity, that is, so-called Edwardseans, millennialism was transformed. C. C. Goen called this phenomenon a "new departure of eschatology" (Goen 1950). Differing from the pessimism and the horrifying image of the end of history and the glory only for the selected, postmillennialism is based upon the idea of a gradual progress of the world, finally reaching a universal salvation after a thousand years of blissful time. During that process, human efforts for the final glorious goal can contribute to its completion. It is within this context that missionary activities, whether domestic or foreign, have been promoted. Then, the Second Coming happens. Thus, by pushing the moment of divine judgment far forward beyond the next thousand years, and changing the stance from pre- to postmillennialism, the American psyche reinforced its unique future-oriented optimism.

WILLIAM BRADFORD

Let us see how Puritans used these characteristic methods of interpreting the temporal process of events in their historical writings. Governor William Bradford's *Of Plymouth Plantation* forms a record of the events of the first Puritan settlement in America. The publication of this history has its own history. Though *Of Plymouth Plantation* can be considered the first book written by a New England planter, the work as a whole was not published until almost two centuries later. Subdivided into two books, Bradford's history was separated around the time of the Revolutionary War, when the second book, which contains the gloomy events after 1630, was lost and its contents forgotten. Decades passed before it was rediscovered and published for the first time in 1856 as the *History of Plymouth Plantation.* Before then, some readers assumed that the first book formed the whole work, especially since the first book ends with a sense of completion with the establishment of the Massachusetts Bay Colony. Bradford foresaw the impact the arrival of the Massachusetts Bay colonists would have and changed his narrative stance from one book to the next. Whereas he wrote the first book retrospectively by choosing significant events from the first decade of colonization, he used a more strictly chronological approach in the second book. Furthermore, his use of typology is more obvious in the first book than in the second.

William Bradford was born in Austerfield, Yorkshire. Attracted to the nascent Congregational Church from his youth at Scrooby, he became a stalwart member of a Separatist group. When King James I began severely persecuting these nonconformists, Bradford, together with other Separatists, fled first to Amsterdam and then to Leiden. In order to maintain their identity and survive as a Separatist community, they contracted with a New England company to ship various goods from the New World to England. In exchange, they received transportation to America, albeit with very unfavorable conditions. Bradford started keeping his records earlier, but he began compiling his account into a history in 1630, when Massachusetts Bay Colony was established on a totally different power and scale. As a small and fragile community, Plymouth Plantation was profoundly affected by this event. In order to defend and reconfirm their identity as an independent community, Bradford felt it necessary to write out the origin and development of their own endeavor. Thus, the first book covers the period of the plantation from its preparatory stage until 1630. His use of typology clarifies how Plymouth Plantation manifested Providence. The often-quoted passage from the ninth chapter of the first book, for instance, is clearly typological. With a reference to Pisgah, the name of the mountain from which Moses looked over the distant view of the promised land, Canaan, Bradford clearly parallels the Plymouth colonists with Moses and his followers.

Bradford minimized his use of typology in the second book. In particular, his references to biblical passages for the sake of typological reasoning are largely suppressed. In the latter half of the book, he described several extraordinary natural phenomena, including an earthquake, an eclipse, the great hurricane, a meteor, and pestilence. Readers of the Old Testament know quite well that such natural phenomena are described within the context of God's wrath, but in no case did Bradford interpret these phenomena in terms of Providence. Although it should have been quite easy and natural for him to employ them typologically, he does not refer to the Old Testament, nor does he try to define the meaning of those phenomena within the framework of providential cause and effect. Concerning the great 1638 earthquake described in chapter 29, for example, he leaves the explanation of its influence upon meteorological phenomena to the "naturalist" by saying, "whether this was any cause [of famine of that year] I leave it to naturalists to judge" (Bradford 1970, 303).

When Bradford started writing the second book, his way of looking at Plymouth Plantation had drastically changed. His refusal to take the establishment of the Plymouth Plantation as the antitype of Old Testament types reflects his changed outlook. In some isolated moments, he thought that the achievement of the Plymouth Plantation was an antitypal fulfillment. In a note entitled "A Late Observation," for example, he quoted many passages from the Old Testament, demonstrating how the Plymouth colonists' efforts, sufferings, and final liberation parallel those of the Israelites: "Do you not now see the fruits of your labours, O all the servants of the Lord? That have suffered for His truth, and have been faithful witnesses of the same, and the little handful amongst the rest, the least amongst the thousands of Israel?" (Bradford 1970, 351).

The initial power of the Massachusetts Bay Colony in 1630, combined with various internal troubles of the Plymouth Colony, prompted Bradford to question his colony's purpose. Perhaps as early as 1632, Bradford was deeply discouraged by the dispersal of his people. With the increase of the population in Massachusetts Bay Colony, and the growing demand for "corn and cattle" there, Plymouth planters realized they had to disperse in order to produce crops sufficient to meet their demands. It became more and more difficult to hold the Plymouth Plantation together. In Duxbury, for example, the people wanted to be dismissed from Plymouth to worship for themselves. Commenting on the situation at Duxbury, Bradford observed, "And this I fear will be the ruin of New England, at least of the churches of God there, and will provoke the Lord's displeasure against them" (Bradford 1981, 254).

Other incidents—the move to Nauset, the death of Miantonomo, the death of William Brewster, the bestiality incident, and finally the departure of his closest confidant, Edward Winslow, for England—overshadowed Bradford's initial enthusiasm and hope. He did not or could not think any more that his people were paralleling the chosen people of Israel (Bradford 1981, xxii). Perhaps he began thinking that the chosen people were the Massachusetts Bay colonists. Bradford's use of typology greatly differs from that of other earlier New England typologists such as John Winthrop or Edward Johnson. These Massachusetts Puritans have a strong sense of being "chosen," as fulfilling the types of Old Testament promises, whereas Bradford's typology never looked for New England to fulfill itself as antitype to Old Testament types. His is constructed upon the basis of repetition or parallel, not upon the framework of prophecy and fulfillment.

Also, when we think about Plymouth Plantation, it is highly important to differentiate between myth and historical fact. Readers of *Of Plymouth Plantation* may notice how different Bradford's account is from the traditional stories about Plymouth that have become a part of the popular culture. Bradford does not describe Plymouth Rock or suggest a festive atmosphere surrounding the first Thanksgiving. Bradford's account of this autumnal gathering is quite simple and makes no mention of any friendly relationship with the Indians. These associations were constructed later in the late nineteenth century; they were not a part of the original writings (Seelye 1998). If we put aside these celebratory associations conjured up by the intentional mythmaking efforts of, say, Henry Ward Beecher or Sarah Josepha Hale, and read the original document as it is, the impression is one of failure. Plymouth Plantation did not get the royal charter initially. Its patent, an alternative legal basis, was renewed, but that did not legally protect its status as a plantation. With the revocation of the charter given to Massachusetts Bay Colony, Plymouth also lost its legal status in 1684 and was absorbed by Massachusetts Bay Colony when its charter was renewed in 1691. Thus, at the time of American independence, when all other plantations formed states, Plymouth Plantation had lost its identity and became part of Massachusetts.

JOHN WINTHROP

The leader of the Massachusetts Bay Colony, John Winthrop was born in Suffolk, England, attended Trinity College, Cambridge, and then, after studying law at Gray's Inn, became an attorney. Being a devout and fervent believer in Puritanism, Winthrop, together with other Puritans, obtained a royal charter from Charles I for the Massachusetts Bay Company and decided to leave behind what he saw as the corruption of the Church of England. He was elected governor of Massachusetts Bay Colony in 1629 and led from the flagship *Arbella*. The following fleet consisted of eleven ships, on which some 700 people were on board, so far the largest immigrant group to the New World. Reaching Boston in 1630, he used his strong leadership to found a solid community based upon Puritan faith (Moseley 1992).

It is Winthrop who coined the memorable phrase "the city upon a hill." Before reaching Massachusetts, he read a lay sermon to fellow members of the colony entitled "A Modell of Christian Charity," in which he asserted that their colony would be established in this wilderness with a special mission under contract with God to become a city upon a hill. In this famous so-called ur-text of American historical writing, he used a comparison between the Old Testament and their endeavor: "Soe shall wee keepe the unitie of the spirit in the bond of peace. The Lord will be our God, and delight to dwell among Us as his owne people, and will command a blessing upon us in all our wayes, soe that wee shall . . . finde that the God is Israell is among us" (Winthrop 1988, 23). Winthrop's own understanding that the entire world pays heed to the Puritan endeavor is obvious. The Puritans' confidence in God is based upon a self-conscious understanding of themselves based upon biblical typology. "A Modell of Christian Charity" is often considered the starting point of American exceptionalism. Alternatively, Winthrop may simply reiterate beliefs common among contemporary Puritans, beliefs in the mutual love of a devout community.

It has been said that Winthrop wrote this sermon during his voyage to the New World and read it to the people aboard the *Arbella* just before landing. At least, this is the interpretation Perry Miller set forth in his influential essay *Errand into the Wilderness* (1952). Connecting the special mission of Massachusetts Bay Colony with the phrase "city upon a hill," Miller demonstrated how the colony was intended to become a model of the world.

But was it really so? How extensively did other colonists share Winthrop's ideal, especially those aboard the other ships? Was this sermon printed soon and distributed to all members of the colony? Discussing Winthrop's renowned lay sermon, Darrett Rutman observed, "Speaking aboard the *Arbella,* his was but one small voice, one mind, among hundreds; his dream was not necessarily that of the whole membership of settlers, nor of those who would arrive in the commonwealth in the year ahead. On the contrary, to judge by action in the New World, his was the exceptional mind" (Rutman 1965, 22).

Indeed, although handwritten copies were made, the sermon was not printed soon, nor was it widely circulated among the colonists. The assumption that Winthrop's sermon was well known among the Massachusetts Bay colonists stems back to Perry Miller, who asserted that it was read aboard the *Arbella* before its passengers landed. The copy of the sermon Miller must have used is "the only known seventeenth-century manuscript . . . with a cover note, obviously added later" (Winthrop 1996, 1). It reads, "Written On Boarde the Arrabella, On the Attlantick Ocean. By the Honorable John Winthrop Esquire. In His passage, (with the rest of the Company of religious people, of which Christian Tribes he was the Brave Leader and famous Governor;) from the Island of Great Brittaine to New-England in the North America. Anno 1630." Miller should have been more skeptical about the credibility of this note on the manuscript's front page.

Four decades after Miller's essay, the background of the writing and publication of Winthrop's sermon was investigated by Hugh J. Dawson. According to him,

Winthrop did not write the sermon on the *Arbella* on the Atlantic; he wrote it before departing from England (Dawson 1991). The original intent of the sermon concerns how to enhance "Christian Charity" for constructing a new community. In such ways, just as Bradford's writing on Thanksgiving was quite lavishly interpreted to construct a mythic dimension in a later age, Winthrop's "city upon a hill" was conjured up quite differently from the original intent. Winthrop's appeal for this community is expressed as follows: "Wee must entertaine each other in brotherly Affection, wee must be willing to abridge our selves of our superfluities, for the supply of others necessities. Wee must uphold a familiar Commerce together in all meeknes, gentlenes, patience and liberality. Wee must delight in eache other, make other's conditions our owne, rejoyce together, mourne together, labour and suffer together" (Winthrop 1988, 23). His idea of status in the community is feudalistic in maintaining and emphasizing class differences between the rich and poor: his idea of community is not democratic at all.

Unlike "A Modell of Christian Charity," Winthrop's journal is quite prosaic. Using a chronological method, he started recording events on a daily basis. He likely began the journal soon after completing the sermon. Thereafter he recorded events day by day and let the record stand as it was. In other words, he did not compile the whole and then rewrite it into a narrative history. The customary title, *The History of New England from 1630 to 1640*, comes from Winthrop's nineteenth-century editor. As a matter of fact, when the first volume of the three-volume edition appeared in 1825, it was more faithfully titled "Journal of the Transactions and Occurrences in the Settlement of Massachusetts and the Other New England Colonies from the Year 1630 to 1644." The work was titled *History* when the last two volumes were published because Winthrop began to call the work a history in the later portions of his account. Winthrop's chronological approach to history writing did not exclude his own interpretation or "spiritualization." Reflecting his characteristically Puritan mind, he saw God's will behind the quotidian. When it came to the most banal, natural events, he recognized a special Providence, too, just as Hamlet does.

The classic example from Winthrop's *History* comes from October 1640 and concerns the eating habits of some mice: "About this time there fell out a thing worthy of observation. Mr. Winthrop the younger, one of the magistrates, having many books in a chamber where there was corn of divers sort, had among them one wherein the Greek testament, the psalms and the common prayer were bound together. He found the common prayer eaten with mice, every leaf of it, and not any of the two other touched, nor any other of his books, though there were above a thousand" (Winthrop 1996, 34). Without providing an explicit interpretation, John Winthrop implied that the destruction of the Book of Common Prayer, a symbol of the Anglican Church, was a Puritan wish fulfilled. Though he supplied no interpretation, the fact that he recorded the incident as "a thing worthy of observation" reveals his intentions.

Neither of these histories written by William Bradford or John Winthrop was published in their entirety in the seventeenth century. Although the First Book of *Of Plymouth Plantation* was circulated, the Second Book remained obscure for decades. And Winthrop's history was not published until 1825. In the early seventeenth century, three additional historical works dealing with Plymouth Plantation were published and widely read: the anonymous *Mourt's Relation, New Englands Memorial* by Nathaniel Morton, and the most influential historical work describing the Massachusetts Bay Colony, Edward Johnson's *History of New England: Wonder-Working Providence.*

Because Johnson was an English landowner who had embarked on a military career, his initial motivation to emigrate to the New World is questionable. After a short stay in the Massachusetts Bay Colony, where he was granted a freemanship, he went back to England. He returned to New England with his family in 1636. Assuming a central role in founding the church and community of Woburn, Massachusetts, Johnson dedicated himself to town affairs and the Massachusetts Bay Colony for the remainder of his life. His *History of New England,* which is more widely known by its running title, *Wonder-Working Providence,* was published in London in 1654. It consists of three books, each covering roughly seven years, from 1630 to 1651. Although he did not write much about Plymouth Plantation beyond a few brief comments, one of his remarks touches upon the widespread epidemic among the Indians in 1618. Concerning the timing of their arrival at Plymouth, Johnson drew the reader's attention to the significance of the pestilence, which had almost destroyed the Indians' population just before the arrival of the Separatists:

> The summer after the blazing Starre (whose motion in the Heavens was from East to West, pointing out to the sons of men the progresse of the glorious Gospell of Christ, the glorious King of his Churches) even about the yeare 1618. A little before the removeall of that Church of Christ from Holland to Plimoth in New England, as the ancient Indians report, there befell a great mortality among them, the greatest that ever the memory of Father to Sonne tooke notice of, chiefly desolating those places, where the English afterward planted. (Johnson 1910, 40)

Here, Johnson's Puritan mentality prompted him to interpret a natural phenomenon—the appearance of a comet and its direction of flight—as the prophecy of the spread of the gospel. And the pestilence was also taken by him to have spread to cause the sudden decrease of Indian population, which allowed comparatively easy settlement for the Separatists without severe conflict with the native population. The Second Book deals with two crucial events for the young colony, the Antinomian controversy caused by Anne Hutchinson in 1636 and the Pequot War in 1637. Describing these events, Johnson fully utilized biblical typology to confirm his vision of the community, that is, to show how the establishment of New England fulfills prophecy contained in the Old Testament. In chapter 15 of *Wonder-Working Providence,* for instance, Johnson wrote:

> Then oh! you People of Israel gather together as one Man, and grow together as one Tree. Ezek. 37 and 23. For Christ the great King of all the Earth is now going

forth in his great Wrath and terrible Indignation to avenge the bloud of his Saint. Ezek. 38 and 19. vers. . . . What wonderous workes are now suddenly to be wrought for the accomplishment of these things! Then judge all you . . . whether these poore New England People, be not the forerunners of Christs Army . . . be not the very Finger of God, and whether the Lord hath not sent his people to Preach in this wilderness, and to proclaime to all Nations, the neere approach of the most wonderfull workes that ever the Sonnes of men saw. (Johnson 1910, 125)

This is the passage in which Johnson's "exhortation" to all the people "to endeavor the advancement of the Kingdom of Christ" is expressed. Referring to the Old Testament passages, he demonstrated how the deliverance the Israelites sought would be accomplished by "these poore New England People." The relationship between Old Testament types and the antitypal fulfillment brought forth by New England, particularly Massachusetts Bay Colony in this case, is the framework on which Johnson presented the history of New England. Johnson's understanding of the history of New England significantly influenced historians of the succeeding generations, specifically Increase Mather, William Hubbard, and Cotton Mather.

Typological versus Chronological

When we deal with the historians belonging to the second generation, the different approaches to history writing become clear by comparing the writings of two pastors in the 1670s, Increase Mather and William Hubbard. Increase Mather, the son of Richard Mather, was the most eloquent and influential preacher among the second-generation pastors in Massachusetts Bay Colony. As a community leader, he committed himself to the problem of the Half-Way Covenant. He strongly opposed it, going so far as to attack his own father openly. Richard Mather's untimely death, which is believed to have been caused by this vehement controversy, severely stigmatized his son. Increase Mather was twice sent to England to renew the charter, once at the time of the Commonwealth government and next during the reign of King William. Throughout his life, he was acutely aware of the declining tendency of New England society and occasionally read so-called Jeremiad sermons. One of his most well known sermons in this category is *The Danger of Apostasy* (1677).

As a devout Puritan, Increase Mather never failed to scrutinize his own daily life, which appears poignantly in his diary. For instance, in an entry recorded on the night of April 29, 1675, he wrote:

29) Causes of Humiliation this day. 1. My old sins. 2. Present passages. Unsuitable trade of spirits to the sad awful dispensations of Providence. 3. Troubles like to

come on New England from abroad. 4. The Indians are up in armes having killed 7 english men and burnt 20 Houses in Swansey.

Request to God in ct. 1. that more of his spirit may be given to me, as to gifts and graces. 2. That his presence may be with me from day to day. 3. that Hee would lengthen our days of Tranquility. 4. subdue the Heathen, blessing present expedition for that end. (Mather 1900, 348)

It is not difficult to imagine how these diary entries could be edited to form an autobiography later. Even while charting their individual endeavors and achievements, Puritan autobiographers still sought to explain why they, as a community, came to New England. Similarly, Puritan biographers situated their subjects within the development of the community. History, however, shifts its focus from a particular person to the community as a whole, trying to understand its origins and progress, as the historical writings of Increase Mather clearly reveal.

His writings of the late 1670s and early 1680s should be read in conjunction with the writings of his intellectual and religio-political rival, William Hubbard. An uneasy tension lurks beneath the surface of their writings. In their works, these two often vehemently argued with each other, asserting their own opinions and attacking the other's ideas. Each of them left a historical analysis of the battle with Indians, King Philip's War, which was fought in 1675–1676 and lasted eleven months.

William Hubbard, born in England in 1621, was a member of the first class of Harvard College, the class of 1642. Unlike his classmates, he did not become a preacher right after graduation. In fact, fourteen years passed before he finally decided to preach. This lengthy period of gestation helped Hubbard develop an open-minded attitude toward the changing society of New England. Unlike Increase Mather's strict adherence to the religious and moral standards formed by the first generation, Hubbard was more permissive in accepting the new tendencies of the society. During the late 1670s through the early 1680s, Mather and Hubbard competed for the public's attention with their sermons and historical writings concerning King Philip's War. In order to follow the process, let us start with Increase Mather's jeremiad sermon *The Day of Trouble Is Near*, preached on February 1674 (Mather 1986).

The 1670s was a decade when various social problems became conspicuous, and they deeply affected Increase Mather. In his "Autobiography," he wrote about the concerns underlying *The Day of Trouble Is Near*: "About this time, considering the sins of the Countrey, and the Symptoms for divine displeasure, I could not rest in my spirit without giving Publick solemn warning of judgment near at hand." *The Day of Trouble Is Near* warns against "declension," recognizes the prophecy of the impending war against the Indians, and pleads for the necessity of reformation to avoid the calamity. As a typologist, Increase Mather drew numerous parallels between the historical events in the Old Testament and those of contemporary New England. For instance, as he explained why Israel, the Church of God, had to go through suffering, he supported his argument by using typology: "David, speaking in the Person, and as a Type of Christ, saith, Thou has shared me great and sore troubles, Psal. 71.20. And again; Psal. 25. 17. the troubles of my heart are inlarged, O bring thou me out of my distresses." In this way, David and his antitype Christ had to go through sufferings, so, Mather continued, "believers must undergo troubles and distresses also" (Mather 1962, 301–302).

Speaking of the impending day of trouble and its signs, Mather quoted the book of Isaiah and then drew a historical parallel between the biblical text and New England's condition: "And thou Lord of Hosts with Thunder, and with Earthquake, and great noise, with storm, and tempest, and the flame of devouring fire. Hath it not been so with us? We have been visited with great noise, and with devouring flame, that is with terrible Thunders and lightenings and with Earthquakes, which are often Prognostick of State-quakes, and Heart-quakes, not far off?" As for the reason of divine displeasure, he blamed "pride," especially "spiritual pride." He also attacked what people were wearing, their "carnal, shameful, foolish Pride, in Apparel, fashion, and the like" (Mather 1986, 24–25). His concern with the sins of pride shows up repeatedly in his later sermons, too. Though harsh and unforgiving in his tone, he did not forget at the end of *The Day of Trouble Is Near* to emphasize that all this horrifying doom could be averted if people would humbly repent their sins. In other words, the focus of this sermon was a plea for reformation: "Let us amend our wayes and our doings, and the Lord will cause us to dwell in this place. . . . Certainly we need Reformation. Where is the old New-England Spirit, which once was amongst us? Where is our first love? . . . Now if the Lord help us to reform whatever is amiss, he will still do us good, notwithstanding all our sins, which have provoked him, and cause him to frown upon us" (Mather 1986, 31).

King Philip's War broke out a year and a half after this sermon. Increase Mather received news of the onset of the war with mixed feelings. He must have felt fear and worry concerning the war and its impending calamity, but simultaneously he was justified in his role of prophet and as a "God's Watchman." Just like an Old Testament prophet, his prophecy had been fulfilled. Encouraged and self-confident, he concentrated on his effort to bring about a reformation. He brought the matter to the General Court and listed numerous evils to be corrected. On November 3, 1675, the General Court decided to name thirteen "Provoking Evils" in order to stop the backsliding of the society and, by doing so, to avoid God's wrath and judgment, which had been shown to them in the form of the Indian War. Those evils included such social problems as neglect of religious regulations, alcoholism, sexual deviancy, excessive fashion, and so forth. The deputies on the General Court intervened on Mather's behalf, but the magistrates and the governor, representing the wealthier class of society, disliked Mather's strict pessimism. On November 9, Mather wrote in his diary, "Reformation doth not go forward. Magistrates too slow in that matter." Moreover, in the entry of November 28, his anger and irritation against the magistrates and governor became even stronger: "Magistrates have no Heart to doe what they might in order to [effect] Reformation, especially the

Governor. Nor will they call upon the churches to renew their covenant with God" (Mather 1900, 357, 359).

That the magistrates and governor viewed Mather unfavorably can be seen in the selection of the preacher for the election day sermon for the next year. It must be remembered that magistrates and deputies alternated in choosing the election sermon preacher. In 1676 the magistrates decided who would preach the election day sermon. To Mather's bitter disappointment, they chose William Hubbard. When Hubbard published his sermon, "The Happiness of a People Is the Wisdome of Their Rulers," he dedicated it to Governor John Leverett, as if to show off his popularity among the magistrates and the governor.

Hubbard's sermon refutes many of Mather's ideas. Responding to Mather, Hubbard sought the reason of divine displeasure not in the heinous attitudes of the people themselves but in "pride" as a root of it: "Let all due testimony be borne against this kind of pride, so abounding; but it is another sort, spiritual pride, that is so offensive in the sight of God, and is indeed the root whence the other springs, with many other heinous evils that are apt to provoke the Lord to jealousie" (Hubbard 1984, 56). Although on the surface, this attack on pride sounds similar to Mather's, Hubbard's attack on "spiritual pride" as the root of the matter implicitly criticized Mather's list of Provoking Evils. Concerning the opening of a synod, Hubbard was not optimistic about its value. Both his skepticism and his criticism against Mather's pleas are apparent in the subject pronoun of the following sentence: "Some are already to attribute too much to the power or use of Synods, which make others, on the other hand ascribe too little to them." Instead, he recommended "moderate" and "peaceable" councils. The magistrates welcomed Hubbard's complacent sermon.

During this period, the frustrated Increase Mather put much effort into writing a history of King Philip's War, *A Brief History of the War with the Indian* (Slotkin and Folsom 1978). As part of this work, he condensed his argument for the reformation into "An Earnest Exhortation." The theme of Mather's *Brief History of the War* is clear and simple. Relying upon the doctrine of Providence, Mather tried to interpret every incident of King Philip's War in terms of divine will, particularly by pointing out some connections between the battle and his effort for reformation. For example, when the colonists won a battle, Mather did not forget to insert some information as to the reason of the success, say, a fast that had been observed locally. When they lost the battle, Mather stressed that deeper humiliation was needed. In such ways, the cause and effect of the battle was explained from the viewpoint of God, as Mather believed it to be. According to Michael Hall, Increase Mather "wanted to place the war in the context of a providential world view in which the war served some purpose of God's and in which the Indians were the agents of that purpose" (Hall 1988, 119). The whole course of the war is, according to Mather's interpretation, focused on whether the reformation of religion could be made or not. Thus, for instance, telling about the incident at Plymouth Plantation on June 30, 1676, Mather recorded the renewal of the covenant as a reason for the colonists' victory:

> Squaw-Schem with about ninety persons, hearing that Plimouth Forces were approaching them, came and tendered themselves to Major Bradford, wholly submitting to mercy, so that this day were killed, taken, and brought in no less than an hundred and ten Indians. And the Providence of God herein is the more observable, in that the very day before this, the Lords People in Plimouth did unanimously consent to renew their Covenant with God, and one another, and a day of Humiliation was appointed for that end. (Slotkin and Folsom 1978, 130)

Alternatively, Hubbard in his *Narrative of the Troubles with the Indians* gave the description of the same event in the following manner:

> Yea, further, a Squaw Sachim of Sakonet, one of Philips Allies, having first sent three Messengers to the Governor of Plimouth too sue for life and liberty, promising submission to their Government on that condition; but understanding the Plimouth Forces were abroad, before her Messengers were returned, she with her People, about ninety in number, rendered themselves up to Major Bradford, so that above one hundred and ten were killed, and taken upon composition that day. (Hubbard 1972, 97)

Hubbard clearly did not render any providential significance in his description of the event. His interpretation did not reach immediately for a divine explanation of human events but sought natural and rational reasons instead. As Kenneth B. Murdock observed, "Hubbard was groping for a way of reading history which should not rely too heavily on extraordinary Providence" (Murdock 1943, 37).

Another typical example of the difference between Mather and Hubbard can be seen in their description of the battle at Hatfield on October 19, 1675. According to Douglas Leach, this battle at Hatfield is the most significant one among a series of battles fought in the Connecticut Valley during late autumn of 1675. After the harsh attack on Springfield, which was partially burned on October 4 and 5 of that year, the morale of the towns in the upper Connecticut Valley was low. In addition, the information collected by a scout revealed that another major attack was imminent. Following several small battles, in which eight or nine English scouts out of ten were killed, the Indians began to attack Hatfield. After the severe battle, however, the English fought back and succeeded in dispersing the Indians, who retreated through the river. Thus, the fight at Hatfield on October 19 partly compensates for the Springfield disaster, teaching the Indians that their foes could fight effectively given the proper circumstances (Leach 1958). Concerning this battle, Hubbard gave a candid description in his *Present State of New-England*:

> On the sudden seven or eight hundred of the enemy came upon the Town in all quarters, having first killed or taken two or three of the Scouts belonging to the Town, and seven more belonging to Capt. Mosely his Company: But they were so well entertained on all hands where they attempted to break in upon the Town, that they found it too hot for them. Major Appleton with great courage defending

one end of the Town, and Capt. Mosely as stoutly maintaining the middle, and Capt. Pool the other end; that they were by the resolution of the English instantly beaten off, without doing much harm. (Hubbard 1972, 43)

Although as a good Puritan minister, he did not forget to mention "the good providence of Almighty God," Hubbard's description of the battle is strategic, clear in numbers, and objective. On the other hand, Mather's description of the same battle begins with the topic of reformation. "For that day when there was a vote passed for the Suppression and Reformation of those manifest evils, whereby the eyes of Gods Glory are provoked amongst us, the Lord gave success to our Forces, who that day encountered with the Indians at Hatfield. The English lost but one man in the fight (albeit some that were sent forth as Scouts were killed or Captivated) the Enemy fled before them, and ran into the River" (Slotkin and Folsom, 1978, 106).

In such ways, the historical writings of Increase Mather and William Hubbard show a clear difference in terms of their stance. The difference can be understood as a contrasting attitude toward the past. One is based upon providential and ty-pological interpretation, the other on objective and natural reasoning. In the history of Puritan history writing, such a difference was already embodied in the First and Second Books of William Bradford's *Of Plymouth Plantation*. The clash would continue among third-generation historians Cotton Mather and Thomas Prince.

THIRD-GENERATION HISTORIANS

The most ambitious attempt at history writing in early New England is Cotton Mather's *Magnalia Christi Americana* (1702). Subtitled the *Ecclesiastical History* of *New England from Its First Planting in the Year 1620 unto the Year of our Lord, 1698*, this voluminous compendium of 600 folio pages consists of seven books, each of which contains various types of historical writing. Among all colonial New England histories, this book is the greatest in terms of both scope and range of historical subjects. Since Cotton Mather was not writing this book from scratch but editing several of his former writings to yield one work, it does not form a stylistic or structural whole, yet it remains audacious in its attempt to synthesize New England history.

Cotton Mather, the son of Increase Mather and grandson of John Cotton and Richard Mather, was the most influential among the third-generation preachers. After earning his B.A. at the age of sixteen and his M.A. at nineteen from Harvard, he began his active career as a preaching minister and a prolific writer. The total number of the books and pamphlets authored by him is more than 450. Cotton Mather is in this sense one of the most outspoken and strongest leaders in the colonial period. Among his numerous historical writings, *Magnalia Christi Americana* is the most important. The entire book, written from 1693 through 1697, mixes various genres—biography, church history, hagiography, sermon. Among them, biography occupies more than half of the book as Mather recounted the lives of the Puritan leaders. Like medieval hagiography, the *Magnalia* retold the lives of the Puritan leaders as saintly models of exemplary behavior.

Using a typological framework, Mather established a relationship between the promised types in the past and the fulfillment of them to be realized in the future. In doing so, he depicted America as the place where the ecclesiastical history would occur. Depicting the life of William Bradford, for instance, he draws a typological comparison with Moses as a leader of the people. In book 2, under the title "The Shields of the Churches: New England's Governors," Mather describes the life of Bradford as prefigured by that of Moses:

> The leader of a people in a wilderness had need be a Moses; and if a Moses had not led the people of Plymouth Colony, when this worthy person was their gover-nour, the people had never with so much unanimity and importunity still called him to lead them. Among many instances thereof, let this one piece of self-denial be told for a memorial of him, wheresoever this History shall be considered: The patent of the colony was taken in his name, running in these terms: "To William Bradford, his heirs, associates, and assigns. But when the number of the freemen was much increased, and many new townships erected, the General Court there desired of Mr. Radford, that he would make a surrender of the same into their hands, which he willingly and presently assented unto, and confirmed it according to their desire by his hand and seal, reserving no more for himself than was his proportion, with others, by agreement. (Mather 1977, 207)

In the same manner, Mather chose Nehemia, the ruler of Jerusalem, as a typological comparison to John Winthrop:

> But whilst he thus did, as our New-England Nehemiah the part of a ruler in man-aging the public affairs of our American Jerusalem, when there were Togijahs and Sanballats enough to vex him, and give him the experiment of Luther's observation Omnis qui regit est tanguamsignum, in quod omnia jucala, Satan et Mudus dirigunt, he made himself still an exacter parallel unto that governour of Israel, by doing the part of a neighbour among the distressed people of the new plantation. . . . Indeed, for a while the Governour was the Joseph, unto whom the whole body of the people repaired when their corn failed them; and he continued relieving of them with his open-handed bounties, as long as he had any stock to do it with. (Mather 1977, 216–217)

In the Puritan typological tradition, Cotton Mather is the most conspicuous typologist among all New England historians. Taking *Paradise Lost* as an inspiration, Mather foresaw his *Magnalia* as a great American epic. History for him was not something that took place in the far distant and European past, but what happened in New England over the previous eighty years. With high expectations for the current state of New England, he considered that its history was entering its final stage. In the last pages of the *Magnalia* in a speech entitled "Things to Come," he wrote, "From relating of things past, it would no doubt be very acceptable to the reader if we could pass to foretelling of things to come." Apparently surpassing the scope of history, he dared to prophesy the future of their society. In other words, he finished the book with the image of the promised America yet to come. And the image itself was the vision of the imminent Second Coming: "The mighty angels of the Lord Jesus Christ will make their descent, and set the world a trembling at the approaches of their almighty Lord." In such ways, he focused upon the wonder-filled images of the completion of history based upon premillennialism.

Another third-generation preacher, Thomas Prince also made an important contribution to New England historiography. His *Chronological History of New England* is a significant work showing the intellectual climate of mid-eighteenth-century Boston. He was born in a seashore town, Sandwich. Educated at Harvard and graduated in 1709, he spent a few years at the West Indies and Madeira and then went to London and preached eight years in Suffolk. He returned to Boston in 1717 and became a pastor of Old South Church, to which he dedicated the rest of his life. He assembled a vast collection of precious books and manuscript material concerning New England history, which were preserved at the church. At the time of Revolutionary War, the British army destroyed a portion of it, but the surviving documents were later preserved in the Boston Public Library (Hayes 2001). Among his various historical writings, the best-known work is the informative *Chronological History of New England.* The first volume appeared in 1736. The second volume, entitled *Annals of New England,* appeared in 1755. Originally, it was planned to cover the years 1602 through 1730, but it only reached to 1633. The significance of this work lies in the author's method of describing the historical development of New England. At the outset of the work, he clarified his stance:

> However being still solicited, and no other attempting; at length in 1720, I deter-
> mined to draw up a short Account of the most remarkable Transactions and
> events, in the Form of a mere Chronology; which I apprehended would give a
> Summary and regular View of the Rise and Progress of our Affairs, be a certain
> Guide to future Historians, make their Performance easier to them, or assist
> Mr. Neal in correcting his Second Edition; and which I supposed would not take
> above Six or eight Sheets, intending to write no more than a Line or two upon
> every Article. (Prince 1736, III)

It is true that in spite of this introductory remark, he did interpret the events as other Puritan historians did. Referring to the pestilence that had killed many Indians two years before the first Puritans arrived in 1620, Prince wrote: "However, by their being guided Hither, they then unknowingly escaped the much greater Danger of falling among the Multitudes of Savages at that Time filling the Countries about Hudson's River, and are landed in a Place of greater Safety; where a general Pestilence had 2 or 3 Years before, exceedingly thin'd the Natives and prepar'd the way for this feeble Company" (Prince 1736, 84). To be sure, he thought they were "guided," but unlike

Edward Johnson or Cotton Mather, he never brought in the intervention of Providence, but rather limited himself in providing cause and effect of the event.

CONCLUSION

Thus far, we have dealt with representative historians of early Puritan New England. Based upon their theological understanding of time, all share the same attitude toward Providence. As Thomas Prince started his chronology from the Creation, time has started its flow and proceeds to the completion of history. Meanwhile, they all recognized that interpreting the historical process was an important role of the historian. Some interpreted history by using the typological method, while others put strong emphasis on the eschatological development of history leading to the millennium, which was considered to be imminent in New England.

What cannot be forgotten is that there is an alternative way of interpreting history. William Bradford in his later age, William Hubbard, and Thomas Prince eschewed the typological interpretation of history. They were more objective and open-minded to the process of cause and effect. Just as Bradford introduced the description of events year by year in book 2 of *Of Plymouth Plantation,* Thomas Prince used chronology as a proper method of his history. It can be said that in Puritan history, there is a clash between two ways of interpreting historical events: typological or chronological. The former considered the founding of New England as completing the progress of reformation, while the latter maintained more reasonable and logical interpretations without such presupposition. The chronological histories paid more attention to the process of reasonable cause and effect. Later in the eighteenth century, the Enlightenment ethos took control over typological interpretation. But the typological way of interpretation did not die out completely: it remained vital as a mythmaking power. It recurred during the Revolutionary era, a time of mythmaking, and it has recurred again when the origins of the United States have been commemorated. Like an underground current, typology, as a form of historical interpretation, still resurfaces occasionally, especially in times of crisis.

REFERENCES

Bercovitch, Sacvan. 1972. *Typology and Early American Literature.* Amherst: University of Massachusetts Press.

Bradford, William. 1970. *Of Plymouth Plantation,* edited by Samuel Eliot Morison. New York: Knopf.

———. 1981. *Of Plymouth Plantation, 1620–1647,* edited by Francis Murphy. New York: Modern Library.

Brown, Ira V. 1952. Watchers of the Second Coming: The Millenarian Tradition in America. *Mississippi Valley Historical Review* 39: 441–458.

Dawson, Hugh J. 1991. John Winthrop's Rite of Passage: The Origins of the "Christian Charitie" Discourse. *Early American Literature* 26: 219–231.

Goen, C. C. 1950. Jonathan Edwards: A New Departure in Eschatology. *Church History* 28: 25–40.

Hall, David D. 1989. *Worlds of Wonder, Days of Judgment: Popular Religious Belief in Early New England.* New York: Knopf.

Hall, Michael G. 1988. *The Last American Puritan: The Life of Increase Mather, 1639–1723.* Middletown, CT: Wesleyan University Press.

Hawthorne, Nathaniel. 2006. *Five Novels,* edited by Kevin J. Hayes. New York: Barnes and Noble.

Hayes, Kevin J. 2001. How Thomas Prince Read Captain John Smith. In *Finding Colonial Americas: Essays Honoring J. A. Leo Lemay,* edited by Carla Mulford and David S. Shields, 367–378. Newark: University of Delaware Press.

Hubbard, William. 1972. *The Present State of New England: Being a Narrative of the Troubles with the Indians, 1677,* edited by Cecelia Tichi. Bainbridge, NY: York Mail-Print.

———. 1984. The Happiness of a People Is the Wisdome of Their Rulers. In *Election Day Sermons, Massachusetts,* edited by Sacvan Bercovitch. New York: AMS Press.

Johnson, Edward. 1910. *Johnson's Wonder-Working Providence, 1628–1651,* edited by J. Franklin Jameson. New York: Scribner's.

Leach, Douglas Edward. 1958. *Flintlock and Tomahawk: New England in King Philip's War.* New York: Macmillan.

Maclear, J. F. 1975. New England and the Fifth Monarchy: The Quest for the Millennium in Early American Puritanism. *William and Mary Quarterly,* 3rd ser., 32: 223–226.

Mather, Cotton. 1977. *Magnalia Christi Americana, Books I and II,* edited by Kenneth Ballard Murdock. Cambridge, MA: Belknap Press of Harvard University Press.

Mather, Increase. 1900. *Diary by Increase Mather, March, 1675–December, 1676: Together with Extracts from Another Diary by Him, 1674–1687,* edited by Samuel A. Green. Cambridge, MA: John Wilson and Son.

———. 1962. The Autobiography of Increase Mather, edited by Michael G. Hall. *Proceedings of the American Antiquarian Society* 71: 271–360.

———. 1986. *Departing Glory: Eight Jeremiads.* Delmar, NY: Scholars' Facsimiles and Reprints.

Miller, Perry. 1952. *Errand into the Wilderness: An Address.* Williamsburg, VA: William and Mary Quarterly for the Associates of the John Carter Brown Library.

Moseley, James G. 1992. *John Winthrop's World: History as a Story; the Story as History.* Madison: University of Wisconsin Press.

Murdock, Kenneth B. 1943. William Hubbard and the Providential Interpretation of History. *Proceedings of the American Antiquarian* 52: 15–37.

Prince, Thomas. 1736. *A Chronological History of New-England in the Form of Annals.* Boston: S. Gerrish.

Rutman, Darrett Bruce. 1965. *Winthrop's Boston: Portrait of a Puritan Town, 1630–1649.* Chapel Hill: University of North Carolina Press.

Seelye, John. 1998. *Memory's Nation: The Place of Plymouth Rock.* Chapel Hill: University of North Carolina Press.

Slotkin, Richard, and James K. Folsom, eds. 1978. *So Dreadfull a Judgment: Puritan Responses to King Philip's War, 1676–1677.* Middletown, CT: Wesleyan University Press.

Smith, David E. 1965. Millenarian Scholarship in America. *American Quarterly* 17: 223–260.

Winthrop, John. 1908. *Winthrop's Journal, "History of New England," 1630–1649,* edited by James Kendall Hosmer. 2 vols. New York: Scribner's.

———. 1988. A Modell of Christian Charity: Written on Board the Arrabella, on the Atlantick Ocean. In *An Early American Reader,* edited by J. A. Leo Lemay, 14–24. Washington, DC: United States Information Agency.

———. 1996. *The Journal of John Winthrop, 1630–1649,* edited by Richard S. Dunn, James Savage, and Laetitia Yeandle. Cambridge, MA: Harvard University Press.

CHAPTER 5

NEW ENGLAND POETRY

RONALD A. BOSCO AND

JILLMARIE MURPHY

Until the 1960s, the dominant critical view of colonial New England verse held that it was deficient in poetic sensibility. This supposed deficiency was attributed to the Puritans' reliance on what was commonly called the "plaine stile," the narrative form to which William Bradford announced he would adhere in his *History of Plymouth Plantation* to demonstrate his "singular regard unto the simple trueth in all things" (Bradford 1912, 1: 1), but then proceeded to ignore as he spun out one of the finest prose epics of New World settlement composed in the seventeenth century. Although *The Whole Booke of Psalmes* (*Bay Psalm Book*) defined the standards for Puritan poetry, the writings of Anne Bradstreet, Michael Wigglesworth, and Edward Taylor show that those standards were violated by most early New England poets. In their "plaine" translations of David's psalms from the original Hebrew, Puritans Thomas Weld, John Eliot, and Richard Mather chose "Conscience rather then Elegance." As their rendition of Psalm 23 demonstrates, "Gods Altar" was perfectly safe from their human "polishings":

> The Lord to mee a shepheard is, want therefore shall not I.
> Hee in the folds of tender-grasse, doth cause mee downe to lie:
> To waters calm me gently leads[:] Restore my soule doth hee:
> he doth in paths of righteousness: for his names sake leade mee.
> Yea though in valley of deaths shade I walk, none ill I'le feare:
> because thou art with mee, thy rod, and staffe my comfort are.

> For mee a table thou hast spread, in presence of my foes:
> thou dost annoynt my head with oyle, my cup it over-flowes.
> Goodness and mercy surely shall all my dayes follow mee:
> and in the Lords house I shall dwell so long as dayes shall bee.
> (Miller and Johnson 1963, 2: 556–557)

Many previous commentators have felt the need to apologize for the Calvinist strain evident in pre-Revolutionary writings or to demean those writings as a regrettable prelude to the superior literary productions of the new republic. Samuel Kettell's *Specimens of American Poetry,* for example, ignores Cotton Mather's counsel to young ministers in his *Manuductio ad Ministerium* (1726) that they become acquainted with poetry not only because it had been in popular demand since the earliest days of settlement but also because it could improve the appeal of, and the range of learned reference in, their homilies. Kettell does not acknowledge Mather's wish that the ministers' "Souls" would be poetical. Instead, he introduces Mather, whose poems open the anthology, as an illustration of the "primitive simplicity" of early New England life with its "unvaried" regimen of "study, fasting and prayer," and, finally, death. Citing Mather's well-earned reputation as the author of several hundred published volumes of theology, history, natural science, and sermonic discourse, Kettell confessed that his poems were "distinguished by little else than the hardness of their style, and the want of that . . . quality in which we recognize the spontaneous ebullitions of a mind 'smit with the love' of song" (Kettell 1967, 1: 13). Among the four poems by Mather he printed was one on the death of a son and another on the death of a daughter. In both, Mather adheres to the non-Romantic bias Kettell attributed to him. The poem on his son, for instance, ends with the traditional Puritan consolation that death represents the cessation of pain in this world:

> Afflictions for the present here
> The vexed flesh will grievous call;
> But afterwards there will appear,
> Not grief, but peace, the end of all—

In the poem on his daughter, Mather uses her death as an occasion to restate his faith in Christ:

> I do believe that every bird
> Of mine, which to the ground shall fall,
> Does fall at thy kind will and word;
> Nor I, nor it, is hurt at all.
> Now my believing soul does hear
> This among the glad angels told;
> I know, thou does thy Maker fear,

From whom thou nothing dost withhold!
(Kettell 1967, 1: 14–15; Mather 1989, 40–41)

Unfortunately for Mather's reputation—Romantic or otherwise—Kettell overlooked a lovingly personal poem he wrote on the death of his first wife, Abigail, in
1702, which appeared in Mather's *Meat out of the Eater* (1703), the same source from
which Kettell drew the poems on his children:

> Go then, my Dove, but now no longer *Mine!*
> Leave *Earth,* and now in *Heavenly Glory* Shine.
> *Bright* for thy Wisdom, Goodness, Beauty here;
> Now *Brighter* in a more *Angelick Sphaere.*
> Jesus, with whom thy Soul did long to be,
> Into His *Ark,* and Arms, has taken thee.
> Dear *Friends* with whom thou didst so dearly Live,
> Feel *Thy one Death* to *Them* a *Thousand* give.
> Thy *Prayers* are done; thy *Alms* are spent; thy *Pains*
> Are *Ended* now in *Endless* Joyes and Gains.
> The *Torch* that gave my *House* its pleasant *Light,*
> Extinguish'd leaves it now *dark* a *Night!*
> I faint, till thy last words to mind I call;
> Rich words! Heav'n, Heav'n will make amends for all.
> (Mather 1989, 44)

Although he ignored Bradstreet, included an excerpt from Wigglesworth's
"The Day of Doom," and was unaware of Taylor, whose poetry would not be discovered for another century, Kettell was ultimately far more generous in his appreciation of Puritan poets than were his successors over the next 150 years. In
Handkerchiefs from Paul (1927), a collection of then generally inaccessible Puritan
poems drawn from manuscripts and published texts, Kenneth Murdock created a
modern working anthology of Puritan poetry, but at a high price for the reputation of New England's early poets. Introducing *Handkerchiefs from Paul,* he told
readers that "the world's great poetry is no whit increased by bringing these forgotten works . . . to light. They deserve printing not for any appeal which they make to
sophisticated students of *belles lettres,* but for their historical implications, for the
sidelights they shed upon Puritan character and taste." Murdock informed readers
that if they could tolerate the "harshness," "lack of music," and "stark crudeness of
the colonial verse-writers," then the collected poems would give them "a glimpse
of the deep emotion which demanded expression of writers unequal to their task"
(Murdock 1927, lxii, lxiv).

As critics have for nearly two centuries, today's readers will approach New England's early poets for the antiquarian—almost escapist—charm their verses offer
to the modern imagination, or for the articles of faith evident in the works of some

poets that appear to accord with those of modern believers, or, if they have been schooled in the great Metaphysical and Cavalier traditions of English poetry, for the rare creative flights of symbolism, personal expression, and religious and social commentary expressed by them. These are all legitimate responses to early New England poets and their art, which, in any case, do not require our apologies. Thus, in stating that Puritans took preeminent delight in sermons and adapted their poetry to that norm, David Leverenz is correct, but only partially so (Leverenz 1980, 5). If we accept Perry Miller's claim that the Puritans' creation of humiliation, feast, and fast days along with the jeremiad as their elucidating genre served them as "an engine of Americanization," then the poetry early New Englanders created was at least the jeremiad's equal as an engine of self-culture (Miller 1953, 26). Written by individuals who were not professional poets in our sense of the term "professional," but who were concerned with balancing the attractiveness and necessities of this world against their idealized glories of the next, with creating a workable society in the New World wilderness, and with expressing the poetry inherent in the human heart, early New England poetry was intentionally devotional, confessional, homiletic, self-referential, and biographical. As Wigglesworth's "God's Controversy with New-England," composed in 1662 in a time of "great drought," or Benjamin Tompson's *New Englands Crisis* (1676), published shortly after the outbreak of King Philip's War, illustrate, early New England poetry was also historical and written with the purpose of "improving upon" the meaning of momentous events. And as Bradstreet's "The Flesh and the Spirit" and "The Vanity of all Worldly Things," Wigglesworth's contemplative reflections in *Meat out of the Eater; or, Meditations Concerning the Necessity, End, and Usefulness of Afflictions unto God's Children* (1670), and Taylor's *God's Determinations Touching his Elect* (ca. 1680) admirably demonstrate, early New England poetry served Puritans as an open forum for the elucidation of Calvinist doctrine.

All reading is an exercise in interpretation and appropriation, which confirms Arthur Miller's justification for his selective use of historical fact to suit the aesthetic purpose of *The Crucible:* "One finds . . . what one seeks" (Miller 1971, 41). Miller's comment recognizes the influence that the intellectual and imaginative predispositions of readers and critics exert on historical materials, and it is instructive for reading poetry composed in a distant historical period. We are now in a position to approach the era's leading poets with fresh eyes guided by modern, reliable texts. Beginning in the 1960s, complete scholarly editions of the poems of Bradstreet, Mather, Taylor, Tompson, and Wigglesworth have appeared in print, and these, complemented by substantial anthologies of early American poetry, have supported an outpouring of original scholarship (Cowell 1981; Eberwein 1978; Jantz 1962; Meserole 1985; Silverman 1976). Several recent studies form groundbreaking examples of the modern recovery of early New England's poetic voices and literary genius (Daly 1978; Hammond 1993a, 1993b, 2000; Scheick 1988, 1992; White 1985).

ANNE BRADSTREET

The first English woman known to have written poetry in the New World and America's first published poet, Anne Bradstreet was warmly regarded in her time as a poet of rare merit. Many of the terms under which Bradstreet is read and praised today were introduced as early as the first printing of *The Tenth Muse Lately Sprung Up in America, By a Gentlewoman of Those Parts* (London, 1650). Nathaniel Ward, among those who wrote verse tributes for this edition, recognized her devotion to and imitation of the sixteenth-century French poet Guillaume de Salluste, Sieur Du Bartas, who was a favorite of leading seventeenth-century English poets. Ward also cautioned his male peers to beware of female poets:

> The Auth'ress was a right Du Bartas girl. . . .
> I muse whither at length these girls will go;
> It half revives my chill frost-bitten blood,
> To see a women once do ought that's good;
> And shod by Chaucer's boots, and Homer's furs,
> Let men look to't, lest women wear the spurs.
> (Bradstreet 1967, 4)

A generation later, Cotton Mather credited Bradstreet as a poet whose works provided "a grateful Entertainment unto the Ingenious." By drawing a parallel between her inheritance of a powerful intellect and imagination from her father, Governor Thomas Dudley, and the inheritance of the same a century before Bradstreet by the English prose writer and poet Margaret Roper from her father, Sir Thomas More, he suggested that the "spurs" of literary accomplishment had long been worn by women "in both Englands" (Mather 1702, 17).

Even though Kettell ignored Bradstreet, other nineteenth-century critics were cognizant of her unique position in the history of American poetry. James Anderson treated her as a serious poet whose sole—but not fatal—flaws were her strict indoctrination "in puritan principles" and "steady" profession of them "throughout the whole of her life" and her tendency to imitate Du Bartas and sixteenth- and seventeenth-century English poets, rather than rely on her own imagination to supply her with subjects worthy of her art. As one of the first critics to recognize the influence of North America's natural environment on her imagination, Anderson praised Bradstreet's "appreciation of the beauties of nature." Seizing on "Contemplations" as an expression of a poetic walk "through the August temple of creation," he argued that it "proves that she was a genuine poet, and affords perhaps the most favourable specimen of her poetical genius" (Anderson 1862, 1: 156–184). In 1867, John Harvard Ellis published an edition of Bradstreet, which attracted renewed interest in her writings. Characterizing her poems as "quaint and curious" but containing "many beautiful and original ideas, not badly expressed," Ellis urged readers to bear in mind the "unpropitious circumstances" in which she wrote: the absence of a "genial coterie of gifted minds . . . near to cheer and inspire her," a "circle of wits to sharpen and brighten her faculties," and "rich works of art" that might have shaped her tastes (Bradstreet 1932, XLII).

Modern critics have consistently characterized Bradstreet's production of verse and her poetry itself, in spite of prevailing religious and cultural forces that worked against the idea of a female poet, as revolutionary in concept and in the impression her writings leave on readers. Bradstreet's family and friends encouraged her art throughout her life, which in itself was an anomaly for the seventeenth century; without her knowledge, her brother-in-law John Woodbridge carried the manuscript of her poems to London, where he supervised its printing as *The Tenth Muse* and composed an introductory epistle to the "Kind Reader" that opened the volume. However, it is not just her unusual position as the first American Puritan lyricist to be published, nor the fact that she wrote poetry at a time when women were expected to be devoted wives and mothers, not aspiring creative writers, that has created such an enduring fascination with Bradstreet; modern scholars generally agree that she is one of the most important poets of seventeenth-century New England precisely because her spectacularly executed poetry offers a woman's perspective not otherwise available in the masculine, doctrine-driven environment in which she lived and against which she composed her poetry.

Writing in the 1960s, Josephine K. Piercy divided the body of Bradstreet's poetry into two broad categories that defined her opus, first according to the dominant phases of her career and then according to content. Under the headings "The Apprentice" and "The Craftsman," Piercy followed the disposition of earlier commentators to group Bradstreet's early, long, and sometimes labored imitative poems such as "The Four Elements," "Of the Four Humours," and her survey of the Assyrian, Persian, Grecian, and Roman epochs in "The Four Monarchies" into a period representing her poetic apprenticeship, and the more brief and often personal writings she composed throughout her life—"An Elegy upon Sir Philip Sidney," "In Honour of Queen Elizabeth," "A Dialogue between Old England and New," "The Flesh and the Spirit," "Upon the Burning of Our House," "As Weary Pilgrim," and numerous pieces on her husband, children, and grandchildren—into her lifelong struggle to master her craft and her voice. Like the "Pilgrim" in "As Weary Pilgrim," Piercy saw Bradstreet following a poetic path that "led steadily upward: from rebellion to assurance, from immaturity to maturity" (Piercy 1965, 41). Piercy's recognition of the poet's capacity for "rebellion," which modern readers have increasingly recognized as the surest sign of her intellectual and imaginative maturity, represented a significant shift away from earlier criticism. From the 1960s, this shift has become the new center of Bradstreet studies (Stanford 1966; Requa 1974; Rosenmeier 1977; Mawer 1980; Saltman 1983; Hammond 1993b). Collectively, these studies unveil a poet who early on had learned to speak in a clear, self-assured voice and whose tone reflects her self-assurance and resistance to Puritan ideology.

On the surface a seemingly submissive and faithful Christian, in her poetry Bradstreet often looks askance at the narrowly defined theological, political, and gendered power structures of Puritan New England. Opposed to the asceticism sometimes advocated by Wigglesworth or the stylized metaphysical verse Taylor composed primarily for his own edification, Bradstreet transformed the tensions inherent in birth and death, the flesh and the spirit, the material and the spiritual, this world and the next, man and God.

When Piercy described Bradstreet as "a Puritan woman of deep spiritual faith," she reminded readers that her subject's "highly intelligent and well-educated mind was capable of questioning and even of rebellion" against the dominant ideologies of her day (Piercy 1965, 17). Bradstreet's ability to negotiate poetically the distance between her spiritual faith and her impulse toward rebellion is evident throughout the body of her writings. Although it appears most prominently in the works she composed after the birth of her children and especially after the death of some of her grandchildren, where her spiritual faith is represented by her questioning of Puritan doctrine, this ability is also evident in poems such as "In Honour of Queen Elizabeth," where Bradstreet skillfully defends Elizabeth's and her own talents in spite of the fact that they are the talents of women:

> Nay masculines, you have thus taxed us long,
> But she, though dead, will vindicate our wrong.
> Let such as say our sex is void of reason,
> Know 'tis a slander now but once was treason.
> (Bradstreet 1967, 198)

In "An Elegy upon Sir Philip Sidney," Bradstreet stakes a claim for the survival of her lines in tribute to Sidney alongside his own dignified verses, saying, "Let none disallow of these my strains / Whilst English blood yet runs within my veins" (Bradstreet 1967, 190). Her claims for being heard and preserved come through loud and clear because they are made in lines ingeniously intermingled among others full of adoration for a much loved queen and a heroic poet.

The careful reader of Bradstreet's poems is always rewarded by discoveries of the freshness, sensibility, individualism, and feminized Puritanism. In "The Prologue," Bradstreet opens with a humble exposition of her poetic ability:

> To sing of wars, of captains, and of kings,
> Of cities founded, commonwealths begun,
> For my mean pen are too superior things:
> Or how they all, or each their dates have run
> Let poets and historians set these forth,
> My obscure lines shall not so dim their worth.

However, she deftly leads the reader through an elaborate series of conceits in which she continues to downplay her poetic talent, stating, "My foolish, broken, blemished Muse so sings, / And this to mend, alas, no art is able, / 'Cause nature made it so irreparable." She contrasts herself to Demosthenes—"that fluent sweet tongued Greek, / Who lisped at first, in future times speak plain"—and asserts her right to be a poet: "I am obnoxious to each carping tongue / Who says my hand a needle better fits." Skillfully, she casts the blame upon those who would criticize her as a female poet: "For such despite they cast on female wits: / If what I do prove well, it won't advance, / They'll say it's stol'n, or else it was by chance." She then cleverly—and winningly—asks the reader to:

> Let Greeks be Greeks, and women what they are
> Men have precedency and still excel,
> It is but vain unjustly to wage war;
> Men can do best, and women know it well.
> Preeminence in all and each is yours;
> Yet grant some small acknowledgement of ours.
> (Bradstreet 1967, 15–16)

Many of Bradstreet's poems show her appreciation of everyday experience. A large part of her appeal is the universal human impulse evident in her distinction between the doctrinal and the human sides of her spirituality, which in Puritan times could be, and often were, at irreconcilable odds. Such distinction is apparent in "To My Dear and Loving Husband," thirteen highly charged lines in which Bradstreet contemplates the perfect physical and spiritual union she enjoys in her married life:

> If ever two were one, then surely we.
> If ever man were loved by wife, then thee;
> If ever wife was happy in a man,
> Compare with me, ye women, if you can.

After moving to an unexpected materialistic trope as a measure of the depth of her love for her husband—"I prize thy love more than whole mines of gold / Or all the riches that the East doth hold"—Bradstreet then turns to the natural, physical world for an image to express the sheer passion she feels for her husband: "My love is such that rivers cannot quench, / Nor ought but love from thee, give recompense." Only in the concluding four lines of the poem—and then explicitly only in the last line of those four—does Bradstreet acknowledge the obligation she also feels, or which she knows her culture expects her to address, to translate the physical and spiritual union represented by her marriage in this world into the idealized union she and Simon Bradstreet may hope to enter in the next:

> Thy love is such I can no way repay,
> The heavens reward thee manifold, I pray.
> Then while we live, in love let's so persevere
> That when we live no more, we may live ever.
> (Bradstreet 1967, 225)

"To My Dear and Loving Husband" is not unique among Bradstreet's works. In three poetic "letters" composed to her husband during periods of his absence from their home, she finds a place where she can express intensely personal but thoroughly human feelings of profound loneliness mingled with feelings of love and desire that are otherwise invisible in poems produced in seventeenth-century New England. In what appears an unassuming set of verses from a mother to her children as they are growing older and flying from her "nest," Bradstreet expresses the deepest of maternal emotions behind thinly veiled metaphors drawn from nature. In contrast to the elaborate and highly religious prose verse "To My Dear Children," at the conclusion of "In Reference to Her Children, 23 June, 1659," composed some thirteen years before her death, she reveals a mother's more earthbound hopes for how she wishes to be remembered by her children as they enjoy their lives as husbands or wives and parents after her death:

> When each of you shall in your nest
> Among your young ones take your rest,
> In chirping language, oft them tell,
> You had a dam that loved you well,
> That did what could be done for young,
> And nursed you up till you were strong.
> And 'fore she once would let you fly,
> She showed you joy and misery;
> Taught what was good, and what was ill,
> What would save life, and what would kill.
> Thus gone, amongst you I may live,
> And dead, yet speak, and counsel give:
> Farewell, my birds, farewell adieu,
> I happy am, if well with you.
> (Bradstreet 1967, 234)

Helen Saltman delivers a masterful reading of "Contemplations" as "no ordinary Puritan spiritual autobiography" in which "the poet dwells on . . . theological concepts . . . that support the Puritan doctrine of rebirth and salvation" (Saltman 1983, 226). Used as a model through which to read most of the poems that Piercy included as examples of Bradstreet's mature verse, Saltman's approach invites an interpretation of Bradstreet's lifelong motivation as a mature poet to spin out in verses on the everyday an extended spiritual autobiography. Bradstreet's religious meditations such as "The Flesh and the Spirit" and "As Weary Pilgrim," her "Dialogue between Old England and New," and her elegies on the deaths of those close to her all reveal the poet balancing between human attachment to the personal and the material of this world and initial resistance, but eventual acquiescence, to the laws of a divine plan that assure the enduring Christian rebirth and salvation after this life.

"Contemplations" is, as Saltman argues, Bradstreet's most sustained foray into this form of Puritan spiritual autobiography; however, the poet's exhaustive survey of nature's splendors across more than 200 lines of close observation ends essentially where it begins. In stanza 2 of "Contemplations," Bradstreet remarks,

> I wist not what to wish, yet sure thought I,
> If so much excellence abide below,
> How excellent is He that dwells on high,
> Whose power and beauty by his works we know?
> (Bradstreet 1967, 205)

Twenty-seven stanzas later, her question has been thoroughly answered: The seemingly inexhaustible wonders of creation barely begin to describe the excellence and power of "He that dwells on high." But instead of being satisfied with this knowledge, in the final five stanzas of the poem, the poet is so distressed that she breaks off her literal contemplations and lunges into a form of jeremiadic discourse more appropriate to Michael Wigglesworth. The disconnection between the near Romanticism of stanzas 1 through 28 and the poetic preoccupation with humankind's frailty, vanity, ignorance, and sinfulness in stanzas 29 through 33 is staggering. In stanza 30, for instance, Bradstreet writes,

> And yet this sinful creature, frail and vain,
> This lump of wretchedness, of sin and sorrow,
> This weatherbeaten vessel wracked with pain,
> Joys not in the hope of an eternal morrow;
> Nor all his losses, crosses, and vexation,
> In weight, in frequency and long duration
> Can make him deeply groan for that divine translation.
> (Bradstreet 1967, 213)

What is happening here? How does a mediation on the splendors of nature as emblematic of the excellence of God's divine plan result in a poetic concession to humankind's apparent rejection of the possibility of "divine translation" to the even better world beyond this?

Although modern critics have offered various cogently argued interpretations of "Contemplations," Saltman's reading finds Bradstreet confessing here her own human frailty and inability to wean herself from the attractions of this world. This is one of Bradstreet's finest, most human poetic moments. She is not rejecting the possibility of "divine translation" to a better world, but she is exposing her share in the personal struggle evident in all Puritan spiritual autobiography, where even the most dutiful Calvinist, knowing what doctrine dictates, ultimately yields to the dictates of the human heart until, approaching death, that heart is finally humbled and broken. Only in "To My Dear Children" and "As Weary Pilgrim" do we witness Bradstreet fully achieving the spiritual awakening that announces her readiness to leave this world behind. Until actually facing death, Bradstreet, as with most Puritan spiritual autobiographers, prefers the hardship and anguish of this world, balanced as she knows they are by opportunities for human love, friendship, and passion, and this, as "Contemplations" shows, is the essential struggle of all Puritans' existence.

MICHAEL WIGGLESWORTH

In "A Funeral Elogy, Upon that Pattern and Patron of Virtue . . . Anne Bradstreet," John Norton II memorialized Bradstreet shortly after her death. Professing his inadequacy to the task, Norton directly addressed his subject, "To write is easie; but to write on thee, / Truth would be thought to forfeit modesty," and expressed the hope that, because "Virtue ne'er dies, time will a Poet raise / Born under better Starrs" to sing "thy praise" (Meserole 1985, 462). He then described the ways in which Bradstreet's inspired art and virtuous life would test the ability of any elegist to convey adequately. In contrast to Norton's confidence in Bradstreet's enduring fame based on the exemplary quality of her art and life, Cotton Mather felt the need to identify in a series of puns the qualities through which Michael Wigglesworth might best be remembered. Whereas Norton's emphasis was on Bradstreet's character, which had nurtured not only her own family but also her extended family of readers in Old England and New, Mather's was strictly on his subject's dual professions of physician and minister and on the instructional poetry he composed during an extended period of severe psychological and sexual distress he suffered from the early 1660s through the late 1670s, which prevented him from fulfilling his professional obligations to the people he served in Malden, Massachusetts. Mather printed these lines on "The Excellent Wigglesworth, Remembered by some Good Tokens" in *A Faithful Man, Described and Rewarded* (1705), the sermon he preached at the poet's funeral:

> His Pen did once Meat from the Eater fetch;
> And now he's gone beyond the *Eaters* reach.
> His *Body*, once so *Thin*, was next to *None*;
> From Thence, he's to *Unbodied Spirits flown*.
> Once is rare skill did all *Diseases* heal;
> And he does nothing now *uneasy* feel.
> He to his *Paradise* is Joyful come;
> And waits with Joy to see his Day of Doom.
> (Mather 1989, 95)

It is doubtful that Wigglesworth's contemporaries foresaw his rise to fame as New England's premier poet and the author of *The Day of Doom,* a slender volume of poems that, from the time of its appearance in 1662, outsold all printed works in the colonies except for the Bible and the *Bay Psalm Book* prior to the American Revolution. But as one indication of his poetry's appeal in the eighteenth century, legend has it that Edward Taylor's first wife, Elizabeth, perfumed her lips nightly with selections from Wigglesworth's writings before falling asleep; more concretely, although "God's Controversy with New England," composed in 1662, did not appear in print until 1871, seven complete editions of *The Day of Doom* were printed between 1662 and 1751, and six complete editions of *Meat Out of the Eater*—Wigglesworth's most substantial volume of poems—were printed between 1670 and 1770 (Wigglesworth 1989, 310, 305–306, 312). Today, Wigglesworth is remembered for the title poem from *The Day of Doom* and "God's Controversy with New-England," both of which are usually printed in full or in part in college-level anthologies of American literature; except for a few treatments, Wigglesworth's *Meat Out of the Eater* has been almost entirely ignored since the eighteenth century (Crowder 1962; Wigglesworth 1989; Hammond 1993a).

Contemporary readers find that Bradstreet's domestic themes and feminist perspective make her verses accessible to the modern imagination and that Taylor's obvious debt to the Metaphysical and Cavalier traditions provides a crucial key to his style; these same readers are often at a loss to comprehend Wigglesworth's purpose or point. Echoing Murdock's view of "The Day of Doom," some believe the poem "is—or seems—comic" (Murdock 1929, x–xi) and nothing more, while others notice in the poem's litany of sinners being cast into the eternal flames of hell an unexpected ring of modernity that led Robert Daly to state after his consideration of the poem, "we need conclude neither that Puritan taste was any more demented than our own . . . nor that [Wigglesworth's poems] had some great merit lost on modern readers" (Daly 1978, 134). Still others, reading "The Day of Doom" and "God's Controversy with New-England" together, hear their homiletic tone straightaway and, even if they cannot identify the doctrinal issues at stake in the poems, believe that something serious was being said about them to the poems' first readers. And, indeed, something was, for Wigglesworth's call to the pulpit in Malden was to serve as the congregation's teacher, not pastor; as such, according to the *Cambridge Platform* of 1648, he was expected "to attend to doctrine, and therein administer a word of knowledge," "execute censures," and preach (Wigglesworth 1989, xx–xxi).

The only sensible way to approach Wigglesworth's poetry is to regard it as a form of homily in verse and to recognize, as did the several generations raised on his verses, that didacticism and orthodoxy were its very strengths. This is as true for the often maligned "stampeding fourteeners" of "The Day of Doom," which made the lessons embedded in the poem's commonplace balladry both entertaining and easy to memorize for its earliest audiences, as it is for the jeremiadic language of "God's Controversy with New-England," which sounded a poetic alarm against the backsliding of second-generation New Englanders and newcomers to the colony from the religious commitment of the colony's original settlers. This is also true for the typically "unread Wigglesworth," poems such as his "Song of Praise," a lyric written about 1673 to commemorate the return of William Foster from captivity under the Moors, or his Song X of "Light in Darkness," Song IV of "Sick Mens Health," and Song III of "In Solitude Good Company" from *Meat Out of the Eater,* which demonstrate the poet's facility with dramatic monologue and dramatic debate. Wigglesworth's contemporaries knew that, regardless of the style of a poem they were reading, they were being instructed by their "teacher," and the didactic quality of his verse was positively reinforced by Jonathan Mitchell in these lines from his "On the following Work, and It's Author," which introduced the first and subsequent editions of *The Day of Doom:*

> A Verse may find him who a Sermon flies,
> Saith *Herbert* well. Great Truths to dress in Meeter;
> Becomes a Preacher; who mens Souls doth prize,
> That Truth in Sugar roll'd may taste the sweeter.
> No Cost too great, no Care too curious is
> To set forth, and win mens Souls to bliss.
> In costly Verse, and most laborious Rymes,
> Are dish't up here Truths worthy most regard:
> No Toyes, nor Fables (Poets wonted Crimes)
> Here be; but things of worth with Wit prepar'd.
> Reader, fall too; and if thy tast be good,
> Thou'lt praise the Cook, & say, 'Tis choicest Food.
> (Wigglesworth 1989, 292)

The fact that Wigglesworth composed what are by modern judgment his two most enduring poems in 1662 was no accident. In that year, New England Puritans attempted to check declension by instituting the Half-Way Covenant, which dramatically relaxed the standards governing formal church membership. Whereas previously individuals had to profess their belief publicly and be baptized in order to gain access to the civil privileges associated with membership in the local congregation, the Half-Way Covenant provided the children and grandchildren of church members with a form of partial church membership that preserved a congregation's numerical authority in the community, even though half-way members could not vote within the congregation. From the outset, the Half-Way Covenant was a failure, and in "The Day of Doom" and "God's Controversy with New-England"—the last of which he likely circulated in manuscript among his Malden congregants—Wigglesworth instructed his congregation on the pitfalls of compromising church standards for any purpose whatsoever. Conservative at heart, in "The Day of Doom" he critiqued the sense of "carnal" or worldly security that the Half-Way Covenant encouraged. Of the poem's 224 stanzas, the first 218 celebrate the unmasking of sinners and all form of backsliders far and wide, critique their ingenious arguments in defense of their wickedness and laxness, and portray their casting into the eternal fires of hell by a Christ whose exacting sense of righteousness is never moderated by his application of mercy. Although it takes 1,744 lines for the "Saints" to finally express their immense joy at being saved and be ushered into heaven, Wigglesworth's purpose was less to represent the splendors of salvation—which in any case had been preached from New England's pulpits for over forty years—than it was to expose the pervasiveness of declension in communities that, from the outset, had been established to promote godliness in the New World wilderness. Nevertheless, for those who eventually memorized "The Day of Doom" after reading it or hearing it read or recited aloud—which Wigglesworth clearly intended by setting the poem in ballad meter—the rejoicing of the "Saints" at the poem's end must have lingered long and fondly in their memory:

> The Saints behold with courage bold,
> and thankful wonderment,
> To see all those that were their foes
> thus sent to punishment:
> Then do they sing unto their King
> a Song of endless Praise:
> They praise his name, and do proclaim
> that just are all his ways.
> (Wigglesworth 1989, 65)

The popularity of a poem such as "The Day of Doom" throughout the settled regions of the New World for more than 100 years after its initial publication is not too difficult to understand. Although it was written by a Calvinist, belief in some form or other of Christianity, not just Calvinism, made the poem accessible and its harsh lessons persuasive to a remarkably diverse body of readers spread out over three generations. By contrast, "God's Controversy with New-England" was a thoroughly Calvinist poem written specifically for a New England audience at the time of a specific crisis. Believing that the divine mind was discernible in human affairs as well as in natural events, Puritans generally, and the preachers of jeremiads from the 1660s through the opening decades of the eighteenth century specifically, scoured the persons and landscapes around them for signs of God's disposition toward them. Throughout the 1650s, the leaders of New England's colonies from the earliest days of settlement one by one died off, and disconcerting as their passing might have been to believers, preachers typically read each passing as one more sign among many that God was increasingly displeased with the rising secularism of his formerly religious plantation. In 1662, New England experienced the second or possibly the third year of a great drought, and Wigglesworth seized upon the convergence of that event with the passage of the Half-Way Covenant as an occasion to compose the New World's most compelling jeremiad in verse.

"God's Controversy with New-England" features one prominent voice, that of an Old Testament–style Jehovah who has lost all patience with his people. After several introductory stanzas that narrate Jehovah's transformation of a "waste and howling wilderness, / Where none inhabited/But hellish fiends, and brutish men / That Devils worshiped" into "a fruitfull paradeis" (Wigglesworth 1989, 90, 95) designed to be the home of godly people, the poem shifts into a litany of Jehovah's complaints against those people for their rejection of the strict Covenant to which the colony's founders had originally subscribed, their multiple violations of every one of the Ten Commandments, and their increased devotion to the material world while turning a deaf ear to the righteous lessons of their ministers. Arguing that the drought that has continued to plague New England has the capacity to return the "paradeis" that was his gift to the founders to the "waste and howling wilderness" the founders discovered on their arrival, Jehovah utters these dread-inspiring, tightly worded statements of his intentions, unless New Englanders mend their ways:

> Now . . . hearken and encline your ear,
> In judgment I will henceforth with you plead;
> And if by that you will not learn to fear,
> But still go on a sensuall life to lead:
> I'le strike at once an All-Consuming stroke;
> Nor cries nor tears shall then my fierce intent revoke . . .
> Beware, O sinful-Land, beware;
> And do not think it strange
> That sorer judgements are at hand,
> Unless thou quickly change.
> Or God, or thou, must quickly change;
> Or else thou art undon;
> Wrath cannot cease, if sin remain,
> Where judgement is begun.
> (Wigglesworth 1989, 99, 101)

EDWARD TAYLOR

If someone were inclined to interpret the cultural history of late seventeenth-century New England through the lens of Wigglesworth's poetic imagination, that person would have to admit that the poet's dire predictions of New England's decline and fall in "God's Controversy with New-England" came to pass with remarkable speed; in fact, one of the reasons "The Day of Doom" remained popular among Puritan and non-Puritan readers for so long may have been that it served them as a ready handbook of how their behavior was inexorably leading them toward a divine Judgment Day that was first going to be played out in the systematic reversal of their fortunes in the material world they so loved. In the final third of the seventeenth century, New England's ministers transformed themselves into latter-day Jeremiahs on entering their pulpits, not only on those occasions when they preached sermons for specially called days of fast, prayer, or humiliation, but also on celebratory days such as the annual election day, on public spectacle days when colonial criminals were humiliated or executed for their transgressions, and on regular Sabbath and lecture days. And during this thirty-year period, those ministers did not have to look very far for hard evidence of how, as Wigglesworth wrote, "Wrath cannot cease, if sin remain, / Where judgement is begun." A "Reforming Synod" of ministers that convened in Cambridge, Massachusetts, in 1679 published a comprehensive listing of "Personal Afflictions," "mortal Contagions," "Seasons of Destruction," "devouring Fires," and like judgments sent against half-way believers by a wrathful God as complements to King Philip's War that had ravaged the colonies in the mid-1670s; those judgments continued as complements to the first signs of the presence of witches in New England in the 1680s and the crippling of the Puritan theocracy by the Crown's imposition of a royal governor on the colonies in the 1690s. In "When as the wayes of Jesus Christ," a powerful but unread poem that he composed around 1665, Wigglesworth predicted the reversals that would befall Puritan New Englanders for the next thirty years, and he laid the blame squarely on the Half-Way Covenant.

This was the prevailing climate in New England's Puritan culture at the time Edward Taylor began his public ministry late in 1671 in the newly settled wilderness town of Westfield, Massachusetts, where he would serve until his death in 1729, and throughout a personal ministry he undertook in concert with his public one in an extraordinary body of meditative, doctrinal, and occasional poetry he composed for his own edification in private manuscript journals that would not be recovered for more than two centuries after his death. A second-generation Puritan minister and physician, Taylor was born in Leicestershire, England, in or about 1642, emigrated to the Massachusetts Bay Colony in 1668 on a several-month-long voyage during which he divided his time between reading the Bible and tending to his seasickness, entered Harvard a few months later, graduated in 1671, and settled in Westfield by the year's end. On his voyage, Taylor carried with him letters of introduction to Increase Mather, who then headed Boston's ecclesiastical leadership, and the colony's mintmaster. John Hull; their friendship toward him not only facilitated his admission to Harvard and his call four years later to Westfield's pulpit but also established his credentials as a theologically sound Calvinist who respected the original Covenant and could be counted on to promote its values for a new generation of believers through his scholarly preaching, defense of "civil and religious Liberty," opposition to King James and Massachusetts's colonial governor Sir Edmund Andros, and advocacy of "King William and the Revolution of 1688." Described by Ezra Stiles, his grandson and the president of Yale, as a "man of small stature, but firm; of quick Passions, yet serious and grave[;] Exemplary in Piety, and for a very sacred Observance of the Lord's Day" (quoted in Taylor 1960, XLVI–XLVII), from his

distant wilderness post, Taylor quietly exerted a significant influence on New England culture in his defenses of conservative Puritan theology, politics, and sense of
social decorum throughout his long career. However, it is for his poetry that Taylor
is admired today; indeed, although he wrote poetry for himself, not for the public,
and intended that his manuscripts should be destroyed after his death, if Taylor's
heirs had yielded to that intention, a major chapter in the history of American poetic theory and practice would have been lost.

The recovery of Taylor's poetry from manuscript is the single greatest achievement of early American literary scholarship, and that achievement is extending into
the twenty-first century as new comprehensive editions of the poetry continue to be
prepared and as the substantial body of original scholarship on Taylor's aesthetics
and theology continues to grow. To date, two full generations of scholars and their
students have devoted entire careers to the recovery and analysis of Taylor's poetry;
their story begins in the 1930s, when Thomas H. Johnson found his "Poetical Works"
manuscripts in the Yale University Library, where they had languished in virtual obscurity since Ezra Stiles deposited them there in the late eighteenth century (Taylor
1966b). Johnson published a selection of texts from the Yale manuscripts in 1939.
After Johnson, Donald E. Stanford prepared from the Yale manuscripts and manuscripts of Taylor's poetry that he discovered in other libraries what is still considered the standard (though incomplete) edition of Taylor's poetry in 1960. Two years
later he published a microform edition of Taylor's *Metrical History of Christianity*,
which runs to more than 20,000 lines. Significant recoveries of Taylor's poetry have
continued (Taylor 1981, 2003). As these scholars have published texts from Taylor's
poetry manuscripts which they have assiduously pursued in archives in the United States and abroad, others have prepared editions of his personal and theological writings from newly discovered or rediscovered manuscripts—*Christographia,
Diary, Harmony of the Gospels, Treatise Concerning the Lord's Supper, Upon the Types
of the Old Testament* (Taylor 1962a, 1964, 1966a, 1983, 1989)—and have thereby created
contexts for reading Taylor's poetry in light of his preaching record, theological
views, and important aspects of his personal life not otherwise revealed in the lines
of the poems themselves.

Less as a function of its relatively recent introduction into the canon of early
American literature than of the enormous body of interpretative scholarship it has
encouraged, at first glance Taylor's poetry appears impossibly daunting to students
as well as many scholars. Whereas Bradstreet's and Wigglesworth's writings can be
initially approached with a basic "working" knowledge of the time in which the poets
lived and their motivations for writing poetry, Taylor's poems challenge newcomers
with their stylistic debt to the English Metaphysical and Cavalier traditions, their
highly nuanced approaches to Calvinist doctrine, and their form as an expression
of spiritual autobiography quite unlike that associated with either Bradstreet's and
Wigglesworth's poems or the prose autobiographical writings of their contemporaries. As starting points for their own inquiries, modern readers will find recent

bibliographic studies indispensable (Hammond 1993a; Guruswamy 2003). Yet even with these resources in hand, several cautions sounded by two eminent Taylor scholars are worth repeating here. Donald E. Stanford commented on the "adjustments" modern readers have to make in their interpretative habits when approaching this writer who appears before them without the advantage of two centuries of "intervening ... scholarship and critical judgment to help in understanding and appreciating" his poetry: first, they have to place themselves "imaginatively in the world of seventeenth-century Puritan Calvinism, where the devil is taken seriously and literally and a few saints are battling a great many sinners"; second, they have to be "willing to accept the artificial rhetorical style of the seventeenth-century metaphysical poets, which often seems confused and awkward" compared with the more popular Romantic poets (Stanford 1972, 59). Twenty years later Thomas M. Davis reinforced the first of Stanford's cautions, remarking, "perhaps the most fundamental misreading of Taylor's work is to be unaware of the subtle but clear stages of development in the poetry, for they signal and reflect basic changes in his attitudes toward his poetry and toward his own spiritual state" (Davis 1992, 13). The one consolation all readers can take from their own first approaches to Taylor is that no one has yet uttered the proverbial last word on the meaning of his poems, on the extent to which the poems serve as a measure of the depth of his own mind and imagination, or on the extent to which they offer a window into the material and spiritual culture in which Taylor lived and about which he wrote.

Because current scholars have moved well beyond the carping of early critics who felt his meditative verses were not equal in style or depth to those produced out of the English traditions that served as their model, the Taylor we approach today is respected as the most aesthetically interesting and intellectually satisfying poet of colonial New England. Readings of his poems are invariably distributed across the three categories of poems Taylor produced; those categories are evident in the arrangement of his poems in Stanford's edition, in his explanation of the range of Taylor's poetic interests (Stanford 1972), and in virtually all anthologies of American literature in print today.

By far the largest and most provocative category of Taylor's poems is his *Preparatory Meditations,* which he composed in two series of more than 200 poems between 1682 and the mid-1720s as investigations into, and expositions of, his own intellectual, emotional, and spiritual states as he prepared to officiate over the sacrament of the Lord's Supper before his congregation. The second category of Taylor's poetry encompasses his *God's Determinations Touching his Elect; and The Elects Combat in their Conversion, and Coming up to God in Christ Together with the Comfortable Effects Thereof.* Though a few scholars, conditioned perhaps by the representation of selections from *God's Determinations* in anthologies, have treated the work as a gathering of separate poems, most Taylor scholars read *God's Determinations* as a sustained poem on the related subjects of explaining God's ways to sinners and instructing those who hope to number among the elect in the way to salvation through Christ. Undated in manuscript, Davis offers compelling evidence that Taylor wrote *God's Determinations* between 1679 and 1682 as a direct and potentially public response to the events of the 1670s (Davis 1992, 27–28). However one reads *God's Determinations*, when it is read in conjunction with a reading of "The Day of Doom," it spectacularly highlights the differences between Taylor and Wigglesworth as teachers. For while Wigglesworth spends most of his poetic energy and invective in describing the unmasking and condemnation of sinners, Taylor quickly dispatches the damned to hell in order to develop lessons on how God variously brings the elect to salvation by providing them with the grace needed to persevere in their conversion. Finally, for want of a better title, the third and fairly substantial category of Taylor's poetry consists of his "occasional poems," which encompass elegies, homiletic and meditative poems that improve upon commonplace events in nature and human experience for the lessons they may impart, and the *Metrical History of Christianity* (Taylor 1962b). Taylor's editor describes the *Metrical History* as "a dogged, determined performance composed in a style that is frequently crude and dull," but revealing "a few flashes of genuine poetry here and there" (Stanford, 1972, 88). Yet most scholars agree with Jane Donahue Eberwein's dismissal of Taylor's versification of church history and its celebration of Protestantism's "triumph ... over the infidel atrocities of heathens and Catholics" in the *Metrical History* as a "bigoted, barbarous," and "most distasteful poetic effort" (Eberwein 1978, 64).

The overwhelming majority of readings of Taylor's poetry concentrate on the *Preparatory Meditations* or use them as the starting point for explorations into, for instance, *God's Determinations*, Taylor's use of typology, or his foreshadowing of originality in the American poetic voice. In his remarkable reading of Taylor's poetry, Davis states that the *Preparatory Meditations* are his "best poetry," and he identifies those composed as the poet's spontaneous reaction to "the stuff of his world," not those written in deference to his "periodic external duty" of preparing a bimonthly sermon in anticipation of administering the Lord's Supper, as the best of all (Davis 1992, 199). Hammond calls the *Preparatory Meditations* "vehicles for Taylor's private exploration of his own struggles as an earthly pilgrim seeking signs of inner congruence with the saintly metaself" (Hammond 1993b, 164), while Raymond A. Craig argues that Taylor's "mixing" of "spiritual and temporal" language in the meditations transforms the rich biblical allusion of his poems into serial "images of personal vision" that mark him as the most sophisticated of the Puritan poets and contribute to that "peculiar elegance" in Taylor that reveals "what is poetic about Puritan poetry" (Craig 1997, 96). In his study of the American poetic psyche, Albert Gelpi reads Taylor's meditative verses as "foreshadowing an indigenous poetic tradition," which, he notes, after listing the "gold, gems, perfumes, liquors, brocades, [and] incense ... that were clearly not part of his life at Westfield," forced the poet "into the privacy of his imagination where his passionate nature ... articulate[s] the Puritan vision of the city on a hill" (Gelpi 1975, 15, 42–43). William J.

Scheick makes this point even more forcefully, stating that in spite of "the influence of Calvin on his thought," Taylor explores an optimistic worldview in order to affirm "an older, more humanistic tradition" that looks back to Augustinian thought with its "respect for the rational faculty and . . . high regard for nature." Scheick contends, "What emerges from the *Preparatory Meditations* is a portrait of Taylor's incessant endeavor to assert his self and to appraise that self's relation to the 'Sacred selfe'" (Scheick 1974, 4, 161).

As these brief summaries of critical opinion suggest, there is no absolutely agreed upon reading of Taylor's poetry or understanding of his significance in the American poetic tradition. Taylor himself defies absolute correctness in the reading of his meditations, when in the "Prologue" he parallels their subtle variableness to that of God's will as exemplified in all creation:

> Thy Crumb of Dust breaths two words from its breast,
>   That thou wilt guide its pen to write aright
> To prove thou art, and that thou are the best
>   And shew thy Properties to shine most bright.
>   And then thy Works will shine as flowers on Stems
>   Or as in Jewellary Shops, do gems.
> (Taylor 1960, 1)

Similarly, in Meditation 63 from the Second Series, he imagines himself in the Canticles' "Garden of Nuts," singing "Heart ravishing tunes, sweet Musick for our King," drawn from the multiple wonders of creation that appeal to his fancy and pique his poetic imagination:

> If, Lord, thou opst, and in thy garden bring
> Mee, then thy little Linet sweetly Will
> Upon thy Nut tree sit and sweetly sing
> Will Crack a Nut and eat the kirnell still.
> Thou wilt mine Eyes, my Nose, and Palate greet
> With Curious Flowers, Sweet Odors, Viands Sweet.
> Thy Gardens Odorif'rous aire mee make
> Suck in, and out t'aromatize my lungs.
> That I thy garden, and its Spicie State
> May breath upon with such ensweetned Songs.
> My Lungs and Breath ensweetned thus shall raise
> The Glory of thy garden in its praise.
> (Taylor 1960, 195)

Nevertheless, there are some thematic constants in Taylor's poetry that will serve readers as guideposts to his poetic interests. Throughout the meditations, *God's Determinations,* and occasional poems, Taylor repeatedly assumes a sinner's self-accusatory posture until, through a series of rhetorical turns, he humbles himself before God and announces himself ready to accept his punishment and act through whatever grace he may enjoy in order to persevere toward salvation through Christ. Taylor's fear of not being accepted into God's grace is palpable throughout the meditations. In Meditations 23 through 40 from the First Series, for instance, he treats Christ and Christ's visible church on earth as his "spouse" and lawyerly "advocate," stating that he is willing to offer all that he has, and especially his poetic talent, in service to God for a good hearing through Christ on his dreadfully woeful case. In those meditations, as in Meditation 54 from the Second Series, Taylor confesses his spiritual worthlessness and the progressive unworthiness of his verses to merit even the slightest consideration from God. Fearful that he will never be worthy of union with the Almighty, he utters these questions in a near whimper, "My Gracious-Glorious Lord, shall I be thine? / Wilt thou be mine?" Believing that he hears his Lord answer positively, a relieved Taylor concludes, "Then happy, happy mee," and promises that his poems will be infused with the heavenly gold of grace to sing the Lord's praises forever: "Lord, so be it. My rusty Wires then shall / Bee fined gold, to tune thee praise with all" (Taylor 1960, 178). This pattern is played out fully in Meditation 26 from the Second Series, where he begins with the self-accusation, "Unclean, Unclean: My Lord, Undone, all vile / Yea all Defild" before posing the question, "What shall thy Servant doe?" Further questioning his worthiness to be counted among the "fold" of the elect, Taylor acknowledges that as a "Bag of botches, Lump of Loathsomeness: / Defild by Touch, by Issue: Leproust flesh," he is incapable of becoming "Pure, Cleane, and bright, Whiter than whitest Snow," and seems destined to remain "fowle" forever. Personalizing the meditation's opening question, he asks again, "What shall I doe?" Fearing that he will find God's "Church Doors . . . shut," thus shutting him out forever from "Church fellowship" and such opportunities for divine grace as that fellowship may provide, over the next three stanzas of the poem Taylor confesses the depth of his sin and his unworthiness to be heard even in prayer; then, humbling himself before God, he implores,

> Oh! wash mee, Lord, in this Choice Fountain, White
> That I may enter, and not sully here
> Thy Church, whose floore is pav'de with Graces bright
> And hold Church fellowship with Saints most cleare.
> My Voice all sweet, with their melodious layes
> Shall make sweet Musik blossom'd with thy praise.
> (Taylor 1960, 130–131)

The mystical process that Taylor follows in the meditations from self-accusation to belief in the possibility of his salvation—no matter how tentative—is also apparent in *God's Determinations*, where it is often depicted "as the soul's exertion to accept the fact that it has been chosen" (Grabo 1988, 27). As an exploration of how to discern and maintain one's position among the elect, *God's Determinations* is an evolutionary poem in which the narrator, Christ, and Satan dramatically enact the saint's difficult journey from conversion, to rationalization, to, finally, consecration.

Designed to educate its audience in the subtleties of Calvinist doctrine and to instill courage in those ambivalent church members who are lingering on the threshold of complete conversion to Christ's church, *God's Determinations* has been defined as a "morality play," seeing each of its characters as representations of various allegorical figures (Lewalski 1979, 391). This is most obvious in the poem's "Dialogue between Justice and Mercy" sequence, where through their lines of dialogue Justice and Mercy serve as symbolic characters, but it is also apparent throughout the poem in dialogical exchanges among the figures of the Soul, Christ, and Satan. The central figure in *God's Determinations* is Christ, who, as in the meditations, provides the answer to the question that most plagues the earthbound saint: "How can I discover and persevere in my place among the elect?" "Christ's Reply," which serves as a response to "The Souls Groan to Christ for Succor" against the wiles of Satan, humankind's "Dreadfull Enemy," depicts the Savior's relationship to the visible church and the individual saint engaged in mortal struggles in both spousal and parental terms; speaking in a voice that sounds very much like a nurturing mother addressing her lost and wandering child, Christ says,

> Peace, Peace, my Hony, do not Cry,
> My Little Darling, wipe thine eye,
> Oh Cheer, Cheer up, come see.
> Is anything too dear, my Dove,
> Is anything too good, my Love
> To get or give for thee?

This seeming maternal voice continues, counseling the lost soul to repent and accept purifying grace:

> And though thy sins increase their race,
> And though when thou hast sought for Grace,
> Thou fallst more than before,
> If thou by true Repentance Rise,
> And Faith makes Me Thy Sacrifice,
> I'l pardon all, though more.
> (Taylor 1960, 414, 416)

Taylor's representation of Christ here as a gentle, loving maternal figure is juxtaposed not only to the "broken tootht," barking Satan who "seeks to aggrivate thy sin / And screw them to the highest pin, / To make thy faith to quaile" (Taylor 1960, 414–415), but also to an archetypal Old Testament–style angry and vengeful paternal God who is ready to exact horrific punishments on those who transgress his commandments. Yet unlike God the Father of Wigglesworth's "Day of Doom" or the Jehovah of his "God's Controversy with New-England," the heavenly Father and Son of Taylor's *God's Determinations* offer hope, to which the poet responds with his now well-tuned song of praise in "An Extasy of Joy Let in by [Christ's] Reply":

> Christ, to his Father saith, Incarnate make
> Mee, Mee thy Son; and I will doe't:
> I'le purify his Blood, and take
> The Coare out of his Throate.
> All this he did, and did for us, vile Clay:
> Oh! Let our Praise his Grace assaile.
> To free us from Sins Gulph each way,
> He's both our Bridge, and Raile.
> Although we fall and Fall, and Fall and Fall
> And Satan fall on us as fast.
> He purgeth us and doth us call.
> Our trust on him to Cast.
> My Lumpish Soule why art thou hamper'd thus
> Within a Crumb of Dust? Arise,
> Trumpet out Praises. Christ for us
> Hath slain our Enemies.
> Screw up, Deare Lord, upon the highest pin:
> My soul thy ample Praise to sound.
> O tune it right, that every string
> May make thy praise rebound.
> (Taylor 1960, 420)

CONCLUSION

Louis L. Martz observed almost a half century ago that as we read "more deeply and more widely" in Taylor's poetry, we will become conscious of the "tenacious intelligence" that speaks to this poet's deserved significance in the American literary canon: "a bold, probing, adventurous intellect that deliberately tries to bend the toughest matter toward his quest for truth" (Taylor 1960, XVIII). As Martz rightly predicted, our close reading of any decent selection of Taylor's poems is easily rewarded with our repeated sightings of his "quest for truth" and with our enhanced awareness, too, of a concession to personal humility in his quest that characterizes not only his writings but also Bradstreet's and, to a lesser degree, Wigglesworth's. In Taylor's case, even the occasional and somewhat artificial poems he wrote outside of his *Preparatory Meditations* and *God's Determinations* reveal his searching intellect and fertile imagination. In "Upon a Spider Catching a Fly," for instance, he compresses into a fifty-line poem a homily on the implications of a natural scene in which a spider (developed as a thinly disguised Satan) wisely chooses a fly over a wasp (one of God's saints infused with irresistible grace) to ensnare in its web of certain destruction (death in the eternal flames of hell); similarly, in "Huswifery," a poem based on the activity common in seventeenth- and eighteenth-century New England homes of spinning fabric for household use, Taylor symbolically re-creates himself as a spinning wheel to be turned by God's designing hand to create useful godly cloth in this world in anticipation of the glorious robes worn by the elect in the next (Taylor 1960, 465–467). Even a poem as emotionally wrenching as "Upon Wedlock, and Death of Children," in which he treats another commonplace reality in colonial New England—the loss of one's children in a wilderness environment that guaranteed a high rate of infant mortality—Taylor draws useful, if not entirely comforting, lessons for himself that complement Bradstreet's responses to the death of her grandchildren. Like Bradstreet, Taylor is driven to distraction by the unnaturalness of one of his children's "tortures, Vomit, screechings, groans, / And six weeks Fever" that pierced his heart "like stones," but unlike Bradstreet, he writes his way to reconciliation over the loss of this and other of his children, stating,

> . . . take, Lord, they're thine.
> I piecemeal pass to Glory bright in them.
> I joy, may I sweet Flowers for Glory breed,
> Whether thou getst them green, or lets them seed.
> (Taylor 1960, 469–470)

Such poems demonstrate Taylor's mind and imagination at work in the commonplace as well as in the near-sublime, in the "Excellence" of every aspect of God's creation and human experience in it. In 1708—or about halfway through his public ministry to the people of Westfield and his private, poetical self-ministry—he wrote in Meditation 80 from the Second Series:

> This Curious pearle, One Syllable, call'd LIFE,
> That all things struggle t'keep, and we so prize
> I'd with the Edge of sharpen'd sight (as knife)
> My understanding sheath'th anatomize
> But finde Life far too fine, I can not know't
> My sight too Dull; my knife's too blunt to do't.
> And if you say, What then is Life? I say
> I cannot tell you what it is, yet know
> That Various kinds of Life lodg in my clay.
> And ery kinde an Excellence doth show[.] . . .
> (Taylor 1960, 229)

The "Excellence" that Taylor portrayed throughout his poems is an "Excellence" that Bradstreet and Wigglesworth appreciated and wrote about as well. In the Calvinist world in which they wrote, whatever failures Taylor or they conceded about their respective perceptions of the world in which they lived or their desire to join the host of the saved in heaven, they each attributed to the infallibility of their too human intellects and the defect of their too human hearts. Yet with comprehensive editions of the writings of each at our disposal, and with a growing body of informed scholarship to assist our reading of their poems, we are in a position to approach their writings afresh and size up for ourselves the extent to which they each contributed to "the American poetic vision." And their poems are not the only ones at our disposal to encourage and direct this undertaking. As noted at the outset of this chapter, contemporary critical editions of poems by Wigglesworth, Cotton Mather, and Benjamin Tompson, along with the verses of many other early New Englanders gathered in Meserole's and Silverman's collections, are waiting for us as their newest readers. The opportunities these scholarly resources offer are significant. In Wigglesworth's case, for instance, the substantial body of poems he included in *Meat Out of the Eater* has been virtually untouched since the mid–eighteenth century; similarly, in the collections by Meserole and Silverman, modern readers will find remarkable gatherings of poems on early New England history, on everyday life in early New England, and elegiac poems, which, as Jeffrey A. Hammond said recently, constitute the genre of early American verse most in need of our recuperation from critical invisibility.

REFERENCES

Anderson, James. 1862. *Memorable Women of the Puritan Times.* 2 vols. London: Blackie and Son.

Bradford, William. 1912. *History of Plymouth Plantation, 1620–1647,* edited by Worthington Chauncey Ford et al. 2 vols. Boston: Massachusetts Historical Society.

Bradstreet, Anne. [1867] 1932. *The Works of Anne Bradstreet in Prose and Verse,* edited by John Harvard Ellis. Reprint. New York: Peter Smith.

———. 1967. *The Works of Anne Bradstreet,* edited by Jeannine Hensley. Cambridge: Belknap Press of Harvard University Press.

Cowell, Pattie, ed. 1981. *Women Poets in Pre-Revolutionary America.* Troy, NY: Whitston.

Craig, Raymond A. 1997. The "Peculiar Elegance" of Edward Taylor's Poetics. In *The Tailoring Shop,* edited by Michael Schuldiner, 68–101. Newark: University of Delaware Press.

Crowder, Richard. 1962. *No Featherbed to Heaven: A Biography of Michael Wigglesworth, 1631–1705.* East Lansing: Michigan State University Press.

Daly, Robert. 1978. *God's Altar: The World and the Flesh in Puritan Poetry.* Berkeley: University of California Press.

Davis, Thomas M. 1992. *A Reading of Edward Taylor.* Newark: University of Delaware Press.

Eberwein, Jane Donahue, ed. 1978. *Early American Poetry: Selections from Bradstreet, Taylor, Dwight, Freneau, and Bryant.* Madison: University of Wisconsin Press.

Gelpi, Albert. 1975. *The Tenth Muse: The Psyche of the American Poet.* Cambridge, MA: Harvard University Press.

Grabo, Norman S. 1988. *Edward Taylor.* Rev. ed. Boston: Twayne.

Guruswamy, Rosemary Fithian. 2003. *The Poems of Edward Taylor: A Reference Guide.* Westport, CT: Greenwood.

Hammond, Jeffrey A. 1993a. *Edward Taylor: Fifty Years of Scholarship and Criticism.* Columbia, SC: Camden House.

———. 1993b. *Sinful Self, Saintly Self: The Puritan Experience of Poetry.* Athens: University of Georgia Press.

———. 2000. *The American Puritan Elegy: A Literary and Cultural Study.* New York: Cambridge University Press.

Jantz, Harold S., ed. [1943] 1962. *The First Century of New England Verse.* Reprint. New York: Russell and Russell.

Kettell, Samuel, ed. [1829] 1967. *Specimens of American Poetry, with Critical and Biographical Notices.* 3 vols. Reprint. New York: Benjamin Blom.

Leverenz, David. 1980. *The Language of Puritan Feeling: An Exploration in Literature, Psychology, and Social History.* New Brunswick, NJ: Rutgers University Press.

Lewalski, Barbara Kiefer. 1979. *Protestant Poetics and the Seventeenth-Century Religious Lyric.* Princeton, NJ: Princeton University Press.

Mather, Cotton. 1702. *Magnalia Christi Americana: or, The Ecclesiastical History of New-England, from Its First Planting in the Year 1620. unto the year of Our Lord, 1698.* London: for T. Parkhurst.

———. 1703. *Meat out of the Eater: or, Funeral Discourses, Occasioned by the Death of Several Relatives.* Boston: for Benjamin Eliot.

———. 1705. *A Faithful Man, Described and Rewarded.* Boston: B. Green, for Benj. Eliot.

———. 1726. *Manuductio ad Ministerium: Directions for a Candidate of the Ministry.* Boston: for T. Hancock.

———. 1989. *Cotton Mather's Verse in English,* edited by Denise D. Knight. Newark: University of Delaware Press.

Mawer, Randall R. 1980. "Farewell Dear Babe": Bradstreet's Elegy for Elizabeth. *Early American Literature* 15: 29–41.

Meserole, Harrison T., ed. 1985. *American Poetry of the Seventeenth Century.* University Park: Pennsylvania State University Press.

Miller, Arthur. 1971. *The Crucible: Text and Criticism,* edited by Gerald Weales. New York: Viking.

Miller, Perry. 1953. *The New England Mind: From Colony to Province.* Cambridge, MA: Harvard University Press.

Miller, Perry, and Thomas H. Johnson, eds. [1938] 1963. *The Puritans: A Sourcebook of Their Writings.* 2 vols. Reprint. New York: Harper and Row.

Murdock, Kenneth B., ed. 1927. *Handkerchiefs from Paul.* Cambridge, MA: Harvard University Press.

———. ed. 1929. *The Day of Doom.* New York: Spiral Press.

Piercy, Josephine K. 1965. *Anne Bradstreet.* New York: Twayne.

Requa, Kenneth A. 1974. Anne Bradstreet's Poetic Voices. *Early American Literature* 9: 3–18.

Rosenmeier, Rosamond R. 1977. "Divine Translation": A Contribution to the Study of Anne Bradstreet's Method in the Marriage Poems. *Early American Literature* 12: 121–135.

Saltman, Helen. 1983. "Contemplations": Anne Bradstreet's Spiritual Autobiography. In *Critical Essays on Anne Bradstreet,* edited by Pattie Cowell and Ann Stanford, 216–237. Boston: Hall.

Scheick, William J. 1974. *The Will and the Word: The Poetry of Edward Taylor*. Athens: University of Georgia Press.

———. 1988. The Poetry of Colonial America. In *Columbia Literary History of the United States*, edited by Emory Elliott, 83–97. New York: Columbia University Press.

———. 1992. *Design in Puritan American Literature*. Lexington: University Press of Kentucky.

Silverman, Kenneth, ed. 1976. *Colonial American Poetry*. New York: Hafner.

Stanford, Ann. 1966. Anne Bradstreet: Dogmatist and Rebel. *New England Quarterly* 39: 373–389.

Stanford, Donald E. 1972. Edward Taylor. In *Major Writers of Early American Literature*, edited by Everett Emerson, 59–91. Madison: University of Wisconsin Press.

Taylor, Edward. 1960. *The Poems of Edward Taylor*, edited by Donald E. Stanford. New Haven, CT: Yale University Press.

———. 1962a. *Edward Taylor's Christographia*, edited by Norman S. Grabo. New Haven, CT: Yale University Press.

———. 1962b. *A Transcript of Edward Taylor's Metrical History of Christianity*, edited by Donald E. Stanford. Cleveland, OH: Micro Photo.

———. 1964. *The Diary of Edward Taylor*, edited by Francis Murphy. Springfield, MA: Connecticut Valley Historical Museum.

———. 1966a. *Edward Taylor's Treatise Concerning the Lord's Supper*, edited by Norman S. Grabo. East Lansing: Michigan State University Press.

———. 1966b. *The Poetical Works of Edward Taylor*, edited by Thomas H. Johnson. Princeton, NJ: Princeton University Press.

———. 1981. *Edward Taylor's Minor Poetry: The Unpublished Writings of Edward Taylor*, edited by Thomas M. Davis and Virginia L. Davis. Boston: Twayne.

———. 1983. *Edward Taylor's Harmony of the Gospels*, edited by Thomas M. Davis, Virginia L. Davis, and Betty L. Parks. 4 vols. New York: Scholars' Facsimiles and Reprints.

———. 1989. *Upon the Types of the Old Testament*, edited by Charles W. Mignon. 2 vols. Lincoln: University of Nebraska Press.

———. 2003. *Edward Taylor's Gods Determinations and Preparatory Meditations: A Critical Edition*, edited by Daniel Patterson. Kent, OH: Kent State University Press.

Tompson, Benjamin. 1676. *New Englands Crisis, or, A Brief Narrative of New-Englands Lamentable Estate at Present, Compar'd with the Former (but Few) Years of Prosperity Occasioned by Many Unheard of Cruelties Practised upon the Persons and Estates of its United Colonyes*. Boston: John Foster.

White, Peter, ed. 1985. *Puritan Poets and Poetics: Seventeenth-Century American Poetry in Theory and Practice*. University Park: Pennsylvania State University Press.

Wigglesworth, Michael. 1989. *The Poems of Michael Wigglesworth*, edited by Ronald A. Bosco. Lanham, MD: University Press of America.

CHAPTER 6

··

CAPTIVITY LITERATURE

··

LORRAYNE CARROLL

Captivity narratives present examples of several literary genres familiar to early American readers. From those that described conditions for captives in South and Central America, such as Hans Staden's tale (1557) and Cabeza de Vaca's relation (1542), to the North American captivities of early English settlers, such as John Smith's famous relation (1624), captivity narratives provided rich details about travels in exotic or wild locales and about cross-cultural interactions between European explorers or settlers and the indigenous peoples whose lands they colonized. Captivity texts appeared in many different forms: book-length narratives, appendixes to sermons, poems, passages in travel accounts, evidentiary or anecdotal texts folded into a historical study, letters, newspaper items, or novels and short fiction. They exhibit stunning breadth of purpose, functioning as conversion tales, proto-ethnographic texts, compendiums of historical and geographic data, sermons, travelogues, commercial advertisements, political propaganda, and accounts of current events. This range of forms and functions demonstrates how captivity texts might address the concerns of their contemporary readers. For modern students of the captivity genre, this diverse and intriguing canon serves as a capacious window into early American life.

THE EMERGENCE OF CAPTIVITY NARRATIVES

From the earliest captivity narratives that emerge from contexts of discovery and exploration to nineteenth-century frontier narratives, these stories present tales of families sundered, communities destroyed, and borders shifting and vulnerable to attacks by both native peoples and their European allies. Much of their force derives from the fear and uncertainty attendant on the captive's position in hostile, little-known North American locales. For many European readers, the captivity tales offered dramatic and distinctively personal representations of unfamiliar lands and their peoples. Although early captivity narratives, such as the seventeenth-century Puritan texts, generated conventions that recur in later publications, the variety of captives and their experiences make it difficult to generalize about the effects of captivity tales, especially those dedicated to telling the stories of European captives. Captivity narratives "disrupt the notion that there was ever a single, identifiable British, still less 'European' perspective on the non-European world" (Colley 2002, 15). The diverse ways in which accounts represent experiences of captivity cannot be reduced to claims made by the better-known texts.

Attention to authors' perspectives and the contexts of publication provides a sense of the genre's multiple meanings. While the captives, especially in first-person accounts, may align their voices with those of powerful contemporary institutions of church or state, captivity texts should not be reduced to one formulation, such as a propaganda text in the project of European colonization. Many of these accounts do reinforce pernicious, ethnocentric images of natives as primitives, but some also (and simultaneously) present images of sophisticated and effective native practices—in warfare, political negotiation, and spiritual exercises. A useful index of different perspectives in captivity literature can be found by comparing the captivities of the Jesuit missionaries in New France and some of the accounts of New England colonists. For example, the story of Father Isaac Jogues's capture, torture, and murder by Iroquoian people (1655) contrasts sharply with Mary Rowlandson's relation of her brief captivity among the Narragansetts, Nipmucs, and Wampanoags during King Philip's War (1676). Jogues expresses a piercing sorrow at the lot of his fellow captives, his "companions" who are both French and Huron. He laments, "the way to the Christian faith [is] closed by these Iroquois" (Sayre 2000, 99). Rowlandson is no missionary; she has only harsh words for the "Praying Indians," those natives purportedly converted by English ministers such as John Eliot. For Rowlandson, who, during her capture, sees some of the supposed converts dressed in the clothes of murdered Englishmen, they are duplicitous "preying" Indians. Regarding their perspectives on natives, the Jogues and Rowlandson accounts exemplify the diverse attitudes held by both Europeans and native peoples during these early years as they developed and negotiated inter- and intracultural relationships.

As the processes of colonization, settlement, and displacement continued in early America, captivities became more common. Although never a routine experience, enough colonists were taken captive and enough of their stories were published that captivity texts emerged as a recognizable genre. They have become key documents in studies of early American history and culture. One measure of their importance is the serial publication of the *Garland Library of Narratives of North American Indian Captivities*, a 111-volume collection containing 311 titles (Washburn 1975–). Tracing the relationships among European and native peoples from the earliest days of contact well into the twentieth century, this comprehensive collection illustrates many sharp transformations in native-European interactions, from alliance, peaceful cohabitation, and mutual support to misunderstanding, betrayal, and the ultimate breakdown of warfare.

Furthermore, captivity texts reveal some of the complex negotiations between the dominant discourses of powerful European forces, such as the colonial governments and religious institutions, and the personal versions of captivity each narrative displays. Women's captivity narratives, while sometimes reflecting prevailing gender roles, often challenge those roles. Notably, the endurance of female captives under harsh and debilitating conditions of captivity countered popular views of women. These dominant images, often created and disseminated by cultural authorities such as religious leaders, presented women as passive as well as morally and physically weaker than men. In light of these gender distinctions, women's captivity narratives function as subversive texts because they portray the women captives acting effectively, reasonably, and, occasionally, with shrewdness to ameliorate the conditions they and their families endure during captivity.

Whether based on the experiences of women or men, all captivity texts derive their narrative power from the image of the suffering captive. They emphasize individual experiences of privation, loss, injury, death, occasional escape, and redemption—both physical and spiritual. As greater numbers of English captivity narratives were published throughout the late seventeenth and early eighteenth centuries, "redemption" became a governing metaphor in the language of captivity. For example, John Williams's *The Redeemed Captive Returning to Zion* (1707) explicitly links the secular and religious meanings of the term when he describes both the temporal and the spiritual plight of English residents of Deerfield, Massachusetts, captured in a French and Indian raid of 1704 (Haefeli and Sweeney 2003). Because they experienced captivity among both French Canadian Catholics and their native allies, the Deerfield settlers' bodies and souls were at risk; they might be threatened with death, but, for Williams, a more dangerous fate awaited those who converted to Catholicism in Canada.

The Redeemed Captive is noteworthy for several reasons: Williams was a well-known minister with established connections to the Boston elites; the Deerfield attack resulted in a large number of captives, including Williams's daughter

Eunice, who chose not to return to English society; the narrative is comparatively long, a publication that stood alone rather than as an appendix to or entry into a larger text; and it was republished many times throughout the eighteenth century (Demos 1994). As in a conventional conversion narrative, the interpretation of the religious dimensions of captivity was meant to lead readers to spiritual transformation. In this manner, *The Redeemed Captive* reiterates and amplifies themes from Mary Rowlandson's captivity narrative, the most well known work of its kind in American literature.

MARY ROWLANDSON

The Sovereignty and Goodness of God, by Mary Rowlandson (1682) recounts the captivity of Mary White Rowlandson, the wife of Joseph Rowlandson, minister to the congregation in Lancaster, a western frontier settlement in the Massachusetts Bay Colony. Rowlandson was taken in the February 10, 1675/6 attack on Lancaster, a time she characterizes as "the dolefullest day that ever mine eyes saw" (Rowlandson 1997, 68). While her husband was in Boston on a mission to secure troops to protect the town, Rowlandson and the other settlers from Lancaster and surrounding settlements watched as a Narragansett and Nipmuc raiding party destroyed their crops, burned their houses, and killed their family members and neighbors. Rowlandson had three children, Joseph, Mary, and Sarah; Joseph and Mary were separated from her, but Sarah, who was around six years old, was wounded and remained with Rowlandson until the child died eight days later. Rowlandson was able to see first Mary, then Joseph during her travels, but since each belonged to a different master, Rowlandson spent the rest of her captivity without her family. Over the course of twenty "removes," or treks from one area to another across the central Massachusetts countryside in late winter, she depicts her sufferings and dramatizes the events of her captivity. Near the end of her captivity, she meets Metacom (King Philip), the chief prosecutor of the war on the native side, discusses her return, and is then redeemed by agents from the colonial government in Boston for the relatively high sum of twenty pounds (Lepore 1998).

While recognizing the importance of *Sovereignty* to any discussion of early American captivity narratives, recent scholarship has attempted to look beyond Rowlandson's account, both back toward those earlier narratives written in languages other than English, and forward to the writings of later captives, who had been taken under quite different social and political circumstances. Yet *The Sovereignty and Goodness of God* remains the most significant early American captivity narrative, the template against which subsequent texts are gauged. Editor Neal Salisbury claims, "For most readers over the past three centuries, the distinctive quality of Rowlandson's narrative lies in the combination of her unique experience and her powerful depiction of that experience" (Rowlandson 1997, 5). Furthermore, the work's primacy in the captivity canon is related to its status as first, female, and famous.

Scholars have long noted the importance of *Sovereignty* as an inaugural text. For example, Roy Harvey Pearce's *Savagism and Civilization* (1965) and Richard Slotkin's *Regeneration through Violence* (1973) treated early New England captivity narratives as examples of Puritan responses to fear and insecurity occasioned by the violent interactions between English settlers and various Algonquian peoples living in northeastern North America, and each discusses *Sovereignty* at length. Warfare, intermittent in the early seventeenth century and then more sustained in the later seventeenth and eighteenth centuries, shaped the experiences of all peoples competing for land and resources in the region. Since warfare and its consequences formed a central feature of life in the English colonies, and since captivity was a common occurrence in the warfare, narratives describing the experiences of captives offered a means of making a generalized social anxiety particular and personal. Individual accounts of captivity gave order to the war by confining the often chaotic, confusing, and obscure details of fighting and capture to a coherent narrative with recognizable plot devices and, crucially, a resolution. Because the stories presented real captives as informants, the captives' voices confirmed the authenticity of the accounts. Written in the first-person voice, and, as such, differentiated from the earlier ministerial histories of Anglo-native warfare, Mary Rowlandson's text was the first lengthy self-representation of an individual's captivity published in the New England colonies.

As the preface to the work argues, "not the generall but particular knowledge of things make deepest impression upon the affections" (Rowlandson 1997, 66). This emphasis on particularity, the individual experience of captivity, not only underwrites the text's claim to authenticity but also offers a specific example of proper Puritan conduct. Rowlandson's continuous recourse to her Bible, characterized in numerous scriptural quotations, mirrors the narrative's depiction of her own interior, spiritual journey. The physical rigors of her "removes" produce an image that gives readers both a broad view of war and a deeper purview of a conscience in struggle. This image of Rowlandson as a hinge figure, experiencing and articulating both outward suffering and inward turmoil, initiates the genre's reliance on psychological commentary as a requisite complement to the description of captors and countryside. In addition, most scholars agree that "Amicam," the pseudonymous author of the preface, was Increase Mather (Derounian 1998, 39; Minter 1973, 343; Sayre 2000, 128). For these reasons, Rowlandson's text stands as the model of early American captivity narratives in English; *Sovereignty* established conventions that would recur in many subsequent captivity narratives.

More recent scholarly interest in Rowlandson's text emerged with the rise of feminist studies. Scholars have long noted the paucity of women-authored texts in the early American canon; by the end of the seventeenth century, only four texts attributed to women had been published in the New England colonies (Koehler 1980), and Rowlandson's was "the first published narrative by an Anglo-American woman" (Sayre 2000, 129). The others are two brief letters and Anne Bradstreet's *Several Poems* (1678). Searching for examples of women's voices and experiences in early American literature, feminist scholars found in Rowlandson's complex narrative a source for investigations into the ways gender, race, and class influence a subject's self-construction and her representation of important historical events.

Besides offering a rare female voice, *The Sovereignty and Goodness of God* became, almost from its initial run, the colonial equivalent of a best seller. There are no extant copies of the first (Boston) edition of 1682, but a second (Cambridge) edition was produced within the same year, as was a third (London) version, published as *A True History of the Captivity and Restoration of Mrs. Mary Rowlandson* (Derounian 1988). All these editions appear to have been printed with a copy of the last sermon of Rowlandson's husband, the Reverend Joseph Rowlandson. Although this kind of ministerial linkage became common in later captivity narratives, *Sovereignty* inaugurates the convention that captivity narratives appear with exculpatory or explanatory frames prepared by religious or secular authorities. In the case of *Sovereignty*, the preface and appended sermon bracket the work and imbue it with multiple voices.

The preface's conventional use of both scripture and commentary indicates that Mather sought to fuse homiletic (sermon) forms with his practice of recording and interpreting current events. The result is an exhortation warning readers to attend to God's interventions in "redeeming" Rowlandson: "I am confident that no Friend of divine Providence will ever repent his time and pains spent in reading over these sheets, but will judg[e] them worth perusing again and again" (Rowlandson 1997, 67). This model of explaining to readers what they must "take" from the text resonates with homiletic practices of "opening" a biblical verse and then explaining to the congregation what to make of it (Stout 1986). Similarly, in the narrative itself, several passages use scripture to ground the reader's understanding of events as they are related.

Mather's preface and Rowlandson's account both take colonial authorities in Boston to task, thereby situating the text within contemporary debates concerning the Massachusetts Bay Colony's responsibility toward its outlying settlements. These arguments arose because deliberations on how best to conduct the war against Metacom and his allies most often occurred in Boston, and general funds were issued by authorities there. Reliance on Boston authorities often delayed the militias that were supposed to defend frontier settlements like Lancaster. As in many subsequent captivity narratives, *Sovereignty*'s story of English defeat and capture includes a strong measure of political critique. Mather's condemnations and Rowlandson's complaints together create a powerful brief against the colony's leaders whose mistakes caused the sufferings detailed within the narrative.

While the rhetoric and politics of Puritan New England are significant elements of *Sovereignty* and important topics for critical study, the work's multiple voices raise the question of attribution. It is impossible to determine which passages in Rowlandson's text Mather had a hand in (Fitzpatrick 1991). This indeterminacy had provoked much critical discussion about the work's composition: did Mather prompt Rowlandson to write? Did Rowlandson write "therapeutically" to relieve herself of harrowing memories of her captivity (Derounian 1987)? One scholar argues that Rowlandson wrote the narrative and allowed it to be published in order to save her reputation: since no one could know how she comported herself outside Puritan surveillance, Rowlandson might have needed to fashion a story to maintain her "credit" in the home community (Toulouse 1992).

Additional discussions about the meanings and cultural significance of *Sovereignty* use its text to query broader issues of Puritan polity and practices. For example, Mitchell Breitwieser (1990) argues that the narrative offered Puritan readers a model for how to mourn the painful losses they experienced during continued warfare while practicing a religion that discouraged other responses besides complete resignation to God's will. For Breitwieser, contemporary readers of the narrative could find in Rowlandson's vacillation between grief and resignation—her carving out of a space of resistance and questioning—a way to cope with their own sufferings and their own relationships with their God. Castiglia (1996) argues that Rowlandson's narrative stages a drama of "white womanhood" crossing over into native society and finding there a place from which to critique her home culture. Almost all scholars who read *Sovereignty* remark on its representation of Rowlandson's relationship to her captors and note that her responses range from hatred and contempt to gratitude. Within this range, there is ample opportunity for readers to interpret the cross-cultural meanings of the text.

The potential for misinterpretation of the text concerned Increase Mather even as he wrote its preface, in which he attempts to teach readers how to understand the ensuing narrative and, in so doing, encourages them to view Rowlandson with pity and, notably, with commiseration: "Who is there of a true Christian spirit, that did not look upon himself much concerned in this bereavement, this Captivity in the time thereof, and in this deliverance when it came, yea more than in many others?" (Rowlandson 1997, 66). As Michelle Burnham notes, many captivities construct stories that exhort readers to identify with captives and thereby trigger "the process of sympathy, which requires a crossing of the boundary between reader and text" (Burnham 1997, 44). Readers of *Sovereignty,* according to Mather's preface, should be "much concerned" in the sufferings of Mary Rowlandson and must not only feel but also simultaneously understand the events that constitute her captivity, those "laid out and portrayed before their eyes" (Rowlandson 1997, 66). By inviting, even compelling, readers to commiserate with Rowlandson and interpret her story correctly, the preface offers a clue to interpret the text's "dueling textual voices" (Fitzpatrick 1991, 3).

In the preface Mather shuttles between a description of Rowlandson's miseries and an exegesis of those miseries. He sets the scene in the initial pages, describing the attack, but his narrative of these events abruptly halts when he recalls that it is not his "business to dilate on these things, but only in a few words introductively to preface to the following script, which is a Narrative of the wonderfully awfull, wise, holy powerfull, and gracious providences of God, towards that worthy and precious Gentlewoman ... in casting of her into such a waterless pit, so in preserving, supporting, and carrying through so many such extream hazards, unspeakable difficulties and disconsolateness, and at last delivering her out of them all" (Rowlandson 1997, 65). Mather shows how Rowlandson's experiences fit into the providential scheme: the temporal events of the attack and subsequent captivity cannot be read outside of providential dispensation, the Calvinist belief that God had ordered all events before human history began. Mather even plays on the double meaning of "dispensation" within the Puritan lexicon to argue that, because Rowlandson's experiences were exceptional, God granted her a "dispensation" by saving her from harm (Carroll 1996, 68).

This dialogic writing recurs throughout the text, when narrative elements are constantly interrupted by commentary or scriptural quotation. Rowlandson's description of the first moments of the attack provides specific, graphic details: "Thus were we butchered by those merciless Heathen, Standing amazed, with the blood running down our heels" (Rowlandson 1997, 69). Her sister, watching the scene, cries out, "Lord, let me dy with them," and is immediately struck by a bullet. Rather than maintaining the narrative focus on the scene of carnage and confusion, however, the text digresses to a story of how Rowlandson's sister's early years were marked by doubts about her salvation, followed by her conversion, which was occasioned by a verse from Corinthians. The passage continues with Rowlandson's own reflection on how meaningful the verse was to her sister. This digression culminates with a phrase that recurs so often throughout the text that it takes on an incantatory effect: "But to return" (Rowlandson 1997, 70). As with the preface's shift from observation to interpretation, the narrative itself stages its own internal dialogue so readers can be led to understand the significance of the text's descriptive passages.

If they had any questions about the reasons for the publication of *Sovereignty* the preface did not address, readers might find answers near the end of the narrative, where the text turns from action to declamation. After mentioning that a "General Court" convened by her captors determined that she could be ransomed back into English hands, Rowlandson interrupts the narrative flow, using spatial metaphors to characterize this switch in narrative modality: "But before I go any further, I would like to take leave to mention a few remarkable passages of providence, which I took special notice of in my afflicted time" (Rowlandson 1997, 104). What follows is a list of four numbered points that address an array of the captive's concerns, from castigating the failures of the "English Army" in its prosecution of the war to providing details about Native American food preparation. This kind of ethnographic detail became a staple of later captivity narratives, but it is important to note that, within the logic of *Sovereignty,* the detail serves to reinforce the text's prescriptions for how someone should read it. Instructed by Mather's preface, and trained by the narrative's own self-referential style, readers could gain the fullest benefit of Rowlandson's text through a combination of sympathetic connection with Rowlandson and attention to the interpretive interjections. For seventeenth-century readers, the significance and utility of *Sovereignty* lay in the complex narrative apparatus that challenged them to "Peruse, Ponder, and from hence lay up something from the experience of another, against thine own turn comes, that so thou also through patience and consolation of the Scripture mayest have hope" (Rowlandson 1997, 68).

Increase Mather's exhortation to "peruse" and "ponder" Rowlandson's text marks his prescience regarding the narrative's novelty and usefulness as an instrument for instruction. His perspicacity has been borne out not just in the work's popularity among contemporary readers but also in its value for later readers who interpret *Sovereignty* in light of their own contemporary concerns, such as the feminist scholars who find the text's foundation in a (purportedly) woman's voice a challenge to Puritan patriarchal discourse. Moreover, many of Rowlandson's readers in 1682 would find that *Sovereignty* inaugurated a genre, not that of captivity narratives per se but of specifically Puritan captivity narratives, ones either attributed to or focused on women and then published by male ministers. These texts sought to remind backsliding congregations about their slippage from orthodox practices, a problem identified by ministers as "criolian degeneracy," and to reinvigorate their commitment to the divine plan that brought them or their forebears to New England. Women formed the majority of the Massachusetts Congregationalist Church, the Puritan religious organization, so they functioned as key exemplars in both Increase Mather's and his son Cotton Mather's project to halt the degeneration of orthodox observation. Evidence of this interest in the representational value of women can be found in Cotton Mather's conduct book for women, entitled *Ornaments for the Daughters of Zion* (1692), in which he characterized the church as "figured by a Woman."

COTTON MATHER AND THE CAPTIVITY NARRATIVE

Cotton Mather was assistant minister of his father's congregation at the North Church in Boston and the most prolific published author of the early American period. He saw himself as a zealous providential agent in the campaign against spiritual—and often temporal—"degeneracy." His contributions to the captivity genre include his history of the "sorrowful decade" of Anglo-French-native warfare (King William's War) that raged from 1689 to 1699, *Decennium Luctuosum* (1699). With much gruesome detail, *Decennium* presents numerous accounts of captivity, recounting instances of family separation, torture, privation, death, and, most important, conversion. The many examples of English settlers captured in attacks reinforce the point that all English colonists must turn to Providence to save them from physical and spiritual dangers. While *Decennium* is a history, it exemplifies the distinctively Puritan model of historiography by using both biblical typography and contemporary accounts to reinforce the key concept of providential design; it is decidedly not a secular history. As such it draws on several earlier specimens of Mather's homiletic writings to tell the story of the war and to help readers make sense of the war—to meditate on these events as a means toward their own spiritual edification.

Cotton Mather's sermon, preached on May 6, 1697, and soon after published as *Humiliations Follow'd with Deliverances,* served as one source for *Decennium.* The printed sermon includes the stories of two captives, Hannah Swarton and Hannah Duston. Mather adds an appendix to the sermon proper concerning the events of Hannah Swarton's captivity, "A Narrative of Hannah Swarton, containing a great many wonderful passages, relating to her Captivity and Deliverance." Swarton's narrative is a first-person account of her capture, at Casco (now Portland), Maine, in 1690. Unlike Mary Rowlandson's captivity, Swarton's lasted several years, and she spent most of it not with her Algonquian captors but with French settlers in Canada who bought her from the natives.

Several features of the Swarton text make it a significant entry within the captivity canon. First, it is clearly a work of Mather's hand; as such, it shows him imitating his father's practice of shaping a woman's voice for his ministerial ends. Discussing the narrative, Mather's bibliographer remarks, "Evidently Cotton Mather was Hannah Swarton's 'ghost writer'" (Holmes 1940, 2: 492). A close reading of the narrative within the context of Mather's oeuvre confirms the evaluation. This impersonation raises the intriguing question of why Mather chose to write as a woman in a society where cultural authority inhered in men, especially in ministers such as Mather. Recurring to the ways in which women "figured" the Puritan Church, Swarton's story, like Rowlandson's, offers readers an informant whose voice is rarely heard in public and is therefore more highly valued as a rarity, someone with "particular knowledge" of divine dispensation.

The sermon proper functions as a jeremiad and seeks to convince readers that the depredations caused by warfare with the natives manifest God's anger at the laxity in church members' behavior. Specifically, the sermon illustrates the ways in which New England congregations must account for the "humiliations" that this warfare inflicts on frontier settlements far from ministerial oversight—what Mather later called the "ungospelized plantations" (Mather 1702a). A careful comparison between the language of the sermon and the narrative demonstrates the utility of appending Swarton's story to the sermon. Each of the points Mather raises in his jeremiad is aptly illustrated by one of Swarton's experiences: for example, Mather chastises the congregation for not conducting regular fasts, and the Swarton narrative resonates with this point when it positions Swarton as someone who, during her initial time in captivity, did not eat when she should have and later "pined with want" (Mather 1697, 52).

A second key concern of the Swarton text emerges when Swarton arrives in Canada. Studies of captivity narratives often consider "Indian" captivity and discuss the rich material generated by remarkable culture crossings without examining the issue of French captivity as another, equally intriguing, crossing (Bumstead 1983; Carroll 2004; Castiglia 1996; Ebersole 1995; Strong 1999). Unlike the captivity accounts Mather would compose for *Decennium,* this narrative is not so much an Indian captivity narrative as a French one. The majority of the narrative is spent telling the story of how Swarton survives, and experiences conversion, while she serves in a French household. Notably, Swarton, a poorly educated frontier woman, engages in a debate with the French priests who attempt to convert her to Catholicism. In this manner, the Swarton narrative displays the hostilities between European powers, and their religious agents, because the story provides a stage for Mather's theological debate with French priests through his instrument, Swarton. Thus the Swarton text offers readers a fuller understanding of the specifically European contexts that drew various native peoples into conflicts and so dramatically shaped life on the New England frontiers.

Another noteworthy feature of "A Narrative of Hannah Swarton" is its affiliation with the other Hannah in the published sermon, Hannah Duston. While the valuable data located by Emma Coleman (1925) reveal that most of those taken in raids and forcibly marched to Canada were "redeemed" by agents from the English colonies, occasionally some captives escaped. The most notorious of these escaped captives was Hannah Duston (variously spelled Dustin, Dustan, or Dunstan).

In *Humiliations Follow'd with Deliverances,* Mather offers an "improvement" to the story of Duston, who had been captured at her home in Haverhill, Massachusetts, in late March and who escaped back to English domains by the end of April, a week before the sermon was preached. In the attack on Haverhill, Duston had been roused out of bed, having just given birth a short time earlier to a daughter. One of the attackers immediately murdered the infant, a common occurrence in these raids because infants made travel difficult. Duston was seized, along with another Haverhill resident, Mary Neff, and they were forced to march through the forest toward Canada. During the march, they were joined by another English captive, a boy named Samuel Lennardson, who had been taken from Worcester. Up to this point, Duston's story is, by contemporary standards, a conventional captivity narrative. Like Swarton, she might have been "carried to Canada" and subsequently redeemed. However, she, along with Neff and Lennardson, managed to escape. Yet Duston's signal accomplishment was not escape but the means by which she secured it. Traveling up the Contoocook River (in present-day New Hampshire), Duston awakened Neff and Lennardson, stole the captors' hatchets, and killed ten of the twelve native people holding her captive. (They spared a young boy, and an older woman escaped.) Of the ten, five were children. Duston, Neff, and Lennardson then scalped the corpses, a practice encouraged by a law awarding bounties for native scalps (a law that happened to be rescinded during their captivity).

Duston's actions differentiate her from Swarton in several respects, and each offers some insight into the cultural work of captivity narratives in the hands of Cotton Mather. Whereas Swarton's narrative appears as an appendix and is composed in the first person, the "improvement" on Duston's captivity occurs within the body of the sermon, as an exemplum, and is rendered in the third person, set off graphically within quotation marks. The sermon's disposition of the two captives' accounts indicates that Mather viewed them both as instruments for instructing his congregation on the various and sometimes bloody modes by which providential design is made manifest. Within the rapidly changing and contentious religious culture of late seventeenth-century New England, these captivity narratives served several purposes: reminding congregants of their failure to carry out their religious duties, inciting readers to defend English settlements from native attack, and warning them of the dangers of French Catholicism. For both Mathers, women captives provided apt emblems of divine providence's work to preserve the "chosen" people of the Puritan settlements.

It is important to note, too, that while Mather returned to the Swarton narrative one more time, by reprinting a variant version of his "appendix" in *Magnalia Christi Americana* (1702b), he reproduced the Duston story in both *Decennium Luctuosum* and *Magnalia*. Many later New England historians were drawn to the Duston story because of its notorious and problematic "heroine": Daniel Neal, Thomas Hutchinson, Timothy Dwight, Leverett Saltonstall, and others, wrote about Duston, and each struggled with her actions. Duston reappears in such nineteenth-century literary works as John Greenleaf Whittier's short story "A Mother's Revenge" (1831); Nathaniel Hawthorne "The Duston Family" (1836), which praises Duston's husband for saving the older children and attacks her for killing and scalping; and *A Week on the Concord and the Merrimack Rivers* (1849), in which Henry David Thoreau uses the captivity tale to introduce his meditation on the practice of writing history.

The status of captivity narratives as historical texts has been confirmed recently by contemporary historians who work with them to reconstruct and interpret the social, political, and intellectual histories of early America and its European colonizers (Colley 2002; Demos 1994; Haefeli and Sweeney 2003; Sayre 1997; Snader 2000). But, as Cotton Mather's inclusion of captivity accounts in both *Decennium* and *Magnalia* proves, from the time of their original publication, these texts were viewed as specimens of historical writing, authoritative texts that relied on credible informants to underscore the narratives' truth claims. Statements insisting on the veracity of the text often appeared in titles, such as the title to the 1682 London edition of Rowlandson's account, *A True History of the Captivity and Restoration of Mrs. Mary Rowlandson;* prefaces also attested to the text's value as an accurate account of personal experience.

QUAKER CAPTIVITIES

While the Mathers were busy composing and publishing histories containing captivity accounts, they were instrumental in foregrounding the image of the captive as informant, one whose lived experiences revealed some of the workings of providential history. But given the Mathers' positions as Puritan ministers, their histories spoke mainly to the specific congregations in the New England colonies and in England. Captivity accounts were also composed in other communities of dissident religious practitioners such as the Society of Friends or Quakers. These captivity narratives also attempted to fashion a history for their readers, not the providential history of the Puritans but an alternative version that addressed the growing sense among Quakers that their institutions and beliefs needed a historical frame.

One early captivity narrative in English that did not take place in New England was published by the Society of Friends in Philadelphia in 1699. Entitled *God's Protecting Providence,* it recounts the experiences of Jonathan Dickinson, a wealthy Quaker merchant, as he traveled with his family and a well-known Quaker missionary, Robert Barrow, from the West Indies to Philadelphia. Dickinson's captivity followed a shipwreck off the Florida coast in 1696; during this time he apparently kept a journal that served as the basis for *God's Protecting Providence* (Dickinson 1945). If Puritan captivity accounts gave New England readers a sense of the landscape and native peoples that shaped their lives, Dickinson's Quaker narrative offered the far more exotic locale of southern Florida, at that time a Spanish territory far removed from the daily experiences of Philadelphia readers. *God's Protecting Providence* portrays Dickinson as a heroic, authoritative, and sensible captive, one who negotiates assuredly with his captors and manages to solicit credit from the Spanish governor of St. Augustine to provision the group's return to Philadelphia. Dickinson is the model of the emerging Quaker man of business, and his text alternates between the story of his competent actions and a hagiographic appreciation of Barrow, the elder, beloved missionary, whose death near the end of the narrative provokes a textual apotheosis.

Dickinson's captivity narrative served at least two purposes for the Society of Friends as it moved from radical sect to mainstream institution. It illustrated how a Quaker, under duress, capably manages the problems associated with temporal life (Dickinson) while it also offered a model of Quaker piety and resignation in death

(Barrow). In addition, the narrative might be viewed as an example of the Society of Friends' purposeful creation of its own history, through documentation, a history that was fairly recent, given the Society's origins in the mid–seventeenth century. Another captivity narrative, one set on the New England frontier, and published almost thirty years later, further illuminates the Quakers' use of the conventions of the captivity genre.

Elizabeth Hanson's account of her capture and travel through what is now New Hampshire to French settlements in Canada shares many features with *Sovereignty* and "A Narrative of Hannah Swarton." As in the Puritan captivities, Hanson was taken from her house with her children, separated from some of them, and subjected to terrible suffering on the trail. Like Duston, she had recently given birth, but Hanson was nursing her infant along the journey; like Swarton, she finished her journey as a servant in a French household. The general contours of the Puritan captivity story thus recur in Hanson's account, *God's Mercy Surmounting Man's Cruelty* (1728) but with some distinctive differences. These differences between Hanson's narrative and the earlier Puritan texts demonstrate that, in Quaker hands, captivity accounts served various purposes directly related to Quaker concerns about the Society's self-representation.

If Dickinson's text presented a heroic male and saintly elder, then *God's Mercy* created a "heroine" of astonishing passivity. Elizabeth Hanson's recounting of her captivity never produces a spirited debater like Swarton or a capable gentlewoman like Rowlandson, who could hold her own in conversation with the formidable Metacom. Rather, Hanson's passive acceptance of her native master's cruelty seems to mark her as unusually resigned, almost receding from her own story (Ulrich 1983). Hanson's text does offer a number of strange parenthetical observations that explain, for example, what she means when she uses native terms. One of the most striking examples of the apparent narrative disconnection between what is described and the emotions it might elicit is when Hanson recounts an instance of scalping that she witnessed and then gives a precise definition of the practice in parentheses right after it. These ethnographic details seem to indicate that Hanson's captivity, although a story of her experiences, served as an important Quaker entry into the field of publications concerning native practices, as well as a record of a Friend's "sufferings," the Quaker term for hardships endured by Friends in the early, more radical, days of the group.

Those early days of Quaker women disrupting Puritan services or traveling through New England preaching and proselytizing for the Society seem to haunt the Hanson text. She was taken from her homestead in Cocheco, New Hampshire, not far from the settlement in Dover where, years earlier, Quaker women had been whipped at the cart's tail for preaching in the town. Hanson, the passive captive, appears to undo the gender trespass of these earlier women to offer a model of a more subdued and gender-appropriate captive, one who is finally ransomed from Canada like many of her Puritan sisters. With Hanson, the Society of Friends fashioned its own informant and thus established, in addition to the heroic Dickinson, a distinctively female Quaker presence in the canon of captivity texts that served as a version of historical writing.

Hanson's text again raises the question about attribution in these texts, especially those ascribed to women (Derounian-Stodola and Levernier 1993; Colley 2002). Just as the Rowlandson captivity narrative has generated much debate about the boundaries between Increase Mather's composition and Rowlandson's own production, many of the later captivity narratives, like Swarton's, exhibit features that call into question the provenance of the first-person authorial voice. Hanson's text, for example, acknowledges that the story is "taken from her own mouth" in its prefatory material, a statement that seems to indicate that Hanson "told" the story to an amanuensis (probably an itinerant Quaker preacher). Cotton Mather's "ghostwriting" of Swarton's narrative, and some of the later eighteenth-century first-person captivity narratives, such as Susannah Johnson's, exemplify the problem of reading these texts as direct compositions by the woman captive herself (Carroll 2004). While the tricky question of attribution poses problems for historians who seek facts about wars, cross-cultural interactions, colonial politics, social practices, and religious conflicts, the uncertainty does offer a space for inquiring into the meanings of the text as it is composed within specific contexts of publication and distribution. Though it becomes difficult to argue about a particular woman's agency or resistance to oppressive forces as portrayed by "her" voice in the narrative, readers may turn to a wider interrogation about the roles of gender and class position in fashioning the specific version of the female captive's voice the text offers.

THE CAPTIVITY NARRATIVE AND THE INTERCOLONIAL WARS

As with any literary genre, captivity narratives gradually developed a set of features that made the texts recognizable to readers as a genre. From the seventeenth-century texts, readers might come to expect a deeply religious strain in the accounts, but they would also presume to find an array of other conventions: descriptions of native life; a credible, sympathetic captive voice and/or an authoritative rendering of the meanings of the captive experience; particular motifs of suffering, such as images of hunger and exposure; detailed renderings of specific tortures like running the gauntlet (a ritualized beating by the inhabitants of a native settlement upon the captives' arrival); portrayals of different kinds of deaths—by tomahawking, burning, shooting, sickness—sometimes followed by scalping; the dissolution (and occasional reconstitution) of families and communities; and, as in the earlier texts, a resolution usually achieved by "redemption" and return. Many of the captivity narratives of the middle to late eighteenth century display several of these features, but they also make evident that the social, political, economic, and religious contexts that shaped earlier captivity texts had changed, and these later works reflect some of those transformations.

A majority of eighteenth-century captivity narratives relate events that occurred during the French and Indian Wars, otherwise known as the Second (1702–1713), Third (1744–1748), and Fourth (1754–1763) Intercolonial Wars. Because these wars involved disparate native groups who served as allies for either British or French forces (occasionally for both), and because the territories under dispute ranged from the eastern North American coast well into present-day Ohio, numerous frontier settlements were affected. Narratives from this period record captivities from various places in New England, New York, Pennsylvania, and Ohio, as well as some set in southern locales. Several captives taken by natives in Massachusetts in the Third Intercolonial War (King George's War) published their stories almost as soon as they returned from Canadian captivity. Like John Williams, from whose narrative he takes his title (*The Redeemed Captive*, 1748), the Reverend John Norton not only described his capture by natives and his sufferings during the long march to Canada but also recorded his ministerial duties within the community of English captives in Montreal. Norton's account, structured as a journal with daily entries, includes the following information: "May 25. Died Mr. Nehemiah How, of No. 2 [the settlement's designation], aged about fifty-six; taken at Great Meadow, October 11th, 1745" (39). Readers of Norton's narrative might also turn to *A Narrative of the Captivity of Nehemiah How, Who Was Taken by the Indians at the Great-Meadow-Fort Above Fort Dummer* (1748) to read a first-person account supposedly written by How but, of course, posthumously published. As the confluence of the Norton and How texts demonstrates, eighteenth-century readers might encounter similar motifs and conventions in different texts as well as the same captive "characters."

Other accounts from the intercolonial wars indicate how widespread the hostilities were, and data on their publication show that these texts enjoyed a diverse, widespread readership. For example, William Fleming's captivity narrative was republished several times in 1756, in Philadelphia, in New York, and in Boston. One of the Philadelphia editions advertises the text as "A narrative of the sufferings, and surprising deliverance of William and Elizabeth Fleming . . . as related by themselves"; this edition claims as well that it was "Printed for the benefit of the unhappy sufferers, and sold by them only" (Fleming 1756b). While this Philadelphia edition claimed that the text was meant to function as a fund-raiser, the title page of the Boston edition suggested that Fleming's story was supposed to serve as a recruitment tool, rallying soldiers for service on the western frontiers. The Boston text asserted that Fleming's relation was "a narrative necessary to be read by all who are going in the expedition, as well as every British subject. Wherein it fully appears, that the barbarities of the Indians is [are] owing to the French, and chiefly their priests" (Fleming 1756c). The Fleming text was published in German, too (Fleming 1756a). The German text, like the captivity account of Marie LeRoy and Barbara Leininger (1759), accommodated the large German-speaking population in Pennsylvania. These aspects of this work's publication attest to its value for a diverse readership. While it is still a commonplace to find scriptural passages on the title pages and interspersed throughout these texts, captivity narratives of this period no longer aimed exclusively at New England audience sharing the same religion or those who might be interested in events confined to a certain geographic area; by the mid–eighteenth century, they became a popular genre with a more secularized and more transregional appeal.

John Gyles's *Memoirs of Odd Adventures* (1736), another popular account, exemplifies some of these changes in tone and style. *Memoirs* may be viewed as a transitional work in the captivity canon because it displays elements of both earlier and later captivity texts. Like the earlier narratives, it is set in New England. (Gyles was from the same area in New Hampshire as Elizabeth Hanson, although he was not a Quaker.) The introduction proclaims: "These private memoirs were collected from my minutes, at the earnest request of my second consort; for the Use of our family; that we might have a memento ever ready at hand to excite in ourselves gratitude and thankfulness to God; and in our offspring, a due sense of their dependence on the Sovereign of the universe, from the precariousness and vicissitudes of all sublunary enjoyments" (Gyles 1869, 3).

The language here replicates standard Puritan rhetoric concerning the captive's thankfulness for divine dispensation, but the body of the text offers surprisingly entertaining, and often humorous, commentary on the creatures and landscapes Gyles encounters while a captive of the natives. Gyles treats an array of topics, from the conventional discussion of "abusive and barbarous treatment" by the Indians to fantastic stories, such as the one about a "Gulloua" bird that seizes a boy and carries him to her nest. Gyles describes the sexual practices of the St. John's River tortoises with a homey simile obviously meant to amuse: "in their Coition or Treading they may be heard half a Mile, making a noise like a Woman washing her Linen with a batting-Staff" (Gyles 1736, 26). Gyles also incorporates literary works, both ancient and modern, into the narrative, quoting Homer as well as Dryden, and he uses footnotes, such as the one that explains what a moose is. These features indicate that the text was intended as a witty and erudite relation, not one focused primarily on spiritual concerns.

An important distinction between Gyles's *Memoirs* and earlier captivity narratives may be found in the gap between the dates of Gyles's captivity and the date of publication. Gyles was taken in August 1689 and returned to Boston in June 1698. He was therefore a contemporary of Swarton and Duston, as well as of the other captives mentioned in Cotton Mather's *Decennium Luctuosum*. Yet Gyles's text was not published until 1736. The gap between captivity and publication raises several questions. Why did Gyles wait? What prompted the publication in 1736 (not earlier or later)? Perhaps Gyles objected to the kind of ministerial control that the Mathers had over the printing press at the time of his return in 1698, and he did not wish to have his story shaped or vetted by a Puritan divine. Perhaps, by 1736, Gyles saw publication as an opportunity for fame and fortune, hoping to make some money from the book although, because there were no copyright laws at the time, that is an unlikely reason. These questions may persist, but Gyles's text at least demonstrates that, as early as 1736, some captivity narratives were being used to create a sense of history and historical distance in the lives of their writers and readers, while others retained the strong religious focus and immediacy of the earlier texts.

The numerous captivity texts published and reprinted during the 1750s and 1760s reflect the expanding scope of the genre as well as its popularity. Peter Williamson's captivity (1757) had forty-one printings (Snader 2000, 25). This narrative contains an expanded consideration of "captivity" beginning with Williamson's kidnapping from Scotland at the age of eight, and it recounts his various experiences with many different versions of captivity; Colley argues that the text demonstrates Williamson's penchant for refashioning himself through these different contexts (Colley 2002, 188). Like the account of Henry Grace (1764), self-published in Basingstoke, England, Williamson's narrative demonstrates the continuous, and growing, transatlantic contexts of captivity texts—stories of return from Indian captivity as well as return to the heart of the colonial empire.

The imperial wars of these decades generated captivity texts that, like the earlier narratives, attempted to instruct readers about the significance of the larger struggles between Britain and France by personalizing the stakes. Born a Quaker, but a convert to Presbyterianism, Robert Eastburn escaped from his captivity among the French and Indians of Canada. His text is deeply spiritual, almost a reversion to the kinds of religious rhetorics that characterized the seventeenth-century Puritan narratives and aligned these texts with conversion testimonies. While the many scriptural references in this text resonate with Rowlandson's account, Eastburn's relation focuses on the threats of French Catholicism and his rejection of French proselytizing, as did Swarton's impersonated text. He recounts the missionary efforts of French priests in order to castigate, like the Mathers before him, the "prophane pretended Protestants" who ignore their spiritual duties (Eastburn 1758, 8). Eastburn's account represents an example of a recursive quality in the French and Indian War texts that seeks to mobilize religious sentiment to explain the political and military contexts of imperial warfare.

Eastburn's narrative also demonstrates that earlier concerns with the status of the authors of captivity texts deepen over the eighteenth century. A "recommendatory" preface by the Reverend Gilbert Tennent offers guarantees of both Eastburn's veracity and the text's religious significance. Tennent's remarks illustrate the potential questions about authenticity that authors of captivity narratives anticipated due to the expanding print culture of the eighteenth century. Although Tennent claims that Eastburn, a deacon in the Presbyterian Church, "needs no Recommendation of others, where he is known," he acknowledges that "the following Sheets, are like to spread into many Places, where he is not known," and therefore this circulation outside of customary acquaintance requires Tennent's imprimatur. In explicitly addressing the problem of print's wider dissemination, and the concomitant difficulty of confirming authorial reliability, Tennent's preface foreshadows the almost universal practice, in the texts of the 1780s and 1790s, of including attestatory materials declaring the captive's honesty and dependability.

The Captivity Narrative After the Novel

The uncertain provenance of many captivity texts, as well as the impersonation of captives via first-person discourse, accounts for their explicit self-authenticating language. By 1793, for example, the explosion of narratives depicting captivities set in both past and more recent wars made possible a popular anthology, *The Affecting History of the Dreadful Distresses of Frederick Manheim's Family.* This publication asserts on its opening page, "All the instances are authenticated in the most satisfactory manner;—some by deposition, and others by the information of persons of unexceptionable credibility" (Anon. 1793). These instances are brief relations: of the nine entries, four purport to be first-person accounts, all by men, all taking place in the western wilderness (including a reprint of the 1757 Peter Williamson captivity, here entitled "Adventures and Sufferings of Peter Wilkinson"). In this anthology, only Jackson Johonnot's relation features language associated with belief in providential dispensation, probably because Johonnot was born and raised in the Congregationalist stronghold of Falmouth (now Portland), Maine. The other accounts, like Johonnot's, are set in Pennsylvania and the western territories. Several appear as letters either by the captive ("Sufferings of John Corbly's Family") or about one (the tale of Experience Bozarth, "Extraordinary Bravery of a Woman"). The anthology stakes its authentication on the "unexceptionable credibility" of each entry's eyewitness testimony; for example, one entry literally reproduces official testimony, "Deposition of Massey Herbeson." First-person accounts, personal letters, and legal forms notwithstanding, eighteenth-century readers had good cause to question a captivity text's accuracy or truthfulness. Many of the period's captivity texts depict shocking scenes of murder, scalping, and torture in such florid language that even the most credulous consumer of fiction might suspect exaggeration if not outright fabrication.

Although some entries in the Manheim collection might strain credulity, an even less believable, but certainly popular, narrative appeared in *Bickerstaff's Almanack* of 1788. The "Panther Captivity" tells the story of an unnamed young woman who elopes, is captured, and then is forced to watch as her lover is tortured to death by their native captors. In just a few pages, she escapes to a cave in the forest, kills its inhabitant—a giant—and settles in for "nine long years" with only a "faithful dog" for a companion. The "Panther Captivity" provides a catalog of features that characterize the intersection of captivity narratives and the sentimental fictions of the period. It is an epistolary account, represented as a letter from one of the men who discovered the "Lady" while hunting, who signs himself "Abraham Panther." The "Lady" makes clear that her most distressing experience was not witnessing her lover's gruesome murder but fending off the sexual advances of the giant: "I must either accept of his bed or expect death for my obstinacy" (Derounian 1998, 89). This focus on the sexually vulnerable female aligns the "Panther Captivity" with contemporary seduction novels, such as *Charlotte Temple* and *The Coquette*, while harking back to the spiritual vulnerability asserted by earlier captives like Rowlandson and Swarton (Kolodny 1981; Davidson 1986).

The blurring of factual and fictional captivity texts presents multiple problems (Derounian 1994). Ann Eliza Bleecker's *The History of Maria Kittle* (1790–1791) offers a case study in misidentification and concurrent scholarly confusion. Because of its epistolary form, scenes of shocking violence, overwrought emotionalism, and sentimental ending, critics had long considered this text a fiction, albeit a story that drew heavily from contemporary captivity literature. For example, in the initial attack, the letter writer retells the story of the death of Maria Kittle's pregnant sister-in-law, Comelia. Although the deaths of pregnant women, and especially the murder of infants, are a commonplace in even the earliest captivity narratives, in *Maria Kittle*, Comelia's body and the unborn infant's are mutilated, an event described in horrifying detail. Additionally, at the end of the "Letter to Miss Ten Eyck," *Maria Kittle* is reunited with her husband by an accidental encounter on the streets of Montreal, another passage composed in the highly sentimentalized language associated with contemporary novels. Sharon M. Harris argues, however, that *Maria Kittle* was based on incidents in the life of Maria Kittle (or "Kittlehuyn"), who lived in the same upstate New York area as Bleecker and that Bleecker's own distressing experiences during the Revolutionary War inform the narrative's details and enhance its dramatic and emotional force (Harris 2003, 2).

Two famous captivity narratives of the same era as Kittle's also demonstrate the strong affiliations between historical writing and sentimental fiction that emerged in the early Republic. Both Susannah Johnson's narrative (1796) and the accounts of Jemima Howe's captivity employ the ruse of a first-person, female captive's voice to portray events in the history of the French and Indian War from the perspective of the new United States (Gay 1792; Humphreys 1788). Although both Johnson and Howe were indeed captives, taken during the 1750s, carried to Canada, and then ransomed back to British colonial society, their narratives were written by men (Carroll 2004). Published as personal testimony and, therefore, composed to "sound like" women's writing, these texts indicate ways in which gendered language is imagined, written, and manipulated to produce a certain effect, here, the sense that, as informants, Johnson and Howe are credible and compelling witnesses to (and victims of) historical events.

Through the last half of the eighteenth century, captivity narratives assumed the more varied formats available in the expanding print culture, and they were fashioned to advance diverse ends. For example, Jeremy Belknap included Jemima Howe's captivity in his *History of New-Hampshire* (1784–1792) while the "Panther Captivity" appeared in an almanac, and Ashbel Stoddard published "The Returned Captive: A Poem. Founded on a Late Fact" in six lines of verse. Newspapers, such as New Hampshire's *Farmer's Weekly Museum,* became important venues for the publication of captivity accounts, running articles about battles on the western Pennsylvania and Ohio frontiers, the tribulations of captured soldiers, and the difficulties of reintegrating captive children back into Euro-American society (Carroll 2004). Earlier in the century, during the Intercolonial Wars, London newspapers featured similar captivity stories from the colonies, a practice that provided Benjamin Franklin with the opportunity to publish an instructional but specious captivity text.

The "Extract from an Account of the Captivity of William Henry in 1755" was published in the *London Chronicle* in two issues during one week in June 1768. This two-part article purports to be a reprint of sections from a published narrative of one William Henry, a captive who remained with the Senecas for more than six years until his escape. The *Chronicle* provides bibliographic information on the text, asserting that the account had been printed in a quarto edition in Boston in 1766. Intriguingly, both sections begin partway through the "Account," digesting information that would, by convention, reproduce the horrors of attack and initial captivity experiences. Rather, the articles alternate Henry's first-person relations with third-person interjections that provide details missing in Henry's telescoped and interrupted account. Henry asserts that his proficiency in learning languages made him a favorite of his village's "chief man," and this linguistic ability and his previous education at a religious academy provide Henry with the tools to engage in philosophical disputation with the old native warrior and counselor, Canassatego (Franklin 1959–, 15: 149). In this model of debate, the "Account" not only reproduces the captivity convention of the captive's debate with her or his captors, such as Swarton's parrying with the French priests, but also harkens to the seventeenth-century "Dialogues" designed by John Eliot to proselyze the Massachusetts natives. Moreover, the narrative supports prevailing representations of natives as superstitious and spiritually unenlightened, even credulous, people, but it employs irony to subvert these stereotypes. For example, Canassatego's story of how selfishness and lack of collaboration harmed the people of the Five Nations leads to his explicit criticism of the ways in which the English and French conduct exchange with each other. The tale of the Five Nations' internecine struggles and the critique of European practices raise troubling questions about the moral basis of trade relations.

The "Account of William Henry" ends with an arch comparison of the "miserable darkness these poor creatures labour under" with "the unerring oracles that we possess, and the histories contained in them" (Franklin 1959–, 15: 157). Clearly ironic, the conclusion to the narrative "excerpts" exaggerate culturally powerful captivity conventions regarding native inferiority and European precedence in all things moral, historical, and civil. With this parody, however, captivity conventions prod readers into turning a critical eye on their own prejudices and presumptions about cross-cultural relations.

CONCLUSION

The utility of literature as a means of identifying and castigating hypocrisy emerged powerfully in the captivity narratives of the American Revolution. While many texts still addressed the cross-cultural events of Indian captivity and continued to describe captives' experiences among the French, the Revolutionary War provided contexts for other kinds of captivity. Political transformations, such as the recent alliance with the French in the war against the British, dictated a change in emphasis in these Revolutionary-era texts. Ethan Allen's extraordinarily self-promoting *A Narrative of Colonel Ethan Allen's Captivity* (1779), for example, depicts the British as treacherous elites intent on reducing the proud spirit of America's revolutionary soldiers. In this blustering tale of his time spent as a prisoner of the British, Allen fashions himself as a native, indeed "Native," American hero, dressed in buckskins and besting the British at every turn. He appropriates the Indian role and inverts long-standing captivity conventions to make himself a "wild man" (Ziff 1991).

After the Treaty of Paris, as United States' shipping grew, naval engagements reproduced culture-crossing conventions, broadening the focus from Native Americans to Barbary pirates. These captivities copied many of the earlier conventions and transferred the images of threatening "tawnies" from the forests of North America to the North African peoples of Algeria, and other Tripolitanian states (Baepler 1999; Colley 2002). Royall Tyler's picaresque novel, *The Algerine Captive* (1797), and Susanna Rowson's play *Slaves in Algiers* (1794) both demonstrate the ways in which captivity forms and conventions of the seventeenth century were transformed and adapted to late eighteenth-century political concerns as well as to literary tastes.

The Algerine captivities also exemplify captivity literature's expanding transatlantic sphere. Briton Hammon, "a Negro man," records in his captivity narrative (1760) the sufferings he underwent after a shipwreck and capture by natives in Florida. Hammon describes his imprisonment in Cuba by Spanish navy agents who sought to press him into service aboard a Spanish ship. Like the better known and much longer narrative of Olaudah Equiano (1789), Hammon's narrative offers a dynamic view of the multiple culture crossings that captives experienced in various locales. Equiano's text moves across many territories, including the west coast of Africa, Central America, North America, Caribbean islands, and Europe. While Hammon's tale focuses on his Indian and Spanish captivity and escape back into English society, Equiano's extends the meanings of captivity to encompass not only capture by natives but also the most common African experience of captivity, lifetime enslavement.

By the end of the eighteenth century, captivity narratives remained a recognizable genre, but their forms and meanings had shifted away from earlier emphases on religious conversion toward more secularized and blatantly politicized representations. As Equiano's text illustrates, captivity literature continued to consider fundamental moral and ethical questions, especially regarding the construction and interpretation of racial differences. The early attention to gender differentiation in the captivities changed with the rise of female authorship. No longer a rarity, the "particular knowledge" of female captives rendered in print addressed less sacred and more profane issues that threatened a woman captive, especially emphasizing sexual rather than spiritual vulnerability. Romantic discourses of subjectivity and identity revised and adapted some of these captivity figures, combining the cross-cultural concerns of Indian captivity with the imagery of sexual threat more often found in the period's gothic novels. Charles Brockden Brown's novels *Wieland* (1798) and *Edgar Huntley* (1799) both draw extensively on this combination of captivity conventions and gothic imagery to construct an atmosphere of terror and dread, features that resonated with some of the uncertainties of life in the new United States.

Captivity literature remained popular throughout the nineteenth century. Appearing as novels, plays, poetry, broadsides, sermons, educational texts, and newspaper accounts, as well as personal or official histories, these texts often presented themselves as peculiarly American productions. The diversity of captive voices, whether fictive or factual, testifies to the literature's enduring appeal. The roots of nineteenth-century slave narratives as well as those of the less well-known convent captivities (Schultz 1999) were firmly planted in the fertile imaginative terrain of Mary Rowlandson's and Increase Mather's New England landscape.

REFERENCES

Allen, Ethan. 1779. *A Narrative of Colonel Ethan Allen's Captivity from the Time of His Being Taken by the British, near Montreal, on the 25th Day of September, in the Year 1775, to the Time of His Exchange, on the 6th Day of May, 1778: Containing Voyages and Travels . . . Interspersed with Some Political Observations*. Philadelphia: Robert Bell.

Anon. 1793. *The Affecting History of the Dreadful Distresses of Frederick Manheim's Family.* Exeter, NH: H. Ranlet.

Baepler, Paul, ed. 1999. *White Slaves, African Masters: An Anthology of American Barbary Captivity Narratives.* Chicago: University of Chicago Press.

Belknap, Jeremy. 1784–1792. *The History of New-Hampshire.* 3 vols. Philadelphia and Boston: for the author.

Breitwieser, Mitchell. 1990. *American Puritanism and the Defense of Mourning: Religion, Grief, and Ethnology in Mary White Rowlandson's Captivity Narrative.* Madison: University of Wisconsin Press.

Bumstead, J. M. 1983. "Carried to Canada!": Perceptions of the French in British Colonial Captivity Narratives, 1690–1760. *American Review of Canadian Studies* 13: 79–96.

Burnham, Michelle. 1997. *Captivity and Sentiment: Cultural Exchange in American Literature, 1682–1861.* Hanover, NH: University Press of New England.

Carroll, Lorrayne. 1996. "My Outward Man": The Curious Case of Hannah Swarton. *Early American Literature* 31: 45–73.

———. 2004. "Affecting History": Impersonating Women in the Early Republic. *Early American Literature* 39: 511–552.

Castiglia, Christopher. 1996. *Bound and Determined: Captivity, Culture-Crossing, and White Womanhood from Mary Rowlandson to Patty Hearst.* Chicago: University of Chicago Press.

Coleman, Emma L. 1925. *New England Captives Carried to Canada between 1677 and 1760.* Portland, ME: Southworth.

Colley, Linda. 2002. *Captives: Britain, Empire, and the World, 1600–1850.* New York: Anchor Books.

Davidson, Cathy. 1986. *Revolution and the Word: The Rise of the Novel in America.* New York: Oxford University Press.

Demos, John. 1994. *The Unredeemed Captive: A Family Story from Early America.* New York: Knopf.

Derounian, Kathryn Zabelle. 1987. Puritan Orthodoxy and the "Survivor Syndrome" in Mary Rowlandson's Indian Captivity Narrative. *Early American Literature* 22: 82–93.

———. 1988. The Publication, Promotion, and Distribution of Mary Rowlandson's Indian Captivity Narrative in the Seventeenth Century. *Early American Literature* 23: 239–261.

———. 1994. The Indian Captivity Narratives of Mary Rowlandson and Olive Oatman: Case Studies in the Continuity, Evolution, and Exploitation of Literary Discourse. *Studies in the Literary Imagination* 27: 33–46.

———, ed. 1998. *Women's Indian Captivity Narratives.* New York: Penguin.

Derounian-Stodola, Kathryn Zabelle, and James Levernier. 1993. *The Indian Captivity Narrative, 1550–1900.* New York: Twayne.

Dickinson, Jonathan. 1945. *Jonathan Dickinson's Journal or God's Protecting Providence,* edited by Evangeline Walker Andrews and Charles McLean Andrews. New Haven, CT: Yale University Press.

Eastburn, Robert. 1758. *A Faithful Narrative, of the Many Dangers and Sufferings, as well as Wonderful Deliverances of Robert Eastburn During his Late Captivity among the Indians.* Philadelphia: William Dunlap.

Ebersole, Gary. 1995. *Captured By Texts: Puritan to Post-modern Images of Indian Captivity.* Charlottesville: University Press of Virginia.

Equiano, Olaudah. 1789. *The Interesting Narrative of the Life of Olaudah Equiano, or Gustavus Vassa, the African.* London: for the author.

Fitzpatrick, Tara. 1991. The Figure of Captivity: The Cultural Work of the Puritan Captivity Narrative. *American Literary History* 3: 1–26.

Fleming, William. 1756a. *Erzehlung von den Trübsalen und der Wunderbahren Befreyung so Geschehen an William Flemming und dessen Weib Elisabeth.* Germantown: Christoph Saur.

———. 1756b. *A Narrative of the Sufferings and Surprising Deliverance of William and Elizabeth Fleming.* Philadelphia: James Chattin.

———. 1756c. *A Narrative of the Sufferings and Surprizing Deliverance of William and Elizabeth Fleming.* Boston: Green and Russell.

Franklin, Benjamin. 1959–. *The Papers of Benjamin Franklin,* edited by Leonard W. Labaree et al. 37 vols. to date. New Haven, CT: Yale University Press.

Gay, Bunker. 1792. *A Genuine and Correct Account of the Captivity, Sufferings and Deliverance of Mrs. Jemima Howe.* Boston: Belknap and Young.

Grace, Henry. 1764. *The History of the Life and Sufferings of Henry Grace.* Reading, UK: for the author.

Gyles, John. 1736. *Memoirs of Odd Adventures, Strange Deliverances, &. in the Captivity of John Gyles, Esq.* Boston: S. Kneeland and T. Green.

———. 1869. *Memoirs of Odd Adventures, Strange Deliverances, etc.* Cincinnati: for William Dodge.

Haefeli, Evan, and Kevin Sweeney. 2003. *Captors and Captives: The 1704 French and Indian Raid on Deerfield.* Amherst: University of Massachusetts Press.

Hammon, Briton. 1760. *A Narrative of the Uncommon Sufferings, and Surprizing Deliverance of Briton Hammon.* Boston: Green and Russell.

Hanson, Elizabeth. 1728. *God's Mercy Surmounting Man's Cruelty, Exemplified in the Captivity and Redemption of Elizabeth Hanson.* Philadelphia: S. Keimer.

Harris, Sharon M., ed. 2003. *Women's Early American Historical Narratives.* New York: Penguin.

Holmes, Thomas J. 1940. *Cotton Mather: A Bibliography of His Works.* 3 vols. Cambridge, MA: Harvard University Press.

How, Nehemiah [attributed author]. 1748. *A Narrative of the Captivity of Nehemiah How, Who Was Taken by the Indians at the Great-Meadow-Fort Above Fort Dummer, Where He Was an Inhabitant, October 11th, 1745.* Boston.

Humphreys, David. 1788. *An Essay on the Life of the Honorable Major-General Israel Putnam.* Hartford: Hudson and Goodwin.

Johnson, Susannah. 1796. *A Narrative of the Captivity of Mrs. Johnson.* Walpole, NH: Davide Carlisle, Jr.

Koehler, Lyle. 1980. *A Search for Power: The "Weaker Sex" in Seventeenth-Century New England.* Urbana: University of Illinois Press.

Kolodny, Annette. 1981. Turning the Lens on "The Panther Captivity": A Feminist Exercise in Practical Criticism. *Critical Inquiry* 8: 329–345.

Lepore, Jill. 1998. *The Name of War: King Philip's War and the Origins of American Identity.* New York: Knopf.

LeRoy, Marie, and Barbara Leininger. 1759. *Die Erzehlungen von Maria Le Roy und Barbara Leininger welche vierthalb Jahr unter den Indianern gefangen gewesen, und am 6ten*

May in in dieser Stadt glücklich angekommen. Philadelphia: Peter Miller and Ludwig Weiss.

Mather, Cotton. 1697. *Humiliations Follow'd with Deliverances.* Boston: B. Green, & F. Allen for Samuel Phillips.

———. 1699. *Decennium Luctuosum: An History of Remarkable Occurrences, in the Long War, which New-England Hath Had with the Indian Salvages.* Boston: B. Green, and J. Allen, for Samuel Phillips.

———. 1702a. *A Letter to Ungospellized Plantations.* Boston: B. Green, & J. Allen.

———. 1702b. *Magnalia Christi Americana: or, The Ecclesiastical History of New-England, from Its First Planting in the Year 1620. unto the Year of Our Lord, 1698.* London: Thomas Parkhurst.

Minter, David L. 1973. By Dens of Lions: Notes on Stylization in Early Puritan Captivity Narratives. *American Literature* 45: 335–347.

Norton, John. 1748. *The Redeemed Captive: Being a Narrative of the Taken and Carrying into Captivity the Reverend Mr. John Norton.* Boston: Samuel Kneeland and Timothy Green.

Pearce, Roy Harvey. 1967. *Savagism and Civilization: A Study of the Indian and the American Mind.* Baltimore: Johns Hopkins University Press.

Rowlandson, Mary. 1997. *The Sovereignty and Goodness of God, Together with the Faithfulness of His Promises Displayed,* edited by Neal Salisbury. Boston: Bedford/St. Martin's.

Sayre, Gordon. 1997. *Les Sauvages Americains: Representations of Native Americans in French and English Colonial Literature.* Chapel Hill: University of North Carolina Press.

———, ed. 2000. *American Captivity Narratives.* Boston: Houghton Mifflin.

Schultz, Nancy Lusignan, ed. 1999. *Veil of Fear: Nineteenth-Century Convent Tales.* West Lafayette, IN: NotaBell Books.

Slotkin, Richard. 1973. *Regeneration through Violence: The Mythology of the American Frontier, 1600–1860.* Middletown, CT: Wesleyan University Press.

Snader, Joe. 2000. *Caught between Worlds: British Captivity Narratives in Fact and Fiction.* Lexington: University Press of Kentucky.

Stout, Harry S. 1986. *The New England Soul: Preaching and Religious Culture in Colonial New England.* New York: Oxford University Press.

Strong, Pauline. 1999. *Captive Selves, Captivating Others: The Politics and Poetics of Colonial American Captivity Narratives.* Boulder, CO: Westview.

Toulouse, Teresa. 1992. "My Own Credit": Strategies of Evaluation in Mary Rowlandson's Captivity Narrative. *American Literature* 64: 655–676.

Tyler, Royall. 1797. *The Algerine Captive: or, The Life and Adventures of Doctor Updike Underhill, Six Years a Prisoner among the Algerines.* Walpole, NH: David Carlisle. 2 vols.

Ulrich, Laurel Thatcher. 1983. *Good Wives: Image and Reality in the Lives of Women in Northern New England, 1650–1750.* New York: Oxford University Press.

Washburn, Wilcomb E., ed. 1975–. *Garland Library of Narratives of North American Indian Captivities.* 111 vols. to date. New York: Garland.

Williams, John. 1707. *The Redeemed Captive, Returning to Zion: A Faithful History of Remarkable Occurrences, in the Captivity and the Deliverance of Mr. John Williams.* Boston: B. Green, for Samuel Phillips.

Williamson, Peter. 1757. *French and Indian Cruelty.* York: N. Nickerson.

Ziff, Larzer. 1991. *Writing in the New Nation: Prose, Print, and Politics in the Early United States.* New Haven, CT: Yale University Press.

CHAPTER 7

....

JONATHAN EDWARDS AND THE GREAT AWAKENING

....

THOMAS S. KIDD

In 1757, trustees asked Jonathan Edwards to become the president of the College of
New Jersey, and in reply he gave a number of reasons for why he might not be their
best choice. In addition to having a personality sometimes marked by "disagreeable
dullness and stiffness," he admitted that he could probably "write better than I can
speak." With regard to his educational preparation, the polymath Edwards told the
trustees that he was "deficient in some parts of learning," including algebra and
the Greek classics. One gets the impression that Edwards figured he knew most
everything else there was to know (Edwards 1998, 726–729). The prickly, introverted
Edwards was enormously learned, yet he used his knowledge in the service of populist, evangelical heart religion. He became one of the most important leaders of the
First Great Awakening of the 1740s in New England, and one of the most influential
articulators of evangelical Calvinism ever. Edwards defended Calvinist Christianity
and the religion of the new birth with a logical brilliance few have ever matched, and
he should be viewed as an exceptionally capable advocate for a religious movement
that transformed American Christianity from the mid-eighteenth century.

Although many of the American colonies had been founded primarily for economic reasons, the New England colonies of Massachusetts and Connecticut stood
out for their distinctly religious character. English Puritans fleeing persecution in
the homeland settled these colonies and maintained a strong Calvinist consensus
there through their early decades. The Puritans strongly emphasized an individual's
devotion to God, as well as loving, holy living within godly societies and churches.

By the later decades of the seventeenth century, Puritan pastors began to perceive that the colonies were in religious decline, and the influence of non-Puritan outsiders and the allure of commercial profits seemed difficult to contain. While the Puritans of New England had insisted on very precise standards of theology and Congregational church polity, the years after the Glorious Revolution of 1688–1689 forced New Englanders into a more ecumenical pan-Protestant mode. They, along with Britons at home, faced a long series of wars with Europe's Catholic powers, especially France and Spain. A new charter for Massachusetts in 1692 required the toleration of all Protestant churches, and suddenly New Englanders became quite invested in the success of the British Protestant monarchy and empire. The era of Puritanism had come to an end (Kidd 2004).

But did the end of Puritanism mean that religion had gone into an irreversible decline? The move from English Puritanism to British Protestantism did not necessarily indicate spiritual degradation, but many pastors suspected that their societies had substantially failed in their devotion to God. Everywhere the pastors turned, the judgment of God seemed to threaten them, in the forms of natural disasters, financial and political crises, and especially attacks from French Catholics and allied Native Americans in northern New England. A genre of Puritan sermons, the "jeremiads," called for moral reform in the face of such troubles. Pastors listed the many sins of the colonists and warned that if they did not repent, God's wrath would become ever more devastating. By the second and third decades of the eighteenth century, however, a number of pastors began to call not just for simple moral reform but for an outpouring of the Holy Spirit, which would revive languishing devotion, reenergize the churches, and deliver New England from the various temporal dangers.

Among the pastors who led these early calls for revival were Jonathan Edwards's grandfather and ministerial predecessor, Solomon Stoddard of Northampton, Massachusetts, and Edwards's father, Timothy Edwards of East Windsor, Connecticut. Stoddard passed on a considerable evangelical heritage to Edwards, as Edwards noted in *A Faithful Narrative of the Surprising Work of God* (1737). He described Stoddard as "renowned for his gifts and grace; so he was blessed, from the beginning, with extraordinary success in his ministry in the conversion of many souls. He had five harvests, as he called them." These "harvests" came in 1679, 1683, 1690, 1712, and 1718 (Edwards 1995, 58). Stoddard himself told his congregation in 1687, "I have made it my business to gain Souls to Christ" (Stoddard 1687, sig. A4). In this business he may have been the most successful of any New England preacher in his generation. Stoddard relied on the Lord's Supper as a "converting ordinance," or a preparatory ritual that could lead unconverted seekers to Christ. On this point Stoddard differed from his clerical colleagues in the Boston area, who believed that the Supper was meant only for the converted (Schafer 1963, 332–340). Stoddard had to defend his policy of open communion against various attacks from the church establishment, and he argued that he would not hesitate to "clear up a Truth that has not been received, whereby a door is opened for the revival of Religion" (Stoddard 1709, sig. A3). Edwards was particularly impressed that during each of Stoddard's harvests, "the bigger part of the young people in the town seemed to be mainly concerned for their eternal salvation" (Edwards 1995, 58).

Stoddard developed the most elaborate evangelical theology of conversion prior to Edwards. As an orthodox Calvinist, Stoddard believed that the Spirit of God drew sinners to salvation, but he also observed that powerful preaching was the means God often used to woo people. Thus Stoddard recommended that preachers should warn of the threat of damnation, on one hand, and offer the hope of salvation through Christ's grace, on the other. This view no doubt heavily influenced his grandson Jonathan's preaching. Stoddard argued that the dread of damnation was the most, and perhaps the only, effective means to lead sinners to true "humiliation," or a sense that their sin was deplorable in light of God's holiness. God awakened conviction of sin in the elect, followed by the hope that Christ's grace was sufficient to deliver them from the judgment of God. The brutal wars that plagued the Connecticut River Valley during his ministry in Northampton surely colored Stoddard's preaching on damnation. Although the Puritans had originally come to New England with the supposed intent of evangelizing local Native Americans, they tended more often to provoke and bully the Indians over land rights and other issues. When the Native Americans resisted, as they did during King Philip's War of 1675–1676, the English colonists used the most brutal practices of war imaginable to subdue them. Understandably, many Indians in northern New England allied with the French and periodically raided frontier towns in western and northern New England. The Deerfield raid of 1704, for instance, decimated Northampton's close neighbors to the north. Northamptonites, faced with the ever-present threat of French Catholic and Native American attacks, could easily accept Stoddard's reminders of their imminent peril (Demos 1994).

Likewise, Timothy Edwards, husband of Stoddard's daughter Esther, was "an expert on the science of conversion," according to historian George Marsden. Unlike Stoddard, Edwards required applicants for full membership to give a public "relation" of their conversions, some of which have survived as testimony to his revival ministry. He led four or five revivals in his East Windsor congregation before the 1734–1735 Northampton awakening, according to Jonathan Edwards's adult memory. At least two of these took place in the years just after 1710 and profoundly affected Jonathan. In 1716 the young Edwards wrote to his sister Mary that "there hath in this place been a very remarkable stirring and pouring out of the Spirit of God.... About thirteen have been joined to the church" (Marsden 2003, 26, 33). Timothy Edwards's awakenings were followed by more regional revivals in the coming years, punctuated especially by a prodigious stir in towns along the Connecticut and Thames rivers from 1720 to 1722.

Edwards's background, then, prepared him well to become the evangelical giant he was. His "Personal Narrative" traced the beginnings of his own conversion to "a time of remarkable awakening in my father's congregation" when he was nine years old. He began to pray fervently, five times a day, and met with other boys in the congregation for devotions. Edwards and his friends "built a booth in a swamp, in a very secret and retired place, for a place of prayer." Though one can see that this was no ordinary boy, Edwards never considered his piety a natural inclination, and soon the immature fervor dulled. As he bluntly put it, he "returned like a dog to his vomit, and went on in the ways of sin" (Edwards 1995, 281–282).

Edwards saw conversion as a believer's experience of rising out of spiritual deadness and embracing the joy of being chosen by God for salvation. Obviously, this was not something that all could do, for not all were chosen. For the elect, however, rejecting the misery of self-glorification was a long process, punctuated by moments of spiritual breakthrough. One of those breakthrough moments might be described as "conversion," but not in the sense that it settled all questions of eternal destiny. Edwards did not think believers normally enjoyed what later evangelicals called "assurance," at least not immediately. Instead, if one takes Edwards's own recollection of his spiritual travels as a model, the saint was likely to have several critical conversion moments, each followed by seasons of deadness. There was a single point in time, however, when God regenerated the soul of the saint. The believer might not be able definitively to pinpoint that moment, but for the truly saved, the spiritual trajectory was always upward, toward delighting in the ways of God, and away from idolatry (Marsden 2003, 28, 519). So it was for Edwards.

Even as he attended Yale for his pastoral training, Edwards was not convinced of his own salvation. The main problem blocking Edwards's conversion was his inability to accept the doctrine of God's sovereignty, especially in salvation. If God was entirely sovereign over the created order, then certainly that must mean that he controlled the eternal destiny of humans, the pinnacle of creation. To Edwards this was no mere theological proposition, for it was intimately involved with the question of his own fate. His salvation was evidenced by an admission that he would no longer contest God's supreme authority. This was not assent to dry doctrine, but an emotional repudiation of sin, and embracing of God's ultimate power. The elect enjoyed God's sovereignty, and pursuing salvation meant seeking a "delightful conviction" of the omnipotence of God (Edwards 1995, 283).

When he was seventeen, and still an intense, unpopular student at Yale, he experienced the first of his spiritual breakthroughs. He recalled reading 1 Timothy 1:17, "Now unto the King eternal, immortal, invisible, the only wise God, be honor and glory forever and ever, Amen," upon which "there came into my soul . . . a sense of the glory of the Divine Being." Overwhelming feelings of joy concerning God's omnipotence stirred him. Soon he went to his father and told him about his experience, and Timothy encouraged his son to feed this new spiritual sensitivity. Jonathan then walked out to his father's pasture and wrote that as "I looked up on the sky and clouds; there came into my mind, a sweet sense of the glorious majesty and grace of God, that I know not how to express. I seemed to see them both in a sweet conjunction: majesty and meekness joined together: it was a sweet and gentle, and holy majesty; and also a majestic meekness; an awful sweetness; a high and great, and holy gentleness." Edwards had stepped out of his father's house and into a wonderful new world of spiritual delights in God (Edwards 1995, 284–285). He earnestly devoted himself to bringing others into this new world.

At twenty-six, Edwards took over the Northampton pulpit from his deceased mentor Solomon Stoddard, who, like Timothy Edwards, helped Jonathan develop an expectation of revivals in the congregation. Northampton had gone through its five or six significant harvests under Stoddard, the most recent only two years earlier as a response to a significant earthquake in 1727 that had generated revivals across New England. At that time "there were no small appearances of a divine work amongst some," and perhaps twenty people converted, but "nothing of any general awakening" transpired (Edwards 1972, 146). Since then, however, many of the congregants had neglected their spiritual duties. Edwards was concerned about the state of the church's youth, despite being fairly young himself. He seemed unable to identify with their indulgences or frolics. Certainly Edwards was a kind of killjoy in an earthly sense, but in a spiritual sense nearly all he cared about was people's joy and happiness. Edwards believed that true delight was found in God. In 1729, many young people in his congregation did not seem concerned about their intense pastor's pleas for them to forsake carousing for the holy ways of the Lord. Those same youths would in several years become pliant in Edwards's pastoral hands, but only temporarily (Kidd 2007).

In the meantime, when theological liberalism was seeping into certain New England pulpits and Harvard classrooms, Edwards's brilliant orthodoxy made him a favorite among the emerging evangelical cohort in Boston. Edwards's debut as a leading Anglo-American evangelical came in July 1731 when he delivered a public lecture in Boston the week of Harvard commencement. His sermon, soon published as *God Glorified in the Work of Redemption*, offered little that was new theologically, but it marked out a clear stance against the enticements of rationalist Arminianism. Arminians had won many fashionable Anglo-American pulpits, arguing that man had free will to choose salvation. Surely God would not predestine anyone to damnation, the rationalists said. We must have the moral ability to choose God, even if our sin does earn us damnation when we reject God. Without free will, human salvation and damnation seemed not only irrational but immoral.

Edwards would have none of this "rationality," and *God Glorified in the Work of Redemption* made clear that redemption (and, by implication, the renewal of hearts in revival) depended totally on God. The way of salvation in Christ, the faith to believe, and the power for holiness all came from God alone. Thus, God, not man, got all the credit for the great things he accomplished in the salvation of the elect. Moreover, God chose not to redeem some, and because all deserved damnation in the first place, God's free choice was not immoral (Kidd 2007). "When man is made holy, it is from mere and arbitrary grace; God may forever deny holiness to the fallen creature if he pleases, without any disparagement to any of his perfections," Edwards averred (Edwards 1999, 71). For Edwards, the conversion of any soul depended on God's decision, and the pastor's duty was to remain available for God to use as a tool in the work of redemption.

As a pastor, Edwards's first great moment of usefulness came in 1734–1735. His published account of that revival, *A Faithful Narrative of the Surprizing Work of God,* is our best record of what happened. Though the narrative is heavily colored by Edwards's perspective, it nevertheless gives a fairly systematic account of what seems to have been a stupendous stir. He first began to notice a change among the young people in 1733, what Edwards called a new "flexibleness" in their attitudes toward his preaching. He insisted that they give up their "mirth and company-keeping" on Sunday evenings, and he began to see a willingness to comply. Edwards also organized neighborhood meetings (the settlements encompassed by the Northampton congregation were far-flung) of fathers concerning the governance of their children. Surprisingly, the fathers reported that the children needed no extra chastening to get them to remain faithful to the Sabbath. The youths themselves were convinced by Edwards's preaching (Edwards 1972, 147).

The first trickle of the revival torrent began in the village of Pascommuck, about three miles from Northampton, but still part of Edwards's parish. There, several people "seemed to have been savingly wrought upon." There needed to be a catalyst to make a serious breach in the people's complacency, however, and it came in the form of untimely deaths. A young man "in the bloom of his youth" fell ill with "a pleurisy" and was dead in two days. Then, a young married woman fell ill, but before dying she secured assurance of her salvation and passed away "very full of comfort." Edwards, determined to strike while the iron was hot, began encouraging dismayed young people to organize into small group meetings for "social religion" (Edwards 1972, 147–148).

In December 1734 the excitement broke loose with numbers of conversions that Edwards found surprising. One young woman, "one of the greatest company-keepers in the whole town," came to Edwards with the news that God had converted her. He thought that "what she gave an account of was a glorious work of God's infinite power and sovereign grace; and that God had given her a new heart, truly broken and sanctified." Edwards initially was unsure what effects this transformation might have on her friends, but it produced better results than he could have imagined: "God made it . . . the greatest occasion of awakening to others, of anything that ever came to pass in the town." She received visits from many of the young people inquiring about what happened to her, and many of these friends too were converted (Edwards 1972, 149).

What had begun as a movement of God among the young people now became "universal," and everyone, young and old, seemed only to talk of religion and salvation. Many more began attending the private meetings in homes for discussing spiritual topics, and church assemblies became energized with fervent singing. The fleeting pleasures of carousing and joking were now replaced by what Edwards called "spiritual mirth" in his *Faithful Narrative* (Edwards 1972, 149, 152).

Edwards's account mentioned thirty-two communities besides Northampton that experienced awakening in 1734–1735. About half were in Massachusetts, and half in Connecticut, as the revival ran north and south along the course of the Connecticut River, in communities that depended on the river for trade and transportation. Churches at Windsor and East Windsor, including Timothy Edwards's church, which had experienced awakening in 1720–1722, again felt the Spirit move in 1735 (Crawford 1991, 125). The results in Northampton itself were stunning enough, however. Edwards was always cautious about definitively pronouncing anyone "saved," but he guessed that about 300 people had been converted in six months. This meant that the church had grown to 620 communicant members, almost all the adults in Northampton. Truly this awakening had become "universal," as Edwards put it, for it touched all ages of men and women. Edwards noted that Stoddard's revivals had often affected disproportionate numbers of young women, but now the numbers of men and women, young and old, were remarkably even. The revival had jumped racial boundaries, too, as Edwards noted in his *Faithful Narrative* that "several Negroes . . . appear to have been truly born again" (Edwards 1972, 157–159).

Edwards's separate mention of "Negroes" reminds us that he was very much a person of his time, believing in a hierarchical world in which devoted Christians might own slaves. Indeed, starting in the early 1730s, the Edwards family seems usually to have owned at least one slave (Marsden 2003, 255). Eighteenth-century Christians of European descent normally saw African Americans and other nonwhites as human, however, meaning that they had souls needing eternal salvation, just as whites did. Edwards and his fellow evangelicals did comparatively more than colonial American Anglicans, who dominated the southern colonies, to evangelize the slaves, perhaps having less to fear regarding slave insurrection should Christianity give the slaves ideas about their dignity and need for freedom.

In the South, white evangelicals had to contend with the issue of slavery more directly, and no other evangelical before the American Revolution wrote more prolifically about his work among slaves than Virginia's evangelical Presbyterian minister Samuel Davies. Davies and other Virginia Presbyterians and Baptists included slaves in the life of their churches (although seldom in any leadership positions), and Davies wrote admiringly in 1756 that "sundry of [the slaves] have lodged all night in my kitchen; and sometimes, when I have awaked about two or three a-clock in the morning, a torrent of sacred harmony poured into my chamber, and carried my mind away to Heaven. In this seraphic exercise, some of them spend almost the whole night" (Davies 1757, 16). Like many other key pastors who led the Great Awakening, Davies and Edwards owned slaves and sought their spiritual, but not social, liberation. Some of Edwards's northern disciples would become antislavery, but in the South, the evangelical antislavery cause crumbled under the weight of social pressure to condone human bondage.

Despite the remarkable changes it had wrought, Edwards's 1735 revival at Northampton cooled in the second half of the year. That awakening, however, proved to be the beginning of a much larger movement that touched not only most of New England but also many other parts of the American colonies. The excitement of the First Great Awakening, which saw its height from 1740 to 1742, was keyed not primarily by Edwards but by the young Anglican itinerant George Whitefield, who used innovative marketing and advertising techniques to generate huge interest across Britain and America for his revivals (Lambert 1994). He also became a brilliant, passionate orator partly through the adaptation of acting methods he learned as an unconverted youth in England's theaters (Stout 1991). Whitefield was not theologically insightful in the way that Edwards was, but they both shared Calvinist evangelical convictions and took the religion of the new birth to the people at large. By the early 1740s, however, Whitefield had probably become the most recognizable name in Britain and the colonies, save perhaps for King George II.

In America, the effects of the revivals of the 1740s were deep and widespread, particularly in Edwards's New England. Itinerants like Whitefield and New Jersey's Gilbert Tennent spoke before large, eager audiences about the necessity of conversion, or the new birth. They often criticized established ministers as insufficiently supportive of the revivals, and at times even implied that these opposing ministers were actually unconverted. More indelicate and radical ministers like Long Island's James Davenport sometimes even called out unconverted ministers by name and prayed publicly for them to be saved. From the start, the evangelical movement was committed to revivals and the new birth, but evangelicals also immediately began to split between moderates and radicals. The moderates supported the awakenings but believed that they should only energize the existing churches, not transform the ecclesiastical status quo. Radicals endorsed unlimited itinerancy, even by uneducated preachers. They put a heavy emphasis on the Spirit-filled experiences of the laity and believed that anyone who was truly converted would know it instantly (Kidd 2007). The converted, moreover, could perceive whether others (including ministers) were truly converted or not.

Jonathan Edwards played a mediating role in the contest between moderate and radical evangelicals. Early on, he seemed to lean toward the radical wing, as seen in the tumult surrounding his most spectacular sermon of the First Great Awakening, *Sinners in the Hands of an Angry God* (1741), delivered at Enfield, Connecticut. Edwards designed *Sinners* to be an "awakening sermon" that would shake the ungodly out of their self-righteous delusions. The topic was not unusual for Edwards or other Calvinist preachers, and Edwards almost certainly did not use any performative tactics like Whitefield's to generate a response. He was reputed to be solemn but intense in his style (Marsden 2003, 220–221). So what was it about *Sinners* that led to such a spectacularly emotional response, with congregants falling to the floor and crying out for mercy?

We should not imagine that Edwards's sermon produced an unusually emotional response, in the awakenings' broader context. The week before the Enfield sermon Edwards had been involved with very similar meetings at the nearby town of Suffield, Connecticut. Some of the lay radicals from Suffield and other nearby towns were likely in the audience at Enfield. Edwards may simply have given these followers what they wanted: an explosive, awakening sermon that generated an enthusiastic response (Winiarski 2005). Scholars, however, agree that much of the sermon's power lay in its rhetoric. *Sinners in the Hands of an Angry God* was brilliant, vivid, and terrifying. Edwards's warnings of judgment made the congregation scream for fear of hell.

Sinners used at least twenty metaphors to picture God's wrath building up against rebellious sinners, including a furnace burning, black storm clouds approaching, floodwaters surging against a dam, and, most famously, the spider dangling over fire: "The God that holds you over the pit of hell, much as one holds a spider, or some loathsome insect, over the fire, abhors you, and is dreadfully provoked; his wrath towards you burns like fire; he looks upon you as worthy of nothing else, but to be cast into the fire; he is of purer eyes than to bear to have you in his sight; you are ten thousand times so abominable in his eyes as the most hateful venomous serpent is in ours," Edwards warned. For the sinner damned to hell, "there will be no end to this exquisite horrible misery. When you look forward, you shall see a long forever . . . you will know certainly that you must wear out long ages, millions of millions of ages, in wrestling and conflicting with this almighty merciless vengeance; and then when you have so done . . . you will know that all is but a point to what remains" (Edwards 2003, 401, 411, 415). All of Edwards's listeners that day would have affirmed that this judgment awaited unforgiven sinners, but perhaps the doctrine had grown stale with familiarity. Edwards's vivid images may have awakened some previously passive residents, while other visitors may have come expecting to have another emotional encounter with God, and gotten their wish.

Soon Edwards found himself in a position as the key defender of the revivals' legitimacy, even as he began to back away from some of the most radical aspects of the awakenings. At Yale's commencement in 1741, he launched his first great defense of the awakenings in his address *The Distinguishing Marks of a Work of the Spirit of God*. Edwards began his examination of the revivals with a list of aspects that "are not signs that we are to judge of a work by." This clever approach allowed him indirectly to dismantle all the objections that conservative critics of the revivals had raised. Were the revivals new and unusual? Surely this was no reason to dismiss them as illegitimate, Edwards argued, for many of God's greatest acts in redemptive history featured effects no one had previously seen. Did penitents demonstrate extraordinary bodily and vocal exercises in the meetings? It was no wonder that they did so, since many had gained new insights into the judgment and mercy of God.

Edwards may have been thinking of the great outcry at Enfield two months earlier. "If we should suppose," he reasoned, "that a person saw himself hanging over a great pit, full of fierce and glowing flames, by a thread that he knew to be very weak . . . what distress would he be in . . . would not he be ready to cry out in such circumstances?" (Edwards 1972, 228, 231). Those at Enfield had cried out, and Edwards considered their response reasonable.

Likewise, Edwards contended, the presence of "great impressions" on the imagination did not make the revivals bogus. He did worry about the affected giving too much weight to so-called prophetical visions, but overall he considered the mental images a likely means of God to convict or comfort. Yes, some of the penitents "have in some extraordinary frames, been in a kind of ecstasy, wherein they have been carried beyond themselves, and have had their minds transported into a . . . kind of vision." He knew that to some opponents these reports signaled reckless enthusiasm or religious frenzy. Edwards knew better. As he said in *Distinguishing Marks*, "I have been acquainted with some such instances; and I see no manner of need of bringing in the help of the Devil into the account we give of these things" (Edwards 1972, 235–237).

He also conceded that the revivals occasionally produced "imprudences and irregularities," "delusions of Satan," and "gross errors or scandalous practices," but so did all great new movements of God. Finally, he insisted that it was no shame to the revival that its leaders sometimes focused "very much on the terrors of God's holy law, and that with a great deal of pathos and earnestness." Hell was real, and many were going there for eternity. Why should ministers not sound the alarm? "If I am in danger of going to hell, I should be glad to know as much as possibly I can of the dreadfulness of it," he noted drily (Edwards 1972, 241, 243–244, 246–247).

Having concluded that most justifications for dismissing the revivals were unreasonable, he proceeded to "shew positively, what are the sure, distinguishing, scripture evidences and marks of a work of the Spirit of God." Authentic religious experiences might manifest themselves in various ways, but Edwards argued that they would always produce enduring, godly effects. The work of the Spirit raised the "esteem" of Jesus, while working against "the interest of Satan's kingdom." It created a "greater regard" for the scriptures (Edwards 1972, 248–250, 253). It encouraged true love for both God and man. He admitted that Satan could temporarily mimic these signs of the Spirit, but he thought that these lasting features would eventually distinguish true and false works.

Based on these standards, Edwards concluded that the late work "is undoubtedly, in the general, from the Spirit of God." He appealed again to his own experience in the revivals: "I am one that, by the providence of God, have for some months past, been much amongst those that have been the subjects of that work that has of late been carried on in the land." Here he subtly contrasted himself with critics. Had they been there when the outcries began? Had God converted anyone through their preaching? "I look upon myself called on this occasion to give my testimony

[that] this work has all those marks" of the Spirit. I know, Edwards implied, because I have been there to see it. He had long been familiar with revivals at Northampton, he reminded them, going back to Solomon Stoddard's tenure. There had, of course, been the celebrated revival in his parish in 1735, but the work of God in 1741 was "much purer than that which was wrought there six years before" (Edwards 1972, 260, 263–264, 270).

Having made such a bold defense of the revivals, Edwards proceeded to threaten the critics of the awakenings. Never one to hold back when he believed himself to be on God's side of an issue, Edwards warned the Yale audience that attempts to slander the late work of God could meet with divine retribution. Specifically, Edwards posited that the critics' carping against the revivals could make them guilty of the "unpardonable sin against the Holy Ghost," that fearsome but mysterious sin that Jesus mentioned in Matthew 12: 31–32. The revivals' opponents thought this charge revealed Edwards's "partiality" and "rashness," as the rebuttal tract *The Late Religious Commotions in New-England Considered* put it (Rand 1743, 38, 40). Edwards concluded *Distinguishing Marks* with warnings to the friends of the revival to rein in their enthusiastic excesses and to be particularly wary of preferring "impulses and impressions" to the clear guidance of the scriptures. To do so would be to "leave the guidance of the pole star to follow a Jack-with-a-lanthorn." In a caution certainly directed at Davenport and his followers, he spoke against "passing censures upon others that are professing Christians, as hypocrites and ignorant of anything of real religion." He further advised the revivals' defenders to avoid "too much heat and appearance of an angry zeal" (Edwards 1972, 275, 282–283, 287). Having just implied that the revivals' critics had committed the unpardonable sin, Edwards, one might argue, needed to take his own advice against angry censuring. *Distinguishing Marks* did nothing to placate doubters, or rein in radicals, but it staked out a moderate evangelical position and forced private naysayers into the open.

Edwards's *Distinguishing Marks* set the stage for his weighty book *Some Thoughts Concerning the Present Revival of Religion* (1743), which expanded his defense of the First Great Awakening, despite the revivals' excesses. The key antirevivalist leader in Boston, Charles Chauncy, responded to Edwards with *Seasonable Thoughts on the State of Religion in New-England* (1743), which denounced the revivals as fatally corrupted by the spirit of enthusiasm. Where Edwards had seen enthusiasm as a nonessential by-product, Chauncy saw the revivals as shot through with animal passions and gauche displays of emotion. Their debate over the Great Awakening framed the antirevivalist and moderate evangelical positions, respectively.

While Chauncy's critique raised serious questions about the practice of revivalism, there was no stopping the evangelical movement in America, and Edwards was becoming established as its chief defender and philosopher. When the awakenings in New England petered out after 1743 and became enmeshed in squabbles over the radicals' right to separate from established churches, Edwards took a more philosophical turn in his defenses of Calvinism and evangelical religious experiences.

While Edwards saw theological Arminianism and the belief in human free will as among the most pernicious threats against New England's orthodoxy, he equally feared that Chauncy's brand of cool, rational Christianity would needlessly disparage the emotional aspect of true religion. Thus, Edwards followed his defenses of the awakenings with *A Treatise Concerning Religious Affections* (1746), which asserted bluntly that "true religion, in great part, consists in holy affections" (Edwards 1995, 141). Belying his own heavily intellectual Calvinism, Edwards put emotional experience at the heart of authentic Christianity. Edwards argued that those who had been chosen by God had their affections transformed, so that they delighted in God and his holiness. These saints did not prove their election by ecstatic experiences: those feelings might, or might not, be part of truly godly affections. Instead, the elect inevitably demonstrated their salvation by their long-lasting delight in God and his ways, for no carnal man could maintain an authentically holy life.

Edwards knew that there were many hypocrites in the churches who did not actually share in these holy affections, and in Northampton he wanted to maintain the purity of his church membership as best he could. This desire eventually led to his dismissal from his Northampton church in 1750. New Englanders had long struggled with the uncertain status of baptized but unconverted members. Since the 1660s, as part of the Half-Way Covenant, many New England churches had allowed baptized but unconverted parents to have their children baptized, too. Edwards's predecessor Stoddard had accepted the Halfway Covenant, as well as the practice of open admission to the Lord's Supper for all who demonstrated an outwardly godly life, even those who had not experienced conversion. Edwards rejected these policies, believing they introduced corruption into the church body. Parents desiring baptism for their children would now have to be full, converted church members, and only such members could take the Lord's Supper, as well (Marsden 2003, 354). Although the logic of these changes was rigorously consistent, they aggravated key members of the congregation who already harbored resentments against the prickly Edwards, and he was voted out in summer 1750.

As remarkable as Edwards's expulsion seems to us now, it reminds us that Edwards was not simply an intellectual giant but also a pastor. These two callings did not ultimately mix well in Northampton, and Edwards might well be regarded as a failure in his pastoral career. Ironically, his dismissal opened the way for Edwards to compose his most innovative philosophical works after he removed his family to the relative isolation of a Native American mission at Stockbridge, Massachusetts. The literature on Jonathan Edwards has tended to ignore his social context, particularly during his tenure at Stockbridge. We should remember, however, that as a missionary pastor in Stockbridge Edwards tailored his Calvinist evangelicalism to his Indian congregation. It appears that this requirement helped Edwards develop a keener sense that all people were not only equally sinful but equally in need of an infusion of divine grace to be saved. Although Edwards had a typically dim view of human nature, his belief in original sin led to a strange kind of

Christian egalitarianism, particularly with regard to his Native American congregants (Wheeler 2003, 740).

Although his pastoral responsibilities in Stockbridge did influence his treatises of the 1750s, his increased time for writing and reflection also helped him produce new, even more mature and challenging elaborations of his earlier theology. His theology of Calvinist evangelicalism focused heavily on the glory of God as revealed in God's sovereign rule over the universe, and especially the election of some souls to salvation. Edwards believed that all humans were born as depraved, debilitated sinners whose hearts loathed God. The only way for any of these sinners to be saved was for God to change them into people who loved him. For the sake of his own glory, God chose some humans to be transformed and renewed, becoming creatures who delighted in God and his saving mercy through Christ. Edwards himself testified that as a youth he revolted against the idea of God's sovereignty over man's salvation, and as we have seen, Edwards dated his own conversion to the time when the sovereignty and glory of God became to him a "delightful conviction."

Much of Edwards's writing from the 1750s can be understood as an attempt to defend the sovereignty of God against the attacks of enlightened critics, many of whom Edwards called "Arminians," or those who believed that humans had the freedom within themselves to choose to be saved. The critics of strict Calvinism in Edwards's era often argued that election appeared to make God into an arbitrary ogre, giving only a select few the chance to be saved. Again, if people could not choose to be saved, then how could a just God fairly damn them for eternity? In his *Freedom of the Will* (1754; actually published under the more instructive title *Enquiry into the Modern Prevailing Notions of that Freedom of the Will, Which is Supposed to be Essential to Moral Agency, Vertue and Vice, Reward and Punishment, Praise and Blame*), Edwards argued that predestination remained consistent with praise and blame. He believed that the will always responded to its strongest desire, and that the will's disposition could not be self-determined. Therefore, humans could freely choose to do what they wanted. It was just that they always wanted to do evil, unless God intervened and changed their desires. The Arminian notion that people could determine what their will desired was nonsense, he declared, and supposed that humans had a sort of power to create themselves and their will as they saw fit (Holifield 2003, 121).

Moreover, Edwards believed that the Arminians had failed to distinguish between natural and moral inability. For natural inability, creatures could not be blamed: you cannot blame a criminal for being unable to break through his jail cell's iron bars, for instance. But you could blame that prisoner if he could not accept an offer of release, because it was conditioned on apologizing for his offenses, and his stubborn heart could not let him do it (Edwards 1995, 220–221). The former was natural inability, and the latter was moral inability. Similarly, humans all had the natural ability to accept God's gift of salvation, but unless God changed their will, no one would choose to be saved, because the unregenerate will always choose against God.

Edwards also argued that an irreversible disposition of the will was consistent with praise and blame, because God was incapable of sinning, yet Christians praised him for his goodness. If someone must be able to sin, or their virtuousness is not commendable, then "Jesus Christ was very far from being praiseworthy for those acts of holiness which he performed, these propensities being so strong in his heart" (Edwards 1995, 215). Jesus was holy because that was all he wanted to be. He had no desire to sin. Likewise, unconverted humans only act selfishly and sinfully, because that is all they want to do. Praise is therefore due to the former, blame to the latter.

Other critics argued, however, that it would be unreasonable and unfair for God to impute Adam's sin to his descendants, which represented the traditional Calvinist view of the doctrine of original sin. In *Original Sin* (1758), Edwards emphasized that Adam's sin left all humanity with a disposition toward evil, instead of holiness. Edwards admitted that some unconverted persons seemed to live a reasonably moral life, but he believed their motivations were impure. Regardless of how many actual sins one observed being committed, the state of human hearts inclined toward sin. Thus, sin was not just a matter of broken laws but of enslaved wills. History demonstrated, and scripture confirmed, that everyone's moral character had a "corrupt or depraved propensity" (Edwards 1995, 227). All humans found themselves in this state because Adam had sinned in the Garden of Eden and lost the ability to choose to live in obedience to God. God imputed the guilt for Adam's sin to all humanity, according to Edwards, not just because he represented all humans but also because God did not deal with humans individually with regard to sin. As a matter of fact, all humans did commit Adam's sin, because Adam and his descendants are one. This difficult argument was abandoned by most of Edwards's followers, but the idea of the human propensity toward sin remained a hallmark of Edwardseans (Holifield 2003, 144).

Edwards also focused on the potential for regenerated humanity's goodness in two treatises he completed before his death, but which were not published until 1765. In the *Dissertation Concerning the End for Which God Created the World*, Edwards argued that God had created the world for his own glory, because the universe was designed to exalt the highest excellency, that is, God. Did that make God selfish? No, Edwards argued, because God alone, far above all inferior created beings, should seek his own glory. For God to seek his own glory inevitably meant that he would express that glory in love. God created the world to communicate love to the created beings in it, just as the Godhead (Father, Son, and Spirit) had eternally demonstrated love for one another, and shown the glory of God in doing so. Although *The End for Which God Created the World* is not now one of Edwards's better-known treatises, its radically God-centered universe may better encapsulate Edwards's thought than any other writing (Marsden 2003, 460–463).

Edwards wrote *The End for Which God Created the World* alongside the better-known *Nature of True Virtue*. Moral philosophers in Anglo-America at Edwards's time were consumed with the nature of virtue, but Edwards did not believe that true virtue could be found outside of a will transformed by God. He did believe that natural virtues, like self-love, gratitude, and fidelity to conscience, served as ballast for a decent society. He thought it was a mistake, however, to conflate these secondary virtues with true virtue, which manifested itself in glorifying God. Love for humanity was a secondary good, but "true virtue must chiefly consist in love to God; the Being of beings, infinitely the greatest and best of beings" (Edwards 1995, 252). Moral philosophy was foolish to seek true virtue in people's supposedly innate moral sense, because ethical behavior that did not fundamentally seek God's glory was paltry and selfish, at best.

When Edwards was called to become the president of the College of New Jersey in 1757, he told the trustees that he had in mind two more "great works" that likely would have served as capstones for his whole theological corpus. He called these projects *A History of the Work of Redemption* ("a body of divinity in an entire new method") and *The Harmony of the Old and New Testament* (Edwards 1998, 727–728). Based on earlier writings, notes, and Edwards's own description, we may surmise that the first would have defended the view that history and theology together revealed God's glory and expressed the unfolding of intra-Trinitarian love. The second would have defended the coherence of the whole scripture as a testimony to God's sovereignty and Christ's atonement for sinners (Marsden 2003, 488). Edwards would not complete either project, however. Only weeks after arriving in Princeton, Edwards received a smallpox inoculation that was intended to give him a mild case of the disease, in order to develop immunity. Instead, however, the risky procedure resulted in a full-blown case of smallpox, to which Edwards succumbed on March 22, 1758.

Despite the undeniable power of Edwards's thought, his reputation has not always held up in scholarly or ecclesiastical circles. During the late eighteenth century and early nineteenth century, generations of his successors in New England defended and refined Edwards's theological legacy. One of Edwards's key disciples, Samuel Hopkins, developed the concept of "disinterested benevolence" as the essence of true virtue. People motivated by disinterested benevolence would act on behalf of the weakest and most vulnerable in society, leading some advocates of the so-called New Divinity to support the antislavery movement in ways that Edwards himself never would have countenanced (Minkema and Stout 2005).

The ideology of disinterested benevolence also helped fuel the nineteenth-century missions movement. Edwards's primary contribution to the history of missions (despite his tenure in Stockbridge) came through his *Life of David Brainerd* (1749), which in the nineteenth century became the most popular and frequently reprinted of all his works. The saintly Brainerd that Edwards depicted gave up everything to go as a missionary among New Jersey's Native Americans, ignoring the progressive decline of his health from tuberculosis. Brainerd's self-denial, evangelistic activism, and relentless quest for greater holiness inspired legions of Americans and Britons who answered the call to go to the ends of the earth as missionaries

(Conforti 1995, 63). It was not uncommon to hear of missionaries whose personal libraries in the field included only the Bible and Edwards's *Life of Brainerd*. In 1836, H. H. Spalding, a missionary to the American West, gave a copy to a mountain man, who liked *Life of Brainerd* so well that when another mountain man offered him ten dollars for it, he refused the offer, saying he "would not sell it for 2 hundred" (Spalding and Whitman 1936, 120).

Despite Edwards's growing influence in some nineteenth-century contexts, his Calvinist theology began to fall out of favor by the mid–nineteenth century, especially in New England, where he was once so revered. In the early twentieth century, Progressive historians deplored Edwards's thought, seeing him as a tragic genius, or worse. But by the mid–twentieth century, signs of a major scholarly recovery of Edwards began to appear, highlighted by the inspired but often erroneous intellectual biography of Edwards by Perry Miller in 1949. The atheist Miller, sobered by the rise of totalitarianism, the horrors of war, and the use of the atomic bomb, saw Edwards as a brilliant neo-orthodox critic of human pretension and folly, who as a teenage savant grasped all the implications of, and problems with, dawning modernity. Miller also helped start Yale University Press's monumental Works of Jonathan Edwards series, which after fifty years is nearing completion in print, and which recently has spawned the new Jonathan Edwards Center at Yale University.

Scholarly interest in Edwards reached a near-deafening crescendo in 2003, the 300th anniversary of Edwards's birth. That year saw major academic and churchly conferences devoted to Edwards and the publication of George Marsden's definitive biography, *Jonathan Edwards: A Life*. Marsden tried explicitly in the book to "bridge the gap between the Edwards of the students of American culture and the Edwards of the theologians" (Marsden 2003, 502). Whereas Miller and similar historians had admired Edwards but not shared his theological commitments, Marsden and other evangelical historians have recommended Edwards's thought while also painting him as a flawed man of his time. Marsden believed Edwards's view of the God-centered universe was still worthy of consideration, even by skeptical academics.

For Marsden, Edwards's Calvinist theology provided a realistic and compelling account of the human condition before God. A more recent biography by Philip Gura suggests, however, that it has not been Edwards's Calvinism but his evangelical piety that has made him such a hero among many American believers. "Except for a small number of cognoscenti," wrote Gura, it was not Edwards's abstract theology that achieved his fame. Instead, Edwards's views and descriptions of "personal religious experience" keyed his enduring popularity (Gura 2005, 229). No wonder, then, that Edwards's most popular texts have been those that depicted the spiritual lives of ideal figures such as David Brainerd, or the emotional effects of revival, like *Religious Affections* and *A Faithful Narrative*.

Gura's view of Edwards's popularity seems quite plausible. Although evangelicalism largely embraced Calvinism at its outset, in no small part because of Edwards's influence, in its populist forms it largely abandoned Calvinism by the time of the Civil War. Recent efforts to recover Edwards and the Calvinist legacy within American evangelicalism have only begun to chip away at the dominance of popular Arminianism. But the idea of the heart transformed by God's grace has remained an essential element, even to the present, within the seemingly endless varieties of charismatic and evangelical Christianity across the world. For these hosts of believers, Edwards's insights on piety, religious emotion, and revival often serve as guidelines (sometimes unknowingly) for their own experiences. Many low-church, anti-intellectual, individualistic, and even Pentecostal believers have lately found a friend in Edwards. One example may suffice: Guy Chevreau's *Catch the Fire* (1995), a defense of the so-called Toronto Blessing, one of the most remarkable outbreaks of charismatic revival in recent decades, spends much of its text adapting Edwards's lessons in *Religious Affections* to the Toronto Airport Fellowship's "holy laughter" and other signs and wonders.

Many scholars of Edwards, or Reformed theological devotees, might cringe at this use (or abuse) of their great master, but in order to understand Edwards fully we must comprehend him as a figure of enormous intellectual power who served the cause of evangelical heart religion. Edwards believed that a person with mistaken theology—one, for instance, who believed in human free will—could not respond with proper affections toward God, for he would not accept God in all his stark, frightening reality. Only if a person properly apprehended the dire straits of sinful humanity before a holy, sovereign God could one also fully delight in grace from that same God. "True religion consists in holy affections" was probably the most influential idea of his career. Those affections were not for the elite and booklearned alone but were a gift to all those who embraced the truth about God in hearts transformed through grace. Everyone from the king to the slave might experience this kind of divine agency. These concepts stand among the chief reasons that Edwards remains popular among such a wide variety of scholars and religious groups. Rarely has such a celebrated intellectual endorsed such a leveling, heart-oriented, or God-centered creed.

REFERENCES

Chauncy, Charles. 1743. *Seasonable Thoughts on the State of Religion in New-England: A Treatise in Five Parts.* Boston: Rogers and Fowle, for Samuel Eliot.

Conforti, Joseph A. 1995. *Jonathan Edwards, Religious Tradition, and American Culture.* Chapel Hill: University of North Carolina Press.

Crawford, Michael. 1991. *Seasons of Grace: Colonial New England's Revival Tradition in Its British Context.* New York: Oxford University Press.

Davies, Samuel. 1757. *Letters from the Rev. Samuel Davies.* 2nd ed. London: R. Pardon.

Demos, John. 1994. *The Unredeemed Captive: A Family Story from Early America.* New York: Knopf.

186 DEVOTIONAL LITERATURE

Edwards, Jonathan. 1972. *The Great Awakening: A Faithful Narrative; The Distinguishing Marks; Some Thoughts Concerning the Revival; Letters Relating to the Revival,* edited by C. C. Goen. New Haven, CT: Yale University Press.

———. 1995. *A Jonathan Edwards Reader,* edited by John E. Smith, Harry S. Stout, and Kenneth Minkema. New Haven, CT: Yale University Press.

———. 1998. *Letters and Personal Writings,* edited by George S. Claghorn. New Haven, CT: Yale University Press.

———. 1999. *The Sermons of Jonathan Edwards: A Reader,* edited by Wilson Kimnach, Kenneth Minkema, and Douglas Sweeney. New Haven, CT: Yale University Press.

———. 2003. *Sermons and Discourses, 1739–1742,* edited by Harry S. Stout, Nathan O. Hatch, and Kyle P. Farley. New Haven, CT: Yale University Press.

Gura, Philip F. 2005. *Jonathan Edwards: America's Evangelical.* New York: Hill and Wang.

Holifield, E. Brooks. 2003. *Theology in America: Christian Thought from the Age of the Puritans to the Civil War.* New Haven, CT: Yale University Press.

Kidd, Thomas S. 2004. *The Protestant Interest: New England after Puritanism.* New Haven, CT: Yale University Press.

———. 2007. *Awakenings: The First Generation of American Evangelical Christianity.* New Haven, CT: Yale University Press.

Lambert, Frank. 1994. *"Pedlar in Divinity": George Whitefield and the Transatlantic Revivals.* Princeton, NJ: Princeton University Press.

Marsden, George M. 2003. *Jonathan Edwards: A Life.* New Haven, CT: Yale University Press.

Minkema, Kenneth P., and Harry S. Stout. 2005. The Edwardsean Tradition and the Anti-slavery Debate, 1740–1865. *Journal of American History* 92: 47–74.

[Rand, William.] 1743. *The Late Religious Commotions in New-England Considered: An Answer to the Reverend Mr. Jonathan Edwards's Sermon, Entitled, The Distinguishing Marks of a Work of the Spirit of God.* Boston: Green, Bushell, and Allen, for T. Fleet.

Schafer, Thomas A. 1963. Solomon Stoddard and the Theology of the Revival. In *A Miscellany of American Christianity: Essays in Honor of H. Shelton Smith,* edited by Stuart C. Henry, 328–361. Durham, NC: Duke University Press.

Spalding, H. H., and Marcus Whitman. 1936. Spalding and Whitman Letters, 1837. *Oregon Historical Quarterly* 37: 111–129.

Stoddard, Solomon. 1687. *The Safety of Appearing at the Day of Judgment: In the Righteousness of Christ, Opened and Applied.* Boston: Samuel Green, for Samuel Phillips.

———. 1709. *An Appeal to the Learned: Being a Vindication of the Right of Visible Saints to the Lord's Supper.* Boston: B. Green.

Stout, Harry S. 1991. *The Divine Dramatist: George Whitefield and the Rise of Modern Evangelicalism.* Grand Rapids, MI: Eerdmans.

Wheeler, Rachel. 2003. "Friends to Your Souls": Jonathan Edwards' Indian Pastorate and the Doctrine of Original Sin. *Church History* 72: 736–765.

Winiarski, Douglas. 2005. Jonathan Edwards, Enthusiast? Radical Revivalism and the Great Awakening in the Connecticut Valley. *Church History* 74: 683–739.

PART III

THE AUGUSTAN AGE
IN AMERICA

CHAPTER 8

AUGUSTAN AMERICAN VERSE

CHRIS BEYERS

The narrator of Henry Brooke's *The New Metamorphosis* remarks that Michy, the poem's hero, is off to "Antigua, Jamaica / Barbado's, Bermude, or the Lands of Tobacco," as if these places were interchangeable, but Michy discovers the perils of ignoring local conditions when he loses his entire investment. Brooke's spirited work is one of numerous poems written from about 1700 to around 1770 by poets who considered themselves loyal British citizens living in the colonies. However, "the colonies" is a term somebody living in England might have used. The colonists themselves usually identified with a specific colony. For example, the title page of Ebenezer Cook's *Sotweed Redivivus,* playing off the common subtitle of almanacs, says the poem is "calculated to the meridian of Maryland." And Richard Lewis set his greatest poem on the road between Patapsco and Annapolis. The Schuykill Swains (Thomas Godfrey, Nathaniel Evans, Francis Hopkinson, and others) locate their meditations next to the river with that name.

POETRY AS PERFORMANCE

Colonial Augustan poets sought to produce "polite" verse and participate in what they considered the great tradition of British belles lettres. Colonial poets often said they were imitating Alexander Pope, Virgil, and Horace. Joseph Addison, John Dryden, and John Milton were also frequently mentioned. A reader acquainted with James Thomson, Abraham Cowley, Samuel Butler, and John Pomfret's "The Choice" will find much familiar in colonial poetry—so much so that later critics have often complained that colonial verse is derivative. Consider the opening to Robert Bolling's "To Miss Nancy Blair of Williamsburg in Virginia":

> Say, why like a little fawn
> Bounding o'er the dewy lawn
> Seeking where its dam hath stray'd
> Dost thou fly me, little maid?
> (Bolling 1764a, 92)

Since nothing in these lines (or subsequently in the poem) is peculiarly American, poems such as this have often been dismissed as unoriginal. The poem could have as easily been written in London as in Williamsburg—but that was exactly the point. Bolling wanted to fit in with British poets, and his many publications in Great Britain confirm his success on his own terms. Moreover, time and again, poets asserted their writing adhered to the principles of an "approved Judge," as Lewis puts it in the preface to *The Mouse-Trap,* his translation of Edward Holdsworth's *Muscipula.* For this reason, translation and imitation held a very high place on both sides of the Atlantic. Alexander Pope's fortune was made not from *An Essay on Man* or *The Rape of the Lock* but from his translations of Homer, and James Thomson was called the English Virgil for *The Seasons.* The first belletristic work published in Maryland was *The Mouse-Trap.* Lewis calls his work a "Performance," and the text appears with the Latin original and Lewis's English rendition on facing pages, so the reader could judge the performance (Lewis 1728, 63–64). Similarly, Bolling's imitation of Horace prints numbers in the margins corresponding to numbered sections of its model, while Thomas Cradock's *Maryland Eclogues* are glossed with passages from Virgil (Bolling 1762; Cradock 1983). The many verse paraphrases of psalms published in magazines and newspapers have this aspect of performance, as their writers surely believed readers familiar with the original.

Poetry as performance implies an audience, conceiving writing as a social act appropriate to the intercourse of everyday life. Elizabeth Fergusson inscribed a poem on a fan and sent it to her friend Juliana Ritchie, as well as Ritchie's witty reply (Stabile 2004). Sarah Kemble Knight did not think it improper to intersperse short lyrics in her prose travel narrative. Cook argued economic policy in *Sotweed Redivivus,* and William Smith's proposal to the New York House of Representatives, *Some Thoughts on Education* (1752), concludes with a lengthy poem.

Whatever the audience, virtually every colonial Augustan thought that, in the words of Joseph Breitnall, poetry's function was to "gladden and instruct the World" (Rose 1740, 12). In *The Sugar-Cane,* James Grainger asserts that "instructing the reader" is the "nobler end of all poetry" (Grainger 1764, 2). Poetry's didactic function is also asserted when Cook likens *Sotweed Redivivus* to a hornbook. Martha Brewster claimed that she "had but a single Aim / My Self and nearest Friends to Entertain," but this was not the case even for her own collection, which includes such instructive poems as "An Essay on the Four Ages of Man" and "On the Last Judgment" (Brewster 1758).

Conversely, Mather Byles's encomium to Milton, "Written in *Paradise Lost,*" does not stress instruction:

> Now Hell is open'd, and I see the Flames
> Wide-waving, blazing high, and flutt'ring dance:
> Now clanking Chains amaze my listn'ing Ears,
> And hideous Spectres skim before my Sight
> Or in my wild Imagination Stare.
> (Byles 1744, 26)

One might think a Congregational minister and grandson of Increase Mather would address the epic's doctrinal aspects (such as its Arianism), but Byles stresses the aesthetic and affective, as does Nathaniel Evans in his definition of true poetry:

> There is a pleasing *Je ne scay quoi* in the productions of *poetic* genius, which is easier felt than described. It is the *voice of nature* in the *Poet,* operating like a charm on the soul of the reader. It is the *marvellous conception,* the noble *wildness,* the *lofty sentiment,* the *fire* and *enthusiasm* of spirit, the *living imagery,* the *exquisite choice of word,* the *variety,* the *sweetness,* the *majesty* of numbers, and irresistable *magic* of *expression.* (Evans 1772, VII)

Evans's enthusiasm strongly suggests the influence of Longinus. Distant though this is from a Popean emphasis on wit and reason, it shares with the poetics of that influential Augustan a central tenet: originality is not an important criterion for judging poetry. In fact, even Byles and Evans believed that poetry ought to say "what oft was *Thought,* but ne'er so well *Exprest,*" as Pope expressed it in *An Essay on Criticism.*

Augustan poets thus found themselves in a bind: they were to instruct, yet they were to tell readers what they already knew. John Parke's introduction to *Lyric Works of Horace* quotes Addison's remarks on Pope to elaborate this notion: "As for those [precepts] which are the *most known,* and the most *received,* they are placed in so beautiful a light, and illustrated with such apt allusions that they have in them all the graces of *novelty;* and make the reader, who was *before* acquainted with them, still more convinced of their truth and solidity" (Parke 1786, XVIII). Those poets who claimed originality tended to say that they were applying what was already known to a new place. Grainger explained that the "novelty" of his poem on the subject of cultivating sugarcane would "enrich poetry with many new and picturesque images" but adds, "the general precepts are suited to every climate" (Grainger 1764, 1).

Similarly, Cook's calculating his satires to Maryland's meridian implies universal principles locally applied.

Though some had delved into Longinus and expected to be amazed, typically Augustan readers delighted in predictability. Most agreed with Samuel Johnson that poetry's "great pleasure" stems from "the known measure of the lines and the uniform structure of the stanzas, by which the voice is regularized and the memory relieved" (Johnson 1925, 47). The "sweetest Numbers," Jane Colman Turell wrote in her verse tribute, "On the Incomparable Mr. Waller," come from the "justest Standard of our English Verse" (Turell 1735, 83). In other words, readers took pleasure in recognizing what they read. Social performance, then, meant satisfying an audience's expectations and comporting oneself in a pleasing way in print.

The reader, time and again, was thought to sit in judgment. In *Some Critical Observations upon a Late Poem, Entituled, The Breeches,* William Smith professed to be surprised that the author allowed his name to appear: "I could scarce have believed any Man so foolishly ambitious, as to imagine he could recommend himself to the Publick by so mean a Performance" (Smith 1750, 5). William Dawson's preface to *Poems on Several Occasions* concludes with these words: "It is therefore my sincere Request to the candid Reader, that he will peruse the following Poems with the utmost Strictness and Severity; and if he finds them unworthy of his Approbation, the Author takes this Opportunity of being the first in giving his Vote, that he never hereafter publish any more" (Dawson 1920, iv).

How much of this is merely conventional modesty and how much a real fear of negative opinion is hard to reckon. Still, colonial writers often acknowledged that they felt the burden of living up to the standards of British high culture. Poems in the *translatio studii* genre project a *future* glory for the colonies; even the poems that depict Britain as a fading kingdom took for granted the glory of Britain's not-so-distant past. The difference between the colonies and the mother country is the foundation of the satire in Cook's *Sot-weed Factor* (1708) and an engine that drives nearly every work on local themes.

Poets often commented on the poverty of their surroundings. The speaker of Bolling's "To My Flute" spoke for many when he said he felt "exil'd" in a "solitude / Dull seat of boors and planters rude" (Bolling 1764b, 101–102). George Webb's celebration of genteel culture in *Batchelors-Hall* is prefaced with the comment "every rude essay towards wit and politeness ought to be encouraged in so young a country as ours" (Webb 1731, 4). A shepherd in Nathaniel Evans's "Daphnis and Menalcas" worries that poets in the colonies will "ne'er feel the muse's fire": "O Pennsylvania!" he continues, "shall no son of thine / Glow with the raptures of the sacred nine?" (Evans 1772, 1). No doubt Evans's performance is supposed to dispel these fears, but while a London poet might fear that he or she lacks the poetic impulse, that same poet would never say it may not be available on English soil. Even poets asserting that the colonies were a fine place for the arts felt the sting of negative assumptions from across the Atlantic. In *Some Critical Observations,* for example, William Smith complains that "the unhappy Prepossession of some *Europeans*" was that "all *Americans* are Fools, or little better" (Smith 1750, 5).

Like their European contemporaries, Augustan poets in the colonies believed the "polish'd Arts" could help control "wild Passions" and "humanize the Soul," as James Sterling asserts in the prologue to *The Tragedy of the Orphan and Lethe* (Sterling 1760a). Writers like Sterling and Lewis wrote works that model politeness with the aim of creating high culture and improving moral development. Lawrence E. Klein has pointed out the political implications of Shaftesbury's gentlemanly calls for politeness, but Shaftesbury's full name and title—Anthony Ashley Cooper, Third Earl of Shaftesbury, Baron Cooper of Pawlett, Baron Ashley of Wimborne St. Giles, helps demonstrate that gentility was within the pale of existing class system (Klein 1994).

Alternatively, Cradock's *Eclogues* depicts a much more mobile society:

> Our haughty Lord, tho' now so wondrous great
> Once on Tobacco, and on Hogs did wait:
> First toil'd like me, was next an Overseer;
> So by Degrees grew what you've found him here.
> (Cradock 1983, 151)

Still, such a person was likely to have European prejudices. One of the card-playing women in *Sot-weed Factor* says to the other,

> D———m you, says one, tho' now so brave,
> I knew you late a Four-Years Slave;
> What if Planters Wife you go,
> Nature design'd you for the Hoe.
> (Mulford 2002, 570)

Four years was a typical term of indenture. Likewise, an unsigned poem in the *Maryland Gazette* entitled "The Tale of the T[ur]d" narrates the tale of a baker who tries to make excrement palatable. But no matter how he dresses it, it still stinks. The moral, says the author, is that "all the Power of Art or Education" will not "intirely wash away the Dirt of the Journey-Man's palm." As a matter of fact, relatively few eighteenth-century American poets did not have dirty palms in their immediate ancestry. Thus, colonial Augustan poetry provides the drama of writers attempting to take paradigms of gentility and culture that emerged from one society and transplant them in a very different society. Shaftesbury jockeyed for the rights of a class that already had considerable privilege. The colonies, on the other hand, featured "gentlemen" without an estate and centuries of breeding assuming those same rights.

Devoted to reproducing British high culture, colonial Augustan poets often wrote verse that, to a twenty-first-century eye, seems to offer glimpses of the "authentic" awash in a sea of convention. Modern readers may prefer these lines from

Annis Boudinot Stockton, describing her vigil watching over her husband during his fatal illness—

> While through the silence of this gloomy night,
> My aching heart reverb'rates every groan;
> And watching by that glimmering taper's light,
> I make each sigh, each mortal pang my own.

—which feel heartfelt, over the consolation with which the poem ends—

> Yes, the Redeemer comes to wipe the tears,
> The briny tears, from every weeping eye.
> And death and sin, and doubts, and gloomy fears,
> Shall all be loss in endless victory.
> (Stockton 1995, 101)

—which feels merely conventional. Similarly, we can be pardoned for admiring the intense longing and loneliness of Brewster's "A Letter to My Daughter, Ruby Bliss"—in which the speaker expresses grief over her daughter's leaving home—more than its advice on pleasing subservience. But as we experience these feelings, we should be aware that the writers would insist that our priorities are backward, and that their religious and domestic pieties are no less heartfelt than the expression of strong emotion.

Moreover, as John Markland's *Typographia* makes clear, sometimes the poet's view of himself as performer overshadows anything said. *Typographia,* a poem celebrating the introduction of printing in Virginia, invokes Pindar and his "fiery-footed steeds impatient of the Rein" (Markland 1730, 6). This allusion and the rhyming lines of irregular length show the influence of Cowley's *Pindarique Odes* (1688).

The ode eventually turns to praising William Gooch, saying of Virginia's lieutenant governor that "His calm, yet awful Look / Majestic, yet serene / The very Pow'r of Prejudice remov'd" so that "Ev'n Party-Rancour dy'd away, / And private spleen"; in fact, all "Factions end, and Murmurs cease" (Markland 1730, 9–10). While Gooch seems to have done a good job placating differing interests, he did not actually end *all* factions, prejudice, and spleen. Two years later, he would pen a pamphlet supporting his tobacco purity act, aimed at planters who burned tobacco in protest and refused to follow the law.

There is a sense that even Markland feels he went overboard. "I have said nothing herein," he says in the preface, "which, I am confident, will not be readily asserted to, by all who have the Happiness to live under the present Administration, in this Colony." But then he qualifies:

Unless, perhaps, this Exception be taken, that where a disinterested and unprejudic'd Patriotism (for I will not be asham'd of the Word) of a Governor to his People, and a reciprocal Affection and Obedience of them to Him is to be describ'd, the Author of this Piece may have wanted a Scale of Thought and Comprehension equal to the Heights of the Merits of the One, or the cordial Duty of the other; and that on such a Subject it were better to be silent, than to say too little. (Markland 1730, iii–iv)

Well, if there are those who take exception to Markland's claim that Gooch removed all spleen, then that would seriously undermine that claim, would it not? But such an analysis misreads the poem. To understand *Typographia* (and much of Augustan colonial poetry), we have to remember that Markland understood himself on a social stage. His narrator performs two things: first, the Cowleyan Pindarique ode; second, patriotism. The Pindarique, generally understood as hyperbolic, demands that the subject be the highest, and thus the governor must be ideal. Markland felt his role as a patriot likewise demanded unqualified praise.

TRANSCENDENT VALUES AND CONTRACTARIAN LOGIC

David Shields suggests dividing Augustan colonial poetry into two camps: men of wit and men of sense. Colonial poets can also be divided into those poets who supported the "court" party (royal and proprietary interests) and those who supported the "country" party (merchants, lower houses of state legislatures, and others who felt the court hindered their interests); those writing for a specific coterie and those seeking wider publication; and so on. Perhaps the most salient difference is between those works that extol transcendent values versus those that explore contractarian logic.

Typographia provides a convenient starting point:

> ... with contending Zeal
> The *Prince* and *People* strive,
> The *Prince* to make his *People* thrive,
> Their Grievances to heal;
> And all their good and adverse Fortune shares;
> *They* in Return to *Him,*
> Pay mutual Rev'rence and Esteem,
> And all his Pow'r, his Honour, Happiness, is theirs.
> (Markland 1730, 7)

Although the mutuality between ruler and ruled may seem like a contract, Markland's rhetoric suggests that he is thinking along the lines of the Great Chain of Being, a network of relationships that parallel each other in type but not in scope: God is to the universe as the king is to the empire, as the lord is to his men, as the father is to the family. Everyone serves the other out of a sense of duty and love. Providence guarantees the system. Such a concept sanctions existing social and political relations, since they are created by God and mirror his ways.

A contractarian like Cook might ask, "Yes, but where is the surety?" There is in Markland's idea no earthly system of penalties to redress a breach of faith, and, to a committed contractarian, only a fable of balanced interests. The system functions only in an ideal world of selfless labor. Contractarian logic assumes that everybody is out to make the best deal for themselves even if it is at the expense of their trading partners. In fact, the possibility of betrayal underlies all contracts, and, partly for that reason, contractarian Augustan poets were often disgusted utilitarians.

The opening of Lewis's descriptive poem "A Journey from Patapsko to Maryland, April 4 1730" shows the uncomfortable fit between transcendent values and colonial conditions. The sun rises on a small plantation, where

> Safe in yon Cottage dwells the *Monarch-Swain,*
> His *Subject-Flocks,* close grazing, hide the Plain;
> For him they live—and die t'uphold his reign.
> Viands unbought his well-till'd Lands afford,
> And smiling *Plenty* waits upon his Board;
> *Health* shines with sprightly Beams around his Head,
> And *Sleep,* with downy Wings, o'er shades his Bed;
> His *Sons* robust his daily Labours share,
> Patient of Toil, Companions in his Care
> (Lewis 1988, 561)

Critics have praised the poem for its portrayal of the Maryland landscape, a claim bolstered by contemporary comment on the poem. Edward Kimber calls Lewis's description "just and fine" (Kimber 1998, 52). When the poem appeared in the *Pennsylvania Gazette,* it was prefaced with the assertion that the "Picture" the poem presents "would suffer no disadvantage by an immediate comparison with the Original." However, these writers only praise Lewis for his beautiful natural description. Kimber's *Itinerant Observations in America,* in contrast, addresses issues like the different rates of exchange in the colonies and, in fact, does a better job than Lewis of describing real conditions.

A literalist Maryland reader of 1730 would surely ask, "If this is supposed to be a real plantation, where is the tobacco? Where are the slaves, overseers, and indentured servants?" By the 1730s Maryland was in the midst of a fundamental economic and social shift. The low price of tobacco and the large-scale importation of slaves transformed a rather atomic society based on smaller plantations to a more centralized one of large plantations. Because tobacco is a labor- and land-intensive crop, only large landholders could take advantage of economies of scale. While indentured servants were cheaper than slaves, their terms of indenture were up after a set number of years, whereas slaves—and all their children—were owned for perpetuity. Further, tobacco exhausted the soil, so tobacco fields had to be rotated and large tracts of land lie fallow. Finally, the price of tobacco fluctuated but was generally low. In order to make a significant profit, a planter had to sell a lot of tobacco. All these factors produced an economic logic of larger plantations worked by slaves; smaller family farms like the one described in Lewis's poem were constantly in danger of failure.

Lewis's ideal plantation is subject to none of these strains. It is self-sufficient with "unbought" viands and does not have to worry about market fluctuations: its inhabitants do not appear to buy or sell. It produces wool and venison, useful products, instead of the stinking weed. Further, it is presided over by a "Monarch-Swain" and his willing servants who all follow the rules of self-sacrifice and obligation outlined by Markland. The sons dutifully share the father's toil.

In the colonies, there was an endemic problem of labor, since a great deal of work was performed by slaves and indentured servants. With no remuneration, slaves had incentive only to work enough to escape punishment. Indentured servants, too, had little motivation. Although terms of indenture varied, typically servants had already received the lion's share of their payment (transportation to the colonies). After their term, they might receive a new shirt, a pair of shoes, and a nominal payment or some acres of land. Small wonder, then, that the main advertisers in colonial newspapers were large landholders placing notices about escaped slaves and servants.

Thus, there was an unfortunate dynamic of employers trying to extract as much work as possible out of laborers who had little motivation to work. This comedy is well within the ken of contractarian writers like Cook and Bolling, but against the nature of transcendentalists like Lewis. Lewis dealt with the problem of labor by positing a farm very unlike the majority of farms in the colony and placing it outside the economic system. In this ideal landscape, even the sheep willingly give their lives for their monarch, just as in Lewis's poem extolling the social good of shipbuilding, "To Mr. Samuel Hastings," envisions the trees taking "Pleasure" in giving up their place in the forest in order to "fly to distant Lands o'er deepest Floods" (Lewis 1730). By making commodities free agents happily participating in an economy that literally destroys them, Lewis erases the laborers who cut down the trees and the farmhands who slaughter the sheep.

The labor problem taxed the ingenuity of poets writing colonial georgics, provoking, for example, grammatical convulsions in Charles Woodmason's "The Indico" (1757). This is how he describes chopping down trees: "Arm'd with destructive Steel thy Negroes bring / With Blows repeated let the Woodlands ring" (Mulford 2002, 500). The mood here is imperative, as the speaker instructs a planter on preparing to plant indigo. Untangled, the sentence says, "Have your Negroes bring destructive steel so that the woods ring with its repeated blows." Unlike Lewis, who turns commodities to agents, Woodmason turns agents to commodities, as the lines literally portray slave labor as the planter's passive tool. The steel does the real work; the slaves just bring it to the woods. Poetic license thus effaces the entanglements of self-interest typical of human society.

More typically, poets fell back on the Great Chain of Being. Sterling's "Verses Occasioned by the Success of the British Arms in the Year 1759," for instance, openly acknowledges what Lewis and Woodmason elide:

> The *Planter* there amidst his swarthy Slaves,
> Proscribes the Ground where yet the Forest waves;
> The Slaves obedient to their new Lord's decree,
> The keen edg'd ax apply to ev'ry Tree . . .
> (Sterling 1760b)

The key word in the passage is "Lord," which suggests feudal and religious sub-servience. As the poem progresses, the speaker worries about the trees' "Groans" and not the conditions of the slaves' obedience; it is all justified in the end, though, when order is brought to the wilderness. As the planter surveys his plantation, "all in chearful Plenty smile": everyone benefits from attending to the planter's cares.

Similarly, Cradock's tenth eclogue concerns Worthy, a jilted planter. Seeing the master brooding over lost love, everyone on the plantation likewise broods: "His faithful Overseer his Task forgets/And every Slave at his misfortune frets." This empathy seems odd when considering the predatory master-slave relationship indicated later in the poem, when Worthy wishes he had been born an overseer so that he could have assuaged his hurt feelings with a "Convict-Girl" or "Black *Bess*," even though he admits he finds that latter's appearance "hideous" (Cradock 1983, 199).

Nowhere is the labor problem more manifest than in book 4 of Grainger's *The Sugar-Cane*, which deals with slavery. The book begins by giving advice for how to choose the best slaves (for instance, it counsels that slaves from certain parts of Africa will commit suicide rather than accept servility) and how to accustom them to hard work. It then addresses the slaves directly, asking them to compare their relatively healthy toil to the lot of Scottish miners. Such an imprecation can only act as apostrophe, of course, since slaves were denied education. Grainger is trying to argue his way out of an obvious discrepancy—if people prefer death to labor, then the transcendent contention that all benefit seems ridiculous. Grainger would have the slaves think like Lewis's trees and sheep, willingly giving their lives to a system bent on destroying them.

HENRY BROOKE'S *THE NEW METAMORPHOSIS*

Henry Brooke's *The New Metamorphosis* (1702) depicts the collision between transcendence and contract in a particularly telling way. Shields calls the work

Hudibrastic, and certainly the poem, like *Hudibras,* is a mock epic that mixes noble diction and ribald action. However, instead of Butler's racy iambic tetrameter, Brooke uses anapestic tetrameter with frequent iambic substitution in the first foot. As a result, the poem unfolds with all the dignity of that other poem in the same meter—the nursery rhyme about the old woman living in a shoe. *Metamorphosis* has a balladic air, a reduction and inversion of Homer's dactylic hexameter. However, Brooke's target is not Homer but the characters' failure to maintain transcendent values.

The poem's endnote explains that a young merchant went to the New World to make a fortune by trading but "carried nothing home with him, but a bald Eagle," and then invented the story to explain how he had lost everything (Shields 1988, 24). The poem begins by describing the young man's parents. True epic heroes have divine ancestors and legendary hometowns; Peltander and Membrana live in Southwark (notorious for its prostitution, jail, and asylum), ironically described as famous for "eminent Schools / Of faith and good pay the Kingsbench and the Rules." Peltander excels in the "liberal Arts / Of scraping and saving." Lest any reader take this to mean he is merely careful with money, the narrator later calls Peltander a "Miser" (Shields 1988, 20–23).

Every night Peltander throws himself on a bed of straw and the "fleabitten breast" of his consort, whose name puns off "member," which can mean penis. As a result of "tumbling together and heaven knows what"—actions true epics omit—Michy, the poem's hero, is born. Brooke means to emphasize that Michy is the offspring of the spirits of penny-pinching and lust. His name is a further irony. Shields says it is a nickname for Michael, though probably Brooke wants his readers to compare the biblical prophet Micah, who blames troubles on a "harlot," uses the bald eagle as an image, and rails against false merchants, faithlessness, and untrustworthy sons.

After Michy grows up, Peltander and nineteen of his kinsmen "pawn'd all to the skin" raise twenty pounds, which they give to Michy to invest. After "dropping some tear for his gold, or his Son," Peltander sends him off to buy tobacco cheaply in the colonies and sell for a profit elsewhere. Michy squanders his money on the eagle, a cheap horse, and dissipation. To cover his tracks, he claims that, after he made his money, he got drunk, visited a prostitute, and refused to pay her. She complained to Venus, who converted Michy's tobacco to an eagle (Shields 1988, 21–23).

It is hard to see how this tale, even if it were believable, could restore Michy's reputation. The story, indeed, is more reflective of the contractarian logic that Brooke associates with the colonies. Michy is called on to be a factor, a middleman who does not, himself, produce anything. In fact, the narrator tells us that to raise capital, Peltander and his family acted as middlemen to their own possessions, for pawning only sells what has already been sold and produces nothing new. Peltander and his nineteen relatives hope to make money by taking advantage of the different exchange rates in the British Empire's economic sphere.

When he arrives in the colonies, Michy reverts to type, following his lusts and pinching pennies. His dealings with the prostitute exemplify contractarianism:

> A Minion of Venus presents in his way,
> And Michy was frail, and consented to stray.
> The time and the place and the sum were agreed,
> And my Gallant had all his affections cou'd need;
> But his Mistress (poor heart) for demanding her pay,
> Was dismis'd with a kick, and my Spark slunk way
> (Shields 1988, 23)

Because the poem does not consider the real state of prostitution—where women are forced into the trade through poverty, addiction, and abuse—it can conceive of prostitution as a contract, whereby a woman rents out her body for a price. The passage's irony comes from blending the rhetoric of contract with that of romantic courting. And this is precisely the rhetoric of prostitution. Any male who has ever found himself in the wrong section of town in the evening can attest to the fact that prostitutes do not say, "I will endure your sexual advances for money, you disgusting pig"; instead, they say something like, "Hey, good looking! Want to be my boyfriend?" The john pretends to believe that the prostitute is attracted, and she pretends to enjoy his attentions. This false sympathy is also at work in more socially respectable selling, especially among those salesmen working for commission. It is a fiction that everyone engages in but no one believes.

When Michy breaks his contract with the prostitute, he loses the fruits of his other contract. Of course, Michy's broken contract with Venus's minion is a fiction; his real act of faithlessness is as steward of the money of his father and nineteen kinsmen. It might seem that the piece's moral is to fulfill your contracts, yet Brooke's note to his poem calls it a "Fable without a Moral" (Shields 1988, 24). The poem is without a moral because Brooke does not believe there should be contracts at all. To see this more clearly, it helps to state plainly what the poem ironically portrays. A father should fear for his son's safety as he watches him leave for a long and potentially perilous venture, but Peltander is at least as interested in the fate of his investment. Entrusted with capital from his relatives, a son should resist the urge to squander it. If he seeks female companionship, it should be the disinterested kind based on real affection. At every juncture, characters pursue self-interest to the detriment of others. Even the relationship between Peltander and Membrana seems based on fulfilling personal desire, and the story's satire stems from the characters' lack of selfless action.

In all, *Metamorphosis* depicts a man who grows up in a world where everyone pursues self-interest but covers it up in a genteel and transparently false rhetoric. He travels to an overtly mercantile world where contracts are made plain, and when he breaks his contracts, he loses everything. These contracts are only necessary because of the debased nature of the people described. At nearly every juncture an alternative, more noble system of value would be preferable.

EBENEZER COOK

Since the narrator of Cook's *Sot-weed Factor* is unnamed, perhaps we ought to call him Michy, since his tale entirely concerns the stretch of the story Brooke disdains to tell. The poem opens with its speaker lamenting that "Fate" has "Condemn'd" him with "Friends unkind and empty Purse," forcing him to come to Maryland and trying to make his fortune by acting as a factor in the tobacco trade (Mulford 2002, 563). There are any number of reasons that a person from early eighteenth-century Britain might have an empty purse, including restrictions on his religion, economic deprivation, and unpopular political beliefs. From the evidence of the poem, it seems a fair guess that profligacy depleted the narrator's purse and presumption alienated his friends. At any rate, from the speaker's point of view, the poem opens with two broken contracts: the first, between the goodwill (and, presumably, loans or advantageous economic liaisons) one might expect from friendship; the second, between the speaker the world. The speaker assumes that the world owes him something; when he does not get it, he feels condemned.

The first time the factor sees Maryland's planters, he remarks that they have a "Hue as tawny as a Moor: / Figure so strange, no God design'd / To be a part of Humane Kind" (Mulford 2002, 564). Although Cook and his fellow Marylanders considered themselves British citizens, to the English speaker they are the Other. When he subsequently compares the planters to the kin of Cain, he inadvertently uses an argument used to justify slavery (dark skin was asserted to be the mark God put on Cain), while continuing the theme of broken contracts with the well-known biblical story of brother killing brother.

A "surley Peasant" soon asks him "from whom [he'd] run away," assuming that the factor is an escaped indentured servant. The narrator is angered that the world does not recognize his innate nobility. This comedy is repeated when the factor is told by a planter that he is welcome "whether you come from Gaol or a Colledge" (Mulford 2002, 564). The planter offers him a homely meal and lodging, which the factor accepts with bad grace; his scorn for his food is obvious to his host, who comments on it as the two share rum.

The native brew is too strong for the factor, and he goes off to bed, meeting up with "one who pass'd for a Chamber-Maid," though the factor notices her "sluttish Dress." She explains that she is an indentured servant who had come to the colonies because she was "Kidnap'd and Fool'd" and thus she "hither fled, / To shun a hated nuptial Bed." The factor supposes that she had been caught "supping e'er the Priest said Grace," that is, copulating before wedlock (Mulford 2002, 565). Cook may mean that the servant was tricked by a Lothario and disowned by her family or, perhaps, offered the choice of a disgusting husband or indentured servitude. Whatever the story, it implies broken and unfair contracts drove her to her situation. Her blushes indicate moral conscience, but our narrator no more feels pity for her plight than he feels gratitude for his free meal.

After an uncomfortable night, the factor borrows a horse and, with the planter's son for a guide, rides to Battle-Town. On the way, they argue over the origin of Native Americans. The son opines that the Native Americans are descended from the Chinese, while the factor offers the equally improbable hypothesis that they are wayward Phoenicians. The factor stops the narrative to comment that "when that both had talk'd their fill / We had the self same Notion still," and that the controversy was as irresolvable as religious debate. This discussion is then juxtaposed to raucous arguments at the country court. The lawyers' histrionics contrast with the civil discussion about race, though it is important to realize that little is at stake in the former disputation. The factor dismisses the lawyers' arguments as "nonsense, stuff and false quotation" (Mulford 2002, 568). His words pretty much describe the substance of his dispute with the planter's son. Together, the two examples show that human unreasonableness turns "reason" into a rhetorical exercise.

After court, the factor again drinks too much and looks for a place to sleep. Finding the beds at the inn taken, he happens upon an upper room used to store grain and settles into "quiet sleep" (Mulford 2002, 569). When he awakens, he discovers his shoes, hat, wig, and stockings have been stolen. The factor considers this another example of Maryland depravity, but the reader may take another message. When the factor removes himself from the hullabaloo of Battle-Town, he finds peace but also the Hobbesian truth that people band together not because they like each other but for mutual protection. The isolation that permits quiet sleep also assured the thief that he could escape undetected.

After a furious and fruitless search, the factor wakes up his host, who finds he must immediately race outside because the factor neglected to feed his borrowed horse, and "not content all Night to stay / Ty'd up from fodder, [the horse] ran away." Like the drunken merchants, the horse is simply pursuing its appetite. The factor comments that he thus lost "both Horse and Man" (Mulford 2002, 569–570). Of course, the planter's son is hardly his "man"—his manservant—at all; the factor's sense of superiority causes him to mistake generosity for subservience.

Seeing the factor's plight, another planter invites him to his house. The factor buys new clothes, goes to the house, and drinks until midnight. He sleeps until noon, wakes up to a sumptuous meal, again drinks excessively, and passes out under a tree. He wakes up at night and makes his way to the fireside, where he sees a group of women playing cards. One woman cries, "Dealing's lost is but a Flam, / And [she] vow'd by G—d she'd keep her *Pam*" (Mulford 2002, 570). Having received the most valuable card in the game, she is not about to give it up just because of a bad deal. This foreshadows the factor's later troubles and again points to the violations of contractarian logic the work satirizes. Card games are but agreements among the players about the relative values and rules, and a player insisting on keeping something valuable despite the rules is demanding a private interest impossibly against the interests of others.

The speaker wakes up the next day and goes into town to conduct his business. Finding a Quaker businessman, he trades his "*English* Truck" for "ten thousand weight / Of *Sot-weed* good and fit for freight" (Mulford 2002, 571). In doing this, he has participated in the mercantile economy, for what is "Truck" to one group may be valuable to another; tobacco, for instance, was plentiful in the Maryland but not grown in England. English mercantile economics differ from free-market capitalism, because the Board of Trade tried to ensure that the various participants did not compete by producing the same commodities. George Lillo's popular British play *The London Merchant* (1731) states the transcendent abstraction used to justify mercantilism. In the play, an idealized merchant explains that Providence has "bestowed some good peculiar to itself" in every place in the world. "It is the industrious merchant's business to collect the various blessings of each soil and climate," he argues, and to distribute the excess commodity of one country to another that does not produce it. Intercourse among nations enriches all and "promotes humanity" by "diffusing love from pole to pole" (Lillo 1731, *passim.*).

This, however, is not what the factor finds when he makes his deal. He has his commodities put aboard the Quaker's ship and waits for the tobacco to be brought to him. Unfortunately, he neglected to obtain any surety, and the Quaker sails off without delivering the tobacco. The factor made an advantageous deal without anticipating what the Quaker's interests might lead him to do. The London merchant says that he is in the cooperative endeavor of diffusing love, but the Quaker is in the competitive endeavor of maximizing profits.

Having found his goods taken from him, the factor seeks redress in a Maryland court. Although he heaps abuse upon his lawyer, he actually wins his case, only to be compensated in "Country pay": for example, "Pipe staves, corn, or Flesh of Boar," commodities plentiful in England. It is a fitting irony. Throughout, the factor asserts his own point of view without considering others; in the end, he is compensated by an agreement that only serves the other person. Disgusted, he returns to England and hurls a curse, wishing upon the colony's traders "the Fate they well deserve," which is to be "From Trade, Converse, and Happiness exil'd" (Mulford 2002, 572). In short, he wishes to banish Marylanders from participating in a Lillo-esque world that did not exist.

Thus it is that nearly every incident in *Sot-weed Factor* revolves around contractarian logic, and this is also true of Cook's other long narrative, *A History of Bacon's Rebellion in Virginia* (1731). The poem tells the story of Nathaniel Bacon's insurrection against William Berkeley, the governor of Virginia. Cook's poem casts the battle as between a "testy knight" (Berkeley) and a "waspish squire" (Bacon). Fairly early in the poem, the narrator comments, "Promises are scarce worth minding" and not "binding" when "Grounded on mental Reservation / Or made without Consideration" (Wroth 1934). Even more than *Sot-weed Factor*, *A History of Bacon's Rebellion* is a comedy of double-dealing, full of noble declamations followed by acts of duplicity, pride, and cowardice.

In the narrative, Native Americans take over a colonial fort and, besieged, send six negotiators to arrange a peace. However, Berkeley has them killed. The Native Americans reckon that ten colonial lives are equivalent to one Native American life. After they kill sixty colonists, they again attempt to negotiate, but Berkeley's court views negotiating with savages as beneath its dignity, and besides, some "for Honour or for Pay / Made Sword and Pistol their Vocation" (Wroth 1934, 312–313).

Disgusted by his government's inability to resolve the matter, Bacon raises his own force and begins a series of raids on the Native Americans. Berkeley gets him to stop partly by promising him a seat in the state legislature, only to jail Bacon when he comes to town. Bacon escapes by claiming his wife is sick, promising to return after the illness. He quickly raises forces to fight Berkeley.

Eventually, the governor sends a captain of a merchant ship, Thomas Grantham, to meet with Bacon's men (Bacon by this time has died of illness). Grantham "long had traded in the Parts / [and] Knew Planters Tempers and their Hearts" (Wroth 1934, 324). He points out that the governor summoned troops from England to help quell the insurrection; further, while everybody is fighting, crops are rotting in the fields, and this could ruin both planters and merchants. When he also promises a pardon from the governor, the insurgents relent. After everybody returns to work, many of the insurrectionists are hung. Thus, peace is possible only when everybody's self-interest is taken into consideration, and the rebels, like the factor, learn the fatal lesson that any contract needs a surety.

It is easy to see why Cook has so often been looked upon as a moralist, and certainly his poems lampoon moral failings. However, there are deep ambiguities that trouble straightforward moralist readings. For example, it seems self-evident that the factor's parting shot, that no Maryland woman is "Chast," is false, yet some of Maryland's residents would have said the claim is only slightly exaggerated. In Cradock's *Eclogues,* for example, Cut-Purse brags that he has cuckolded his overseer, and Scape-Rope says he has done the same thing to his master. Lest a reader mistake these claims for braggadocio, Cradock comments that such is "common among the lower Tribe of Planters' wives" (Cradock 1983, 165). So, when the factor meets the half-dressed woman, is her verbal modesty meant to seduce, or should we credit her story? Should we believe the allegation by one of the card players that the other is a prostitute?

It is not the case that everything Cook's unreliable narrator says is false. The narrator is sometimes mistaken, sometimes accurate, sometimes exaggerated; sometimes he makes dubious statements that echo the opinions of other people, and the truth of some of what he says is ambiguous. Brooke's Southwark engendered base people who act in ridiculous ways; it is as clear where Brooke's sympathies lie as it is in Cradock's eclogues. Brooke and Cradock give negative examples, and we can understand a better system of values simply by inverting the assertions. Cut-Purse and Scape-Rope are proud of their adultery, and they ought to be ashamed of it. But in Cook's major satires, firm ground is harder to come by, and what ought to be morally, self-importantly noble sentiments will not suffice. This tawdry world where everyone will always pursue self-interest is all we have, Cook seems to be saying, and the only way to make our way in it is by making careful contracts with sureties. If we do so, then, as in the end of *A History of Bacon's Rebellion,* everybody can get to work for prosperity's sake.

Instead of a Hobbesian view, perhaps a closer model would be that of Bernard Mandeville, whose *Grumbling Hive* (1705) and its revision and extension, *Fable of the Bees* (1714), dismiss moral injunctions, arguing that conspicuous consumption is the wheel that turns trade, however much it is spurred by luxury, vanity, and vice. The vast industry needed to satisfy moral failings consequently leads to employment, wealth, funding for the arts, and everything that makes a country great. A similar argument is made in *Sotweed Redivivus,* Cook's sequel to *Sot-weed Factor.* In the preface, Cook remarks, "It's industry, not a nauseous Weed, / Must cloath the Naked and the Hungry feed" (Steiner 1900, 36). The poem proper debates various plans to increase prosperity. Significantly, though Cook finds tobacco nauseous, he does not advocate eradicating it (though he would diversify agriculture), because he knows that people become planters to make money, not to diffuse universal love by trading healthy commodities. The poem assumes that economic planning can occur only with negotiation among the various interests, and Cook's consistent theme is how often promises are not worth minding. *Sotweed Redivivus* ends with a planter literally standing on shifting sands, looking hopefully outward as a stream rolls away from him—suggesting that nothing is certain in this world except human desires and the urge to satisfy them.

Robert Bolling's "Neanthe"

Bolling's "Neanthe" (1763) is written in the same jaunty Hudibrastic way as Cook's major poems and shares their contractarian concerns. Set in Pungoteague on the Chesapeake Bay, it begins by introducing a planter who lives solely for "lucrative

Pursuits" until his "frail Nature" leads him to pursue pleasure (Lemay 1982, 113). The poem thus ironically defines virtue as self-denial for financial gain. The narrator explains the planter's descent into pleasure was inevitable:

> Ah! Pleasure is invincible;
> Let Virtue mutter, what she will!
> Why then against her keep the Field?
> God can but damn us; tho we yield.
> (Lemay 1982, 114)

Given the pervasive irony of "Neanthe," the reader is initially encouraged to take these lines as evidence of the narrator's flawed viewpoint.

Following his desires, the planter seduces a maiden, promising that he will marry her if she becomes pregnant. When she does, she "from her Contract wou'd not flinch: / He scorn'd to be behind an Inch," and marries her one day before a baby girl, Neanthe, is born. The planter's faith in honoring the contract earns him the narrator's epithet, "The honest man of Pungoteague" (Lemay 1982, 114). As in *Metamorphosis*, there is an ironic mixing of the rhetoric of contract and that of courting.

Neanthe's parents' "rigid Industry" and "close Economy" enable them to "scrape together an Estate" and earn their neighbors' esteem due to their comparative wealth. They judge Neanthe "no small Catch." Like Michy in *Metamorphosis*, Neanthe is the product of her parents' appetite. The narrator asserts she is "Possess'd of every native Grace." She has a red, freckled face, oily black hair, a nose like a potato, bushy black eyebrows, red eyes, sharp teeth, a moustache, large breasts, and a protruding belly. She is about four feet tall and three feet around. She has two other outstanding qualities. The first is her competence with food:

> None on the shoals, like her, cou'd nab
> Or, brought to table, scoop a Crab:
> The Cockle none detect, like her,
> Or daintier Cockle-broth prefer:
> The bloated Oyster none so well
> Extort from the reluctant Shell
> (Lemay 1982, 114–115)

A child of appetite, Neanthe is particularly good at getting every last morsel of meat from shellfish, a skill those around the Chesapeake Bay pride themselves in to this day. Bolling undoubtedly knew that doing this involves a great deal of cracking, sucking, and slurping.

Neanthe's other conspicuous quality is her "divine and powerful Scent" that gives men "such keen Twitches, / They scarce contain them in their Breeches." She is quite eager to meet men under the hedgerow, quickly "compose her Haunches," and satisfy their mutual desires. She seems perpetually in heat. She tells her lovers that she "wou'd do any thing, but wed," asserting a very male control over her own sexuality. Dolon of Anacock and Euphenor of Matsapreak, on the other hand, want "to give Neanthe Chains," that is, to marry her and assume ownership of her body. (Lemay 1982, 116–117). Is it any wonder she despises marriage? As the embodiment of desire, she demands free expression.

It cannot be said that Dolon and Euphenor want to marry Neanthe so that they can copulate with her. They "freely" had their "Solace" with Neanthe. Presumably, other young men in Pungoteague also wanted Neanthe chained up for their personal pleasure, but they would be disqualified due to their social standing. Dolon and Euphenor are "Lads of Worth" who are "Blest by Fortune in Descent / In Bloom of Youth and opulent." Dolon's family has made its fortune by selling bullfrogs, while Euphenor's family plunders shipwrecks: they are the type of low gentry mentioned by Cradock. The pretension to English gentility is further mocked by the speaker's assertion that Dolon and Euphenor have an "antient Friendship," which in England might mean the two families have been friendly for centuries but in Pungoteague probably means something like a decade (Lemay 1982, 116–117).

At any rate, like Palamoun and Arcite in Chaucer's *Knight's Tale,* their similar desire for Neanthe causes their friendship to end. The two meet, and Dolon claims he has talked to a wizard who knew a method of discerning "For whom the Gods allot the prize," a kind of contest. Dolon explains their actions will be emblematic, like that of a man sticking pins in a voodoo doll:

> For tis a mode, well known of old
> Whoe'er a chard wou'd well unfold
> (To quell a foe, or Mistress win)
> He must, in Emblem, act the Scene
> To send the first across the Styx,
> He, with a pin, his Image pricks
> (Lemay 1982, 118)

This last line begins a series of sexual puns. The two men are to shoot firelocks (a kind of gun) at the moon. The discharge (the fiery emission, not the bullet) that comes closest to the moon wins:

> Against that Sister of the Sun [i.e., the moon]
> Present the Muzzle of your Gun
> If thence a greater Flame arise
> Than from between my shaggy Thighs
> (In Turn when I prepare to blaze
> Against her with my rival Rays)
> Neanthe's yours I will agree,
> Mine, otherwise, the Fate decree.
> (Lemay 1982, 119)

It is really an ejaculation contest. Since both men's attraction to Neanthe is entirely sexual, why shouldn't the most sexually capable man get the prize? It is worth noting that Neanthe is not consulted in the matter. Dolon and Euphenor treat Neanthe as a commodity and not, as she asserts, a free agent.

After Euphenor shoots, Dolon inserts a rocket in his buttocks and shoots it off, which of course goes much higher than the firelock's detonation. Euphenor is initially despondent but soon discovers the ruse. Outraged at "the Breech of Faith," he attacks Dolon (Lemay 1982, 120). Here the contractarian logic is most evident— Euphenor is willing to accede when he thinks he has lost fairly but outraged when he learns the terms of a contract are not met.

The fight is full of gouging and low blows. "You English wou'd abhor that Plight," explains the narrator, "Who strain no Tackling, gouge, or bite," but such is the practice in Pungoteague, who have had their "Manners mended" by the Irish. That is to say, colonial manners do not match those of higher British culture. The conflict is unbridled and open, so much so that Euphenor kills Dolon, appropriately enough, since it was Dolon's faithlessness that caused the dispute in the first place. When Neanthe hears the news, she begins to resemble Emelye of *The Knight's Tale,* because it turns out she had been in love with Dolon all along. His death will leave a "Gap, unfilled," a "tremendous Void." Although surely Lemay is right that her grief is filled with sexual puns, just as surely we are to see that she indeed feels something for him. She laments, "Ah, had he farted less . . . / He might his Wishes have possess'd / And I, with him, had lived most blest" (Lemay 1982, 121, 124). Unable to contemplate living without her lover, she hangs herself in despair.

This turn of events is startling, because the reader had been led to believe that Neanthe had no tie to any man. However, it suddenly becomes clear that she inherited her father's fidelity as well as his appetite. Under the conventional morality of Cook's factor, of course, sexual promiscuity is equated with faithlessness (his final curse, after all, yokes these two); however, under contractarian logic, the two are reconcilable, since she never promised constancy to her lovers. Her Dido-like death in effect proves that she is the factor of her own body and not the commodity of others.

The poem concludes with a strange elegy to Neanthe that praises her beauty, wit, eyes, singing ability, and wisdom; she is a "Maid" as never seen before but in Greece (Lemay 1982, 126). Ironies attend the praise: she dances like a "Paphian queen," an epithet of Aphrodite that often implies illicit sexuality; her "Syren's Throat" also suggests sexuality, and the comparison to Helen is equally ambiguous—is Helen the innocent victim she portrays herself as in the *Iliad* or the scheming harlot of the misogynist tradition?

All these are typical Hudibrastic ironies. What is truly odd is that very little in the elegy has anything to do with Neanthe. Readers had not been given any evidence of her wit (or lack of it), her dancing, her singing, and so forth. One might have expected some ironic comment on her smell and expertise with food, but the elegy does not mention these things.

Because the elegy was probably the most frequently published sort of poem in the eighteenth century, it is perhaps inevitable that there were some parodies.

Benjamin Tompson's *Grammarian's Funeral* (1708), for instance, describes how the different parts of speech mourn the passing of a great teacher of grammar, though the poem seems more an exercise of wit than a work of satire. More satiric are Nathaniel Gardner's *Gentleman's Lamentation for the Loss of His Dog Bacchus* (before 1760) and Joseph Green's *A Mournful Lamentation for the Sad and Deplorable Death of Old Mr. Tenor* (1750). Both lampoon sentimental attachment to inappropriate objects (a dog and a specie of currency), yet the poems praise actual qualities of the departed: Old Tenor "gave the rich their costly wine / The poor their flip and toddy," and when Bacchus heard church music, he "rais'd his notes above the rest" (Green 1750). *The Funeral Sermon, on Michael Morin* (Anon. 1748) satirizes inappropriate rhetoric. Morin's actions, such as chasing cows out of the churchyard with a pitchfork and breaking up a dogfight, are asserted as heroic. The reader is supposed to see that Morin deserved an elegy more along the lines of the humble epitaph of Thomas Gray's "Elegy Written in a Country Churchyard."

The satire in "Neanthe" runs much deeper than in the other mock elegies. It is not that the poet is trying to put the deceased's life in the best light; aside from some sexual puns, it has *no* relation to the life of Neanthe. While certainly elegies were written to comfort the bereaved, they also had a social value of promoting desirable traits. The elegy at the end of "Neanthe," however, commends the subject for actions she never performed and for personal qualities she never had. Since Neanthe was a product of her surroundings, it would seem that nobody in Pungoteague has these qualities. The narrator pointedly remarks that Neanthe's parents hired a poet to write the elegy, which speaks to the motivation behind many such productions: the desire for economic advantage from the survivors (and, in the case of governors, replacements) through fulsome praise.

So, "Neanthe" would have us see, it is not just that rhetoric of elegies can be exaggerated, but that the entire enterprise is, or can be, false. And this takes us back to the poem's initial assertion about the universal triumph of self-interested pleasure over selfless virtue. Even the polite, respectful, and religious performance of an elegy, it would seem, can ultimately be traced to a desire to satisfy personal desires. The greatest irony of the poem is that the assertion that pleasure trumps all human values is, ultimately, *not* ironic.

RICHARD LEWIS'S "A JOURNEY FROM PATAPSKO TO ANNAPOLIS"

In "A Journey from Patapsko to Annapolis, April 4 1730," Lewis imagined an ideal plantation that better fit the patterns of English pastoral poetry than the actual conditions of colonial Maryland. Such an ideal existence is fitting only for farmers and not for the speaker, whose greatest meditations happen not on the plantation in Patapsco or in the town of Annapolis but in a world where he is virtually the only person. Likewise, in "Hastings," the speaker arrives at his most profound vision in a midnight reverie that happens apart from the labor the poem celebrates. These poems enact metaphorically the actual composing process of *Muscipula,* which was written, Lewis tells us in the introduction, during respites from his "very fatiguing Employment" as a teacher (Steiner 1900, 65).

While Lewis's contemporaries praised "A Journey from Patapsko to Annapolis," they also recognized that it demonstrated an unusual freedom. When the English publication the *Bee* printed the poem, the editor took pains to assure readers that the poem did not express apostasy or atheism: "Doubts which arise in the Author's Mind . . . are no more than what we could prove (if it was necessary) have perplex'd and disturb'd the Minds of some of the wisest of Men. These Doubts and Apprehensions are finely express'd, as are those Reflections by which he gets the better of them" (quoted in Carlson 1937, 310). Cradock, however, was not so sure. Although in a note to his *Eclogues,* he expressed sympathy that Lewis was "very poor," he also scornfully remarks that Lewis "was a fine gentleman, and laught at Religion with the rest" (Cradock 1983, 169). "The rest," the eclogue makes clear, are the "Sons of Reason"—Cradock names the Deist thinkers Matthew Tindal, Anthony Collins, Thomas Morgan, Thomas Woolston, and Shaftesbury. For Cradock, Deism had very little to do with teleology or the quietism of Pope's affirmation, "Whatever is, is Right" in *An Essay on Man.* It had everything to do with the kind of rationalism that scoffed at sacred mysteries, undermined faith, and viewed organized religion as a sham.

"A Journey from Patapsko to Annapolis" made even sympathetic readers nervous because of the uncertainty it finds in everyday experience. Consider, for example, the poem's many descriptions of sunlight. Early in the poem, "lightsome Beams" fall on "Foliage," and "trembling shine in many-colour'd Streams." This light is more complex than, for instance, Pope's "unchanging *Sun*" (in *An Essay on Criticism*) that "Clears, and *improves* whate'er it shines upon, / It *gilds* all Objects, but *alters* none" (Pope 1969, 46). While both poets say that heavenly illumination beautifies the world, Pope's sun transcendently reveals what is there and is itself immutable; Lewis's sun rays are modified by the earth and characterized by constant change. Lewis several times remarks on refracting light, and, near the poem's center, clouds eclipse the sun.

The unstable light acts as a metaphor for a point of view that finds traditional verities precarious. For example, about halfway through the poem, the speaker ascends to the "Summit of a *Mount*" to behold the prospect. He observes a river that "reflects" the plants and trees on its banks like a "smooth Mirror." The speaker remarks he is "well pleas'd" with the sight. Anyone familiar with descriptive poetry will recognize the passage's symbolic meaning. The speaker has labored so that he can survey the grander scheme of things from a better perspective. The reflecting stream is an analogue of the reflective mind. The outer world is perfectly transmitted into the speaker's thoughts, which pleases him. However, he is soon disquieted when a hawk swoops down to seize a fish:

> The Stream, disturb'd, no longer shews the Scene
> That lately stain'd its silver Waves with green;
> In spreading Circles roll the troubled Floods,
> And to the Shores bear off the pictur'd Woods.
> (Lewis 1988, 564)

As the stream bears the image of death to its surroundings, the agitated reflection mirrors the speaker's agitated thoughts. The sudden, apparently random death troubles the speaker's confident notions of natural serenity. He now cannot look at the natural world without recognition of what Tennyson would later call "nature red of tooth and claw." Allegorically, this unavoidable fact will always disturb his reflections.

This view differs markedly from the simpler, more confident hopes of Lewis's contemporaries. For example, when Lewis's speaker finds himself in a violent thunderstorm, he "beholds with Grief" the way that the storm's actions "deform" the "*noon-tide* Beauties of his *Life*" (Lewis 1988, 566). In contrast, when Mather Byles, in "The God of Tempest," sees "wild Confusion" and "harsh Disorder" in a storm, he has no moment of lost hope because he believes the storm presages apocalypse: the speaker prays to Christ to hasten and "come in Flame" in order to "break all Nature's frame" (Byles 1744, 6–7). Likewise, when contemplating the stars, Lewis's speaker meditates on his own insignificance when compared with the universe's immensity. He worries that metaphysics may just be the product of "*Self-Love*," and that immortality is a simply "*fancied* Feast" (Lewis 1988, 567). Contemplating the same stars, the astronomer in Francis Hopkinson's *Science* "learns th' important Laws by which they move; / Sits in the Center, wrapt in Thought profound" and comes to understand the "Cause" that determines the changing seasons (Hopkinson 1762, 11). Like Byles, Hopkinson finds that meditation leads to greater certainty without a detour through doubt. Indeed, in 1740 "Enroblos" published a poem in *American Weekly Mercury* that he says is based on a "Hint" from "Journey," though it is actually a fairly close imitation, including quoting lines from Lewis's mockingbird description (Lemay 1972, no. 557). Enroblos attempts to defuse the controversial aspects of "Journey" by citing scripture for support, doubting reason's ability to explain what we would today call natural selection, and placing its speaker in a specific political context that, the speaker asserts, removes doubt.

For all the uncertainties "Journey" entertains, the *Bee* was right that the poem is about the restoration of hope. The poem's final line indicates the ultimate way that doubt can be removed. The speaker prays to God that he may learn to "*know myself, and honour Thee*" (Lewis 1988, 568). Self-knowledge will allow the speaker to find the innate ideas placed in his mind by the Creator, the epistemology at the heart of Deist rationality. This direct connection to the supreme being and faith in personal reason irked readers like Cradock because it did not admit outside authority into the equation: the speaker does not read the Bible, consult a minister, or wait for Sunday to arrive (April 4, 1730, was the Saturday after Easter) and go to church. Instead, he meditates on the natural world and his own nature, and reasons it out.

Still, this is hardly laughing at religion. In fact, making fun of anything is contrary to the politeness Lewis's writing modeled (for instance, he takes pains in the notes to *The Mouse-Trap* to explain that the poem does not ridicule the Welsh). In other realms of human experience, he shows a great respect for authority: he envisions a patriarchal family farm in "Journey," and the prefatory poem to *The Mouse-Trap* counsels Marylanders to protect proprietary privilege. On its most fundamental level, "Journey" is performing the role of Gentleman Thinking. It claims the freedom of thought claimed by Shaftesbury while modeling how such liberty should lead to greater piety and humility. Unlike Shaftesbury, however, the speaker has no estate at Wimborne St. Giles to return to. Lewis, as Cradock reminds us, was very poor yet still a gentleman. His works tend to protect a privilege that does not seem to have benefited him very much, and in this respect he seems very much like the patriarch's sheep and Hastings's lumber.

The speaker's gentility is based solely on his education, his manners, and his ability to think. Outside of settlements, the speaker finds he can attain greatness of mind by dint of his own intellectual abilities, and he takes his place in a meritocratic, perhaps egalitarian, republic of thought. It is a lonely republic, to be sure, but a fine place for unfettered speculation. Still, as the poem's title indicates, at day's end, he will enter the town and perforce comply with all its social and political dealings. Yet he still will be Gentleman Thinking. While a contractarian like Cook offers a more obvious critique of the world, he does not suppose another is possible, and so seeks to alert us to humanity's fallen nature and mend what he can. While Lewis's social and political views are conservative, his habit of mind, with its tendency to doubt, meditate, and imagine something better, has a latent radical edge to it. And when mainstream poets started to apply Lewis's skepticism to colonial political arrangements, the Augustan age in British America began to end.

REFERENCES

Anon. 1748. *The Funeral Sermon, on Michael Morin.* New York: James Parker.

Bolling, Robert. 1762. Lib. IV. Ode 3. Horace. Imitated. *The Annual Register: or, A View of the History, Politics, and Literature for the Year 1762*, edited by Edmund Burke, 206–207. London: J. Dodsley.

———. 1764a. To Miss Nancy Blair of Williamsburg in Virginia. *Universal Magazine* 34: 92.

———. 1764b. To My Flute. *Universal Magazine* 34: 101–102.

Brewster, Martha. 1758. *Poems on Divers Subjects.* Boston: Edes and Gill.

Byles, Mather. 1744. *Poems on Several Occasions.* Boston: S. Kneeland and T. Green.

Carlson, C. Lennart. 1937. Richard Lewis and the Reception of His Work in England. *American Literature* 9: 301–316.

Cradock, Thomas. 1983. *The Poetic Writings of Thomas Cradock, 1718–1770,* edited by David Curtis Skaggs. Newark: University of Delaware Press.

Dawson, William. 1920. *Poems on Several Occasions by a Gentleman of Virginia,* edited by Earl Gregg Swem. New York: C. F. Heartman.

Enroblos [pseud.]. 1740. O Heavenly Muse My Darling Breast Inspire. *American Weekly Mercury,* nos. 1051–1052 (February 19–26).

Evans, Nathaniel. 1772. *Poems on Several Occasions, with Some Other Compositions.* Philadelphia: John Dunlap.

Grainger, James. 1764. *The Sugar-Cane.* London: R. and J. Dodsley.

Green, Joseph. 1750. *A Mournful Lamentation for the Sad and Deplorable Death of Old Mr. Tenor.* Boston.

Hopkinson, Francis. 1762. *Science: A Poem.* Philadelphia: Andrew Steuart.

Johnson, Samuel. 1925. *Johnson, Prose and Poetry,* edited by A. M. D. Hughes. Oxford: Clarendon Press.

Kimber, Edward. 1998. *Itinerant Observations in America,* edited by Kevin J. Hayes. Newark: University of Delaware Press.

Klein, Lawrence E. 1994. *Shaftesbury and the Culture of Politeness.* New York: Cambridge University Press.

Lemay, J. A. Leo. 1972. *A Calendar of American Poetry in the Colonial Newspapers and Magazines and in the Major English Magazines through 1765.* Worcester, MA: American Antiquarian Society.

———. 1982. Southern Colonial Grotesque: Robert Bolling's "Neanthe." *Mississippi Quarterly* 35: 97–112.

Lewis, Richard. 1728. *The Mouse-Trap: or, The Battle of the Cambrians and Mice, A Poem.* Annapolis: for the author, by W. Parks.

———. 1730. To Mr. Samuel Hastings. *Pennsylvania Gazette* (January 13).

———. 1988. A Journey from Patapsko to Annapolis, April 4, 1730. In *An Early American Reader,* edited by J. A. Leo Lemay, 560–569. Washington, DC: United States Information Agency.

Lillo, George. 1731. *The London Merchant: or, The History of George Barnwell.* London: for J. Gray.

Markland, John. 1730. *Typographia.* Williamsburg, VA: William Parks.

Mulford, Carla, ed. 2002. *Early American Writings.* New York: Oxford University Press.

Parke, John. 1786. *The Lyric Works of Horace, Translated into English Verse.* Philadelphia: Eleazer Oswald.

Pope, Alexander. 1969. *Poetry and Prose of Alexander Pope,* edited by Aubrey Williams. Boston: Houghton Mifflin.

Rose, Aquila. 1740. *Poems on Several Occasions.* Philadelphia: Benjamin Franklin.

Shields, David S. 1988. Henry Brooke and the Situation of the First Belletrists in British America. *Early American Literature* 23: 4–27.

Smith, William. 1750. *Some Critical Observations upon a Late Poem, Entituled, The Breeches.* New York: James Parker.

———. 1752. *Some Thoughts on Education.* New York: J. Parker.

Stabile, Susan. 2004. *Memory's Daughters: The Material Culture of Remembrance in Eighteenth-Century America.* Ithaca, NY: Cornell University Press.

Steiner, Bernard C., ed. 1900. *Early Maryland Poetry.* Baltimore: Maryland Historical Society.

Sterling, James. 1760a. Prologue to *The Tragedy of the Orphan and Lethe. Maryland Gazette,* no. 774 (March 6).

———. 1760b. Verses Occasioned by the Success of the British Arms in the Year 1759. *Maryland Gazette,* no. 765 (January 3).

Stockton, Annis Boudinot. 1995. *Only for the Eye of a Friend: The Poems of Annis Boudinot-Stockton,* edited by Carla Mulford. Charlottesville: University Press of Virginia.

Tompson, Benjamin. 1708. *Grammarian's Funeral.* Boston.

Turell, Ebenezer, ed. 1735. *Reliquiae Turellae, et Lachrymae Paternae: The Father's Tears over His Daughter's Remains.* Boston: S. Kneeland and T. Green.

Webb, George. 1731. *Batchelor's-Hall.* Philadelphia: Benjamin Franklin.

Wroth, Lawrence C., ed. 1934. The Maryland Muse by Ebenezer Cooke. *Proceedings of the American Antiquarian Society* 44: 267–336.

CHAPTER 9

PICARESQUE TRAVEL NARRATIVES

DANIEL ROYOT

Stendhal compared narrative art to reflections in a mirror held at random along a road. Among the numerous American diaries produced in the first half of the eighteenth century, the works of William Byrd II, Edward Kimber, Sarah Kemble Knight, and John Lawson best exemplify the experiences of a privileged, perceptive, and witty observer on a journey through the backcountry, frontier settlements, and the wilderness. Temporarily removed from their familiar surroundings for either work or pleasure, such travelers were prone to account for day-to-day happenings with the steady view of informing and entertaining the reader. They thus made the most of their southward or westward explorations in a style often akin to picaresque literature. The narrator was, however, no picaro recollecting sinful ups and downs in a stratified society, but a gentleman or a lady attentive to the manners of fellow colonists or Native Americans, from "savage" squaws or medicine men to uncouth country bumpkins and arrogant planters. In such cases the routes through towns, villages, and backwoods led no farther west than the Appalachian Mountains. But each of those four voyages of discovery gratified contemporaries at home and abroad with the pictorial quality of exotic sites, dramatic scenes, and comic portrayals. Such artistic landscapes of colonial America also bore witness to an ironic sense of relativity when the diarists moved away from civilization and were confronted with unexpected situations in a remote environment. In the burgeoning Age of Reason, their humor was also a safeguard against the awe-inspiring specters, omens, and witches that had long inflamed colonial minds with lurid mirages.

TOWN VERSUS COUNTRY: SARAH KEMBLE KNIGHT'S PROGRESS, FROM ERRAND TO PEREGRINATION

Born in 1666, Sarah Kemble was a New Englander who spent most of her life in Boston. Her father was a wealthy trader and her mother, Elizabeth Treice, belonged to an old and respected Massachusetts family. Their daughter Sarah most likely heard sermons and jeremiads in Congregational churches. She married Richard Knight sometime before 1689. He was then an old man who had already made a career as a shipmaster and London agent for a Boston firm. Sarah had a daughter by him in 1689 before being widowed in 1706. She had already gained some independence by being a shopkeeper and landlady in a house on Moon Street in Boston, aside from an employment as a court scrivener. After her daughter married into the wealthy family of John Livingston of New York in 1714, Knight moved to New London, Connecticut, where she devoted herself to innkeeping, farming, and land speculation. She left an important estate at the time of her death in 1727 (Bush 1995).

In 1704 Sarah Kemble Knight was called upon to settle the estate of her deceased cousin Caleb Trowbridge in New Haven, Connecticut. Her interest in legal matters could easily be expected in a Puritan environment stubbornly given to litigation. At the age of thirty-eight, she had the self-possession, business acumen, and relative emancipation from bigotry spared her the naive outlook of a New England Candide. The text of her *Journal* covers two periods, first from October 2 through October 7, second, several days between December 6 and January 6, 1704–1705. To complete her task, she accompanied a relative to New York before returning to Boston. For five months, she jolted along unknown trails, nearly fell from her horse into a torrent, and steered across a river in flood. Roughing it in the colonial Northeast amounted to a strenuous, risky expedition for several reasons. Her route encountered treacherous streams to be crossed at hazard whether by ferry or canoe or on horseback. The overland trip was somewhat safer in the fall, rivers being lower than in spring, when freshets often made them impassable. Knight's picaresque ride to New York excluded navigation, which had long been the prevalent means of communication among westering New Englanders. In the early eighteenth century, horse riding thus only partially conformed to the popular image of an errand in the hinterland between two poles of civilization. Postal riders were used to such routes, but most travelers needed local guides to help them establish their schedules, especially by locating inns on the way.

The diary of Knight's journey to the Hudson and back may sometimes evoke the soliloquy of the goodwife of Bath in *The Canterbury Tales*. But between Boston and New York, the wilderness did not lend itself to a safe, thoroughly enjoyable pilgrimage as in Chaucer's times. It was unusual to see a woman traveling on her own, hiring guides at each stage of her journey. No doubt Knight was not only a strong-willed personality, unimpressed by sexist contentions on the forbidden fruit, but also well-read in the records of indictments and pleas. As an "inky lady," she was likewise prepared to transcribe faithfully her experiences during the rough-and-tumble of her trip. Her generation had gone through the witch trials and learned how to cast off the lingering religious fanaticism shared by Cotton Mather and his disciples. At the turn of the century, the New England churchgoer was not necessarily far estranged from Bunyan's Christian, whose path echoed with pastoral idylls in *The Pilgrim's Progress*. Walter Raleigh and Erasmus were still familiar authors in the Bay Colony among the offspring of the Yorkshire yeomen. While the Mathers were losing favor among the merchant class, women gained power in the congregations. Meanwhile, there was a widening gap between peasant folk life and the highbrow culture of the still dominant clerics. Besides, a new population of run-away servants, deserters, pirates, and drunkards crowded harbors. The uproar of the Harvard squabbles could of course never reach those distant areas.

In her *Journal*, Knight refers to visits paid to ministers on her journey. Whatever the nature and extent of her faith, she had preserved links with the clergy in mature years, which were still assets in the nascent Enlightenment. She would have deserved to serve as a model for Benjamin Franklin's Silence Dogood on account of her commonsensical approach to haphazard occurrences, strange encounters, and local idiosyncrasies. By 1704 Knight was already aware of the didactic significance of her diary for female readers, so far reluctant to undertake such a journey alone. The daughter of the Billings innkeeper is vocal on the subject: "I never see a woman on the rode so dreadfull late, in all the days of my versall life" (Knight 1994, 54).

Although the *Journal* was often advertised as an exclusive panorama of provincial New England, it sheds light on a broader segment of colonial America (Margolies 1964). The autobiographical tone has nothing in common with the determinism of Puritan annals, and nowhere in Knight's misadventures is to be found evidence of predestination. Her straightforward, often blunt account of mishaps hardly ever conveys the obtrusive, stringent morality of sermons. She remains conscious that her ironic distance challenges the conventions prevailing in personal narratives concerned with a spiritual quest.

After leaving the comforts of Dedham in the early part of her journey, Knight fathoms the wilderness at dark. In the gloom, her guide's shade resembles "a globe on a gate post" as he rides before her. Such a physical replica of Sancho Panza is playfully likened to a "prince disguised" when he tells her about his adventurous life. By humorously referring to the mythical knight-errant in *Parismus* and the *Knight of the Oracle*, she further debunks the swaggering rascal longing for social recognition. Yet she implicitly admits that such eccentric scamps are indispensable to find one's way in the backwoods especially when he leads her safely to Billings, a welcome recess in a hazardous voyage of discovery.

As Knight expresses her fears in the "lonesome woods" on the second night of her trip, she dramatizes her experience, while stressing that it might arouse terror in a male's mind. Meanwhile, she never assigns a dominant role to her guides apart from topographic information. After enhancing her own image for the courage displayed, she may at times confess to her improvidence, hence belatedly substantiating conventional wisdom about woman's frailty. She transcends the Puritan literature of guilt-ridden self-examination, hardly ever looking to the Bible for an explanation of her attitude toward a potential devilish presence in the dark forest. Nor does she find clues in theology to her nightmarish visions: "Nothing but Light can dissipate those fears. / My fainting vitals can't lend strength to say; / But softly whisper, O I wish 'twere day" (Knight 1994, 56–57).

The Bostonian wayfarer eventually finds within herself the cause of her predicament. When she finally discovers a clearing after an exhausting ride in the forest, she extols the beauty of the place in the moonlight rather than thank God for a divine rescue from the evils lurking in the wilderness. On the third day she and her guide cover thirty miles without finding accommodation. To answer her recriminations, he informs her that they will soon reach Mr. Devills. She is not slow to indulge in puns about going to the Devil, speeding to his habitation like "the rest of deluded souls that post to the Infernal den." In a mock-heroic tone she transfigures her plight into a Christian conversion narrative, a takeoff on Dante's *Divine Comedy* or *The Pilgrim's Progress.* The yarn then turns into a hoax with the poem written as an incantation to exorcize the haunted mansion:

> Tis Hell, tis Hell! and Devills here do dwell:
> Here dwells the Devil—surely this's Hell.
> Plenty of horrid grins and looks severe,
> Hunger and Thirst, but pity's banish'd here—
> (Knight 1994, 59)

In another episode Knight praises the prosperous town of Fairfield while deriding the venal cares of its inmates, for whom spiritual pursuits are nonexistent. Hence the anticlimactic, Swiftian allusion to local resources among the New World Philistines: "They have abundance of sheep, whose very dung brings them great gain, with part of which they pay their Parson's salary. And they Grudge that, preferring their Dung before their minister" (Knight 1994, 72).

Knight's enraptured contemplation of nature does not blind her to grim social realities such as a wretched hut whose floor is the bare earth. This picture of poverty reveals a miserable couple and their two children at pains to survive. Yet her ironic, uncompromising view of the common run of humanity is never concealed under smug humanitarianism. Her satire may even be biting in some cases.

She finds no saving grace in many of the country bumpkins whose descendants will be wily Yankees matching their wits against suspicious strangers a few generations later. While the rising class of the Boston merchants of her times is replacing lineage with money as the new criterion for high society respectability, the peasant class painstakingly keeps a higher status than the Native Americans, who represent the underworld doomed to antihonor as in the original picaresque tradition. Nurtured on captivity narratives, colonists like Knight deemed Indians cruel, barbarous, and treacherous, delighting to torment men and women, flaying some alive as William Bradford noted in *Of Plymouth Plantation*. Native Americans are "the most savage of all the savages" she has ever met. She blames them for atavistic polygamy, idolatry, promiscuity, immorality, and immaturity. Although they take unfair advantage of English leniency, they are eventually duped. In a deadpan manner the diarist suggests who the trickster is: "They trade most for rum, for which they hazard their very lives; and the English fit them generally as well, by seasoning it plentifully with water." A born gossip, Knight cannot refrain from alluding to the "foolish sex" having interracial affairs with the natives. But when she says that such trivial matters "are not proper to be related by a female pen," her cant is all the more titillating because factual evidence is not given. Typical of her comic anecdotes is also the case of an Indian implicated in the theft of a hogshead and brought before a judge to be cross-examined. Once the community has managed to erect a bench made with pumpkins, the Malefactor is called: "You sirrah, why did you steal this man's hogshead? Hogshead, replies the Indian, me no stomany. No? says his worship; and pulling off his hat, patted his own head with his hand, says, Tatapa-You, Tatapa-you, all one this, Hogshead all one this. Ha! says Netop, now me stomany that" (Knight 1994, 64–65).

Helpful though they may be as guides, some of the subhuman "creatures" of white stock have borrowed their savage habits from neighboring natives. Despite the fluidity of the colonial frontier, Knight's conventions postulate a Euro-American society that is divided into two broad categories. She ranks herself among the upper class but never utters disparaging judgments in the abstract. She can become more harshly critical when siding with the young, who are punished by the courts for "a harmless kiss," or openly subversive to admonish judges for condemning a generous slave owner for a breach of contract with his nagging black man (Knight 1994, 63–65).

In the *Journal* comic action is generated from low characters, mostly country rubes, servants, guides, and innkeepers, whose comic potential is based on convenient stereotypes. Anecdotes serve to draw scathing caricatures of local inhabitants whom she dealt with. In a store, a tall country fellow keeps chewing his cud before advancing to the middle of the room, making an awkward nod and spitting a large deal of aromatic tincture. Then he stands staring round him like a cat let out of a basket: "Like the creature Balaam rode on, he opened his mouth and said: have you any Ribinen for hatbands to sell I pray?" The alleged swashbuckler is now reduced to absurd proportions in an anticlimactic punchline. In the same place, Knight delights in making fun of Joan Tawdry, an awkward, bashful customer who obsequiously drops about fifty curtseys to the merchant who is her stern creditor. Viewed from the standpoint of a wit, those characters are incurably clumsy, gross in intellect, and totally without the deftness of mind needed to succeed in social life. In Connecticut, Knight sees both sham self-righteousness and vulgarity in the people. Although she recognizes their "large portion of mother wit," she regrets their lapses into ridicule for want of a proper education. But for her innate prejudices, she would have come close to a perceptive view of inchoate New England humor and perhaps discovered a versatile persona lurking behind the comic mask. Later the village oracle would become a popular figure by adopting an innocent pose to express the racy wisdom of the commoner.

Knight's narrow cross section of rural society includes fellow countrymen brazenly attempting to intrude on her privacy. Her characterization is thus centered on absurd troubleshooters often reduced to caricatures but brimful of vitality. Whereas Puritan chroniclers divided mankind into saints and sinners, Knight saw more folly than vice in such samplings of the colonial population. She discloses negative signs, but unlike the archetypal picaro, she does not see society from below. Keeping aloof from the protagonists, she singles out episodes that strengthen her superior point of view, her comments being more condescending than indignant. Because she finds her boorish hosts and guides hilarious, she hastens to communicate her fun rather than her anger.

While New France Catholics found holiness in wine, Satan reigned over rum and beer in Calvinistic New England. But the *Journal* suggests that Knight has no time for invective or denunciation when she is attempting to find a guide in a tavern, although she only sees men "tyed by the Lipps to a pewter engine." The colloquial, pungent speech of such low characters is unpredictable and outside the expectations of social decorum as drinking frees up their outrageous similes and hyperboles. For instance, while Knight is trying to get some sleep in an inn, several drunkards discuss the origins of the Indian name "Narragansett." As their arguments are absurdly strung together, this logic of non sequiturs lends itself to mounting violence. While the opponents come to fisticuffs, she gives an outlet to her resentment by writing lines about the brawl. Poetic diction naturally emphasizes the incongruity of the otherwise beastly scene.

> I ask thy Aid, O poetent Rum!
> To Charm these wrangling Topers Dum.
> Thou hast their Giddy Brains possesst—
> And I, poor I can get no rest.
> (Knight 1994, 53, 580)

The *Journal* stresses salient traits of backcountry personality, parsimony, low cunning, dismal naïveté, uncontrollable curiosity, loutishness, and impudence.

It helps set the lineaments in popular fancy about innocent travelers cozened by rustic sharpers. At Dedham the hostess asks Knight to hire her son but requires an exorbitant salary. There is no end of bargaining, which induces Knight to believe that she "was got among the Quaking tribe." Meanwhile, her narrative art preserves the turns of speech of rural talk while she depicts the clownish antics of the New England rogues. The picaresque element is in the contrast between the diversity of confrontations and the redundance of motivations such as vanity and greed. At Billings, it is not covetousness but vainglory that urges the hostess to impress her guest by ostentatiously wearing rings. Knight's satiric thrust would have delighted Nathaniel Ward when she concludes that a sow would have produced a similar effect. Elsewhere the Boston lady measures up the status of the innkeepers by commenting on their recipes, which leads to devastating dismissals: "I desired a fricasee, which the Frenchman undertaking, managed so contrary to my notion of cookery, that I hastened to bed supperless." There is some self-mockery in the role of country woman played in the narrative by the itinerant bourgeoise at Norowalk. The servant comes to her room, compared to a kennel, which she scratches up as if she were in a barn among husks. But exhausted as she is Knight comments: "down I laid my poor carcass" (Knight 1994, 67). In another instance, her comic distance applies to her own attitude as she describes her anguish before riding across a "fierce" river. Retrospectively the comic deflation of her own terror introduces a tall tale element by overdoing her predicament. She first sees herself drowning, and then hopefully rescued "like a holy sister just come out of a spiritual bath in dripping garments." The anticipation of danger is expressed through hyperbole when the glimmering light of the stars makes nature look terrifying: "Each lifeless trunk with its shattered lims appeared an armed enemy and every little stump like a ravenous devourer" (Knight 1994, 55). Here, the interplay between appearance and reality results in a shift of focus as though she was emulating Don Quixote tilting at windmills. She has some qualms about her daring, but her Puritan sense of guilt subsides into Deistic casuistry while the awesome specters are shattered by concrete observation. Her vision is suddenly illuminated by the moon, causing her to forget her past toils and inspiring her with soothing thoughts.

The narrator eventually invites the reader to confront the wilderness and see through whatever occult powers might have threatened to overwhelm the alien-ated ego in the age of witches and demons. By rationalizing her experience, she now perceives the universe as an object and cuts off the ties keeping the New Eng-lander prisoner of ancestral fantasies. "Fair Cynthia," the "pagan goddess" who is "the conductress of the night," transfigures the dark forests into an urban para-dise filled with buildings and churches with their steeples, balconies, and galleries (Knight 1994, 55). Fair Cynthia's wand has therefore changed the obscure wilder-ness into a futuristic Boston. Poetic diction becomes subversive through ironic reversal, thus substituting flamboyant images for the austere, forbidding plain style of the Puritan killjoy.

Ultimately the road leads to Manhattan, the climax of Knight's undertaking. She realizes that her wilderness passage was not a guided tour of the pit but an instructive struggle through a terra incognita. New York provides an outlet for the lingering sense of regression left by a dismal environment sheltering Indianized barbarians. It seems Knight now breathes some fresh air in the urban setting. The light-handed tone of her descriptions shows how comfortable she feels among the stately buildings and their privileged inmates. In the picaresque tradition the anti-hero rises on the social scale to reach the upper crust only momentarily, before his downfall. In the *Journal,* Knight has now nothing left at stake. She combines business with sightseeing in a city where she meets her equals and is well entertained. She makes no ethnic discrimination between the English and the Dutch except for the freedom of the latter with the Sabbath. She not only envies their religious emancipation but marvels at their jewels, especially the earrings, a welcome contrast with the tawdry paraphernalia on show in backwoods inns. As opposed to a picaresque adventure, Knight does not interpret her overall experience in terms of success or failure. Despite the ban on theater in Puritan Boston, European observers might have deemed the diarist indebted to the Restoration comedy of manners. In the *Journal* everything violating upper-class norms and expectations is subject to ridicule. Back in Boston, Knight exults at recollecting frightful episodes as if she were expected to dramatize her five months' voluntary exile for the family circle on her return in January 1705. Perhaps a merrier and wiser woman, she thanks her "Great benefactor for thus graciously carrying forth and returning in safety His unworthy handmaiden" (Knight 1994, 75). In her discourse, Providence almost identifies with the Great Clockmaker while her concealment of pride under humility is in skillful connivance with her fellow bourgeois reader.

Like Cotton Mather in *Magnalia Christi Americana,* Knight pointed to the difficulties of a rough and hard wilderness wherever morality seemed to stop at the edge of a clearing. In the meantime, far remote from New England, new lands were challenging the pioneer spirit of English adventurers eager to transform the wild into a pastoral Eden.

John Lawson: A Condottiere Among the Indians

Little is known about John Lawson's youthful years in London. Whatever his origins he was well trained in science and belonged to a middle-class family, being held himself as a gentleman among his relations. In May 1700 he left from Cowes to sail across the Atlantic Ocean. After a short stay in New York he went to South Carolina in August. It was a colony in full expansion whose major city, Charles Town, appealed to him for its nice planning and architecture. The tidewater region was inhabited within sixty miles west of the coast, and the virgin land that lay beyond could be reached by using the waterways. Lawson was assigned to survey sites for new settlers by the Lords Proprietors. He set off on December 28, 1700, with a party of six Englishmen and four Indians. They paddled up the Santee River, journeyed on foot in the hinterland, and encountered several native tribes such as the Congarees and the Waxhaws (Breytspraak and Breytspraak 1992; Holloman 1991).

In January 1701, the explorers reached the location of present-day Charlotte, where they met the Sugarees and the Catawbas. Then they took a trade route to the north. In early February, the main party decided to head for Virginia from Keyauwee Town. On his side, Lawson chose to go through Carolina with another member of the group. By the time he rallied Occaneechi, present-day Hillsborough, he hired an Indian guide, Enoe Will, to show him the way to the coastal settlements. Beyond the falls of the Neuse River, Lawson found the winter quarters of several hundred Tuscarora hunters. With an Indian escort, he made his way to the plantation of Richard Smith at the Pamlico River, after crossing the Tar River by the end of February. Altogether 500 miles had been covered within sixty days in the wilderness.

Lawson picked up a site on a hill close to a stream to build his home. He bought sixty acres on the north bank of the Pamlico to develop the town of Bath, which counted a dozen houses and fifty residents. The county had been established in 1696. One of the planters, David Perkins offered sixty acres of his land to Lawson and other landowners, then commissioners of the incorporated town. Seventy lots were soon sold to local planters. Lawson fully committed himself to economic development and social life, particularly as a clerk of court. He was also instrumental in the building of a mill for the exclusive use of residents. The colony was, however, living through many hardships. Religious conflicts stemmed from legal discriminations against dissenters like Quakers, while the Anglican Church was striving for hegemony. But Lawson eluded the period of tension that culminated in 1710. A year before, he had sailed back to London to revise the manuscript of his *A New Voyage to Carolina* (1709). As an agent for North Carolina in the English capital Lawson was kept busy settling the problem of the boundary line with Virginia. In 1711, he cooperated with Baron Christopher von Graffenried to gather a group of Swiss and Palatine emigrants who were intending to plant a colony. The joint venture resulted in the foundation of New Bern on the Neuse and Trent rivers (Dill 1986). In 1711, Lawson had been back to Carolina for a year when the Tuscarora Indians attacked settlers for retaliation on improper trading operations. Lawson convinced his partner to participate in an expedition up the Neuse River. Both were captured and taken as hostages. Graffenried was freed and returned to Bath alone. Lawson was tortured, then executed in the Indian town of Catechna. The fierce counteroffensive by the English troops spared few tribes. A thousand Tuscaroras were sold into slavery. The remaining population left Carolina to rally the Iroquois Confederacy in the north.

John Lawson was endowed with protean gifts as a diarist. As a surveyor he had prominent skills that enabled him to become the deputy of the colony's surveyor-general. His extensive knowledge of botany and zoology qualified him to write abundant notes on the flora and fauna of the region. In London he had been trained by James Petiver, an apothecary whose huge collection of plants was unrivaled. *A New Voyage* is primarily a promotion tract intended for potential colonists. But it also honestly rationalizes expectations with guiding lines about areas for settlement and prospects of cultivation, accurately documenting the topography of tidewater Carolina. Accordingly, the wide popularity immediately gained by the book was due to scientific accuracy and rigorous observation. As in Captain John Smith's accounts, Lawson emphasizes the practical problems of travel and husbandry while detailing terrain, climate, and crops. He feels the need to narrate the new and give plot and purpose to landscapes, plantations, and the wilderness. From a literary point of view *A New Voyage* reflects Lawson's preoccupation with the objective renderings of multifarious experiences and, on the other hand, his urge to communicate a sense of wonder through stirring events and unparalleled adventures. Retrospectively, his tragic fate made readers aware that his confrontation with native tribes had not been just a fantasy.

Almost all the native nations of Carolina vanished within the first five decades of colonization. In 1670 the population numbered about 10,000 in twenty-eight coastal and inland tribes belonging to four linguistic families (Muskhogean, Iroquois, Algonquin, and Siouan). By 1700 nine tribes amounting to a thousand individuals lived between the Santee and the Savannah rivers. They spoke either Muskhogean or Siouan. Low-country inhabitants spent the summer in villages along the rivers. They covered up to fifty miles to winter in the hinterland. Being seasonal farmers and hunters, they grew corn, beans, and squash and relied on dried or smoked venison in case of penury. In their matrilineal society, polygamy was banned. The tribal chieftain was a man or a woman elected for a life term. Most powers, however, lay in the hands of a council representing families and clans. Intertribal wars broke out at times to test the fighting spirit of young warriors. Scalps were welcome trophies in local conflicts that were not intended to annihilate the enemy.

Native American culture was often misinterpreted to support the cause of the colonists. A Huguenot minister, Paul L'Escot, paradoxically praised the Indians for their civility toward Europeans while still considering them as idolatrous barbarians. The Lords Proprietors had no mind to deprive them of their land. They valued their alliance against Spanish territorial expansion, whether or not they shared the prevailing beliefs in the noble savage. Initially the Lords Proprietors were suspicious of migrants eager to buy land directly from Indians, but geopolitical issues soon determined more complex attitudes. Until 1700, the Low-Country Kiawahas sought support from the English settlers against the bellicose Westoes, who were supplied with arms by Virginian colonists. The Lords Proprietors painstakingly maintained a balance between antagonistic interests before their commitment to the dreaded

Westoes alienated them from many settlers. A long period of unrest began with the arrival of the Yamasees from Georgia to the Low Country in 1685. They supplanted the Savannahs near Charles Town and exerted a strong influence on the Indian policy of the government against both the Spanish and the Tuscaroras, who rebelled after being despoiled of their lands.

When Lawson reached Carolina, the Santee River, situated forty miles north of Charles Town, was accessible in two days on horseback after getting across three large swamps and six tributaries. Named Rio Jordan in early sixteenth-century Spanish cartography, it had been located by Jean Ribault and René de Laudonnière, two Huguenots who, encouraged by Admiral Gaspard de Coligny, had tried to seize part of Florida in the 1560s, before they built Charlesfort, about sixty miles south of Charles Town, in the bay of Port Royal. It was on the south bank of the Santee that a group of Huguenot refugees settled in the 1680s. John Lawson counted seventy families in 1700 when he described the peaceful French people he met on his return from the church whose pastor was Pierre Robert, a Swiss citizen. At the turn of the eighteenth century, after their twenty years' exile, the French Huguenot community was faced with a difficult choice: either join the Anglican Church or remain independent. The Charles Town urban residents preferred to remain in the bosom of Calvinism, whereas the rural colonists turned to Anglicanism.

The narrator of *A New Voyage* decries travelers who are unable to give reasonable accounts of what they meet because they are uneducated, low-down individuals in the service of merchants. Dedicating his work to his aristocratic Carolina employers, he rates his own observations by comparing them with the journals of the French missionaries and gentlemen whose monarch encourages emulation by supporting the best efforts in the wilderness. Lawson may have in mind the contributions of historians and geographers such as Pierre Boucher, Father Jean de Brébeuf, Nicolas Denys, and Louis Hennepin, who wrote about New France, from Canada to Louisiana, in the second half of the seventeenth century. Lawson prides himself on his comprehensive view of Carolina, including Native Americans whose speech and customs have been too long ignored by his fellow countrymen. His often irenic views of prospective relationships with the Indian communities were to prove tragically false when he met his death in captivity after being tortured like Jean de Brébeuf.

In *A New Voyage* Lawson introduces himself as a scientist and a surveyor, thereby dismissing any "falsity or hyperbole" that would be detrimental to the impartiality of the account. Such a statement of aims is far removed from the confessions of a picaro who owes his survival to makeshift in a society given over to pretense and lust. For the narrator the colony was at first planted by "a genteel sort of people" who made good use of the advantages offered in the warm South. Heliotropism was thus considered as an asset in the process of colonization. A few decades later, Buffon and Voltaire updated his estimate when they disparaged the few acres of snow in Canada to favor Louisiana. Lawson's viewpoint is determined by the general policy of the Lords Proprietors, especially in his favorable presentation of the Huguenot community, as he praises the religious freedom enjoyed by all congregations. The fact that in 1565, French Protestants were mass-slaughtered in the Spanish town of St. Augustine in Florida strengthens ties with the English colonists whose hatred of papists is ingrained in mentalities. Lawson's devastating picture of the Spanish presence in Florida conforms to the strategy consisting in forming alliances with Indians who have "groaned under the yoke" of His Catholic Majesty (Lawson 1709, 11, 2, 4).

Carolina is appraised as a land of plenty enjoying a peaceful coexistence between merchants and gentlemen, planters and slaves, Huguenots and Anglicans. Lawson lays aside preconceived ideas to learn what Indians can teach him about their vision of life. His didactic purpose conditions the success of colonial ventures as Indians interpret nature for the newcomers, dispensing in the practical knowledge of food, clothing, and medicine. Lawson's Carolina is not a promised land but a land of opportunity for pioneers to seize. Seldom invoking the Bible, he views his exploration through mostly utilitarian spectacles and defines his mission in secular rather than sacred terms. He makes it clear that he deliberately chose to confront the wilderness with his passion for discovery. It is no easy task as natural obstacles are set in the way of the explorers upon their departure. The ebb tide leaves only shallow waters for Lawson's craft to sail upstream from the coast through the swamps. After circling around islands, the party enters the Santee River. The narrator's mention of the chilly weather contrasts with his previous enraptured pictures of palmettos evoking a Bermudian paradise. The picaresque element is introduced through paradigms expected in adventure stories, such as the interplay of appearance with reality. For instance, the terrorized members of the expedition hear a great noise like a gun report as if two parties were engaged against each other, but find it to be Sewee Indians firing cane swamps to drive out the game. Indians are not immune to comic discomfiture either. For example, hunters chasing the deer who disguise themselves to look like their prey sometimes come up so close together with a stalking head that they kill each other. Lawson's narrative also involves self-mockery when one of his men who is top-heavy walks a narrow pole over a creek and falls into the water up to the chin. While laughing at the incident, the narrator comes to the same misfortune. Throughout *A New Voyage* he sometimes mixes fancy with fact and supplies the raw material with which folk imagination can build a fresh conception of the wilderness. The Carolina cornucopia sometimes harbors amphibian monsters like alligators. But it also provides travelers with turkeys weighing forty pounds, together with raccoon and goose meat, whether barbecued or stewed. Hunting privileges are enjoyed by both the rich planter and the poor laborer, for anyone can live off the fat of the land. But the water available may at times color the excrements as black as coal (Lawson 1709, 10, 16, 13).

Lawson's depiction of native mentalities reflects his open-mindedness but also emphasizes the differences between peoples close to one another in space yet standing in the same relation as history to prehistory. While trying to bridge the gap between whites and Indians, he shows himself dispassionate, often by understating comments on astounding happenings. His minute descriptions of funeral rituals on burial mounds concentrate on the handling of flesh and bones, thereby revealing ethnological objectivity rather than an irrational interest in the primitive sense of sacredness. Although Lawson's portrayal of Indian mores questions assumptions about born pilferers and cruel heathens, his characterization sometimes leaves room for animadversion and allows comic relief in otherwise earnest developments. In an anecdote about the devastating effects of rum in the Indian communities, he satirizes the naïveté of primitives unable to evaluate the size of the Atlantic. Some of the most clever of them once observed that the ships laden with liquor came to the same harbor and imagined they had covered only a short distance. So canoes were built and a fleet gathered to carry pelts to England, where Indians could buy twenty times the value for every skin sold abroad. They secretly set sails but were soon caught in a storm, then rescued by an English ship and sold into slavery (Lawson 1709, 12).

Despite their helplessness when faced with European civilization, within their own society Indians cling to traditions and practices that reveal a coherent set of values. Even though the Sewees have tragically suffered from the smallpox spread by the Europeans, their medicine men have kept outstanding skills to cure the sick: "An Indian hath been often found to heal an Englishman of a malady, for the value of a matchcoat, which the ablest of our English pretenders in America after repeated applications, have deserted the patient as incurable" (Lawson 1709, 10–11).

The narrator concludes that God has supplied all countries with specific remedies for their peculiar diseases. His statement anticipates Montesquieu's trust in a world order determined by geology and climate in which human beings naturally find their place. Such an idyllic image of native health care has naturally little in common with Smollett's caricatures of quack doctors. Lawson refrains from calling superstition the use of magic by the Sapona king, a staunch ally of the English, who lost an eye when a barrel of gunpowder blew up in front of him. As a conjurer he can manage to drive away a strong hurricane raised by the devil when law and order are threatened. Such is the case when ferocious Iroquois warriors are captured by the Saponas who intend to burn them alive. The Iroquois are known for cutting the toes of prisoners because the impression of their half feet makes it easy to trace them if they escape. The Iroquois remain insensitive and defiant, expecting that the same fate will later attend their enemies. Meanwhile, the neighboring Totero tribal chiefs intervene to have the captives freed to repay them for the mercy previously shown by the Iroquois toward Totero prisoners (Lawson 1709, 49, 53). Once the request is granted, it remains for the Sapona king to appease the devil who was dissatisfied with the absence of retribution.

In a deadpan manner Lawson deals with the issue of native promiscuity as if he were inspired by the libertines. For him, neither noble nor ignoble, the savage merely shares the civilized man's lust. A slave of appetite and sloth, never emancipated from animal passion according to the Puritan stereotypes, the Indian is in fact the victim of the *lues venerae* spread by the colonists. Lawson blatantly ascribes gonorrhea altogether to the immoderate drinking of rum and eating of pork, the difference of climates, and the contamination of Indian women by Spanish soldiers. For him the disease extended to Europe by the time the solitary widows of His Catholic Majesty's conquistadores were entertained by the French, giving the Monsieurs "a large a share of their pocky spoils." Lawson nevertheless recognizes "how much frailty possesses the Indian woman betwixt the garter and the girdle" and also ascribes her degradation to both native chiefs and traders. The Santee River is a New World Sodom and Gomorrah where neither virginity nor continence is a cardinal virtue. Not only are husbands pleased to offer their wives to guests or neighbors, but the king of the Kadapus always keeps two or three trading girls in his cabin. As the sovereign pimp of the nation he gladly receives his due from rampant prostitution (Lawson 1709, 19, 51, 44).

A genuine picaresque episode occurs when a member of Lawson's party proudly exhibits all his beads to an Indian girl singled out to become his temporary bride. Then paradoxes crop up in the narrator's evocation of the wedding. The bridesmaids are "great whores," and all nubile girls generously offer their services to the guests. When the English bridegroom awakes in the night after the orgy, his spouse has fled with his beads and shoes so that "like a pilgrim" he has to walk barefoot (Lawson 1709, 41).

Tolerant but aloof, Lawson does not see himself redeeming Carolina from its wilderness state, nor does he wage a Manichaean battle between the light of gospel and pagan darkness. He is no messianic theologian, but as a close observer of native spirituality, he suggests that Indian religion includes the Flood, the immortality of the soul, as well as good and evil. Granted that Indians are still unable to understand the meaning of heavenly bliss, Lawson concludes that French Jesuits are right in trying to convert Indians, neither angels nor beasts, to the Bible: an ultimate, provocative paradox on Huguenot territory.

WILLIAM BYRD II, THE ROGUISH GENTLEMAN

By the early eighteenth century not all gentlemen faced the wilderness from the pioneer's perspective. William Byrd II was born in Virginia on the site of present-day Richmond on March 28, 1674. His father, William Byrd I, a wealthy landowner, Indian trader, and public official, sent him to England at the age of seven. William Byrd II spent his formative years in London, where he acquired the manners of the gentry. In 1692 he entered the Middle Temple and was called to the bar three years later. He was acquainted with William Congreve and William Wycherley among the wits of the times. A theatergoer, Byrd was thus familiar with the characters of the Restoration comedy. In 1696 he returned to Virginia and entered a political career but was soon back to London, where he represented Governor Edmund Andros in a controversy with Commissary James Blair about the new College of William and Mary. Appointed agent for Virginia in London in 1698, Byrd antagonized the new governor Francis Nicholson over the military support requested by New York against the Five Nations. He also struggled to safeguard the interests of tobacco and cotton plantations. At the death of his father in 1704, he inherited the 26,000-acre estate at Westover. In May 1706 he married Lucy Park, a temperamental young lady with whom he had four children. Her rakish father, one of the Duke of Marlborough's aides-de-camp during the battle of Blenheim, had just been rewarded with the governorship of the Leeward Islands when Byrd sent him a letter asking permission to court his daughter. While retaining his links with the English establishment, Byrd fully committed himself to Virginia politics and was appointed to the council in 1709. Lord George Hamilton being an absentee governor, several lieutenant governors had ruled the colony in his place. The governorship that Byrd had tried to buy with several recommendations went to Colonel Alexander Spotswood in July 1710. Peace reigned for some time. For instance, there was no discord between the new lieutenant governor and the council when an army was mustered for the defense of Virginia after the Tuscaroras killed John Lawson in 1711. Spotswood was, however, determined to stem the power of the councillors, reform the system of tax collection, control the General Court and monopolize the Indian trade. Having to settle the debts of his deceased father-in-law, Byrd seized the pretext to sail to England in 1715. In London he endeavored to have Spotswood recalled by using his influence in aristocratic circles. But personal problems claimed much of his time in the meantime (Marambaud 1971).

His wife Lucy died of smallpox in 1715. Byrd, who was a renowned womanizer, could not long remain a sorrowful widower. He had a good number of affairs, calling his paramours "Sabina" or "Charmante" and himself, "Enamorato l'Oiseau" in his love letters. He eventually married Maria Taylor, a twenty-five-year-old heiress, in May 1724, before returning to Virginia in 1726. She bore him four children.

Meanwhile, Governor Alexander Spotswood was not only concerned with advancing the frontier but also intent on increasing his own landed property. In 1716, he gathered a handful of fellow Virginians to thrust his way into the wilderness across the Blue Ridge to the Shenandoah, which he named Euphrates. Among his companions were John Fontaine, a Huguenot serving as chronicler for the expedition. Upon his return to Westover, Byrd was again in full swing. He belonged to a coterie of sturdy, merrymaking Cavaliers who shared Spotswood's expansionist prospects but were denied the membership in the Order of the Golden Horseshoe that distinguished enterprising Virginians eager to explore and settle the wild country. In 1728, Byrd, however, managed to gain control of the commission appointed to survey the disputed boundary line between Virginia and North Carolina. As a libertine in search of outlandish experiences he was equally desirous to stage himself by transcribing them in colorful accounts. The gentleman-turned-explorer enjoyed the exhilarating prospect of living outdoors, immersed in nature. At the age of fifty-four, he preferred bivouacking to the comforts of a plantation to rejuvenate himself.

On March 5, 1728, Byrd took the lead of an expeditionary force including North Carolina representatives. He had enlisted as chaplain Peter Fontaine, John's brother, who was expected to baptize and marry colonists as well as watch over the souls of the lusty surveyors. The westward journey did not follow the route of Spotswood's earlier expedition but also reached well beyond the confines of settled areas through the Great Dismal Swamp, to the Roanoke and Dan rivers. The mission ended in November 1728 after a log of 240 miles over nine months.

As the travelers headed for the westernmost part of Virginia, their excitement grew. On October 11 they sighted the Appalachian Mountains. As they climbed higher, grandiose vistas opened on the way. Byrd was familiar with the aesthetic outlook of his time on pastoral nature. As a gentleman he would feel the thrill of open space without the risk of lapsing from civilization into the primitive state. He was, however, well aware that some individuals could be overwhelmed by the backwoods environment and surrender to savage habits. Yet he was by no means influenced by the malaise of some of his pious contemporaries in an American desert compared to the devil's den. In a more secular mood he was prone to consider, like William Cooper, that it was essential to cause the wilderness to bloom and fructify.

Byrd's expedition was reported in two parallel accounts, the *History of the Dividing Line* and *The Secret History of the Line,* which was first destined for a private audience. It chronicles the daily lives of truculent, blustering characters in a festive comedy entailing sexual license and heavy drinking. The pastoral myth is constantly undermined by the intrusion of disjunctive picaresque elements, as lofty geopolitical strategies boil down to loudmouthed bickerings. Byrd is as averse to North Carolinians as Sarah Kemble Knight was to the Connecticut residents. At stake is the possession of a stream that would give North Carolina access to Albemarle Sound, making it easy for its planters to bypass the Virginian ban on shipping their tobacco from the Chesapeake.

As its title suggests, *The Secret History* claims to disclose hidden stratagems and unavowed motives to gratify inquisitive readers interested in the seamy side of history. Mock-heroic incidents subvert the epic grandeur expected from such a voyage of discovery. The narrative often turns out to be about a picaresque progress involving a band of scoundrels rounded up in a haphazard enterprise like a bunch of satyrs driven on by Bacchus. After Ebenezer Cook in *The Sot-weed Factor* (1708), Byrd introduces coarse, slyly deceitful colonists in a satiric allegory revealing that the wilderness may not be worth rhapsodic hymns. The participants are all nicknamed according to some salient feature like Firebrand or Humdrum. The cast therefore duplicates the real names of the commissioners and surveyors. As a humorist Byrd has chosen laughter rather frontal onslaught to puncture shams and expose transgressors. As a gentleman he stoops to conquer the minds of conniving readers by filtering the agonizing scenes of brutality and degradation he has stumbled over and transmuting them into a hilarious spectacle.

Byrd adopts both a voice and a mask. As first-person narrator he observes his material from above but also projects himself into the character of Steddy and contrives significant episodes through third-person autobiographical sequences. Being instrumental in reconciling conflicting attitudes, Byrd thus transcribes his own speech: "Here Steddy thought proper to encourage the Men by a short harangue to this effect. 'Gentlemen, we are at last arriv'd at this dreadfull place, which til now has been thought impassable'" (Byrd 1994, 98).

As a diarist Byrd shares the planters' condescending views of the common run of humanity. His ironic distance toward the alleged easy virtue of peasant girls is expressed in epigrams such as "Amongst other Spectators came 2 girls to see us, one of which was very handsome, and the other very willing." Squaws emulating southern belles are ridiculed: "The Ladies had put on all their Ornaments to charm us, but the Whole Winter's Dirt was so crusted on their Skins, that it required a strong appetite to accost them" (Byrd 1994, 93, 113). The quip should not necessarily be read at its face value because Byrd was obviously joking. In fact, he often advocated miscegenation, considering that after two generations the Métis would be integrated. Intermarriage was for him a way to reclaim Indians from barbarity as, he thought, the French did in Canada and Louisiana to make allies.

Byrd's erectile humor belongs to eighteenth-century male libertinism whatever the race of the female object, hence the following evocation of forced sex rings with smutty double entendre: "A Damsel who came to assist in the Kitchen wou'd certainly have been ravish't, if her timely consent had not prevented the Violence. Nor did my Landlady think herself safe in the hands of such furious Lovers, and therefore fortify'd her Bed Chamber and defended it with a Chamber-Pot charg'd to the Brim with Female Ammunition" (Byrd 1994, 124).

Named Lubberland, Byrd's Swiftian dystopia is crowded with boorish men and slovenly women who have migrated from North Carolina to Virginia. To his mind, this white trash should be replaced by stalwart yeomen from England or Germany. While comic shafts playfully target the ignorant rabble, a harsher satiric allegory is intended to upbraid vice that dissembles as virtue. It applies to double-faced characters in the picaresque tradition of merciless disclosure. Those rascals generally prove unworthy of their tasks while cynically deceiving whoever trusts them. It thus belongs to the narrator to divulge the truth about their duplicity, step by step.

Among the commissioners, Firebrand (Richard Fitzwilliams) is the butt of ridicule. An inveterate troublemaker, constantly angered at society, he is the evil genius of the expedition, a figure of misrule and a traitor to Virginia. At a crucial moment the obnoxious timeserver defects with the Carolinians, changing the course of events and threatening to end the surveying process to benefit North Carolina at the expense of the Virginia territory. Firebrand and his faction even harass and sometimes rape girls in their hosts' houses. Like Astrolabe, Orion is an incompetent surveyor. The sycophantic, cowardly knave of Firebrand is hated by the group, as suggested in this episode: "Orion slept so sound that he had been burnt in his Blanket, if the Centry had not been kinder to him than he deserved" (Byrd 1994, 95). Boastful and provocative, Byrd's scapegoats remain poor hunters and lovers but unceasingly give evidence of the imp of the perverse in human nature. For example, Firebrand's henchmen jeer at Humdrum (Peter Fontaine), the virginal chaplain who is dubbed "Dean Pip." Though less aggressive, other commissioners are likewise ranked as caricatures: Plausible (Moseley) is deceitful; Shoebrush (Lovick), a former valet de chambre, is good-humored but servile; Puzzlecause (Little), a Harvard-educated preacher, has degenerated into an awkward oversexed rake.

The Carolinians are the villains because they do not want the line to be extended to the Appalachian Mountains, whereas Steddy means to finish the job to comply with the king's projects of western expansion. The symbolic "Line" anticipates Frederick Jackson Turner's concept of the frontier as a dynamic force of penetration into the wilderness. It means that the delineation of the temporary boundary between civilization and the wilderness is an incentive to the conquest of the American terra incognita, the frontier being in permanent motion. When the party is rid of Firebrand, it celebrates its renewed integrity like the knights of the Round Table who have expelled the felon from Avalon. They create the Order of Maosti, a parody of Spotswood's Order of the Golden Shoe. Having now triumphed over disrupting evil forces, they can proceed on their route like crusaders.

In Byrd's frontier fable, his entourage stands for pioneer virtues. Meanwell (Dandridge) is a reliable aid. So are the rank-and-file surveyors sternly carrying the chains across swamps, quicksand, and rattlesnakes. Steddy is Byrd's alter ego. Embattled against raw pretensions, he possesses a civilized presence that remains a bulwark against colonial entropy. As mounting tension breaks out into scuffles, Firebrand happens one day to grasp the leg of a chair to strike Meanwell. But Steddy valiantly wards off the blow. He is in His Majesty's service as loyal and outspoken as Ivanhoe. The narrator being a scandalmonger, Steddy embodies communitarian values. With reference to the group their coexistence seems to imply both identification and rejection, fascination and revulsion, thus paving the way for nineteenth-century southern folk humor.

As the expedition goes deeper into unexplored areas, the picaresque subsides into an obsessive quest of the "Line." Firebrand and his villains first duplicated Congreve's wicked bachelors and double dealers in the canebrakes. The hardships suffered by the surveyors in the desert of the Dismal Swamp are now transfigured into an hyperbolic tall story: "They were reduced to such Straights that they began to look upon John Ellis's Dog with a longing Appetite, and John Evans who was fat and well liking, had reasons to fear that he wou'd be the next Morsel" (Byrd 1994, 103). At last feeding on bear meat thanks to Indian Ned Bearskin's skills, Steddy's men appropriate the strength of the mythic animal through gargantuan feasts.

An Americanized Beowulf, the bear becomes a symbol of pagan nature, whose greatness measures the greatness of his opponent. The mother bear encountered in the forest is even more humane than anyone of the Carolinians. Bearskin is to the amused but tolerant narrator what Queequeg is to Ishmael or Jim to Huckleberry Finn. The Native American is a rising folk hero whose culture deserves attention because it holds some coherence, even though there is nothing ecstatic about Bearskin's cosmology, as exemplified in some of the clownish deities to be met in the Indian world beyond death: "On the Borders sits a hideous Old Woman whose head is cover'd up with Rattle-Snakes instead of Tresses, with glaring white Eyes, sunk very deep in her Head" (Byrd 1994, 144).

While the Hudibrastic spirit reigns among the braggarts, Steddy proceeds to a secular land of promise anticipating Jefferson's garden of the world, rather than recalling the Puritan city upon the hill. Meanwhile, the Appalachian Mountains are nicknamed "pimple wart" and "maiden's breast." The best among Byrd's swashbucklers are a civilizing force and not a destructive one in the backwoods. They want nothing more than to tame the chaos to survive and rejoice like Rabelais's outsize characters in their triumph over frustrating isolation. They stand by the reality principle like Thomas Morton, who around the Maypole of Merry Mount in his New Canaan revived the Bacchanalias to challenge the strictness of conscience prevailing in William Bradford's Plymouth Plantation. The Cavaliers who celebrate the zest of life are the enemies of all abstractions, moral principles, and joylessness. They are hedonists who live for the moment, and their lust for life casts off inhibitions. Pitted against the wilderness, they can go through harrowing adventures with only a dim sense of danger.

Similarly, Rabelais's Gargantua and Pantagruel share the energy of a world in which the abnormal, the natural, the cosmic, and the comic are bound together in rituals celebrating the triumph of vitality. Byrd sometimes makes mayhem a cause of enjoyment through his treatment of orgiastic saturnalia and farcical profanity. His highbrow English acquaintances would have probably disclaimed the crude metaphors and madcap hyperboles pervading *The Secret History*. Stemming from the subsoil of Augustan satire, his humor strikingly evolved into a native brand, exorcizing the terrors bred by the colonial frontier. When Byrd died in 1744, as Pierre Marambaud points out, the frontier was still the source of imminent danger and future wealth.

EDWARD KIMBER, THE RAMBLING OBSERVER

Edward Kimber was born in 1719. At first a Baptist minister, his father Isaac had turned to writing, being a journalist before becoming the editor of the *London*

Magazine in 1732. Like father like son: no doubt Edward was immersed in bookish occupations at an early age. In his brilliant edition of *Itinerant Observations in America,* Edward Kimber's travel narrative published in installments during the mid-1740s, Kevin J. Hayes mentions that the author was strongly influenced by the evocative power of the American landscape in Richard Lewis's poem "Journey from Patapsco to Annapolis," reprinted in the *London Magazine* in 1733. A year later, Kimber already contributed pastoral verse inspired by Alexander Pope's poetic diction.

Kimber responded to the call of the wild when he left England in September 1742. As in the case of John Lawson, the heliotropic impulse was strong enough for him to shorten his stay in chilly New York and head for Georgia on a hazardous voyage dramatically recorded in *Itinerant Observations.* From the harbor of Senepuxent in Maryland where he landed, Kimber's inland trip took him to Williamsburg, before his departure from Yorktown for Frederica, Georgia, on St. Simon's Island, where he arrived in early January 1743.

Spain's hold on Florida had been weakened by the establishment of Georgia in 1733, an English proprietary colony under the authority by General James Oglethorpe and the Trustees. Georgians had migrated to the mouth of the Altamaha, founded Frederica, and occupied the province of Guale. Spanish officials shored up the land and water approaches to St. Augustine especially to protect the St John's River, a strategic waterway. Meanwhile, Oglethorpe had enlisted Creek, Cherokee, and Chickasaw tribes. The war broke out in the spring of 1740 when a force of more than 2,000, including English troops and their Indian allies, invaded Florida but withdrew when reinforcements from Cuba arrived. Spain counterattacked in 1742 with a flotilla carrying 2,000 men. They landed on St. Simon's Island but were driven back at Bloody Marsh. Kimber joined Oglethorpe's regiment in an expedition to St. Augustine in 1742 that amounted to a few skirmishes, the killing of a polecat, and five scalps.

Kimber's report on the expedition dated July 29, 1743, was published anonymously by the *London Magazine* in 1744. Self-image enhancing resulted in lyrical outbursts on the exotic landscapes of Florida in a jingoistic style that lionized Oglethorpe. Kimber's tour of the New World led him then to Savannah and Charles Town, only a few months before his return to London in July. His diary drafted over two years offered scant factual evidence for a book-length travel narrative intended to cover the American scene.

The structure of *Itinerant Observations* did not follow the day-by-day chronology but reorganized time and space, allowing Kimber to focus on specific moments, as happens with the description of Simon's Island, which occurs in media res. Whereas an anonymous letter in the *London Magazine* had announced a broad panorama of the North American colonies by a young gentleman who had made several voyages across the Atlantic, the achievement was not equal to the expectation, at least in volume. Perhaps the advertisement was no humbug but self-deceit on the part of an ambitious young man who had overreached himself.

The anonymous commentator intruded again to vindicate missing pages on Carolina for diplomatic reasons. As Hayes puts it, "Kimber, like any good Grub Street writer, made sure that what he wrote got printed. . . . If he had written about Carolina in detail, it seems unlikely he would have neglected to see the writings in print" (Kimber 1998, 16). What Kimber did not see he could easily imagine. In his later literary career he wrote seven ramble novels in which plots were strung together with series of comic situations implying stereotypes such as tramps, servants, thieves, and con men. Kimber also used the journalistic method of the reversed pyramid, which consists in singling out and highlighting first a significant event of the story to bait the reader by offering a dramatic close-up effect before returning to the beginning of the development.

Itinerant Observations is not a promotion tract but a mosaic of vignettes to be enjoyed separately. The locations are described with graphic accuracy, making it obvious that the visual quality is due to serious documentation as illustrated in the mapping of Frederica. In support of English propaganda, Kimber refers to the furious and fanatic Spaniards, as if he were personally involved in the defense of the territory. Meanwhile, digressions are strangely obtrusive, as in the statement about the difficulties of horse riding in America. Kimber cannot help capitalizing on his outlandish though brief experience to give an exotic taste of frontier life. Then shifting from the urban setting to nature, the tone is romanticized by the narrator now overwhelmed with the beauty of the hickory, the cypress and the "robes of antique Moss." The local color is also suffused with mysticism and pathetic fallacy, almost anticipating Chateaubriand's vision of the American South in Atala, as illustrated in "the prowling Wolf" and "the discontented Bear." The additional hint that danger is always lurking in the backwoods further identifies the narrator as an intrepid adventurer. The pictorial quality of the evocations of the fauna and the flora is not often sustained in the toponymy, as happens in Lawson's abundance of foreign names, which amplifies the sense of faraway places. At times, the itinerant observer even uses poetic diction such as "the finny race" or the "Strain of saddening Philomel," which surprisingly transmutes the exotic into the familiar (Kimber 1998, 29–31). At times Kimber's dual vision of Georgia and England even emerges as a palimpsest. As the traveler becomes acquainted with the colonists, his aim is to recapture the atmosphere of the English environment on the plantations. The passage on his visit of an orphan house displays humanitarian ideals in nature's haven, in the mood of Oliver Goldsmith's social pity in The Vicar of Wakefield, published some twenty years later.

It is in Savannah that Kimber undertakes to deal with colonial politics, first conspicuously supporting General James Oglethorpe, commander in chief of His Majesty's forces. In the 1740s, the majority of the Georgia immigrants were funded by the Trustees under the leadership of Oglethorpe, who since 1732 had been offering tracts of land aside from tools and provisions. The pioneers settled in different places according to their ethnic origins, the English being in Savannah and the Scots at Darien. One-third of the population, having neither financial support nor assistance, objected to the prohibition of both slavery and rum by the House of Commons with the Trustees' approval. Among the reasons for such legislation was the offer made by the Spaniards to grant freedom to defecting slaves who would enlist in their regiments. The Malcontents were a group of settlers, mostly slave-holders, organized by Patrick Tailfer, who circulated a petition to amend the laws. A pamphlet entitled *A True and Historical Narrative of the Colony of Georgia* by Tailfer and several Malcontents denounced policies resulting in the impoverish-ment of planters and the increase of squatters (Tailfer 1971). By 1750, the Malcontents eventually won when slavery and open land ownership were legally authorized.

In *Itinerant Observations,* as the Georgia episodes close, the focus shifts back to Kimber's earlier departure from England. The action is thus set in motion af-ter the somewhat static presentation of a single scene. The picaresque narrative style slowly pervades the account of the voyage from New York to Senepuxent in Maryland. Kimber's human geography gains in variety just as an apothegm warns innocents abroad: "A Traveller should never depend upon any Thing, but his own Sight, or the Experience of a Friend, for the Character of a Vessel and its Com-mander" (Kimber 1998, 37).

Homespun metaphors add to the skeptical outlook of the narrator, "a Vessel in bad Trim" being compared to "an unhappy Marriage." All the ingredients of a rough sea crossing readily dramatize the context, such as a leaky ship, a sick captain, seven stultified black slaves, and mutinous drunken sailors. The first American shore discovered is the bleak site of snow-covered Long Island, a "large Desert" where "tuneful Warblers" hop over a barren ground (Kimber 1998, 38). In the midst of a severe storm off the coast of New Jersey, the narrator-actor is involved in the rescue of the sinking ship. A virtual skipper among helpless mates, Kimber does not even spare his readers the derelict of a phantom ship and, in the wake, the mutilated body of a sailor devoured by sharks. It is almost a wreck that reaches Senepuxent while the transfigured narrator assumes a heroic stature. Part of Kimber's picaresque in-spiration is to contrive some misadventure to break from unnerving pastoral land-scapes. Later in Virginia he steps into a small punt to reach a shallop lying at anchor a mile from the coast. On the way, swimming porpoises disturb hogs loaded on board, and the boat capsizes. It then takes pages for Kimber to ponder over human destiny in the hands of Providence.

The Maryland episode is mostly devoted to an appraisal of colonial lifestyle. As in Lawson's and Byrd's accounts, Kimber's epicurean tastes are essential elements in his evaluation of the New World. The nature of local products is judged with reference to homeland consumption as exemplified in the respective qualities of persimmon and medlar. Although the prosperity of planters is described in glowing terms, the seamy side of colonial society is brought to light through observations on courthouses "where as much idle Wrangling is on Foot, often as in any Court in Westminster Hall" (Kimber 1998, 47). Kimber's analysis of southern society seems to be less based on eyewitness evidence than dependent on general information. His view of planter society as a semifeudal system is, however, perceptively developed, especially by voicing the opinions of keen observers, well aware of prevailing values in eighteenth-century England. The planter class is praised for its refinements, the character of the Virginia belle being rapturously extolled. Toward slavery, Kimber's humanitarian concern urges him to blame ruthless planters and favor paternalism. He takes it for granted that the caste barrier between whites and blacks originates in the racial inferiority of Africans and, in particular, finds fault with interracial relations tolerated between children. Racial exclusiveness does not affect Kimber in the same degree regarding Native Americans, his comparative study of Indians and whites being derived from the idea of a culture gap to be bridged. For him, just as primitive tribes peopled the English backwoods when Diana and the satyrs were evoked in antique mythologies, American Indians indulge in pagan rituals and privilege hunting at the expense of agriculture, although living side by side with civilized colonists. Yet Kimber trusts that Christianization has already considerably hastened their transmutation. In this respect, Kimber like Lawson seems to be closer to the policies of Catholic New France to convert the heathens and make allies of them.

Kimber's picaresque imagination is spurred on by the status of articled servants, especially ex-convicts. He inserts an anecdote about a boy shipped to Maryland and sold to a brutal master whose daughter will become the wife of the emancipated white slave. When the old master is recognized and submitted to by his former victim, he prefers suicide to the prospect of becoming a servant himself. Throughout *Itinerant Observations*, Kimber strives to combine the range of picaresque experience with the structure of romance. Had he been supplied with enough material he would have loved to write the secret story of a rambler overseas. This tendency is often perceptible in eighteenth-century libertine fiction. Fanciful realism then transcends historical reality, suggesting that writing about stimulating experiences is more valued than the experience itself. It reflects a literary dichotomy clearly also observable in Byrd's twofold production of history and satire about his adventures along the Virginia boundary line.

Kimber wrote several ramble novels such as the popular *Life and Adventures of Joe Thompson* (1750) and *The Juvenile Adventures of David Ranger* (1756), in which he produced spurious memoirs of actor David Garrick. *Itinerant Observations* offers him less opportunity to stretch common experience, except for his adventures at sea and a few lines on Oglethorpe's defense of Frederica. In many eighteenth-century ramble novels, plots provided a succession of comic accidents in the style of *Lazarillo de Tormes, Till Eulenspiegel, Joseph Andrews,* and *Gil Blas.* Such occurrences were abundant in Byrd's inspiration. The loose, haphazard structure of *Itinerant Observations* would have lent itself to digressive elements, had the author been less sanctimonious about colonial manners and thereby willing to break taboos as Lawson and Byrd do in their works. On the other hand, Kimber legitimately kept to the ethical functions of a truthful travel narrative in a faithful confrontation of colonial America when his imagination did not run wild.

REFERENCES

Breytspraak, Charlotte, and Jack Breytspraak. 1992. Historical Profile: John Lawson. *Journal of the New Bern Historical Society* 1: 29–31.

Bush, Sargent, Jr. 1995. Sarah Kemble Knight (1666–1727). *Legacy* 12: 112–120.

Byrd, William. 1994. *The Secret History of the Line.* In *Colonial American Travel Narratives,* edited by Wendy Martin, 77–172. New York: Penguin.

Dill, A. T. 1986. Graffenried, Christoph, Baron von. *Dictionary of North Carolina Biography.* Vol. 2, *D–G,* edited by William S. Powell, 34–36. Chapel Hill: University of North Carolina Press.

Holloman, Charles R. 1991. Lawson, John. *Dictionary of North Carolina Biography.* Vol. 4, *L–O,* edited by William S. Powell, 327–328. Chapel Hill: University of North Carolina Press.

Knight, Sarah Kemble. 1994. *The Journal of Madame Knight.* In *Colonial American Travel Narratives,* edited by Wendy Martin, 49–75. New York: Penguin.

Kimber, Edward. 1998. *Itinerant Observations in America,* edited by Kevin J. Hayes. Newark: University of Delaware Press.

Lawson, John. 1709. *A New Voyage to Carolina; Containing the Exact Description and Natural History of that Country: Together with the Present State thereof. And A Journal of a Thousand Miles, Travel'd thro' Several Nations of Indians.* London.

———. 1967. *A New Voyage to Carolina,* edited by Hugh Talmage Lefler. Chapel Hill: University of North Carolina Press.

Marambaud, Pierre. 1971. *William Byrd of Westover.* Charlottesville: University Press of Virginia.

Margolies, Alan. 1964. The Editing and Publication of *The Journal of Madam Knight. Papers of the Bibliographical Society of America* 58: 25–32.

Tailfer, Patrick, et al. [1741] 1971. *A True and Historical Narrative of the Colony of Georgia.* Reprint. Freeport, NY: Books for Libraries Press.

CHAPTER 10

DR. ALEXANDER HAMILTON

KEVIN J. HAYES

Stopping in Philadelphia during his colonial American odyssey in 1744, Dr. Alexander Hamilton spent a night with Henry Fielding's recent work, *The Adventures of Joseph Andrews* (1742), the first comic novel in the history of English literature. He enjoyed the work immensely. Even before he finished it, he called *Joseph Andrews* "a masterly performance of its kind and entertaining; the characters of low life here are naturally delineated, and the whole performance is so good that I have not seen any thing of that kind equal or excell it" (Hamilton 1948, 23). He retired early the next night to finish the book. Reflecting on his experience, Hamilton thought his time well spent. Perhaps it should be unsurprising to see how much he enjoyed *Joseph Andrews*: Hamilton is the Henry Fielding of American literature. His great travel narrative, the *Itinerarium*, rivals Fielding's *Journal of a Voyage to Lisbon* (1755) for wit, charm, descriptive power, and personal insight, and *The History of the Ancient and Honourable Tuesday Club*, the fictionalized proceedings of the Annapolis club that Hamilton founded, is to American literature what *The History of Tom Jones* (1749) is to English literature. Much as Henry Fielding is one of the great figures of eighteenth-century British literature, Dr. Alexander Hamilton is one of the great figures of eighteenth-century American literature. Unlike Fielding, who established a sizable contemporary following, Hamilton, save for his pseudonymous contributions to the *Maryland Gazette,* was read solely by a close-knit group of friends.

THE RECOGNITION OF DR. ALEXANDER HAMILTON

In 1809, Dr. Upton Scott, the last surviving member of the club Hamilton founded, lent the manuscript of the *History of the Tuesday Club* to the Baltimore Library. In a letter accompanying the loan, Scott remembered the work's author as "a man of strict honor and integrity, of a friendly, benevolent disposition and a most cheerful, facetious companion amongst his friends, whom he never failed to delight with the effusions of his wit, humor and drollery, in which acquirement he had no equal." As Scott's remarks suggest, Hamilton was appreciated in Annapolis, but outside those who knew him personally, he had no literary reputation. The manuscript of the *History of the Tuesday Club* remained in the Baltimore Library, gathering dust for decades. It went virtually unread until the Reverend Dr. John G. Morris prepared a paper about the club for the Maryland Historical Society. Morris recognized the historical value of the *History* but failed to appreciate its literary importance. Describing its contents, he wrote, "A great mass of learned nonsense is displayed in the treatment of these several chapters and the most irrelevant subjects are dwelt on at great length; facts are manufactured and history is made false; quotations are cited and authors referred to of whom no body ever heard" (Morris 1873, 150–151). Morris's remarks form the earliest published criticism of the *History*.

Otherwise Hamilton's writings remained unknown until a manuscript of the *Itinerarium* surfaced in Italy during the early twentieth century. William K. Bixby, the great St. Louis collector of Americana, acquired the manuscript and commissioned Albert Bushnell Hart to prepare an edition, which appeared in 1907. In his introduction, Hart said, "Among the numerous journals and narratives of travel during the Colonial period, few are so lively and so full of good-humored comment on people and customs as the *Itinerarium* of Dr. Hamilton" (Hamilton 1907, ix). Literary histories provide one way to track Hamilton's subsequent reception history. Though the Hart edition was printed for private distribution, it was soon recognized as an important work of early American literature. In his chapter on travel writing for *The Cambridge History of American Literature,* George Parker Winship quotes liberally from the *Itinerarium*. Though most impressed with Hamilton's depiction of contemporary book culture, Winship also appreciated the *Itinerarium* as a whole, observing, "Dr. Hamilton, one of the most entertaining of American travellers, appears to advantage even beside the urbanity of Byrd and the sprightliness of Mrs. Knight" (Winship 1917, 13).

Despite Winship's efforts to canonize the *Itinerarium* as an American literary classic, the work was largely forgotten in the coming decades. The next major history of American literature, Robert E. Spiller's *Literary History of the United States,* does not mention Hamilton at all. In 1948, the same year Spiller's *Literary History* appeared, Carl Bridenbaugh published a new edition of the *Itinerarium,* which found favor with its reviewers. Hugh Lefler called it "the best travel account of colonial

America"—high praise from the editor of John Lawson's *New Voyage to Carolina*. In his review, Lawrence C. Wroth observed, "In his journal a procession of colonial types passes before the eye of the reader in a degree of fullness found in no other American document of the period." In his literary history of colonial Maryland, J. A. Leo Lemay called the *Itinerarium* "the best single portrait of men and manners, of rural and urban life, of the wide range of society and scenery in colonial America." Lemay predicted, "In the future, Hamilton will rank as a major American writer of neoclassic prose" (Lefler 1950; Wroth 1949; Lemay 1972b, 229, 213).

These heartfelt appreciations had minimal impact on Dr. Hamilton's reputation, however. In the *Columbia Literary History of the United States,* Hamilton received a total of two sentences (Simpson 1988, 129). The same year this literary history appeared, Elaine Breslaw published *The Records of the Tuesday Club,* an early version of the work that would become the *History,* and John Bary Tally published a book-length study of the music composed and performed by Hamilton and the other members of the club. Two years later Robert Micklus published his magisterial three-volume edition of the *History* and *The Comic Genius of Dr. Alexander Hamilton,* a book-length critical study of Hamilton. Micklus's efforts prompted a reprint of Bridenbaugh's edition of the *Itinerarium* (Hamilton 1992). Still, in the next major national literary history, Bercovitch's *Cambridge History of American Literature,* Hamilton received little more space than he had received in the original *Cambridge History of American Literature* (Shields 1994, 321–323).

In recent years, Hamilton has started to earn more attention in the scholarly community. Micklus published an abridged edition of the *History* ideal for classroom use in 1995. Another book-length study, Wilson Somerville's *The Tuesday Club of Annapolis as Cultural Performance,* appeared the following year. Detailed critical essays have followed (Imbarrato 2001; Beyers 2005). Beyond the realm of literary studies, Hamilton has been cited in works treating African American musical traditions, colonial American foodways, gender roles in early America, maritime life, material culture, and public life (Radano 2003; McWilliams 2005; Vickers and Walsh 2005; Hood 2003; Thompson 1999). These various studies indicate that Lemay's prediction is gradually coming true: Hamilton is now achieving the recognition he deserves as one of the major authors of early American literature.

LIFE

Born in Edinburgh on September 26, 1712, Alexander Hamilton, at thirteen, matriculated at the University of Edinburgh, where his father, William, was principal and professor of divinity. Studying there, Hamilton came under the influence of Charles Mackie, the university's first professor of history (Breslaw 2004). Mackie taught Western civilization, the history of Scotland, and British, Greek, and Roman antiquities. He instilled a sense of seriousness and dedication in his students. Lecturing in Latin, he emphasized the importance of historical accuracy and impartiality (Smitten 2004). Though a sprawling mock history, Hamilton's *History of the Tuesday Club* nonetheless shows Mackie's influence in terms of its emphasis on chronology and its keen awareness of historiography. Mackie was also a dedicated clubman, serving as a mason as well as a member of the Old Revolution Club and the Rankenian Club. Among his students and his fellow clubmen, Mackie encouraged conviviality and goodwill to create an atmosphere that fostered learning and mutual improvement.

After taking his M.A. from the university in 1729, Hamilton decided to study medicine. He received his medical degree from the University of Edinburgh in 1737, writing his thesis on bone disease, *De Morbis Ossium* (Micklus 1990). In medical school, he and some fellow classmates formed a student organization, which would eventually become the Royal Medical Society of Scotland. He also became a standing member of Edinburgh's Whin-Bush Club. The club's poet laureate was the distinguished Scottish poet Allan Ramsay, who composed some lines of verse for Hamilton's induction. Hamilton enjoyed the weekly gatherings of the Whin-Bush Club, but before another year had passed, he decided to emigrate to America, where he would have a much better chance of establishing a medical practice than he had in Scotland. The decision was not unusual. Generally speaking, Hamilton observed, Scots, "being of a bustling, pushing disposition, cannot rest at home, where nothing is to be got, but range about to all parts of the world, [and] Improve their fortunes" (Hamilton 1990, 1: 80).

In 1738, Hamilton reached Annapolis, Maryland, where he established a medical practice and gradually earned a reputation as the city's most eminent physician. He also became involved in social and political life. He joined the Ugly Club of Annapolis in 1739 and remained an active member until the club disbanded in 1744 shortly before he left on his northward journey. The coincidence suggests that Hamilton himself had been the driving force behind the Ugly Club. In 1743, he was elected to the office of common councilman, a position he retained until his death. In the early 1740s, Hamilton began to show signs of tuberculosis. To improve his health, he prescribed a rigorous adventure. He would spend a summer touring the American colonies to the north. He left Annapolis in late May and did not return until late September. The *Itinerarium* forms the record of that journey.

THE *ITINERARIUM*

Starting from Annapolis on May 30, 1744, Dr. Hamilton was accompanied by his Negro slave Dromo, a Sancho Panza to Hamilton's Don Quixote. Overall,

Dr. Hamilton cut quite a figure. His flamboyant attire included a lace hat, a green vest, ruffles, a brace of pistols, and a smallsword. Evincing his characteristic good humor, he made fun of his personal appearance within the pages of the *Itinerarium* by recording some conversation on the subject, one of many such snippets that make the *Itinerarium* such a delight (Hamilton 1948, 139). At the sight of him, a Boston woman asks a mutual friend, "What strange mortall is that?"

"'Tis the flower of the Maryland beaux," the friend replies. "He is a Maryland physitian."

"O Jesus! A physitian!" the woman responds. "Deuce take such odd looking physicians."

Besides contributing to its humor, this brief exchange indicates the literary sophistication of the *Itinerarium*. Characterizing the episode, Robert Micklus observed, "Hamilton inverts the typical perspective of travel writers: here the observer becomes the observed, and all get to play the optical game of eighteenth-century traveler—the observance of oddity" (Micklus 1990, 91).

Traveling north the very first day of his trip, Hamilton met one "Mr. H——t." Throughout the surviving manuscript of the *Itinerarium*, Hamilton obscured many proper names in this fashion, using a technique contemporary novels often used. Not all the names in the *Itinerarium* can be recovered. This one can. Mr. H——t was Hamilton's friend Samuel Hart, who would later be elected an honorary member of the Tuesday Club. Hart, who was going the opposite direction, turned around and escorted Hamilton to his home. Hart was a good host, and the evening proved to be delightful. After dinner, they "conversed like a couple of virtuosos" (Hamilton 1948, 4).

Brief as it is, Hamilton's description of their evening embodies key themes that recur throughout the *Itinerarium*. Writing in a time before science became a profession or, indeed, before the word "science" entered the English language, Hamilton was using the term "virtuoso" to refer to the amateur gentleman-scientist, a man with sufficient wealth and leisure to have time for scientific pursuits. The virtuoso might observe the natural world or attempt physical experiments or both. Regardless, he would be sure to discuss his scientific pursuits with others engaged in similar observations and experiments of their own. Here's the tricky part: though conversation let the virtuoso display his interests in science, he had to be careful not to boast too much about his scientific discoveries. In conversation, the virtuoso, like any proper gentleman, had to maintain both modesty and decorum.

As his experience throughout this journey clarifies, the conversation of others was a kind of litmus test for Hamilton. He was "a conversation-loving author" (Koch 1949). The way people conducted themselves in conversation enabled him to discern their personalities. From their speech, Hamilton could discover or thought he could discover the learning, background, and cultural sophistication of those he met on the road (Hoffer 2003, 202). Mr. D——gs, a man he encounters the next day, Hamilton initially identifies as "a virtuoso in botany." The more Mr. D——gs talks, the more he reveals his ignorance. Hamilton observed, "He affected some knowledge in naturall philosophy, but his learning that way was but superficiall" (Hamilton 1948, 5). An unabashed snob, Hamilton took offense when others whom he saw as beneath him in the social scale engaged him in conversation. His indignation rose to a higher pitch, however, when those who could consider themselves his equals or near equals revealed their backwardness in conversation. Taken together, the diary entries that form the *Itinerarium* create a running record of conversations Hamilton had throughout his journey and, as such, form a unique document that brings the many voices of colonial America alive. Yet the conversations in the *Itinerarium* do much more. Situated within a written work whose contemporary audience consisted of a small group of Hamilton's friends, the conversations provide a poignant contrast between oral and written culture and suggest crucial parallels between the two.

Hamilton's enjoyment of the art of conversation and the pleasures of club life complemented one another. A club meeting at Treadway's ordinary, where he stayed his second night on the road, emerges from the *Itinerarium* as a parody of proper clubical behavior. The club is just breaking up as he arrives. An exemplar of the Enlightenment, Hamilton viewed the world with Cartesian coordinates superimposed on it. Most of the drunken club members this evening "had got upon their horses and were seated in an oblique situation, deviating much from a perpendicular to the horizontal plane, a posture quite necessary for keeping the center of gravity within its propper base for the support of superstructure; hence we deduce the true physicall reason why our heads overloaded with liquor become too ponderous for our heels" (Hamilton 1948, 6).

Hamilton compared the physical position of these men with their conversation: "Their discourse was as oblique as their position; the only thing intelligible in it was oaths and God dammes; the rest was an inarticulate sound like Rabelais' frozen words a thawing, interlaced with hickupings and belchings" (Hamilton 1948, 6). This simile introduces another filter through which Hamilton viewed the world: the literary tradition provided him with a wealth of images and ideas he used to interpret what he saw. In this case, Rabelais's *Gargantua and Pantagruel* provided an episode allowing Hamilton to articulate his experiences to his close-knit circle of readers, who, as educated gentlemen, were familiar with Rabelais's writings. The reference also let Hamilton pay homage to a crucial literary influence. The *Itinerarium* and, even more so, the *History of the Tuesday Club* reflect the profound influence Rabelais had on Hamilton's prose style, an influence that deserves closer study.

The first week on the road took Hamilton the rest of the way through Maryland and lower Pennsylvania (Delaware) and into Pennsylvania. One day he stopped for dinner at a Pennsylvania tavern, where his fellow dinner guests engaged in what Hamilton facetiously called "a learned dispute." They were debating the difference between a declaration and proclamation. Hamilton listened for a while, but he left the table at the argument's peak. He explained: "They grew very loud upon it as they put about the bowl, and I retired into a corner of the room to laugh a little, handkeerchef fashion, pretending to be busied in blowing my nose; so I slurd a laugh with nose blowing as people sometimes do a fart with coughing" (Hamilton 1948, 15–16). Seen in light of Hamilton's intended readership, his remarks show him abandoning the conversation of the moment and anticipating how he might retell the episode for his friends. His fellow members of the Ugly Club, for example, greatly enjoyed "Coarse homespun Similes, gross metaphors and allusions, pronounced with a harsh tone of voice and a horse laugh" (Hamilton 1990, 1: 106).

Hamilton's frequent dissatisfaction with conversations along the road occasionally make his journey resemble a mythic quest, good conversation being his holy grail. By the time he reaches New Jersey, he longs for more than the overly presumptuous friendly greetings he has been hearing along the road. Upon meeting the Reverend Mr. Joseph Morgan, a hoary-headed man who was reputedly one of the greatest scientific minds in New Jersey, Hamilton hoped for some enlightened conversation. Morgan had been corresponding with the Royal Society of London for decades, and he had even written what one modern reader has called "a remarkably good Utopian novel," *The History of the Kingdom of Basaruah* (Morgan 1715; Stearns 1970, 497–499). Astrology, Morgan's first topic of conversation, quickly makes Hamilton skeptical. Discussing the influence of the stars, Morgan, as Hamilton observed, put "a great deal more confidence than I thought was requisite." Morgan proceeded to discuss several other scientific subjects. When he reaches medicine, Hamilton could see that Morgan was "a great pretender" (Hamilton 1948, 36). Apparently New Jersey offered little opportunity for intellectual conversation. On to New York.

Hamilton spent several days in New York City. One evening he got involved in a conversation about "the differences of climates in the American provinces with relation to the influence they had upon human bodies." Now here was an intellectual conversation Hamilton could both learn from and contribute to. The *Itinerarium* describes the part he played in this discussion: "I gave them as just an account as I could of Maryland—the air and temperature of that province, and the distempers incident to the people there." The learned conversation continued in earnest for some time, but Hamilton abbreviated his account of it. The only other remark he recorded comes from a man from Curaçao, who related "that in a month's time he had known either 30 or 40 souls buried which, in his opinion, was a great number in the small neighbourhood where he lived." Hamilton ended his account with a commentary on the Curaçao man's observation: "I could scarce help laughing out at this speech and was just going to tell him that I did not think it was customary to bury souls anywhere but in Ireland, but I restrained my tongue, having no mind to pick a quarrell for the sake of a joke" (Hamilton 1948, 47–48).

In his narrative, Hamilton is negotiating a space between those with whom he conversed and his intended readers. During this conversation, he maintained decorum and withheld his joke, but he included the joke as part of his written text to amuse his Annapolis readers. In the *Itinerarium,* Hamilton is a man in search of poignant conversation, but this joke suggests that he wanted something more. In addition to intellectual stimulation, he also wanted humor and conviviality. Ideally, he wanted both, to enjoy serious conversation yet to be free to interject humorous remarks whenever the whim happened to strike.

He liked matching wits with others, but he often found the men he met during his travels inadequate to the task. One Mr. H——d, for example, pretended to be learned, but he was really "fit to shine no where but among your good natured men and ignorant blockheads." Once Mr. H——d demonstrated his skill at applying proverbs, he somewhat redeemed himself. Hamilton observed, "He dealt much in proverbs and made use of one which I thought pritty significant when well applied. It was *the devil to pay and no pitch hot?* An interrogatory adage metaphorically derived from the manner of sailors who pay their ship's bottoms with pitch." This proverbial devil gave Hamilton the opportunity to interject another proverb into the conversation: a Wellerism. Hamilton next explained, "I back'd it with *great cry and little wool, said the devil when he shore his hogs,* applicable enough to the ostentation and clutter he made with his learning" (Hamilton 1948, 82–83).

Hamilton is contemptuous of everyone who pretends to have great learning. The Reverend John Miln, to cite another example, is the object of his humorous derision. "In some parts of learning," Hamilton said of Miln, "such as the languages, he seemed pritty well versed. He could talk Latine and French very well and read the Greek authors, and I was told that he spoke the Dutch to perfection." Despite Miln's linguistic proficiency, Hamilton was unimpressed with other aspects of his learning. Ferrying up the Hudson River together, Hamilton described him in the process of reading. Miln, he wrote, "read a treatise upon microscopes and wanted me to sit and hear him, which I did, tho' with little relish, the piece being trite and vulgar, and tiresome to one who had seen Leewenhoek and some of the best hands upon that subject. I soon found Miln's ignorance of the thing, for as he read he seemed to be in a kind of surprize att every little trite observation of the author's. I found him an intire stranger to the mathematicks, so as that he knew not the difference betwixt a cone and a pyramid, a cylinder and a prysm" (Hamilton 1948, 52–53). Catching Miln in the act of reading in public, Hamilton saw deeply into his character. Miln wished to display himself as a learned man who took an interest in the sciences and other fields of knowledge beyond those required for his calling. While he may have given the less-educated ferryboat passengers such an impression, he did not impress this Edinburgh-trained physician (Hayes 2000, 42).

For all its criticism, the *Itinerarium* ultimately displays the complexity and variety of colonial culture. Often it reads like a Whitmanesque celebration of American diversity as Hamilton depicts the different people he encounters: the Pennsylvanians who boast about the stoniness of their roads; the dancing, finical, humpbacked barber; the servant who has the audacity to get into a fistfight with his unwieldy, potbellied master; the comical fellow who is tolerably well-versed in the quirps and quibbles of the law; the Dutch-speaking African woman who mouths off to Dromo; the young Boston man who mimics cats, dogs, cows, and hens, hitting high enough notes to bring his virility into question; the inquisitive rustic willing to purchase air to cure his fevers; and the drunken doctor who dares to spout against Boerhaave.

Furthermore, the *Itinerarium* shows that what we now consider the American national character was already well developed by Hamilton's day. On his return trip through Pennsylvania, he remarked that the Philadelphians "have that accomplishment peculiar to all our American colonys, viz., subtilty and craft in their dealings" (Hamilton 1948, 193). Hamilton's wording suggests that the inhabitants of colonial North America shared personal characteristics that distinguished them from people in other lands. At the work's end, he reiterates the point: "I found but little difference in the manners and character of the people in the different provinces I passed thro'. . . . As to politeness and humanity, they are much alike" (Hamilton 1948, 199). Hamilton's work shares great affinities with the subsequent humor of the old South, narratives by educated gentlemen fascinated with the language and personalities of the American population. His definition of the colonial character is much the same as what we now consider the American character. Colonists from Annapolis to Albany were self-sufficient, proud, innovative, malleable, sturdy, sly, sharp, and eager for profit.

His quest for good conversation was only occasionally successful, but it was really unnecessary. Returning to Annapolis, he was returning to a choice group of friends he could count on for delightful conversation. Since the Ugly Club had disbanded earlier that year, however, Hamilton needed to form a new club to help assure regular opportunities for conversation and conviviality.

The History of the Tuesday Club

Home from his American odyssey, his health partly recovered, Dr. Hamilton soon met with a handful of friends to form the Ancient and Honorable Tuesday Club of Annapolis. As one of its cardinal rules, the club established a law, which became known as the "Gelastic Law." It was designed to avoid the contentiousness that had doomed the Ugly Club: "That if any Subject of what nature soever be discussed, which levels at party matters, or the Administration of the Government of this province, or be disagreeable to the Club, no answer Shall be Given thereto, but after Such discourse is ended, the Society Shall Laugh at the member offending, in order to divert the discourse" (Hamilton 1988, 7–8). The Gelastic Law worked well: the conviviality of the Tuesday Club persisted for years.

As club secretary, Hamilton was responsible for taking the minutes, but he went well beyond what the role of club secretary required: he reworked the proceedings of the club multiple times. He revised the "Minutes" into the *Records of the Tuesday Club* (Hamilton 1988). After compiling the *Records,* he then drafted the first two volumes of the *History* but abandoned the draft history without revising the third volume. Instead, he returned to the beginning of the first volume of the draft history to rewrite the final three-volume version. In the final revision, which he titled *The History of the Ancient and Honorable Tuesday Club,* Hamilton gave the club members their typenames: Hamilton himself became Loquacious Scribble; Maryland printer and litterateur Jonas Green became Jonathan Grog; Upton Scott became Jeronimo Jaunter; Charles Cole, the club president, became Nasifer Jole. Even honorary members and visitors to the club received typenames. Samuel Hart became Ignotus Warble, and Benjamin Franklin, appropriately enough, became Electro Vitrifice. Much of the *History,* therefore, went through four different versions: "Minutes," *Record,* draft history, and *History.* Throughout the revision, Hamilton adequately performed the role of "a proper and able Historiographer," which, he believed, was "to connect and form into an uniform Rhapsody affairs and facts of such Singular Importance" (Hamilton 1990, 1: 395). He also copiously illustrated both the *Records* and the *History* with his own humorous pen-and-ink-wash drawings.

With the publication of the *Records* and the *History* in quick succession during the late twentieth century, the *Records* were initially seen as merely an interim version of the *History,* a document that was important solely for what it could say about the composition of the *History.* Two decades after its publication, *Records* is now being seen as a document with its own intrinsic value. The fictional qualities of the *History* that so delight literary enthusiasts can form a barrier for historians, some of whom prefer the factual over the fanciful. As one recent commentator has remarked, "It is their very banality that makes the *Records of the Tuesday Club of Annapolis* compelling as a resource for historians inclined to theory" (Rice 1996, 220).

Yet *Records* are not without literary qualities. Indeed, as Chris Beyers has suggested, it is a mistake to read the work as a straightforward account of the club meetings. The work may start out that way, but gradually *Records* becomes something considerably more sophisticated. Letters to the club that Hamilton incorporated, he subtly rewrote to satirize what the correspondents were saying. He also interjected editorial comments critiquing President Cole and others. In addition, numerous speeches from club members he included show his hand in their composition. Sometimes, as Beyers observes, Hamilton rewrote speeches to mean the complete opposite of what their speakers intended (Beyers 2005).

The self-reflexive nature of the *History of the Tuesday Club* forms one of its most modern characteristics. In other words, this so-called history often takes the subject of history writing as a topic of discussion. Hamilton disagreed with those who thought that a history should maintain a clear and distinct focus. He observed,

> We shall meet with some Histories, where there is nothing but a dry relation of facts, without any useful reflections, or observations interspersed, which are Indeed the Salt of History, and afford it a Savor which makes it agreeable to the palat of every Judicious reader, without this, it would look like the York-shire Squire's Story of himself and his friend, which consisted chiefly of—and so quoth he, and so quoth I, and so we agreed on this, and so we differed on that, and so I went there, and so he came here, and so—and so—and so etc. (Hamilton 1990, 1: 129)

Hamilton's remarks anticipate Laurence Sterne's celebration of digressions in *Tristram Shandy*. True to what he says, Hamilton does not hesitate to include numerous digressions throughout the *History*. Indeed, as one reader has remarked, "It could be argued that the Tuesday Club as such is no more than a literary peg on which to hang a sequence of literary, philosophical, rhetorical, and farcical disquisitions and digressions, frequently mocking established literary and social forms" (Clark 1992, 155).

Hamilton's persona, Loquacious Scribble, begins book 1 of the *History* with "Of History and Historians." The delightful first chapters of each book nearly always follow the same pattern. He picks a subject—illustrious personages, witty sayings, the theater, insignias, rebellions—and then provides the subject's history, tracing it from the ancients to the Dark Ages (which seem especially dark to Hamilton), through the Renaissance, into recent times and across the ocean to America. Inevitably, the history of each subject culminates with the founding of the "ancient and honorable Tuesday Club of Annapolis in Maryland, now the Club of Clubs, and the only true ancient Club upon Earth" (Hamilton 1990, 1: 37). Placing the Tuesday Club on such a pinnacle, Hamilton mocks the notion that modern civilization can recapture ancient greatness. Though his attitude is tongue-in-cheek, it nevertheless reiterates a prevalent colonial American literary theme: in the New World, it is possible to begin civilization afresh and achieve classical excellence.

As Hamilton revised the draft history into the *History*, he made additions that further stressed the parallel between the Tuesday Club and ancient civilization. Even the changes that heighten the parody emphasize the theme. Celebrating the club's fourth anniversary, for example, Scribble compares its laws with Roman and Greek laws but hesitates to call them as great as the ancients. In the draft, Sir John Oldcastle frowned and exclaimed, "Sir, I make bold to affirm, that we of this here Club, are as great as any body" (Micklus 1980, 1564). Hamilton rewrote Sir John's remark: "Sir!—Sir!—I make bold to affirm, that we of this here Club, are as great, and as wise as any body, not excepting either Greeks or Trojans" (Hamilton 1990, 1: 343). In the character of Sir John, Hamilton creates the naive, drum-beating, bullheaded, jingoistic American partisan, a humorous type that reappeared throughout nineteenth- and twentieth-century American literary humor (Hayes 1993, 298). Sir John anticipates such figures as the senator in Joseph Heller's *Catch-22*, who exclaims upon learning of Major Major's plan to study English history: "What's the matter with American History? It's as good as any history in the world!"

Hamilton often brings up, if only to lampoon, the *translatio* theme—the idea that the course of civilization moves westward with the course of the sun and will therefore reach its zenith on the American strand. He notes that his Annapolis club is nothing but the Tuesday (or whin bush) Club of Lanneric, Scotland, "translated to America" (Hamilton 1990, 1: 111). After one anniversary celebration, Scribble sends Jonathan Grog's "Anniversary Ode" to the club's London agent, Captain Comely Coppernose, and asks him to insert it in a London magazine, "with a Suitable short preamble, drawing a parallel between the genius of the Incomparable Colley Cibber, and our American Bard . . . as that great Luminary of Parnassus, the British Laureat Cibber, is about to *set in the east,* and finish his glorious course, after having regaled us with many unparalleled odes, so, *In the west there now rises a sun,* that we hope will be as bright as Colley's, to wit, the Genius of the Poet Laureat of the ancient Tuesday Club of Annapolis in Maryland, whose mellifluous muse, will Surely qualify him to succeed the now Superannuated British Laureat" (Hamilton 1990, 2: 158). The Old World was aging and decrepit; the New was young, vibrant, and ready to replace the Old. By the time he wrote in the mid–eighteenth-century, *translatio* had been a central theme of American literature for more than a hundred years. Hamilton's playful derision emphasizes the prevalence of this colonial American motif.

With the founding of the Tuesday Club, ancient glory was restored, but the excesses of civilization almost immediately caused it to degenerate. "Luxury" has been called the *History*'s chief villain (Micklus 1990). Making the bombastic Loquacious Scribble the enemy of luxury and the champion of simplicity, Hamilton lampoons both luxury's presumed dangers and primitivism's supposed advantages. When the club was formed, the charter members ruled that only one simple dish—a gammon of bacon, for example—should be served at their meetings, but soon luxury crept in and club members began serving multicourse meals to outdo one another. Only by reverting to the single-dish rule, Scribble contends, can the club regain its ancient greatness. When it is his turn to serve as high steward, Scribble practices what he preaches by serving hominy. Long accustomed to fricasses and ragouts, several members grumble at Scribble's meal. He defends his choice with a typically long-winded oration: "Homony, I affirm, to be a good wholesome and Simple Dish, very well adapted for nourishment, and The more Simple our food is, the more kindly and agreeable it is to our Stomachs, in the opinion of all learned, wise and Judicious men, let us look back into the first ages of the world, many Centuries before any Records can be found, of this here ancient and honorable Club, to those blessed times, those halcyon days, which were called the Golden age, in which men lived long and happy, then all their food was Simple" (Hamilton 1990, 2: 207–208). Scribble asserts that hominy, the American Indian dish, was also an ancient favorite, and he provides a pseudo-etymology of the word, explaining that it was derived from Greek, Latin, and English words. Hamilton himself was well aware of the word's Indian origin; his humorous wordplay establishes a parallel between the ancients and American Indians, a recurrent American literary motif since Thomas Hariot's *Brief and True Report of Virginia.* Besides echoing earlier American literature, Hamilton anticipates works to come. His paean to hominy anticipates one of the greatest works of early American poetry, Joel Barlow's "The Hasty Pudding."

There are some references to contemporary colonial events in the *History* but far fewer than those in the *Itinerarium.* The transportation of felons to Maryland, for example, was a pervasive concern in the late 1740s and early 1750s, and convict crime frequently received attention in the pages of Jonas Green's *Maryland Gazette.* Transported felons appear in the *History* only as a Jonathan Grog conundrum: "Why is a Convict wroth, Just landed from England, like a man of taste, Just married to a fine Girl?" The answer: "Because he is *transported*" (Hamilton 1990, 2: 156).

One of the lengthiest references to colonial events outside Annapolis occurs when the club members decide to have a club medal struck. Loquacious Scribble eloquently compares Maryland's Tuesday Club with Virginia's Knights of the Golden Horseshoe, those men who accompanied Governor Alexander Spotswood into the mountains in 1716. He justifies the digression because "America is the Scene of our History." Hamilton's allusion to the Knights allows him to discuss the character of the Virginians: "His majesties ancient colony of Virginia is stocked with Inhabitants, which Consist of two Classes, the Grandees and the Common people, the first Class are fond of pomp Show and extravagance, and make a Shift to cast a fine dash in dress and equipage, without any certain estates to support it, as for the plebs, we only observe that they are very poor and very miserable, and therefore highly dispised by the Grandees" (Hamilton 1990, 1: 217–218). Although Hamilton pokes fun at his Virginia neighbors, the characterization shows that the colonists across the Chesapeake had also developed their own personality, which was similar enough to the Marylanders' to make a good comparison. The lengthy passage regarding the Golden Horseshoe was not part of *Records.* Adding the story in revision, Hamilton further emphasized indigenous American themes (Hayes 1993, 300).

Hamilton's American references refer less to specific events and more generally to the culture. Even though he was often condescending toward popular beliefs and behavior, he retained a fascination with contemporary folklore. The interest in proverbs that shows in the *Itinerarium* resurfaces in the *History.* For example, critiquing verse written by club members praising their president's bountiful table, with its "partridge pies and pies of apple" and "lusty Gammon,/With generous wine and punch of Lemon," Hamilton found appropriate the following proverb: "*They could not fare well but they must cry roast meat*" (Hamilton 1990, 2: 51). In other words, they cannot enjoy good fortune without boasting. For Hamilton, proverbs had both current and lasting value. He used them to spice up his conversation and his prose, but he also recognized the importance of recording proverbs for posterity. Bartlett Jere Whiting has recorded the proverbs Hamilton used in the *Itinerarium* (Whiting 1977). Cataloging the proverbs in the *History* remains an important scholarly task.

The *History* contains examples of virtually every type of proverb, including the *blason populaire*. Decades earlier, Joseph Addison had used the name "Tom Folio" in *The Tatler*, but he referred to a specific person, the well-known book collector Thomas Rawlinson (Addison 1870, 4: 186). Hamilton initially suggests that the name originally may have referred to an actual person, but his detailed definition shows that it had since become a *blason populaire:* "Tom Folio is another worthy of this class, who is often mentioned, in conversation, it is uncertain when and where he lived, but we have reason to believe, that he was a profound Critic in title pages, and had treasured up in his head a voluminous catalogue of books, since it is a common appellation, bestowed upon all such (since his time) as talk much of books which they have never read, dipt into or understood, such people being properly stiled Tom Folios" (Hamilton 1990, 1: 123).

As Hamilton's inclusion of such proverbs demonstrates, the *History* has much documentary value. Though a fictionalization of the Tuesday Club's activities, the *History* records many aspects of contemporary culture that have otherwise gone undocumented. *Völksbucher* or chapbooks, the cheaply printed books ubiquitous in early America, have almost escaped written record. They were so common that few bothered to write about them. People bought such books to read and use, and they continued reading and using them until they fell apart, at which time the books became tinder for starting fires, wrapping paper for dried goods, or, quite frankly, lavatory paper (Hayes 1997a, 4–5). The *History* forms one of the fullest accounts documenting the fate of these books in early America. To such cheaply printed materials

> not . . . only the Tobacconists and spice Shops, but even the Houses of office, have been of late years so Infinitely Indebted, who, had they not been supplied from these vast piles of waste paper, would have been at a Sad loss how to wrap up their grocery and haberdashery, and besides, many honest well meaning Christians, must have run the risque of befowling their fingers, in using the tender leaves of vegetables, which are not of so tough a nature, as that same other Historical Stuff is, besides the risque they must have run, of getting that most grievous distemper called the piles, by means of the Corrosive down that often abounds upon the leaves of the said vegetables, which like so much low Itch, would vellicate in a dreadful manner, the Tender plicae of the Rectum, where it terminates in the anus. (Hamilton 1990, 1: 22–23)

Besides proverbs and chapbooks, other genres of folklore are represented in the pages of the *History*. Though disdainful of superstitious people, Hamilton recognized that their superstitions could serve to season his history. One time he mentions people who "make a bad omen of two Straws across, a Salt Seller overset, a Jacket button awry, or a Coffin, as they call it, in the candle, or a Stocking wrong side out, or the glowing of ones face, or the Itching of ones elbow, or the noise of the worm Called the Death watch" (Hamilton 1990, 1: 70). Hamilton banishes superstitious people from the club, but he cannot mask his curiosity about their beliefs and his fascination with the way they are formulated.

He also records instances of tall tales and tall talk. Though the superstitious are banished from the club, talk talkers are welcome. Clubman George Neilson, for example, was known for his tall tales: "He dealt much in the marvelous, as many Great travellers do, among the other prodigies he had seen in his travels, he would talk of Churches twenty miles Long, of Spiders as large as a Sheep, of men 15 or 20 feet high, of Scots Lairds worth £20000 Sterling a year, and among his own exploits, he used to relate, how he once spited 24 woodcocks on the wing, at one Shot upon the ramrod of his Gun, and strung them all exactly thro' the Eyes, and such like Stories" (Hamilton 1990, 1: 79).

Though both the *Itinerarium* and the *History* fit solidly into the early American tradition, they are very different works. The *Itinerarium* is remarkable for the way it captures the diversity of the colonial American people Hamilton encountered on his trip. Unlike the *Itinerarium*, the world of the Tuesday Club is largely self-contained, a society unto itself. Hamilton rarely included the kinds of subtle distinctions between the people of different colonies that he made so brilliantly in the *Itinerarium*. But the themes of the *History*—recapturing classical greatness on the American strand, the westward movement of civilization, the ancient simplicity of the Indians—are what make it a uniquely American book.

Conclusion

Among well-to-do gentlemen in colonial America, it was often considered unseemly to publish their written compositions—in both senses of the word "publish," that is, to have them printed and also to have them made public. The fact that the *Itinerarium, Records,* and *History* all remained in manuscript throughout Hamilton's lifetime suggests that he, too, recognized the impropriety of publishing. Instead, all three works circulated in manuscript largely among members of the Tuesday Club. The *Itinerarium* was read by others outside the club yet within its author's general circle of friends. But Hamilton was not averse to publishing some of his writings given the opportunity. Once his friend and fellow club member Jonas Green started the *Maryland Gazette* in 1745, Hamilton quickly used the paper as a forum to start a literary war between members of his literary coterie—the Annapolis Wits—and a group of neighboring versifiers, the Baltimore Bards. The controversy, which took the form of both satirical poems and mock advertisements, extended into the following year (Lemay 1972b, 229–230). In terms of Hamilton's relation to print culture, the mock advertisements may be the most interesting: they show him cleverly manipulating the conventions of the newspaper press for satirical purposes.

His most significant contribution to the press is an essay he contributed to the *Maryland Gazette* on June 29, 1748. He wrote under the pseudonym of Don Francisco de Quevedo Villegas, a seventeenth-century Spanish author whose works were known to many colonial readers, including William Byrd, William Dick, and John Montgomerie (Hayes 1997b, no. 857; Hayes 2000, no. 552). Quevedo was best known for the dream visions he wrote, and, appropriately, Hamilton's essay is structured as a dream vision. Lemay calls this work the finest periodical essay in the literary history of colonial Maryland and possibly the finest colonial American essay published to that time excluding those of Benjamin Franklin (Lemay 1972b, 233–234). In it, Hamilton summarizes, satirizes, and criticizes the first three years of the *Maryland Gazette.* The essay amounts to a literary history of the newspaper (Lemay 1966). Hamilton's satirical portrayal of contemporary Maryland authors mocks their delusions of fame. As Lemay observes, "Since Hamilton himself was a major writer for the paper, the essay is partially self-mocking, ridiculing his own vanity and foolishness in hoping for literary fame" (Lemay 1972b, 238).

Though Hamilton's contributions to the *Maryland Gazette* would seem to contradict the unwritten rules among contemporary colonial gentlemen against publishing their writings, Hamilton, ironically, wrote for publication largely to lampoon the very act of writing for publication. Overall, he had a good sense of what belonged in manuscript and what belonged in print. He and his fellow club members wrote numerous collaborative poems that Hamilton incorporated in the *History,* yet only one appeared in the *Maryland Gazette* (Lemay 1972a, no. 995). Hamilton may have published some writings to castigate those who sought literary fame through the printed word, but he obviously gloried in the literary notoriety his manuscript works earned him among the close group of friends who formed the Tuesday Club. He never stopped revising and expanding the *History of the Tuesday Club.* He kept working on it until May 11, 1756, when he finally succumbed to tuberculosis.

REFERENCES

Addison, Joseph. 1870. *The Works of Joseph Addison,* edited by George Washington Greene. 6 vols. Philadelphia: Lippincott.

Beyers, Chris. 2005. Race, Power, and Sociability in Alexander Hamilton's *Records of the Tuesday Club. Southern Literary Journal* 38: 21–42.

Breslaw, Elaine G. 2004. Hamilton, Alexander. In *The Oxford Dictionary of National Biography,* edited by H. C. G. Matthew and Brian Harrison, vol. 24, pp. 755–756. New York: Oxford University Press.

Clark, Peter. 1992. Review of Alexander Hamilton, *The History of the Ancient and Honorable Tuesday Club,* edited by Robert Micklus. *William and Mary Quarterly,* 3rd ser., 49: 153–157.

Hamilton, Dr. Alexander. 1907. *Hamilton's Itinerarium: Being a Narrative of a Journey from Annapolis, Maryland through Delaware, Pennsylvania, New York, New Jersey,*

Connecticut, Rhode Island, Massachusetts and New Hampshire from May to September,
1744, edited by Albert Bushnell Hart. Saint Louis, MO: William K. Bixby.

———. 1948. *Gentleman's Progress: The Itinerarium of Dr. Alexander Hamilton, 1744,* edited
by Carl Bridenbaugh. Chapel Hill: University of North Carolina Press.

———. 1988. *Records of the Tuesday Club of Annapolis, 1745–56,* edited by Elaine G. Breslaw.
Urbana: University of Illinois Press.

———. 1990. *The History of the Ancient and Honorable Tuesday Club,* edited by Robert
Micklus. 3 vols. Chapel Hill: University of North Carolina Press.

———. [1948] 1992. *Gentleman's Progress: The Itinerarium of Dr. Alexander Hamilton, 1744,*
edited by Carl Bridenbaugh. Reprint. Pittsburgh: University of Pittsburgh Press.

Hayes, Kevin J. 1993. A Colonial American Masterwork. *Resources for American Literary
Study* 19: 294–300.

———. 1997a. *Folklore and Book Culture.* Knoxville: University of Tennessee Press.

———. 1997b. *The Library of William Byrd of Westover.* Madison and Philadelphia:
Madison House and Library Company of Philadelphia.

———. 2000. *The Library of John Montgomerie, Colonial Governor of New York and New
Jersey.* Newark: University of Delaware Press.

Hoffer, Peter Charles. 2003. *Sensory Worlds in Early America.* Baltimore: Johns Hopkins
University Press.

Hood, Adrienne D. 2003. *The Weaver's Craft: Cloth, Commerce, and Industry in Early
Pennsylvania.* Philadelphia: University of Pennsylvania Press.

Imbarrato, Susan Clair. 2001. Genteel Confusion: Reading Class Structure in Dr. Alexander
Hamilton's *Itinerarium.* In *Finding Colonial Americas: Essays Honoring J. A. Leo Lemay,*
edited by Carla Mulford and David S. Shields, 153–169. Newark: University of Delaware
Press.

Koch, Adrienne. 1949. A. Hamilton, Voyageur. Review of *Gentleman's Progress: The Itinerarium of Dr. Alexander Hamilton,* edited by Carl Bridenbaugh. *New York Times,* February
20, p. 2.

Lefler, Hugh T. 1950. Review of *Gentleman's Progress: The Itinerarium of Dr. Alexander Hamilton,* edited by Carl Bridenbaugh. *Mississippi Valley Historical Review* 36: 689–690.

Lemay, J. A. Leo. 1966. Hamilton's Literary History of the *Maryland Gazette. William and
Mary Quarterly,* 3rd ser., 23: 273–285.

———. 1972a. *A Calendar of American Poetry in the Colonial Newspapers and Magazines
and in the Major English Magazines through 1765.* Worcester, MA: American Antiquarian Society.

———. 1972b. *Men of Letters in Colonial Maryland.* Knoxville: University of Tennessee
Press.

McWilliams, James E. 2005. *A Revolution in Eating: How the Quest for Food Shaped America.*
New York: Columbia University Press.

Micklus, Robert, ed. 1980. *Dr. Alexander Hamilton's The History of the Tuesday Club.*
Newark: University of Delaware.

———. 1990. *The Comic Genius of Dr. Alexander Hamilton.* Knoxville: University of
Tennessee Press.

[Morgan, Joseph.] 1715. *The History of the Kingdom of Basaruah: Containing a Relation of
the Most Memorable Transactions, Revolutions and Heroick Exploits in that Kingdom,
from the First Foundation Thereof unto This Present Time.* [New York: William
Bradford.]

Morris, John G. 1873. History of the Annapolis "Tuesday Club." *American Historical Record* 2: 149–155.

Radano, Ronald. 2003. *Lying Up a Nation: Race and Black Music.* Chicago: University of Chicago Press.

Rice, Grantland S. 1996. Review of Alexander Hamilton, *Records of the Tuesday Club of Annapolis, 1745–56,* ed. Elaine G. Breslaw. *William and Mary Quarterly,* 3rd ser., 53: 219–221.

Shields, David S. 1994. British-American Belles Lettres. In *The Cambridge History of American Literature. Vol. 1, 1590–1820,* ed. Sacvan Bercovitch, 309–343. New York: Cambridge University Press.

Simpson, Lewis P. 1988. Thomas Jefferson and the Writing of the South. In *Columbia Literary History of the United States,* ed. Emory Elliot, 127–135. New York: Columbia University Press.

Smitten, Jeffrey R. 2004. Mackie, Charles. In *The Oxford Dictionary of National Biography,* edited by H. C. G. Matthew and Brian Harrison, vol. 35, pp. 638–639. New York: Oxford University Press.

Somerville, Wilson. 1996. *The Tuesday Club of Annapolis (1745–1756) as Cultural Performance.* Athens: University of Georgia Press, 1996.

Stearns, Raymond Phineas. 1970. *Science in the British Colonies of America.* Urbana: University of Illinois Press.

Thompson, Peter. 1999. *Rum Punch and Revolution: Taverngoing and Public Life in Eighteenth-Century Philadelphia.* Philadelphia: University of Pennsylvania Press.

Vickers, Daniel, and Vincent Walsh. 2005. *Young Men and the Sea: Yankee Seafarers in the Age of Sail.* New Haven, CT: Yale University Press.

Whiting, Bartlett Jere. 1977. *Early American Proverbs and Proverbial Phrases.* Cambridge, MA: Belknap Press of Harvard University Press.

Winship, George Parker. 1917. Travellers and Explorers, 1583–1763. In *The Cambridge History of American Literature: Colonial and Revolutionary Literature; Early National Literature, Part I,* edited by William Peterfield Trent et al., 1–13. New York: Macmillan.

Wroth, Lawrence C. 1949. Review of *Gentleman's Progress: The Itinerarium of Dr. Alexander Hamilton,* edited by Carl Bridenbaugh. *William and Mary Quarterly,* 3rd ser., 6: 123–126.

CHAPTER 11

INDIAN VOICES IN EARLY AMERICAN LITERATURE

JOSHUA DAVID BELLIN

The Indian peoples whom English colonists encountered did not possess written languages, and it was not until the nineteenth century that significant numbers of Indian authors began to publish writings in English. What this means is that Indian "voices" in early American literature are *mediated;* they come to us not from the Indians themselves but through non-Indian writers. And these writers, whether or not they tried to present the Indians' words accurately, were limited by a number of factors. First, and most obviously, they were required to translate the Indians' words from their original languages into English. As anyone who has studied a second language knows, it is tremendously difficult to capture the essence of one language in the words of another; even under the best of circumstances, much will be "lost in translation." Couple this with the fact that translators were frequently working with oral speeches that had to be taken down on the spur of the moment—and that the speakers were seldom able to check the accuracy of the translations—and it is easy to see that Indian voices in early American literature are unlikely to be precise transcripts of what the Indians actually said (Krupat 1992; Low 1995).

But another factor, more subtle than the first, affects the reliability of Indian voices in early American literature: the issue of cultural bias. It was not only Indian languages that differed markedly from those of Europeans; Indian religions, social and economic arrangements, and other beliefs and practices differed as well. At the simplest, this meant that Europeans frequently did not understand what Indians said in the terms that the Indians meant them; Europeans unconsciously "translated"

Indian concepts into concepts familiar to themselves (Cheyfitz 1991, 3–21). At the same time, such biases often led to ridicule or condemnation; rather than thinking of Indian cultures as simply *different* from theirs, Europeans thought of Indian cultures as *inferior* to theirs (Berkhofer 1978; Pearce 1953). It goes without saying that biased translators make poor translators: they are likely to be careless and ungenerous with the other's language, and may even intentionally misrepresent the other's words.

This leads to a final factor that affects Indian voices in early American literature. The writers who recorded the Indians' words were not disinterested parties: they had motivations for recording Indian speech, and these were frequently at odds with the Indians' interests. Some writers wished to convert the Indians to Christianity; some hoped to gain Indian lands; still others sought to prove the inferiority of Indian cultures. Whether intentionally or not, such writers were inclined to represent the Indians' words in ways that supported European agendas, regardless of whether these were shared by the Indians.

Taking these factors into consideration, it is obvious that we cannot accept Indian voices in early American literature as straightforward records of what the Indians said. Rather, we must take care to place these voices within their historical contexts, to consider the circumstances under which they were recorded. If, however, we must be skeptical, we should not be dismissive; we should not assume that all Indian "voices" were fabricated by European authors to serve ends hostile to the Indians' own. To be sure, in all early American literature—particularly that which was produced after the American Revolution—there is a tendency toward such fabrication. Yet when we place Indian voices in their historical contexts, a more complex picture emerges, a picture of Indians fighting to be heard within the texts that threaten to silence them. In the nineteenth century, Indian authors began to develop their own literature, one that is frequently critical of European policies. The mediated voices of Indian peoples from previous centuries can help us, as they may have helped these later authors, to locate a distinctly Indian perspective on American life and literature.

INDIAN DIALOGUES

One of the most extensive collections of Indian "voices" in early American literature comes from the missionaries who sought the Indians' conversion to Christianity. Europeans often named Indian conversion as one of their principal reasons for emigrating to the New World; colonial charters often listed conversion as a primary goal of settlement. Missionary reports published in England thus served a number of purposes: notifying their sponsoring societies of the successes they had enjoyed, soliciting funds, assuring royal patrons that the religious mission of the colony was being upheld, and explaining the place of the mission within the larger history of the church. One of the best ways of fulfilling these ends, the missionaries found, was to record the words of the Indians; English readers, it seems, were eager to hear Indian voices as a way of charting the progress of the gospel among them (Stevens 2004).

The most substantial body of Indian voices from seventeenth-century English mission literature appears in the writings of John Eliot of the Massachusetts Bay Colony. The pastor of Roxbury, Massachusetts, Eliot learned the language of the local Indians from a Montauk Indian, Cockenoe, who had been captured in the Pequot War of 1637; in 1646, Eliot preached his first sermon to the Indians in their own tongue. Aided by Indian translators, Eliot published the New Testament in the Massachusett language in 1661, followed by the Old Testament in 1663—the first Bible published in the colonies, typeset by one of Eliot's converts, James Printer (Meserve 1956). In 1651, Eliot founded the town of Natick, where his Indian converts, or "Praying Indians," assembled to form a new civil and religious society; by 1674, the "Praying Towns" numbered fourteen, with a population of some 1,100 inhabitants (Bowden 1981, 116–133; Morrison 1995). But in the following year, the Wampanoag sachem (chief) Metacom, or "King Philip," led a coalition of tribes against the colonists, and in the violence of King Philip's War (1675–1676), these towns were decimated, only four surviving (Lepore 1998).

During the years of the mission's greatest success, Eliot and his supporters wrote a series of tracts, beginning with *The Day-Breaking, if Not the Sun-Rising of the Gospel with the Indians in New-England* (1647) and concluding with *A Brief Narrative of the Progress of the Gospel amongst the Indians in New-England* (1670). In these works, published in London, the missionaries provided ample records of the Indians' words; not only did they quote natives who resisted the mission, but later tracts, such as *Tears of Repentance* (1653), contained the conversion narratives of Indians who had joined the Praying communities. Thus these works, known as the Eliot Tracts, constitute the fullest account of English missionary activity in the seventeenth century and of Indian responses to the missionary program.

The Indian voices in the Eliot Tracts, however, reveal all the problems named here. Though Eliot's skills as a linguist may have been considerable, he himself admitted how difficult translation could be (Guice 1991). As he wrote in *Tears of Repentance*: "oft I was forced to inquire of my interpreter (who sat by me) because I did not perfectly understand some sentences. . . . I have been true and faithful unto their souls, and in writing and reading their Confessions, I have not knowingly, or willingly made them better, than the Lord helped themselves to make them, but am verily perswaded on good grounds, that I have rather rendered them weaker (for the most part) than they delivered them; partly by missing some words of weight in some Sentences, partly by my short and curt touches of what they more fully spake, and partly by reason of the different Idioms of their Language and ours" (Eliot 2003, 282–283). Eliot deserves high marks for honesty, but by the same token, he leaves us in doubt concerning the fidelity of the translations; lacking the original speeches, we have only Eliot's record of what these speakers said (Murray 1991, 127–130).

At the same time, it is impossible to avoid the issue of cultural bias in the writings of the Eliot mission. The Puritans believed that Indian religions were no less than devil worship; in the first of the tracts, Eliot confronted an Indian powwow or medicine man, asking him, "If God bee the author of all good, why doe you pray to . . . the devill?" (Eliot 2003, 97). Throughout the tracts, Eliot and his peers miss no chance to demean Indian beliefs while exalting their own; indeed, of the laws for the Praying Indians that Eliot listed in a later tract, *The Clear Sun-shine of the Gospel Breaking Forth upon the Indians in New-England* (1648), the majority involve the levying of fines against traditional customs (Eliot 2003, 115–116). No matter how faithfully Eliot may have tried to convey the Indians' words, his bias against Indian culture almost certainly prevented him from understanding Indian utterance in the Indians' own terms.

As a final complication, it is by no means certain that Eliot *did* try to convey the Indians' words as faithfully as he claimed. Some historians accept Eliot at his word, believing that he was motivated by a simple desire to save souls; others, however, suggest that Eliot and his brethren were more concerned with their colony's reputation in England than with their converts' spiritual state, while still others argue that the Puritans used the mission as a way of furthering English control in the region (Cogley 1999; Bross 2004; Jennings 1975, 228–253). If so, then not only might Eliot have misinterpreted Indian words due to linguistic deficiencies and unconscious bias, but he might have intentionally misrepresented those words in order to serve agendas that worked against the Indians' interests or had little to do with the Indians at all.

To read the Eliot Tracts is thus to confront head-on the problems that all Indian "voices" in early American literature raise. Yet these problems, however daunting, are at the same time invaluable, for they point us toward the historical circumstances in which Indian voices were recorded. If, then, we cannot trust these voices without question, we can see in them a dramatization of the most pressing issues that faced Indian communities during this period: issues of secular and sacred conflict, loss of land and political power, and—not least—the difficulty of speaking in a world in which Indians had such limited access to the means of publication. A critical reader, then, will view the problems inherent in the Eliot Tracts not as insurmountable obstacles but as opportunities to gain insight into Indian-European encounter in the colonial era.

One way to enter this arena is through the confessions the Praying Indians delivered as they sought admission to the church. (Puritans generally required such public demonstrations of religious conviction as a preliminary to church membership.) In these speeches, recorded in *Tears of Repentance,* the Praying Indians appear as individuals grappling with a new, alien faith. The confession of one Indian, Nishohkou, is typical:

> I am dead in sin, Oh! that my sins might die, for they cannot give life, because
> they be dead: before I prayed to God, I did commit all filthynesse, I prayed to
> many gods, I was proud, full of lusts, adulteries, and all other sins. . . . Sometimes
> I think I am like unto Satan, because I do all these sins, and sin in all things I do;
> if I pray I sin, if I keep Sabbath I sin, if I hear Gods Word I sin, therefore I am
> like the Devil. Now I know I deserve to go to Hell, because all these sins I have
> committed: then my heart is troubled, and I say, Oh God and Christ pardon all
> my sin, for I cannot pardon my sins my self. (Eliot 2003, 287–288)

Though the modern reader may be shocked by the depth of self-loathing evident here, in actuality such expressions were consistent with Puritan theology, which dictated that only by accepting one's utter worthlessness could one embrace Christ as savior (Cohen 1986). What may have differed for the Praying Indians was that they were required to confess not only their *own* sinfulness but that of their societies; Nishohkou's reference to "praying to many gods" and his equation of himself with the devil seem to accord with Puritan beliefs about the hellishness of Indian religion (Salisbury 1974). Confessions such as Nishohkou's thus suggest that the Praying Indians had adopted the missionaries' prejudices—or, perhaps, that Eliot had placed these words in his converts' mouths to further the mission's ends.

A more complex portrait emerges, however, when we view the confessions in relation to other Indian "voices" in the mission literature. According to *Clear Sunshine*, the Indians did much more than passively accept, or parrot, Puritan doctrine: "There have been many difficult questions propounded by them, which we have been unwilling to engage ourselves in any answer unto, until we have the concurrence of others with us" (Eliot 2003, 135). One of the tracts, *The Glorious Progress of the Gospel amongst the Indians in New England* (1649), contains a list of such questions, including the following puzzlers: "Doth the Devill dwell in us as we dwell in an house?"; "Seeing we see not God with our eyes, if a man dream that he seeth God, doth his soule see him?"; "If God made hell in one of the six dayes, why did God make Hell before Adam had sinned?" In the same list, too, there appears a question that concerns less Christian preaching than Christian practice: "Doe not Englishmen spoile their soules, to say a thing cost them more then it did? and is it not all one as to steale?" Elsewhere, such suspicion of English motivations is directed against the mission itself; in *The Light Appearing More and More towards the Perfect Day* (1651), an Indian sachem takes the mission to task: "*Myoxeo* asking [a Praying Indian] how many Gods the English did worship, he answered one God, whereupon *Myoxeo* reckoned up about 37. principal gods he had, and shall I (said he) throw away these 37. gods for one?" (Eliot 2003, 155–156, 178). Implicit in Myoxeo's question is the charge that the mission, seeking to replace "many gods" with one, seeks to transform a world shared by Indians and colonists to one dominated by the English alone (Ronda 1977).

As the mission progressed, that critique became more insistent. In 1671, shortly before King Philip's War, Eliot published *The Indian Dialogues*, a fictionalized account of the labors of the past three decades. Intended, it seems, as a primer for the Indian missionaries he hoped to send into the field, the book consists of three "dialogues" between Praying Indians and their unconverted kin, with the converts bent on securing new proselytes for the mission. Yet even here, the critique of colonialism is evident. One of the Indians, for example, spurns the converts' advances, stating, "Our forefathers were (many of them) wise men, and we have wise men now living. . . . Are you wiser than our fathers? May we not rather think that *English* men have invented these stories to amaze us and fear us out of our old customs, and bring us to stand in awe of them, that they might wipe us out of our lands?" (Eliot 1980, 71). Aside from the obvious stab at European expansion, this suspicion that Christian stories were invented to wipe the Indians out of their lands suggests that the Indians may have seen the connection between literacy (or literature) and colonialism.

Even more strikingly, Eliot concludes the book with a dialogue between two converts and King Philip himself, who expresses grave doubts: "If I should pray to God, and all my people with me, I must become as a common man among them, and so lose all my power and authority" (Eliot 1980, 121). This dialogue ends just short of Philip's conversion; even in a work of fiction, it seems, Eliot could not fully overcome the sachem's misgivings. A story current in Eliot's day held that Philip had once rejected the missionary's offers: "he took a *button* upon the *coat* of the reverend man, adding, 'That he cared for his gospel, just as much as he cared for that button'" (Mather 1855, 566). Another report, relayed by John Easton of Rhode Island during King Philip's War, further suggested Philip's distrust of the missions: "[He] had a great fear to have ani of ther indians should be Caled or forced to be Christian indians. [He] saied that such wer in everi thing more mischivous, only disemblers, and then the English made them not subject to ther kings, and by ther lying to rong their kings" (Easton 1913, 10). If none of these accounts can be accepted as the actual voice of King Philip, all suggest a long-standing tradition of Indian resistance to colonialism under the guise of missionary benevolence.

Throughout the following century, missionaries reported persistent Indian opposition to Christianity. In 1753, John Sergeant quoted the Shawnees: "The Indians have one way of honoring and pleasing [God], and the white people have another; both are acceptable. . . . Christianity need not be the bond of union between us" (Hopkins 1911 100). Samuel Kirkland found the Senecas similarly suspicious of his overtures: "This white man . . . brings with him the white peoples *Book*. . . . Brothers, you know this book was never made for *Indians*. Our great Superintendent Thaonghyawagon in *Upholder of the Skies* gave us a *book*. He wrote it in our heads and in our minds and gave us rules about worshipping him" (Kirkland 1980, 23–24). Focusing, again, on the Christian *book* as an agency of colonialism, this speaker rejects not only the gospel message but the gospel text.

By the final third of the eighteenth century, such critiques would coalesce around the figures of Indian revivalist prophets, who counseled their people to reject Christianity and to return to their original ways of living (Dowd 1992). One of these prophets, a Delaware named Neolin, reportedly told his people "to quit all Commerce with the White People and Clothe themselves with Skins"; too, Neolin countered the missionaries with a scripture of his own, "Portrayed on a Dress'd Leather Skin," to "shew [the Indians] the right way to Heaven" (Kenny 1913, 188, 171). The inspiration for the Ottawa chief Pontiac, who formed an alliance of Indian tribes to curb British expansion in the 1760s, Neolin can be seen as a descendant of leaders such as King Philip, who perceived the connection between spiritual, secular, and scriptural power in the struggle for the continent.

Yet in seeking spiritual precedent for a revitalized Indian front, Neolin looks back not only to Philip but also to the Praying Indians. For while it could weaken traditional beliefs, Christianity, it seems, could rejuvenate Indian communities as well. Thus in a sermon recorded in *A Further Accompt of the Progresse of the Gospel amongst the Indians in New-England* (1659), Waban, a leader of the Natick community, advised his people to "goe to Christ the Phisitian; for Christ is a Physitian of souls; he healed mens bodies, but he can heale souls also: he is a great Physitian, therefore let all sinners goe to him" (Eliot 2003, 333). This reference to Christ as "physician" suggests that the Praying Indians may have found it possible to fuse the Christian savior with the traditional healer, the very figure the missionaries most reviled. From the Indian perspective, then, conversion appears not as an act of submission but as a quest for autonomy, less confrontational than Philip's but no less pragmatic (Axtell 1988; Van Lonkhuyzen 1990; Wyss 2000, 17–51). Both Philip's rejection of the missions and the converts' acceptance of them, in other words, laid the groundwork for later Indian peoples who spoke for Indian self-determination in the face of Euro-American territorial and religious dominance.

THE AFFAIR OF THE LAND

From the beginning of the colonization of America, it had seemed to Europeans that Indians had no legitimate claim to the land; believing that only private ownership conferred title, Europeans considered Indian practices, where lands were held in common for the use of hunting and agriculture, to be illegitimate and unproductive. As *Mourt's Relation* put it: "They are not industrious, neither have art, science, skill or faculty to use either the land or the commodities of it; but all spoils, rots, and is marred for want for manuring, gathering, ordering, etc. As the ancient patriarchs, therefore, removed from straiter places into more roomy . . . so is it lawful now to take a land that none useth, and make use of it" (Anon. 1985, 79). According to this model, Indians could easily dispense with such "unused" lands; ultimately, many colonists believed, the Indians could be led to see the unprofitableness of their way of living and to embrace private landholding. Thus, Europeans reasoned, colonization would benefit both parties: Europeans would gain lands for settlement, and Indians would begin the process of moving from the "savage" to the "civilized" state (Cheyfitz 1991, 41–58).

Indians, it is perhaps needless to say, saw the matter differently. To them, land was both community heritage and sacred space, and if it was to be parted with, this must be done with a full recognition of their rights. Thus a tentative pattern of diplomacy developed: where the balance of power between Indians and settlers was relatively equal, Europeans were required to treat with Indians for the sale of lands; but once that balance shifted in favor of the colonists, meaningful diplomatic relations were suspended, and Indians were forcibly removed from their lands (Washburn 1971). Following the English victory in King Philip's War, this is precisely what had happened in New England: Indian peoples had been restricted to territories under colonial jurisdiction (such as the Praying Towns). In other regions, however, powerful coalitions of Indian tribes, including the Iroquois League in New York and the Creek Confederacy in the Southeast, retained sufficient strength to command treatment as sovereign entities. Particularly before the end of the Seven Years' War (1756–1763), when England and France vied for control of North America, maintaining alliances with Indian tribes was vital to European interests. Thus in formal councils, Indian and European representatives worked out territorial arrangements while forging and renewing political and military ties (White 1991, 223–314).

The resulting treaty literature, a vast body of writings scattered throughout government papers as well as published separately by colonial printers, comprises a substantial record of Indian "voices" in eighteenth-century American literature (Drummond and Moody 1953; Wroth 1928). Treaty councils were elaborate affairs, lasting days and even weeks, with feasts, gift exchanges, and other ceremonies preceding the negotiation of terms; during the negotiations, speakers recalled past alliances, commented on present policies, and debated future actions, while interpreters stood by to record their words (and, sometimes, gestures). At the same time, whereas Eliot and other missionaries demanded that the Indians enter the English world, treaty councils generally worked in the opposite direction, the need to secure Indian support dictating that these meetings follow the Indians' own rules for ceremony and address. Europeans thus joined in Indian rituals such as the smoking of pipes, listened while speeches were read from wampum belts (strings of shells or beads that served as aids to memory), and employed Indian kinship terminology in their own addresses. This does not mean that the treaty literature—any more than the missionary literature—accurately conveys the voices of the Indian participants. Rather, it means that this literature represents another place in which the contexts of Indian-European encounter are exhibited, another place in which the struggle for land, power, and representation is played out.

These qualities are displayed in one of the fullest eighteenth-century records of treaty proceedings: Cadwallader Colden's *History of the Five Indian Nations,* published in New York in 1727, then expanded for a London edition in 1747. In this work, Colden, who held various posts in the colonial administration of New York, covers the diplomatic history between the English and the Iroquois: the Senecas, Mohawks, Oneidas, Onondagas, and Cayugas. (A sixth tribe, the Tuscaroras, joined the league in 1713.) The *History* begins with an acknowledgment of the pivotal role the Iroquois play in British contests with France: "The following Account of the *Five Indian Nations* will shew what dangerous Neighbours the *Indians* have once been; what Pains a neighbouring Colony (whose Interest is opposite to ours) has taken to withdraw their Affections from us; and how much we ought to be on our Guard." As these comments suggest, Colden's position toward the Iroquois is one of wary respect: a "barbarous People, bred under the darkest Ignorance," they are uncertain if essential allies. Thus his book is meant to demonstrate how these "dangerous neighbors" may be turned to the British cause: "by this may be seen the Advantage of using the *Indians* well, and I believe, if they were still better used (as there is Room enough to do it) they would be proportionably more useful to us" (Colden 1747, IV–V, 5).

Colden's treatment of the Iroquois speeches that constitute a sizable portion of his history reveals a similar calculation. At first notice, he appears enamored of Iroquois eloquence, writing that it exposes a glimmer of the "bright and noble Genius" that shines through the "black Clouds" of Indian barbarity. Yet as later comments indicate, Colden, who confesses himself "ignorant of their Language," sees oratory as inseparable from "savage" society; lacking a supreme ruler, the Iroquois must resort to speech making to carry out what, among Colden's own people, is achieved by royal edict: "Where no single Person has a Power to compel, the Arts of Persuasion alone must prevail. As their best Speakers distinguish themselves in their publick Councils and Treaties with other Nations, and thereby gain the Esteem and Applause of their Country-men, (the only Superiority which any one of them has over the others) it is probable they apply themselves to this Art, by some Kind of Study and Exercise." If, then, English speakers condescend to this barbarous "art," they do so only to secure British interests: participating in council oratory is another means of assuring that the Five Nations will "become a People, whose Friendship might add Honour to the *British* Nation" (Colden 1747, V, 14, VIII).

Yet if Colden views the treaty council in a manner similar to Eliot's Praying Towns—as a place to win Indian "converts" to the English side—his *History* discloses a more complex process, one in which the Iroquois jockey to protect their own interests and, indeed, to "convert" the English in turn. Thus in the speeches, frequent references to the "covenant chain"—the Anglo-Iroquois alliance forged in the seventeenth century (Richter 1992, 134–142)—reveal Iroquois efforts to secure

English support: "Hear now," a Mohawk speaker addresses the colonists, urging that past conflicts be reconciled, "let a strong Stream run under the Pit, to wash the Evil away out of our Sight and Remembrance. . . . The Covenant must be kept; for the Fire of Love of *Virginia* and *Maryland* burns in this Place, as well as ours, and this House of Peace must be kept clean" (Colden 1747, 49–50). Though the concept of the covenant chain was of both Iroquois and English extraction, the expressions recorded here—in particular, that of "washing the evil away out of our sight and remembrance"—are drawn from the most important political ceremony of the league: the Ritual of Condolence. Performed upon the death of a sachem to comfort the bereaved and to elect a new leader, the Ritual of Condolence was also employed to renew external alliances (Richter 1992, 39–41). Thus in a late eighteenth-century ritual led by a Mahican Indian, Hendrick Aupaumut, in council with the league's western allies, one hears the echo of Colden's treaty discourse:

> Our good ancestors did hand down to us a rule or path where we may walk.
> According to that rule I now wipe off your tears from your eyes and face that you
> may see clear. And since there has been so much wind on the way that the dust
> and every evil things did fill your ears, I now put my hand and take away the dust
> from your ears, that you may hear plain—and also the heavy burden on your
> mind I now remove, that you may feel easy, and that you may contemplate some
> objects without burden. (Aupaumut 1827, 87)

For the Iroquois, it seems, the Condolence was a way to bring allies into the league politically and symbolically: to construe others, that is, in league terms. Tracking the Condolence in Colden's *History* suggests, then, that his text records a process in which each party seeks not only to gain its own interests but to represent the other within its own systems of belief (Pomedli 1995).

This process of intercultural negotiation becomes even more prominent in the expanded edition of the *History,* in which Colden reproduces contemporary treaties between the Iroquois and the colonies. One such treaty, from 1742, finds the speakers debating the meaning and use of the land, with an Onondaga orator, Cannasatego, arguing: "We know our Lands are now become more valuable: The white People think we do not know their Value; but we are sensible that the Land is everlasting, and the few Goods we receive for it are soon worn out and gone." He is rebuffed, however, by the lieutenant governor of Pennsylvania, George Thomas, who asserts: "It is very true, that Lands are of late become more valuable; but what raises their Value? Is it not entirely owing to the Industry and Labour used by the white People, in their Cultivation and Improvement? . . . What you say of the Goods, that they are soon worn out, is applicable to every Thing; but you know very well, that they cost a great deal of Money; and the Value of Land is no more, than it is worth in Money" (Colden 1747, 64, 66–67). This debate hinges on variant senses of the word "value"; where Cannasatego accords land a "value" greater than that of other objects, Thomas sees the land as another "valuable"—salable—commodity. Thus, though both men appear to be discussing the same thing, in fact each views that thing in a different way. As such, this treaty not only calls attention to the difficulties of cross-cultural communication and translation but also suggests the competing beliefs and practices that lay at the heart of Indian-European conflict.

A similar debate over culturally distinct views of the land emerges in a later treaty, held at Lancaster in 1744 between the Iroquois and the colonies of Maryland and Virginia. Once more, Cannasatego speaks for a sense of land as inalienable legacy as against the commissioners' sense of land as alienable property:

> When you mentioned the Affair of the Land Yesterday, you went back to old Times, and told us, you had been in Possession of the Province of *Maryland* above One Hundred Years; but what is One Hundred Years in Comparison of the Length of Time since our Claim began? since we came out of this Ground? For we must tell you, that long before One Hundred Years our Ancestors came out of this very Ground, and their Children have remained here ever since. You came out of the Ground in a Country that lies beyond the Seas, there you may have a just Claim, but here you must allow us to be your elder Brethren, and the Lands to belong to us long before you knew any thing of them. (Colden 1747, 103–104)

For Cannasatego, it appears, "Maryland" is misnamed: far from being the property of a British sovereign, it is the birthright of the Iroquois people, guaranteed by ancient origins. Yet as Cannasatego also seems to recognize, his people's claims were imperiled by the very act through which his words were recorded: "We are," he concludes, "liable to many other Inconveniencies since the *English* came among us, and particularly from that Pen-and-Ink Work that is going on at the Table (*pointing to the Secretary*)" (Colden 1747, 105). As with the critique of the Bible in the mission literature, this passage suggests that the struggle between Indians and Europeans took place on both material and textual planes. The treaty literature, that is, shows Indians engaging Europeans in debate not only over land but also over literacy; the "issue of the land" resolves into an issue of representation, of who has the right—or the writing—to name and claim the land.

Intriguingly, a passage within the Lancaster treaty suggests that Iroquois rites, if not writing, may have played a role not only in American literature but in the invention of the American nation. As the council winds down, Cannasatego remarks: "Our wise Forefathers established Union and Amity between the *Five Nations;* this has made us formidable; this has given us great Weight and Authority with our neighbouring Nations. We are a powerful Confederacy; and, by your observing the same Methods our wise Forefathers have taken, you will acquire fresh Strength and Power" (Colden 1747, 149). This and similar speeches have given rise to the theory of Iroquois "influence" on the United States Constitution; some scholars suggest that, as the new nation was forming, the Iroquois League provided the founders with a model for a constitutional republic (Grinde and Johansen 1991). As with all issues concerning Indian voices in American texts, this thesis cannot be positively proved; it is possible, for example, that colonial writers inserted such speeches into Iroquois orators' mouths to provide precedent for their own dreams of union. But it is also possible that, among the many streams that flowed into the making of the nation, one stream had an Iroquois source. If so, then the language of the Condolence, of Iroquois belief and ritual, may yet be heard: "We now . . . plant the Tree of Prosperity and Peace. May it grow and thrive, and spread its Roots" (Colden 1747, 141).

TELLING STORIES

The close of the American Revolution marks a watershed both in the relationship of Euro-Americans to Indians and in the role of Indian voices in early American literature. Whatever part Indian peoples may have played in shaping the new nation, that nation treated Indians as anything but cherished "elder brethren": the Treaty of Paris (1783), by which the United States gained formal independence, regarded those Indians who had supported the British as conquered nations; as such, the young republic took the opportunity to claim massive land cessions, with little regard for the actual complexities of Indian alliance during the Revolution (Calloway 1995). The Seneca chief Cornplanter, reporting the Americans' words in 1783, captured the new nation's attitude: "We are now Masters of this Island and can dispose of the lands as we think proper or most convenient to ourselves" (Calloway 1994, 284). Though Indian resistance to United States expansion would last until the end of the next century, the process of dispossession had entered its final phase: Indians were now in theory, if not wholly in fact, wards of the nation, to be "disposed of" as the nation saw fit. Throughout the remainder of the eighteenth century and into the nineteenth, United States policy would be to shatter the institution of the tribe, to assimilate Indians to Euro-American "civilization," and—failing that—to remove Indians beyond white-occupied lands, where, many politicians and planners predicted, Indians would finally vanish as a people.

At the same time, and perhaps as a consequence of the Indians' lost autonomy, Indian voices in early American literature reveal a shift during this period: from (ostensibly) factual records of Indian speech to fanciful examples of American "eloquence." Euro-American writers, that is, begin to perceive Indian voices primarily as material for a distinctly American literature, and only secondarily (if at all) as utterances concerning real events. One way to chart this change is to notice that in Revolutionary literature, Indian voices are commonly presented as if they issue from a vacuum: translators and the contexts in which translation occurs recede, and readers are left with Indian "voices" that *appear* to be unmediated. But as this chapter has demonstrated, the fact of mediation, if it introduces uncertainty, also signals the historical circumstances within which Indians spoke. Losing such context does not, then, lead the reader closer to the Indians' voices; quite the contrary, it takes the reader farther away, into a fantasy realm where, impossibly, Indians speak directly to the reader within the works of non-Indian authors.

Some Revolutionary-era writers, to be sure, resist this impulse; for example, naturalist William Bartram, who traveled among the southeastern Indians from 1773 to 1777, continues to present Indian voices in the context of disputes over the land:

> The surveyor having fixed his compass on the staff, . . . the Indian chief came up, and observing the course he had fixed upon, spoke, and said it was not right. . . . The surveyor replied, that he himself was certainly right, adding, that that little instrument (pointing to the compass) told him so, which, he said, could not err. The Indian answered, he knew better, and that the little wicked instrument was a liar; and he would not acquiesce in its decisions, since it would wrong the Indians out of their land. (Bartram 1955, 58)

This episode reminds us that, if literature itself was one of the "wicked instruments" by which Europeans sought the Indians' dispossession, one can always reconstruct the historical contexts that gave rise to Indian utterance (Hallock 2003, 149–173). Yet in the bulk of Revolutionary-era literature, such contexts are suppressed. Thus it is during this period that the problems of the Indian "voice" in early American literature become most pronounced: whereas previously, even in such largely fictionalized exercises as *The Indian Dialogues,* Indian voices were presented within actual situations of cultural contact, Indian speakers now appear as the inventions of Euro-American ventriloquists for whom Indians are usable fictions, not substantial considerations.

This process is observable in an essay that appeared in the year of the Treaty of Paris: Benjamin Franklin's "Remarks Concerning the Savages of North-America" (1783), written while Franklin was living abroad as minister to France. Franklin, who had earlier published Indian treaties, including the Treaty of Lancaster, presents Indian oratory in terms similar to Colden's: "all their Government is by the Counsel or Advice of the Sages. . . . Hence they generally study Oratory; the best Speaker having the most Influence" (Franklin 1987, 969). Yet when he offers examples of such oratory, he does so in a way that transforms serious debates into humorous sketches, thereby diverting attention from the historical conflicts to which Indian speeches had originally referred.

Nowhere is this clearer than in Franklin's anecdote of an Indian speaker whose rebuttal of a missionary is couched more as fable than fact. Franklin writes of a minister who, "having assembled the Chiefs of the Susquehanah Indians, made a Sermon to them, acquainting them with the principal historical Facts on which our Religion is founded, such as the Fall of our first Parents by Eating an Apple, the Coming of Christ to repair the Mischief, his Miracles and Suffering, etc. When he had finished, an Indian Orator stood up to thank him. What you have told us, says he, is all very good. It is indeed bad to eat Apples" (Franklin 1987, 971). The jocular orator then proceeds to tell a story of his own: "In the Beginning our Fathers had only the Flesh of Animals to subsist on, and if their Hunting was unsuccessful, they were starving. Two of our young Hunters having killed a Deer, made a Fire in the Woods to broil some Parts of it. When they were about to satisfy their Hunger, they beheld a beautiful young Woman descend from the Clouds, and seat herself on that Hill which you see yonder." Having propitiated the spirit with venison, the hunters return to find "Plants they had never seen before, but which from that ancient time have been constantly cultivated among us." The episode concludes:

> The good Missionary, disgusted with this idle Tale, said, what I delivered to you were sacred Truths; but what you tell me is mere Fable, Fiction and Falsehood. The Indian offended, reply'd, my Brother, it seems your Friends have not done you Justice in your Education; they have not well instructed you in the Rules of common Civility. You saw that we who understand and practise those Rules, believed all your Stories; why do you refuse to believe ours? (Franklin 1987, 971–972)

In many respects, Franklin's story touches on the bases of Indian-European conflict: religious intolerance, competition over the land, and the question of the speaker's authority are all evident (Bellin 2001, 116–123). But in contrast to earlier records—including the treaty deliberations Franklin himself had published—the Indian tale of "Remarks" is offered simply as an amusing skit, divorced from the contexts that might have given rise to such a story. Franklin's nameless orator, that is, becomes a stock character: the artless Indian who is taken aback by "civilized" rudeness. As such, however, Franklin's essay may parody the colonial apparatus and its missionary wing; his orator lacks the quality of situated critique found in the Eliot Tracts or the treaty literature. Ironically, though Franklin's orator chides the missionary for treating Indian stories as "fiction," Franklin himself denies his Indian mouthpiece an independent voice.

A similar process is evident in the most famous Indian oration of the Revolutionary era: the speech of Chief Logan, or Tahgahjute, recorded in Thomas Jefferson's *Notes on the State of Virginia* (1785). Unlike Franklin's anonymous orator, Tahgahjute was an actual person, an Oneida (or perhaps Cayuga) warrior misidentified as a "Mingo" (an ethnic slur, from Delaware *mengwe* or "sneaky people," and not the name of an Indian tribe). In 1774, after members of his band were massacred by British soldiers, Tahgahjute renounced his friendship for the British and undertook a series of retaliatory strikes against local settlers. When Lord Dunmore, the royal governor of Virginia, set out to treat with him, Tahgahjute refused the invitation, delivering instead to one of Dunmore's lieutenants an impassioned, defiant speech. First published in the *Virginia Gazette* in 1775, the speech, as recorded by Jefferson, reads:

> I appeal to any white man to say, if ever he entered Logan's cab in hungry, and he gave him not meat; if ever he came cold and naked, and he clothed him not. During the course of the last long and bloody war, Logan remained idle in his cabin, an advocate for peace. Such was my love for the whites, that my countrymen pointed as they passed, and said, "Logan is the friend of white

men." I had even thought to have lived with you, but for the injuries of one man. Col. Cresap, the last spring, in cold blood, and unprovoked, murdered all the relations of Logan, not sparing even my women and children. There runs not a drop of my blood in the veins of any living creature. This called on me for revenge. I have sought it: I have killed many: I have fully glutted my vengeance. For my country, I rejoice at the beams of peace. But do not harbour a thought that mine is the joy of fear. Logan never felt fear. He will not turn on his heel to save his life. Who is there to mourn for Logan?—Not one. (Jefferson 1982, 63)

Immensely popular in its own time and in the century following, Logan's oration was also the subject of intense debate: it was attacked as a forgery (largely by defenders of Michael Cresap, whom Tahgahjute mistakenly blamed for the massacre), leading Jefferson, in subsequent editions of *Notes,* to append a series of affidavits testifying to the speech's genuineness. To this day, critics dispute how closely the published versions capture the original address (O'Donnell 1979; Sandefur 1966). Noting not only the echo of the Gospels but the presence of nonnative elements such as the substitution of "country" for tribe, some scholars dismiss the speech as pure fabrication (McElwain 2001). But whatever the case may be, most significant for our purposes is the fact that in Jefferson's text, the speech is severed from the conditions under which it may have been spoken and used for purposes that have nothing to do with its speaker. To understand this, it is critical to observe that as with Franklin's essay, *Notes* was first published in Paris, where Jefferson was living as a delegate to treat with the European powers. This in turn explains why Logan's speech appears within a larger discussion in which Jefferson refutes a theory popular among European philosophers: the theory that North American animals, vegetables, and human beings were smaller, less vigorous, and less virile than their counterparts in Europe.

Given this history, it becomes apparent that Jefferson reproduces Tahgahjute's speech not to defend his claims—much less the claims of Indian peoples generally—but to prove that *America* is as strong, vital, and vocal as the Old World (Sheehan 1973; Gray 2000). Jefferson's introduction to the speech indicates his purpose: "I may challenge the whole orations of Demosthenes and Cicero, and of any more eminent orator, if Europe has furnished more eminent, to produce a single passage, superior to the speech of Logan, a Mingo chief" (Jefferson 1782, 62). In a tactic popular among the American revolutionists—the most famous example being that of the costumed revelers at the Boston Tea Party—Jefferson thus dons an "Indian" persona to champion the "native" American (Deloria 1998, 10–70; Kamrath 2005). Yet in so doing, he reduces Indian voices to figments of the nonnative mind; he initiates a process that continues today in the use of "Indian" names and images for aspects of American popular and national culture (Steele 1996).

At the same time, Jefferson's transformation of Tahgahjute, the victim of colonial violence, into Chief Logan, the voice of the American nation, anticipates a process that would mushroom in the nineteenth century: the creation of fictional narratives and staged melodramas by writers such as James Fenimore Cooper, Lydia Maria Child, and John Augustus Stone, all of whom invented heroic yet tragic Indians whose fate it was to pronounce pathetic speeches, then disappear before the superior might of the American nation (Bank 1993; Maddox 1991). A direct line can be traced from Revolutionary poet Philip Freneau's "Prophecy of King Tammany" (1782), which has the historical Delaware chief Tamenund speak a bitter curse against his conquerors before vanishing into "dark oblivion's shade" (Freneau 1902–1903, 2: 189), and the famous concluding lines of Cooper's *The Last of the Mohicans* (1826), in which the same figure sums up his people's doom:

> "It is enough!" he said. "Go, children of the Lenape; the anger of the Mannitto is not done. Why should Tamenund stay? The pale-faces are masters of the earth, and the time of the red-man has not yet come again. My day has been too long. In the morning I saw the sons of Unâmis happy and strong; and yet, before the night has come, have I lived to see the last warrior of the wise race of the Mohicans!" (Cooper 1986, 350)

In this fictive lament, the Indian voice, far from countering colonialism, is recruited as its spokesman. Thus in the nineteenth century, it seemed that what Indians had feared all along had come to pass: Euro-Americans had invented stories with the power to wipe them out of the land.

Yet just as Indian "voices" appeared destined to become figments of the colonialist imagination, a remarkable event occurred: literate Indians began to publish works of their own. One of the first of such writers was a Mohegan (not Mohican) Indian, Samson Occom. Born in 1723, Occom converted to Christianity during the Great Awakening and was later schooled by minister Eleazar Wheelock. After years of traveling in the colonies and abroad to raise funds for Wheelock's proposed Indian missions, Occom broke with his mentor in 1768, objecting to the latter's design to use the money to found Dartmouth College. Occom worked as an itinerant preacher until 1785, when his long-planned Christian Indian community of Brothertown was established in upstate New York; for the remainder of his life, he fought to save Indian lands in Connecticut and New York from white encroachment (Peyer 1997, 54–116). In his writings, Occom expresses his anger at the missionaries who had supposedly saved him; thus in his "Short Narrative of My Life," penned after his 1768 falling-out with Wheelock but not published during his lifetime, he describes the withdrawal of his already meager salary:

> I Can't Conceive how these gentlemen would have me Live. I am ready to (forgive) their Ignorance, and I would wish they had Changed Circumstances with me but one month, that they may know, by experience what my Case really was; but I am now fully convinced, that it was not Ignorance. . . . So I am *ready* to say, they have used me thus, because I Can't Influence the Indians so well as other missionaries; but I can assure them I have endeavoured to teach them as well as I know how;— but I *must Say,* "I believe it is because I am a poor Indian." I Can't help that God has made me So; I did not make my self so. (Occom 1994, 112–113)

In this passage, Occom unveils the racism beneath the missionaries' piety: though they preach that all souls are equal before God, in practice they see Indian souls as less valuable than their own. Occom's most famous work, a 1772 sermon delivered at the execution of an Indian convicted of murder, makes this point more emphatically: "we wrestle not against flesh and blood, but against principalities, against powers, against the rulers of darkness of this world, against spiritual wickedness in high places" (Occom 1994, 100). Using Christian terminology to incriminate Christians, Occom voices an Indian's indictment of colonialism, of "spiritual wickedness in high places" (Brooks 2003, 51–63; Gustafson 2000, 90–101).

In the nineteenth century, this tradition of Indian protest literature flourished in the works of writers such as William Apess (Pequot), Elias Boudinot (Cherokee), and Sarah Winnemucca (Paiute). All these writers were Christian converts; all were critical of the injustices Indians suffered in a nominally Christian nation. Too, all were advocates of Indian self-determination; like the Praying Indians of John Eliot, all sought to use the dominant culture's tools to secure the existence of Indian communities (Walker 1997; Weaver 1997). Apess in particular bridges the seventeenth century and the nineteenth; in his final work, "Eulogy on King Philip" (1836), delivered 60 years after the declaration of America's independence and 160 years after the defeat of Philip's forces, Apess extols Philip as the hero of surviving Indian peoples:

> as the immortal Washington lives endeared and engraven on the hearts of every white in America, never to be forgotten in time—even such is the immortal Philip honored, as held in memory by the degraded but yet grateful descendants who appreciate his character. . . . Justice and humanity for the remaining few prompt me to vindicate the character of him who yet lives in their hearts and, if possible, melt the prejudice that exists in the hearts of those who are in the possession of his soil, and only by the right of conquest. (Apess 1992, 277)

Revering Philip as a founding father, one who fought for Indian liberty against the oppressive regime of colonialism, Apess uses the means of literacy to protest the wrongs and to protect the rights of Indian peoples. At the same time, by recovering Philip's voice for Indian purposes, Apess refuses to allow Indian words to become mere playthings of white authors and audiences (Dannenberg 1996; Gussman 2004; O'Connell 1997). In this respect, the writings of Apess and those who followed him reveal that though Indian voices in early American literature can never be fully recovered, these voices speak to us still.

REFERENCES

Anon. 1985. *Mourt's Relation: A Journal of the Pilgrims of Plymouth,* edited by Jordan D. Fiore. Plymouth, MA: Plymouth Rock Foundation.

Apess, William. 1992. Eulogy on King Philip. In *On Our Own Ground: The Complete Writings of William Apess, a Pequot,* edited by Barry O'Connell, 275–310. Amherst: University of Massachusetts Press.

Aupaumut, Hendrick. 1827. A Narrative of an Embassy to the Western Indians, edited by B. H. Coates. *Memoirs of the Historical Society of Pennsylvania* 2: 63–131.

Axtell, James. 1988. *After Columbus: Essays in the Ethnohistory of Colonial North America.* New York: Oxford University Press.

Bank, Rosemarie K. 1993. Staging the "Native": Making History in American Theatre Culture, 1828–1838. *Theatre Journal* 45: 461–486.

Bartram, William. 1955. *Travels of William Bartram,* edited by Mark Van Doren. New York: Dover.

Bellin, Joshua David. 2001. *The Demon of the Continent: Indians and the Shaping of American Literature.* Philadelphia: University of Pennsylvania Press.

Berkhofer, Robert. 1978. *The White Man's Indian: Images of the American Indian from Columbus to the Present.* New York: Vintage.

Bowden, Henry Warner. 1981. *American Indians and Christian Missions: Studies in Cultural Conflict.* Chicago: University of Chicago Press.

Brooks, Joanna. 2003. *American Lazarus: Religion and the Rise of African-American and Native American Literatures.* New York: Oxford University Press.

Bross, Kristina. 2004. *Dry Bones and Indian Sermons: Praying Indians in Colonial America.* Ithaca, NY: Cornell University Press.

Calloway, Colin G., ed. 1994. *Early American Indian Documents: Treaties and Laws, 1607–1789. Vol. 18, Revolution and Confederation.* Bethesda, MD: University Publications of America.

———. 1995. *The American Revolution in Indian Country: Crisis and Diversity in Native American Communities.* New York: Cambridge University Press.

Cheyfitz, Eric. 1991. *The Poetics of Imperialism: Translation and Colonization from "The Tempest" to "Tarzan."* New York: Oxford University Press.

Cogley, Richard W. 1999. *John Eliot's Mission to the Indians before King Philip's War.* Cambridge, MA: Harvard University Press.

Cohen, Charles Lloyd. 1986. *God's Caress: The Psychology of Puritan Religious Experience.* New York: Oxford University Press.

Colden, Cadwallader. 1747. *The History of the Five Indian Nations of Canada, Which Are Dependent on the Province of New-York in America, and Are the Barrier Between the English and French in That Part of the World.* London: T. Osborne.

Cooper, James Fenimore. 1986. *The Last of the Mohicans,* edited by Richard Slotkin. New York: Penguin.

Dannenberg, Anne Marie. 1996. "Where, Then, Shall We Place the Hero of the Wilderness?": William Apess's *Eulogy on King Philip* and Discourses of Racial Destiny. In *Early Native American Writing: New Critical Essays,* edited by Helen Jaskoski, 66–82. New York: Cambridge University Press.

Deloria, Philip. 1998. *Playing Indian.* New Haven, CT: Yale University Press.

Dowd, Gregory Evans. 1992. *A Spirited Resistance: The North American Indian Struggle for Unity, 1745–1815.* Baltimore: Johns Hopkins University Press.

Drummond, A.M., and Richard Moody. 1953. Indian Treaties: The First American Dramas. *Quarterly Journal of Speech* 39: 15–24.

Easton, John. 1913. A Relacion of the Indyan Warre, by Mr. Easton, of Roade Isld., 1675. In *Narratives of the Indian Wars, 1675–1699,* edited by Charles H. Lincoln, 7–17. New York: Scribner's.

Eliot, John. 1980. *John Eliot's Indian Dialogues,* edited by Henry W. Bowden and James P. Ronda. Westport, CT: Greenwood.

———. 2003. *The Eliot Tracts, with Letters from John Eliot to Thomas Thorowgood and Richard Baxter,* edited by Michael P. Clark. Westport, CT: Praeger.

Franklin, Benjamin. 1987. *Writings,* edited by J. A. Leo Lemay. New York: Library of America.

Freneau, Philip. 1902–1903. *The Poems of Philip Freneau, Poet of the American Revolution,* edited by Fred Lewis Pattee. 3 vols. Princeton, NJ: Princeton University Library.

Gray, Edward G. 2000. The Making of Logan, the Mingo Orator. *The Language Encounter in the Americas, 1492–1800: A Collection of Essays,* edited by Edward G. Gray and Norman Fiering, 260–277. New York: Berghahn.

Grinde, Donald A., and Bruce E. Johansen. 1991. *Exemplar of Liberty: Native America and the Evolution of Democracy.* Berkeley: University of California Press.

Guice, Stephen A. 1991. John Eliot and the Massachusett Language. In *1990 Mid-America Linguistics Conference Papers,* edited by Frances Ingemann, 120–137. Lawrence: University Press of Kansas.

Gussman, Deborah. 2004. "O Savage, Where Art Thou?": Rhetorics of Reform in William Apess's *Eulogy on King Philip. New England Quarterly* 77: 451–477.

Gustafson, Sandra. 2000. *Eloquence Is Power: Oratory and Performance in Early America.* Chapel Hill: University of North Carolina Press.

Hallock, Thomas. 2003. *From the Fallen Tree: Frontier Narratives, Environmental Politics, and the Roots of a National Pastoral, 1749–1826.* Chapel Hill: University of North Carolina Press.

Hopkins, Samuel. 1911. *Historical Memoirs Relating to the Housatonic Indians.* New York: William Abbatt.

Jefferson, Thomas. [1954] 1982. *Notes on the State of Virginia,* edited by William Peden. Reprint. New York: Norton.

Jennings, Francis. 1975. *The Invasion of America: Indians, Colonialism, and the Cant of Conquest.* New York: Norton.

Kamrath, Mark L. 2005. American Indian Oration and Discourses of the Republic in Eighteenth-Century American Periodicals. In *Periodical Literature in Eighteenth-Century America,* edited by Mark L. Kamrath and Sharon M. Harris, 145–178. Knoxville: University of Tennessee Press.

Kenny, James. 1913. Journal of James Kenny, 1761–1763, edited by John W. Jordan. *Pennsylvania Magazine of History and Biography* 37: 1–47, 152–201.

Kirkland, Samuel. 1980. *The Journal of Samuel Kirkland: Eighteenth-Century Missionary to the Iroquois, Government Agent, Father of Hamilton College,* edited by Walter Pilkington. Clinton, NY: Hamilton College.

Krupat, Arnold. 1992. On the Translation of Native American Song and Story: A Theorized History. In *On the Translation of Native American Literatures,* edited by Brian Swann, 3–32. Washington, DC: Smithsonian Institution Press.

Lepore, Jill. 1998. *The Name of War: King Philip's War and the Origins of American Identity.* New York: Vintage.

Low, Denise. 1995. Contemporary Reinvention of Chief Seattle: Variant Texts of Chief Seattle's 1854 Speech. *American Indian Quarterly* 19: 407–421.

Maddox, Lucy. 1991. *Removals: Nineteenth-Century American Literature and the Politics of Indian Affairs.* New York: Oxford University Press.

Mather, Cotton. 1855. *Magnalia Christi Americana,* ed. Samuel G. Drake. 2 vols. Hartford, CT: Silas Andrus.

McElwain, Thomas. 2001. "Then I Thought I Must Kill Too": Logan's Lament: A "Mingo" Perspective. In *Native American Speakers of the Eastern Woodlands: Selected Speeches and Critical Analyses,* edited by Barbara Alice Mann, 107–121. Westport, CT: Greenwood.

Meserve, Walter T. 1956. English Works of Seventeenth-Century Indians. *American Quarterly* 8: 264–276.

Morrison, Dane. 1995. *A Praying People: Massachusett Acculturation and the Failure of the Puritan Mission, 1600–1690.* New York: Peter Lang.

Murray, David. 1991. *Forked Tongues: Speech, Writing and Representation in North American Indian Texts.* Bloomington: Indiana University Press.

Occom, Samson. 1994. A Short Narrative of My Life. In *Native American Autobiography: An Anthology,* edited by Arnold Krupat, 105–113. Madison: University of Wisconsin Press.

O'Connell, Barry. 1997. "Once More Let Us Consider": William Apess in the Writing of New England Native American History. In *After King Philip's War: Presence and Persistence in Indian New England,* edited by Colin G. Calloway, 162–177. Hanover, VT: University Press of New England.

O'Donnell, James H., III. 1979. Logan's Oration: A Case Study in Ethnographic Authentication. *Quarterly Journal of Speech* 65: 150–156.

Pearce, Roy Harvey. 1953. *Savagism and Civilization: A Study of the Indian and the American Mind.* Berkeley: University of California Press.

Peyer, Bernd C. 1997. *The Tutor'd Mind: Indian Missionary-Writers in Antebellum America.* Amherst: University of Massachusetts Press.

Pomedli, Michael M. 1995. Eighteenth-Century Treaties: Amended Iroquois Condolence Rituals. *American Indian Quarterly* 19: 319–339.

Richter, Daniel K. 1992. *The Ordeal of the Longhouse: The Peoples of the Iroquois League in the Era of European Colonization.* Chapel Hill: University of North Carolina Press.

Ronda, James P. 1977. "We Are Well as We Are": An Indian Critique of Seventeenth-Century Christian Missions. *William and Mary Quarterly,* 3rd ser., 34: 66–82.

Salisbury, Neal. 1974. Red Puritans: The "Praying Indians" of Massachusetts Bay and John Eliot. *William and Mary Quarterly,* 3rd ser., 31: 27–54.

Sandefur, Ray H. 1966. Logan's Oration: How Authentic? *Quarterly Journal of Speech 46:* 289–296.

Sheehan, Bernard W. 1973. *Seeds of Extinction: Jeffersonian Philanthropy and the American Indian.* Chapel Hill: University of North Carolina Press.

Steele, Jeffrey. 1996. Reduced to Images: American Indians in Nineteenth-Century Advertising. In *Dressing in Feathers: The Construction of the Indian in American Popular Culture,* edited by S. Elizabeth Bird, 45–64. Boulder, CO: Westview.

Stevens, Laura M. 2004. *The Poor Indians: British Missionaries, Native Americans, and Colonial Sensibility.* Philadelphia: University of Pennsylvania Press.

Van Lonkhuyzen, Harold W. 1990. A Reappraisal of the Praying Indians: Acculturation, Conversion, and Identity at Natick, Massachusetts, 1646–1730. *New England Quarterly* 63: 396–428.

Walker, Cheryl. 1997. *Indian Nation: Native American Literature and Nineteenth-Century Nationalisms*. Durham, NC: Duke University Press.

Washburn, Wilcomb E. 1971. *Red Man's Land/White Man's Law: A Study of the Past and Present Status of the American Indian*. New York: Scribner's.

Weaver, Jace. 1997. *That the People Might Live: Native American Literatures and Native American Community*. New York: Oxford University Press.

White, Richard. 1991. *The Middle Ground: Indians, Empires, and Republics in the Great Lakes Region, 1650–1815*. New York: Cambridge University Press.

Wroth, Lawrence C. 1928. The Indian Treaty as Literature. *Yale Review*, n.s., 17: 749–766.

Wyss, Hilary E. 2000. *Writing Indians: Literacy, Christianity, and Native Community in Early America*. Amherst: University of Massachusetts Press.

CHAPTER 12

SCIENTIFIC DISCOURSE

SUSAN SCOTT PARRISH

Many years after the event, William Bradford, the leader of Plymouth Colony, re-membered the Puritans' 1620 landfall in strategically dismal tones: "What could they see but a hideous and desolate wilderness, full of wild beasts and wild men[?]" He continued, alluding to the moment in the book of Exodus when the Israelites finally were granted a view of the promised land after their long, purifying exile in the Sinai Desert: "Neither could [the Puritans], as it were, go up to the top of Pisgah to view from this wilderness a more goodly country to feed their hopes; for which way soever they turned their eyes (save upward to the heavens) they could have little solace or content in respect of any outward objects. For summer being done, all things stand upon them with a weatherbeaten face, and the whole country, full of woods and thickets, represented a wild and savage hue" (Bradford 1952, 62). As Bradford represented it, the physical world of outward objects was so unfamiliar and even hostile as to drive the colonists' eyes heavenward, in search of the Chris-tian's true promised land of spiritual permanence. Whether or not this memory of reluctant founding is accurate, we as a nation have since embraced the vision of our origins as one of spiritual purification so that we might sanctify a history that has been much more worldly, if not materialist, in its unfolding.

THE TRANSATLANTIC CONTEXT

Writing around the same time as Bradford, back across the Atlantic, was another Englishman whose alternate philosophy would ultimately win out in shaping the modern Western world: Francis Bacon. If Bradford in this passage emphasized the holy Word and turned his eyes away from his repugnant surroundings, Bacon and his English and, eventually, American followers championed the worth of the physical world and the knowledge gained through the human encounter with new and distant territories. While the quest for spiritual, even antimaterial, purification has played a role in North American history, much more truly central to this history have been investigations of, extractions from, and identifications with the natural world. Many of the people engaged in such pursuits, moreover, did not see them as ungodly—as set against religion per se; instead, God seemed to sanction the Englishmen's plantation and "improvement" of what appeared to them to be wasted land.

While Bradford reacted to the unfamiliarity of nature in the Western Hemisphere by turning his eyes away from it, many colonists and authors reacted to this environmental difference with an intense curiosity. More than this, the need to understand the American climate or soil or native flora often amounted to a matter of personal life and death, or the success or failure of a colonial venture. Nature was a vital concern. And it was a vital concern not only for disoriented English newcomers but also for indigenous people (whose natural world was remade by these strange newcomers from across the ocean) and for Africans (who had to orient themselves anew while enslaved to aliens in an alien place). For survival and economic viability, English settlers and investors needed to learn about what resources could be harvested from this New World. In the North, they extracted beaver pelts, cod, and timber, and built ironworks; in the South, after discovering a dearth of precious metals, they grew crops of tobacco, rice, and indigo, and harvested timber and deer pelts. Throughout the colonies, settlers had to figure out what the growing seasons were like and how to make this unfamiliar land highly productive. Settlers and travelers surveyed and mapped coastal and inland territory for navigation and westward expansion. Indians had to change their farming and hunting practices to adjust to English encroachment or to traders demanding large quantities of pelts. Africans had to adapt their agricultural knowledge to new crops and often terrible working conditions.

Unlike in our own day, all these groups believed that human health was tied to the natural world. The English believed that physical health depended on the balancing of four types of fluids in their bodies called humours. One could control this balance through diet and forms of purging (purposeful vomiting, bleeding, evacuation), but such a balance was believed to depend also on the local air, water, and earth. A new environment produced new effects on the body. An altered body, in turn, produced an altered mind. Because this belief in environmental determinism was so widespread in all ranks of colonial society, the English were extremely energetic about diagnosing how this new place was changing their own natures. Many were certain that the new climate degraded the English body and mind; they called such a phenomenon "criolian degeneracy," "Creole" being the term for Old World people born in America. Indians were powerfully struck by how their health declined upon contact with Europeans: possessing no antibodies to fight off European and African diseases, Indian populations dwindled; it seemed to them as if their natural and spiritual worlds were extraordinarily out of balance, and the knowledge possessed by their traditional healers shockingly outmoded. Africans likewise saw a high mortality rate, due to conditions on the Middle Passage and on the plantations; they worked quickly to understand the healing and toxic aspects of their new environments, often acting as key sources of botanical information for the English.

Knowledge of the natural world—what we would today call "science"—was thus essential to survival and prosperity in colonial America. Colonization of America between 1500 and 1800 therefore encouraged the growth of numerous branches of science: oceanography, geography, botany, mineralogy, zoology, climatology, and ethnology. Europeans reached America because their knowledge of geography and astronomy and their navigational technology were improving. This new fifteenth-century ability to travel greater distances caused new encounters both biological and human, which in turn spurred the growth of modern institutions and technologies: museums for collecting distant specimens, state-sponsored scientific societies, better technologies for investigation (microscopes, telescopes, and air pumps), conceptual systems for classifying the newly collected information, and printing and engraving technologies that made this information available for dissemination. Francis Bacon, writing a century after Columbus's landfall in the Caribbean and the subsequent Spanish exploitation of that discovery, codified for English people this new orientation toward physical knowledge of global proportions. Now that an entire hemisphere had been "found," nothing on this earth seemed beyond the reach of the penetrating minds of men.

Expressing this sense of how the New World spurred on human scientific knowledge as never before, the Italian chronicler of Spain's endeavors in America, Pietro Martire d'Anghiera, wrote in 1520 that, unlike the Eastern Hemisphere, "owre mooste frutefull Ocean and newe woorlde, engendereth and bringeth furthe dayly newe byrthes wherby men of great wytte, and especially such as are studious of newe and marvelous thinges, may have sumwhat at hand wherewith to feede their myndes" (Anghiera 1555, 113). A century later, Bacon turned this novel mental hunger, or curiosity, into a modern scientific program for England and wrote: "above all things it must be looked after, that [this program's] extent be large, and that it be made after the measure of the Universe, for the World ought not to be tyed unto the straightness of the understanding (which hitherto hath been done) but our Intellect should be stretched and widened, so as to be capable of the Image of the World, such as we find it" (Bacon 1670, 3). Bacon wanted Englishmen to stop relying on what classical authors had written about nature; instead, he urged his readers to explore every inch of the earth and sky with their eyes, hands, and instruments, and to experiment with substances in laboratories until they understood their properties. He spoke of empirical science as a mental conquest of the world but also believed that the world itself could enlarge the minds of men.

In the early 1660s, after the end of the Puritan interregnum with King Charles II now restored to the throne, Englishmen at the universities who wanted to realize Bacon's vision of hands-on, experimental, and globally expansive science—then called natural history or natural philosophy—received the king's backing to found the Royal Society of London for Improving Natural Knowledge. They eventually acquired a building equipped with laboratories, printed their own journal, solicited patronage from the nobility, and commenced an international correspondence network. Their goals were both intellectual and economic. Some members seemed simply to want to know more about how the natural world worked—they possessed a kind of pure scientific curiosity. Though these men were cautious that this noble endeavor would be corrupted by turning it toward profit-making schemes, there was, in actuality, a connection between England's rising imperial ambitions and its scientific visions. In the same decade that the Royal Society was founded, the English finally gained control over the entire eastern seaboard of North America from Nova Scotia to the Carolinas and controlled many lucrative islands in the Caribbean. The monarch wanted to manage these colonies more centrally and make them more profitable. Exhaustive knowledge of their physical properties was part of the imperial and the scientific program.

In 1670, the secretary of the Royal Society, Henry Oldenburg, wrote a letter to John Winthrop Jr., governor of Connecticut and fellow of the Royal Society. In the letter, Oldenburg offered his vision of colonial science:

> I hope the New English in America will not be displeased with what they find the Old English do in Europe, as to the matter of improving and promoting useful knowledge by observations and experiments, and my mind presages mee, that within a little time wee shall heare, that the ferment of advancing real Philosophy, which is very active here and in all our neighboring countrys, will take also in your parts, and there seize on all that have ingenuity and industry for the farther spreading of the honour of the English nation, and the larger diffusing of the manifold advantages and benefits to thee must proceed from hence. I am persuaded, Sir, you will lay out your talent for that purpose and instill the noblenesse and usefulnesse of this institution and work, with your best Logick and Oratory, into the minds of all your friends and acquaintances there, especially of those pregnant Youths, that have begun to give proof of their good capacityes for things of that nature. I doubt not, but the savage Indians themselves, when they shall see the Christians addicted, as to piety and virtue, so to all sorts of ingenuityes, pleasing experiments usefull inventions and practises, will thereby insensibly, and the more chearfully subject themselves to you. (Anon. 1963)

Oldenburg is not speaking down to his colonial correspondent in this letter. He hopes that these Englishmen in New England can operate in the front lines of the combined missions of science, empire, and Christianity. For the "nobility" of the English nation to move westward across the ocean, it must take hold of the souls and minds of both colonists and their Indian subjects. Science, hand in hand with religion, could bring a worthy and pleasant form of subjugation, according to Oldenburg. A far-reaching scientific network made possible through the growing British Empire would both help the colonists "improve" wild territories by making them yield commodities for an Atlantic market, redirect Indian energies toward "usefull . . . practices," and advance English science by supplying it with exotic specimens and information.

Science was not American in this time period. It was transatlantic. As one can see from the quotation above, virtually all the colonial scientific pursuits and writings were tied to London, and to Royal Society members. These London-based naturalists or virtuosos understood that to make their knowledge global, they had to have competent collectors and correspondents sending them new material all the time from all over the world. Correspondents in America were particularly valuable because they possessed "English minds" but were extensively occupying exotic physical territory. Besides encouraging the colonists, the Crown also funded various Englishmen to take scientific gathering trips in the New World. Royal Society members would encourage ship captains and their wives to collect specimens for them during their ports of call; they encouraged those traveling through the colonies to make use of local slaves, Indians, and female midwives for botanical information, often commenting that these groups knew more than colonial doctors. Finally, colonial leaders like Winthrop who were well connected to London through politics, trade, or early schooling were encouraged to become members of the Royal Society and constantly send information and specimens from their American locales. Because natural history in this time was premised on the scientist's immediate encounters with nature, the seeing, touching, collecting, describing, and image making of people in America were crucial to English knowledge of the Western Hemisphere. While much of the scientific rhetoric of this period projects an image of knowledge flowing outward from the imperial center of London to civilize and "improve" the wild hinterlands, it is striking to note in more private correspondence how dependent the Londoners felt on the colonial frontiers to provide them with material and information.

What is an important part of the story for the history and sociology of science is that because correspondents in London wanted American specimens and information so urgently, they were quite open to whichever human sources could get them those materials. Because of this, nonelite white men (farmers and artisans), women, Indians, and Africans were frequently the origin for specimens and information: seeds, butterflies, roots, curative plants, aquatic animals, and birds, as well as anecdotes about healing, inexplicable physical events, migrational patterns, and behavior of animals all came from these sources. Usually only the elite white men wrote to the Royal Society—and certainly only they were official members—but they willingly revealed how much they were indebted to their lower-ranked townsmen and women, slaves, neighboring Indians, or female family members. Knowledge about nature in America drew its roots, then, from England, Scotland, Africa, and America itself; it also inherited some of its premises from classical thinkers like Aristotle. However, the final site of this knowledge—where it reached print or became established in a collection—was, almost until American Independence, London or Edinburgh, Amsterdam or Göttingen.

Such, therefore, was the complex transatlantic world of colonial American science. All this information is crucial to comprehending the literature produced in connection with such activities. Otherwise we might project backward in time our own contemporary, highly specialized and professionalized practices of science and technology. Because science was not professionalized then, and because people who practiced it were leisured nobility, physicians, merchants, ministers, plantation owners, or well-to-do women in these households, the boundaries of scientific discourse were much more blurred than today. What we might call "polite" or recreational science overlapped with more institutionally connected or even state-sponsored endeavors. Therefore, we need to include many different genres to do justice to this period's literary encounters with nature. Almost every genre of writing then practiced was touched by a consideration of the natural world. It was not just writing about America that was environmentally attuned. In subsequent periods of American literary history, the natural world remained a more pervasive thematic concern than in other national literatures. We see the beginnings of this trend, and the reasons for it, in the colonial period. The genres more or less directly concerned with the natural world were the report or account, the "history and present state," the natural history, travels, letters (both familiar and written to the Royal Society), and almanacs.

THE REPORT OR ACCOUNT

The earliest form of English scientific writing was in fact a combination of travel narrative, promotional tract, descriptive atlas, and natural history. These texts were glowing inventories of and spatial aids for locating the existing and potential natural commodities of the New World in places the British hoped to colonize. The most influential of these included Thomas Hariot's *Briefe and True Report of the New Found Land of Virginia* (1588) and Captain John Smith's *Generall Historie of Virginia, New-England and the Summer Isles* (1624). When these were written, the

English were just beginning to attempt colonization—going beyond their piratical adventures in the Atlantic waters off the American coasts. Behind Spain in laying claim to and reaping a sustainable profit from New World territories, some English decided it was time to interest their countrymen in westward expansion. They had to counter rumors and images that had been streaming out of the Atlantic experience—of cannibals, strange animals, burning heats, infectious airs, and generally dismal living conditions—by publishing more positive and yet convincing reports written by eyewitnesses. Moreover, they wanted to publish directives for "adventurers" willing to invest in colonization to make such an effort successful. Thomas Hariot explained that this report would counter the slanderous accounts about Virginia that were being circulated: "I have therefore thought it good being one that have beene in the discoverie and in dealing with the naturall inhabitants [the Indians] specially imploied; and having therefore seene and knowne more then the ordinarie. . . . [that] you may generally know and learne what the countrey is, and thereupon consider how your dealing therein if it proceede, may returne you profit and gaine; bee it either by inhabiting and planting or otherwise in furthering thereof" (Hariot 1972, 5)

Here was a detailed advertisement and a "how-to" for plantation and investment. His book consisted of three sections of inventories: the first on commodities that could be yielded (silk, flax, hemp, furs, etc.), the second on indigenous plants and animals that might sustain the English inhabitant (corn, turkeys, herring, etc.), and the third a general advice manual with a lengthy description of native "manners." Every description was calculated to suggest an atmosphere of natural plenty, a plenty moreover that the English had in the past associated only with Near Eastern and Mediterranean locales. Virginia, Hariot reasoned, could yield exotics like silk, grapes, olives, and pearls, being in the same latitudinal band with the countries that currently produced such profitable commodities. He promised that "there will rise as great profite in time to the Virginians, as there of doth now to the Persians, Turkes, Italians and Spaniards" (Hariot 1972, 5–8).

To convey a sense of natural superabundance, Hariot employs a syntactical style of addition. Of corn, for example, he writes that "it is a graine of marveilous great increase; of a thousand, fifteen hundred and some two thousand fold . . . of the stalkes some beare foure heads, some three, some one, and two: every head co[n]taining five, sixe, or seve[n] hundred graines within a fewe more or less" (Hariot 1972, 13). Not only is Hariot submitting the natural world to a numerical standard—actually counting the kernels on an ear of corn!—to appeal to his economically concerned readers, but he purposefully chooses to estimate output numerically by giving not just one number; instead, he offers every possible yield amount, in an additive string of numbers that are calculated to convey a general sense of material "increase." Promotional inventories and instructive maps such as these were written about various fledgling colonies throughout the colonial period as investors tried to line up other financial backers and settlers willing to risk their lives and assets to make a given territory profitable. As late as 1767, for example, when revolutionary agitation against British imperial rule had already begun, London promoters were attempting to draw settlers into the frontier territory of Florida, recently won from the Spanish, with William Stork's *Account of East-Florida*. These promotional accounts were what we might think of as scientific in that they assessed the natural properties and the human behavior of a place; they were also what we would call rhetorical because they positioned those assessments to encourage investment and settlement. Hariot did so in particular by tapping into his English readers' long-held notions of oriental and Mediterranean plenty, as well as his readers' new trust in the truth of numerical language.

"History and Present State"

A genre related to these reports and accounts was that of the "History and Present State." The first one of these written by a colonial was Robert Beverley's *History and Present State of Virginia* (1705). It was divided into four sections: the first addressed political history and present government; the second described the "Natural Productions . . . suited to Trade and Improvement"; the third told of indigenous culture; and the last assessed the "present State of the Country." Written by a member of the colonial elite who resented the economic and political restraints on his class by London politicians and merchants beginning in the late 1600s, this book promoted the inherent promise of the land while it told a tragic political tale of imperial mismanagement. The science in the text then has a promotional bent to it because Beverley wanted to prove that any faults with Virginia lay in human error rather than in environmental defect. Echoes of Hariot's syntax and imagery appear in Beverley's description of animal abundance: "As in Summer, the Rivers and Creeks are fill'd with Fish, so in Winter they are in many Places cover'd with Fowl. There are such a Multitude of Swans, Geese, Brants, Sheldrakes, Ducks of several Sorts, Mallard, Teal, Blewings, and many other Kinds of Water-Fowl, that the Plenty of them is incredible" (Beverley 1947, 153). How different from William Bradford's representation of that "desolate wilderness, full of wild beasts and wild men"! Instead of an indistinguishable and repellant totality of wildness, Beverley allures his London readers with a copious list of distinct particulars. Nature here is not diabolical but, rather, providential; nature gives humans what they need to survive. In Beverley's *History*, as in Genesis, God has stored the earth with animals of every kind for human use.

It should be said that eighteenth-century science in general manifested such a providential worldview. In the earlier seventeenth century, English Christians tended to look for God's dramatic interventions in human affairs through natural cataclysms like comets, hurricanes, and earthquakes, and through what they called preternatural occurrences such as babies born with birth defects. Around the turn of the eighteenth century, however, partly owing to the global cataloging of European imperial science, Englishmen more and more remarked upon God's stable handiwork and ceased to believe in "monsters" (or, that biological aberrations were a message from God). They parceled this handiwork up into specimens and commodities for scientific and mercantile improvement. Some historians see this shift as a process of "disenchantment," whereby the Enlightenment did not so much advance knowledge as strip the cosmos of its mystery and spiritual animation (Horkheimer and Adorno 1972, 3). English naturalists on both sides of the Atlantic, to the contrary, represented their work as a devout explication of God's Creation.

Natural History

The most polished and comprehensive scientific print genre was the illustrated natural history. In this genre, as in those previously mentioned, the author kept a rather low profile; as one botanist wrote in his 1682 natural history: "Yet not I, but Nature speaketh these things" (Grew 1682). The genre was a descriptive catalog that laid out all available specimens in prose and illustration. The goal was to be as compendious as possible, to present a virtual museum of specimens to the reader. Though one could argue that the natural history genre served a promotional agenda by anatomizing the colonies as in the other genres, the prose tends to be more neutral and less tinged with economic forecasts of investors' returns. These books were often quite expensive to produce. They were printed in multivolume folio editions, full of hand-colored engravings. Typically the author financed the book's publication in advance through a group of wealthy subscribers whose names would be listed in the front of the first volume, amounting to a prestigious "who's who" of elite patrons of the British scientific enterprise. It was difficult for colonials to muster such patronage from across the Atlantic.

Thus the most influential natural histories of the American colonies were written by traveling Englishmen with homes in London: Sir Hans Sloane's two-volume *Voyage to the Islands Madera, Barbados, Nieves, S. Christophers, and Jamaica, . . . Wherein Is an Account of the Inhabitants, Air, Waters, Diseases, Trade, etc. of That Place* (1707–1725) and Mark Catesby's two-volume *Natural History of Carolina, Florida, and the Bahama Islands* (1731–1743). The contents of Catesby's natural history were typical of the genre. He gives brief political histories of the places under consideration, then describes the physical surroundings: the mapped boundaries, air, soil, water, aborigines, agriculture, cultivars, and beasts. After this lengthy preface comes the illustrated catalog of specimens. An example of the kind of prose required in such a genre is his description of the buffalo, which begins: "These creatures, though not so tall, weigh more than our largest Oxen. The skin of one is too heavy for the strongest man to lift from the ground: their limbs are short, but very large: their heads are broad: their horns are curved, big at their basis, and turned inward: on their shoulders is a large prominence or bunch: their chests are broad: their hind parts narrow, with a tail a foot long, bare of hairs, except that at the end is a tuft of long hairs" (Catesby 1771).

Such a description, accompanied by the illustration, is meant to make this distant animal palpable to an English reader: a comparison is made to a local animal, physical contact is imagined, and then a series of simple declarative phrases follow (all joined together by the basic "to be" verb connector). This prose is meant to convey a self-evident truthfulness. Though the entire *Natural History* amounts to a kind of descriptive list or collection (as in Hariot and Beverley) and reflects a sense of English mental ownership of the places and creatures described, natural history at its best approaches the English scientific ideal of "disinterestedness"—knowledge for the sake of knowledge alone—more than those genres with a promotional or political agenda.

Catesby had traveled in the colonies from 1712 to 1719 and from 1722 to 1726; therefore, his illustrations and verbal descriptions were based on empirical observation and on-the-spot sketches. Numerous colonists, however, resented that a traveler's representation of American nature would so far eclipse their own and, in their mind, better understanding. For example, the South Carolina physician Alexander Garden—who though born and educated in Edinburgh, considered himself an American—fumed on a number of occasions to his European correspondents about Catesby's incompetence. To the great eighteenth-century Swedish taxonomist Carl Linnaeus, Garden wrote in 1760:

> Please to observe the Albula, our Mullet; and you will immediately perceive that [Catesby] has not only forgotten to count and express the rays of the fins, but that he has, which is hardly credible, left out the pectoral fins entirely, and overlooked one of the ventral ones. . . . It is sufficiently evident that his sole object was to make showy figures of the productions of Nature, rather than to give correct and accurate representations. This is rather to invent than to describe. It is indulging the fancies of his own brain, instead of contemplating and observing the beautiful works of God. (Smith 1821, 1: 300–301)

Garden's statement reveals much about what scientific writing was supposed to be: correct and accurate descriptions as opposed to showy inventions. It was meant to conduct God's creations transparently to the viewer without any indulgent fancy on the part of the naturalist. While the English had once accused the French of producing just such foppish writing, the Americans were now accusing the haughty English of affecting an unnatural form of scientific prose.

THE TRAVEL NARRATIVE

The travel narrative was a genre with much overlap with those mentioned previously, and one that also contained scientific information. If the report or account, "history and present state," and natural history genres tended to provide spatial inventories with little authorial intervention, as if nature was somehow describing itself, the travel narrative told a spatiotemporal story of one human's experience. Because that experience needed to take place in a country remote from the reader to make it worth reading, descriptions of the curiosities and hardships of an alien natural world were typically an important part of the narrative. Some travel narratives, like Sarah Kemble Knight's journal of 1704, for example, were more interested in describing (and lampooning) the social rather than physical geography. As the rise of popular science in the eighteenth century provided a more precise awareness of and language for physical particulars, many travel narratives capitalized on this widespread curiosity by adding such information. Physical details also proved to the reader that the narrator had really "been there" and was not merely inventing a far-fetched romance.

William Byrd II's manuscript *History of the Dividing Line Betwixt Virginia and North Carolina* (ca. 1730s) provides examples of how writers served to authenticate their travel experiences and bolster their authorial status by offering descriptions of nature. Partly a satire of uncouth frontier life that by contrast displayed the civility of Byrd (the discerning observer), his narratives also aspired to reveal new specimens of flora and fauna on the western edge of the British Empire. "Among the shrubs," he wrote, "we were showed here and there a bush of Carolina tea called Japon, which is one species of the Phylarrea. This is an evergreen, the leaves whereof have some resemblance to tea, but differ very widely both in taste and flavour. We also found some few plants of the spired leaf silk grass, which is likewise an evergreen, bearing on a lofty stem a large cluster of flowers of a pale yellow. Of the leaves of this plant the people thereabouts twist very strong cordage" (Byrd 1841, 12).

In this passage, Byrd displays his on-the-spot sensory access to new botanical specimens and his insider's social access to the human improvement of the specimen, that is, making cordage; he also proves that he is aware of the printed taxonomies of Europe ("one species of the Phylarrea"). He knows how American nature fits into European knowledge systems. This type of useful knowledge was sprinkled in with what might be called entertaining social commentary of life in the wilds of America. On the following pages of his journal, Byrd described "a marooner, that modestly called himself a hermit, though he forfeited that name by suffering a wanton female to cohabit with him. His habitation was a bower, covered with bark after the Indian fashion. . . . But as for raiment, he depended mostly upon his length of beard, and she upon her length of hair, part of which she brought decently forward, and the rest dangled behind quite down to her rump, like one of Herodotus' East Indian pigmies" (Byrd 1841, 13).

Byrd was a member of the Royal Society, brought live specimens there (the rattlesnake and opossum) in the 1690s, and had his "Account of a Negro-Boy That is Dappel'd in Several Places of His Body with White Spots" published in their journal in 1695. He experimented with new cultivars (ginseng) and attempted to improve the land of Virginia with wetlands drainage and mining works. In other words, he was an exemplary virtuoso of his day. Byrd knew, though, that if his travel narrative was to be widely entertaining—and there is evidence that he hoped to have it published with illustrations in London—it would have to answer to the public's many kinds of curiosity: a straight-faced desire to know the works of nature but also a winking, even prurient desire to know all the ways of men.

Letters

Though these print genres may be more familiar nowadays, it was actually the manuscript letter that was the most common carrier of scientific news both within the colonies and across the Atlantic. The letter, moreover, was the inexpensive form most available to colonial Americans who lived far away from large-scale scientific patronage. The bulk of these letters were between people who had a like-minded fascination with the natural world. They may have been very local within the colonies. The wealthy South Carolina plantation owner Eliza Lucas Pinckney, for example, wrote in 1742 to a female friend then living a day's journey away in Charleston about the early morning appearance of a comet: "By your enquiry after the Comett I find your curiosity has not been strong enough to raise you out of your bed so much before your usual time as mine has been. But to answer your querie: The Comett had the appearance of a very large starr with a tail and to my sight about 5 or 6 foot long—its real magnitude must then be prodigious. The tale was much paler than the Commet it self and not unlike the milkey way" (Pinckney 1972, 31).

Pinckney had received some education in England and was intellectually encouraged by her father and her husband. She was aware of transatlantic scientific trends and quelled her sense of provincialism by showing to her correspondent—a wealthy young lady visiting from London—that she possessed the metropolitan trait of curiosity. She studiously observed and noted the particularities of this celestial phenomenon and hypothesized about the comet's real dimensions, aware of the difference between appearance to the human eye and physical actuality. Pinckney brought rare Carolina birds with her to London and presented them to the Dowager Princess of Wales. Once settled again outside of Charleston, she sent flowering plants back to England. She also experimented with indigo as a crop and eventually helped to make that commodity profitable for her colony and king. Though some of these activities may seem unscientific now, they shaded very subtly into institutional science. Specimens and letters sent between friends often passed on to the Royal Society, or to important individual collectors who would then publish or display the new information.

John Bartram is a good example of someone whose scientific activities gradually shifted from private, humble, and local to public, prestigious, and transatlantic. A Pennsylvania farmer without formal education, Bartram had a talent for finding and cultivating American plants. Through contacts in Philadelphia, he struck up a correspondence with the most active plant collector of his day in London, Peter Collinson, a wool merchant and member of the Royal Society. Though not aristocratic, Collinson funneled exotic plants both to aristocratic collectors and to the society. At first, knowing Bartram's lack of pedigree, he assumed that Bartram was useful only as a physical collector of specimens and told Bartram not to take the time to describe these specimens. Bartram, undaunted, did write long descriptions of plants and other physical phenomena and asked Collinson to send him books so that he could further educate himself. Slowly, Collinson came to recognize Bartram's talent and dedication. With many warnings about how Bartram should dress himself, Collinson put Bartram in touch with important scientific figures in Philadelphia, New York, Virginia, and South Carolina. Bartram visited and corresponded with all these men and women throughout his career. Eventually, Collinson presented Bartram's letters to the Royal Society, where they were read aloud and printed in its journal. Bartram sent presents—of bullfrogs and plants—to the king of England and the queen of Sweden and was ultimately made "King's Botanist to the Colonies," an appointment that came with an annual salary of fifty pounds. Despite English beliefs about the link between intelligence and noble bloodlines, or, to put it another way, that social inferiority disposed people toward unreliable reporting, Bartram, in large part because of his advantageous access to exotic American novelties, could break through class barriers and hence help mitigate the importance of class distinctions within science.

Indeed, his unpolished writing style came to seem, to his English correspondents, a guarantor of the truthfulness of the information conveyed. Bartram apologized for his scientific prose; he wrote in 1755 to Collinson: "now dear Peter I have sent A confused heap of broken links [I fear] it will puzzle the[e] all to make A tough chain of such brittle materials" (Bartram 1992, 384). Collinson assured him, however, that his verbal "Hodge podge digests very Well with Mee," and that Bartram's noble patron, Robert Lord Petre, "admires thy natural way of writing." At other moments, Bartram could be defensive (rather than apologetic) about the integrity of his writing: "good grammar and good spelling," he wrote in 1754, "may please those that are taken with A fine superficial flourish than real truth but my chief aim was to inform my readers of the true real distinguishing characters of each genus" (Bartram

1992, 473). Bartram was trying to describe the physical appearance of plants that were distant from his readers. Though he was apologetic on the grounds of his limited education, he also came to perceive an English scientific prose aesthetic that he seemed perfectly to fulfill.

As language reformers at the Royal Society had been writing since the 1660s, things were meant to direct language; language was not meant to overdress and hence obscure the true character of the physical world. The English had accused France and other Catholic countries of producing ornate writing that obscured the clear communication of facts. English science would be the first to produce a pared-down, naked prose, its defenders claimed. Therefore, Bartram and other colonial writers, who felt rather tender about their uncouth American birth and often apologized about what one writer in 1736 called his "Indian scribble," came to discover that their less embellished writing was very desirable (Tinling 1977, 493). As the example of Alexander Garden's chastisement of Mark Catesby showed, colonial authors eventually came to believe (at least as they expressed it to each other) that their direct access to exotic nature and their direct writing style were what made them even better naturalists than their London patrons.

One notable exception to this rule was the Massachusetts Puritan minister Cotton Mather, who sent quantities of letters to the Royal Society in the early 1700s that were so full of linguistic excess, outmoded belief in the supernatural, and citations to ancient authors, and so lacking in simple physical description, that many were never printed, to Mather's great distress. One of his London correspondents complained of all of Mather's "Puns, Anagrams, Acrosticks, Miracles, Prodigies, Witches, Speeches, Epistles, and other Incumbrances" (Oldmixon 1708, ix). Mather failed to understand that he was writing in a scholastic, erudite manner that was no longer in fashion and that, indeed, the new scientific activities themselves had rendered obsolete. Mather was in the right place to be in the front lines of scientific truth making—he had heard, for example, about smallpox inoculation from African slaves in the port of Boston even before the Royal Society had heard of such a cure from an English woman returning from Turkey—but he lacked the kind of prose that conveyed factuality.

The interchanges between John Bartram, Cotton Mather, and their London correspondents are really the tip of the iceberg of a vast debate about American prose, or, to put it better, about modern prose, which many Americans saw themselves as typifying. The world of physical objects became ever more fascinating to the modernizing English mind, beginning in the seventeenth century, as global trade, colonization, science, and a new wealthy merchant class all came into being in interconnected ways. In London, the physical objects people could encounter were ever more varied and exotic: coffee, tea, sugar, tobacco, potatoes, beaver hats, or American Indians making diplomatic tours. From east and west, new objects of fascination—human, animal, and vegetable—sailed in. As exotic objects rose in prominence, language was often required to be more object-centered. Thus, in many ways, the scientific imperative of exhaustive but unembellished description came to influence modern prose significantly. Because America was the exotic place that held the most English people, it was writing by the English in America that stood at the vanguard of this new direction of the English language.

ALMANACS

If letters were the most frequent bearers of scientific news within the colonies and across the Atlantic, they involved only a relatively small group of committed individuals. The medium that was the most widespread purveyor of scientific information to the colonial populace, on the other hand, was the almanac. Almanacs were inexpensive yearlong calendars that became a staple of colonial printing presses as early as 1646. In modest but literate households, the almanac may have been the only text on the premises other than the Bible. Single-sheet (or "broadsheet") almanacs were posted in taverns and other public venues, so that even individuals unable to purchase the yearly calendar found it to be an integral part of their lives. At their most basic, almanacs were calendars that noted the particular daily times for the rising and setting of the sun, the high and low points of the tides, distances between towns, and civic or religious information such as court or election days. Another typical feature of a basic almanac was the "Man of Signs," a pictured body on which was diagrammed the influence of the various astrological signs on different organs and body parts. The printer or compiler of the almanac needed the mathematical and astronomical skills to be able to calculate the preceding information, and so was a kind of local scientific expert in an applied rather than abstract or experimental manner. Such information was useful to farmers, fishermen, sailors, and travelers. As the medium grew during the colonial period, printers—often producing within a competitive marketplace—innovated and elaborated upon the basic form: they included poetry on top of each month's calendar, prognostications about weather and fortune, as well as aphorisms and important historical dates (the beheading of King Charles I, for example) within the calendar pages to fill up every available white space. Printers began to add more pages to the calendar matter, in which they would include anecdotes and short narratives, as well as many kinds of charts and lists deemed useful: currency conversions, chronologies of English royalty, various aristocratic ranks within England, and, after the Revolution, key facts about the new structures of governance.

Not only would the calculation of the astronomical information have been a scientific act, but many of the poems and brief narratives sought to describe the natural world, its divine creation, and its effects on the human body, and hence contributed to colonial scientific discourse. One influential compiler of almanacs, Nathanael Ames, in his *An Astronomical Diary, or, An Almanack* (1732), defended the cultural importance of the scientifically oriented poetry contained within his publication; though some might criticize these poems as inappropriate, he averred, "I hope they will acknowledge that the consideration of the Distances, Places, Motions, Center, and Magnetism of the Heavenly Bodies, and how inviolably they obey the Laws of some Omniscient Contriver, in their exact Revolutions, according to their several Periods, is sufficient to lead my Thoughts this way to admire the Omniscient Mind." Rather than an unpredictable and anger-prone Jehovah, God was invoked as an "Omniscient Contriver," who received "inviolable" obedience from the natural sphere. The Christian observer's job was to witness such perfect obedience in motion.

In "An Essay on Regiment," which appeared in his *Almanack of* 1754, Ames asked why humans are so subject to disease once they turn thirty. He blamed overindulgence and lack of exercise: "Nature in her secret Distribution of the circulating Fluid requires, those Compressions, Extensions and other Kinds of Motions necessary to separate the several Humours, and cast them into their proper Channels, to retain the Balsamick and throw off the redundant excrementious Particles of the Blood." Our bodies were created by God a perfect "Machine," he continued, but at some point a "forbidden, (if not an heterogeneous Substance) . . . broke the divine Harmony"; in antediluvian days, people could survive for 900 years, but since then, our blood, the key fluid that maintains all the other organs, has been complicated by "animal Substances" and has shortened the "divine Warranty." The accommodations of reasoning you see here—as Ames reconciles biblical "facts" with humoral theory in order to tender sound practical advice—is typical of practical science in this period. An almanac reader could use both the more pagan, lowbrow "Man of Signs" as well as this Christian, scientifically theoretical model by which to manage his or her bodily health.

What makes almanacs an especially fascinating medium is that those which have been preserved frequently contain copious handwritten notes. Readers marked up their calendars, correcting the printer's weather predictions or recording personal events or unfolding civic history; others interleaved the printed pages with blank pages upon which to keep a line-a-day diary. These quick jottings typically recorded daily weather next to more monumental events such as the birth or death of a child. On some pages, we find careful records about natural events, both local and global, that demonstrate how the practices of (what we might call private) natural history were rather common among colonial Americans. A Salem, Massachusetts, resident, William Bentley, wrote in his copy of Isaiah Thomas's *Almanack* of 1804 on the page for February: "an Earthquake felt at Madeira" (February 9); "A meteor observed at Richmond Virginia brilliant at 8 in the evening passing in a NW direction" (February 18); and "weather severe in Holland & Low Countries" (February 28). A Bostonian, Samuel Baldwin, in an unidentified 1749–1750 *Almanac,* recorded on its front leaf: "June 14 1750 I was diverted with a sight very remarkable: viz. a wild Creature and four footed about the bigness of a large Cat. having white and gray hairs Long visage teeth in the upper[,] and under[,] having a tale something like a musk Squash whose young ones grow at the tets: having a false belly over them." Without knowing its name, Baldwin was closely inspecting and describing the physiology of the female opossum, just as better connected colonists were doing in letters to the Royal Society in these years. Scientific practice and discourse was not exclusive in this period in the colonies. The almanac shows how the most popular colonial print medium was a venue for the diffusion of semi-learned knowledge as well as a container for privately witnessed natural facts.

CONCLUSION

The sciences discussed so far are what practitioners then called natural history. They involved collecting, describing, categorizing, naming, and dissecting plants, animals, humans, minerals, and fossils, as well as accounting for earthly and bodily phenomena like the circulation of blood or the appearance of a giant bone buried underground. It was in these sciences that the colonists could make the most obvious and ready contribution because of their proximity to so many specimens never before seen by Europeans. Because of this situation, they were encouraged to be contributors and even partners in the knowledge-making process. Moreover, when they offered as their source for their specimen or information an Indian or enslaved African, such sources paradoxically made the information appear even more real or natural because it came from people who Europeans saw as closer to nature and hence more likely to know its secrets. Though Indians and Africans did not write scientific documents in English in the eighteenth century, their expertise gained from thorough empirical contact with American nature was often the origin for what would later become European printed facts.

The sciences that people in America had a much harder time breaking into were the more theoretical and experimental ones. Europeans were willing to acknowledge American expertise about American specimens, but they were disdainful about the American capacity to theorize about what they called the "first causes" of nature's mechanisms. Still more, the ability to move from theorizing about a natural process to manipulating that process for human use seemed too advanced for a colonial society just recently hacked out of the wilderness. The case of the Scots-born lieutenant governor of New York, Cadwallader Colden, provides a good example of this double standard. He was a welcome correspondent of the great European collectors of his day; Linnaeus even championed the botanical work of

Colden's young daughter Jane, who first identified two new species and suggested, in a Scottish scientific journal in 1756, the establishment of a new order of plants to correct Linnaeus's system. When Cadwallader Colden attempted to have his theory of gravity accepted in London, however, his colonial status stood in the way. His treatise, *An Explication of the First Causes of Action in Matter, and, of the Cause of Gravitation,* was published in America in 1745; when it was reprinted in London without Colden's permission, elite members within the Royal Society balked. Peter Collinson confided to Benjamin Franklin in 1747 that "one was so meane Spirited as to Say He did not believe it was Doc Coldens Work but that the Ship wrack papers of Some Ingenious European had fell into his hands." An "eminent mathematician" from London chimed in: "I am amazed how this Book got to New York, for I am satisfied it came originally from Hence [London] and was once under a Cover with other things—and the pacquet has been Gutted" (Colden 1918–1937, 368, 371). An American could know about America but could not define eternal and universal laws of nature.

It was Benjamin Franklin's experiments with electricity that finally began to shift the balance away from Eurocentrism in the theoretical and experimental sciences. Traveling exhibitors of electricity were popular in the colonies in the second half of the eighteenth century. These performances were as much spiritual and political theater as they were scientific demonstration. Coming out of this culture of electricity, if you will, Franklin was a master at turning his scientific knowledge into a political spectacle. One of his exhibits involved taking a portrait of King George II of England and electrifying the removable crown that sat on the monarch's head. Participants would be asked to dislodge the crown from the head of their king in order to feel the shock. The message was clear: republican ingenuity and curiosity existed in a charged and potentially painful relation with traditional monarchical authority. Scientific know-how and political independence were linked. When in July 1776 American revolutionaries read the Declaration of Independence standing on the deck of the observatory from which ingenious Americans had recently viewed the transit of Venus as part of a global team of observers, those revolutionaries were likewise making the connection between knowledge and independence.

Thomas Jefferson wrote in this Declaration that "Nature and Nature's God" sanctioned the Americans' separation from Great Britain, and that the American people found the "truths" that impelled them to this separation to be "self-evident." To discern universal truths and to understand the order of nature were enlisted by Jefferson as political marks of national maturity. He enlisted these marks because the practices of science had achieved such a high status in the modern world of 1776. Moreover, this separation from England was "natural" and hence reasonable because it was based upon the discernment of "facts." Jefferson's allusions to science were meant to assure the world that this political outcome was arrived at through the scientific perception and deduction of rational men able to govern themselves, not by the fists of an angry and brutal mob of ungrateful colonial degenerates.

In the wake of the Revolutionary War, Americans found themselves looking for a foundation for their national culture and seeking out the true nature of their identity as a people. Not wanting to merely perpetuate European traditions, many looked for indigenous signs of cultural belonging. Such a project made knowing American nature—or performing popular and professional science in the United States—a patriotic act of nation formation. Geography textbooks and maps, almanacs that described local physical features, panoramic paintings of the western frontier, novels set in the wilderness, the Lewis and Clark expedition to find a northwest passage to the Pacific and an American trade route to Asia—all these were meant to make the United States both powerful and natural as a nation.

REFERENCES

Anghiera, Pietro Martire d'. 1555. *The Decades of the Newe Worlde or West India, Conteyning the Navigations and Conquestes of the Spanyardes, with the Particular Description of the Moste Ryche and Large Landes and Ilandes Lately Founde in the West Ocean,* translated and edited by Richard Eden. London: Guilhelmi Powell.

Anon. 1963. *Letters and Communications from Americans, 1662–1900.* London: Royal Society.

Bacon, Francis. 1670. *A Preparatory to the History Natural and Experimental.* London: Sarah Griffing and Ben. Griffing, for William Lee.

Bartram, John. 1992. *The Correspondence of John Bartram, 1734–1777,* edited by Edmund Berkeley and Dorothy Smith Berkeley. Gainesville: University Press of Florida.

Beverley, Robert. 1947. *The History and Present State of Virginia,* edited by Louis B. Wright. Chapel Hill: University of North Carolina Press.

Bradford, William. 1952. *Of Plymouth Plantation, 1620–1647,* edited by Samuel Eliot Morison. New York: Knopf.

Byrd, William. 1841. *The Westover Manuscripts: Containing The History of the Dividing Line,* edited by Edmund Ruffin. Petersburg, VA: Edmund and Julius C. Ruffin.

Catesby, Mark. 1771. *The Natural History of Carolina, Florida, and the Bahama Islands.* 2 vols. London: Benjamin White.

Colden, Cadwallader. 1918–1937. *The Letters and Papers of Cadwallader Colden.* 9 vols. New York: for the New York Historical Society.

Grew, Nehemiah. 1682. *The Anatomy of Plants: with an Idea of a Philosophical History of Plants; and Several Other Lectures Read before the Royal Society.* [London]: W. Rawlins.

Hariot, Thomas. 1972. *A Briefe and True Report of the New Found Land of Virginia.* New York: Dover.

Horkheimer, Max, and Theodor W. Adorno. 1972. *Dialectic of Enlightenment,* translated by John Cumming. New York: Herder and Herder.

Oldmixon, John. 1708. *The British Empire in America.* London: J. Nicholson, B. Tooke.

Pinckney, Eliza Lucas. 1972. *The Letterbook of Eliza Lucas Pinckney, 1739–1762*, edited by Elise Pinckney. Chapel Hill: University of North Carolina Press.

Smith, James Edward, ed. 1821. *A Selection of the Correspondence of Linnaeus, and Other Naturalists from the Original Manuscripts.* London: Longman, Hurst, Rees, Orme, and Brown.

Tinling, Marion, ed. 1977. *The Correspondence of the Three William Byrds of Westover, Virginia, 1684–1776.* 2 vols. Charlottesville: for the Virginia Historical Society by the University Press of Virginia.

PART IV

CONTEXTS OF READING

CHAPTER 13

....

NEWSPAPERS AND
MAGAZINES

....

CHRISTINE A. MODEY

On December 5, 1767, John Dickinson wrote to Boston lawyer and patriot James Otis, with whom he had served in the Stamp Act Congress in October 1765. The letter flatters Otis, praising his "indefatigable zeal and undaunted Courage" in defending Americans' rights, and honors Massachusetts generally for "Vigilance, Perseverance, Spirit, Prudence, Resolution, and Firmness" in successfully opposing the Stamp Act (Adams 1972, 1: 3–4). Dickinson enclosed a manuscript copy of his *Letters from a Farmer in Pennsylvania to the Inhabitants of the British Colonies.* The *Letters* had, three days before, begun serial publication in the *Pennsylvania Chronicle,* a newspaper edited and printed in Philadelphia by William Goddard. The first letter, which appeared on December 2, 1767, caused an immediate sensation and was reprinted within the week by Philadelphia's other two newspapers, the *Pennsylvania Journal* and the *Pennsylvania Gazette.* Within three weeks, the *Letters* were being reprinted in Boston (whether from the manuscript in Otis's possession or from a Philadelphia newspaper publication is uncertain). By January 27, 1768, nineteen of the twenty-three colonial newspapers were reprinting the *Letters.*

Collected in American pamphlet editions in Philadelphia, Boston, New York, and Williamsburg, the *Letters* were reprinted in London (with a preface by Benjamin Franklin), in Dublin, and in a French translation, published in Paris with an Amsterdam imprint. Dickinson became a colonial celebrity: his portrait was engraved, his figure cast in wax, and his likeness used for a figurehead on a ship bearing his name (Flower, 1983, 76). The *Letters* were the most popular American political writing to appear prior to Thomas Paine's *Common Sense* in 1776. Unlike *Common Sense,* however, which first appeared in pamphlet form—the favorite vehicle of political rabble-rousers since the English Civil War—the *Letters* first appeared in a newspaper. Their publication reflected the maturation of the colonial American newspaper, from its beginnings as a quasi-official record of events to a political instrument that mobilized the first "American" public.

When they originated in the American colonies, newspapers were not intended or used for criticism of the government or for propaganda in the way Dickinson and his audience had come to accept. Rather, newspapers evolved over the first half of the eighteenth century from conveyers of impartial news reports to vehicles of revolutionary propaganda, eventually becoming the dominant agent in American print culture and in the American public sphere in the decades prior to the Revolution. Their development illustrates the interrelation of face-to-face and printed exchanges of information, the consolidation and adaptation of English periodical forms, the transatlantic audience imagined by their publishers and readers, and the increasing politicization of American public discourse. Newspapers' increase in political influence paralleled their increase in number over the century: from the first weekly newspaper in Boston in 1704 to the fifty-eight distributed among fourteen states in 1783.

English newspapers originated in other news organs that had existed for several centuries, particularly privately circulated manuscript newsletters, written by a paid correspondent or a "newswriter" to promote trade and facilitate politics. Popular in the fifteenth and sixteenth centuries, newsletters were usually addressed to a private recipient interested in court happenings or foreign commercial and political news but often took on a public life of their own when read aloud by a town crier or posted in a tavern. At about the same time as newsletters were circulating throughout Europe, newsbooks or news pamphlets, containing information on a single topic of interest, also circulated. Often, such pamphlets were partisan, particularly during the Civil War and Interregnum, when numerous rival newspapers thrived in London. The Restoration sparked a renewed curiosity about political events, while simultaneously prompting a need for government control of circulation of potentially seditious information. Therefore, from 1665 to 1694, only one official newspaper was published in London: the *London Gazette,* which became the model for later English newspapers, both colonial and provincial. The lapse of the Licensing Act in 1695, coupled with commercial development and a growing literary community, facilitated the growth of newspapers in England (Clark 1994, 15–16).

While the presses of the metropole were still subject to the Licensing Act and regulated by the Stationers' Company, scofflaw English publisher Benjamin Harris published *Publick Occurrences, Both* Foreign *and Domestick,* in Boston on September 25, 1690. Ephemeral attempts had been made to publish "news" in America before this time: for example, a single issue of the *London Gazette* on the death of Charles II was reproduced in Boston in February 1684/5; in 1689, a news sheet about Increase Mather's mission to London to renew the Massachusetts charter was printed; in the 1690s, occasional news items were published in broadside format, but none prior to Harris's were intended to have ongoing publication (Amory and Hall 2000, 350–351). Harris had fled London in 1686 after having spent time in the pillory and in prison for violating the Licensing Act; prior to that, during a lapse of the act, he had been prosecuted for seditious libel. During the final revival of the act, between 1685 and 1694, Harris "set up shop as a publisher, opened the London Coffee House, and engaged the printers of [Boston] to print books and an almanac" (Clark 1994, 71). Harris indicated his intention to publish his paper monthly or "if any Glut of Occurrences happen, oftener."

The reasons Harris offers for publishing the paper—and the reasons for its subsequent suppression by colonial authorities—reveal Massachusetts colonists' thinking about the role of the press in the late seventeenth century. Harris's first two purposes—to create a record of the "Memorable Occurrences of Divine Providence" and to help his readers to understand "the Circumstances of Public Affairs," both at home and abroad, not only because they ought to be informed about world events but because such knowledge may be important for the conduct of business—both seem obvious reasons for publishing a paper. His remaining reasons, however, reveal more about the specific circumstances of late seventeenth-century New England and suggest a particular view of the conflicting natures of oral and print discourse. The paper is being published, writes Harris, "that some thing may be done towards the Curing, or at least the Charming of that Spirit of Lying that prevails amongst us." Harris also pledges to publish only what he believed to be true, to correct any demonstrable errors, and to expose in print the name of anyone who is "a malicious Raiser of a false Report." Harris's concern with publishing the truth suggests that the fixing of news into print would counter the rumors and "false Reports" that circulated by word of mouth in New England: a newspaper would use the publicity of the truthful printed word to counter the falsity of the private spoken word. Nevertheless, the printed sheet reveals that Harris was dependent, as were later newspaper editors, on face-to-face exchanges, particularly with ships' captains and others he might encounter at the London Coffee House. In late seventeenth-century Boston, the printed page was a fragile tissue overlaying the contentious world of oral discourse. And if the tissue did not receive official sanction, it was easily destroyed.

Harris's emphasis on and commentary about the war and about the king of France provoked the paper's suppression four days after its publication and also caused the government to issue an order that nothing else could be published in the colony without a license. Harris returned to London in 1695, and newspaper publishing in Boston ceased for almost a decade. Boston printers, however, did continue to issue occasional broadsides, reprinting news from London papers. The

Boston postmaster, Duncan Campbell, began to exchange colonial and foreign news with "correspondents in other colonies" (Clark 1994, 73). A Glaswegian bookseller, Campbell had become the Boston postmaster in 1693. In 1700, he began sending newsletters to Governor Fitz John Winthrop of Connecticut, continuing a tradition extending back as far as 1666; evidence also exists of similar correspondences between London, New York, Philadelphia, and Boston. When Duncan Campbell died in 1702, his son John succeeded him and continued the practice of writing and sending newsletters. Often, the newsletters, or manuscript copies of them, would be posted or read aloud in coffeehouses or taverns (Sloan 2004). The content of the newsletters was primarily European and Atlantic news rather than local events. It was, perhaps, assumed that people could get their local news from informal oral news networks, despite the constant danger of "false reports"; news from other colonies and overseas, however, for those not in immediate contact with or geographic proximity to travelers, depended upon the written or printed word.

Though Charles E. Clark argues that newspapers were not merely the transliteration of newsletters into print but rather the creation of a public document in place of a private one, John Campbell's publication of the first ongoing newspaper in the American colonies, the *Boston News-Letter*, on April 24, 1704, may have been a result of increasing public demand for the information his newsletter included (Sloan 2004). As postmaster in a large and busy port city—Boston had a population of 7,000 in 1700—Campbell was uniquely positioned to have access to information both from incoming ships and from the mails. As postmaster, he also enjoyed franking privileges. When the demand for the newsletter began to overwhelm Campbell's ability to duplicate it by hand, he arranged to have it printed by Bartholomew Green and sold by bookseller Nicholas Boone, who also took in advertisements for the paper (Sloan 2004). Campbell's newsletter was, in the words of Arthur M. Schlesinger, "too great a novelty" to achieve immediate success, and he had to be supported financially by the legislature in the early years, which naturally gave his newspaper a quasi-official status and encouraged circumspection in reporting. As befits its origin as an official letter to the governor of a neighboring colony, Campbell's *News-Letter* was designed to meet the needs of the social, political, and economic elite of Boston and reflected the perspective of the colonial government and the "mainstream clerical leadership." Eventually, merchants came to rely on it, and it became the longest running of the colonial papers (Schlesinger 1965, 51–52; Clark 1994, 83). According to Clark, Campbell's printing of the newsletter changed the very nature of colonial information networks, making them both commercial and public. In the manuscript newsletter, he was a "simple intelligencer," writing for a private audience; in the printed newspaper, Campbell became the creator and marketer of a product while also becoming "an early and crucial agent in the transformation, by depersonalization and enlargement, of the public sphere" in Boston (Clark 1994, 79).

Campbell's *Boston News-Letter*, as well as its first competitor, the *Boston Gazette*, founded in 1719, had a somewhat different purpose than Harris's abortive attempt at a paper: unlike Harris, who wanted to inform a local audience of local events to prevent false reports, Campbell wanted to link "provincial Americans with the metropolitan center of their pan-Atlantic English world," the aim of the vast majority of American papers over the next thirty-five years (Clark 1994, 79). With its imitation of the form of the *London Gazette* and its extensive reprinting of English and foreign news, the *Boston News-Letter* helped to create an "Anglicized" communal identity, a way for readers to think of themselves as provincial English subjects, clearly oriented toward the metropolis of London (Clark 1994, 83). The first issue of the *Boston News-Letter* perfectly demonstrates this emphasis. The main article, reprinted from an issue of the *London Flying-Post* from the previous December, concerned the threats to Protestantism posed by Catholics, particularly James VIII of Scotland and French immigrants to England. The same issue of the *Boston News-Letter* also reprinted Queen Anne's address to the houses of Parliament concerning the activity of Catholics in Scotland and Parliament's readiness to defend Protestantism. Inclusion of these news items seems calculated to engage the sympathies of both the Puritan and Anglican communities of Boston in common cause with their counterparts in England, particularly because the colonies themselves were the site of the second of the French and Indian Wars, the Queen Anne's War. Campbell proceeds by indirection, representing the point of view of the metropole without mentioning events in the colonies themselves, not even the raid on Deerfield, Massachusetts, in February 1704. Emphasis on English news may also have been necessitated by the available channels of communication: for a variety of reasons, it was easier to get news from England than from within the colonies themselves (Steele 1986).

Never printed in an edition larger than 300 copies, the *Boston News-Letter* remained colonial America's only newspaper for fifteen years. To judge from the dunning notices published in the *News-Letter*, Campbell had difficulty attracting subscribers and advertisers and getting subscribers to pay, the perennial problem of newspaper and magazine publishers throughout the eighteenth and much of the nineteenth century. In 1719, at the age of sixty-five, Campbell was replaced as postmaster by William Brooker, who attempted to take over publication of the *News-Letter*. Campbell refused to surrender the paper, so Brooker started the second newspaper in America, the *Boston Gazette*, on December 21, 1719, an event that benefited both papers. Two newspapers were better than one: the appearance of Brooker's *Gazette* as the "official" newspaper allowed Campbell's *News-Letter* to include more personal opinion and more emphasis on the workings of the local government (Sloan 2004). Being the official paper seems not to have had substantial benefits, for either Brooker or his successor, Philip Musgrave: "There is no evidence that Campbell's relationship with the province authorities, whether executive or legislative, changed very much after he left the postmastership or that Musgrave ever achieved important 'beats' over the *News-Letter* as a result of official privilege" (Clark 1994, 121). Both Musgrave and Campbell were brought before the colonial legislature to account for errors in their papers; both were required to submit copies of their papers to official approval before publishing. Both seemed on better terms with the governor than with the popular body, and both were opposed, on its appearance, by the *New England Courant,* which was allied with the popular party of Elisha Cooke (Clark 1994, 121). The two publishers seem to have had equal access to official news from the assembly and to foreign news from the London papers and from ship captains. Being the officially sanctioned paper did not really seem to matter, unless a journalist decided to take on officialdom.

With the advent of the *New-England Courant* on August 7, 1721, however, newspaper publishing immediately became more contentious in Boston. Two events precipitated the founding of the *New-England Courant:* James Franklin's loss of the business of printing the *Boston Gazette* to Samuel Kneeland, and the controversy in Boston over smallpox inoculation (Thomas 1970, 235; Clark 1994, 124). James Franklin was encouraged to publish the *Courant* by Boston Anglicans, who wanted to challenge the preeminence of Cotton Mather and the Puritan establishment; the smallpox inoculation controversy provided a convenient pretext (Williams 1999, 112). The *New-England Courant* differed from its Boston competitors in at least two significant ways. First, it published more local news and essays on controversial subjects; it was unafraid to attack the Massachusetts ruling classes. A second, related innovation was its editing and publication by a group of friends, a "club," who contributed original items, often belletristic and imitative of the kinds of moral essays published in the *Spectator* and the *Tatler.* The tone of the *Courant* was often facetious, sometimes satiric. The printer's original intention was to publish every two weeks; the second number, however, indicates that he had been encouraged to publish weekly instead. Taking aim at his fellow newspaper publishers, he writes, "This Paper will be published once a Fortnight, and out of meer Kindness to my Brother-Writers, I intend now and then to be (like them) very, very dull."

As Charles E. Clark points out, the *New-England Courant* managed to wield the forms of polite letters in the service of antiestablishment politics. David Sloan views the *New-England Courant* as an organ of High Church Anglicanism pitted against the surrounding Puritanism. Clark also characterizes the *Courant* as antiestablishment, almost inevitably encountering problems with the Puritan authorities. Its opponents included Increase Mather, who published a notice in the *Boston Gazette* on January 29, 1721/2, denouncing the *New-England Courant* as "a Wicked Libel" for listing him among its supporters. The inoculation controversy, which the *Courant* engaged from its first number and which was also debated in the *Gazette,* was part of a larger factional controversy (Sloan 2004; Clark 1994, 125). In its appeal to the popular party, the *Courant* differed from the *News-Letter* and the *Gazette,* which were similar politically—respectful of the governor, slightly in disagreement with the popular assembly, in harmony with the Puritan church and Harvard College— and shared similarly elite audiences. "There is a certain pleasant irony," Clark writes, "in the recognition that the first American newspaper to deal largely in the polite letters of Augustan England was also the first to identify itself to any degree with some of the segments of society that the *News-Letter* and *Gazette* mostly ignored. It used a device whose origins and essential nature were learned and genteel to attack learning and gentility, and to espouse causes identified mainly with the common sort of people" (Clark 1994, 123).

Observing the forms of gentility, however, was not enough. A censure against the *Courant* was issued by the council on July 5, 1722, requiring that it be read by the secretary before publication. Failing to suppress Franklin's libelous writings, in January 1722/3, the council referred the matter to the Massachusetts House of Representatives, which took similar action. Franklin was prohibited from publishing the paper "except it be first supervised by the Secretary of this Province" (Thomas 1970, 237, 239). Franklin refused to submit to this supervision and continued to publish the *Courant* under his younger brother Benjamin's name, even after Benjamin had departed for Philadelphia. In 1723, James Franklin was imprisoned, an event that, coupled with other members' preoccupation with other professional duties, marked the beginning of the *Courant*'s decline (Clark 1994, 137–140). The *Courant* finally ceased publication in June 1726. By 1729, twenty-five years after the appearance of the *Boston News-Letter,* several papers were being published in cities along the eastern seaboard: the *Boston Gazette,* the *New-England Weekly Journal,* and the *Boston News-Letter* in Boston; the *New-York Gazette* in New York; the *American Weekly Mercury* and the *Pennsylvania Gazette* in Philadelphia; and the *Maryland Gazette* in Annapolis.

THE BUSINESS OF NEWSPAPERS

As evidence from the newspapers of the period amply demonstrates, newspaper publication was a marginal endeavor at best. For a paper to succeed, the right social conditions had to prevail, including a fairly high rate of literacy among the population. When newspapers were founded in Boston, the male literacy rate might have been as high as 70 percent, rising to 85 percent by 1760. Adequate population density was also required: 10,000 to 15,000 people in the colony, with at least 1,000 in the printer's hometown. Moreover, the printer needed access to channels of communication, as well as readers who required the information conveyed by those channels: port cities had access to news on arriving ships and adequate commercial activity to support newspapers (Humphrey 1992, 18, 21).

Benjamin Franklin, perhaps alone among colonial newspaper publishers, was able to turn newspapering into a profitable enterprise, but only in conjunction with other printing businesses and official sinecures and an expansive network of printers, former apprentices, and journeymen whom he encouraged in their trade elsewhere in the colonies (Amory and Hall 2000, 270). The professional status of colonial printers was more ambiguous but also more flexible than that of their counterparts in England, according to Stephen Botein; in America, they were neither "mechanics" nor "principals," neither mere tradesmen nor true merchants. In London, where the book trade was diversified and printing was becoming consolidated in a few large printing houses, printers felt the status of their trade slipping (Botein, 1975, 140, 132, 134–135). In the colonies, however, printing enterprises were smaller and entrepreneurial. Printers could rarely support a family unless the printer had government work and a successful newspaper; indeed, three-fourths of printers in the years between 1700 and 1765 printed newspapers. Few substantial books were published in the colonies (it was more economical to import them from England and became more so as bookbinding developed in the colonies), so printers often kept general stores, bound books, ran coffeehouses, served as postmasters, and so forth to make ends meet (Botein, 1975, 143–147; Schlesinger 1965, 54).

Printers who decided to undertake newspaper publication faced numerous obstacles. First among them was obtaining the necessary equipment. Presses and types were expensive and only obtainable from England for much of the colonial period. Trade disputes and nonimportation agreements, though they encouraged native manufacture of some printing equipment and supplies, prevented the acquisition of printing equipment from England. Military activities also disrupted printing, and most newspaper printers found themselves dunning for payment of subscriptions and struggling to attract advertising (Humphrey 1992, 23, 28). Circulating the newspapers posed other problems. Postal regulations, up to 1758, allowed postmasters to exclude materials at will—including their competitors' newspapers—and mail their own free of charge. Postriders often charged customers prohibitive fees for carrying newspapers. And, although postal frequency on the eastern seaboard improved under postmasters Benjamin Franklin and William Hunter in the 1750s, the mails remained slow and uncertain in the South (Schlesinger, 1965, 54, 7).

In towns too small, or in colonies too sparsely populated, to support rival newspapers, newspaper printers relied upon public patronage, and pressure could be exerted on a printer to publish or to suppress a piece of writing. Because of a printer's dependence upon government work to support his livelihood and his inability to attract adequate advertising revenue, the relationship between a printer and government could be close, often compelling the printer, particularly in the South where newspapers grew more slowly, to make his newspaper an organ of the government: "Like the London Gazette, which for a hundred years had been the official organ of government, these southern weeklies remained adjuncts of the state. Almost all were founded by printers who enjoyed public subsidies, and most of them continued to benefit from government support in one way or another." Newspaper printers could not afford to alienate any portion of the local leadership, so they often walked a fine line between reportage and propaganda (Bailyn and Hench 1980, 103–114).

FREEDOM OF THE PRESS

The case of James Franklin's *New-England Courant* illustrates some aspects of press freedom, particularly that poking fun at colonial authorities could land a printer in prison. The Licensing Act's lapse in 1695 did not automatically lead to a free press, in England or in the colonies; in fact, colonial legislatures often attempted to license colonial presses even as freedoms expanded in England. Freedom of the press, particularly as it pertains to newspaper publishing in the American colonies in the years prior to the American Revolution, developed from a condition of government controls on the press, primarily through prosecution for seditious libel, to a freer press in which community standards exerted informal control over what was published.

"Neither freedom of speech nor freedom of press," writes Leonard Levy, "could become a civil liberty until people believed that the truth of their opinions . . . was relative rather than absolute; until kings and parliaments felt sufficiently strong and stable to be able to ignore political criticism; and until the people considered themselves as the source of sovereignty, the masters rather than the servants of the government" (Levy 1985, 5). In post-Restoration England, none of these conditions prevailed; dissent was equivalent to rebellion, for which the government had several mechanisms of control, including the Licensing Act of 1662. The act of 1662, enforced primarily through the Stationers' Company, controlled both production and distribution of books, with the purpose of preventing the circulation of heretical or seditious materials. The act was the British parliament's last attempt at prior restraint of the press. Richard Buel Jr. attributes Parliament's refusal in 1694 to renew the Licensing Act as a sign of "modern libertarianism," particularly the development of religious toleration and recognition that the state cannot impose or enforce religious orthodoxy (Bailyn and Hench 1980, 64–65).

Without the mechanism of prior restraint, the government sought other means of press control, most prominently prosecution for libel, a charge that might be brought against a printer for publishing "blasphemous, immoral, treasonable, schismatical, seditious or scandalous" works, regardless of their truthfulness. Parliament could also prosecute a printer for contempt of its authority and arrogation of its privileges. What Parliament could do in England, colonial legislatures could do in America, and anyone who spoke against the government could be brought, like James Franklin, before the legislature to "make inglorious submission" for his words (Levy 1985, 12–18).

Unlike Franklin, most printers of the early eighteenth century were unwilling to risk alienating a powerful portion of the populace. Nor did printers see political advocacy as part of their jobs. "Freedom of the press" meant, in the colonies, that the printer should allow everyone equal access to his press and himself remain politically neutral (Botein 1975, 177–178; Bailyn and Hench 1980, 19). Despite this principle and the law of seditious libel, other forces in the colonies tended toward increasing press freedom, including growing conflicts between colonial legislatures and royal governors. In 1721, for example, the Massachusetts legislature refused to renew a licensing law, not because it valued freedom of the press per se but because it was concerned that prior restraint might limit the legislature's ability to criticize the governor and because it did not want to give the governor "an exclusive licensing power" (Levy 1985, 30). This attitude reflects English libertarian thought, which "defined a free press not merely as one open to all persuasions but, more important, one that could be counted upon to keep a watchful eye on the encroachments of executive power" (Bailyn and Hench 1980, 116). In addition, following the line of reasoning adopted by John Trenchard and Thomas Gordon's *Cato's Letters* and the *Independent Whig,* colonists may have felt that truth would rise to the surface and that any truly legitimate government could not be threatened by a free press (Bailyn and Hench 1980, 66). Early libel trials, including those of William Bradford in 1692 and Thomas Maule in 1696, suggested that libertarian ideas were gaining a foothold in the colonies. By the time John Peter Zenger was prosecuted for libel for publishing attacks on New York governor William Cosby, the definition of "free press" was shifting to mean a press that published criticism of the government (Botein, 1975, 177–205).

The Zenger trial is probably the most famous libel trial to take place on American soil. Often singled out as setting a new precedent for press freedom, in fact, it failed to set any legal precedent. What it did, however, was to indicate that popular opinion was with Zenger—that the public drew a distinction between "true" liberty and liberty under the law and recognized "the nonsensical nature of the law of seditious libel" (Levy 1985, 37). Zenger, a former apprentice of William Bradford, was approached by the opponents of Governor William Cosby to undertake a paper that would be the voice of the opposition. Almost from the first, the newspaper beat the drum of press freedom. After publishing an attack on Cosby, accusing him of neglecting to safeguard New York from the French ship *Le Caesar,* Zenger reprinted an item from *Cato's Letters* on press freedom. Cosby made no reply in the *Gazette* for some time, but eventually the Cosbyites began to complain about Zenger and to seek a way to try him for libel.

Zenger was arrested on November 17, 1734. When Cosby failed to get a grand jury to indict Zenger for seditious libel, he filed an "information" against him on January 28, 1734/35, and Zenger was brought to trial on August 4, 1735. Andrew Hamilton of Philadelphia was recruited as his defense attorney. Hamilton, arguing that truth was a defense against libel, easily convinced the jury of Zenger's innocence. In pursuing this line of defense, Hamilton argued from logic but not from current English law practice. Hamilton assumed that citizens had the right to criticize rulers and that English laws did not apply to the American situation: governors were not monarchs and should be open to criticism. Hamilton's contention that American sovereignty rested in the people through the legislatures was not a great legal defense, but rather great rhetoric, based on what "should be" (Katz, 1963, 22–25, 28). That the jury accepted this argument indicates the degree to which popular opinion favored increasing press freedom.

The verdict of the Zenger trial was widely publicized, and both supporters and opponents recognized that what had been achieved was not a new legal precedent but the popularizing and validating of Whig political theory (Katz 1963, 28). Though Zenger's verdict failed to change the law, common law prosecutions for libel died out after his verdict. The press was not totally free, of course; legislatures continued to invoke the equivalent of parliamentary privilege to control the distribution of information about their proceedings and the effect was "dampening . . . on the free expression of opinion on legislative measures and matters" (Levy 1985, 48). The Zenger verdict, however, did advance the acceptance in the colonies of two important aspects of Whig theory: that truth could be a defense from libel and that juries should render verdicts in libel cases on both fact and law. This affirmed the argument William Bradford had set forth forty years earlier. Later defendants who could prove the truth of facts reported in the newspaper were freed, though the "truth" of unpopular opinions rarely provided an adequate defense (Levy, 1985, 128–130).

While Zenger's case may not have been the free press watershed it is often considered, it occurred at a time in American print history when the uses of the press were shifting. While, in the early years of the eighteenth century, newspapers informed the people about government business and news in other colonies and overseas, they became increasingly likely to persuade. The free press in the American colonies came to be seen, over the course of the eighteenth century, as a bulwark against overzealous executive power, a vehicle for promoting the good of society (Bailyn and Hench 1980, 70), and an instrument for unifying a widely distributed people in a common cause. From the 1740s, the newspaper press was more political, more partisan, and more likely to take the side of "the people" against "the crown," as exemplified by the 1742 trial of Thomas Fleet for printing seditious material: when it turned out that Fleet's report was accurate, popular pressure demanded the suit be dropped (Levy 1985, 32–33). Official control over the press in the colonies diminished, partly because of growing geographic distribution of both population and printers and partly because American juries were unwilling to convict printers for libel (Bailyn and Hench 1980, 69, 73–74). At the same time, the first colonial American magazines were established, pointing not so much toward the growing political unrest (though certainly they came to advance political opinions) as toward a desire among Americans to create, for themselves, a symbol of English culture.

MAGAZINES

Like newspapers, colonial American magazines imitated British models. While newspapers served a utilitarian function like so much of the product of the colonial

American press and therefore quickly took on their own character, the magazines Americans produced—short-lived though they were—bespeak the colonists' orientation toward the metropole more strongly than any other product of the colonial press. The production of a literary magazine—and almost all of the twenty or so magazines published in America between 1741 and 1789 were literary—indicates what Jack P. Greene has described as "a self-conscious effort to anglicize colonial life through the deliberate imitation of metropolitan institutions, values, and culture" (Greene 1988, 175).

American magazine editors openly acknowledged their debt to the *Gentleman's Magazine* (established 1731) and the *London Magazine* (established 1732). Both magazines were available to American readers. Some wealthy Americans had their own subscriptions to the magazines. Others had access to the magazines through libraries, clubs, or coffeehouses. The letter book of the Charleston Library Society, for instance, reveals regular requests for not one but two copies of "Magazines of Each Sort" as well as the monthly reviews (Raven 2002, 237). The Library Company of Philadelphia listed the *Gentleman's Magazine* from 1731 to 1741 and *Philosophical Transactions* from 1734 to 1744 among its collection. Indeed, British magazines, rather than American ones, were the main magazines available to American readers until after the Revolution, when American magazine publication expanded rapidly (Amory and Hall 2000, 360). Prior to that time, American magazines were few and far between.

Still, the magazines of colonial America were significant to their readers as a sign of cultivation and an outlet for native literary production. They remain useful to modern literary scholars, as Frank Luther Mott points out, because they provide insight into the social and cultural, and sometimes the political, history of their times. Colonial magazines were founded not only in the hopes of making a profit but also because their publishers and editors wished to showcase American talents and culture abroad and to promote England's understanding of the colonies; the magazines sought a transatlantic readership and saw themselves as informing the larger world (Mott 1939, 2–3, 21–23; Amory and Hall 2000, 436). While magazine publishers' hopes for riches were rarely realized—they faced too many difficulties in overcoming delinquent subscribers, attracting adequate advertising, finding efficient and effective means of distribution, and acquiring sufficient supplies of paper, ink, and type—their productions reflect a growing American self-awareness and the development of "a common Anglophone culture in the western Atlantic" as the Revolution approached (Mott 1939, 13–21; Greene 1988, 174).

Philadelphia, rather than Boston, witnessed the birth of the first American magazines, an indicator of the mid-Atlantic's rising commercial and literary influence. Benjamin Franklin and Andrew Bradford raced to see who would bring out the first magazine in 1740/41, and Bradford won, his *American Magazine; or A Monthly View of the Political State of the British Colonies* appearing on February 13, 1741. Franklin's *General Magazine, and Historical Chronicle, for all the British Plantations in America* followed on February 16. Neither magazine survived long: Bradford's lasted three months, Franklin's six.

Appearing in his *American Mercury* newspaper on October 30, 1740, Bradford's prospectus announcing his plan to publish a magazine for the American colonies reveals much about how he (and presumably his fellow colonists) thought about the public prints. First, it declares a broad reach: the magazine would include a re-cord of government activities in all the American colonies, as well as in the West Indies, descriptions of the colonies' "Situation, Climate, Soil, Productions, Trade, and Manufactures," accounts of trials, notices of exchange rates and prices, foreign news, and records of "Party-Disputes." Second, it reflects the predominant colonial view of a free press. Bradford asserts that his paper will offer anyone "ready Admittance to a fair and publick Hearing at all Times." The magazine itself will strive to present argu-ments without editorial comment: "we shall *inviolably* observe an exact Neutrality." Nevertheless, Bradford promises that his magazine will provide the opportunity for "the Oppressed" to convey their opposition to "illegal Acts of Power" at no expense to themselves and that such expression will be heard not only in the colonies but also in the "Mother-Country, for whose Inspection considerable Numbers of this Maga-zine will be monthly Printed-off." Bradford's comments suggest that as early as 1740, the American colonists saw some British actions as arbitrary exercises of power and a free press as a way to remedy them. Further, it is clear that Bradford imagined both an intercolonial and a transatlantic audience. Philadelphia was the ideal location for such an enterprise, being centrally located among the colonies and on both Atlantic and West Indian trading routes. Bradford concludes his prospectus with the meta-phor of a stage: "The Reader is desired to consider the Undertaking, as an Attempt to *Erect*, on *Neutral Principles*, A Publick Theatre in the *Center* of the *British* Empire in *America*, on which the most remarkable Transactions of each Government may be *impartially* represented, and fairly exhibited to the View of all His Majesty's Subjects, whether at-Home or abroad, who are disposed to be Spectators."

Two weeks later, on November 13, Franklin advertised his planned magazine in the *Pennsylvania Gazette*, openly acknowledging, like Bradford, his imitation of the British models. In the advertisement, Franklin notes that John Webbe, the editor he had recruited for the magazine, had gone to Bradford, disclosed Franklin's plan, and negotiated a better arrangement for himself as editor of Bradford's *American Magazine*. Demonstrating characteristic business bravado, Franklin promised the magazine for January, two months earlier than Bradford's proposed publication date, and declined to solicit subscriptions, as his rival had, instead suggesting that the magazine would earn its own way: "our Readers . . . will then be at Liberty to buy only what they like; and we shall be under a constant Necessity of endeavouring to make every particular Pamphlet worth their Money." Intended to be the same size as Bradford's, the *General Magazine* would, nevertheless, cost nine pence (Pennsylvania currency) per issue, rather than Bradford's shilling. Though his content was to be similar to Bradford's, with the addition of extracts from new books and pamphlets published in the colonies, Franklin's advertisement suggests that he joined the race for the first magazine in the colonies with some enthusiasm, implying that he had really been the first one to think of it: the magazine "was long since projected," his correspondence network established, and the types (always an issue) acquired.

The three issues of Bradford's *American Magazine* turned out, in Mott's words, to be "about as heavy as any similar number of pages in all the considerable library of the periodical literature of its century" (Mott 1939, 72). Though it imitated the *Gentleman's Magazine*'s practice of including a woodcut illustration of its city above the masthead, unlike the British model, it was dominated by proceedings of the legislative assemblies and included no original belles lettres. Franklin's *General Magazine*, on the other hand, included a considerable amount of poetry (little of it original), and its prose was dominated by the paper currency crisis and the revivalism of George Whitefield, who returned to Philadelphia in 1740 after his successful revival meetings there in 1738. Both magazines ceased publication within six months, and no more were attempted until 1743, when three magazines were founded in Boston: the *Boston Weekly Magazine*, the *Christian History*, and the *American Magazine and Historical Chronicle*.

The first "really important colonial American magazine" was the *American Magazine and Historical Chronicle*, edited by Jeremy Gridley in Boston and published by Gamaliel Rogers and Daniel Fowle (Mott 1939, 25). A magazine in the true sense of the word—a compilation of interesting or useful material—it drew heavily on British magazines of the period and included reports of parliamentary debates, accounts of treaties with Native Americans, and book extracts, as well as "Poetical Essays" and a catalog of books, with emphasis on local publications. The "historical chronicle," imitating (and sometimes extracting from) a similar feature in the *Gentleman's Magazine*, occupied several pages near the back of each issue and included British, Continental, and American news. The *American Magazine and Historical Chronicle* also aimed for a wide readership; Rogers and Fowle had agents in towns all over the northern and mid-Atlantic colonies, including Philadelphia, New York, Newport, and New Haven. Gridley was a politically conservative Deist and thus maintained a cool attitude toward the religious controversies of the Great Awakening, events that another magazine, *Christian History*, was meant to record. The *Christian History*, the first religious periodical in America, was founded as a public relations vehicle for the religious revivals in New England by Thomas Prince, pastor of Boston's Old South Church, who hoped that a dispassionate history of the revival would create understanding among those who greeted religious enthusiasm with skepticism. He also tried to provide a religious history of New England, a chronicle of the events leading up to the current controversy. The *Boston Weekly Magazine* lasted for only three issues. But the story of these early magazines in Boston indicates that, although the American colonists might have wished to imitate British models and to create an Anglicized culture on the western edge of the Atlantic, their magazine productions were affected very much by the local milieu, including evangelical religion, and often tended to copy British magazines rather than to imitate them.

More than a decade passed between the end of the *American Magazine and Historical Chronicle* and the first issue of another major American periodical. In the meantime, four magazines—none lasting more than a year, and two lasting only a couple of months—were founded in New York. William Bradford's *American Magazine and Monthly Chronicle*, however, which was published in Philadelphia beginning in October 1757, "bears comparison with any year's file of the *Gentleman's* or the *London Magazine*," according to Mott, although it survived for only one year (Mott 1939, 26). The preface to the first issue notes that "the important concerns of these colonies were but little studied and less understood in the mother-country." Like other magazines of the time, the *American Magazine* was founded for a particular purpose—it was primarily concerned with promoting the war with France; one of its regular contributors signed himself "the Antigallican"—but also included European history, American history, philosophy, science, and contemporary events. Articles included both extracts from British magazines and original contributions from members of the faculty of the College of Philadelphia. The magazine's founder, the Reverend William Smith, was particularly concerned to organize militias in the colonies, a topic that dominates the magazine. A regular feature, "Monthly Essays," provided an opportunity for four midcentury essayists, writing pseudonymously, to showcase their talents. According to Richardson, the *American Magazine* was unlike most magazines; it ceased publication because its contributors moved on to other pursuits rather than because it lacked public support (Richardson 1931, 106, 122).

Although many newspapers and magazines in the first half of the eighteenth century were founded for engaging in transatlantic political controversy, creating an imitation of the British public sphere, or connecting Americans to cultural life in the metropole, newspapers were largely local in their coverage of colonial news. In other words, colonial newspapers covered local happenings and British and Continental news to a much greater extent than they covered intercolonial news. Though colonial newspaper printers before the mid–eighteenth century routinely exchanged papers with printers in other towns, it took the Stamp Act crisis to form American printers into a "true mass-media editorial voice" on a matter of public importance, to show them their power to influence public opinion, and to create the first "mass media" event (Sloan and Williams 1994, 124, 142).

The Stamp Act Crisis

The Stamp Act, passed by Parliament on March 27, 1765, to go into effect on November 1 of the same year, was intended to raise much-needed revenue to finance the prosecution of the Seven Years' War in the American theater and the defense of newly acquired territories. Among other provisions, it taxed paper and charged a halfpenny for each copy of a half-page newspaper and a penny on the "next larger size." Moreover, it charged an exorbitant two shillings for each advertisement; printers typically charged their customers only three to five shillings. In addition to printers, merchants and lawyers were also targeted: taxes from three pence to six pounds were charged on a variety of legal and business forms (Schlesinger 1965, 68). Because it affected the most powerful men in the American colonies, as well as those with access to the press, the Stamp Act mobilized and unified public opinion, ultimately bringing an end to the policy of press neutrality that many printers had tried to maintain throughout the first half of the century. Just as neutrality had seemed a prudent business practice then, taking a side in the political controversy (and making a profit from it) was the course chosen by many printers now. Neutrality simply became untenable (Botein 1975, 214).

Between Parliament's passage of the act and its becoming law on November 1, 1765, the issue was widely lamented in the colonial press. Arthur M. Schlesinger describes the initial response to the taxes as "daze and indecision." Printers made an extra effort to collect payment for subscriptions from their delinquent subscribers; others announced that they would have to raise subscription rates to offset the additional costs (Schlesinger 1965, 69–70). Then, a variety of arguments were formulated in response to the act. Some, such as John Adams, argued that the tax was an attempt to shackle American minds by depriving them of information and knowledge (Brown 1996, 57–58). Others argued that the taxes amounted to an infringement of press freedom, as well as an unconstitutional internal tax. Newspapers controlled by the Sons of Liberty and other patriots kept up a constant barrage against the act during the summer of 1765.

Anticipating the act's going into effect, many publishers announced the suspension of publication of their newspapers, often accompanied by an engraving of a tombstone or inside black borders, for mourning. In the end, however, few papers were actually suspended, and those that were, primarily in the South, resumed publication after a short hiatus, often because the printer had been threatened with physical punishment by a patriot mob (Schlesinger 1965, 78–79). Printers had two basic approaches if they decided to defy the Stamp Act: they could publish openly without stamps, or they could publish without an imprint, hoping that anonymity would protect them. Opposition to the Stamp Act was nearly unanimous in the colonial press; essays and articles about the act were widely reprinted in papers throughout the colonies. Though government officials knew that much of what the papers published constituted seditious libel, officials declined to prosecute them; public opinion so strongly favored the printers that government was unlikely to convince a jury to convict.

Bowing to popular opinion, Parliament repealed the Act on March 18, 1766, and word of its repeal reached the colonies in May. The American press had gained a sense of its own power to shape public opinion, and printers had been confirmed in their sense of themselves as influential men; the government had realized that in conflicts between the colonists and the British parliament, seditious libel could no longer be used as a weapon and that they would have to retaliate in kind, using the Tory press (Schlesinger 1965, 84). Freedom of the press, rather than remaining a principle by which to maintain press neutrality, had become a principle by which to promote the public good.

The unification of public opinion in response to the Stamp Act did not indicate a wish for the colonies' separation from England; it did, however, affirm the role of the press as an effective vehicle for registering displeasure with England. So, when the Townshend Duties went into effect in 1767, John Dickinson wrote his *Letters* in protest and became an American political celebrity. The press's role in disseminating liberal Enlightenment ideals had been established.

NEWSPAPERS AND MAGAZINES DURING THE AMERICAN REVOLUTION

Unsurprisingly, American colonists, cut off from English news by nonimportation agreements prior to and during the Revolutionary War and eager for information regarding protests and fighting in other colonies, felt the need for more domestic news sources. The number of American newspapers and magazines published in America doubled between 1765 and 1785, from 55 to 109 (Bailyn and Hench 1980, 329). In addition, their geographic distribution increased. Compared with the first half of the eighteenth century, when newspaper publishing was concentrated in Boston, New York, and Philadelphia, with isolated newspapers in Maryland, Rhode Island, South Carolina, and Virginia, in 1775—the year that saw more newspaper publication than any year prior to 1783—4 papers were published in Connecticut, 1 in Georgia, 3 in Maryland, 10 in Massachusetts, 1 in New Hampshire, 1 in New Jersey, 5 in New York, 2 in North Carolina, 8 in Pennsylvania (including 2 German-language papers), 2 in Rhode Island, 3 in South Carolina, and 5 in Virginia (2 in Norfolk, 3 in Williamsburg), all titled the *Virginia Gazette* (Lathem 1972, 9–13). Between 1764 and 1783, 137 papers were published in forty-four locations; about half of these were in Massachusetts, New York, and Pennsylvania, and half elsewhere (Bailyn and Hench 1980, 347). These figures suggest that, as the colonial communications network improved and as colonists thought of themselves less as isolated English subjects and more as Americans, they felt the need for a local paper to make common cause with other Americans in other colonies.

If the first flowering of American magazines in the 1740s and 1750s had attempted to establish an English identity on the western edge of the Atlantic, American magazines now worked to create an American identity. After nearly a decade in which no magazine of lasting significance was published, three important, if short-lived, colonial magazines were founded just prior to and during the war: Isaiah Thomas's *Royal American Magazine* (1774); the *Pennsylvania Magazine* (1775), founded by Robert Aitken and edited by Thomas Paine; and Hugh Henry Brackenridge's *United States Magazine* (1779). Published in Boston, the *Royal American Magazine* italicized "American" in its title and styled itself the "Universal Repository of Instruction and Amusement." The magazine emphasized its Americanness by devoting pages to American history and by expressing its patriotism and appreciation for all things American. It included a wide range of articles, including an open letter, in its first issue, to the "literati of America" advocating the organization of the American Society of Language in order to perfect the English language in America; polite essays on marriage and "female education"; "poetical essays"; and instructions on dyeing wool, growing indigo and madder, and printing cotton (arts necessitated, perhaps, by the nonimportation agreement). The magazine, in keeping with its purpose as a "repository of such interesting events as occur from one month to another," included a department called "Historical Chronicle," which provided a history of America for the current month, though the first issue had to go back in time to catch readers up on the nonimportation agreements that preceded Philadelphia's successful refusal of a shipment of East India tea in December 1773. In addition, Thomas Hutchinson's *History of the Colony of Massachusetts Bay* was printed in parts as a supplement to the magazine itself. The title of the *Royal American Magazine* epitomizes the magazine's double nature: it both wanted to imitate the British models of polite literature ("Receipt for a Modern Love Letter," "Against Idolatry and Blasphemy") and to advance the cause of American patriots by promoting both a political cause and a cultural identity, formed not only by what later became characterized as "American literary nationalism" but also by the promotion of all sorts of "native genius" and America's limitless possibilities.

Robert Aitken and Thomas Paine's *Pennsylvania Magazine; or, American Monthly Museum* included some similar material, though with more emphasis on the genteel and the scientific than on the historic and patriotic. The first number included some news items, announcements of deaths, a "meteorological diary," and "prices current." It also included a series of essays, character sketches, a description and engraving of an electrical machine, poetry, and selections from new publications. These selections are accompanied by an apology. Without imported British magazines from which to extract, the beleaguered editors have to find writers to produce original materials; in the "present perplexities of affairs," few have time or interest to write for a magazine. Indeed, when the magazine reached the end of its first volume, "The Publisher's Preface" notes these difficulties again, adding to the list America's deplorable lack of "curious remains of antiquity," the discovery of which provides material for European magazines. To this list, Hugh Henry Brackenridge, writing in December 1779, at the end of his magazine's first volume, added that the depreciation of currency made it impossible for him to continue the *United States Magazine; a Repository of History, Politics, and Literature,* the magazine he had begun in January 1779 with high hopes.

The high hopes Brackenridge entertained for his magazine centered on its potential to provide education to those inhabitants of the United States who had no other means of acquiring one. Noting that "the path to office and advancement" was open to everyone, Brackenridge went on to argue that everyone had an obligation to fit himself for public office. Many would never be able to get the required education from "the best writers, or the conversation of men of reading and experience," but all could avail themselves of "some publication that will itself contain a library." Like the similar magazines also published during the 1770s, Brackenridge's *United States Magazine* intended to cover a wide range of topics—history, politics, philosophy, trade and commerce, law, current events—and to both amuse and instruct. By reading this magazine, Brackenridge promised, "the honest husbandman and the industrious laborer and mechanic" will be fit not only to fulfill the duties of their offices, but also to enjoy the company of learned men. Not only do magazines provide educational material, they also provide opportunities for those with a little leisure to publish an essay or two and for those who are still inexperienced writers to try out their skills. In other words, the magazine creates a world of conversation in itself, where those educated by magazines can also write for magazines. Brackenridge refers to this phenomenon when he calls the magazine "the literary coffeehouse of public conversation."

The evidence of Brackenridge's essay, and perhaps all three magazines of the Revolutionary era, suggests a blurred dividing line between oral and print culture. Certainly, periodicals created in imitation of the *Gentleman's Magazine* and the *London Magazine,* as well as those that imitated aspects of the *Spectator* and the *Tatler,* such as James Franklin's *New-England Courant,* reveal that magazines could imitate the products of coffeehouse culture even if they were created quite apart from it. In these cases, the coffeehouse conversation served as a metaphor for the production and reception of periodical works in a new American republic of letters that was, in fact, geographically distributed. In other cases, again including the *New-England Courant* and the *Transactions of the American Philosophical Society* and various periodicals of the early Republic, a magazine or newspaper grew out of a face-to-face meeting into print. Far beyond the simple print-to-print transfer of early newspapers that relied heavily on extracts, the late eighteenth-century periodical could conceive itself as a recollection, a reification of both oral and written discourse. Brackenridge, like many of the editors that followed him in the early national period, is looking forward, in the middle of the Revolution, to the meaning of republican government and its demands on American citizens and making an argument for the role of periodical literature in the service of republican virtues.

REFERENCES

Adams, John. [1917–1925] 1972. *Warren-Adams Letters, Being Chiefly a Correspondence among John Adams, Samuel Adams, and James Warren.* Reprint. 2 vols. New York: AMS Press.

Amory, Hugh, and David D. Hall, eds. 2000. *A History of the Book in America.* Vol. 1, *The Colonial Book in the Atlantic World.* New York: Cambridge University Press.

Bailyn, Bernard, and John B. Hench, eds. 1980. *The Press and the American Revolution.* Worcester, MA: American Antiquarian Society.

Botein, Stephen. 1975. Meer Mechanics and an Open Press: The Business and Political Strategies of Colonial American Printers. *Perspectives in American History* 9: 125–225.

Brown, Richard D. 1996. *The Strength of a People: The Idea of an Informed Citizenry in America, 1650–1870.* Chapel Hill: University of North Carolina Press.

Clark, Charles E. 1994. *The Public Prints: The Newspaper in Anglo-American Culture, 1665–1740.* New York: Oxford University Press.

Flower, Milton E. 1983. *John Dickinson: Conservative Revolutionary.* Charlottesville: University Press of Virginia.

Greene, Jack P. 1988. *Pursuits of Happiness: The Social Development of Early Modern British Colonies and the Formation of American Culture.* Chapel Hill: University of North Carolina Press.

Humphrey, Carol Sue. 1992. *"This Popular Engine": New England Newspapers during the American Revolution, 1775–1789.* Newark: University of Delaware Press.

Katz, Stanley Nider, ed. 1963. *A Brief Narrative of the Case and Trial of John Peter Zenger, Printer of The New York Weekly Journal.* Cambridge, MA: Harvard University Press.

Levy, Leonard W. 1985. *Emergence of a Free Press.* New York: Oxford University Press.

Lathem, Edward Connery. 1972. *Chronological Tables of American Newspapers, 1690–1820.* Barre, MA: American Antiquarian Society.

Mott, Frank Luther. 1939. *A History of American Magazines, 1741–1850.* Cambridge, MA: Harvard University Press.

Raven, James. 2002. *London Booksellers and American Customers: Transatlantic Literary Community and the Charleston Library Society, 1748–1811.* Columbia: University of South Carolina Press.

Richardson, Lyon N. 1931. *A History of American Magazines, 1741–1789.* New York: Nelson.

Schlesinger, Arthur M. 1965. *Prelude to Independence: The Newspaper War on Britain, 1764–1776.* New York: Vintage.

Sloan, [William] David. 2004. John Campbell and the Boston News-Letter. AEJMC Newspaper Division. http://www.aejmc.net/ newspaper/WDSloan-BostonNews.html.

Sloan, William David, and Julie Hedgepeth Williams. 1994. *The Early American Press, 1690–1783.* Westport, CT: Greenwood.

Steele, Ian K. 1986. *The English Atlantic.* New York: Oxford University Press.

Thomas, Isaiah. 1970. *The History of Printing in America, with a Biography of Printers and an Account of Newspapers,* edited by Marcus A. McCorison. Barre, MA: Imprint Society.

Williams, Julie Hedgepeth. 1999. *The Significance of the Printed Word in Early America: Colonists' Thoughts on the Role of the Press.* Westport, CT: Greenwood.

CHAPTER 14

....

PRINT AND MANUSCRIPT CULTURE

....

CARLA MULFORD

On January 15, 1723, a special committee drawn from members of the Massachusetts Council and the House of Representatives made public their findings regarding James Franklin's newspaper, the *New-England Courant*. They averred "That the tendency of the said Paper is to Mock Religion, and bring it into contempt, That the Holy Scriptures are therein Prophanely abused. That the Reverend and Faithful Ministers of the Gospell are injuriously reflected on: His Majesty's Government Affronted: The Peace and good Order of His Majesty's Subjects of this Province disturbed by the said Courant." Their recommendation, in effect, was to shut down the press unless Franklin submitted his materials to authorities in advance of printing each issue of his weekly newspaper. Their strictures clarified that he should be punished for past printing offenses and proscribed from future ones. They recommended that "for prevention of the like Offenses" in the future James Franklin be forbidden to publish the *New England Courant* without governmental approval (Ford 1919–1967, 4: 208–209).

Such a move would not only silence James Franklin and his press but take away his livelihood, which seems to have been the goal of the committee, the Massachusetts Council, the Massachusetts House of Representatives, and, especially, the Mathers and others involved in the church hierarchy and government. Indeed, shutting down Franklin's press had long been the aim of the Mathers. For his part, Cotton Mather obsessed about the paper's open criticism of ministerial power. He wrote in his diary, December 1721: "Warnings are to be given unto the wicked Printer, and his Accomplices, who every week publish a vile Paper to lessen and blacken the Ministers of the Town, and render their Ministry ineffectual" (Mather 1957, 2: 663).

From his paper's inception, James Franklin and a small cohort of writers had offered news, fictional pieces, gossip, satires, and memorandums from other papers. Much of the material was intended as entertainment, but a good deal of Franklin's paper criticized prominent political and ministerial authorities (including the Mather family), their elitism, their support of inoculation for smallpox, their preaching about piety and community, and their anxiety about keeping power in the hands of churchmen rather than "knaves," "scribblers," and others who were writing for the public press. To Increase Mather, the paper was "a *Cursed Libel*," "a *Wicked Paper*" likely to bring down the heavens' wrath upon New England because of its absence of respect for the authorities of church or government (Mather 1723). In effect, by printing materials that were entertaining or controversial, or both, James Franklin found a useful way to sell his newspapers and pamphlets.

We might, as some scholars have done, attribute to politics and to the cause of testing the freedom of the press Franklin's continued publication of materials critical of ecclesiastical and civic governance, but we ought to be mindful that his livelihood entailed selling papers, and sell papers he did. The amount of ink spent detracting from and defending James Franklin's *New-England Courant* is an index to the anxiety about his impact on those in civil offices. In New England as in old, where the state and state religion had a tenuous hold over a diverse population, draconian measures, such as attempting to ensure the demise of dissident voices, were considered the sole means by which civil unrest could be averted.

New England civil authorities would brook no dissent in their community. In working to shut down James Franklin's press, they were seeking to implement restrictive measures common in England. As if no action had been taken against him, Franklin challenged them by printing his newspaper on January 21, the week after the House had passed the order for supervision over his press. For local news, he reproduced the motion made and agreed to on January 14 by the House and Council to suppress the open publication of his paper. By reproducing the statement made against him, he provided an impudent rebuke of the authorities, enabling readers to participate in the rebuke by purchasing and reading his newspaper. In J. A. Leo Lemay's view, such an action showed the fearlessness of the Franklin brothers, James and Benjamin, as they challenged the authorities' actions. James Franklin was getting his papers sold while legitimately challenging the rights of any colonial legislature to regulate printing. Local authorities called for his arrest, and young Benjamin Franklin took over the newspaper's publication (Lemay 2006, 1: 186; Clark 1991).

The example of James Franklin's *New-England Courant* provides a useful glimpse into issues related to print and the book trades, the circulation of news, and literary culture in New England's formative years. By looking into his work on the *Courant*, we witness the ecclesiastical, civic, cultural, and pragmatic problems faced by those interested in promulgating intellectual inquiry and literary culture. In civic and ecclesiastical terms, authorities sought assurance that their views (and the implementation of those views) would dominate pertinent social matters and that dissent would have no public forum beyond informal conversations in homes and businesses. In cultural terms, authorities sought to retain power over whose voices would be welcome and whose unwelcome amid an increasingly diverse population. In pragmatic terms, authorities could regulate commerce and culture more easily if dissent were quelled immediately.

Printers and publishers were dissatisfied with the idea that they should print nothing without the authorities' approval and frequently returned to arguments like John Milton's in *Areopagitica* (1644) that truth would win out, if the people had a chance to encounter dissenting positions and formulate their own opinions on matters civic and ecclesiastical. Likewise, printers and publishers found they could assist in formulating cultural norms by appealing to certain groups of readers among a diverse reading public. The world of print enabled greater numbers of people to find materials that would appeal to their own cultural attitudes and tastes, not just the attitudes and tastes of the ruling elite. Finally, the concept of the freedom of the press met the pragmatic needs of printers, who could make reasonably good livelihoods as long as they were permitted to print whatever might prove sufficiently interesting to potential readers who would purchase their papers and pamphlets. Controversy in print sold well, printers and publishers realized, especially controversy associated with criticism of leaders of church and state.

The situation was more complicated than a simple contest between authorities and printers and publishers. Print culture requires readers. Readers' opinions might not necessarily have concurred with all that they read, and owning printed matter might have had its own symbolic import beyond the printed content. The act of buying a newspaper cannot be taken to mean that the reader concurred with the newspaper's content. It can only be taken as indicating the purchaser's curiosity. In matters of local controversy, people like to seem "in the know," so owning any particularly controversial newspaper might have had its own status symbol of a person's being "informed." James Franklin's paper was one of a handful that survived well beyond its first year. But in North America, scribal or manuscript culture existed side by side with print media well into the early nineteenth century.

Print was merely one artifact the growing consumer society in colonial America consumed, for a variety of reasons concerning culture and commonwealth. By examining the relationship between early American literature and the printing press, we can recognize the extent to which literary culture developed amid a contested cultural terrain, one marked by books and newspapers as much as it was by the circulation of manuscripts, as in a totally scribal culture. With regard to the scribal dimension, it is important to understand that through much of British colonial America, printing presses were not established until the late seventeenth or early eighteenth century. Local literary culture among some people was, in effect, a scribal culture dependent on the circulation of manuscripts, whether for ecclesiastical or civic education, the circulation of general news, shipping news, the latest local or parliamentary legislative agreements, or entertainment. Indeed, for a long time, scribal writings were circulated alongside printed writings.

Together, print and manuscript helped create a market of readers and thus helped shape early American literature. Three main areas deserve consideration: (1) the coincidental historical circumstances of the advent of print amid scribal cultures in Europe but especially in England, the push by Britain for colonization of North America, and the formation of a gentlemanly cultural value of truthfulness in Britain; (2) the complications in colonial America, when print was introduced amid scribal circulation of news; and (3) the impact of print and manuscript culture on early American literature, especially imaginative writings.

HISTORICAL CONSIDERATIONS

With the advent of print technology in fifteenth-century Europe, church and state officials began to realize the expansive possibilities of print as a vehicle for fostering and indeed regulating ecclesiastical and civil discipline. Almost as soon as the printing press emerged as a reliable technology, these officials interested themselves in what was being printed, and by whom. The freedom of printers and publishers to print and circulate materials critical of church and state had long been questioned in England, especially under the heavy hand of Henry VIII, who in 1530 labeled "blasphemous and pestiferous" several Protestant books that, he argued, would "stir and incense [the people] to sedition, and disobedience against their princes, sovereigns, and heads" (quoted in Amory and Hall 2000, 8). Henry wanted to see the press print materials supporting his own views on matters, not others' views (Guy 1988). As David D. Hall has remarked, in the early modern era, opposition to the state was not considered legitimate, so "the early modern civil state treated . . . criticism and dissent that appeared in print as 'sedition.'" In addition to suppressing criticism and dissent, the British state "was no less anxious about the flow of news, which it wished to regulate for its own benefit" (Amory and Hall 2000, 4). Whether printers purveyed news, rumors, letters, orations, poems, or gossip—all unregulated print was considered potentially subversive.

Anxiety about the printed word prompted the search by civic authorities for a process of regulation from the time of the Reformation forward. Beginning in England in 1557 and with notable exceptions in the 1640s and then from 1679–1685, the central mechanism by which the state regulated print and the book trade was through the Stationers' Company, chartered by the Crown. Titles were registered by printers, licenses procured from ecclesiastical or civil authorities, and printers' names attached to title pages, according to the charter of the Stationers. The Licensing Act of 1662 reinforced the original charter of the Stationers, but this system of licensing was never fully effective, especially during the 1640s, when civil war wracked Britain, and the late 1670s through the 1680s, when the authority of king versus Parliament was seriously tested.

The seventeenth-century print-licensing acts and the repeated contests over religion and civil authority led to a successful underground book trade in England and on the Continent and a flourishing trade in handwritten materials or scribal publications circulated in manuscript form. Suppression by the state actually stimulated demand, particularly of those titles proscribed by church and state. In the book trade, both printers and booksellers took advantage of the market possibilities that could occur when overzealous authorities sought to repress print and its readers and sometimes produced clandestine books and pamphlets with false publishing information. There was a market for such printed matter especially in times of civic or religious crisis. The trade in handwritten materials was outside the realm of licensing statutes, so this trade was of a different kind and could not be regulated, except by interception. Scribally "published" materials of this kind—handwritten and hand-copied books, letters, notes, memorandums—were difficult to regulate, as the means for circulation were private rather than public. Scribally prepared materials circulated through sometimes clandestine and sometimes not-so-clandestine routes, so anxiety about what was being circulated increased among civil and ecclesiastical officials, especially during these years of religious and civil divisions.

When speaking about the advent of printing in England, then, we do well to recognize that the history of books and manuscripts is much more interesting when we look beyond the books entered into the Stationers' Register during the sixteenth, seventeenth, and eighteenth centuries and consider, in addition, the circulation of handwritten materials that were part of the culture (Eisenstein 1979; Ezell 1999). The English colonists, among them a bevy of nonconformists heading to establish their own ecclesiastical-civil commonwealth in America, were among those who might have been considered particularly suspect by the Crown, so the books the settlers carried, the speech acts and handwritten words they were creating, and the materials they were circulating all interested authorities in England.

As the colonists were setting sail for America, religious contests were under way in England and Europe. Sometimes, questioning authority was cause for incarceration. Concerns of the marketplace tended to dominate the mission of those who set sail for Virginia, whereas concerns about forming the Puritan God's commonwealth in New England drove those settlements along the northeastern seaboard. This is not to say that Virginia had no religious settlers. Virginia's settlers were Anglicans, and they interested themselves in establishing the Church of England in Virginia.

But it is to suggest that the joint stock chartering of the Virginia Company was an effort for England to gain for itself riches similar to those Spain and Portugal had acquired through colonization. Although the dominant goal of New Englanders was to establish the ecclesiastical and civil dominion of the Puritan, dissenting church, those with mercantile or adventuring interests also came to the region. Disputes over the truthfulness of colonists' accounts reveal the fractures in civil and ecclesiastical authority that were bound to occur when different people set sail for an unknown coastline on sometimes competing missions.

The history of scribal and printed publication in colonial America reveals the contest of voices and the varying versions of "truth" that resulted from a collision of competing interests. Stories of colonization exemplify what Stephen Shapin has identified as a fundamental concern in early modern times: the culture of truthfulness. In *A Social History of Truth*, Shapin described the extent to which English gentlemen valued truthfulness: they were "prepared and able to identify veracity and mendacity in the contest of practical action" and sought to do so in the public context of others of their group (Shapin 1994, xxi). Shapin's position is related directly to the rise of the new science, but it can be argued, using the colonists' writings as evidence, that truthfulness was a key measure by which writers asserted their existence, even across class boundaries. The earliest writers' seeming obsession with making sure their version of the story would become the accepted version among those in their group reveals the extent to which scribal publication and then print technology facilitated the culture's obsession with truth.

By examining the contested versions of settlement in Virginia and New England, for instance, we glimpse the appeals to truth many writers adopted. The writings evince for us the problems the settlers and indigenous peoples faced, the competing interests and appeals some used to audiences back home in an effort to assure that their versions of the situation would dominate (at least among people in their circles), and the ways in which print (if the handwritten manuscripts were eventually published) might work to counteract manuscript records about some situations, especially as the events have receded into history. Of the many Virginia examples, none stands out so well as that of Captain John Smith, who wrote repeatedly of his exploits in Virginia and the failures of those originally sent to lead the Virginia Company's colony. "The new president [Edward Maria Wingfield] and [John] Martin," Smith wrote, "being little beloved, of weake judgement in dangers, and less industrie in peace, committed the managing of all things abroad to Captaine Smith: who by his owne example, good words, and faire promises, set some to mow, others to binde thatch, some to build houses, others to thatch them, himselfe alwayes bearing the greatest taske for his owne share, so that in short time, he provided most of them lodgings, neglecting any for himselfe" (Mulford 2002, 180).

Attempting to get reinstated for future voyages, Smith worked hard to establish himself as the colony's leader in times of trial, and the specificity of his written narratives suggests to many readers today the reliability of his accounts when they are set against those written by some others. But Smith was born to neither a gentleman's nor an aristocrat's station, as Edward Maria Wingfield was, so Smith's accounts, however truthful they might have been, were not received as well as he might have hoped.

Wingfield wrote his own *Discourse of Virginia,* which circulated among aristocratic circles in England. According to him, the "truth" is that Wingfield worked the hardest to bring order, decency, and common sharing to the colony. Using (as Smith did) the common method of speaking of himself in the third person, presumably to assure authority and disinterest in the account, Wingfield created nearly a day-by-day record of events as the colony unfolded, including, for instance, a record of the complaints against him when he attempted to prevent the colonists' access to wine because he was trying to save it for sacramental use. In September of the colony's first year, Wingfield reported that those in the "Council did again fall upon the President for some better allowance for themselves and [for] some few [of] the sick, their privates." Expressing concern about the welfare of the whole group, not just those gentlemen in the Council, Wingfield said that he became unpopular and was deposed from being president precisely because he was a good one, seeking the well-being of all: "The President protested he would not be partial; but, if one had anything of him, every man should have his portion according to their places," he averred, adding, "If the President had . . . enlarged the proportion according to their request, without doubt in [a] very short time he had starved the whole company." In an appeal to the justice of his case, Wingfield concluded, "He would not join with them, therefore, in such ignorant murder without their own warrant" (Mulford 2002, 190).

Appeals to truthfulness and honor, self-sacrifice and bravery are hallmarks of both Smith's and Wingfield's accounts. By appealing to a set of values commonly held among gentlemen, whether in the colonies or in England, Smith and Wingfield both were seeking the approbation of company leaders for their version of events that occurred during colonization. That Smith caused his account to be printed in London seems to indicate a growing sense, if only among those outside aristocratic circles, that publication might work not just to circulate information as widely as possible but to create a greater potential for acceptance as "truth." Wingfield chose the aristocrat's method of circulating his manuscript in private. Such a method could create a reputation of honor, wherein one did not sully the truth by circulating it in the marketplace, where the presumably nondiscriminating multitude could grab hold of the printed word and use it for contrary purposes. The situation of Smith and Wingfield provides a perfect example of the contested nature of truth and how the contest was waged with or without the uses of print. To some readers in high places, Wingfield's appeals to trustworthiness gathered greater validity because he did not make his claims in print, whereas Smith could be perceived as pandering to the mass of people by publishing his writings and enabling the people to judge for themselves. Smith does indeed appeal directly to the mass of readers in many places in his writings, taking advantage of what print offered him—a readership—over the cultural situation in which Wingfield operated, one of manuscript circulation primarily among peers.

In addition to more formal accounts like those made by Smith and Wingfield, handwritten letters helped shed light on the culture of the day and the problems that confronted settlers, whether they were wealthy gentlemen or indentured servants. If authored by someone of high status, the materials would circulate among gentlemen back in England and thus provide additional "authorized" accounts of important matters related to the colonization process. In an account about his forthcoming marriage to Pocahontas, daughter of Powhatan, for instance, John Rolfe insisted to Sir Thomas Dale that his intentions were purely from the selfless goal of spreading the gospel truth to Pocahontas and her people. Appealing to the Christianity and honor of his countryman in seeking to explain his decision to marry an Indian woman, Rolfe said that after much struggling about his situation, he considered his own conscience at ease. In writing to Dale, he was seeking "grave and mature judgement, deliberation, approbation, and determination" on the subject: "And did not my ease proceed from an unspotted conscience, I should not dare to offer to your view and approved judgment these passions of my troubled soul, so full of fear and trembling is hypocrisy and dissimulation" before God. Rolfe clearly was agonizing over how his decision would be received in England and what his friends would think. His letter sought Dale's approval of the match and his kind construction of it when speaking among friends. "Knowing my own innocence and godly fervor in the whole prosecution hereof, I doubt not of your benign acceptance and clement construction," he said. Rolfe's letter repeatedly expressed his anxiety about what he called "the vulgar sort," who might accuse him of "the filth of impurity," and so he spoke in terms of his sacrificing himself to God's will in his marriage to Pocahontas:

> Now if the vulgar sort, who square all men's actions by the base rule of their own filthiness, shall tax or taunt me in this my Godly labor, let them know it is not any hungry appetite to gorge myself with incontinency. Sure, (if I would, and were so sensually inclined) I might satisfy such desire—though not without a seared conscience, yet with Christians more pleasing to the eye and less fearful in the offence unlawfully committed. Nor am I so desperate in estate that I regard not what becometh of me. Nor am I out of hope but one day to see my country; nor so void of friends, nor mean in birth, but there to obtain a match to my great content.
> (Mulford 2002, 196–197)

Rolfe wanted to assure his friend that he was behaving with propriety and sanctity, two values common in his era. His repeated allusion to carnal desire—and its expressed absence in this case, as he insisted—suggests a cultural concern about speaking truthfully about purity of motive, even as it seems to reveal to some readers today, in protesting the contrary, that Rolfe might have been fascinated with cross-cultural intermingling. Like Wingfield's account of the events in Virginia, Rolfe's transmittal of his views via letter might suggest that he wished them to be private, whereas in fact, the letter is composed in a way to suggest an assumption that it would be circulated among sympathetic friends and acquaintances. Such appeals by way of letter rather than by print, in other words, might have formed a fuller testament to truthfulness than any published document might have offered.

Print enabled Captain John Smith to have a voice remembered and made available for readers today, and it is Smith's story about Pocahontas—told in repeated and embellished versions—that resides in the public consciousness. It might be that readers today know Smith's accounts—and have converted them into a myth of Indian love of the colonizers—precisely because they were published. Readers' views today, it would seem, are conditioned by an attitude that has privileged printed materials above manuscript. Yet in the early modern world, print was sometimes considered suspect precisely over the point of honor and truthfulness: an honorable person would not need to protest to the masses about the truthfulness of his account; an honorable person would have people in high station who were positioned to circulate his narrative among those who counted in the government. Especially in matters of colonial politics and the English Crown or charter companies—as opposed to writings of the imagination, as, for instance, Anne Bradstreet's volume of poems *The Tenth Muse, Lately Sprung Up in America* (1650)—scripted materials carried significantly greater weight over published ones.

Contests for power and domination of viewpoints—including the "truth" value behind these viewpoints—occurred in nearly every new settlement in the earliest years of the English colonization process. Another example of the complexities of settlement and writing about settlement lies in the competing narratives about the contest among the first settlers at Plymouth. The accounts, where writers make repeated appeals both to God and to leaders back home that they be accepted as telling the real truth behind events, clarifies the battle that ensued in the New England settlements between those whose purpose for sailing was to establish their God's commonwealth on earth and those who sailed as adventurers for financial gain. In the hands of William Bradford and John Winthrop, the narratives of settlement clarify that God's providence guided the settlers when they succeeded and chastised them when their affairs, particularly with American Indians, went awry.

In the hands of Thomas Morton, whose reasons for sailing were fundamentally for personal profit, the story of the settlement has to do with the bounty of the lands and forests, a bounty that the Puritans, Morton argued, sought to control for their own selfish purposes. Morton was uninterested in the Puritan idea that paradise came through salvation by an angry God; in Morton's view, the countryside was a kind of paradise on earth: "In the month of June, Anno Salutis 1622," he wrote,

> it was my chance to arrive in the parts of New England with 30 servants and provision of all sorts fit for a plantation; and while our houses were building, I did endeavor to take a survey of the country. The more I looked, the more I liked it. And when I had more seriously considered of the beauty of the place, with all her fair endowments, I did not think that in all the known world it could be paralleled for so many goodly groves of trees, dainty fine round rising hillocks, delicate fair large plains, sweet crustal fountains, and clear running streams. . . . For in mine eyes t'was Nature's masterpiece, her chiefest magazine of all where lives her store. If this land be not rich, then is the whole world poor. (Mulford 2002, 251–252)

Thomas Morton was engaging in a mode of writing common to literature of promotion that would appeal to adventurers and, in his mockery of Puritans, to his Anglican churchmen. Instead of appealing to spiritual matters and the Separatists' sense of God's bounty as a gift, Morton appeals to the here-and-now production value of the land. Morton's narrative, interspersed with light and sometimes bawdy verse and complaints about "the precise Separatists" who seemed bent on keeping him from having fun among the Indians, shows the tensions between the competing values of godliness and monetary gain. In an effort to bring home his points to a sympathetic, Anglican audience, Morton created an account of the Puritans' attack against him at Ma-re Mount as a satiric rendering of the Puritans' sternness in religion, their authoritarian approach to living among Indians, their concern that the settlements in New England be godly, and their presumed jealousy over any transactions that might leave the godly Plymouth people financially and physically weakened. Morton was imprisoned by the Puritans and sent back to England, only to be acquitted. In frustration, he returned to New England but was arrested again. By joining with a sufficient number of Anglicans upset with the Massachusetts Bay Company, he finally challenged the charter held by the company.

In the end, the Massachusetts Bay Company retained its charter, but not until Morton's *New English Canaan,* published in 1637, had succeeded in making a mockery of the goals of the Puritan settlers by celebrating the bounty of the lands they were overtaking for their own seemingly ascetic mission. Whose "truth" emerged— that is, whether Morton's view of the land the Puritans dominated or the Puritans' view of their sufferings because of Morton—has remained open for interpretation for centuries now. What we do understand is that Morton's published account would have had high entertainment value among the Anglicans in England who were his primary audience.

From the moment the reports arrived in London of the first North American settlements, the authenticity of settlers' accounts was difficult to determine, often because accounts differed significantly from one another. Each writer seems to have wished his account to be accepted as the "truth" of the events that occurred, so each writer worked to create in his audience a sympathetic understanding. All accounts reaching government officials and those involved with the originating company charters were originally handwritten; no presses were set up when the colonies were first established. Such scribal materials sometimes were written with the author's expectation of full circulation—as, it seems, in the case of John Rolfe—and sometimes with the author's assumption that the account would be held private by the recipient. What happened with the accounts, once they reached England, could not be controlled by the authors or, sometimes, even by the first recipients. We have no real information, for instance, about Richard Frethorne, whose indenture papers for the Virginia voyage seem to have been signed by his parents and whose surviving letters home reveal his powerlessness to improve his situation. Frethorne's handwritten letters provide much greater insight into the real hardships faced by everyday people than the letters and manuscripts sent by Captain John Smith and Edward Maria Wingfield.

Frethorne's letters home to his parents reveal a learned person's understanding of the rhetoric of address but a very poor person's clear understanding that he probably would not come out of his indenture alive. He opened his letter of March 20, 1623, to his "loving and kind father and mother" with an appropriate remark about his "duty remembered to you, hoping in God of your good health"—a formula suitable to begin a letter from a son to his parents. But he immediately disclosed his "most heavy case" of destitution "by reason of the nature of the country, [which] is such that it causeth much sickness, as the scurvy and the bloody flux and diverse other diseases, which maketh the body very poor and weake." After offering a good deal of concrete detail of the problems the settlers were facing, Frethorne pointed out that he had "nothing to comfort me, nor there is nothing to be gotten here but sickness and death, except [in the event that] one had money to lay out in some things for profit." Without attacking his parents' godliness or their ultimate decision to sign the papers indenturing him to laboring in what seemed like a hellish place to him, Frethorne nonetheless directed his parents' attention to someone who had treated him in kindly fashion, almost as if he had been a parent. "Goodman Jackson pitied me," Frethorne wrote, saying that "they be very godly folks, and love me very well, and will do anything for me." But he added, quite poignantly striking at the heart of the matter to his parents, that Goodman Jackson "much marvelled that you would send me a servant to the Company; he saith I had been better knocked on the head" (Mulford 2002, 197–198). Such an appeal would work to force his parents to question their godliness (as they are being compared to someone whom their son perceives as godly) in signing papers condemning their son to such harsh treatment, even as it shows the difficulties faced by laboring people.

The story told by the laborers would of course be a much different narrative than the one told by the leaders, and it is a story that tended to be neglected if not

intentionally suppressed in favor of a more valiant and glorious story of colonization, one speaking to the goals and interests of the colonizers rather than the lives
and efforts of those of lesser station. When speaking about manuscripts and printed
records from the past, it is important to recognize that, for the most part, the laborers' stories were essentially silenced. Whereas Captain John Smith could cause his
narrative to be circulated and then to reach print and Edward Maria Wingfield could
see that his narrative reached certain members of the aristocratic and court circles
in which he circulated, Richard Frethorne had no guarantee that his letters would
reach his parents (having no money to offer someone to secure their passage), and
his parents would have no interest in seeing them published. Thus it is that the stories told across time about the colonial efforts have favored those higher in station
or those who managed to get their writings into print, because these are the records
that, whether printed or circulated in manuscript, became public knowledge. Stories told by laborers to their families, at least until the eighteenth century (when
a greater number of laborers were reading and writing, as in the famous cases of
James and Benjamin Franklin), remained largely absent from the storytelling that
took place publicly in the colonial era.

In addition to the handwritten narratives and letters, other reports were in
circulation, oral reports conveyed by those who worked on the sailing vessels and
those who returned home (back-migration was significant in the earliest years)
and thus created little to no written record of their experiences. These oral accounts existed side by side with the written record. Yet it is worthwhile noting that
by focusing on written works, we are generalizing about people who were educated and people who held property. Such generalizations focus on matters related
to the dominant group and especially to men. In rare situations, we can recover
information about people who did not create their own records, but such information is scant, often based on reportage from a witness rather than the original
speaker, and might be less reliable than a first-person account. It is useful to note,
too, that in many instances, the lives of people—whether laborers, women, Native
Americans, or Africans—sometimes entered the earliest records precisely because
of presumed cultural aberrations or contests regarding their cases, whether it is
the outspokenness of an Anne Hutchinson (whose records exist primarily in John
Winthrop's record of her trial), the problems created by Indians who resented the
English (as evident in the multitudes of writings about the presumed "savages" of
North America), or the problems created when slaves were stubbornly engaged
in seeking freedom from oppression (as evidenced in runaway slave ads, protests
by enslaved Africans, and other means revealing slaves' resistance to subjugation).
In many instances, however, this is the only way literary historians can account
for the lives, experiences, and intellectual activity of most women, Africans, and
Native Americans. Such records by the elite, in other words, reveal that a wide
oral culture must have existed among those whose personal experiences remain
relatively unrecorded, whether in script or print, except when their activities came

under scrutiny by settlers whose records dominate the earliest literature. These peoples are precisely the ones who would eventually benefit, over a century later, from the arrival of print in the colonies.

SCRIPT, PRINT, GOVERNANCE, AND THE CIRCULATION OF NEWS

When printing began in the colonies in the seventeenth century, printers were working in a cultural marketplace already accustomed to the sharing of information—whether pragmatic, philosophical, or imaginative—by oral means (in homes, church meetings, and taverns) and by scribal means (in handwritten letters to family, friends, and business or political acquaintances). Scribal materials in the colonies included handwritten materials related to civil governance and social order (laws, deeds, wills, property transmittals, for instance) and ecclesiastical governance and church order (including expressions of church discipline; testimonies of faith of parishioners; records of marriages, births, and deaths; sermons, catechisms, and so forth). Such writings as these were needed as part of the local and long-distance legal and cultural record keeping necessary to forming and structuring an ongoing community and to reporting back to legal and financial authorities in England about the ongoing activities of those involved in the original charters. As David Hall has acknowledged, "Governments in the seventeenth century depended on information being written down. So did people with property" (Amory and Hall 2000, 57).

But there were other uses for writing in that day, as in ours, so another large fund of materials in script are writings about daily life (narrative accounts such as regional histories, town histories, family histories, and histories of relations with Africans and American Indians) and about colonists' religious or imaginative experiences, whether recorded in poetry and prose, anagrams, acrostics, or other forms of literature. Printers and booksellers often worked in coordination with but sometimes contradicted authorities in the earliest years. Contradiction of the authorities also occurred in scribal writings. Scribal materials did not, as has sometimes been thought, fall into disuse in the first century of printing in the British colonies.

In its earliest years, the colonial book trade was a transatlantic business, with books and pamphlets forming a part of the larger commercial shipments made to the colonies. Indeed, by the middle of the seventeenth century, the North American market offered for sale a significant portion of the books and pamphlets printed in England and Europe (Amory and Hall 2000). In the beginning, vendors of books marketed other commodities that came into their stores. But by the start of the eighteenth century, a differentiated trade emerged, with printing, printed products, paper, ink, and so forth becoming almost a separate province of vendibles for the market. The shift began when booksellers and printers developed a domestic market for printed matter. Whereas the book trades in the earliest years relied on the circulation of goods from beyond American shores, within the first century of English settlement, domestic production of printed matter constituted a sizable portion of the printed materials sold.

The trade differentiated by region, as we might expect, with a higher percentage of printed matter being created and sent into circulation in the northern and middle colonies than in the southern colonies. Initially, local governments patronized colonial presses the most. In effect, the presses were established to assist the tasks of government, and they were used in much the same way they were used in Reformation England: to publish laws and foster public opinion on behalf of governmental measures. The presses, in other words, took over some of the functions of scribal work needed by government officials. In the colonial era, one of the primary functions of scribal materials was the recording of official, government-related activities. In the first half century of Virginia settlement, the General Assembly preferred scribal publication over print, thus facilitating easy creation and repeal of statute law. If laws and proclamations were inscribed in broadside sheets, they could be changed—or lost—at the will of local officials (Amory and Hall 2000, 62–63). Virginia was an unusual case. Most of the original colonies and their leaders—New England, New York, Pennsylvania, Maryland—hired printers to assure laws would be printed and made available to those whose activities they sought to control. If the materials were not printed for the government, they were published for leading members of the community, primarily religious leaders in the northern and middle colonies and members of the planter classes in the South.

Establishing a printing house was costly and difficult, because type and paper originally had to be imported. Isaiah Thomas estimated that before 1700, "there had never been more than two printing houses open at the same time in Boston" (Thomas 1874, 95). Printers would often try to start up presses, but the market for local writers was uncertain at best, and local governments typically favored certain printers and their imprints. One way printers assured that their presses would remain active was by declining to print anything controversial without first consulting government officials. The firm of Green and Allen, for instance, was able to maintain its monopoly from the 1690s by consulting the lieutenant governor or else "their particular Friends and imployers," Increase and Cotton Mather, before running a particular publication through their press. To Richard D. Brown's thinking, "Members of the trade had reason to cooperate with the government, for in each colony the surest line of business was the contract for printing sessions and statute laws, legal forms, and proclamations. To be designated 'government printer' was every tradesman's goal" (Amory and Hall 2000, 367). Those who disagreed with the government or religious leaders in New England usually sought to publish their writings elsewhere—London, New York, Philadelphia—where printers would be outside the jurisdiction of the colony leaders (Amory and Hall 2000, 94–95). This was the strategy Captain John Smith had adopted in the earliest days of the project of colonization of Virginia a century earlier. For the most part, there seems to have been a significant amount of political conservatism practiced by printers, but such presumed conservatism might have more to do with making a living than with sharing the authorities' politically conservative leanings.

Another way of assuring that the press would remain active was a method taken by James Franklin, who by the 1720s determined that the strong arm of the Mathers and governmental spokespersons could no longer control the print marketplace sufficiently well to squelch the market of readers who might be interested in materials beyond those supporting the ruling elite and their religious views. Franklin was interested less in the religiosity of Boston than in the possibility for literary achievement and the creation of an entertaining newspaper. As we have seen with the example of his *New-England Courant*, printers who wished to print from within their colonial boundaries experienced difficulties when they sought to contradict leaders and those of high station whose authority—whether in the colony or in London—would not readily be called into question. But by the early decades of the eighteenth century, the population even in New England was, by Franklin's calculation, sufficiently differentiated that printers who rivaled those supported by the government stood a small chance of succeeding—provided they could stay out of jail.

That printers were willing to go to jail over their publication of materials deemed libelous or slanderous against individuals or the local or imperial government has been taken by some historians to signify a movement toward the political articulation of freedom of the press. On one hand, this assessment seems appropriate: James Franklin was indeed willing to test the social and political system by challenging it, though he understood perfectly well that he might be jailed. But he was also a shrewd businessman who had a brother and a number of other apprenticed printers who could take over his paper in his absence, should his absence be required by law. It is tempting to characterize such challenges to authority as expressions of political freedom and the testing of free speech. Looked at from a slightly wider cultural standpoint, however, the situation seems to suggest a growing secularization in the community that Franklin and printers like him were interested in testing the market for. That is, Franklin's paper included satires, fictional entertainments, and other light fare—in addition to articles the Mathers detested—common in newspapers in England but absent from papers in New England. Franklin seems to have made an assessment that such materials, more secular and cosmopolitan in style and content, would find a ready market among American readers. It is as appropriate to consider Franklin's behavior as one supporting greater cosmopolitanism, a wider sense of a transatlantic readership (and authorship), as it is to consider his behavior a political challenge in behalf of freedom of the press and of the democratization of American culture.

Perhaps those who argue that print essentially enabled a challenging of political freedom and a democratizing of American culture are correct over the longer haul: by the early nineteenth century, reading, writing, and printing were no longer in the hands of elite groups, and they no longer fostered a single view of culture. But when we consider the shorter run—the first century of printing in New England and the Middle Colonies, where printing was more frequent and printers more numerous than in the South—we become aware that print media more or less occurred side by side with scribal media. It would be easy to assume, as some literary historians formerly did, that with the advent of print people would have been happy to relinquish their reliance on the time-consuming scribal medium for passing imaginative writings or practical, political, or local news in order to partake in the newly acquired technology. But such was not the case. Print media did not supplant handwritten media until the nineteenth century. Despite the flourishing of print in the early eighteenth century, scribal writings, both pragmatic and imaginative, were in continual circulation.

In the case of newspapers, scribal media (letters, journals, and other handwritten documents) remained stable vehicles for offering news, information, and entertainment. As Sheila McIntyre has shown, with the advent of a greater number of printing houses and newspapers, letter writing by New England ministers and other leaders in the late seventeenth and early eighteenth centuries tended to increase rather than decrease. This increase can be attributed to the fact that letter writers could, when transmitting their letters or journals, send along the recent local newspapers, or they could assume that their recipients had these newspapers (or other colonies' local papers) at hand. Thus, letter writers could comment on existing news offered in print sources, validate it or invalidate it, interpret it or misinterpret it. Unlike adult readers today, whose intellectual habits have been developed in a cultural system relying on print media as primary vehicles for disseminating information, McIntyre has pointed out, "Early colonial readers did not privilege printed information over oral and scribal forms; indeed, handwritten letters were sometimes more widely disseminated than certain printed publications. Site-based correspondents, who shared news quickly after verifying it, were considered the most trustworthy reporters" (McIntyre 1998, 613–614).

In sum, handwritten materials dominated British colonial culture in the initial stages of settlement. With the introduction of printers and printing presses, colonists had opportunities for sharing news, political pamphlets, sermons, poems, broadsides, and other print matter that complemented but did not supplant information, whether pragmatic or imaginative, shared among writers circulating their manuscripts. Print and manuscript cultures existed side by side for a long time in colonial America. By the mid–eighteenth century, when a sufficient number of presses were established and a suitable number of local authors were trained in reading, writing, and polite, literate culture, printers began to gain interest—if not livelihoods—in printing locally authored materials. It remains for us to examine the impact of print and manuscript culture on the imaginative writings and cultural performances in the eighteenth century.

SCRIPT, PRINT, AND THE PERFORMANCE OF CULTURE

Despite the advent of print in the colonies, scribal publication remained an active component in eighteenth-century cultural commerce. Both script and print facilitated the circulation of materials created by writers of spiritual or imaginative experiences whose works are often considered formative to contemporary practices of American letters. Each colony, having been developed for different reasons, had its own cultural idiosyncrasies when compared with the American colonies as a whole. Yet some general comments about the transformation of American culture can be useful as we attempt to discuss the impact of print and manuscript culture on eighteenth-century literature. First, attitudes about learning changed around the start of the century. Literacy became more widespread. Colleges were established in New England, then Virginia and New Jersey, then Philadelphia. Day schools for most children were promoted as a means not simply to teach children the rudiments of the alphabet so that they could read their Bibles and catechisms but to create a more generally educated citizenry.

In addition to educating English-speaking people, most towns sought to introduce education to people outside the English-speaking community. In Philadelphia, for instance, programs emerged—not without some criticism by German speakers—to educate in English language and lifeways the Germans who were arriving in significant numbers by midcentury. Educational programs were adopted in New England and proposed in the southern areas to assist the assimilation of Indians willing to let their children learn the settlers' culture. Their function was, of course, a disciplinary one, to train Indians how to serve the settlers, but the programs in Indian education nonetheless suggest a general attitude about the necessity of fostering learning. Schools for free and enslaved Africans and African Americans likewise served a disciplinary function while also revealing the conciliating and peaceable gestures of the Society of Friends toward all peoples. In the case of the Society of Friends, their schools assisted their general concern to guide other settlers to consider emancipation a viable and better alternative to slavery.

Second, the educational programs were designed to foster educational ends differing from the religious goals of earlier generations. Like its counterpart at the time in England, American education suited pragmatic and philosophical goals. At first, colonial educational programs had been sponsored by church members and emphasized ecclesiastical training and spiritual striving. The curriculum in England followed the trivium (arts of language and philosophy) and quadrivium (sciences and music). But by the middle of the eighteenth century, educational goals shifted to encompass more modern studies in mechanical and natural philosophy and arts (including the arts of classical and contemporary rhetoric). Training also included reading in English-language texts of a contemporary sort by the end of the century, rather than in the traditionally honored Greek and Roman classics. Overall, the changes were pragmatic, and they usefully engaged a growing populace in the modes of what was considered in Great Britain (dominated as it then was by Scottish Common Sense philosophy) as "polite culture."

These educational effects are evident in the scribal, print, and performance culture of the times. As the eighteenth century continued, the practice of writing for pleasure occurred more frequently. Many more people were creating polite literature, some of them among the educated classes and some among technically skilled artisans and laboring classes. This literature found its way into newspapers and magazines as well as individual pamphlet publications. One of the chief ends of learning among artisan and laboring people by midcentury was self-improvement. The concept of the essential nature of self-improvement drove one of the supreme printer-writers of the era, Benjamin Franklin, much as it drove many of the people with whom he associated. Whether they wrote for print publication or for their own manuscript-circulating circles or whether they were engaging in speaking publicly about or to their own groups, most of the writers and speakers by the end of the century embraced the theme of self-improvement that dominated Franklin's almanac literature and many of his writings outside the political arena.

Materials that circulated hand in hand in the eighteenth century varied widely across the colonies. Three reasons can be identified for the persistence of the circulation of scribal materials despite the opportunity provided by the existence of presses in the colonies. First, if they kept their productions in manuscript form, authors could exert control over circulation, assuming the manuscripts were circulating among trusted friends. Sometimes controlling circulation was essential to an author's ability to refine for accuracy of phrase or data. Manuscript, to some extent, provided an opportunity for control over the use and accuracy of their words.

A second reason that some preferred to keep their materials in manuscript rather than printing them relates to in-group or cultural attitudes about the perceived necessity for privacy. Artisans' groups, private clubs, and Masonic organizations, all of which flourished in midcentury, sought privacy for their members, and so their materials—like their books—tended to circulate privately in the absence of printing. Likewise, privacy was sought by those who perceived themselves to be writing for their specific group, whether ethnically or politically or otherwise distinctive from the general mass of people. While publication suited writings intended for the general population, writings intended for a small private circle could remain in manuscript.

The case of Phillis Wheatley and other educated Africans of her generation complicates the matter of public and private writings. Wheatley was brought to America in a system of slavery that kept her in bondage until she was emancipated after her celebrated tour of England upon the publication of her book of verse, *Poems on Various Subjects, Religious and Moral* (London, 1778). Wheatley's private writings and manuscripts revealed to her friends and associates the struggles she faced as an African and a woman, and they revealed as well her clear understanding of the oppression Africans and Indian peoples were facing in America. Yet her public writings generally attested to her admiration of English and American leaders. The exception to this generalization appeared in print. One of her letters written to Mohegan Indian preacher Samson Occom was published widely in colonial newspapers in 1774 and later. The letter clarified Wheatley's sense of the dominant culture's political and social contradictions about the liberal political notion of liberty in light of their (Wheatley's and Occom's) evangelical sense that liberty comes only to those of true Christian belief: "In every human Breast," Wheatley wrote, "God has implanted a Principle, which we call Love of Freedom; it is impatient of Oppression, and pants for Deliverance; and by the Leave of our Modern Egyptians I will assert, that the same Principle lives in us. God grant Deliverance in his own way and Time, and get him honor upon all those whose Avarice impels them to countenance and help forward the Calamities of their Fellow Creatures" (Mulford 2002, 897).

Wheatley's letter clearly shows her concern about the contradictions faced by people of African, American Indian, and other non-European descent. Outside the eye of the dominant-group population, it could have worked to create solidarity among true nonwhite believers; under the purview of a wider, predominantly white print readership, however, the letter served as an interesting notice of the extent to which print might be used to create public solidarity among non-dominant-group readers. But the time for cultural solidarity among African Americans would not arrive until the nineteenth century. In the eighteenth century, for the most part, members outside the dominant group employed scribal writings to create and attest to a cultural solidarity and an intellectual community that could be discovered and maintained in private groups, outside the eye of the general population.

Finally, authors could reveal their culture and class by keeping their materials in manuscript. This was particularly true for women. While readers in the later eighteenth century seem to have accepted the publication of writings by women (as evidenced in the work of Judith Sargent Murray and Mercy Otis Warren, for example), readers interested in polite culture—or aping the manners of politeness among upper-class people—discouraged the words of intellectual women in print. Thus, for example, Annis Boudinot Stockton frequently was published in her own day, but only later in life did she work to clarify that the publications were hers. Part of her reticence to publish in her own name came from her sense of women of culture: they should not seem to be pandering to general readers; they should remain above concerns of the literary marketplace. Stockton occasionally sent her poems to press by herself, but she much preferred using her brother as her agent or else counting on other men of reputation to submit her poems to printers. The situation Stockton faced was complicated: her private papers indicate she did truly enjoy seeing her writings reach print—even down to telling her brother how to have a particular poem printed—but she was working in a culture that assumed that women in polite circles were uninterested in circulating writings to the multitude. For Stockton, as for many in her circle, writing was a cultural performance, something akin to a dance perhaps as formal as a minuet, wherein everyone knew the steps to take, how to perform them, and how to conclude. People performed gestures of gratitude by writing encomia to those in high station. Annis Stockton created a performance of patriotism in her poems confirming the decisions of those in high office in government. Stockton wrote a poem in support of Alexander Hamilton and the national bank. She was well aware that her work could assist George Washington at crucial moments in his career and wrote several occasional pieces to him that found their way repeatedly into press, sometimes offered by Washington himself or those under his direction. Such cultural performances could assist cultural consolidation in precarious times (Stockton 1995; Amory and Hall 2000, 435–476).

In the last decades of the eighteenth century, during the precarious era of nation building, print became a predominant means of communicating presumed values of national culture to a general population of readers, and history writing and novel writing were key genres in the transformation of the colonies into a new nation. History writing grew in importance as a literary genre, because through the vehicle of history a writer could establish fundamental ideologies of the nation. Competing versions of history based on differing political orientations emerged in this era. Perhaps the best-known historian of the American Revolution was David Ramsay, whose view of what history writing should do mirrored the needs of his society. As Peter Messer has shown, Ramsay's first histories related to the American Revolution (1778, 1785) and centered on the importance of the Revolution as catalyst for social, political, and moral improvement, whereas Ramsay's later version of the history of the American Revolution (1789) worked essentially to define and vindicate "a pre-existing set of values and beliefs that defined what it meant to be an American" (Messer 2002, 205). David Ramsay saw, during his lifetime, the extent to which print could work as a vehicle to secure a particular moral position and to inculcate to a population certain political values that would support a particular national agenda. The function of such history writing was didactic: it worked to teach the population about its presumed goals; it taught readers their place in the nation, a place that would seem, in the later version of his history, to have been the colonies' destiny from their inception.

The use of print as a didactic vehicle was even more apparent in the earliest American novels, which sought to foster a sense of consolidated values among the citizenry: good citizens should read history, practice chastity, develop a reputation for moral probity, and associate only with those whose values were transparent, upstanding, and community-oriented rather than self-serving. To do otherwise could bring disaster to the family and, hence, to the nation. Among the first novels by American citizens printed in the United States were *The Power of Sympathy* (1789) by William Hill Brown and *The Coquette* (1797) by Hannah Webster Foster. Both novels employ the epistolary tradition common in England, and both encourage similar virtues established primarily around the theme of moral probity, in Brown's case, of men especially, and in Foster's case, of both women and men. Long disquisitions on the virtue of studying history and employing conversation to edify one's group are effects of the self-consciously edifying purpose of Brown's novel. And long discussions on the nature of creating and keeping vows to others, in addition to a woman's keeping herself chaste, mark Foster's. In both cases, the authors responded to the call for a national literature that would promulgate values that would conserve and protect American society from immoral outsiders, whether portrayed as extramarital lovers, rakes, or unchaste women. The novels of the era, along with the short stories appearing with greater frequency in the great number of newspapers, especially emphasize the importance of what today are called traditional family values as these would protect the nation from slipping into immorality (Mulford 1996).

In this early era of nationalism, we begin to see what some historians of print have called the democratization of American culture that could result from the world of print. With general literacy rates quite high within the free population, writers were formulating their texts for print-oriented readers with the often-expressed assumption that all should attain knowledge of the world, especially the moral world, in order to become a suitable, contributing member of the citizenry. Thus it is that many historians of print have succeeded in explaining that print enabled a higher number of settlers to become educated and assimilated into the developing national cultural fabric.

CONCLUSION

Interest in scribal publication remained relatively consistent from the founding of Jamestown to the founding of the United States. For a number of reasons, as we have seen, the passing of manuscripts from hand to hand was a preferred method of circulating personal news and imaginative writings. By contrast, print media went through a series of changes, but print culture eventually seems to have ended up where it began. Initially, following what they had experienced in England, those in governance sought to use print media to consolidate and direct state culture and cultural values. When those values were openly questioned, as with the work of James Franklin, for instance, those in power attempted to make it impossible for the printer to survive financially. Yet as we have seen, print was used throughout the colonial era, as Captain John Smith's example attests, as a means for questioning the ruling elite and for challenging existing narratives that the elite were seeking to foster. By the end of the eighteenth century, when concepts of "the nation" were unstable, members of the elite group sought to promulgate a relatively conservative view of culture, and print became the medium through which cultural values were inculcated by an increasingly worried elite group seeking to retain its hold over social attitudes and political agendas. With the exception of Phillis Wheatley, those whose voices went unheard would not employ print as a means to circulate and consolidate their own views about culture and national values until the nineteenth century. It was in the era of the early Republic that readers began to hear more from women, Native Americans, and people of African descent, who were embracing print media to display the extent to which the presumed freedoms and possibilities provided members of the new nation were not equally accessible.

REFERENCES

Amory, Hugh, and David D. Hall, eds. 2000. *A History of the Book in America.* Vol. 1, *The Colonial Book in the Atlantic World.* New York: Cambridge University Press.

Clark, Charles E. 1991. Boston and the Nurturing of Newspapers: Dimensions of the Cradle, 1690–1741. *New England Quarterly* 64: 243–271.

Eisenstein, Elizabeth L. 1979. *The Printing Press as an Agent of Change: Communications and Cultural Transformations in Early Modern Europe.* New York: Cambridge University Press.

Ezell, Margaret M. J. 1999. *Social Authorship and the Advent of Print.* Baltimore: Johns Hopkins University Press.

Ford, Worthington Chauncey, ed. 1919–1967. *Journals of the House of Representatives of Massachusetts.* 38 vols. Boston: Massachusetts Historical Society.

Guy, John. 1988. *Tudor England.* New York: Oxford University Press.

Lemay, J. A. Leo. 2006. *The Life of Benjamin Franklin.* 2 vols. Philadelphia: University of Pennsylvania.

Mather, Cotton. [1911] 1957. *Diary of Cotton Mather,* edited by Worthington Chauncey Ford. 2 vols. Reprint. New York: Frederick Ungar.

Mather, Increase. 1723. Advice to the Publick from Dr. Increase Mather. *Boston Gazette,* January 29.

McIntyre, Sheila. 1998. "I Heare it so Variously Reported": News-Letters, Newspapers, and the Ministerial Network in New England, 1670–1730. *New England Quarterly* 71: 593–614.

Messer, Peter. 2002. From a Revolutionary History to a History of Revolution: David Ramsay and the American Revolution. *Journal of the Early Republic* 9: 289–313.

Mulford, Carla, ed. 1996. *William Hill Brown's The Power of Sympathy and Hannah Webster Foster's The Coquette.* New York: Penguin.

———, ed. 2002. *Early American Writings.* New York: Oxford University Press.

Shapin, Steven. 1994. *A Social History of Truth, Civility and Science in Seventeenth-Century England.* Chicago: University of Chicago Press.

Stockton, Annis Boudinot. 1995. *The Poems of Annis Boudinot Stockton,* edited by Carla Mulford. Charlottesville: University Press of Virginia.

Thomas Isaiah. 1874. *The History of Printing in America, with a Biography of Printers, and an Account of Newspapers.* 2nd ed. Albany, NY: J. Munsell.

CHAPTER 15

EARLY AMERICAN LIBRARIES

SARAH FATHERLY

Books were an important part of British American life from its very beginnings. Faced with choices about what to bring across the Atlantic, some early colonists privileged their books. The writings of Captain John Smith and other Jamestown settlers record the existence of books in England's earliest permanent American colony. Farther north, New England settlers like Plymouth elder William Brewster also brought their book collections with them to the New World (Dexter 1889). As colonial settlements gained firm ground, libraries in seventeenth-century British America emerged most strongly in the form of personal collections and Anglican mission collections. There were some experiments involving governmental oversight of libraries, and the first of the American collegiate libraries took root. Overall, libraries in this early era of colonization emerged largely from the efforts of individuals, be it to enhance their own intellectual resources or to act philanthropically on behalf of a larger audience. The formal organization and administration of libraries was not a part of the official British colonial project in North America, and thus efforts at establishing book collections went forth unevenly across regions. By virtue of Puritan influence and the nature of town settlements, New England led the way in incorporating libraries into the colonial landscape in communal ways. Thanks to the momentum of the Bray libraries, several southern colonies enlarged their book holdings and deployed government to preserve libraries.

PERSONAL LIBRARIES

In the seventeenth century, personal libraries were the province of wealthy and privileged colonists, and only some of that select coterie. After all, having a personal library of any note meant a commitment of time, labor, and money, assets many were loath to spend on books when they could be used to enhance personal comfort or economic well-being. Library owners had to be literate and educated, possess the money to purchase new books and maintain old ones, enjoy leisure time that could be devoted to the collection, and (given the dearth of colonial printing presses) have transatlantic commercial connections useful for acquiring more books. For some individuals, such a serious investment of time and money was well worth the reward.

Excellent examples of personal libraries are available for both the New England and Chesapeake colonies. In New England, John Winthrop II's collection warrants attention for several reasons. When Winthrop journeyed to America in 1631, he brought with him an impressive library that he assiduously added to over the years: by 1640, it was reputed to contain 1,000 volumes, making it the largest library in seventeenth-century British America. Winthrop's collection was also unique in its emphasis on science, one of the owner's intellectual passions. An original member of the Royal Society, Winthrop prized volumes related to astronomy, mathematics, and alchemy (Wilkinson 1963). Until his death in 1676, Winthrop was well known for his generosity in lending books to friends and colleagues. In Virginia, plantation owner and officeholder Ralph Wormeley II amassed a collection that, at just under 400 volumes, was smaller than Winthrop's and more general. Yet in its size and scope, this collection, more than Winthrop's, typified the library of an educated colonial gentleman. On Wormeley's shelves, religious texts and classical literature sat next to titles of history, science, medicine, law, politics, and prescriptive literature, as well as modern belles lettres (Wright 1959, 89).

The tradition of great gentlemen's personal libraries carried on over generations. As the century turned, Massachusetts minister Cotton Mather and Virginia planter William Byrd II both presided over increasingly large and significant private collections that had seventeenth-century foundations. Mather's remarkable collection was built over generations, beginning with the core of books Richard Mather had brought across the Atlantic in 1635 upon his emigration to Boston. Predictably, the Mather collection was especially impressive in its religious and theological titles, but it also included a range of history, travel, classics, natural philosophy, and medicine (Hayes 1994; Tuttle 1910).

The library of William Byrd II soon rivaled that of Mather at approximately 3,500 volumes by the early 1700s. First begun by his father in the late seventeenth century, Byrd's library was notable for not only its size but also its diversity and organization. Byrd carefully shelved his books according to categories that reflected his interests in law, travel, history, medicine, classics, foreign languages, and modern literature. The collection was also distinguished by its impressive Americana materials that included New World travel accounts, histories of individual colonies, and colonial legal codes (Hayes 1997). Byrd's diaries suggest that his books constituted a critical link for him to the high culture world of London where he had been educated, and that he diligently read from his library multiple times a day. This collection was a crucial resource for Byrd as he penned his famous *History of the Dividing Line.*

Although the Byrd library was unusual in the overall size and scope of its holdings, it was fundamentally similar in formation, content, and use to the smaller personal libraries of other wealthy colonists. Those with sufficient means to establish a library of some substance acquired volumes through a variety of avenues, including importing titles directly from agents in England or Scotland, tasking kin and friends abroad to buy books on their behalf, personally purchasing books while traveling in Europe, receiving books as gifts (or bequests), and patronizing colonial booksellers. In terms of content, most personal collections reflected the particular interests of their owners, and large ones especially were often weighted toward owners' specific tastes. Yet most libraries had breadth that took in a range of classics, modern literature, philosophy, history, geography, science, and theology. Whatever the balance of a personal collection, a library was of multiple uses to its owner. On a fundamental level, these libraries signified their owners' social status because such collections were expensive luxuries predicated on learning and financial resources. For many of the colonial gentry, personal libraries signified their cultural identification with British high culture as they tried to build collections that would be considered worthy of the English elite. In a time and place where access to printed information was scarce, book ownership indicated a person's claim to economic, social, and cultural power. Personal collections were also of practical use: a library offered its owner a path to self-improvement, to pleasant leisure, to enlargement of knowledge, and to the creation of original intellectual work (as the experiences of Winthrop, Mather, and Byrd suggest). Owners were not the only ones to benefit from personal libraries as many of them willingly lent volumes to intellectual colleagues and encouraged friends and family members to peruse their collections, an invitation that included women as well as men in many cases.

Of particular note among mid-Atlantic private libraries are those of Philadelphians James Logan and Benjamin Franklin. Emigrating from the West Indies to Philadelphia in 1699, Logan brought with him the foundation of a book collection that would pass the 3,000-volume mark by the mid-1700s. Colonial intellectuals universally admired Logan for his broad knowledge and his taste in books. His collection reflected his special interests in mathematics, languages, Near Eastern studies, and natural philosophy but was still quite broad and diverse in its overall composition. Admired not only for his erudition but also for his generosity, Logan became well known for allowing friends, family, and colleagues to peruse his library and borrow its volumes. This generosity had its ultimate expression in his will, which provided for his private collection to be turned into a public library. In the years following his death, the Loganian Library was readied and finally opened to the Philadelphia public in 1760 (Wolf 1974).

Benjamin Franklin, an admirer of Logan who consulted on the Loganian Library project, amassed an impressive library of his own over his lifetime that aided him in his ambitions to gain standing in colonial and Continental elite circles. Swelling to roughly 4,000 volumes by the 1780s, Franklin's collection was largely amassed while he lived abroad in London and Paris. As might be anticipated, his library was especially strong in experimental and mechanical philosophy, but it also had an impressive concentration of French-language titles. Displaying his well-known penchant for innovation, Franklin created a chair that turned into a ladder and a device for retrieving out-of-reach volumes especially for his library (Wolf and Hayes 2006).

THE START OF COLLECTIVE LIBRARIES

While sizable individual collections existed in both the Chesapeake and New England in the seventeenth and early eighteenth centuries, northern colonists proved especially pivotal in broadening the impact of their libraries and, in so doing, the definition of libraries in British America. In particular, New Englanders were the first Americans to entertain the notion of operating libraries for collective readerships. John Harvard pioneered this trail in 1638 when he bequeathed his personal library of more than 400 volumes to the fledgling college bearing his name. The first known inventory of this collection taken in 1654 suggests that Harvard's library was heavily weighted to theology (constituting not quite two-thirds of the whole) and similarly heavy on Latin titles, with only roughly a third of the volumes in English (Cadbury 1943; Stone 1977, 187). Over the second half of the century, the college slowly realized how to fit its library into academic life and by piecemeal created rules governing its use, maintenance, and location. It was not until 1667, for example, that college overseers formally established regulations for the use of the library that included setting norms for lending periods, access, inventory, and selection of librarians. In 1676, the library moved to Old Harvard Hall, where it was given a designated room that included numbered bookcases where the collection was likely shelved by volume size (Kraus 1973, 144). In 1723, the library issued its first printed book catalog. By then, the collection had more English volumes, as well as a growing number of literature, science, history, and philosophy titles; the catalog totaled the library's size at just over 3,500 volumes (Winans 1981, 8).

At midcentury, New Englanders began linking libraries to larger readerships in another way: they created the initial stirrings of what could be called a public library movement (Shera 1949). Library historians point to Robert Keayne's 1653 bequest of property and books to the town of Boston as the beginning of the long, slow evolution of public libraries in America. While the ultimate use and fate of Keayne's library in public hands is uncertain, the terms of his legacy clearly indicated a new way of thinking about the use of a personal library in the colonies; Keayne wanted his books to be available to local citizens and for them in turn to enlarge the now municipally shared collection. Although Keayne was first in making this gesture, he was not alone. Samuel Eaton left New Haven his personal library in his 1658 will. By the 1650s and 1660s, town leaders elsewhere in New England, including those in Concord and Dorchester, discussed acquiring book collections for the use of their local citizenry.

In all these instances, including Keayne's initial gift to Boston, the results of these efforts were spotty and inconsistent. Little evidence suggests that these private-turned-public collections were well organized or maintained. Moreover, it is unclear whether these volumes were consistently made available to anyone save the person charged with care of the books and other town leaders. These first incarnations of public libraries are thus more important for what they represent than for their actual impact. They represent the beginning of changes in how American colonists thought about libraries: how they might be organized, whom they might serve, and who might oversee them.

It is only fitting that New England was the locus of such new thinking about libraries. In several ways, the region's character provided fertile ground for this sort of intellectual experimentation. Not only did the orientation of regional life around towns make such settlements likely mediums for communal access to printed materials, but the emphasis that Puritanism placed on literacy encouraged New Englanders of varying economic levels to value books. Over the 1630s and 1640s, the area saw a number of British American "firsts" related to intellectual activities, including the founding of a college, the establishment of a printing press, and government-decreed compulsory literacy education.

The key innovations to come out of New England in the early stages of colonization—establishing a college library and using government to provide people with access to printed materials—marked an important stage of development for American libraries. For the first time, the colonial notion of libraries expanded beyond just the private collections of wealthy individuals, although surely the maturation of these trends would not come for another century or more.

A southern contribution to this unfolding chapter of library development came late in the seventeenth century when the Reverend Thomas Bray launched a plan to send book collections to Anglican parishes in Maryland. This plan was the first in a series of proposals Bray drew up beginning in 1695 upon his appointment as overseer for the regulation and organization of the Church of England in that colony. In numerous ways, the collections Bray established provided critical impetus for library development in the southern colonies. Throughout the seventeenth century, the southern colonies had lagged behind their northern neighbors in library advancements. To be sure, the South was home to many fine individual collections, yet little was established in the South beyond those. Indeed, had it not been for the Bray libraries, the establishment of the College of William and Mary library in 1693 (which was subsequently lost to fire in 1705) would likely have been the sole benchmark for southern library development in the seventeenth century. The Bray collections were pivotal in diffusing not just books but ideas about libraries into southern society.

According to Bray's 1695 proposals, which were sent both to London Anglican leaders and to the colonial Maryland Assembly, he aimed to provide Anglican clergy with books that would best equip them to carry out their religious work. He hoped that this scheme would provide colonial ministers going to America each with "a sufficient Library of well-chosen books." In his view, such a collection should include not only theological works but also a range of history, science, government, law, and mathematics (Laugher 1973, 19). By 1697, as his *Essay Towards Promoting All Necessary and Useful Knowledge* indicated, Bray's plans expanded to include sending libraries to other British American colonies and to local parishes in England and Wales. One of the most important features of Bray's plans was that he imagined multiple types of libraries being of use in the colonies. In particular, Bray laid out plans for three separate types of libraries: parochial libraries, provincial libraries, and "layman's libraries." The parochial libraries, the model advocated in his initial 1695 proposals, were to directly aid individual ministers in the execution of their religious work. The collections would be under ministerial control, and the clerics themselves would be responsible for the maintenance of the books. Provincial libraries were to be established in a key town in a colony so that the collection might be accessible to all interested. And layman's libraries were intended to be a series of books given to ministers that could be lent or given to parishioners on request.

Between 1695 and 1704, Bray laid out more than 3,000 pounds to have libraries organized and shipped to America. During this time, he oversaw the establishment of some eighty libraries, including thirty-eight parochial libraries, six provincial libraries (at Annapolis, Bath [North Carolina], Boston, Charleston, New York, and Philadelphia), thirty-seven layman's libraries, and assorted other collections sent to Newfoundland and the West Indies (Laugher 1973, 24, 34). The size of these libraries varied considerably. A parochial library might contain anywhere from 10 to 300 volumes, while a provincial library typically started at just over 200 volumes but might range as high as 1,000 volumes, as did the one at Annapolis (Laugher 1973, 35). The first of the provincial libraries, the Annapolitan Library benefited from a special grant of 100 guineas from Princess Anne and served as a model for the formation of other provincial libraries. Only the Philadelphia library came close to rivaling its size with around 850 volumes (Davis 1978, 2: 513). These and other provincial libraries contained roughly two-thirds theological works and one-third history, geography, philosophy, medicine, and poetry titles. The Boston provincial library proved the exception to this pattern, with a greater theological emphasis. The sizes of layman's libraries are harder to ascertain both because few survived intact and because these collections included volumes given away to parishioners such as prayer books and Bibles.

Bray's activities had a significant effect on the trajectory of American library development. By introducing multiple types of libraries, Bray helped broaden the colonial vocabulary regarding library organizational models. Bray's layman's libraries, for instance, marked the first real attempt in America to support lending libraries of a formal sort. Indeed, in his plans for the enlargement of colonial libraries, Bray imagined libraries sharing collection catalogs and charging small annual subscription fees to facilitate new acquisitions, ideas that presaged eighteenth-century lending library practices. Offering visionary ideas that shaped American understandings of libraries, Bray had an impact on colonists' access to books that is harder to assess. The main beneficiaries of the parochial and provincial libraries—ministers, vestrymen, and political officeholders—were the colonists most likely to have access to printed materials already. The layman's libraries may have introduced tracts into households previously without books.

All the same, Bray's activities left a definite legacy in another important area of American library development: he brought the New England dialogue about the relationship between government and libraries to the colonial South. Particularly in his attempt to secure assistance for provincial libraries, Bray appealed directly to colonial legislatures for aid in protecting and preserving the collections he sent across the Atlantic. Three legislatures—those of Maryland and both Carolinas—took up his charge by parlaying their respective provincial libraries into public libraries of sorts. These legislatures did so by passing laws governing the oversight and use of their Bray provincial libraries. They appointed boards of library commissioners, required that catalogs of books be issued, and outlined rules regarding circulation of volumes. Typical examples of the circulation rules included charging a borrower three times a volume's value if it were lost or damaged and assigning lending periods according the volume size, with folio having the longest circulation period (Laugher 1973, 31). In the case of North Carolina, the legislature's measures were especially proactive because the provincial library it oversaw had initially been a parochial one. In all three cases, colonial legislators helped secure government protection for libraries, although they were not as successful in securing public funding for the expansion or development of these collections. Not all provinces took such an activist approach—in the seaports of Boston, New York, and Philadelphia, lawmakers regarded provincial libraries as the property of the local Anglican parishes and therefore none of their affair. Nonetheless, the door not only to collective library formation but also to government oversight and operation of such libraries was now opened in southern as well as northern colonial America.

LIBRARY COMPANIES

As the eighteenth century unfolded, a new geographic locus of library activity began to emerge as the Middle Colonies matured into a thriving commercial region. Initially, libraries in the mid-Atlantic mimicked those of New England and the Chesapeake. Like their counterparts in the other regions of British America, wealthy colonists in the mid-Atlantic area began amassing personal libraries of substance and value. And here, too, religion played an important role in establishing libraries for collective audiences. Perhaps inspired by the Bray library housed at Christ Church, the Philadelphia Monthly Meeting of the Society of Friends (Quakers) established the first non-Anglican lending library in the region, the earliest records of which date from 1705. The Middle Colonies would contribute far more to colonial library history than merely carrying on the trends of other regions, however. In the increasingly urbane seaport of Philadelphia in particular, colonists in the mid-1700s would take the lead in rethinking the organization, operation, and maintenance of American libraries. In doing so, they would help redefine the nature and purpose of these emerging institutions.

In the middle decades of the eighteenth century, the American colonial library scene changed dramatically as colonists pioneered a new model of collective library establishment and as some enterprising souls transformed book lending into a profitable business. As a result of these activities, the number and types of libraries expanded dramatically across the Atlantic seaboard, sharply improving the ratio of libraries to people. These new types of libraries served a broader audience than the great gentlemen's private libraries, or those of the Anglican mission effort. Yet a person's access to these new organizations was still predicated on their access to some level of wealth whether to pay for shares in a subscription library or lending fees at a circulating one. The other major area of library growth over the heart of the eighteenth century also retained the link between books and privilege as the number of colonial collegiate libraries tripled. By the 1770s and 1780s, all libraries and the social privilege they served struggled to survive the wartime dislocations brought by the American Revolution.

In 1731, a small group of Philadelphians spearheaded by Benjamin Franklin introduced a new type of library into the colonies by creating the Library Company of Philadelphia, America's first subscription library. The impetus for the Library Company came from the activities of Franklin's mutual improvement club, the Junto.

Constituted largely of young, skilled, male artisans, the Junto met regularly at a local Philadelphia tavern to discuss a range of literary, moral, and business topics (Lemay 2006, 332–356). Once the club moved out of the taverns into a meeting room at a member's house, Franklin proposed bringing together their libraries in order to give members access to a wider range of reading materials. Although this effort failed, it nonetheless inspired Franklin to propose the formation of the Library Company to be operated on the subscription model of library popular in Britain. This type of library was collective, yet still private; a limited number of people shared access to the same collection of books based on their ownership of library company shares. The cost of shares plus yearly membership dues provided the library with funds to cover new book acquisition, maintenance of existing volumes, and staffing and collection housing costs. Not just anyone could become a company shareholder. Typically these institutions used some vetting process that often required recommendations from company members and approval of the company's directors.

Franklin's proposed Library Company found fifty backers fairly quickly. The all-male founding members came from a broader social background than had the Junto's affiliates. Included among the company members were still skilled artisans, but they were joined by merchants, landowners, and professional men. Each one invested 40 shillings and agreed to a 10-shilling per annum fee thereafter. By November 1731, organizers chose an initial set of directors and established a schedule for fee payments. With 100 pounds in hand and 25 more pounds to come in annually, the fledgling company immediately turned to creating its initial book order. With the assistance of James Logan, the directors drew up and placed their order with London agent Peter Collinson. When the books arrived in October 1732, they signaled much about this young library and what its members desired from it. The initial set of books was wide-ranging, including titles in history, classics, mathematics, politics, philology, and natural philosophy, as well as etiquette, architecture, geography, and assorted individual volumes on other subjects. Notably absent were theological works. This assortment represented a marriage of practical works with those valued as part of a well-educated person's vocabulary. Library Company of Philadelphia shareholders could no longer bemoan the cost or difficulty in acquiring a well-developed library. Now the cost of a share and yearly fees opened the door to a collection that grew in scale and scope over the eighteenth century. The 1741 catalog (the first surviving published catalog) listed 375 volumes; the 1770 catalog had more than 2,000 entries.

In the wake of the Library Company of Philadelphia's establishment, colonists elsewhere soon formed similar organizations. In Benjamin Franklin's famous words, the Philadelphia library became "the Mother of all the North American Subscription Libraries" (Franklin 1987, 1372). In the two decades following its founding, library companies sprang up in Connecticut, Maine, New Jersey, New York, Rhode Island, and South Carolina. Philadelphia itself became home to three more companies, while five other Pennsylvania towns soon boasted their own library companies as well. Before the Revolution, at least sixty-four subscription libraries existed in the colonies, almost all of which were located in New England and the Middle Colonies (Thompson 1952, 54–55).

Out of these numerous organizations, the Redwood Library (Newport, Rhode Island), the Charleston Library Society, and the New York Society Library emerged as the strongest. All operated on the same model as the Library Company of Philadelphia, and each one had direct ties to Philadelphia. Established in 1747, the Redwood Library bore the name of its main benefactor, Abraham Redwood, who donated 500 pounds for its establishment. Educated in Philadelphia, Redwood made his fortune from mercantile holdings in Rhode Island and the British West Indies. In his famous American travelogue, naturalist Peter Kalm suggested an even more important Philadelphia tie—he claimed that a visit to the Library Company of Philadelphia directly inspired Redwood's largesse. By 1764, the Redwood Library offered members almost 700 titles (McCorison 1965). The Charleston Library Society was founded in 1748 on the heels of its Rhode Island counterpart, and it had links to Philadelphia, too. In this case, one of the founders was Peter Timothy, son of the first librarian of the Library Company of Philadelphia, and in its early years the group shared the same London agent, William Strahan. The Charleston group grew quickly, attracting 129 members within its first two years. By the 1770s, its book catalog indicated not only the expected secular, British titles but also holdings in Americana and fiction (Raven 2002, 185, 193). Founded in 1754, the New York Society Library lagged a little behind the other companies. By that time, New York had witnessed several failed attempts to create some sort of public library, starting with a seventeenth-century Anglican library from Thomas Bray and ending with James Parker's attempts in the 1740s to shore up the Society for the Propagation of the Gospel's Corporation Library. When Parker, who was Benjamin Franklin's printing partner, gave up operation of the Corporation Library, its holdings were divided between storage and City Hall. About 2,000 of its volumes were folded into the New York Society Library collection (Keep 1908).

The emergence of American library companies marked an important shift in how colonists understood and constituted libraries. Most important, these new libraries signaled that colonists were now truly engaged in collective library formation. By the mid–eighteenth century, there was a critical mass of colonists, especially in key urban areas, who wanted to join forces to increase their access to a wide range of reading materials. This is significant not just because it moved library formation away from its traditional locus on the individual. The use of the library company model also meant that for the first time colonists were together shaping libraries to meet their own readership needs. The only collective libraries in America—colleges and church libraries—had all been formed by outside donors or philanthropists with a specific educational or religious project shaping collection contents. With library companies, members chose materials for themselves.

Equally important, the library companies signaled a wider number of individuals having access to diverse book collections. Membership was restricted to some extent along economic lines. Only persons of some means could afford the luxury entailed in library membership costs that included initial stock purchase costs and annual fees, not to mention the education and time to use a company's resources. Stock purchase alone at the Library Company of Philadelphia cost more than six pounds in 1741. Yet if one had the money, joining a library company was a quick and easy way to have a well-stocked bookshelf, an attractive alternative for many men of modest means.

Library companies not only involved more men in libraries, but their patrons also included women. Convention among these libraries held that not only stockholders but also their immediate family were eligible to use the company's books, thus carrying on the tradition of individual libraries of "great gentlemen" being accessible to family and friends. Therefore, while early library company stockholders were almost invariably male, their female kin had access to the collections of these companies. Although a few learned colonial women such as Philadelphian Elizabeth Graeme Fergusson had their own substantive book collections, many others welcomed the chance to use the book stacks of a library company (Hayes 1996, 11–13). Scattered references in women's diaries and letters indicate that some women considered themselves library members in all but name. The Library Company of Philadelphia formalized women's involvement in the 1760s when it welcomed female stockholders in their own right. One interesting implication of this step was that married women stripped of their legal rights under the system of coverture actually gained enhanced legal standing if the library company they belonged to was an incorporated entity. Under the terms of incorporation, all stockholders—regardless of gender or marital status—had legal rights and obligations that included suing and being sued (Fatherly 2000, 141–143).

College Libraries

As library companies flourished, New England and the Middle Colonies also saw an expansion in the number of collegiate libraries. Going into the eighteenth century such collections had numbered three: Harvard, William and Mary, and Yale. Thanks to the Great Awakening and other factors accelerating the foundation of colonial colleges, that number tripled by midcentury as the College of New Jersey (Princeton), King's College (Columbia), the College of Philadelphia, the College of Rhode Island (Brown), Queen's College (Rutgers), and Dartmouth College all took root. Attached to liberal arts institutions focused largely on the training of

Protestant ministers, the collections of these college libraries all emphasized theological works. Yet they also had carefully chosen concentrations in literature, history, science, philosophy, and government, which altogether composed roughly half of each collegiate collection. This was the case despite the quite disparate total size of collegiate libraries that ranged anywhere from a few hundred volumes to Harvard's impressive collection of more than 9,000 titles by 1790 (Kraus 1973, 156).

The overall size of an academic collection was dependent on the funding an institution made available for book buying, as well as the generosity of its alumni and its connections to well-placed individuals and associations. The Harvard library experience exemplifies this lesson. In 1764, fire almost totally destroyed the college's library. In the face of this disaster, 273 friends of the college rallied to replace the collection. Donors included alumni, colonial intellectuals like Benjamin Franklin, local towns and counties, the Society for Propagating the Gospel in Foreign Parts, and the Massachusetts provincial government (Stone 1977, 102).

Some colleges provided fertile ground for additional libraries beyond their main institutional ones. In 1769, Harvard University led the way in forming student literary society libraries. These collections were specifically designed to provide resources for the college debates sponsored by these organizations. Such collections were available to students whenever they desired, thereby alleviating the need to abide by the borrowing restrictions of the main college library. Dartmouth College students followed suit, forming literary societies and accompanying libraries for them beginning in 1783. The other type of academic library to form in this era was the specialized academic library such as those established for medical schools at Harvard University and the College of Pennsylvania.

CIRCULATING LIBRARIES

In the 1760s, even as library companies and collegiate libraries blossomed, an entirely new model of library tentatively surfaced, one destined to become a mainstay of the early American library landscape. In 1762, proprietor William Rind announced his plans to operate the colonies' very first circulating library in Annapolis. Opening its doors in early 1763, this venture aimed to turn book lending into a profit-making business. Rind's operation discarded the library company goal of elevating colonial culture in favor of serving readers and their tastes as they were. The only requirement to patronize Rind's library was the ability to meet his one-year fee of twenty-seven shillings, and he explicitly welcomed both women and men as prospective customers. His operation offered patrons 150 titles from which to choose, including *Pamela* and *Tom Jones,* Montesquieu's *Spirit of Laws,* and works by Pope and Milton

(Kaser 1980, 20–21). While Rind's collection represented the type of books being read by colonists at the time, his selection was limited in its overall size, and it may not have offered enough new or unique titles to attract sufficient customers; Rind's business failed within a year of its opening.

While new on his side of the Atlantic, Rind's idea was well established not only in Britain but also in Europe more broadly. Hints of book rental operations remain in records from Renaissance France and Restoration England. In their eighteenth-century incarnation, such lending ventures popped up next to bookshops and coffeehouses in Germany, France, and Switzerland (Kaser 1980, 15). Circulating libraries appeared in England by the 1740s and quickly found a niche by catering to the growing leisured middle classes. Once fiction became a growing part of the London book trade, these libraries capitalized on offering this new type of material to patrons. The only operative difference between American circulating libraries and those abroad was the colonial dependence on the transatlantic book trade for stock. While American printers existed, it would remain far more cost-effective to purchase books overseas late into the eighteenth century.

Despite Rind's quick failure in Annapolis, other colonial entrepreneurs soon tried their hand at the circulating library business in the 1760s and 1770s. All the circulating libraries established before the Revolution were located in seaport cities, namely, Charleston, New York, Boston, Philadelphia, and Baltimore. While records for circulating libraries are spotty at best, the ten libraries that followed Rind's seem all to have had far larger book holdings to offer customers, with collection size ranging from 800 to perhaps 3,000 volumes. Several also enjoyed great longevity. The longest lived of these businesses lasted upwards of four years, including both Robert Bell's Philadelphia enterprise and George Wood's Charleston operation (Kaser 1980). Both of these operations were likely helped by their location. They were in cities that had long-standing library companies and multiple booksellers, indicating a local appetite for books large enough to be served in multiple ways. Yet location alone did not determine a circulating library's success or failure. Ultimately its survival depended on securing a sufficient number of customers quickly enough to return a profit on the initial investment in books and facilities. The colonial-era circulating libraries most likely to do so, and therefore most likely to succeed over the longer term, tended to follow a set of standard practices. Despite differences in location and proprietors, these libraries regularly printed catalogs, set subscription rates around one pound, established firm circulation periods, publicized hours of operation, and explicitly welcomed both male and female customers. They offered patrons access to more than 1,000 volumes that were weighted to fiction and literature but also included significant amounts of biography, history, and travel writing (Kaser 1980, 39).

The circulating library offered the reading public a new and fundamentally different organizational model of library than that of the library company. One of the key differences between the two types of library was the relationship of the book borrower to the organization: the circulating library patron was a customer, while the library company member was a stockholder and possibly a member of a corporation. This difference meant that patrons occupied quite disparate places in these organizations. In the library company, members helped make decisions about book acquisition, hours of operation, annual dues, employment of staff, and even admittance of other borrowers to the company's stacks. In the circulating library, all these decisions lay solely in the hands of the proprietor. The only control a customer had in the circulating library was the decision of whether or not to patronize the business. And this highlights another important structural difference, namely, the economic configuration of the two types of libraries. Library companies used a joint-stock model to provide members with dividends in the form of better book choices, whereas circulating libraries aimed to turn a financial profit for business owners by meeting patrons' book-borrowing needs.

These structural differences in turn shaped the practices of a circulating library in ways that further set it apart from a library company. Circulating library proprietors were not especially interested in socially vetting their clients. Indeed, Annapolis owner William Rind advertised his operation as designed to "open and extend the Fountains of Knowledge, which are at present shut against all but Men of affluent Fortunes" (quoted in Hayes 1996, 13). While customers still needed literacy and the money for shop fees, indicating they were farther up the social ladder than others, they did not have to be gentry or merchant elites. Circulating libraries lacked any investment in raising or shaping the taste of the reading public; they simply wanted to serve client reading needs. With these priorities in mind, most proprietors pitched their businesses to middling-rank customers, and one important way they did so was through the composition of their book collections. Circulating libraries stocked a higher proportion of literature than did companies, and they offered patrons fiction titles, something most library companies spurned doing. Carrying such volumes gave circulating libraries a niche in a growing market as fiction became an important part of the American reading scene and helped secure women (of middling and upper-rank standing) as customers. By the 1770s, one New York circulating library proprietor explicitly advertised that "the ladies are his customers" (Kaser 1980, 37).

While the character of circulating libraries meant that they often catered largely to a middling rank and/or female customer base, some book lovers patronized these businesses simply because they offered conveniences that library companies did not. Proprietors were quicker to respond to patron desires for flexible hours and rapid turnover of book stock, as well as for a variety of fee schedules, including monthly, quarterly, or annually. Their typical locations in urban commercial areas also made them convenient for male patrons. By choosing to patronize this sort of library, circulating library customers enjoyed easy access to a wide variety of literature and fiction. Their choice did not carry with it the social prestige that accompanied library company membership.

WARTIME DEVELOPMENTS

By 1770, the number of extant collective libraries in colonial America had climbed to seventy-four, a far cry from earlier in the century when that number barely stayed in double digits (McMullen 2000, 25). The growth in this number over the eighteenth century was almost entirely due to library companies and circulating libraries. These libraries were located disproportionately in the New England and mid-Atlantic regions, although Charleston boasted an impressive library company and circulating library, and Williamsburg had the rebuilt academic library of William and Mary. During the 1770s, as tensions between the colonies and Britain heightened, all types of libraries soon faced great challenges to their operation and survival. During the years of the Revolutionary War, many circulating libraries closed up shop; library companies suspended operation; and academic libraries faced military occupation. No new libraries of any type were founded during the war, and existing ones found their transatlantic book shipments suspended for the duration.

The extent to which the war affected a library was in part a question of location but also of organizational type. For circulating libraries, it was at best challenging for proprietors to carry on their businesses in the midst of rampant inflation, the displacement of civilians, and the military enlistment of thousands. Some owners, like Samuel Loudon in New York, did not even try. Loudon closed up shop in the face of military invasion, not to reopen until 1784 (Stone 1977, 305). Others redeployed their talents for the duration. Lewis Nicola, proprietor of a Philadelphia venture, was lucky enough to find employment with the fledgling American military, establishing the collection for a military academy library (Stone 1977, 62). While library companies also faced challenges in serving their patrons in the midst of wartime disruptions, they had no imperative to turn a profit, and this freed them to remain open for their members as long as was reasonable. Once military enlistment, occupation, or dislocation from military encroachments kept library members away, companies then closed until fighting subsided in their region.

Among those companies that remained operational during the war, the Library Company of Philadelphia deserves particular note. As this company kept its doors open, it found itself serving new and different patrons during these unusual times. Located in Carpenter's Hall near the Pennsylvania State House, the Library Company quickly found itself caught up in the tide of Revolutionary politics. As the First and the Second Continental Congress met in Philadelphia, the Library Company extended membership privileges to the delegates. Soon Revolutionary politicians from throughout the colonies were the most frequent visitors. Both geographic proximity and overlap between the Library Company and congressional membership made this invitation logical. Benjamin Franklin, John Dickinson, Francis Hopkinson, and Benjamin Rush all belonged to both groups. Nine members of the Library Company were signers of the Declaration of Independence. When in session, the Continental Congress used the Library Company's books and deposited copies of its proceedings there. Another new group of patrons appeared on the Library Company's doorstep when a nine-month British occupation of Philadelphia began in late 1777. British officers availed themselves of the collection without any negative repercussions for the library's holdings. By the war's end, the Library Company easily transitioned back into serving its shareholders and also opened its doors to delegates to the Constitutional Convention. Other Philadelphia libraries were not so fortunate. In 1777, General Horatio Gates ordered the Loganian Library shut so that ammunition could be stored there. By the war's end, the building was in such poor repair that it never again opened to the public; its books were officially merged with the Library Company of Philadelphia's collection in 1792.

Academic libraries also faced tough times during the war. Seen by both the British and Americans as ideal locations for barracks, headquarters, and storage, American colleges often endured military occupation. As colleges shut down and sent pupils and faculty home, their libraries suffered at best neglect and at worst destruction. Depending on local circumstances, a collegiate librarian might remove an entire collection when that drastic measure seemed both warranted and feasible. The College of Rhode Island, Harvard, King's College, and Yale all sought to protect their collections by this method. Yet removal did not guarantee safety, as King's College soon discovered when it removed its library to New York's City Hall. When the British invaded the region in fall of 1777, soldiers broke in and plundered the academic collection, actions that became the subject of several British military orders demanding the books be returned. While removal proved more successful for other college libraries, it still had its risks. Yale lost books in this fashion, while Harvard ironically gained some thanks to confiscated loyalist property that was turned over to the college (Stone 1977, 106–107).

All things considered, American libraries generally survived the disruptive years of the Revolutionary War in relatively good shape. Many were in a position to resume their services quickly upon the cessation of hostilities in 1782. Over the next two decades, however, libraries—like all American institutions—had to adjust to operating in a changed social and political climate. The transformation of the colonies into an independent nation instilled a desire in many to cultivate an American intellectual culture that was distinct from, rather than emulative of, Britain's high-culture world. This cultural change would affect libraries as they were called upon to adapt to the changing reading tastes of their patrons. Even more important, however, the Revolution had issued a challenge to the logic of social privilege and the notion that the few had a natural right to power. Throughout the colonial era, most libraries had served that logic, protecting knowledge as a form of power meant for those with economic and racial privilege. Even those libraries that served broader constituencies still operated out of this framework, driven as they were by philanthropy. Libraries meant to serve colonists would now have to find their footing in serving citizens of a republic.

THE LATE EIGHTEENTH CENTURY

In the 1780s and 1790s, American libraries faced a new social and political climate. During the years of the Confederation and the early Republic, Americans assigned new value to print culture and to institutions that could provide people with access to those resources. Over the end of the century, more Americans in total achieved literacy than ever before; in the northern states in particular, the free population had achieved near-universal literacy by the turn of the 1800s. The culture surrounding that literacy emphasized it as a necessary first step toward an educated citizenry, in whose hands the fate of the new Republic rested. These changes placed libraries in a position of importance: in service to the virtue of the Republic, they could help bridge the gap between the people and the print world. This shift offered libraries a different operating ethos than they had had in the colonial era. While different types of libraries accepted this challenge each in its own fashion, circulating libraries especially thrived in this era. At the same time, the relationship between libraries and government permanently altered as federal and state governments forged lasting links with libraries.

As institutions predicated on privilege, library companies had to make key alterations in how they operated in the postindependence era. To be sure, there were adherents to the traditionally exclusive and Anglocentric nature of these libraries well into the mid-1800s. But the changing political and social circumstances of the late 1700s encouraged library company directors to adapt their companies to better suit new times. Library companies had by and large been formed to elevate colonial culture broadly and the gentility and intellectuality of privileged colonists specifically. By the 1780s, rather than seeing reading as an instrument of privilege, Americans viewed it as a vital cornerstone to developing a rational and virtuous citizenry who were capable of directing the young Republic. In light of such changes, many library companies began opening their book collections to nonmembers. These companies were still just that—joint stock ventures in which stockholders made key decisions about organizational policy—but now non-stockowners could use library resources. For a fee, nonmembers could borrow books and without charge could use the library's reading room. In the case of the Library Company of Philadelphia, at least, such liberal policies extended to shareholding. Between 1789 and 1793, this institution offered 266 shares as payment to carpenters and other skilled laborers for work performed on the library's new building. Such adaptations in policy earned the Library Company the telling sobriquets of "the City Library" and "the Philadelphia Library" (Wolf et al. 1995, 37, 39). This sort of democratization definitely had its limits, though. In the case of Philadelphia, the city's upper crust continued to dominate the Library Company's board of directors and to resist the acquisition of fiction.

Rather than waiting for the doors of library companies to open, some readers decided to form new libraries to suit their needs. Around 1795, for example, the first women's library society was established in New Hampshire (McMullen 2000, 67). While many women of middling and upper social ranks had availed themselves of colonial-era libraries, the new emphasis on education in the Republic brought new legitimacy to women's reading and to female education more broadly. Prescriptive ideologies such as republican womanhood and the emergence of women's academies brought female readers clearly into public view. The New Hampshire society was an early harbinger of what would become a widespread movement for female library and literary organizations by the 1820s, a movement that would be especially strong in the Midwest. By the early 1800s, other similarly specific types of libraries formed to serve children, young men, mechanics and workingmen, and mercantile men. Typically, these libraries operated on members' annual dues, borrowing fees, and gifts rather than on a joint-stock basis. Denied access to such organizations, African Americans in the North formed their own counterpart libraries in the 1820s and 1830s.

For their part, circulating libraries entered quite easily into the intellectual and economic marketplace of the post-Revolutionary world. This type of library thrived as the total number of ventures grew. Between 1783 and 1800, thirty-nine new circulating libraries were founded across the United States, not just in the traditional library strongholds of New England and the mid-Atlantic but everywhere from Georgia to New Hampshire to the trans-Allegheny West (Kaser 1980, 48). Not only did the total number of these libraries increase, but their business practices also matured, successfully shifting to fit the needs of new customers and new locations. Across regions, some trends in these practices are clear. The median size of collections and the amount of fiction in these libraries increased. Some operations began successfully attaching themselves to other business ventures beyond bookshops; circulating libraries combined with general stores and dry goods operations, and by the early 1800s one even joined forces with a millinery shop. In Pennsylvania, circulating libraries took on a unique level of business specialization when two German-language libraries opened, one in 1785 in the Philadelphia area, followed by another in 1800 in Lancaster (Kaser 1980, 51).

During these decades of expansion and maturation, three circulating libraries are particularly worthy of note. In 1789, proprietor John Dabney opened a lending operation in Salem, Massachusetts. His 1801 catalog of holdings suggests that his library offered customers a sizable stock—1,770 titles in total. Its composition seemed geared for success with circulating patrons, as it was weighted to fiction (41 percent), with strong secondary holdings in literature and science (14 and 13 percent, respectively) and tertiary holdings in geography/travel, history, and biography (7 percent each). No doubt this good-sized, well-balanced stock played a role in Dabney's library achieving its distinguishing feature: it stayed in operation for thirty years. In a business where four years has been considered a lengthy run before the war, Dabney's set a new bar for success in the world of circulating libraries (Kaser 1980). Also notable was William P. Blake's library in Boston, which operated over the

1790s. Blake's establishment rivaled Dabney's overall size (peaking with 1,575 titles in 1798), but it lacked similar breadth. In this difference lies the important function that Blake's business offered Bostonians: his operation probably offered more fiction titles that any other in the area (Kaser 1980, 56). Over the 1790s, Blake's catalogs show a steady climb in fiction; in 1800, fiction titles constituted 63 percent of the total collection. Finally, Hocquet Caritat's 1790s business in New York deserves mention quite simply because it was the largest circulating library in America. Its 1799 catalog included 2,995 titles. Of that total, the library had more titles in literature than its competitors of the time; Caritat had roughly equal holdings in fiction and literature. These two categories combined accounted for 58 percent of the total stock, with holdings in theology, history, and biography all trailing in single digits (Kaser 1980, 51).

As familiar types of libraries made adjustments to better serve their patrons in the republican era, cultural and structural changes in American politics created the conditions for new types of libraries that were explicitly linked to the national project. In 1791, private citizens in Massachusetts led the way in creating a new kind of library they hoped would preserve the unfolding history of the young Republic—the state historical society library. Pioneering this model, the Massachusetts Historical Society began with 100 members and the ambitious vision of preserving the history of the entire United States, not just one state. Americans were keen to document their Revolutionary experiences; libraries were an essential part of all state historical societies from the outset. As memories faded and war veterans aged, state historical societies took up the charge of collecting and interpreting the young country's past. By doing so, they hoped to provide future generations with a touchstone for understanding the origins of the Republic even as they helped create a meaningful past for the fledgling nation.

At the same time that such private ventures went forward, governments themselves moved into library creation and operation in several ways. These activities marked a significant turn in the post-Revolutionary library era as they signaled the redefinition of state power to include library ownership and management. There were some colonial precedents for such government activities. As discussed earlier, in the seventeenth century some New England towns flirted with maintaining collections willed to them, while a few southern legislatures used legal remedies to protect libraries gifted to them by the Anglican Church. In these cases, however, local or provincial governments neither created these book collections nor provided financial backing for their expansion. The eighteenth century saw a few experiments with government-backed libraries of a quite different sort. In 1745, the Pennsylvania Assembly started a library specifically to serve legislators, who had long relied on the Library Company of Philadelphia's collection. It took another decade before the Assembly's library had its own room, a sizable collection, or a librarian (Korty 1965, 62–64). The other experiment linking government and libraries aimed to put state government in the position of creating and operating a public library. In 1779,

Thomas Jefferson introduced a bill before the Virginia General Assembly proposing the establishment of a state library to be located in Richmond. The bill stipulated 2,000 pounds for book and map acquisition plus another 2,000 pounds for librarian compensation. It also laid out specific guidelines for the appointment of librarians and for book use policies, including the stipulation that all reading was to be done on site (Stone 1977, 214). Arguably the middle of the Revolutionary War was not the best time to ask a fledgling state government to lay out thousands of pounds on books and librarians, let alone build a collection from scratch. While failing to pass, Jefferson's proposal anticipated the lively debates of the antebellum era regarding public funding of libraries.

In the late 1780s, the creation of a federal government injected new intentionality and commitment into this sporadic state-library relationship. As officeholders and politicians worked to realize the bureaucratic structure sketched out by the U.S. Constitution, they saw libraries as a necessary resource for governing and making law. In 1789, they made several notable moves in this direction. As part of the creation of the Department of State, its secretary was made responsible for all papers, records, and books for the department, including materials amassed by the Department of Foreign Affairs under the Continental Congress. This directive was taken as authorization for the State Department library. The United States Auditor's library was also begun in 1789, a collection intended to contain public documents and legal materials (Stone 1977, 63). Most important in the pivotal year of 1789, the first proposals regarding the Library of Congress were introduced. Representative Elbridge Gerry of Massachusetts introduced a motion that a committee be formed to explore establishing a book collection that would serve Congress's specific needs. After the motion was tabled for almost a year, a committee was finally appointed, and Gerry reported to Congress on its behalf in June 1790. Given the easy access Congress had to the collections of the Library Company of Philadelphia and then the New York Society Library, nothing much came of this issue until the federal government readied for its move to Washington, D.C. In 1800, a clause of the removal legislation signed by President John Adams provided for a congressional book collection to be purchased and housed in the new city. Official recognition of the Library of Congress came in 1802 with "An Act Concerning the Library for Use of Both Houses of Congress," which spelled out its location, use, and funding.

As the federal government started creating and operating new libraries, state governments also became more intimately connected with library establishment and management. In 1795, North Carolina chartered the nation's first public university and, as part of that institution, a new collegiate library. In contrast to colonial colleges, the University of North Carolina had plans and donations for its library firmly in hand well before classes began. Starting in 1796, a number of state governments began regulating the operation and incorporation of "social" libraries (a category including any library formed by individuals that was not operated for profit). As social libraries mushroomed in number, northeastern states sought to shape the terms under which these organizations might operate and more particularly how they might achieve legal incorporation status. New York's legislation, which was the first of its kind, was quite specific in its stipulations for libraries seeking incorporation: it required a minimum of twenty members and a subscription amount of at least forty pounds; it limited the organization's holding of real and personal property to $500 annually (exclusive of books); and it defined quite tightly the rights accompanying incorporation (Stone 1977, 216). Massachusetts's foray into social library oversight in 1798 was equally detailed, while the other states that soon followed suit tended to be more general in their stipulations regarding the incorporation of social libraries. By the 1830s, Vermont, Connecticut, New Hampshire, and Rhode Island all passed such laws.

CONCLUSION

The story of early American libraries across two centuries is clearly one of growth, whether measured by the number of library types, the total number of libraries, the size of collections, or their longevity. Although that expansion is significant in its own right, it reflects an even more important story about the evolution of American attitudes toward books and reading. Over two centuries, Americans changed the way they understood reading and libraries as institutions that served that activity. For early colonists, libraries were the province of the few who had the most. For those privileged women and men, libraries provided access to materials that helped them cultivate claims to gentility and sociability, sharpen religious understanding, build universal and useful knowledge, and relish leisure time. As barriers to literacy and education weakened over the second half of eighteenth century, more people gained the opportunity to engage in these activities. Then, at the end of that century, the very meanings attached to reading underwent a significant shift from valuing reading as a tool of privilege to seeing it as a task of political responsibility. As a result of this sea change, Americans began viewing library access as a right of citizenship. As libraries adjusted to this new understanding, their operation revealed critical questions that Americans had yet to answer. Were all people equally entitled to library access? And what role should the government play in guaranteeing citizens access to printed materials? Debated in New England since the early 1600s, this issue remained far from resolved.

In 1800, Americans faced a new century that would see the nation expand dramatically in a myriad of economic, geographic, political, and cultural ways. The concomitant impact on libraries included their exponential growth, in terms of number as well as geographic location, and the most substantive commitment ever by state governments to provide their citizens with free access to a network of public libraries. As a result, nineteenth-century Americans came to understand libraries as institutions fundamental to the life of all communities. Though thorny questions about library operation and access remained, this view was possible because it rested on the strong foundations built by British American colonists and by citizens of the early American republic.

REFERENCES

Cadbury, Henry J. 1943. John Harvard's Library. *Publications of the Colonial Society of Massachusetts: Transactions, 1937–1942.* 34: 353–377.

Davis, Richard Beale. 1978. *Intellectual Life in the Colonial South, 1585–1763.* 3 vols. Knoxville: University of Tennessee Press.

Dexter, Franklin B. 1889. Elder Brewster's Library. *Proceedings of the Massachusetts Historical Society,* 2nd ser., 5: 37–85.

Fatherly, Sarah. 2000. *Gentlewomen and Learned Ladies: Gender and the Creation of an Urban Elite in Colonial Philadelphia.* Madison: University of Wisconsin.

Franklin, Benjamin. 1987. *Writings,* edited by J. A. Leo Lemay. New York: Library of America.

Hayes, Kevin J. 1994. Cotton Mather. In *American Book-Collectors and Bibliographers: First Series,* edited by Joseph Rosenblum, 153–158. Detroit: Gale.

———. 1996. *A Colonial Woman's Bookshelf.* Knoxville: University of Tennessee Press.

———. 1997. *The Library of William Byrd of Westover.* Madison and Philadelphia: Madison House and Library Company of Philadelphia.

Kaser, David. 1980. *A Book for a Sixpence: The Circulating Library in America.* Pittsburgh: Beta Phi Mu.

Keep, Austin Baxter. 1908. *History of the New York Society Library with an Introductory Chapter on Libraries in Colonial New York, 1698–1776.* New York: De Vinne Press.

Korty, Margaret Barton. 1965. Benjamin Franklin and Eighteenth-Century American Libraries. *Transactions of the American Philosophical Society,* new ser., 55: 1–83.

Kraus, Joe. 1973. The Book Collection of Early American College Libraries. *Library Quarterly* 43: 142–159.

Laugher, Charles T. 1973. *Thomas Bray's Grand Design: Libraries of the Church of England in America, 1695–1785.* Chicago: American Library Association.

Lemay, J. A. Leo. 2006. *The Life of Benjamin Franklin.* 2 vols. Philadelphia: University of Pennsylvania Press.

McCorison, Marcus A., ed. 1965. *The 1764 Catalogue of the Redwood Library Company at Newport, Rhode Island.* New Haven, CT: Yale University Press.

McMullen, Haynes. 2000. *American Libraries before 1876.* Westport, CT: Greenwood.

Raven, James. 2002. *London Booksellers and American Customers: Transatlantic Literary Community and the Charleston Library Society, 1748–1811.* Columbia: University of South Carolina Press.

Shera, Jesse H. 1949. *Foundations of the Public Library: The Origins of the Public Library Movement in New England, 1629–1855*. Chicago: University of Chicago Press.

Stone, Elizabeth. 1977. *American Library Development, 1600–1899*. New York: Wilson.

Thompson, C. Seymour. 1952. *Evolution of the American Public Library, 1653–1876*. Washington, DC: Scarecrow Press.

Tuttle, Julius Herbert. 1910. The Libraries of the Mathers. *Proceedings of the American Antiquarian Society* 20: 269–356.

Wilkinson, R. S. 1963. The Alchemical Library of John Winthrop, Jr. (1606–1676) and His Descendants in Colonial America. *Ambix* 11: 139–186.

Winans, Robert B. 1981. *A Descriptive Checklist of Book Catalogues Separately Printed in America, 1693–1800*. Worcester, MA: American Antiquarian Society.

Wolf, Edwin, 2nd. 1974. *The Library of James Logan of Philadelphia, 1674–1751*. Philadelphia: Library Company of Philadelphia.

Wolf, Edwin, 2nd, and Kevin J. Hayes. 2006. *The Library of Benjamin Franklin*. Philadelphia: American Philosophical Society and Library Company of Philadelphia.

Wolf, Edwin, 2nd, John C. Van Horne, James N. Green, and Marie Elena Korey. 1995. *At the Instance of Benjamin Franklin: A Brief History of the Library Company of Philadelphia*. Revised and enlarged edition. Philadelphia: Library Company of Philadelphia.

Wright, Louis B. 1959. *The Atlantic Frontier: Colonial American Civilization, 1607–1763*. Ithaca, NY: Cornell University Press.

PART V

EXPRESSIONS OF INDIVIDUALITY

CHAPTER 16

....

DIARIES

....

KEVIN J. BERLAND

Just as no one conversation is quite the same as any other, so the form, structure, method, and purpose of diaries differ enormously. As Steven Kagle has observed, "Almost everyone knows what a diary is until it becomes necessary to define one" (Kagle 1979, 15). The etymology of the term "diary" goes back to the Latin for "daily"; likewise, the almost interchangeable term "journal" originates in the French for "daily." Generally, diaries record events in a regular sequence, most often on a regular daily basis, with the act of writing not far removed in time from when documented occurrences took place. Accounts written long afterward, with plenty of time for reflection and composition, are usually designated as memoirs or autobiographies. Diaries are supposed to be immediate—or at least they convey the sense of immediacy, comprehending both personal eyewitness observation and a register of the diarist's responses and thoughts about the occurrences observed.

The way scholars have approached diaries depends to a large extent on what sort of information they seek, a factor that affects both understanding of genre and qualitative critical evaluations. It has been suggested that literary and historical specialists differ widely in their critical approach to diaries, the former valuing insight into the personality of the diarist and literary style, the latter valuing documentation of the public world beyond the diarist's personal life and imagination (McCarthy 2000, 277). This formula is complicated by the fact that historians have gone through phases during which different sorts of data and different interpretive frameworks seem important. Nineteenth- and twentieth-century historians published the journals of the earliest colonial and "Pilgrim" leaders as documents of value in synthesizing a general prehistory of the United States, such as *Mourt's Relation* (1622). Editors and scholars concentrated on diarists who were prominent members of elite groups, drawing from their personal accounts material relevant to political history. As the tide of history writing turned from documenting elite figures in the last quarter of the twentieth century, editors and scholars became increasingly concerned with those elements of daily life their predecessors often excluded as tedious or commonplace, using them to study private identity, the history of the family, and the record of changing domestic roles and structures. That is, they concentrated on typical or representative people instead of "important" people, in support of an inquiry about what life was like for the ordinary populace. The search for information about daily life has given rise to studies of the "mental world" of individual historical figures, an approach that focuses on the diarist's formation of identity and interaction, and sometimes on a psychological struggle with the outer world. Still others take a feminist approach stressing the gendered nature of domestic life as the arena for women's expression. On the other hand, literary approaches have stressed style, the formal structure of diary writing, and the deliberate or unconscious crafting of a self presented in the pages of the daily record.

If disciplinary distinctions do not get us any closer to explaining why we read seventeenth- and eighteenth-century diaries and journals, this may be because considerations of how modern readers have approached these texts are complicated by the fact that so many of the surviving texts were composed in very different ways, in different forms, and for different purposes.

Everyday Use: Calendrical Form, Manuscript, and Print

Before the current usage settled, people in the seventeenth and eighteenth centuries understood the words "diary" and "journal" in several distinct but related ways, each involving a daily approach to time and experience.

Published annually, almanacs—often called diaries—set out the coming year's astronomical events, usually in a calendar format, with meteorologic predictions and planetary or astrological references. Almanacs were produced in New England as early as the 1640s, and they often appeared in long runs such as Nathan Bowen's series, *The New England Diary, or, Almanack* (Boston, 1722–1737), and Nathaniel Ames's *An Astronomical Diary, or, An Almanack* (1726–1764). By 1750 more than 50 distinct almanacs came out every year, and by 1800 there were more than 125, a publishing phenomenon generating an almanac for nearly every colonial household

(Eisenstadt 1998, 147). The term "diary" was identified with almanacs; among the nearly 500 titles including the word "diary" listed in the Evans bibliography of early American imprints, all but two are almanacs (Evans 1941–1959).

The first almanacs were printed in one large broadside sheet suitable for hanging on a wall, or in an octavo sheet folded to make sixteen pages. Smaller bound almanacs in the form of pocket books, with a steadily increasing number of pages, began to appear in the mid–eighteenth century, and users sometimes inserted blank pages between each printed page. In 1748 the enterprising London printer Robert Dodsley published one of the first books with dated blank pages interspersed with almanac entries, *The New Memorandum Book* (Blagden 1961, 26; McCarthy 2004, 64; Sherman 1996, 171). The first American version appears to have been Philadelphia printer Robert Aitken's *General American Register and Gentleman's Complete Annual Account Book and Calendar for the Pocket or Desk* (1773), though customers were not very receptive (McCarthy 2004, 59).

These almanac-diaries were ubiquitous, and they provided readers with an accessible template for thinking of the present and future in discrete temporal daily units. In numerous instances, people wrote in almanacs, either in the margins or on interleaved sheets of paper. John Winthrop's father Adam kept a journal in an interleaved copy of Allestree's *Almanac* (Shields 1981, 44). Cotton Mather and Samuel Sewall both wrote in the margins of almanacs, as well as in bound volumes (Rosenwald 1986, 330). In the 1760s, Samuel Cooper, minister of Boston's Brattle Street Church, recorded brief notes of his activities on interleaved pages in almanacs (Tuckerman 1901). George Washington also used interleaved copies of the *Virginia Almanac* (Washington 1986, 1: XLI). And Thomas Jefferson kept daily memorandums in interleaved almanacs (Jefferson 1997). Material published in an almanac could provoke personal response, as when someone exasperated by a paragraph about Leeuwenhoek's scientific discoveries in the 1774 *Massachusetts Calendar* wrote "A Damd Lie" and dismissed a further scientific note as "Another" (Stowell 1977, XI). Many other similarly personalized almanacs survive. The space almanacs made available for writing was not always extensive, and even with interleaved blank pages there was little room for what Stuart Sherman calls "narrative expatiation." Almanac diarists tended "to itemize memorable but disparate events rather than to perform each day as prose" (Sherman 1996, 57).

Of course, diarists were always free to record their memorandums on ordinary blank paper (loose or bound), ledgers, notebooks, or any other accessible paper surface. Sometimes a variety of formats occur: Washington shifted from interleaved almanacs to memorandum books and back again. Martha Ballard, the Maine midwife, set up her diary in a blank book with pages she laid out in almanac form. There are fifty-one manuscript pieces to John Adams's *Diary*, most of which were pocket-sized booklets made by folding sheets of paper, sometimes stitching them inside wrappers of marbled paper or newsprint and sometimes leaving them unprotected. The other parts included simple leaves of folded paper, small memorandum books, and larger bound journals (Washington 1986, 1: XLI; Adams 1961, 1: XLI–XLII).

Men and women who kept diaries sometimes used them as source material for later autobiographies. Adams apparently started his own autobiography from memory alone, unassisted by his diaries, letters, and the *Journals of Congress,* but reconnected with his diaries (and other records) as he was writing the second and third parts (Adams 1961, 1: XLVI, LXV). The use of diaries as raw material for the production of memoir and autobiography lies outside the boundaries of this discussion, but it is important to note that it is not always easy to distinguish unrevised diaries from those that have undergone more or less extensive authorial revision.

Some contemporary diaries were published in early America, especially when the diarist was someone of historical significance or prominence, or when the religious character of the diarist could have an uplifting effect on the reader. These were published under the editorial supervision of other parties, a process that rarely involved faithful transcription. Early published diaries and journals were framed, introduced, abridged, annotated, and otherwise edited, and so they bear the mark of the editor as well as the writer.

The word "journal" also initially designated a report or log of daily events. Legislative bodies such as the British parliament and colonial Houses of Assembly kept official handwritten records of their proceedings. These seemed appropriate for a wider audience, leading to print publications beginning (in North America) with *A Journal of the House of Representatives for His Majesties Province of New-York in America* (New York, 1695) and Virginia's *Journal of the House of Burgesses for 1727–1732,* right up to the *Journals of Congress* of the early federal years. Newspapers, too, came to be known as journals because they were published daily (or on a regular calendrical schedule).

On a more personal or individualized basis, journals also record daily business transactions, or the stages of a journey. In either case bare-bones entries could be expanded at the time of notation or later. Seamen kept journals noting sailing conditions: the ship's course, distances traveled, winds, weather, compass variation, currents, waves, the correspondence of charts to actual situations, and so forth (Haselden 1777). The shipboard log, an official running document of voyages maintained by captains or their designates, might include notes on events onboard the ship or in port, often endowed with the writer's personality (Forbes 1923, VIII). Additionally, the sea journal offered seamen a site for all sorts of serious thinking and writing. Peleg Folger, a Nantucket whaling captain, declared: "Many people who keep Journals at sea fill them up with trifles. I purpose in the following sheets not to keep an overstrict history of every trifling occurrence that happens; only now and then some particular affair, and to fill up the rest with subjects Mathematical, Historical, Philosophical or Poetical as best suits my inclination" (Forbes 1923, 390). Shipboard logs and other sea journals provided the temporal superstructure for accounts of voyages largely written after the fact. Explorers and travelers, too, often kept dated notes as they went along, expanding on them later. This seems to have been the method employed by John Lawson in *New Voyage to Carolina* (1709),

William Byrd's *Dividing Line* narratives, Sarah Kemble Knight's *Journal,* Thomas Gage's *The Traveller* (1758), and William Bartram's *Travels* (1791). No doubt, many other travelers based their expanded travel narratives on in-the-field notes: they chronicle events with the dates embedded in the narrative, but the narrative is always considerably expanded with amplification and revision.

Journals—again, the reconstructed and expanded kind—presented chronological accounts of events of historical significance. *Mourt's Relation* is a collocation of letters and journal material published as a history of the Plymouth Colony. Reconstructed journals were often adapted to fit the circumstances of publication, usually framing and expressing a political position. Such is the gist of one chronicle of the capture of Acadie, *A Journal of the Proceedings in the Late Expedition to Port-Royal, on Board Their Majesties Ship, the Six-Friends, the Honourable William Phipps Knight* (1690). This publication serves the imperial project by documenting a moment in the Anglo-French struggle for colonial supremacy. Maintaining the day-by-day journal structure (in an editorially upgraded form) lends such narratives a sense of immediacy. In other chronicles the narration of events has a more specific agenda. In *A Journal of What Passed in the Expedition of His Excellency Col. Benjamin Fletcher . . . to Renew the Covenant Chain with the Five Canton Nations of Indians* (1696), the daily account of negotiations with the Five Nations is subordinated to a different purpose—sycophantically polishing the image of Governor Fletcher. Another politically charged chronicle is Daniel Horsmanden's *Journal of the Proceedings in the Detection of the Conspiracy Formed by Some White People, in Conjunction with Negro and Other Slaves, for Burning the City of New-York in America, and Murdering the Inhabitants* (1744). Horsmanden lays out the major dates of the investigation under datelines:

MONDAY, 2d March

Caesar (*Vaarck's* Negro) was examined by the Justices, and denied every Thing laid to his Charge concerning Hogg's Robbery, but was remanded,

Prince (Mr. *Aubayneau's* Negro) was this Day also apprehended upon Account of this same Felony: Upon Examination he denied knowing any Thing of it. He was also committed.

Upon information that Caesar had shewn a great deal of Silver at *Hughson's,* it was much suspected that *Hughson* knew something of the Matter; so therefore Search was made several Times at his House yesterday and this Day, but none of the Goods or Silver were discovered. (Zabin 2004, 2–3)

This is not an immediate narrative set down as events transpired; Serena Zabin emphasizes that Horsmanden organized and presented material from the 1741 trials over which he presided in support of the court's findings of conspiracy. In this instance journal writing has been completely removed from the original on-the-spot process. No doubt Horsmanden relied on a detailed log of the investigation, court records, and his own notes, but with such complex and directed editorial method any original diary-like elements are altogether submerged. But at the same time, arranging the elements in a daily format suggests the directness and unmediated straightforwardness of the simpler diary form.

There is no paucity of travel narratives and other texts called "journals" in their titles. It is not always possible to determine whether their authors actually began with a personal chronicle of events, a real field journal or diary. But the process of making something new based on an earlier, simpler record was sufficiently well established that satirists and comic writers employed it with mock seriousness, as in Philip Freneau's *A Journey from Philadelphia to New-York, by Robert Slender, Stocking Weaver, Extracted from the Author's Journals* (1787).

Steven Kagle attempts to distinguish between journals and diaries, explaining that "journal" is most often used in titles of work-related texts and official records, while "diary" tends to appear in titles of texts "focusing on internal rather than external concerns, ideas rather than events" (Kagle 1979, 16). But in practice the terms are interchangeable; indeed, exceptions to Kagle's rule outnumber the apposite examples.

Many published lives of prominent men and women advertise that they depend extensively on the personal records of the biographical subject. In prefaces and title pages the editor usually claims to be faithful to the original record: *A Brief Account of the Life of the Late Rev. Caleb Smith . . . . Chiefly Extracted from His Diary, and Other Private Papers* (1763). These gestures implicitly establish biographical authenticity. Similarly, funeral memoirs or testimonials draw on personal records; see, for instance, John Stanford's *The Goodness of God in the Conversion of Youth: a Sermon on the Death of Charles I. S. Hazzard . . . In which Are Introduced, an Account of His Very Early Enjoyment of the Grace of God, and the Exercise of His Mind to the Period of His Death. Transcribed from the Diary Written with His Own Hand* (1799). Stanford offers mourners and other readers an exemplary personal testimony of spiritual seeking embedded in a consolatory sermon. There exists an abundance of such private spiritual diaries and journals extracted and made public for exemplary purposes, or constituting the foundation of a biography, such as Samuel Hopkins's *Life and Character of Miss Susanna Anthony . . . Consisting Chiefly in Extracts from Her Writings, with Some Brief Observations on Them* (1791). Early biographers, too, sometimes made their dependence upon the diaries explicit, particularly when they provided access to the internal workings of the subject's mind. Cotton Mather studied the papers of the prominent churchmen and churchwomen for whom he preached funeral sermons and published religious memorials. To eulogize the Reverend Jonathan Mitchel, Mather turned to Mitchel's diary for evidence of his model humility (Mather 1697, 51, 67). Similarly, in a eulogy for the Reverend John Baily, Mather (1698) cited Baily's diary more than a dozen times. Puritans held that individual Christians passed through a landscape fraught with danger and filled with hope every day. Writing in a diary helped to discover the spiritual significance of daily life. In his eulogy for Jerusha Oliver, Mather notes that she employed her diary to "enter such Passages as concern'd her *Interior State;* and indeed seldome let a Day pass without entring Something or other, that was an Aspiration of Serious Piety: always Ending with that clause; *For the Sake of the Lord Jesus Christ.*" From the record of this modest Christian's struggles Mather collects material suitable for his readers, especially young women. "All that I propose now to do, is only to make a few faithful Extracts from, and useful *Remarks* on, these Reserved *Memorials*" (Mather 1711, 13). Readers of these compiled memorial biographies were given a glimpse into the private ruminations of others much like them, ordinary people facing the spiritual difficulties of everyday life.

THE PURITAN DIARY

A great deal of critical attention has been paid to the diaries and journals of the principal figures involved in settling New England. For some critics, editors, and historians the religious context of these narratives has created some difficulty, most often because an increasingly secular viewpoint tends to dismiss the contexts of radical Christian piety as strange and outmoded. This means that students and scholars embarking on a course of study of Puritan writing must come to terms with the deep antipathy to Puritanism evident in some editions and studies. This antipathy is grounded in a hostile, reductive construction of the Puritan system of belief, which, Margo Todd observes, allows modern readers "to look down with complacency from the heights of their own intellectual towers" on the "confining corridors of faith and piety by rendering them dark, small, and rather shabby." Such constructions distort the past, reflecting "the inadequate perspective of historians on subjects to whom they unabashedly condescend and whom they are more willing to caricature than to try fully to understand. And it reveals a great deal about how historians use and misuse their sources when looking at subjects with that faint amusement that comes from the scholar's conviction of his or her superiority to the actors of the past" (Todd 1992, 237). The editors of the 1911 edition of Cotton Mather's *Diary,* for instance, despise Puritanism and pathologize his spiritual exercises (Mather 1957). It is not necessary to share the beliefs of the Puritans to make sense of their diaries, but it is certainly necessary to understand as much as possible of their background.

As Charles Hambrick-Stowe has noted, Puritan theology "emphasized religious practice and was intended to promote the experience of God and His grace individually and in social groups." This experience often took the form of a pilgrimage, beginning with the first indications of grace in conversion, continuing through daily disciplines preparing for salvation and growing in grace (Hambrick-Stowe 1982, 3, 20). Along the way, however, the pilgrim's most powerful opposition comes from within. Self-examination in a diary allows devout seekers to confront those factors that prevent them from experiencing grace. The record of God's mercies need not be daily, though, as Stuart Sherman points out, Puritans were inclined toward everyday disciplines, giving "the etymologies of 'journal' and 'diary' the force of temporal directive for some self-chroniclers, who produced, for stretches at least, an entry every day" (Sherman 1996, 51).

The Puritan diary, like Puritan daily life, is centered on the doctrine of the depravity of human nature. Salvation was understood to be granted not on the basis of merit, since no man or woman tainted by original sin could earn a way to heaven, but as a free gift of a gracious and miraculously benevolent God. Even those profoundly committed to holy living and inclined to believe in their election found it necessary to struggle constantly with the innate proclivity to sin. Puritans were acutely conscious of the passage of time, concerned with improving the hours because they believed the end of time was approaching. This millenarian view emphasized the gravity of every missed opportunity. The diary helped redeem the time, in biblical terms, by acknowledging Providence's hand in the apocalyptic events in the world at large, and by encouraging diarists to lose no time in working to make their calling and election sure. Diaries thus provided Puritans with an arena in which their personal struggle could be enacted, reviewed, and made the focus of further meditation and struggle. Writing about one's spiritual experiences was a key discipline. Cotton Mather, in his memorial biography of Jerusha Oliver, reproduces a characteristic passage in which the young woman reviews her sinful habits, moving up through a catalog of minor but troublesome matters to very serious charges against herself. This review, and especially its conclusion, clearly demonstrates the meditative function of Puritan diaries:

> What Sins have I been guilty of! O my Sins have been very many!—My Prayers have been sleighty: And I have spent my Time very unprofitably, And I have Read the Holy Word of God sleightily. And I have heard the Word of God sometimes, not with so much Diligence as I should have done. And sometimes I have not attended upon Hearing of Prayer as I should have done. And I have been Proud. And I have been Unthankful. And sometimes I have not Obeyed my Father and Mother as I ought to have done. And I have Eaten things, which were hurtful for me to Eat; and I have Eat more than I have had need to have done. And I have been afraid to go alone to Pray. I used to Pray, when I was a bed. Those were Lazy Prayers indeed! I have omitted those Duties of Meditation and Self-Examination. And I have sometimes omitted to ask a Blessing of God, when I have been going to Eat; and to give Thanks, when I had done Eating. And I have performed this Duty sleightily. And I have been Guilty of one Sin, which is greater than all these; That is, Unbelief. And besides all this, there is that Sin of Sins, my Original Sin; My Nature is Sinful. (Mather 1711, 4–5)

The duty of self-criticism was unremitting, but it was not simply a confessional process or ritual. Rather, it was an ongoing discipline, for without constant vigilance, the individual risked either falling back into habitual tendencies to sin or slipping into complacency. Self-satisfaction was particularly dangerous because it ignored or implicitly denied the degenerate condition of all humankind, and in so doing denied the perpetual need for grace. Thus, complacency was a sin of pride. Complacent Christians vainly overestimated their own sanctity and ungratefully turned away from grace.

It is particularly important for modern readers, schooled in the value of a positive outlook, to understand that what may appear to be absolute negativity was in fact a means to a positive end. The unceasing rediscovery of sin created in searchers sufficient humility to recognize the operations of grace in their lives. Even the often painful practice of confronting one's faults, then, is a positive opportunity. In the diary, regular inventories of personal weaknesses and blessing maintain the diarist in a state of susceptibility to grace.

Puritan minister Thomas Shepherd exhorted his readers to "renew morning and evening by *sad and solemn meditation,* that sense of Gods love to you in Christ, and in every duty he sets you about, and love will love and like the yoke, and make the commandments that they shall not be grievous to you" (Shepard 1747, 42). There is apparent here a sense of spiritual discipline that parallels the Aristotelian definition of virtue as an acquired habit of the soul. Shepard himself maintained a diary named *Meditations and Spiritual Experiences of Mr. Thomas Shepard* in the eighteenth-century edition of Shepard's tracts, *Certain Select Cases Resolved.* The diary is filled with struggle, days when he was overcome with a sense of his unworthiness and with a driving need for self-abnegation: "I saw *how apt I was to think myself something.* And the Lord put me on humbling Work, to see I was Worse than nothing, and to seek no other Advancement or Honour, but Mercy, if I might find that; which I thought was a great, yet holy Ambition." A problem arose for Shepard, as it did for all Puritan divines and leaders, a constant conflict between feeling oneself called to great or important work and the recognition of the limitation of one's own sinful nature. Only grace could lift up a sinner and allow good works to prosper. In the next entry, Shepard wrote:

> March 2. I was cast down with the *Sight of our Unworthiness* in this Church, deserving to be utterly wasted. But the Lord filled my Heart with a Spirit of Prayer, not only to desire small Things, but with an holy Boldness to desire great Things for God's People here, and for my self; viz. That I might live to see all Breaches made up, and the Glory of the Lord upon us. (Shepard 1747, 12)

Like many Puritan diaries, Shepard's records an almost flickering alternation of dark and light as he forces himself to confront all his sins and weaknesses, and then as he senses providential grace in the way his spirit, the listening congregation, and the community contribute humbly to the glory of God. There is always a sense of keeping a spiritual account. Regular meditations on personal shortcomings were necessary both to acknowledge human sinfulness and to demonstrate the understanding that no sinful person can earn salvation, never earned, only given. And signs of this grace only occur when individuals acknowledge their unworthiness. Shepard's regular entries, then, show him hopefully balancing the necessary expenditures of shame with the credit of grace providentially given.

Cotton Mather everywhere recommends the practice of keeping a diary. In a tract designed for soldiers he denies that Christian piety is "inconsistent with the *Profession* of a *Souldier.*" To exemplify this position he offers a story about a valiant pious army captain in the Low Countries. Not only was he courageous, but he was also pious, modest, serious, and prudent. He read deeply in scripture, divinity, and history, "penning down in his private Papers, the memorable Passages, which he found therein Singularly pertinent unto his own Circumstances." This practice of commonplacing supplemented the process of self-examination made possible by regular diary entries: "And he kept a *Diary,* wherein (to use his own Phrase) he had on one side, a Page, *For the Old Man,* on the other side, a Page *For the New Man:* Every Day he noted on the one side, *How far the Interest of Sin decay'd in him;* on the other, *How far he grew in Conformity to Jesus Christ.* This he did, until he dy'd" (Mather 1707, 24). The notion of keeping spiritual accounts is widespread, perhaps originating with John Beadle's seminal Puritan diary (Beadle 1996, xxv–xvi; Webster 1996, 38; Sherman 1996, 59; Shields 1981, 5).

The Puritan diary focuses on the balance between sin and grace in an individual life; it also has its own metanarrative—the operations of providence manifested in the daily affairs of Christians. Returning to the record of personal daily struggles and mercies could also be a valuable discipline. James Allin, for example, recommended frequent rereading of one's diary:

> Look through it, see what special Arguments of Thankfulness to God there are
> in every mercy. . . . There should be never a special deliverance and mercy God
> vouchsafeth you, but you should keep a Record of that mercy, that it might be
> alwayes to be overlooked by you. . . . You find in the old Testament frequently, it
> was the practise of God's people, to erect Monuments of praise for signal Mercies.
> . . . A Christian should keep his Diary, and special Remembrance of Gods good-
> ness. (Allin 1679, 9)

Puritan diaries, then, remind diarists of the operation of grace in their own lives. They also serve to testify to a wider audience.

One notable example of the movement from private discipline to public testimony may be found in the diaries and journals of John Winthrop. Over the years Winthrop's diaries took on a variety of formats and served different purposes. At the age of nineteen he began to keep a spiritual diary (which he called *Experiencia*), a private discipline partly written in cipher. He also maintained notes on sermons and legal briefs. After he was elected governor of the Massachusetts Bay Colony, he kept a more public record. This begins with a sea journal of the fifty-seven days of the voyage from England to Salem, Massachusetts. After his arrival in New England,

Winthrop continued to keep a still more public journal documenting the founding of the colony, apparently to preserve basic materials for a comprehensive history, a development marked by a parallel shift from the first-person pronoun to the third (Shields 1984, 47). His modern editors note that he was working within a fully developed historical and providential framework.

Using paleographic evidence (changes in ink, quill sharpening, etc., indicating how often and at what length he wrote), his editors have plotted the gradual evolution in Winthrop's compositional process. At first he wrote very brief entries once or twice a month, and then a few longer entries detailing providential dispensations. By the end of the second year he began to write longer multiple entries two or three times a month, and as time went by the dating of entries disappeared, and the entries themselves lengthened, taking on more detail and continuity. By the third and last volume, Winthrop was writing long after the events had taken place, probably using a list of memorandums (Winthrop 1996, xxii–xxvii). This evolution from diarist to historian marks a gradual shift beyond the ordinary mode of diary keeping, and yet there is something retained of the reflexive examining and discerning of the operations of Providence in the advances and setbacks of the colony. He interprets the death of six shipwrecked Bostonians "as evidence that God was testing the colonists' corrupt hearts," and sees in the major challenges of the colony—the schisms of Roger Williams and Anne Hutchinson, the Pequot War, and the Antinomian crisis—evidence "that Satan was working hard to destroy Christ's kingdom in New England" (Winthrop 1996, xxii, xxxiii). Winthrop's diary thus marks his movement from the private to the public sphere, and at the same time documents the religious consistency of this movement.

The diary of Samuel Sewall is another classic of Puritan diary writing, a rich resource for the record of personal religious experience, for his change of heart in regard to the Salem witch trials, for his work as a judge, for his early objections to slavery, and for his detailed notices of daily life both in his family and in the community at large (Sewall 1973). His interest in commerce is evident in the records he kept of the arrival of ships and the cost of various commodities, including wine. His concern for community mores is everywhere apparent, from his notes on the proprieties of dress to the proper regard for Native Americans. Sewall's diary has proved invaluable to scholars and historians of every stripe, from those who read in his accounts the story of the founding of New England, to those concerned with documenting the witchcraft trials, to those charting what appears to be a shift in New England thought from religion to commerce, to those intrigued by the evidence of the formation and evolution of Sewall's personality. One excellent example of the projects to which Sewall's record has been essential is the recent revision of the traditional notion of Puritan family life as "joyless, repressive, even brutal." Judith Graham discovers in the diaries plentiful evidence to repudiate this hostile view; she contends that Sewall's diary "suggests that the parent-child relationship in early New England was marked by warmth, sympathy, and love; that the special nature of childhood was a concept that parents understood very well" (Graham 2000, 4).

Thus it becomes increasingly evident that Puritan diaries serve all three functions David Shields indicated as formal varieties of the diary in New England—"the journal of spiritual examination, the diary of memorialized providences, and the chronological epitome of occurrences" (Shields 1981, 4). However, the sample reviewed here indicates that the modes overlap considerably.

QUAKER JOURNALS

Quakers also kept journals documenting their endeavors to live simple lives, their missionary work, their sense of the operation of the inner light in their lives, their public testifying, and especially their persecution and suffering at the hands of other Christian denominations. A large part of Quaker practice was bearing witness to spiritual truth as they understood it, which often brought them into situations in which others found them threatening and seditious. Following the example of the earliest Quaker journals of George Fox, American Quakers recorded the challenges, difficulties, and rewards of a life of bearing witness—the titles often feature the inclusive term "Sufferings"—and circulated their narratives in manuscript as well as in print. There are more than 700 such manuscripts in the collection of Haverford College alone.

The *Journal* of John Woolman is typical of Quaker journals, and, indeed, it exerted an influence on later Quaker diary writing nearly as powerful as that of George Fox. It is a hybrid text, adding to daily entries more comprehensive autobiographical passages and meditations on the religious truths Woolman sought in the world and in his heart. He begins, "I have often felt a motion of love to leave some hints in writing of my experience of the goodness of God." From his early conviction that love of God included love for all his "manifestations in the visible world" emerged a life of preaching and addressing social problems stemming from impious "cruelty to the least creature moving with his life." His tenderheartedness and compassion were particularly attractive to those who read and emulated him. When he was twenty-three and working for a Quaker tailor in England, he was required to draw up a bill of sale for a "negro Woman" belonging to his employer, an action that struck him as "inconsistent with the christian religion" (Woolman 1774, 1, 9, 16). He declined to write any more such conveyances, and gradually his opposition to slavery became an important part of his calling. Woolman was convinced it harmed the souls of slave owners as well as harming the enslaved, and was the first notable Quaker to move beyond a general uneasiness about slavery to active opposition. His opposition was manifested not only in social criticism and preaching, but in practical action. He studiously avoided anything that could support the institution of slavery. His conscience was troubled when he accepted the hospitality of slave owners, and the slave-based West Indian sugar trade struck him as so wicked that he ate no sugar and declined all commerce and transportation connected with it. Woolman also felt called to oppose other forms of cruelty, including war, harsh treatment of domestic animals, poverty, and the oppression of Native Americans. His journal led others to examine their own lives, extending his ministry beyond direct contact.

From the earliest days of the Quaker movement the spiritual gifts of women were recognized, and women's public witness and preaching became an integral part of the testimony. American Quaker women emulated such figures as Margaret Fell, Joan Vokins, and Elizabeth Fry. The journals of Susanna Morris, Elizabeth Hudson, and Ann Moore testify to the urgency of these Quaker women's witness, and to the egalitarianism that not only allowed but encouraged women to participate in and lead the ministry (Bacon 1994).

The distinction between daily, on-the-spot recording of events and retrospective narratives is often blurred. Some Quaker journals appear to consist of serially recorded entries, or to have been generated from such texts. Others were clearly composed after the fact. Differences were also introduced editorially. Quaker journals were published more or less officially, the regional Yearly Meeting commonly exerting editorial privilege. In England, Quaker publications were screened from 1672 onward, and the Yearly Meeting for Pennsylvania and New Jersey appointed an editorial committee in 1709 to oversee publication; its members took measures to suppress texts they deemed inappropriate, and they revised texts to bring them in line with the current sense of doctrine and witness. This editing process could have the effect of containing the strongest and most heterodox positions, such as Elizabeth Ashbridge's uncomfortable claim of prophetic authority (Sievers 2001, 255). Thus, a number of factors may intervene between the immediacy of diary entries and the published witness of Quaker journals.

OTHER PROTESTANT SPIRITUAL JOURNALS

George Whitefield's voyage to Georgia in 1737, *A Journal of a Voyage from Gibraltar to Georgia* (1739), was published in the form of letters addressed to his "Dear Friends." It is warm and personal and evangelical in style, and features a familiar pattern of moralizing the events of his journey:

> The seeing Persons of all Nations and Languages gave me great Pleasure: And the Difference of the Value of their Money and ours, gave me Occasion to reflect on

the Stupidity of those who place their Happiness in that which has no intrinsick Worth in itself, but only so much as we arbitrarily put upon it.

Saw a large Grampus rolling and spouting out Water for a long while, at a short Distance from our Ship: It put me in mind of the Behemoth spoken of by holy *Job*, and of the Leviathan mentioned by the royal Psalmist. *O GOD, who is like unto thee!* (Whitefield 1739, 4, 29)

Whitefield mentions the success of his preaching in Gibraltar among the soldiers and on the long voyage to Savannah. He writes of these almost daily episodes with a mixture of joy at the success of his mission, frequent acknowledgment of Providence, and expressions of humility. Noting the evident success of his sermons against swearing, he piously exclaims, "*Not unto me, not unto me, LORD, but unto thy Name be the Glory!*" (Whitefield 1739, 25). He concludes his account of one busy Sunday by noting the evening ended with devout conversation with his host and hostess and prayer for absent friends, and yet he writes that he "went to bed ashamed I had done so little for God on a Sabbath-Day. But when we cannot do as we would, we must do as we can" (Whitefield 1739, 12). It would be tempting to read this passage, and a few others like it, as if Whitefield had slipped into a more personal mode. Psychologizing critics and biographers might read such passages as signs of his anxiety, a sense of inadequacy to the task he had taken on, or the obsessive quality of his missionary work. However, such readings overlook the fact that the journal is a reader-directed text, designed affectively with consummate writerly skill. It is not so much a matter of self-doubt—rather, it is a public demonstration of humility, staged in such a way that the author avoids the possible charge of vanity for his preaching and good works.

Although the journals are presented with a sense of immediacy, they were not written on the spot. Rather, they were composed through a synthesis of an earlier text and a process of reflection that places events in a pattern of significance. Whitefield reveals his method in a passage recounting the long return voyage from Charlestown to England. The first sight of land moves him to observe a parallel between the conclusion of difficult voyages and attaining heaven. He wakes in the middle of the night, disturbed by the recollection that the ship had run out of provisions—they had "but half a Pint of Water left"—but God providentially supplies their need when the ship's mate returns from shore with supplies, and the ship's crew and passengers thank God for hearing their prayers. Whitefield ponders, interprets, and exclaims: "A little before our Provision came, I had been noting in my Diary, that I believed Deliverance was at hand; for last Night and this Morning, I had the most violent Conflict within my self that I have had at all. Thus God always prepares me for his Mercies. *O that this may strengthen my Faith, and make me willing to follow the Lamb wheresoever he shall be pleased to lead me*" (Whitefield 1739, 38–39). The original diary entry, it seems probable, recorded his hopes and fears as the voyage progressed. To this he later added an interpretive framework stressing grateful·recognition for God's providence, as well as four stanzas of a hymn of thanks, and then he reconsiders his experience, culminating in an exclamatory summary of what he—and his readers—should learn from such events.

Protestant missionaries of various denominations recorded their frontier ministries among the Native Americans. They had been preceded by Jesuit missionaries, whose efforts are documented in that order's records. A Baptist initiative is recorded in David Jones's *Journal of Two Visits Made to Some Nations of Indians on the West Side of the River Ohio, in the Years* 1772 *and* 1773 (1774). Moravian missionaries sent out from Bethlehem, Pennsylvania, were active in the Ohio River Valley from 1762, establishing congregations among the Native Americans (Zeisberger 2005). Quakers were active among the Oneida late in the eighteenth century, their missionary work recorded in William Savery's journal; the Quakers were followed by a Presbyterian mission, recorded in Samuel Kirkland's journal (Tiro 2006). There was a Quaker mission among Cornplanter's Seneca as well; Henry Simmons's journal documents this endeavor (Swatzler 2000). Other missionary journals may be discovered in denominational histories.

From these documents several kinds of historical information may be gleaned. First, they contain valuable insights into the evolution of theological viewpoints, often contrasting with resources stressing doctrine (sermons, tracts, theological works). The journals of David Zeisberger demonstrate the key role he played in altering the Moravian position on missions. Second, missionary journals sometimes afford valuable details of Native American culture, albeit filtered through a Christian perspective. Historians advise using such material with caution because missionary narratives are often fraught with ethnocentric distortions. However, some missionaries may be more reliable than others, especially those with universalist tendencies like the Quakers and Moravians, willing to acknowledge the natural light that extends to people outside the Christian dispensation. Because they attempt to build on extant belief rather than uprooting everything, their perspective may be more tolerant, and their accounts free of the extreme antipathy of many New England divines of the seventeenth century.

WILLIAM BYRD II

William Byrd II of Westover inherited extensive property as well as position in Virginia when his father died in 1705. Transatlantic in culture and disposition, educated in England at Felsted Grammar School and the Middle Temple, and established as a key actor in Virginia politics and commerce, Byrd left behind three diaries covering three periods of his life, offering a fascinating glimpse into the intersection of private and public life in the colonial Chesapeake. The first extant volume covers life in Virginia between 1709 and 1712, when Byrd joined the Virginia Council, served as commander of the militia, executed the duties of receiver general, married, and directed work on his plantation. The second volume sees Byrd back in London between 1717 and 1721, when he acted as an agent for the Virginia House of Burgesses, attended meetings of the Royal Society, sought a second wife, and partook of assorted illicit pleasures. The third volume covers the years 1739–1741, when he was well established at Westover, writing, developing land, surveying, and following many other pursuits typical of an established Virginia planter.

Critics have usually described the diaries as encoded, which is not strictly accurate. Byrd's diaries were written in a peculiar and difficult shorthand, based on William Mason's *La Plume Volante, or, the Art of Shorthand Improv'd* (1719). Though Byrd did not deliberately encrypt his entries, nonetheless the difficulty imposed on the text suggests that he wrote for his own eyes only. No doubt there were reasons to keep some of his subject matter private, especially his uninhibited commentary on friends, neighbors, public figures, and family members. Still more private were the many notes on his sexual activities both licit and illicit. One such entry, much anthologized, occurs on June 30, 1710: "I read a sermon in Dr. Tillotson and then took a little [nap]. I ate fish for dinner. In the afternoon my wife and I had a little quarrel which I reconciled with a flourish. Then she read a sermon in Dr. Tillotson to me. It is to be observed that the flourish was performed on the billiard table" (Byrd 1941, 210–211).

In his *London Diary* Byrd briefly records a variety of sexual adventures: "About eleven I went home and found a great pain in my toe. I kissed the maid and my seed came from me, and neglected my prayers, for all which God forgive me" (Byrd 1958, 71). He notes, "I polluted myself" or "committed uncleanness" with the maid not unfrequently, and sometimes with anonymous women at masquerades or prostitutes in a coach. He also kept a mistress for a while and slept with prostitutes at a tavern or bagnio. Byrd records one such occasion: "Then I went to my kind Mrs. Smith where I met a fine young woman, with whom I ate some rabbit fricassee and then we went to bed together and I rogered her three times and neglected my prayers" (Byrd 1958, 169). During the unmarried years in London Byrd acted the part of a rake, and yet every night he either prayed for forgiveness or admitted ruefully that he had not prayed. He evidently succumbed to temptation and later regretted his loss of self-control, though not enough to prevent him from seeking out further temptations. At the same time he was ardently pursuing a gentlewoman he wished to marry, and he confides to his diary his romantic dreams and fancies of trysts with the object of his affections. The coexistence of the rakish and sentimental strains is one of the most fascinating elements in Byrd's diaries.

The diaries are also an unparalleled source for information about early eighteenth-century Virginia politics, colonial medical practices, private life among elite planters, public life in the closed circle of wealth and political privilege, relations both private and public between colonial and metropolitan culture, and many more topics. Early interpretations stressed Byrd's "cavalier" gentility, his humor, and his frontier endeavors. Much recent critical work on the diaries has concentrated on Byrd's anxiety about achieving a secure identity in the face of a series of psychological crises brought on by generational and domestic issues and by metropolitan disregard of colonial merit (Lockridge 1987). Such scholarship relies on a reading of Byrd's diaries as a register of insecurity; other scholars emphasize the confident way Byrd consolidated economic and political power as a key member of the Virginia patrician class. It must suffice to say that Byrd's diaries contain such a profusion of diverse activities, meditations, and opinions that they will continue to attract the attention of historians and critics, who will produce work emphasizing different aspects of Byrd's multifarious character.

Philip Vickers Fithian

Another diarist associated with Virginia was Philip Vickers Fithian, who served as tutor to the children of Robert Carter from October 1773 to October 1774, after graduating from the College of New Jersey at Princeton. A good proportion of the entries in the diary he kept during this period are very brief notes on travel, the day's activities in the classroom, or the words and activities of the Carter family and the community. In the more extensive passages, however, it is possible to discover much of interest. Fithian himself is an interesting character, an earnest young Presbyterian theology student, well-read, romantically inclined, and capable of perceptive observations about the cultural conditions of late eighteenth-century Virginia. He comments on the character of his pupils and the social life of elite Virginia. He registers shock at the "savage Cruelty" of some overseers, who torture slaves to keep them compliant or to discover a secret. After detailed description of several recommended methods, Fithian concludes, "I need say nothing of these seeing there is a righteous God, who will take vengeance on such Inventions!" The journal also indicates that such views were not limited to northern visitors, quoting with approval Colonel Carter's disgust with "the cruelty and distress which many among the Negroes suffer in Virginia!" Upon hearing of an enslaved coachman kept chained to the box overnight, Fithian deplores the tyranny of the slave owner, doubting whether the ferryman Charon would be willing to transport him across the Styx. Next, abandoning the classical mode for the Christian, he adds, "I query whether he may be admitted into the peaceful Kingdom of Heaven where meekness, Holiness, and Brotherly-Love, are distinguishing Characteristicks?" (Fithian 1968, 38–39, 84–85).

The journal could be mined for various sorts of information, such as the time required for making a long journey, the distance traveled in a day, and the cost of ferry crossings, accommodations, and meals. Entries on his work as a tutor could provide hints about eighteenth-century educational methods. And Fithian's references to newspapers available in Virginia could provide useful evidence in a study of the transmission of current news and the range of newspapers. Sometimes his news is almost current. In February 1774, he read about the Boston Tea Party in the *Virginia Gazette,* less than two months after the occurrence. In an entry for June 18, he notes that a recent London newspaper reported an act of Parliament denying the people of Boston the right to try soldiers or any other accused of a crime, and requiring such offenders be sent back for trial in English courts. A few days later, a neighbor produced a number of the *Pennsylvania Packet* that reported "the Northern Colonies were zealous and steadfast to maintain their Liberties" (Fithian 1968, 64, 122–123). Even though Fithian sometimes felt isolated in Virginia, newspapers kept him abreast of both political and cultural events. Early in 1774 he mentioned an account of Phillis Wheatley's poetry from the *Monthly Review* (published the previous year), and he also transcribes one of her poems from the *Universal Magazine* (Fithian 1968, 72–73).

Another journal documents Fithian's work as a traveling Presbyterian minister for scattered communities in western Virginia and Pennsylvania, and later with the Continental army. Journal entries document conditions in remote settlements, featuring some strong character sketches of the inhabitants:

> Last Evening, after Sunset, I walked with Mrs. Piper to four Neighbour's
> Houses all within half a Mile. She was looking [for] Harvest-Men while her ill-
> conditioned Husband was asleep, perspiring off the Fumes of the Whiskee!—It
> is now seven o Clock. There are two Reapers—Miss Piper is out carrying Drink
> to the Reapers—Her slothful Father is yet asleep. Tim is about House as a kind
> of Waiting Man; an old, liquor-drown'd, impotent, garrulous Man of War's Man.
> (Fithian 1934, 56)

Fithian notes developments in his mission, the success of sermons, the spiritual state of congregations, and the attempts of some communities to convince him to stay as permanent minister. As in the earlier journal, Fithian here records enough detail about his emotional life, his longings, misgivings, and sense of accomplishment to make him an interesting character in his own right. Particularly noteworthy is his faculty of sympathy, which allows him to meditate on the sorrow of the indigenous population displaced by Euro-American settlement:

> As we were returning, in our slim Canoes, I could not help thinking over with my-
> self, how often the Savage Tribes, while they were in Possession of these inchant-
> ing Wilds, have floated over this very Spot. My Heart feels for the wandering
> Natives. I make no Doubt but Multitudes of them, when they were forc'd away,
> left these long-possess'd, and delightsome Banks, with swimming Eyes. It is not a

Triffle, I suppose, that can make an Indian weep; But these were pleasant places. (Fithian 1934, 63)

Another topic to which Fithian returns again and again, and with notable ardor, is the current political situation. On June 1, 1775, he wrote:

The melancholy Anniversary of a tyrannical Manoeuvre of the infatuated, or rather Hell-inspired British Ministry, in blocking up the Port of Boston is ar-rived!—This day twelve-Month their dangerous and cruel Councels began to be executed!—All along the Bladder has been filling with Venom—Now it is distended with Poison,—full, ready to crack, to split with Rage!—Feeble and unavailing Efforts! Three Thousand British Forces were sent, and are now to be joined by two thousand More, with 2 hundred Horse—Five thousand hireling Regulars, at Sixpence Ster: per Day, most of them young and unused to Hard-ships—Five thousand hireling Britons, against the Millions of America's hardy Sons—The Odds is five thousand against thirty hundred thousand; And all those Myriads fighting for what is dear to them as Life, which they will as soon give up to Power! (Fithian 1934, 20)

The exclamatory discourse continues by praising the fertility of the American soil, the flourishing of learning, the arts, military honor, and commerce. It seems probable that this passionate writing reflects the sort of conversation Fithian was having in his travels, but it may also be argued that he wrote for posterity, since high flights of style suggest an appeal to readers other than the diarist. But the patriotic zeal of his apostrophes takes a practical turn: he notes his attempts to master the "Prussian Manual," that is, to learn the disciplines of war as outlined by Frederick the Great. As soon as an independent company of militia formed, he joined, though in his first drills he admits he was "a sad bungler" (Fithian 1934, 21). His involvement grew. In the summer of 1776, he served as chaplain to a brigade of the New Jersey militia; he died of dysentery not long after the Battle of Harlem Heights.

DIARIES OF THE FOUNDERS

It seems reasonable to assume that private writings of the self committed to paper by the nation's founders ought to be of great historical interest. To some extent this is true, but much depends on the personality of the diarist. In the case of George Washington, there is virtually no record of introspection, a quality highly valued by today's diary readers, and sometimes very little commentary on major events, an absence distress-ing to readers hoping for an inside view of historical events. On page after page of his interleaved almanacs he pragmatically noted the state of the weather, the daily work detail on his farm, prices of crops and commodities, and the course of experimenting with various agricultural techniques. In addition to these almanac-diaries, Washington also kept a journal of his 1748 surveying expedition in Virginia's Northern Neck, a record of a voyage to Barbados with his brother a few years later, another journal of his 1754 military embassy to the French forces on the Ohio River, and notes on his presidential tours of the former colonies. He did not keep daily records on a regular basis until 1760; there are regular diaries from 1768 to 1775, but during the Revolution the diaries apparently stopped. Evidence exists that Washington kept diaries during his years as president, but they seem to have disappeared. Some were destroyed and dispersed after his death by relatives and biographers.

Washington's modern editors point out that his letters offer far more personal and confidential detail than the diaries, which served simply as memorandum books where he recorded "Where and How my Time is Spent." Laconic notes preserved the general heads of what happened on a specific day, with no register of how he felt, even at times of crisis, joy, or sorrow. His personal responses appear "in communications to friends, not in the unresponsive pages of a memorandum book" (Washington 1986, 1: XVII–XIX).

Conspicuously missing from Washington's diaries are telling political details. Though he was present at the Second Virginia Convention on March 23, 1775, when Patrick Henry declaimed "Give me liberty or give me death," Washington's diary only notes, "Dined at Mr. Patrick Cootes and lodgd where I had done the Night before" (Washington 1986, 3: 315). Nonetheless, some important elements of Washington's character are discernible. Perhaps the most detailed material available in the diaries deals with his lifelong passion for scientific farming in the experimental mode. Diary entries demonstrate his currency with the state of agricultural science; his experimental projects complement his long-term correspondence with agricultural pioneer Arthur Young. It is possible to reconstruct the progressive gentleman farmer from the diaries, which ought to suggest something important about how Washington defined himself. For his internal and emotional character, and for his public character as general and president, we have to look elsewhere.

The diaries of John Adams, on the other hand, are packed with every sort of information. His earliest diaries feature very brief entries noting the principal activities of most days, the weather, and the company he kept. Readers can trace his activities after he graduated from Harvard in 1756 and went as a schoolmaster to Worcester, and as he studied the law. Many entries are laconic in the extreme; for some time "Kept School" is the only reference to his teaching. From time to time, Adams used the diary to call himself to order:

> Oh! that I could wear out of my mind every mean and base affectation, conquer
> my natural Pride and Self Conceit, expect no more defference from my fellows than
> I deserve, acquire that meekness, and humility, which are the sure marks and Char-
> acters of a great and generous Soul, and subdue every unworthy Passion and treat
> all men as I wish to be treated by all. How happy should I then be, in the favour and
> good will of all honest men, and the sure prospect of heaven! (Adams 1961, 1: 7–8)

Such self-corrective exclamations recur throughout the early diaries. They are equaled in number by aphoristic observations about life written in a polished if conventional style:

> The Stream of Life sometimes glides smoothly on, through flowry meadows and enamell'd planes. At other times it draggs a winding reluctant Course through offensive Boggs and dismal gloomy Swamps. The same road now leads us thro' a spacious Country fraught with evry delightful object, Then plunges us at once, into miry Sloughs, or stops our passage with craggy and inaccessible moun-tains. . . . The Ship, which wafted by a favourable gale, sails prosperously upon the peaceful Surface, by a sudden Change of weather may be tossed by the Tempest, and driven by furious, opposite winds, upon rocks or quicksands. In short noth-ing in this world enjoys a constant Series of Joy and prosperity. (Adams 1961, 1: 18)

Elsewhere Adams recorded the gist of sermons, table talk, and his own extensive reading. In some cases he merely named books he had been reading, but in other cases he wrote down the main points taken from his reading, and even transcribed material in the manner of a commonplace book. Gradually the sententiousness of his entries increased, and at the same time Adams used his diary to record some-times extensive notes on legal matters. Occasionally the seriousness is broken by the appearance of conversations written in dialogue, by bons mots and repartee, and by amusing character sketches of his acquaintances.

We are fortunate that Adams became addicted to diary keeping, for he has left behind an incomparable account of growth into public life. His story is sufficiently well known not to need repeating, but as he became increasingly immersed in the turmoil of the founding of the United States his diaries stayed beside him, and they contain an invaluable record of the founders. Other diarists of the founding, the Revolutionary War, and the early Federal period include James Allen, Dr. Lewis Beebe, Charles Herbert, Samuel Holten Henry Livingstone, Dr. John Morgan, Governeur Morris, Dr. James Thacher, and Dr. Albigense Waldo, to name but a few. James Madison and his family kept a weather diary. Thomas Jefferson kept a weather diary, too, and his memorandum books contain daily records of his ex-penditures throughout his adult life. Seldom do the memorandum books contain insightful personal details.

CONCLUSION

In the early nineteenth century, literary historians sought out factors characterizing their sense of the specifically local character of each colony's literary production. Just as historians focused on the public deeds of prominent men, so did literary historians formulate their notions of colonial style from the diaries and other works of prominent members of the community. Later on, diaries were mined for material supporting succeeding historiographical models and views of the New World: the rich, empty land open for limitless growth, the new land where tyranny had not taken over, the expansionist vision of democratic empire, and manifest destiny, the notion that the key element of the American character could be found along the frontier, and various permutations of the American Dream.

By the middle of the twentieth century, reconstructionist historians were busy examining the past to uncover the processes by which the nation developed its identity. In certain early diaries they found proleptic evidence of things to come, sometimes reading into early colonial narratives a strain of dissatisfaction with British rule. This approach is not unlike examining ancestral portraits to discover congenial resemblances to ourselves, and it usually introduces anachronism, notably the inclusion in the canon of works that anticipate the exceptionalism of later times, and the exclusion of works that align themselves with British traditions. Historians, for instance, have interpreted struggles for economic and political power among colonial elites as early rumblings of revolutionary principle. This problematic meta-narrative has recently been addressed by the growth of transatlantic studies, which, by recognizing that colonial identity was still vitally connected to British culture and nationality, has opened the canon to admit works previously deemed too British to be properly early "American."

The growing influence of cultural studies has meant that diary scholars have been able to cast a wider net than ever before. No longer limited by the implicit directive to attend only to significant historical figures or by established canons of literary taste, critics and historians have turned their attention to issues of gender and sexuality, economic transactions, professions and occupations, and other essential parts of private and public life. The conversations diarists carried out with themselves touched on many topics we are only now beginning to recognize and study.

REFERENCES

Adams, John. 1961. *The Diary and Autobiography of John Adams*, edited by L. H. Butterfield, Leonard C. Faber, and Wendell D. Garrett. 4 vols. Cambridge, MA: Belknap Press of Harvard University Press.

Allin, James. 1679. *Serious Advice to Deliver Ones from Sickness, or Any Other Dangers Threatning Death*. Boston: for John Foster.

Bacon, Margaret, ed. 1994. *Wilt Thou Go on My Errand? Three 18th-Century Journals of Quaker Women Ministers*. Wallingford, PA: Pendle Hill.

Beadle, John. 1996. *A Critical Edition of John Beadle's A Journall or Diary of a Thankfull Christian*, edited by Germain Fry Murray. New York: Garland.

Blagden, Cyprian. 1961. Thomas Carnan and the Almanack Monopoly. *Studies in Bibliography* 14: 23–43.

Byrd, William. 1941. *The Secret Diary of William Byrd of Westover, 1709–1712,* edited by Louis B. Wright and Marion Tinling. Richmond, VA: Dietz Press.

———. 1942. *Another Secret Diary of William Byrd of Westover for the Years 1739–1741, with Letters and Literary Exercises 1696–1726,* edited by Maude H. Woodfin. Richmond, VA: Dietz Press.

———. 1958. *The London Diary (1717–1721) and Other Writings,* edited by Louis B. Wright and Marion Tinling. New York: Oxford University Press.

Eisenstadt, Peter. 1998. Almanacs and the Disenchantment of Early America. *Pennsylvania History* 65: 143–169.

Evans, Charles. 1941–1959. *American Bibliography: A Chronological Dictionary of All Books, Pamphlets, and Periodical Publications Printed in the United States of America from the Genesis of Printing in 1639 Down to and Including the year 1820.* 14 vols. New York: Peter Smith.

Fithian, Philip Vickers. 1934. *Philip Vickers Fithian: Journal, 1775–1776, Written on the Virginia-Pennsylvania Frontier and in the Army around New York,* edited by Robert Greenhalgh Albion and Leonidas Dodson. Princeton, NJ: Princeton University Press.

———. 1968. *Journal and Letters of Philip Vickers Fithian: A Plantation Tutor of the Old Dominion, 1773–1774,* edited by Hunter Dickinson Farish. Charlottesville: University Press of Virginia.

Forbes, Harriette Merrifield. 1923. *New England Diaries 1602–1800: A Descriptive Catalogue of Diaries, Orderly Books and Sea Journals.* Privately printed.

Gage, Thomas. 1758. *The Traveller. Part I. Containing a Journal of Three Thousand Three Hundred Miles, through the Main Land of South-America.* Woodbridge, NJ: James Parker.

Graham, Judith S. 2000. *Puritan Family Life: The Diary of Samuel Sewall.* Boston: Northeastern University Press.

Hambrick-Stowe, Charles E. 1982. *The Practice of Piety: Puritan Devotional Discipline in Seventeenth-Century New England.* Chapel Hill: University of North Carolina Press.

Haselden, Thomas. 1777. *The Seaman's Daily Assistant, Being a Short, Easy, and Plain Method of Keeping a Journal at Sea.* Philadelphia: J. Crukshank.

Jefferson, Thomas. 1997. *Jefferson's Memorandum Books: Accounts, with Legal Records and Miscellany, 1767–1826,* edited by James A. Bear Jr. and Lucia C. Stanton. 2 vols. Princeton, NJ: Princeton University Press.

Kagle, Steven E. 1979. *American Diary Literature 1620–1799.* Boston: Twayne.

Lockridge, Kenneth A. 1987. *The Diary and Life of William Byrd II of Virginia, 1674–1744.* Chapel Hill: University of North Carolina Press.

Mather, Cotton. 1697. *Ecclesiastes: The Life of the Reverend & Excellent Jonathan Mitchel.* Boston: B. Green and J. Allen.

———. 1698. *A Good Man Making a Good End: The Life and Death, of the Reverend Mr. Baily.* Boston: B. Green and J. Allen, for Michael Perry.

———. 1707. *The Souldier Told, What He Shall Do.* [Boston?].

———. 1711. *Memorials of Early Piety: Occurring in the Holy Life & Joyful Death of Mrs. Jerusha Oliver. With Some Account of her Christian Experiences, Extracted from her Reserved Papers.* Boston: T. Green.

———. [1911] 1957. *The Diary of Cotton Mather,* edited by Worthington Chauncey Ford. 2 vols. Reprint. New York: Ungar.

McCarthy, Molly. 2000. A Pocketful of Days: Pocket Diaries and Daily Record Keeping among Nineteenth-Century New England Women. *New England Quarterly* 73: 274–296.

———. 2004. *"A Page, A Day": A History of the Daily Diary in America.* Waltham, MA: Brandeis University.

Rosenwald, Lawrence. 1986. Sewall's Diary and the Margins of Puritan Literature. *American Literature* 58: 325–341.

Sewall, Samuel. 1973. *The Diary of Samuel Sewall, 1674–1729,* edited by M. Halsey Thomas. New York: Farrar, Straus and Giroux.

Shepard, Thomas. 1747. *Three Valuable Pieces. Viz. Select Cases resolved; First Principles of the Oracles of God, or, Sum of Christian Religion . . . and A Private Diary.* Boston: Rogers and Fowle.

Sherman, Stuart. 1996. *Telling Time: Clocks, Diaries, and English Diurnal Form, 1660–1785.* Chicago: University of Chicago Press.

Shields, David S. 1981. *A History of Personal Diary-Writing in New England, 1620–1745.* Chicago: University of Chicago.

Sievers, Julie. 2001. Awakening the Inner Light: Elizabeth Ashbridge and the Transformation of Quaker Community. *Early American Literature* 36: 235–262.

Stowell, Marion Barber. 1977. *Early American Almanacs: The Colonial Weekday Bible.* New York: Burt Franklin.

Swatzler, David. 2000. *A Friend among the Seneca: The Quaker Mission to Cornplanter's People.* Mechanicsburg, PA: Stackpole Books.

Tiro, Karim M. 2006. "We Wish to Do You Good": The Quaker Mission to the Oneida Nation, 1790–1840. *Journal of the Early Republic* 26: 353–376.

Todd, Margo. 1992. Puritan Self-Fashioning: The Diary of Samuel Ward. *Journal of British Studies* 31: 236–264.

Tuckerman, Frederick, ed. 1901. *Notes from the Rev. Samuel Cooper's Interleaved Almanacs of 1764 and 1769.* Boston: David Clapp and Son.

Washington, George. 1986. *The Diaries of George Washington,* edited by Donald Jackson and Dorothy Twohig. 8 vols. Charlottesville: University Press of Virginia.

Webster, Tom. 1996. Writing to Redundancy: Approaches to Spiritual Journals and Early Modern Spirituality. *Historical Journal* 39: 33–56.

Whitefield, George. 1739. *A Journal of a Voyage from Gibraltar to Georgia.* Philadelphia: B. Franklin.

Winthrop, John. 1996. *The Journal of John Winthrop, 1630–1649,* edited by Richard S. Dunn, James Savage, and Laetitia Yeandle. Cambridge, MA: Belknap Press of Harvard University Press.

Woolman, John. 1774. *The Works of John Woolman.* Philadelphia: Joseph Crukshank.

Zabin, Serena R., ed. 2004. *The New York Conspiracy Trials of 1741: Daniel Horsmanden's Journal of the Proceedings, with Related Documents.* New York: Bedford.

Zeisberger, David. 2005. *The Moravian Mission Diaries of David Zeisberger, 1772–1781,* edited by Herman Wellenreuther and Carola Wessel, trans. Julie Tomberlin Weber. University Park: Pennsylvania State University Press.

CHAPTER 17

....

EARLY AMERICAN AUTOBIOGRAPHY

....

SUSAN CLAIR IMBARRATO

Autobiographical writings in early America tell us how individuals lived and imagined themselves within an evolving culture and amid a challenging environment. Explorers, clergy, statesmen, and travelers conveyed their findings and experiences to report discoveries, model exemplary behavior, express gratitude for patronage, or illustrate divine Providence. With an emphasis on personal perspective, autobiography would seem closely aligned with American literature that values and celebrates the self. Rather than emphasize unique identity or promote achievement for its own sake, however, early Americans often wrote about themselves as part of a larger social hierarchy and attributed any success to a greater authority. Although the narratives themselves relate individual efforts and accomplishments, they are not necessarily self-promoting. William Bradford's history is therefore not simply about his life but about life within Plymouth Plantation that, from his perspective, reinforces providential design. The study of early American autobiography involves the study of the conditions for using the first-person voice to express matters spiritual and secular, the general composition of an autobiographical text, and the sources for early American autobiography. In many ways, first-person writings are living history: they show us how a person viewed life and acted within their surroundings. From these eyewitness accounts, early American life becomes more accessible as they document a culture evolving beyond its knowable boundaries.

The specific term "autobiography" is usually associated with the early nineteenth century, during the Romantic period of literature, when, in 1805, British poet and critic Robert Southey (1805) began using it. Michael Mascuch notes an earlier usage: "Precisely when and where modern autobiography emerged is a matter of considerable debate. The term 'autobiography' and its synonym 'self-biography' appeared in the late eighteenth century in a handful of isolated instances in England and Germany" (Mascuch 1996, 19). Georg Misch offers this etymological explanation. The term "autobiography" combines "the description (graphia) of an individual life (bios) by the individual himself (auto)." It is, Misch continues, "a word formed artificially, like the technical terms of science, with the aid of the ancient Greek language" (Misch 1951, 5). Given this evolution, early American writers did not use the term "autobiography" but referred to writings about the self as "memoir" or "history." Benjamin Franklin, for example, described his autobiography as his "Memoirs," "Notes of my early life," "Account of my Life," and "History of my Life." Not until its publication in the mid–nineteenth century, in fact, was it titled Benjamin Franklin's *Autobiography*. Throughout these name changes, whether "account," "history," "autobiography," or "life writing," the individual's story merits attention. As the terms change, so do attitudes toward writing about the self and the overall value and importance of an autobiographical text.

AUTOBIOGRAPHY IN THE LARGER CONTEXT

Whether intended to model civic behaviors or to illustrate providential design, early American autobiography develops at the intersection of geographic, cultural, political, and religious change that values individual accomplishment yet prefers it to be expressed with modesty. In William Bradford's *Of Plymouth Plantation,* for example, he describes the Pilgrims' initial landing in 1620 with a mix of awe and pity: "But here I cannot but stay and make a pause, and stand half amazed at this poor people's present condition; and so I think will the reader, too, when he well considers the same. Being thus passed the vast ocean, and a sea of troubles before in their preparation (as may be remembered by that which went before), they had now no friends to welcome them nor inns to entertain or refresh their weatherbeaten bodies; no houses or much less towns to repair to, to seek for succour" (Bradford 1970, 61). Departing from the narrative of settlement, briefly, to insert this personal perspective, Bradford emphasizes the plight of the Pilgrims through his use of pronouns. He invites the reader into his memory of the initial landing and addresses particularly the second generation of colonists who may neither appreciate or fully understand the sacrifice of their parents nor comprehend the element of divine assistance. Before continuing with a detailed report of their struggles that first winter, Bradford clarifies the source of their very survival: "What could now sustain them but the Spirit of God and His grace?" As a leader and governor of the Puritan settlement, he evokes the first person to bear witness to a greater power rather than to draw attention to his own bravery or leadership. For Bradford, survival was clearly divinely ordained.

For Thomas Shepard, the autobiography reinforces a divine order evident throughout his life. As Michael McGiffert notes, the text "dramatizes what Shepard called 'God's great plot' of reformation and redemption, making vivid the faith in divine design by which Puritans affirmed their sense of the moral order of existence in an age of revolutionary turmoil, defined their parts in the play of God's purpose, and affirmed the cosmic dimensions of their experience" (Shepard 1972, 3). During his migration to America in 1635, when the 200 passengers encountered a terrific storm, Shepard attributes their survival to a higher power: "But when one of the company perceived that we were strangely preserved, had these words, That thread we hang by will save us, for so we accounted of the rope fastened to the anchor, in comparison of the fierce storm." Rather than single out the crew or any one act of bravery, all credit is given to God: "And so indeed it did, the Lord showing his dreadful power towards us and yet his unspeakable rich mercy to us who in depths of mercy heard, nay helped, us where we could not cry through the disconsolate fears we had out of these depths of seas and miseries" (Shepard 1972, 60). Noting how the ship's anchor kept them "strangely preserved," Shepard presents a metaphor of the ship as pilgrim anchored by God's grace. The experience is striking: "This deliverance was so great that I then did think if ever the Lord did bring me to shore again I should live like one come and risen from the dead." Emphasizing the storm's significance, Shepard begins his autobiography with his journey to America, even before the sections on his "birth and life." He thus mentions "terrible storms" and describes "the ship in a storm tumbling suddenly on the one side," which "almost pitched" his wife and child "against a post," but they were saved by "the angels of God who are ministering spirits for the heirs of life" (Shepard 1972, 35). Having established the treachery of the sea voyage, Shepard cast the scene as a reminder of God's dual nature at once "dreadful" and capable of "mercy." Throughout his autobiography, Shepard records additional evidence of God's deliverance, including the "Pequot furies" and "war with Indians and Familists." The main narrative concludes with the death of his first wife, Margaret Toutevile Shepard, in April 1646, three weeks after giving birth, a tragedy he tries to understand: "But I am the Lord's, and he may do with me what he will. He did teach me to prize a little grace gained by a cross as a sufficient recompense for all outward losses. But this loss was very great" (Shepard 1972, 70). As Shepard seeks perspective, he finds solace in a grand divine plan.

For Increase Mather, individual achievement is also referenced as part of a larger scheme. In his autobiography, Mather reports on his educational accomplishments in similar tones of subordination: "In the year 1656 I returned again to Cambridge, and there had my first degree. The Lord made me to profit in learning, and I hope also in spirituals, under precious Mr. Mitchells ministry. Under the shadow of which I sat with great delight" (Mather 1962, 280). Personal accomplishment is thus placed within the established hierarchy, God and teacher, which Mather is certain to recognize. To avoid self-aggrandizement, which might be interpreted as either blasphemous or treasonous, first-person writings provide individual perspective without creating independent agency. For Bradford, Shepard, and Mather, the interconnected relationship between individual expression and social authority was constantly recognized and reinforced. Consequently, writing about personal life within a culture that discourages self-promotion requires a diligent adherence to these expectations as manifest in the numerous expressions of humility and acknowledgments of divine providence.

THE AUTOBIOGRAPHER'S PERSONA

Portraiture from early America, moreover, suggests a seeming contradiction to this presumed humility. For example, Captain John Smith's confidence is displayed in the 1617 engraving possibly by Simon van de Passe; Cotton Mather's sternness is depicted in Peter Pelham's 1727 painting; Benjamin Franklin's purposefulness is evident in more than 500 depictions, and specifically so in Charles Willson Peale's 1785 portrait; Abigail Adams's deliberateness is underscored in Gilbert Stuart's 1800/1815 portrait; Jonathan Edwards's resolve is conveyed in Joseph Badger's portrait (ca. 1750); and Thomas Jefferson's determination is evident in Stuart's 1821 portrait. These representations clearly present strong-willed individuals. And yet, within the larger context of submission to a Great Chain of Being, do such expressions conflict with a competing expectation for humble subordination? More specifically, how do people write about their own lives in a culture that discourages self-promotion? Captain John Smith, never a shy figure, offers one solution by incorporating third-person accounts about himself and deferring to the king and his readers as the superior audience, all the while promoting his exploits and bolstering his leadership. In the introductory letters and verse to Smith's *Generall Historie of Virginia, New-England, and the Summer Isles* (1624), he repeatedly deflects praise, as here in "A Preface of foure Poynts": "This plaine History humbly sheweth the truth; that our most royall King James hath place and opportunitie to inlarge his ancient Dominions without wronging any" (Smith 1986, 2: 43). While deference to higher authority, God, king, and queen, is conventional for this time, both in writing and in speech, it is also a convenient mask behind which an author might maintain expectations of modesty, even though engaged in self-promotion. Understanding these parameters helps explain how early American autobiographical writings can be both about the self yet not self-revealing. It is possible, then, that the self-assured portraiture shows us not simply the individual but the self as a representative leader. Although book 3 of Smith's *Generall Historie* was written by several members of the Virginia colony, the decided use of the third person when referencing Smith highlights this pose. Smith offers himself as the model of cooperation and leadership, and yet avoids accusations of self-aggrandizement by using the third person and framing the narrative as a history rather than a memoir. Extolling the virtues of industry and concern for community welfare, Captain John Smith is indeed a laudable figure, as appropriately depicted in his portrait. The image thus communicates qualities of the leader rather than the importance of the individual.

While assuming the third person allows Smith a convenient mask, using the first-person voice does not necessarily mean that the author is writing about him- or herself in any confessional sense. Instead, evoking the "I" emphasizes the message and empowers the speaker. For example, in the preface *Bonifacius, or Essays to Do Good* (1710), which offers moral instruction and advice, Cotton Mather asserts: "I will not be *immodest,* and yet I will boldly say: The man is worse than a *pagan,* who will not come into this notion of things, A good man is a public blessing [a common good]. None but a *good man,* is really a *living* man; and the more *good* any man does, the more he really *lives. All the rest is death;* or belongs to it" (Mather 1966, 7). Mather confidently asserts his ideas while emphasizing service to the greater good. Drawing from the ministerial tradition, the "I" functions rhetorically rather than as a deliberate disclosure of self. In the second chapter, "Duty to Oneself," Mather suggests constructive ways for people to spend their leisure hours, brought on "when the weather takes them off their business, or when their *shops* are not full of customers." He advises: "Sirs, the Proposal is, *Be not fools,* but *redeem* this *time* to your own advantage, to the best advantage. To the *man of leisure,* as well as to the *minister,* it is an advice of wisdom, *Give thyself unto reading.* Good books of all sorts, may employ your leisure, and enrich you with treasures" (Mather 1966, 7). Choosing the imperative mode, Mather advocates the individual act of reading but, to avoid a self-serving appearance, advises the choice of "Good books." In the third chapter, "Relative to Home and Neighborhood," Mather again takes up the first-person voice to provide advice. Embedded within this chapter, he quotes resolutions from *Paterna,* his own autobiography. He emphasizes his duty and service, holding his actions, not himself, as an example of proper behavior: "I would be solicitous to have my *children* expert, not only at *reading* handsomely, but also at *writing* a fair hand." Affirming the standards of education, as reading and writing, Mather continues with a pledge to oversee their readings: "I will then assign them such *books* to *read* as I may judge most agreeable and profitable; obliging them to give me some account of what they *read;* but keep a strict eye upon them, that they don't stumble on the *Devil's library,* and poison themselves with foolish *romances,* or *novels,* or *plays,* or *songs,* or *jests* that are *not convenient*" (Mather 1966, 46). These arguments for a monitored reading list carry well into the nineteenth century, where fictional accounts will be perceived as dangerous, especially for presumably vulnerable readers, women and children. Mather concludes this resolution with a plan for his children's writing skills, in which they would eventually "*write a prayer of their own composing*," and he promises to "discern, what sense they have of their own everlasting interests" (Mather 1966, 47). Similar to an advice book, Mather's resolutions serve as both family guide and social monitor. While this passage reveals Mather's own tastes and preferences, it is not focused on his life apart from his family or his community. Again, we have assertions of the self without an emphasis upon the individual as a separate self.

Most authors, especially Puritans, were not writing about themselves necessarily to gain a following or to capitalize on their exploits, as a reader today might assume about an autobiography, but instead to provide moral and spiritual instruction. A similar point is evident in Cotton Mather's *Magnalia Christi Americana* (1702). Books 2 and 3 include a series of biographies: "I first introduce the *Actors,* that have, in a more exemplary manner served those *Colonies;* and give *Remarkable Occurrences,* in the exemplary Lives of many *Magistrates,* and of more *Ministers,* who so *Lived,* as to leave unto Posterity *Examples* worthy of *Everlasting Remembrance*" (Mather 1977, 90). Puritan leaders, such as William Bradford and John Winthrop, are subsequently praised for their service to the greater good: "Here was Mr. *Bradford* in the Year 1621, unanimously chosen the *Governour* of the Plantation: the Difficulties whereof were such, that if he had not been a Person of more than Ordinary Piety, Wisdom and Courage, he must have sunk under them. He had, with a Laudable Industry, been laying up a Treasure of *Experiences,* and he had now occasion to use it" (Mather 1977, 205). While Mather's admiration is clear, ultimately, Bradford's strength derives from "more than ordinary" virtues, presumably divinely granted. Regarding John Winthrop, Mather writes, "How *Prudently,* how *Patiently,* and with how much Resignation to our Lord Jesus Christ, our brave *Winthrop* waded through these *Difficulties,* let Posterity Consider with Admiration . . . an Example well worthy to be Copied by all that shall succeed him in Government" (Mather 1977, 215). Embodying prudence, patience, resignation, and bravery, Winthrop garners Mather's praise, stopping short of adulation by holding Winthrop as a model of essential virtues, especially for those considering leadership positions. In each portrait, Mather illustrates the virtuous leader and demonstrates providential history. Kenneth B. Murdock elaborates on this structure: "Like most Puritan biographies, Mather's were fundamentally case-histories." As such, they followed a distinct pattern, "shaped by theological principle in which divine election, vocation, justification, and finally, salvation were crucial aspects of the dynamic operation of God's plan" (Murdock 1949, 119). In his biographies, both diary and biography, Mather offers models of behavior without endorsing self-importance.

To some extent, emphasis upon individual exploits in early American writings varies by regions. In the northern colonies, where Puritan values dominated, the first-person voice is associated with expressions of humility, as in the poetry of Anne Bradstreet and Edward Taylor, and the diary of Samuel Sewall (1973). In the middle colonies, with stronger Protestant and Quaker influences, evidence of industry and duty are often noted, as in the autobiography of Benjamin Franklin and the journal of John Woolman. For southern autobiographers of Anglican persuasion, personal views and accomplishments are more celebrated, as in the histories of Captain John Smith and William Byrd II. Illustrating a range of self-expression, these authors value modesty and commendation, a rich diversity that characterizes early American first-person narratives.

Autobiography and the Contexts of Reading

Most first-person writings were not printed for a contemporary audience but were more likely circulated as manuscript within intimate circles, much like a letter, or preserved as a family history inserted into the family Bible. Information, in general, and family histories, in particular, were more often conveyed orally rather than by printed text. So while a modern audience has the advantage of reading a larger canon of recovered and subsequently printed autobiographical texts, the contemporary interaction between audience and text and between persons and texts was quite limited. Instead, the contemporaries of Captain John Smith or Increase Mather would have known about them more through their deeds or sermons than through a printed text. For many of these early works, publication was delayed by centuries. For example, Benvenuto Cellini's autobiography, which was written in the mid–sixteenth century, was first published in 1728; Thomas Shepard wrote his autobiography in the 1640s, but it was not published until 1832; the autobiography of Increase Mather, written from approximately 1685 to 1715, was not published in its entirety until 1961; and Benjamin Franklin's autobiography, written from 1771 to 1790 was not published in full until the nineteenth century. Knowing that these texts were not written for personal gain or notoriety, but instead to reinforce cultural values, in turn, provides some explanation for their formal tone and elevated style.

The emphasis upon subordinating the self, however, did not discourage writings, whether personal or otherwise. Instead, the Protestant clergy were prolific authors of histories, sermons, essays, biographies, and autobiographies. Clergy may have been a minority in the overall colonial population, but they had a significant impact on the reading materials in early America. Along with the Protestant encouragement of literacy for scriptural interpretation, reading materials were to be instructive and practical. Richard Beale Davis thus notes that books were "assigned a value in terms of usefulness" (Davis 1979, 18). Considering the expense and logistics of migration, personal libraries were also quite limited; as J. A. Leo Lemay explains, "If a colonial family had only two books, they were probably the Bible and the current almanac" (Lemay 1972, 211). David D. Hall concurs and adds a psalm book to this list (Hall 1996, 164). Edwin Wolf substantiates these findings: "The fact cannot be overstressed that the chief reading matter for the majority of people was the Bible . . . . more than 20% of all book importations by bulk consisted of Bibles, Testaments, Psalters, and prayerbooks" (Wolf 1988, 35–36). Reading was thus meant to edify and to teach. Kevin J. Hayes observes, moreover, that devotional, conduct, and domestic manuals served as the main "types of literature read by early American women" (Hayes 1996, 102). This attention to piety and interest in practicality influenced what people were reading and how they wrote about themselves. Hayes further notes the connections between instruction and virtue in children's literature printed in the eighteenth century, so that American editions of James Janeway's *Token for Children* (1671) included Cotton Mather's appendix, "A Token of the Children of New-England: or, Some Examples of Children to Whom the Fear of God Was Remarkably Budding, before They Dyed" (1700), a work "which presented a series of biographies of pious children" (Hayes 1996, 40). Considering these expectations, early American writings were determined as much by topic as by presumptions about the value of books and writing itself.

Early American autobiography also derives from a classical tradition wherein the subject recounts a life of virtue for the benefit of an audience seeking models and inspiration. Examples include Saint Augustine's *Confessions* (ca. 400 B.C.), Montaigne's *Essais* (1580), and Francis Bacon's *Essays* (1597–1625). In such texts, an esteemed figure reviews a life of struggle or shares contemplations that will inspire and console. Mascuch discusses autobiographical lineage and notes that "the identification of the first instance of modern autobiographical practice is no simple task," adding to the preceding list autobiographers Saint Teresa of Avila, Girolamo Cardano, Edward Gibbon, Giambattista Vico, and Jean-Jacques Rousseau (Mascuch 1996, 19). For these essayists and autobiographers, there is a sense of obligation to share the story of one's life, albeit a perspective expressed by the privileged few, as they offer guidance and model reflection. In doing so, an autobiographer tries to convey sincerity and to establish authenticity, as evident in the opening of Benvenuto Cellini's autobiography: "All men of whatsoever quality they be, who have done anything of excellence, or which may properly resemble excellence, ought, if they are persons of truth and honesty, to describe their life with their own hand; but they ought not to attempt so fine an enterprise till they have passed the age of forty" (Cellini 1910, 5). In declarative tones, Cellini showcases the artist's voice while adopting the philosopher's tone. Despite his own colorful history, Cellini frames his autobiography as an obligation taken up by those who have lived long enough to have something of value to communicate.

THE STRUCTURE OF EARLY AMERICAN AUTOBIOGRAPHY

Autobiographies, both spiritual and secular, share a common structure and format. Often, they are framed as if a letter to the writer's family. Thomas Shepard addresses his autobiography to his namesake: "To my dear son Thomas Shepard with whom I leave these records of God's great kindness to him, not knowing that I shall live to tell them myself with my own mouth, that so he may learn to know and love the great and most high God, the God of his father" (Shepard 1972, 33). Benjamin Franklin follows suit and begins, "Dear Son, I have ever had a Pleasure in obtaining any little Anecdotes of my Ancestors . . . . Now imagining it may be equally agreeable to you to know the Circumstances of *my* Life . . . I sit down to write them for you" (Franklin 1986, 1). At the time Franklin was writing in 1771, his forty-one-year-old son, William, was governor of New Jersey, which lends a distinct maturity to the opening sections and underscores autobiography as a valued legacy. John Bunyan's *Grace Abounding to the Chief of Sinners, or, A Brief Relation of the Exceeding Mercy of God in Christ, to His Poor Servant John Bunyan* (1666), which profoundly influenced early American autobiography, is also addressed to posterity, "Children, Grace be with you, Amen." Though it includes some autobiographical material about his childhood, education, military service, and imprisonment, *Grace Abounding* is "intended as a record of the inner religious life of Bunyan," as Roger Sharrock explains, "not as a narrative of his life in the world" (Bunyan 1962, XIII). As a spiritual autobiography, the work is prefaced with a sense of the confessional: "In this Discourse of mine, you may see much; much, I say, of the Grace of God towards me: I thank God I can count it much, for it was above my sins and Satans temptations too. I can remember my fears, and doubts, and sad monthes with comfort; they are as the head of Goliath in my hand." As he continues setting up his text, Bunyan again directly addresses his children to emphasize his didactic intentions and thereby justify writing about himself: "My dear Children, call to mind the former days, the years of ancient times; remember also your songs in the night, and commune with your own heart. . . . Remember, I say, the Word that first laid hold upon you; remember your terrours of conscience, and fear of death and hell: remember also your tears and prayers to God; yea, how you sighed under every hedge for mercy" (Bunyan 1962, 3). With a warning and a guiding hand, Bunyan delivers a message directly to his children, which is also intended to benefit the greater good of society. By grounding his argument and his plea firmly within scripture, Bunyan abides by the convention of the autobiography that aims to inspire and to model. All the while, he avoids calling undue attention to himself and avoids a sense of self-promotion.

In a similar manner of address, Increase Mather's autobiography begins: "Dear children. [You] are all of you so many parts of myselfe; and dearer to me than [all the] things which I enjoy in this world. Wee must not live together [l]ong here below. . . . Now concerning my selfe, I give you a true (and nothing but the truth) Narration of the Lord's dispensations towards me in what here is expressed. I was born at dorchester in New England June 21 in the year 1639" (Mather 1962, 277). Even though he will proceed to write about himself, Mather constantly reinforces divine ways, with special concern for the Doctrine or Preparation. Emory Elliott explains this general intention with particular regard to Increase Mather: "Individual personality was less important than God's general ways of dealing with humanity. Given the autobiographer's inclination to record common human experiences, the unique and surprising acts of divine providence in particular lives have special significance and give Puritan autobiographers, such as Increase Mather, their drama" (Elliott 2002, 211). With care to avoid self-aggrandizing claims of self-importance, Shepard, Franklin, Bunyan, and Mather thus frame their autobiographies as if writing a letter filled with fatherly advice and moral instruction. Following these salutations, texts will then proceed chronologically, beginning with one's early years (birth, parentage, schooling, and mentoring), moving on to significant events in one's life (career, spiritual conversion, military successes, child rearing, travel), and because autobiographies are more often than not "unfinished," they do not always provide a tidy conclusion.

Early American autobiographies will also note if their stories have been written upon request to serve as exemplary models. In some instances, first-person narratives are prefaced by a person of note who endorses the text, allowing an otherwise minority voice legitimacy in the public sphere. Recall the preface to Mary Rowlandson's *Sovereignty and Goodness of God* (1682), for example. Similar instances occur in the preface to Anne Bradstreet's volume of poetry, and later with nineteenth-century slave narratives, such as William Garrison's preface to Frederick Douglass's autobiography. For the disenfranchised, a truthful record will often be verified on the title page, by the inclusion of "written by himself" or "written by herself" or "by the hand of" to authenticate the experience and lend credibility to the narrative.

Franklin also included endorsements to validate his narrative by inserting letters into the beginning of part 2 from Abel James and Benjamin Vaughan, each of whom requests Franklin to record the events of his life. Abel James thus lends this encouragement: "Life is uncertain as the Preacher tells us, and what will the World say if kind, humane and benevolent Ben Franklin should leave his Friends and the World deprived of so pleasing and profitable a Work, a Work which would be useful and entertaining not only to a few, but to millions" (Franklin 1986, 58). From another angle, Benjamin Vaughan urges Franklin to write his story to retain its authenticity: "Your history is so remarkable, that if you do not give it, somebody else will certainly give it; and perhaps so as nearly to do as much harm, as your own management of the thing might do good." Maintaining control over the Franklin life story is key to both autobiographer and reader. Acknowledging autobiography as a didactic, teaching text, Vaughan adds, "your Biography will not merely teach self-education, but the education of a *wise* man" (Franklin 1986, 58–59). For some authors, including such testimonials reinforces the veracity of an autobiography, while for others, they sanction and permit the use of first person.

Though the pattern may be somewhat standard, the selection, emphasis, narration, and intention provide the great variety within autobiographical texts. J. A. Leo Lemay elaborates on this issue: "It is generally thought that the art of an autobiography arises from the author's style and from the selection, arrangement, and interpretation of the facts of his life. In Franklin's case, it might be wise not to be too certain of his facts. There is no question of the truthfulness of the major historical facts recounted in the *Autobiography* or of the honesty of Franklin concerning them." Having established Franklin's overall reliability, Lemay adds, "There is, however, good reason to believe that a number of passages, especially in part I of the *Autobiography,* are deliberate fictions" (Lemay 1972, 238). Given the choices of what to include and which events to emphasize from one's life along with a desire to provide an overall narrative thread, the blending of "truthfulness" with "deliberate fictions" speaks to the almost inherent act of construction, which is, as Lemay reminds, not to undermine the teller but to abide the possible embellishment as part style and part mask.

AUTOBIOGRAPHY AND SELF-FASHIONING

The first-person voice can thus be considered suspect or creative as the author adopts various personae. This act of "self-fashioning," as Stephen Greenblatt identifies the process, "crosses the boundaries between the creation of literary characters, the shaping of one's own identity, the experience of being molded by forces outside one's control, the attempt to fashion other selves" (Greenblatt 1980, 3). Captain John Smith's *Generall Historie of Virginia, New-England, and the Summer Isles* (1624), for example, incorporates several genres, as both a historical narrative and a personal account. In keeping with this idea of masking, Smith refers to himself in the third person, as he relates this history of Roanoke and Jamestown: "The spring approaching, and the Ship departing, Master Scrivener and Captaine Smith devided betwixt them the rebuilding James towne; the repairing our Pallizadoes; the cutting downe trees; preparing our fields; planting our corne, and to rebuild our Church, and recover our Store house" (Smith 1986, 2: 158). Using the third person, Smith avoids self-aggrandizement, all the while that he is promoting himself. Mascuch offers yet another dimension of autobiography as a "cultural practice" and "a performance, a public display of self-identity, even when composed secretly for an audience of one" (Mascuch 1996, 9). Perhaps one of the most well-known sections and one that illustrates both masking and performance occurs when Smith describes his capture by Chief Powhatan and how he was "rescued" by Powhatan's daughter, Pocahontas: "being ready with their clubs, to beate out his braines, Pocahontas the Kings dearest daughter, when no intreaty could prevaile, got his head in her armes, and laid her owne upon his to save him from death: whereat the Emperour was contented he should live to make him hatchets, and her bells, beads, and copper; for they thought him as well of all occupations as themselves" (Smith 1986, 2: 151). Saved by the brave and kind Pocahontas, Smith lives to lead the colony and settle Jamestown. In Joseph Fichtelberg's discussion of Smith's *Generall Historie* in terms of performance and veracity, he notes this scene as the "text's most theatrical moment" with "all the elements of a staged performance before the stately Powhatan and his retainers . . . . In this instance, Smith steals the scene from Powhatan by absorbing his kingly authority. The native council becomes the unwitting audience for the adventurer's exploits" (Fichtelberg 1988, 21). From this perspective, writing about the self invites a reconstruction of real events that position the author closer to the center, enhancing one's value and suggesting a more deliberate sense of purpose. Smith exerts a definite agency in his re-creation of Jamestown, and by calling his record a history, rather than a memoir or an adventure, he presents it as a truthful account. Reading autobiography is thus to some extent an act of faith. One may approach with doubt and cynicism, undermining the author and the content, yet for the early American autobiographer, a fundamental distaste for self-promotion modifies the act of "self-fashioning," lest punitive measures be taken.

Although writing for personal communication, as in letters and journals, increased throughout the seventeenth and eighteenth centuries, formal, printed autobiography was still written primarily by prominent, mostly male, spiritual and secular figures. The extant memoirs reflect not only class status, literacy rates, and public position but also issues of gender, time, and money. For the general populace, labor-intensive domestic duties and the basic logistics of settlement took precedence over writing personal narratives. Consequently, a discussion of early American autobiography may seem to promote the idea of "representative" texts by virtue of the limited sample. As scholars continue to recover the narratives of women and men who were less socially prominent, they expand our understanding of the individual's story in early America. From the captivity narrative of Mary Rowlandson, the slave narrative of Oulaudah Equiano, the travel narrative of Sarah Kemble Knight, the spiritual autobiography of Elizabeth Ashbridge, and the narrative of Samson Occom, first-person accounts become the purview of minority voices as well. Moreover, as many of these texts follow the basic pattern of spiritual autobiography, moving from a condition of sin or enslavement to a state of salvation or freedom, an individual's experience is validated within larger intentions, be they to inform, verify, or testify.

For early American women, letters and journals also provided opportunities for autobiographical narrative, as in the cases of Abigail Adams, Esther Edwards Burr, Sara Cary, Abigail Bilhah Levy Franks, and Eliza Lucas Pinckney, who each maintained extensive correspondences that were part family history, advice book, and autobiography. On December 12, 1735, Franks, for example, writes from New York to her son in London offering this guidance: "I am Mightly Pleased to find you have a right way of thinking in Regard to the many Snares wich Open from One degree of Vice to Another to[o] much Credulity has Very Often proved the ruin of youth and one must be Very Cautious in believing those Exteriour marks of friendship and Virtue too Offten the Subterfuge of the Wicked and Crafty minds" (Franks 1968, 44). Especially when separated by vast spaces and over extended periods of time, letters provided an important opportunity for maintaining family connections, conveying advice, and expressing concern. They also provide a vehicle for personal narrative as evident in the correspondence of all these women.

SPIRITUAL AUTOBIOGRAPHY

Whereas the secular autobiography is often interested in presenting an ideal, constructed version of self, the spiritual autobiography demonstrates how random events are part of God's plan. Everything makes sense because it is geared toward conversion and salvation. The spiritual autobiography of Elizabeth Ashbridge, *Some Account of the Fore Part of the Life of Elizabeth Ashbridge* (1755), for example, exemplifies this process. Written in the 1740s, but not published until after her death, as per the Quaker tradition for autobiographical narratives, Ashbridge's account provides advice as she contrasts her youthful longings for the Truth with a self-portrait as a "Wild and Airy" young woman. Through a series of crises that prepare her for a new, post-conversion life, Ashbridge is married, widowed, bound into servitude, remarried, and treated abusively by her new husband, especially when she becomes interested in the Quaker faith. The transformation from seeker to convert is dramatic as she at first "seemed Like another Creature, and often went alone without fear, and tears abundantly flowed from [her] Eyes." At the moment of conversion she encounters a nurturing and merciful figure: "I heard a gracious Voice full of Love, saying, 'I will never Leave thee, nor forsake thee, only obey what I shall make known to thee.' I then entered Covenant saying: 'My soul Doth Magnify thee the God of mercy, if thou'l Vouchsafe thy Grace the rest of my Days shall be Devoted to thee, and if it be thy Will that I beg my Bread, Ill be content and Submit to thy Providence'" (Ashbridge 1990, 158). With the voice of God perceived as a "voice full of Love," Ashbridge indicates a new confidence in her spiritual musings, even though her quest will continue to meet challenges. The process of conversion that allows her to become a woman of authority parallels the act of autobiography that validates an individual's story.

Jonathan Edwards also balances public and private acts of self-examination and self-expression in his "Personal Narrative." A fourth-generation Calvinist minister, Edwards began writing this autobiographical narrative in the early 1740s, as the religious revivals began to ebb in New England. This act of self-examination itself is not surprising, but the timing and setting do draw attention. Edwards was thirty-six years old and on the verge of congregational turmoil when he decided to write about his conversion experience, an event that took place in the woods alongside the Hudson River, away from the town and its institutional structures. Writing may have given him perspective on the decade-long events and helped to settle questions regarding the authenticity of conversion, his own and his congregation's. For, as David Levin reminds us, the "Personal Narrative" was "written within a year or two after the winter of 1739, apparently in hope of guiding people who were trying to distinguish the signs of grace in a new outpouring of the divine spirit" (Levin 1963, 3). Edwards also may have been responding specifically to inquiries from Aaron Burr, his future son-in-law, and apparently included his narrative in a letter dated December 12, 1740 (Edwards 1998, 747). Although that letter has never been found, we do have Burr's March 1741 response to suggest this intention: "I desire to bless God that he inclined you to write and especially to write so freely of your own experiences; I think it has been much blessed in my spiritual good. Though I have often heard and read of other's experiences, I never [met] with anything that had the like effect upon me. It came in a most seasonable time, and was the means of clearing up several things that I was in the dark about" (Edwards 1998, 747). Whether Edwards intended this piece for himself, a public audience, or a private correspondent, the "Personal Narrative" allowed him to express concerns about his spiritual condition and his ministry (Imbarrato 1998, 33–38).

The public sphere may have been problematic for Edwards, but as the "Personal Narrative" frequently illustrates, his conversion process was an inspired experience. In keeping with the typical mode of autobiography, he introduced himself as a sensitive, thoughtful child: "I had a variety of concerns and exercises about my soul, from my childhood; but had two more remarkable seasons of awakening, before I met with that change, by which I was brought to those new dispositions, and that new sense of things, that I have since had." Even for Edwards, the transformation was erratic, a condition that may have offered some consolation to an outside audience had they been privy to his thoughts. Personal experiences parallel social events, as Edwards describes his childhood as "a time of remarkable awakening in my father's congregation," which left him "very much affected for many months, and concerned about the things of religion, and my soul's salvation" (Edwards 1998, 790). Edwards reinforced the fleeting quality of these initial stirrings by referencing them in terms of seasons and cycles and was careful not to appear overly confident. Daniel B. Shea finds that this succinct opening simply "reveals Edwards's anxiety to get at major issues" (Shea 1965, 22). As such, Edwards does seem aware of an audience that would have taken interest in the mechanics of the conversion process.

Edwards also distinguishes sensory reactions from true conversion as he catalogs the numerous spiritual battles. In his final year at Yale, Edwards felt "very uneasy" about his spiritual health: "It pleased God . . . to seize me with a pleurisy; in which he brought me nigh to the grave, and shook me over the pit of hell" (Edwards 1998, 791). Such displays of God's ultimate power proved humbling. And as a Calvinist who never assumed his own worthiness, Edwards explained: "I used to be continually examining myself, and studying and contriving for likely ways and means, how I should live holily, with far greater diligence and earnestness, than ever I pursued anything in my life" (Edwards 1998, 795). Edwards's determination may seem excessive, but his anxiety was underscored with an admission that he sought salvation "with too great a dependence on my own strength; which afterwards proved a great damage to me" (Edwards 1998, 791, 795). Fearful of the danger of too much self-authority, Edwards remained vigilant. Backsliding followed by affirmation, in turn, complies with the fluctuating patterns of a traditional conversion narrative.

The narrative is less conventional, however, regarding setting and his sense of an immediate audience. For, where the spiritual autobiography is typically addressed to either a direct descendent or a posthumous audience, the "Personal Narrative" falls outside of this confessional, Augustinian tradition by not addressing explicitly a future recipient of his own spiritual legacy. Instead, Edwards framed his narrative as an intimate, private conversation with God amid a natural setting. M. X. Lesser comments on this relationship: "Throughout his life [Edwards] would return to the world of nature, solitary on foot or horseback, to resume the old devotions" (Lesser 1988, 2). Personal contemplation is often associated with natural settings, especially within a romantic sensibility that favors the untamed landscape over the preferred images of a cultivated, contained nature that predominate in the eighteenth century. In finding solace in nature, Edwards appears somewhat rebellious. But as George S. Claghorn observes, Edwards was actually extending the spiritual sphere to all of creation, in that "nature has a positive inspirational role. For Edwards, contemplation of nature took on a sacramental perspective." Nature was indeed a strong, sympathetic presence. In contrast to previous Puritan attitudes that considered nature a force to be controlled or avoided, Edwards found nature restorative: "I very frequently used to retire into a solitary place, on the banks of Hudson's River, at some distance from the city, for contemplation on divine things, and secret converse with God; and had many sweet hours there" (Edwards 1998, 749, 797). His "secret" conversations and the need to retreat from the city represented a different sense of nature. Remarkably, the witch-infested forests of Cotton Mather have become a contemplative landscape for Jonathan Edwards.

As the first-person narrative allowed Edwards to reveal his inner thoughts and spiritual desires, he focused more upon the present moment. The rhythmic cadence of his prose, in turn, mirrors an immediate, sensory interaction. And as the beauty translated him, this relationship to the immediate moment grew increasingly reverent. Where he had previously been "a person uncommonly terrified with thunder," for instance, he recorded a new response: "But now, on the contrary, it rejoiced me. I felt God at the first appearance of a thunderstorm. And used to take the opportunity at such times, to fix myself to view the clouds, and see the lightnings play, and hear the majestic and awful voice of God's thunder." Enraptured by this view, Edwards describes his actions, whereby he would "sing or chant forth my meditations; to speak my thoughts in soliloquies, and speak with a singing voice" (Edwards 1998, 794).

Nature inspired Edwards to express his gratitude openly. As Paul David Johnson notes, Edwards's "singing re-creates the expansiveness of divine immensity within him and, in repetition, creates infinity" (Johnson 1982, 279). As Edwards further developed his relationship with divinity, he temporarily distanced himself from external problems. By slowing down and isolating the moment, Edwards marked time in a more personal context. Unencumbered by controversy, he was free to enjoy divine matters in solitude. Writing the narrative allowed him to recollect these experiences and thereby gain perspective. In this regard, first-person narratives enhance self-understanding and elicit reflection. Claghorn thus notes "the private, human" Edwards emerges "not as an austere and aloof scholar but as an astute readers of persons and situations" (Edwards 1998, 3). When life writing aids writers in understanding the threads of their lives, it potentially brings solace, if not simply renewed perspective. Thus autobiography may be taken up for contemplation, or as Edwards suggests, it is the act of writing itself that reveals how the life is unfolding. To return to Franklin, then, an autobiographer might edit with some freedom, but never stray too far from the basic biographical truth.

SECULAR AUTOBIOGRAPHY

Similar to other first-person narratives, the autobiography of a statesman also includes family history, influential role models, career accomplishments, and early sources of inspiration, while also engaging in a masking of self. Republican ideas were, in turn, especially influential regarding the style of such narratives, as Gordon Wood explains, for individuals were "expected to suppress their private wants and interests and develop disinterestedness—the term the eighteenth century most often used as a synonym for civic virtue" (Wood 1992, 104–105). In doing so, they also addressed a danger identified by Fredric Bogel as "one of self-authorization, of an authority founded on nothing external to the self and its constructions" (Bogel 1987, 191). Modeling behaviors while maintaining hierarchy are key tasks for the politician who engages in autobiography. Thomas Jefferson and John Adams write their memoirs in part as an obligation and also to set the public record straight, while drawing upon classical models of the autobiography as exemplary texts. Similar to Benjamin Franklin's enumeration of his erratum, the autobiography offers Jefferson and Adams a second chance to correct any inaccuracies that have entered the public record.

This concern is particularly prominent for Adams, who explains, "My Excuse is, that having been the Object of much Misrepresentation, some of my Posterity may probably wish to see in my own hand Writing a proof of the falsehood of that Mass of odious Abuse of my Character, with which News Papers, private Letters and public Pamphlets and Histories have been disgraced for thirty Years." For Adams the autobiography allows the opportunity to correct any "misrepresentations" for the sake of family honor. Somewhat surprisingly, the otherwise opinionated John Adams approaches his autobiography with a certain reluctance, explaining, "It is not for the Public but for my Children that I commit these memoirs to writing." In 1802, John Adams, at the age of sixty-seven, thus begins his autobiography: "As the Lives of Phylosophers, Statesmen or Historians written by them selves have generally been suspected of Vanity, and therefore few People have been able to read them without disgust; there is no reason to expect that any Sketches I may leave of my own Times would be received by the Public with any favour, or read by individuals with much interest." In keeping with earlier disdain for self-promotion, Adams modestly deflects any value that might be attached to his narrative. He then offers the standard family lineage: "The Customs of Biography require that something should be said of my origin. Early in the Settlement of the Colony of Massachusetts, a Gentleman from England arriving in America with Eight Sons, settled near Mount Wollaston and not far from the ancient Stone Building erected for the double Purpose of Public Worship and Fortification against the Indians." As a matter of simple facts, he lays out the story of a remarkable life. Adams also wrote in private, without even his family's knowledge. In fact when his son, John Quincy, wrote on November 19, 1804, urging his father to record "an account of the principle incidents" of his life, John Adams responded that he was hesitant to recall his "Mortifications, Disappointments or Resentments" (Adams 1961, 1: LXIX; 3: 253–254). Similar requests from friends such as Dr. Benjamin Rush and F. A. Van were met with denials. For all of Adams's public displays of confidence, he was quite protective of his life story.

In Thomas Jefferson's case, the reluctance is even more pronounced, as his hundred-page autobiography that only partially covers his life from 1743 to 1790 begins simply on January 6, 1821: "At the age of 77, I begin to make some memoranda and state some recollections of dates and facts concerning myself, for my own more ready reference and for the information of my family." Jefferson then proceeds with the conventional tracing of his family lineage: "The tradition in my father's family was that their ancestor came to this country from Wales, and from near the mountain of Snowdon, the highest in Gr. Br. I noted once a case from Wales in the law reports where a person of our name was either pl. or def. and one of the same name was Secretary to the Virginia company" (Jefferson 1984, 3). As with other autobiographers, Jefferson does not simply list dates and events but makes decisions about which events to include and where to expand. In the section preceding the Declaration of Independence, he includes parallel versions to show which of his passages were excised, and makes note of such decisions: "As the sentiments of men are known not only by what they receive, but what they reject also, I will state the form of the declaration as originally reported" (Jefferson 1984, 18).

Jefferson includes several defining political moments that were also quite personal, for example, while in London with John Adams engaged with trade negotiations in 1786, he writes: "On my presentation as usual to the King and Queen at their levees, it was impossible for anything to be more ungracious than their notice of Mr. Adams and myself. I saw at once that the ulcerations in the narrow mind of that mulish being left nothing to be expected on the subject of my attendance; and on the first conference with the Marquis of Carmarthen his Minister of foreign affairs, the distance and disinclination which he betrayed in his conversation, the vagueness and evasions of his answers to us, confirmed me in the belief of their aversion to have anything to do with us" (Jefferson 1984, 57–58). Though publicly Jefferson might have repressed such sentiment, his autobiography allows him to chastise the British for blurring the lines between public and private. Merrill D. Peterson, moreover, observes that despite the "vast corpus of papers, private and public, his personality remains elusive . . . . Jefferson is perhaps the least self-revealing and the hardest to sound the depths of being. It is a mortifying confession but he remains for me, finally, an impenetrable man" (Peterson 1970, VIII). Jay Fliegelman reminds us that "what most post-Freudian readers cannot accept . . . is that Jefferson's self-presentation is not merely a strategy of concealment. Rather, it represents a particular moral and social conception of identity" (Fliegelman 1993, 122). Jefferson and Adams also know that personal disclosure will be publicly scrutinized and use their autobiographies to further establish distinctions between the personal and the public.

CONCLUSION

From the settlements of 1607 to the new nation of 1780, early American autobiography expresses an intimate relationship between the individual and larger cultural forces. Valued artifacts of personal expression, these texts allow us to witness early America from a contemporary perspective, a quality that makes them at once strange and intriguing. We wonder, for example, why they are so absorbed by Providence and why they are so reticent about disclosing personal desires, and yet we empathize with their physical hardships and timeless concerns about family welfare, health, and fortune. Early American autobiographical texts range across class, gender, ethnicity, and creed to anchor our historical understanding of migration, settlement, rebellion, and nation building with important and valuable insight.

REFERENCES

Adams, John. 1961. *The Diary and Autobiography of John Adams,* edited by L. H. Butterfield, Leonard C. Faber, and Wendell D. Garrett. 4 vols. Cambridge: Belknap Press of Harvard University Press.

Ashbridge, Elizabeth. 1990. *Some Account of the Fore Part of the Life of Elizabeth Ashbridge, 1755,* edited by Daniel B. Shea. In *Journeys in New Worlds: Early American Women's Narratives,* edited by William L. Andrews, 117–180. Madison: University of Wisconsin Press.

Bogel, Fredric. 1987. Johnson and the Role of Authority. In *The New Eighteenth Century: Theory, Politics, English Literature,* edited by Felicity Nussbaum and Laura Brown, 189–209. New York: Methuen.

Bradford, William. [1952] 1970. *Of Plymouth Plantation, 1620–1647,* edited by Samuel Eliot Morison. Reprint. New York: Knopf.

Bunyan, John. 1962. *Grace Abounding to the Chief of Sinners,* edited by Roger Sharrock. Oxford: Clarendon.

Cellini, Benvenuto. 1910. *The Autobiography of Benvenuto Cellini,* trans. and edited by J. Addington Symonds. New York: Collier.

Davis, Richard Beale. 1979. *A Colonial Southern Bookshelf: Reading in the Eighteenth Century.* Athens: University of Georgia Press.

Edwards, Jonathan. 1998. *Jonathan Edwards: Letters and Personal Writings,* edited by George S. Claghorn. New Haven, CT: Yale University Press.

Elliott, Emory. 2002. *The Cambridge Introduction to Early American Literature.* New York: Cambridge University Press.

Fichtelberg, Joseph. 1988. The Complex Image: Text and Reader in the Autobiography of Benjamin Franklin. *Early American Literature* 23: 202–217.

Fliegelman, Jay. 1993. *Declaring Independence: Jefferson, Natural Language, and the Culture of Performance.* Stanford, CA: Stanford University Press.

Franklin, Benjamin. 1986. *Benjamin Franklin's Autobiography: An Authoritative Text, Backgrounds, Criticism.* New York: Norton.

Franks, Abigail Bilhah Levy. 1968. *The Lee Max Friedman Collection of American Jewish Colonial Correspondence: Letters of the Franks Family, 1733–1748,* edited by Leo Hershkowitz and Isidore S. Meyer. Waltham, MA: American Jewish Historical Society.

Greenblatt, Stephen. 1980. *Renaissance Self-Fashioning from More to Shakespeare.* Chicago: University of Chicago Press.

Hall, David D. 1996. *Cultures of Print: Essays in the History of the Book.* Amherst: University of Massachusetts Press.

Hayes, Kevin J. 1996. *A Colonial Woman's Bookshelf.* Knoxville: University of Tennessee Press.

Jefferson, Thomas. 1984. *Writings,* edited by Merrill D. Peterson. New York: The Library of America.

Imbarrato, Susan Clair. 1998. *Declarations of Independency in Eighteenth-Century American Autobiography.* Knoxville: University of Tennessee Press.

Johnson, Paul David. 1982. Jonathan Edwards's "Sweet Conjunction." *Early American Literature* 16: 270–281.

Lemay, J. A. Leo. 1972. Benjamin Franklin. In *Major Writers of Early American Literature,* edited by Everett Emerson, 205–243. Madison: University of Wisconsin Press.

Lesser, M. X. 1988. *Jonathan Edwards.* Boston: Twayne.

Levin, David. 1963. *The Puritan in the Enlightenment: Franklin and Edwards.* New York: Rand McNally.

Lowance, Mason I., Jr. 1988. Biography and Autobiography. In *Columbia History of the United States,* edited by Emory Elliott, 67–82. New York: Columbia University Press.

Mascuch, Michael. 1996. *Origins of the Individualist Self: Autobiography and Self-Identity in England, 1591–1791.* Stanford, CA: Stanford University Press.

Mather, Cotton. 1966. *Bonifacius: An Essay upon the Good,* edited by David Levin. Cambridge, MA: Belknap Press.

———. 1977. *Magnalia Christi Americana; or, The Ecclesiastical History of New-England from Its First Planting, in the Year 1620, unto the Year of Our Lord, 1698,* edited by Kenneth B. Murdock. Cambridge, MA: Belknap Press.

Mather, Increase. 1962. *The Autobiography of Increase Mather,* edited by M. G. Hall. Worcester, MA: American Antiquarian Society.

Misch, Georg. [1907] 1951. *A History of Autobiography in Antiquity.* Vol. 1. Reprint. Cambridge, MA: Harvard University Press.

Murdock, Kenneth Ballard. 1949. *Literature and Theology in Colonial New England.* Cambridge, MA: Harvard University Press.

Peterson, Merrill D. 1970. *Thomas Jefferson and the New Nation: A Biography.* New York: Oxford University Press.

Rowlandson, Mary. 1990. A True History of the Captivity and Restoration, edited by Amy Schrager Lang. In *Journeys in New Worlds: Early American Women's Narratives,* edited by William L. Andrews, 27–65. Madison: University of Wisconsin Press.

Sewall, Samuel. 1973. *The Diary of Samuel Sewall: 1674–1729,* edited by M. Halsey Thomas. 2 vols. New York: Farrar, Straus and Giroux.

Shea, Daniel B., Jr. 1965. The Art and Instruction of Jonathan Edwards's Personal Narrative. *American Literature* 37: 17–32.

Shepard, Thomas. 1972. Autobiography. In *God's Plot: The Paradoxes of Puritan Piety. Being the Autobiography and Journal of Thomas Shepard,* edited by Michael McGiffert, 33–77. Amherst: University of Massachusetts Press.

Smith, John. 1986. *The Complete Works of John Smith (1580–1631),* ed. Philip. L. Barbour. 3 vols. Chapel Hill: University of North Carolina Press.

Southey, Robert. 1805. *Madoc.* London: Longman, Hurst, Rees, and Orme.

Wigglesworth, Michael. [1951] 1965. *The Diary of Michael Wigglesworth, 1653–1657: The Conscience of a Puritan,* edited by Edmund S. Morgan. Reprint. New York: Harper and Row.

Wolf, Edwin, 2nd. 1988. *The Book Culture of a Colonial American City: Philadelphia Books, Bookmen, and Booksellers.* New York: Clarendon.

Wood, Gordon S. 1992. *The Radicalism of the American Revolution.* New York: Knopf.

CHAPTER 18

EARLY AMERICAN SLAVE NARRATIVES

APRIL LANGLEY

Recent scholarship has offered important new insights into our understanding of the earliest narratives by American writers of African descent (O'Neale 1993; Zafar 1997; Brooks 2003; Saillant 2003; Carretta 2005). These insights emphasize the value of early American slave narratives and shed light on the successful strategies used by black narrators for telling their stories. Their narrative strategies significantly influenced how such critical issues as religion, politics, commerce, and captivity have been articulated (Gould 2003, 10). Once considered as marginally "black" or "American" or, for that matter, "literature," early American slave narratives reflect the distinct voice of black American identity. They appropriate yet subvert a variety of important literary genres, including captivity narratives, conversion narratives, and spiritual autobiography. Locating eighteenth-century black American narrative within the development of these other genres can provide significant clues to understanding the themes of identity, spirituality, slavery, and freedom, themes that remain central to modern black literary movements (Stepto 1979).

These eighteenth-century American slave narratives represent the earliest attempts to recount black experiences of spiritual, physical, and cultural captivity. They include the following works: Briton Hammon's *Narrative of the Uncommon Sufferings, and Surprizing Deliverance of Briton Hammon, A Negro Man* (1760); Ukawsaw Gronniosaw's *Narrative of the Most Remarkable Particulars in the Life of James Albert Ukawsaw Gronniosaw, An African Prince* (1772), which remained a steady seller for decades after its initial appearance; John Marrant's *Narrative of the Lord's Wonderful Dealings With John Marrant, a Black* (1785); and Olaudah Equiano's *Interesting Narrative of the Life of Olaudah Equiano, or Gustavus Vassa, The African, Written By Himself* (1789), the finest African American narrative before Frederick Douglass's *Narrative of the Life of Frederick Douglass, An American Slave, Written by Himself* (1845). All of these merit further discussion.

BRITON HAMMON

The long title of Briton Hammon's short work provides a good indication of its contents and suggests how it belongs among other forms of narrative discourse in colonial America: *Narrative of the Uncommon Sufferings, and Surprizing Deliverance of Briton Hammon, A Negro Man,—Servant to General Winslow, of Marshfield, in New-England; Who Returned to Boston, after Having Been Absent almost Thirteen Years. Containing an Account of the Many Hardships He Underwent from the Time He Left His Master's House, in the Year 1747, to the Time of his Return to Boston.—How He Was Cast Away in the Capes of Florida;—the Horrid Cruelty and Inhuman Barbarity of the Indians in Murdering the Whole Ship's Crew;—the Manner of His Being Carry'd by Them into Captivity. Also, An Account of His Being Confined Four Years and Seven Months in a Close Dungeon,—And the Remarkable Manner in which He Met with his Good Old Master in London; Who Returned to New-England, a Passenger, in the Same Ship.*

The story of Hammon's departure from New England, arrival in the West Indies, shipwreck off the coast of Florida, capture at sea by Indians, redemption and subsequent imprisonment at the hands of the Spanish in Cuba, encounter with numerous "alien" others (non-Christian, non-Protestant, non-British, non-American), and subsequent freedom and reunion with his master constitutes the earliest published narrative in the English-speaking world by a freed black captive. Beyond questions of race-based bondage in the colonies, Hammon's work opens the door for discussions of cultural, national, and religious self-identification (Zafar 1997, 41). Regardless of Hammon's identification of himself as "a Negro man" in the title, the account of his journey from freedom (with his British master) to slavery (at the hands of Cubans, Catholics, Indians, and others) to freedom (once again in the safe haven of General Winslow and the British colonies) is neither wholly representative of a conventional narration of Indian captivity nor a tale of typical African colonial bondage. While Hammon's captivity narrative embodies the didactic aims of eighteenth-century Christian conversion narratives, it does much more. Both his "*manner* of his being carry'd . . . into Captivity" and his method of relating the "*matters* of fact as they occur" suggest overlapping commercial, political, and religious concerns.

The theme of disobedience, for example, forms an important part of Hammon's *Narrative of Uncommon Sufferings,* much as it does in other early American slave narratives. Speaking about himself in *Narrative of the Lord's Wonderful Dealings,* John Marrant states, "Disobedience either to God or man, being one of the fruits of sin, grew out from me in early buds" (Carretta 2004, 112). Similarly, Hammon suggests that disobedience "either to god or man" triggers the providential forces that led to his capture. Early in *Narrative of the Uncommon Sufferings,* Hammon reveals that it was the sea captain's failure to obey the pleas of "every person on board, to heave over but only 20 Ton of the *Wood*" that resulted in the loss of the "Vessel and Cargo" and the captain's "own Life, as well as the Lives of the Mate and Nine Hands" (Carretta 2004, 20–21). There is no mistaking the biblical parallels between Hammon's recounting of this act of disobedience within the context of a Jonah-like parable. Olaudah Equiano depicts similarly relevant situations with regard to casting objects overboard. On one occasion, Equiano calls such actions both necessary and practical to prepare for an impending battle. Another time he reports that by "tossing many things overboard to lighten her, we got the ship off without any damage." In an act of disobedience, the entire ship's crew engages in mutinous behavior as they side with Equiano and thus thwart their captain's efforts to save the ship by barbaric means. The captain had "ordered the hatches to be nailed down on the slaves in the hold, where there were above twenty, all of whom must unavoidably have perished if he had been obeyed" (Equiano 2003, 76, 149). Making the theme of disobedience prominent, early black narrators such as Hammon, Marrant, and Equiano not only participate in eighteenth-century homiletics on Christian obedience but also extend the development of mainstream discourse on civil disobedience.

Both the manner in which Hammon is captured and the means by which he relates the experience document important aspects of the eighteenth-century slave trade. His narrative offers the opportunity to explore the unique existence of the lives of the people of African descent in early America. As a black narrator, he begins by explaining that he embarks with his master's leave on the seafaring journey that would result in his extraordinary thirteen-year captivity. Since he has identified his racial identity as "a Negro," however, the idea that he has the permission of his "master" to travel suggests a departure from more conventional captivity narratives. While Hammon's race figures less prominently in this eighteenth-century captivity narrative than it would in nineteenth-century slave narratives, it cannot be overlooked. Though his narrative reflects many conventional concerns—the importance of divine Providence, the authority of the British Crown, the propagation of the American Protestant gospel, and the identification of the spiritual and cultural Indian enemy—it deserves to be read in terms of its primary concern, the slave trade.

The captive "Negro man" in *Narrative of the Uncommon Sufferings* parallels the captured Christians in other early American captivity narratives. The "Negro man" cannot elicit the degree of sympathy that the typical narrator (white, English, Christian, female) can, however. Both the black man's race and his uncertain legal status impair reader sympathy. Though Hammon apparently was a free black, he uses the word "master" to refer to his employer, General Winslow, and thus suggests a master-slave relationship. Sometimes his legal status seems unclear in *Narrative of the Uncommon Sufferings*. In *Narrative of the Lord's Wonderful Dealings*, John Marrant, though also a free man, uses the word "master" on several occasions to refer to his employer. In the absence of clarity, even an eighteenth-century audience that understood the dual meaning of the word "master" might have considered the possibility of Hammon being a slave. Slave owners often hired out their slaves to other masters on land as well as at sea. Olaudah Equiano, for example, makes multiples references to the earnings he acquires working aboard a ship, though still a slave to Robert King (Bolster 1997; Reiss 1997, 231; Martin 2004).

Even within eighteenth-century discourse on freedom, slavery, spirituality, and national identification, early black narrators like Hammon enhance narrative complexity. In *Narrative of the Uncommon Sufferings*, the language of slavery interrupts the discourse of Indian savagery (Zafar 1997; Gould 2003). Hammon's account of the Indians' "murdering the whole Ship's Crew" echoes Mary Rowlandson's earlier description of her Indian captors as "those barbarous creatures" who murdered and left a dozen Christians lying in their blood and who "captured and carried off another 24" of whom, Job-like, Rowlandson "escaped alone to tell the News" (Rowlandson 1997, 70). Similarly, Hammon identifies himself as the sole survivor after witnessing the murder of everyone else who waited aboard the sloop with him. Yet there are striking differences between Rowlandson's language—written nearly a hundred years earlier—and Hammon's. Changes in attitude and experience over the intervening century help explain the differences between Rowlandson's decision to remain alive and go along with the Indians and Hammon's initial attempt to escape capture by suicide. During that time, notions of Indian captivity and purposes of Indian captivity narratives had changed drastically (Derounian-Stodola and Levernier 1993, 23; Sekora 1993, 101–103).

Hammon's description of his Indian captors' "prodigious shouting and hallowing like so many Devils" resembles Rowlandson's description of "the roaring, and singing and dancing, and yelling of those black creatures in the night, which made the place a lively resemblance of hell"—with one key difference. Notably, Hammon does not use the term "black" to describe his captors (Rowlandson 1997, 71; Carretta 2004, 21). Given the traditional associations of Indians with "the devil," Rowlandson's language is unsurprising. Hammon's refusal to use similar language in his captivity narrative suggests a change in the dominant constructions of evil. Omitting the word "black" while otherwise using much the same language as Rowlandson, Hammon and, in general, early American narrators of African descent made selective use of dominant white colonial discourse. *Narrative of the Uncommon Sufferings* verifies Hammon's willingness to participate in the language of captivity, at least to the extent that the Indians who murdered and committed other "barbarous" acts were considered vile devils.

Hammon does use the term "black" elsewhere in the narrative, each time with negative connotations. Generally speaking, the Negro narrator's engagement with such key racial signifiers as "black" (through either omission or repetition) suggests a shift in the language of race in the late eighteenth century. Hammon's refusal to extend his description of the Indian "devils" to include men with black skin suggests his awareness of the consequences for a man who was himself a Negro—a black or dark-skinned man—to be identified with such vileness. Alternatively, a black Christian narrator like Hammon who recounts the cost of his skin color for an enslaved black man links the consequences of black skin with unmerited punishment and suggests the extent to which early narratives of black captivity engage discourses of race, religion, and culture.

By making visible race-based African slavery in the context of Indian captivity, early American narratives like Hammon's suggest the inextricable nature of Indian and white colonial "savagery" and "barbarity" as it relates to slavery and captivity. Black writers, as Rafia Zafar has observed, "changed permanently the meanings of the genres they appropriated" (Zafar 1997, 10). By extension, they began large-scale changes in cultural and political discourse that continued well past the Civil War. Furthermore, they have influenced our modern understanding of the "transformative" power of the early black narrative.

UKAWSAW GRONNIOSAW

Henry Louis Gates Jr. has placed great emphasis on the linguistic and literary transformations wrought by early American slave narratives (Gates 1988). The authors who followed Briton Hammon—Ukawsaw Gronniosaw (also known as "James Albert"), John Marrant, Olaudah Equiano—provide further evidence of the powerful shift in mainstream discourse made possible by early black American narratives. Black writers were simultaneously engaged in dialogue with each other and with their white masters. They often marked their texts with a critique of the white literacy. Their writings evince a previously unacknowledged level of intellect and political savvy. Overall, these early black narratives were the works of men who represent an important yet often neglected strain of thought in early America.

A key aspect of early black autobiography is symbolized by what Gates terms the "trope of the talking book." This trope or figure of speech concerns the most important book in early American history, the Bible. In early black narrative, the

Bible is frequently depicted as a text that fails to speak to blacks. As a sign of the master's literate world, reading is inaccessible to blacks. Arguing that the "talking book" links the narratives of Gronniosaw, Marrant, and Equiano, Gates has suggested that these texts speak to one to another through their respective, figurative references.

In his *Narrative of the Most Remarkable Particulars,* Gronniosaw locates in his master's Bible a written text that will not speak to him:

> He used to read prayers in public to the ship's crew every Sabbath day; and when I first saw him read, I was never so surprised in my life, as when I saw the book talk to my master; for I thought it did, as I observed him to look upon it, and move his lips.—I wished it would do so to me. As soon as my master had done reading I follow'd him to the place where he put the book, being mightily delighted with it, and when nobody saw me, I open'd it and put my ear down close upon it, in great hope that it wou'd say something to me; but I was very sorry and greatly disappointed, when I found it would not speak, this thought immediately presented itself to me, that every body and every thing despis'd me because I was black. (Carretta 2004, 38)

Dictated to an amanuensis when Gronniosaw was around sixty, *Narrative of the Most Remarkable Particulars* contemplates this pivotal moment in his life, ironically commenting on his naïveté about the relationship between written and spoken language and about his assumption that his race denied him access to the speaking book. He reveals that blacks first encountered the idea of literacy in the context of religion. His master, who reads prayers on the Sabbath to the ship's crew, confirms the spiritual value of the Bible as a text that must be engaged orally in order to be effective. While Gronniosaw's narrative draws attention to his own illiteracy, it neither affirms nor denies his ability to understand the word as it is "spoken" by his master. Blacks and other illiterate Christians (black and white) learned the Bible by hearing its words read aloud and then repeating them. Gronniosaw's focus in this passage is not on whether he can hear but whether he can make the book speak, to make it address him in the same manner as it does his master. Gronniosaw explains how such a misunderstanding has occurred. The young enslaved African "thought" the book was speaking to his master as he watched him look upon it and move his lips. This type of confusion, especially in the context of Christian conversion, seems reasonable given the pertinent biblical context. The Bible asserts that the attainment of spiritual knowledge occurs through the spoken word. Consider Romans 10:17: "Faith cometh by hearing, and hearing by the *word* of God."

Because the religious aims of a conversion narrative such as Gronniosaw's have chiefly to do with documenting the life of a potential convert to provide evidence of his acceptance into the Christian community, all autobiographical elements that are included should be identified as signs of God's election. John Campbell's *Treatise on Conversion* (1743) is instructive here because it provides a useful context for understanding the conventional aims that structure a conversion narrative: "In the prosecution of our Doctrine, these following Points fall in naturally to be discoursed upon: viz. First, *Conversion*. Secondly, *Faith*. Thirdly, *Justification*. Fourthly and lastly, the *Application* of these briefly and plainly in their Order" (Campbell 1743, 20). Thus narrators first addressed the process by which they were converted.

In Gronniosaw's case his story begins in Bournu (now northeastern Nigeria), as far outside of the reach of the gospel as his Western audiences might imagine. Depicting himself as a Moses-like figure, he establishes his conversion on the basis of one who, in Campbell's words, is "called . . . justified . . . and . . . glorified" (Campbell 1743, 19). Gronniosaw reflects that his "curious turn of mind was more grave and reserved" than that of his brothers and sisters. His own early disposition corresponds to that of serious men like his master, men whose actions (in particular the reading of scripture on the Sabbath) correspond to Gronniosaw's state of mind. Furthermore, his departure for the New World reflects his desire to learn more about this "Man of Power" who "lived above." Providentially, a "merchant from the *Gold Coast*" arrives and offers to take Gronniosaw abroad and return him safely, to show him "houses with wings to [let] them walk upon the water" and "white folks" (Carretta 2004, 35). After a series of misadventures, Gronniosaw is condemned to death and brought before an African king. It "pleased God to melt the heart of the King." In Joseph-like fashion, Gronniosaw is sold into slavery rather than killed. He describes each transaction in the triangular trade from Africa to Europe to the colonies as part of the providential design of an "Almighty" God. Looking back, the elderly Gronniosaw thus relates that he "was glad when my new Master took" those things that symbolized a relinquishing of his royal African birthright, beliefs, and wealth (Carretta 2004, 37–38).

The context of Christian conversion requires a surrender of material for the spiritual wealth in God's kingdom. Years after his initial conversion, when he is free and married with children to his poor but "blessed partner," Betty, Gronniosaw's failure to obtain even such basic necessities as food seems a part of God's providential plan. Even when he and his wife are unable to secure employment and are "reduc'd to the greatest distress imaginable," even when they have nothing to eat but four raw carrots, he retains his Christian faith. Thus, throughout this narrative he reaffirms the moralistic aims of conversion, faith, justification, and application of the tenets of Christian faith—ultimately confirming him and his wife as pilgrims traveling toward their "Heavenly Home" who continue to praise God (Carretta 2004, 49, 50, 53).

Born of the religious fervor of the first evangelical movement of the Great Awakening, narratives of conversion were in their own rights "subversive" texts that undermined the authority of the established clergy. Such narratives did so primarily because the power to articulate conversion became a matter of successfully demonstrating the steps necessary for initiation into God's kingdom. Conversion depended on a relationship between the convert and the divine, not on religious leadership that might be subject to human frailty and corruption. Once set in motion, the deposing of traditional clerical authority would be difficult to reverse. It was in this historical moment that a political as well as a religious awakening was inaugurated.

Despite Gronniosaw's connections to mainstream conversion discourse, both his repeated inflections of "blackness" and his emphasis on the hypocrisy of slaveholding Christians suggest that his narrative is committed to dual purposes. His initial reaction to the Bible's refusal to speak to him marks him as an outsider in terms of both race and religion. In the face of the Bible's refusal to speak, he assumes "that every body and every thing despis'd me because I was black" (Carretta 2004, 38). What could possibly have provoked such a "thought"? And why had it "presented itself" to him with such immediacy? The word "despised" suggests the contempt with which black people were regarded. By the end of the episode, however, it remains unclear why his frustration with his illiteracy would have evoked such strong emotions and sudden realization of color prejudice, especially given his relatively benign depiction of his condition as a black man in the story up to this point.

Elsewhere in *Narrative of the Most Remarkable Particulars,* the reasons underlying Gronniosaw's emotional outpouring in regard to other personal experiences seem clear. Consider the following passage:

> After I had been a little while with my new master I grew more familiar, and ask'd
> him the meaning of prayer: (I could hardly speak English to be understood) he
> took great pains with me, and made me understand that he pray'd to God, who
> liv'd in Heaven; that He was my Father and Best Friend.—I told him that this
> must be a mistake; that *my* father lived at Bournou, and I wanted very much to see
> him, and likewise my dear mother, and sister, and I wish'd he would be so good as
> to send me home to them; and I added, all that I could think of to induce him to
> convey me back. I appeared in great trouble, and my good master was so affected,
> that the tears ran down his face. (Carretta 2004, 39)

Theodorus Jacobus Frelinghuysen, called Mr. Freelandhouse in *Narrative of the Most Remarkable Particulars,* Gronniosaw describes as "a very gracious, good Minister." Though he seems genuinely moved by his slave's predicament, his failure to grant Gronniosaw's request for freedom belies his apparent compassion. (Not until his death did Frelinghuysen free Gronniosaw.) The young African's pleas to return home to his family and friends suggest a desire to be with those who do not despise his blackness. His "immediate" thoughts upon hearing his master's words of religious instruction, as they had been when he first attempted to read the Word of God, turned to those most like him, those he identified with racially and culturally.

Overall, Gronniosaw's *Narrative of the Most Remarkable Particulars* shows how integral literacy, oral culture, slavery, and race are to the story of black conversion. The work captured the attention of contemporary readers. It was first published in Bath, England, in 1770 and was reprinted throughout Great Britain for decades.

William Williams translated it into Welsh in 1779. The first American edition was published at Newport, Rhode Island, in 1774, and in 1797 it was serialized in the *American Moral and Sentimental Magazine.* It continued to be republished in both Great Britain and America in the early nineteenth century as the abolitionist movement expanded. Gronniosaw's personal story touched his readers, provoked their compassion, and prompted them to sympathize with his plight and the plight of enslaved Africans everywhere.

JOHN MARRANT

John Marrant's *Narrative of the Lord's Wonderful Dealings with John Marrant, a Black* stands out among early black narratives in several respects. Marrant tells the story of his experiences as a free black carpenter's apprentice who converts to Christianity, ventures into the wilderness, is captured by the Cherokee and condemned to death, but is saved by his potential executioner's miraculous conversion. The narrative reflects both his open-mindedness and the complexity of his attitude toward Native Americans. The tone and tenor of his remarks differ from those of W. Aldridge, whose words preface *Narrative of the Lord's Wonderful Dealings.* Aldridge uses derogatory language to frame Marrant's experience with the Cherokee people. In contrast to the preface, Marrant's account becomes a counternarrative of Indian and African redemption.

Like Gronniosaw, Marrant graphically depicts the barbaric manner in which white slaveholding Christians subvert the mission of religious conversion. He speaks as an objective, analytical observer who is both insider and outsider, anticipating the perspective Equiano would take. Furthermore, Marrant's narrative offers one of the earliest comparisons between notions of childlike innocence in black and white, which Harriet Beecher Stowe would capitalize on with the character of Little Eva in *Uncle Tom's Cabin.* As a free, American-born, eighteenth-century black narrator who recounts his experiences with Christian conversion and Indian captivity, Marrant is twice rejected but ultimately triumphant. He becomes an itinerant minister to Indian kings and princesses, children, slaves, and masters; chaplain to the first lodge of African masons, which was founded by Prince Hall in Boston; and the first black American to be ordained minister—called to preach to his "kinsmen, according to the flesh" (Carretta 2004, 126).

Marrant's contemplation of his ministerial mission in Nova Scotia may best express the complexity of black life in colonial America. His dynamic role challenges the static views of free and enslaved blacks and changes widely held assumptions about the marginalized people who shaped the American landscape. On the occasion of his departure from his beloved friends in England, Marrant offered the following entreaty for the "earnest prayers" of his "Christian friends":

> that I may be carried safe there; kept humble, made faithful, and successful; that strangers may hear of and run to Christ; that Indian tribes may stretch out their hands to God; that the black nations may be made white in the blood of the Lamb; that vast multitudes, of hard tongues, and of a strange speech, may learn the language of Canaan, and sing the song of Moses, and of the Lamb; and, anticipating the glorious prospect, may we all with fervent hearts, and willing tongues, sing Hallelujah; the kingdoms of the world are become the kingdoms of our God, and of his Christ. Amen and Amen. (Carretta 2004, 127)

Marrant's Christian odyssey began long before his mission to Nova Scotia, however. Wandering the American wilderness after his religious conversion during his teenage years, he established important ties with several Indian nations. After being captured, imprisoned, and set free by Cherokees, he was "received with kindness" by the Creeks, "visited" with the Catawar, and safely "passed among" the Housaw. While divine Providence is presented as an agent in his safe travel, Marrant also demonstrates firsthand knowledge about the importance of nations "at peace with each other." The fact that he is recommended from one Indian nation to another affects his ability to travel beyond Cherokee territory. Far more ominous—couched in the language of conversion but invoking the rhetoric of the Revolution—is Marrant's caution to his white American readers: "When they [the Indian nations] recollect, that the white people drove them from the American shores, they are full of resentment. These nations have often united, and murdered all the white people in the back settlements which they could lay hold of, men, women, and children." In the context of such conflict between Christian whites and those Indian nations not "savingly wrought upon," it becomes difficult to imagine that "Indian tribes may stretch out their hands to God" (Carretta 2004, 119–121).

Marrant's skillful appropriation of the rhetoric of conversion and captivity links the political goals of the "vast multitudes, of hard tongues, and of a strange speech" with the spiritual aim of Christian conversion, that is, to teach the "language of Canaan." This important engagement with and extension of egalitarian Great Awakening theology demands moral accountability from an imperialist slave-holding society on religious grounds. Marrant broadens the Christian community of "fervent hearts, and willing tongues" to include Indian nations among the "the kingdoms of our God." He also insists that such nations be treated similarly with respect to "kingdoms of the world." He demonstrates careful attention to cultural and spiritual conversion and, in so doing, encourages readers to accept Indians as part of the Christian community.

Furthermore, he emphasizes the iconic value of the Bible yet also indicates the importance of literacy for understanding it. Like Gronniosaw, he, too, uses the trope of the talking book. "At this instant the king's eldest daughter came into the chamber, a person about nineteen years of age, and stood at my right hand. I had a Bible in my hand, which she took out of it, and having opened it, she kissed it, and seemed much delighted with it," Marrant observes. "His daughter took the book out of my hand a second time; she opened it, and kissed it again; her father bid her give it to me, which she did; but said, with much sorrow, the book would not speak to her" (Carretta 2004, 119).

Unlike, Gronniosaw's intense reaction to a text that refuses to speak, Marrant staggers the trope of the talking book into two steps, demonstrating the iconic power of the Bible before revealing its inability to speak to those who cannot read. In stark contrast to Gronniosaw's description of himself as a despised being, the king's teenage daughter possesses tender and endearing human emotions. The delight she expresses and the kiss she bestows upon the sacred text once she opens the volume suggest reverent affection born of a virtuous nature. Her second encounter with the book seems similarly delightful, as she once again expresses affection through a deferential kiss. After Marrant tells her that the name of God is recorded in the book and after hearing him read the scriptures, she regrets that she is unable to extract a similar meaning from it.

In the revision of the trope from Gronniosaw to Marrant, what differs most are the emotions expressed upon realizing that the book cannot speak. Whereas Gronniosaw had expressed anger, anger stemming from recognizing his "despised" condition as a black man, the Indian princess expresses sorrow. Both of them experience physical illness after their frustrating encounters with the Bible. Gronniosaw becomes "exceedingly sea-sick," and the princess, "under deep conviction of sin" following intensive prayer, seems beyond "the skill of all their doctors." Following the princess's recovery, a "great change took place among the people" (Carretta 2004, 120). With her recovery, blacks like Marrant are now treated on equal status within this newly converted community of Christian Cherokee brothers and sisters. In this community, the "language of Canaan" Marrant had been looking forward to now prevails. A similar acceptance into the community of newly converted saints is not extended to the displaced African prince Gronniosaw, whose experience in God's "earthly" kingdom continues to be affected by the reality of his blackness and the despised condition to which one of his race has been consigned.

Narrative of the Lord's Wonderful Dealings is both a conversion narrative and a captivity narrative. Marrant's depiction of the spiritual, political, and cultural conversion of Native Americans and blacks implies that his white readers, too, could, in Phillis Wheatley's words, "join th' angelic train" (Wheatley 1989, 53). While Wheatley's words may have originally been meant to include "Christians, Negros, black as Cain" into a presumably "white" heaven, Marrant's experiences in captivity suggest that the spiritual conversion of whites would depend upon the extent to which they were able to adapt to political and cultural ideals of antislavery. On this point, the black narrator's words echo white abolitionist discourse attempting to expose the corruption that the slave trade has wrought on early colonial American society.

OLAUDAH EQUIANO

Olaudah Equiano's *Interesting Narrative of the Life of Olaudah Equiano,* a work James Walvin has called "the classic account of the experience that was the fate of millions of Africans in the era of Atlantic slavery," is not without controversy. In the narrative, Equiano claims to be an Igbo-African who was born in what is now Nigeria; other documentary evidence suggests that he was born in Carolina. Instead of being a true account of his own personal enslavement, Equiano may have composed his narrative from recollections of other slaves he met in America or at sea (Walvin 2004). Rather than impugn Equiano's reputation, the controversy over his narrative has only served to enhance its complexity. In its essence, *Interesting Narrative* questions the meaning of identity. To what extent does the life of an individual represent the life of the group to which he or she belongs? To what extent can black narrators justifiably co-opt the experience of other blacks and claim it as their own? And to what extent can black narrators justifiably make use of fiction in spiritual and secular autobiography?

Life on board ship enabled eighteenth-century black men like Hammon and Equiano to make contact with other African cultures and thus engage in a kind of cultural identification with communities of black people to which they might not otherwise have had access. The experiences of these early narrators both at sea and on land provided models of cross-class, cross-cultural, and interracial relationships that were especially significant in a post-Revolutionary, pre-emancipation world, a world that was weighing the consequences of such diversity in a new country. Jeffrey Bolster maintains, "Voyaging between the West Indies, Europe, and the American mainland enabled seamen to observe the Atlantic political economy from a variety of vantage points, to subvert their masters' discipline, and to open plantation society to outside influences" (Bolster 1997, 26). Equiano offers a model of organizing and understanding African identity within several cultural contexts. *Interesting Narrative* demonstrates how personal awareness framed eighteenth-century black aesthetics of identity.

The matter of using the Lord's name in vain, for example, offers Equiano an opportunity to discuss cultural differences between Africans and Europeans. He asserts that the Igbo people "never polluted the name of the object of our adoration; on the contrary, it was always mentioned with the greatest reverence." Even as the Christian–Afro-American–British Equiano cites "swearing" as an example of the moral inferiority of "more civilized people," he wonders about his own position as someone who is favored by a Christian God and who must acknowledge the reverence "more civilized people" have for God. Furthermore, he questions both the Christian application of charity and the European's capacity for imaginative and rational reasoning. Unwilling to recognize the equality with which God treats all men, whites limited the goodness of God in their conception of him (Equiano

2003, 41, 45). Equiano uses similar examples to draw attention to what had by this time become a powerful tool in antislavery rhetoric, the assertion of an antislavery argument within the context of Great Awakening egalitarianism: heavenly equality could and should be extended to earthly equality.

Equiano's voyage of self-edification and ethnic retrieval began long before he wrote and published *Interesting Narrative* in 1789. His literal and literary journey is fashioned from events that occurred during his passage from and through freedom and enslavement. In the narrative, he passes from physical and geographic freedom in remote Essaka—"unexplored by any traveler"—to similarly remote emotional states of enslavement as manifested by his utter grief at familial and kin separation (Equiano 2003, 32). He recounts with compelling precision the repercussions of his African experience. In one revealing section of his *Interesting Narrative,* he shows how his African identity has been shattered:

> But, alas! ere long it was my fate to be thus attacked, and to be carried off, when none of the grown people were nigh. One day, when all our people were gone out to their works as usual, and only I and my dear sister were left to mind the house, two men and a woman got over our walls, and in a moment seized us both; and, without giving us time to cry out, or make resistance, they stopped our mouths, tied our hands, and ran off with us into the nearest wood. . . . The next day . . . my sister and I were then separated, while we lay clasped in each other's arms. (Equiano 2003, 47–48)

In stark contrast to Equiano's detailed description of the careful manner in which children in his village are reared and protected, this kidnapping scene occurs very quickly. The rapidity with which Africans are stolen away from their nations, their families, and their identities is amplified in Equiano's language, tone, and rhythm. With two ostensibly simple yet powerful words—"But, alas!"—Equiano voices his personal grief at the instant of his capture, the impending danger that awaits him and his sister, and the ghastly fate that looms over entire African nations.

Apart from the trauma caused by his forced removal from village, kingdom, nation, family, and kin, Equiano's depiction of the horrific scene of capture and initial enslavement suggests a more devastating loss, the loss of his identity and the apparent destruction of any means of recovery. Despite such mental and physical self-alienation, dispossession, and displacement, Equiano refuses to surrender, even as he necessarily assimilates his new worldview. Abiola Irele deduces that this sense of loss in Equiano's narrative can be read "as a rhetorical gesture against the state of dispossession" that "attests to an abiding sense of origins and marks a gesture of self-affirmation as African subject" (Irele 2001, 48). In describing the physical up-heaval of being bound, immobilized, and silenced, the narrator inconspicuously reminds his audience of what can neither be silenced nor bound—his memory and his intellect.

The idea of time constitutes an important motif in Equiano's *Interesting Narrative.* His separation from his sister and his enslavement represent time lost; his mental re-creation of his community represents his recovery of historical time, which restores his Igbo worldview and history. This way of viewing time suggests that doom is not the inevitable consequence of the enslavement of Africans in the New World. Equiano insists that "time could not erase" the memory of his African identity. Not only had his culture, as he explains, been "implanted in me with great care," but it had "made an impression on my mind" that subsequent experience "served only to *rivet and record*" (Equiano 2003, 46). Equiano's quest for meaningful dialogue reflects an Igbo consciousness and identity. His integration of balance, continuity, and complementarity into a narrative of rupture and disjunction reflects the Igbo concept of duality, a dominant factor in the shifting narrative tone.

Aware of both African and Western ways of knowing, Equiano exploited both whenever possible. In a way, he resembles other contemporary authors who found it necessary to keep their writing in line with such established conventions of this historical period, conventions such as the concept of the noble African savage. But for Equiano there is far more at stake than demonstrating his humanity via his literary skill. Over the course of his narrative, he provocatively analyzes the progressive stages of dispossession, indoctrination, education, and assimilation in the continually changing systems of classification in the transatlantic slave trade. He explains:

> From the time I left my own nation, I always found somebody that understood me till I came to the sea coast. The languages of different nations did not totally differ, nor were they so copious as those of the Europeans, particularly the English. They were therefore easily learned; and, while I was journeying thus through Africa, I acquired two or three different tongues. In this manner I had been travelling for a considerable time, when one evening, to my great surprise, whom should I see brought to the house where I was but my dear sister. (Equiano 2003, 51)

In the early stages of displacement he emphasizes that he remained in contact with and connected to others who "understood" him. Clearly, he is referring to linguistic understanding, but he also calls attention to the importance of shared systems of cultural knowledge by his use of the term "understood." His physical movement prior to reaching the coast, though quite a distance from Benin and the even more remote Essaka, permitted him to communicate effectively with those of other nations. Communicating with those of different African languages let him reflect upon the nature of community, culture, and kinship, and consider their relationship to language.

Interesting Narrative captured the attention of contemporary readers. After its initial publication in London in 1789, it went through numerous editions. It was reprinted in Dublin, Edinburgh, Halifax, Leeds, and New York. Within a few years of its initial appearance, it was translated into Dutch and German. Written after Equiano was a fully assimilated Afro-American–Briton, *Interesting Narrative* conveys the complex nature of his personal and national identity, especially in light of his experiences as an enslaved and free person both inside and outside of Africa. Much the same could be said about the authors of other early black conversion, captivity, and slave narratives. Written by blacks suspended on land and sea between contradicting views of culture, class, race, politics, and commerce, these narratives assert the identities of their authors even as they question the very meaning of identity and the possibilities of language to convey it.

REFERENCES

Bolster, W. Jeffrey. 1997. *Black Jacks: African American Seamen in the Age of Sail.* Cambridge, MA: Harvard University Press.

Brooks, Joanna. 2003. *American Lazarus: Religion and the Rise of African-American and Native American Literatures.* New York: Oxford University Press.

Campbell, John. 1743. *A Treatise of Conversion, Faith and Justification, &c.: Being an Extract of Sundry Discourses on Rom. V. 5. Delivered at Oxford in the Latter End of the Year 1741, and Beginning of 1742.* Boston: Rogers and Fowle.

Carretta, Vincent, ed. 2004. *Unchained Voices: An Anthology of Black Authors in the English-Speaking World.* Lexington: University Press of Kentucky.

———. 2005. *Equiano, the African: Biography of a Self-Made Man.* Athens: University of Georgia Press.

Derounian-Stodola, Kathryn Zabelle, and James Levernier. 1993. *The Indian Captivity Narrative, 1550–1900.* New York: Twayne.

Equiano, Olaudah. 2003. *The Interesting Narrative and Other Writings,* edited by Vincent Carretta. New York: Penguin.

Gates, Henry Louis. 1988. *The Signifying Monkey: A Theory of Afro-American Literary Criticism.* New York: Oxford University Press.

Gould, Phillip. 2003. *Barbaric Traffic: Commerce and Antislavery in the Eighteenth-Century-Atlantic World.* Cambridge, MA: Harvard University Press.

Gronniosaw, Ukasaw. 1797. "A Narrative of the Most Remarkable Occurances, and Strange Vicissitudes in the Life of James Albert Ukasaw Gronniosaw, an African Prince, as Related by Himself." *American Moral and Sentimental Magazine* 1: 17–23, 32–37, 65–69, 97–102, 148–153, 162–165, 193–199.

Irele, Abiola. 2001. *The African Imagination: Literature in Africa and the Black Diaspora.* New York: Oxford University Press.

Martin, Jonathan. 2004. *Divided Mastery: Slave Hiring in the American South.* Cambridge, MA: Harvard University Press.

O'Neale, Sondra. 1993. *Jupiter Hammon and the Biblical Beginnings of African-American Literature.* Metuchen, NJ: Scarecrow.

Reiss, Oscar. 1997. *Blacks in Colonial America.* Jefferson, NC: McFarland.

Rowlandson, Mary. 1997. *The Sovereignty and Goodness of God, Together with the Faithfulness of His Promises Displayed,* edited by Neal Salisbury. Boston: Bedford / St. Martin's.

Saillant, John. 2003. *Black Puritan, Black Republican: The Life and Thought of Lemuel Haynes, 1753–1833.* New York: Oxford University Press.

Sekora, John. 1993. Questions of Race and Ethnicity: Red, White, and Black. In *A Mixed Race: Ethnicity in Early America,* edited by Frank Shuffelton, 92–104. New York: Oxford University Press.

Stepto, Robert B. 1979. *From Behind the Veil: A Study of Afro-American Narrative.* Urbana: University of Illinois Press.

Walvin, James. 2004. Equiano, Olaudah. In *Oxford Dictionary of National Biography,* edited by H. C. G. Matthew and Brian Harrison, vol. 18, pp. 481–482. New York: Oxford University Press.

Wheatley, Phillis. 1989. *The Poems of Phillis Wheatley: Revised and Enlarged Edition with an Additional Poem,* edited by Julian D. Mason Jr. Chapel Hill: University of North Carolina Press.

Zafar, Rafia. 1997. *We Wear the Mask: African Americans Write American Literature, 1760–1870.* New York: Columbia University Press.

CHAPTER 19

BENJAMIN FRANKLIN

KEVIN J. HAYES

Sailing for England in 1724 aboard the *London Hope* two months prior to his nineteenth birthday, Benjamin Franklin looked forward to seeing London, where he planned to acquire a printing press and related equipment with the letter of credit and letters of introduction Governor William Keith had promised. The governor's promises turned out to be empty ones, however. In England, Franklin discovered that there were no letters. Retelling this episode in his autobiography, Franklin omitted an account of his entry into London comparable to the vivid description of his entry into Philadelphia the year before. Given the date—Christmas Eve—and the disappointment he felt, his arrival in London was no less dramatic. Whereas he had entered Philadelphia with his voluminous trouser pockets stuffed with extra shirts and stockings, he entered London carrying a curiosity of American origin, a fireproof asbestos purse. The difference in baggage hints that Franklin's outlook had brightened considerably during the intervening year. He had entered Philadelphia looking for work; he entered London hoping to befriend the city's literary and scientific elite. You can't make a silk purse from a sow's ear, as Poor Richard might have said. Young Franklin was hoping to turn his asbestos purse into a calling card he could use to introduce and ingratiate himself to London's cognoscenti.

The hopes with which he began the trip seemed almost impossibly remote as he entered London. Without a letter of introduction, he had no way to join London's literary or social world. Without a letter of credit, he had no way of obtaining his printing plant and no way to support himself in London. Thomas

Denham, a Philadelphia merchant who had also sailed aboard the *London Hope*, advised him to find employment with a local printer. He took Denham's advice. Within a week the talented and enterprising Franklin found work with Samuel Palmer, whose printing house was located in a converted part of the church of Saint Bartholomew-the-Great, West Smithfield.

Franklin and James Ralph, his friend and traveling companion, found lodgings adjacent to John Wilcox's bookshop at the sign of the Green Dragon in Little Britain. Franklin befriended Wilcox, who specialized in auctioning large private libraries and whose shop contained a huge quantity of secondhand books. A few years later Wilcox (1730) would auction the fine library of New York governor William Burnet, which had so thoroughly impressed Franklin the previous year. Franklin arranged with Wilcox to borrow books from him for a nominal fee so that he could continue his rigorous self-education at minimal expense. According to one estimate, he borrowed hundreds of books from Wilcox (Lemay 2006, 1: 267).

EARLY WRITINGS

Without Governor Keith's letter of introduction, Franklin set about writing one of his own or, to be precise, something that could function as such, a vehicle letting him display himself as a man of ideas. He wrote and printed *A Dissertation on Liberty and Necessity* (1725), a pamphlet taking issue with William Wollaston's *Religion of Nature Delineated* (1722), the third edition of which he was setting in type at Palmer's shop. Franklin divided his own work into two parts, the first defining the doctrine of philosophical necessity and the second setting forth an original scheme in which man's pleasure and pain equal one another. Franklin's *Dissertation* pessimistically exhibits a philosophical indifference that avoids the grim depths of Wollaston's philosophy yet falls short of the exuberant optimism of other contemporary thinkers such as Lord Bolingbroke (Aldridge 1951).

Franklin repudiated the ideas he expressed in the *Dissertation* in an essay entitled "On the Providence of God in the Government of the World" (1732), but the *Dissertation* remains important in terms of his biography. The pessimism it embodies runs through his later thought (Lemay 1990, 25). In comparison with some of his subsequent writings, the *Dissertation* shows that Franklin's intellectual life moved from the theoretical to the experimental (Aldridge 1951). Furthermore, its closing paragraph signals a direction his writing would take. Admitting that some readers might find his ideas unpalatable, he concluded by applying a suitable proverb: "But, (to use a Piece of *common* Sense) our *Geese* are but *Geese* tho' we may think 'em *Swans;* and Truth will be Truth tho' it sometimes prove mortifying and distasteful"

(Franklin 1987, 71). As his literary career developed, Franklin would realize how valuable such pieces of common sense could be.

Impressed with the young man's industry, Palmer was nonetheless aghast at the unconventional ideas the *Dissertation* expressed. The work did attract some sympathetic readers, most important, a London surgeon named J. Lyons, the author of *The Infallibility of Human Judgment* (1719). Dr. Lyons did not necessarily agree with Franklin, but he recognized the young American's keen mind. He took Franklin under his wing: they met several times and talked much about philosophical necessity. Franklin's ideas significantly influenced Lyons's follow-up study, *Fancy-logy: A Discourse on the Doctrine of the Necessity of Human Actions* (1730).

Franklin briefly mentioned Lyons in his autobiography but did not specify how they met. Most likely, John Wilcox introduced them. Wilcox, who had published the first edition of *The Infallibility of Human Judgment,* knew Lyons personally (Lemay 2006, 1: 286). Being a surgeon, Lyons was well connected with London's scientific elite. He brought Franklin to different taverns and coffeehouses, introducing him to several prominent acquaintances. At the Horns, a pale-ale house in Cheapside, Lyons introduced Franklin to Bernard Mandeville. A physician by trade, Mandeville is best known as the author of *The Fable of the Bees: or, Private Vices, Publick Benefits* (1714). Franklin disagreed with the ideas implicit in Mandeville's paradoxical subtitle, as he showed in his 1751 pamphlet, *Observations Concerning the Increase of Mankind, Peopling of Countries, &c.* (Aldridge 1949, 29). Regardless of their differences of opinion, Franklin found Mandeville a "most facetious entertaining Companion" who formed the soul and center of a congenial club that gathered at the Horns (Franklin 1987, 1346). Lyons also brought Franklin to Batson's Coffeehouse, where he introduced him to Henry Pemberton. A close friend of Sir Isaac Newton, Pemberton promised to introduce Franklin. The meeting with Newton never materialized, however.

Franklin brazenly introduced himself to another prominent member of London's scientific community. The first week of June 1725, he wrote that inveterate collector of curiosities, Sir Hans Sloane, offering to sell him the asbestos purse. The ploy worked. Sloane replied, agreeing to buy the purse and inviting Franklin to his museum (Sweet 1952). Sloane's passion for collecting was infectious. James Salter, after leaving Sloane's employ, had established Don Saltero's Coffeehouse in Chelsea, which Franklin also visited during his time in London. The cabinet of curiosities displayed here was second only to Sloane's in grandeur.

Don Saltero's curiosities, which came from nearly every part of the globe, symbolized the importance of coffeehouse culture to contemporary intellectual life. These curiosities were conversation pieces, objects that gave patrons new topics for discussion and helped them take their thought in new directions. Much the same could be said about contemporary periodical essays. The essays published in the *Guardian,* the *Spectator,* the *Tatler,* and other lesser-known weeklies greatly enhanced the content of the conversations that occurred across the tables of coffeehouses in the metropolis, as well as those scattered throughout the British Empire. Coffeehouse conversation, in turn, generated new essay topics.

Franklin fit comfortably into the London coffeehouse scene not only because of his easy affability and quick wit but also because he had already mastered the defining literary genre of coffeehouse culture, the periodical essay. The Silence Dogood essays, which he had published in the *New-England Courant* in 1722 (when he was sixteen), constitute the first essay series in American literature (Lemay 1972, 205). Written in the persona of a well-meaning widow named Silence Dogood, Franklin's early essays, like those of his English models, amused readers even as they tried to improve society. Many of the same attributes that characterize the finest compositions of Joseph Addison and Richard Steele also characterize the Silence Dogood essays: the invention of an entertaining, likable persona who assumes the role of social and political critic; the liberal use of humor; the preference for Horatian satire over Juvenalian or, in other words, the use of satire that gently cajoles instead of sternly castigating; the philanthropic intent; the timeliness of its topics, which include education and women's rights; a vigilant lookout for hypocrisy; a good sense of contemporary material culture; and a strong emphasis on the freedom of speech.

A few years after returning to Philadelphia, Franklin would create another memorable essay series, which he published in Andrew Bradford's *American Weekly Mercury*. Known by the pseudonym Franklin used for them, the Busy-Body essays have much in common with the Silence Dogood essays but also mark an advance in his writing. They reflect his personal experience, specifically the time he spent reading the books he borrowed from John Wilcox and discussing ideas across the tables of London coffeehouses. Like Silence Dogood, Busy-Body amuses readers while seeking to correct faults prevalent in contemporary society. In this series, unlike the earlier one, Franklin felt no need to invent a background history for his persona. Omitting personal detail, Busy-Body lets his writing style reflect his personality. Silence Dogood is neither erudite nor worldly. Busy-Body, alternatively, has read widely. His writing evinces a cosmopolitanism alien to Silence Dogood. To illustrate his arguments, Busy-Body draws examples from around the world. "Busy-Body, No. 3," for instance, begins with information regarding how virtue was taught in ancient Persia.

"Busy-Body, No. 4" also draws on Near East culture to make its point. Delineating the "*Turkish* Manner of entertaining Visitors," Busy-Body quotes from a work by "an Author of unquestionable Veracity" (Franklin 1987, 103). Busy-Body does not name the source, and its identity has escaped the attention of Franklin's editors, but it was Henry Maundrell's *Journey from Aleppo to Jerusalem* (1703). A major contribution to English travel literature, Maundrell's *Journey* is known for its literary style—informative, yet witty and economic (Butlin 2004). Busy-Body claims to quote his source directly, but Franklin carefully revised Maundrell's account, removing extraneous detail that distracted from the main thrust of the episode. Franklin keeps the focus on the subject of entertainment, quoting the parts about serving sherbet and perfuming the visitors' beards. Maundrell's text may be witty and economic, but Franklin's is wittier and more economic.

ALMANACS AND NEWSPAPER ESSAYS

When Franklin left London in the summer of 1726, he did so in the company of Thomas Denham, who had hired him as a clerk. Franklin's American friend James Ralph remained in London, where he established a reputation as a political pamphleteer and historian. Once they reached Philadelphia, Franklin worked for Denham into the following year, when he returned to Samuel Keimer's printshop, where he had worked upon first reaching Philadelphia. Franklin devoted much of his spare time during the next two years to fostering intellectual activity in Philadelphia. Though he wrote comparatively little during this period, he did band together with several friends who also loved reading to form the Junto, a social organization that took as its mission the moral and intellectual betterment of its members.

Franklin set up his own printing business in 1728, which thrived to such an extent that he was able to establish partners elsewhere in colonial America over the next several years (Frasca 2006). He eventually wrested the failing *Pennsylvania Gazette* from Samuel Keimer. He also started the first German-language newspaper in America, *Philadelphische Zeitung* and, in late 1732, began issuing *Poor Richard's Almanack,* which he would continue for the next quarter century. The newspaper and the almanac were the mainstays of any successful colonial American printer. Franklin made the two more than mere income generators. Filled with pithy news reports and satirical essays, the *Pennsylvania Gazette* became the finest newspaper in colonial America. Filled with hundreds of wise saws and modern instances, *Poor Richard's* became the finest almanac in early America.

Typically, each of Franklin's almanacs begins with a letter to the reader from Richard Saunders, the humble yet lovable almanac maker who remains Franklin's most endearing persona. Scattered throughout each almanac are apt quotations from literature and, of course, Poor Richard's proverbial wisdom. For the literary historian, summarizing twenty-five years of almanacs is a daunting task. For Franklin, it was part of the job. The last *Poor Richard's Almanack,* published in late 1757 for use the following year, essentially constitutes a "best of" *Poor Richard's.*

Richard Saunders begins his last almanac as he had begun earlier ones, with a prefatory letter to his readers. This letter constitutes a more fully developed story than the previous ones. *Father Abraham's Speech* or *The Way to Wealth,* as this letter became known once it was separately published, forms what can be considered the earliest short story in American literature. As he begins his tale, Poor Richard explains what had happened recently when he encountered a large group of people waiting around for a public auction. Several were discussing the pitiful economic conditions of the times. Spying a white-haired old man, one member of the crowd asked his opinion. The old man, Father Abraham, responds, and his speech forms the long middle portion of Poor Richard's opening letter.

As Father Abraham quotes a few sayings he remembered from *Poor Richard's Almanack,* his words attract the attention of others, who gather to hear what else he has to say. The ensuing speech is an amalgam of sayings from Poor Richard. "Sloth, like Rust," Father Abraham observes, "consumes faster than Labour wears, while the used Key is always bright, as Poor Richard says. But dost thou love Life, then do not squander Time, for that's the Stuff Life is made of, as Poor Richard says" (Franklin 1987, 1296). Father Abraham's speech ends as the auction begins, and the people who had listened attentively to what he had said about being thrifty and saving money now ignore his advice and spend their money freely. Father Abraham's speech does influence one person, however, Poor Richard himself, who takes his own advice and walks away from the marketplace without spending a penny. Overall, Franklin incorporated dozens of sayings he had used in previous almanacs as part of *The Way to Wealth.* The result is not necessarily positive. The piling of maxim upon maxim has a cloying effect that caricatures Poor Richard as a zealous moralist who wants to be quoted more than anything (Nickels 1976, 87).

Though Franklin may have ridiculed the persona of Poor Richard in *The Way to Wealth,* his satire was lost on most contemporary readers. People loved the work for its numerous memorable sayings, which they took to heart. *The Way to Wealth* was read by countless thousands over the next several decades. Benjamin Mecom, Franklin's nephew, namesake, and printing partner, recognized the work's value and reprinted it separately in 1758 as a chapbook. Mecom was the first to title the work *Father Abraham's Speech* (Hayes 1999). After Mecom took the initiative, many others began reprinting the work under the title *The Way to Wealth,* sometimes as a pocket-size chapbook and other times as a single broadside sheet that could be affixed to the wall for people to read on a daily basis. For the most part, copies of *Poor Richard's Almanack* were disposed of at the end of each year, but *The Way to Wealth* became a fixture in the home. More than the almanacs themselves, *The Way to Wealth* was responsible for perpetuating Franklin's familiar sayings in the oral tradition (Hayes 1997, 13).

Besides printing and editing the *Pennsylvania Gazette,* Franklin was also its most prolific contributor. His contributions range from brief squibs that fill the paper's spare white spaces to hoaxes to whimsical reflections to humorous yet sharp-edged argumentative essays. Two particular contributions illustrate the artistry and variety of Franklin's contributions to the *Pennsylvania Gazette:* "Meditation on a Quart Mugg" and "Rattlesnakes for Felons."

"Meditation on a Quart Mugg" appeared in the *Pennsylvania Gazette* for July 19, 1733. Its closest antecedent in the English literary tradition is Jonathan Swift's

"Meditation on a Broomstick," which spoofs Robert Boyle's *Occasional Reflections on Several Subjects* (Arner 1993, 69). While deliberately echoing Swift, Franklin was not necessarily spoofing Boyle, whom he greatly respected. Boyle, as Poor Richard says, was "one of the greatest philosophers the last age produced" (Franklin 1987, 1250). Franklin's "Meditation" is considerably more sophisticated than Swift's. Both its structure and its humor are more complex, and its meaning is intentionally ambiguous. Swift's broomstick, for example, is "handled by every dirty Wench, condemned to do her Drugery" (Swift 1973, 421). Franklin's quart mug must "undergo the Indignities of a dirty Wench; to have melting Candles dropt on its naked Sides, and sometimes in its Mouth, to risque being broken into a thousand Pieces, for Actions which itself was not guilty." Using the preposition "of" instead of "by," Franklin created ambiguity and introduced some salacious humor. Subjecting the quart mug to the "Indignities of a dirty Wench," he implied that the mug must undergo the kinds of indignation a dirty wench undergoes, the dripping candle providing sufficiently obvious phallic imagery. Franklin's diction elsewhere in "Meditation on a Quart Mugg" anticipates the discourse of the American Revolution. The quart mug, in Franklin's words, is an "Emblem of human Penury, oppress'd by arbitrary Power," which has nowhere to obtain "Redress of his Wrongs and Sufferings" (Franklin 1987, 217).

"Rattlesnakes for Felons," which first appeared in the *Pennsylvania Gazette* on May 9, 1751 and was reprinted in several newspapers throughout colonial America in the following weeks, recalls another work by Swift, "A Modest Proposal." Like Swift's essay, Franklin's is structured as a classical oration. Franklin had demonstrated his masterful ability to manipulate oratorical conventions a few years earlier with "The Speech of Miss Polly Baker" (Lemay 1976; Royot 2001). Whereas the classical literary heritage provides a way to understand the structure of "Rattlesnakes for Felons," the colonial background provides a way to understand its context. In early 1751, Franklin, as clerk of the Pennsylvania Assembly, read a report from the Lords Commissioners of Trade and Plantations or, more simply, the Board of Trade, the governing body that oversaw colonial affairs. The Board of Trade actually believed that transporting felons to America contributed to the "Improvement and well Peopling" of the colonies. Franklin was incensed by such callousness. These British administrators neither understood nor sympathized with the American men and women they were in charge of governing. Subsequent events reinforced Franklin's indignation. A few months after reading this report, he learned about a gruesome double homicide committed by a transported felon in Maryland, a barbarous act that formed part of a wider crime wave in early America perpetrated by other transported felons.

In April, Franklin reported the news of several recent crimes in the *Pennsylvania Gazette*, ending his report by describing the "*cruel* Sarcasm" perpetrated by the Board of Trade (Hayes 1993). "Rattlesnakes for Felons" appeared the following month. Signing the article "Americanus," Franklin used a persona closely identifying himself with colonial America. Since the British were transporting felons to the colonies, Americanus suggests, colonists should transport rattlesnakes to Great Britain. In his exordium, Franklin quoted the memorable phrase from the Board of Trade, which he reiterated later in the work as he observed: "Our Mother knows what is best for us. What is a little Housebreaking, Shoplifting, or Highway Robbing; what is a Son now and then corrupted and hang'd, a Daughter debauch'd and pox'd, a Wife stabb'd, a Husband's Throat cut, or a Child's Brains beat out with an Axe, compar'd with this 'Improvement and Well Peopling of the Colonies!'" (Franklin 1987, 360). In the coming years, Franklin would repeat the phrase in some of his most memorable works, including "An Edict by the King of Prussia" and "Causes of American Discontents before 1788." To him, the phrase was a continual reminder of the callous insensitivity of the British administrators.

NARRATIVE OF THE LATE MASSACRES

Among the most popular works Franklin published as a printer were contemporary Indian treaties. Issued in quantities far greater than necessary for official business, the Indian treaty became a form of popular literature, both in the United States and in Europe (Wroth 1928). Franklin's friend Cadwallader Colden, who had incorporated numerous speeches from Indian treaties in the revised and expanded edition of his *History of the Five Indian Nations* (1747), made his history resemble classical Greek and Roman histories, which characteristically present great orations at dramatic moments. Franklin's own writings reveal the influence of Indian treaties on his literary style. He often made use of the imagery and figures of speech common to the treaties and occasionally incorporated Indian orations, some real and others invented.

A Narrative of the Late Massacres, in Lancaster County, of a Number of Indians, Friends of this Province, by Persons Unknown (1764), a work that makes significant use of the rhetoric of the Indian treaty, arose from Franklin's indignation with a frontier mob known as the Paxton Boys, who massacred many defenseless Susquehanna Indians in Lancaster County, Pennsylvania. The work begins by mentioning the treaty of friendship William Penn negotiated with these Indians, a treaty "which was to last 'as long as the Sun should shine, or the Waters run in the Rivers.'" According to Native American discourse, the renewal of a treaty was figuratively known as brightening the chain, and Franklin adopted the same figure of speech. He explained, "This Treaty has been since frequently renewed, and the *Chain brightened,* as they express it, from time to time. It has never been violated, on their Part or ours, till now" (Franklin 1987, 540).

Before describing the massacre, Franklin emphasized that the slaughtered Indians were Christians, and he supplied the Christian names and some brief personal descriptions of several. Emphasizing both their Christianity and their individuality, Franklin made their murder more heinous. As it continues, *A Narrative of the Late Massacres* not only echoes other forms of early American discourse but also anticipates modern antiracist rhetoric. Franklin's *Narrative* sounds like a case of conscience, a popular genre of devotional literature among New England Puritans, as it asks, "If an *Indian* injures me, does it follow that I may revenge that Injury on all *Indians?*" Answering this question, he presented an impassioned plea for racial tolerance: "The only Crime of these poor Wretches seems to have been, that they had a reddish brown Skin, and black Hair; and some People of that Sort, it seems, had murdered some of our Relations. If it be right to kill Men for such a Reason, then, should any Man, with a freckled Face and red Hair, kill a Wife or Child of mine, it would be right for me to revenge it, by killing all the freckled red-haired Men, Women and Children, I could afterwards any where meet with" (Franklin 1987, 546).

Franklin shamed the murderous actions of the Paxton boys, whose violent behavior exhibited a level of savagery virtually unparalleled. Instead of behaving savagely ourselves, we Christians, he argued, should set an example when it comes to the knowledge and practice of what is right. For comparison, he used several examples to show how people in different times and different cultures extended their hospitality to everyone, even to their enemies. Taking his first example from Homer, Franklin would seem to be structuring his work as an eighteenth-century progress piece. Though his examples move in a forward and westward path, they do not illustrate progress. Rather, they illustrate continuity. Throughout history, man has consistently behaved in a hospitable manner until, that is, the Paxton boys committed their foul murders.

Some of Franklin's examples in *Narrative of the Late Massacres* come from his reading, but others—the most memorable ones—are his own invention. One anecdote tells the story of a Spanish cavalier who escapes after murdering a "young Moorish Gentleman" and accidentally enters the garden of a neighboring Moor, who extends his hospitality to the Spaniard. Upon learning that the murder victim was his son, the Moor does not avenge the Spaniard because he has already extended his hospitality to him. Another anecdote tells the story of a black named Cudjoe, who worked for William Murray, a white man. When some blacks were seized and forced into slavery, others sought revenge by trying to kill Murray. Answering the door, Cudjoe meets a mob of fellow blacks but staunchly refuses them entry. Franklin dramatized the clash between the mob of blacks and Cudjoe, who tells them, "You must not kill a Man, that has done no Harm, only for being white. This Man is my Friend, my House is his Fort, and I am his Soldier. I must fight for him. You must kill me, before you can kill him" (Franklin 1987, 552–553).

A Narrative of the Late Massacres had a major impact on eighteenth-century literary culture. Once copies of the pamphlet reached England, Franklin's text was reprinted, sometimes in its entirety but more often in abbreviated or excerpted form. In 1764, *A Narrative of the Late Massacres* appeared in the *Universal Museum,* a popular magazine, and also in a literary anthology entitled *The Beauties of the Magazine.* The anecdote about the Spaniard and the Moor and the one about Cudjoe were reprinted often. In 1765, the *Universal Museum* reprinted the first under the heading "Of True Greatness." Another anthology, *The Beauties of History,* reprinted both the stories in 1770 under the heading "Honour." *The Historical Mirror,* a 1775 conduct manual that drew examples from history to illustrate several different virtues, also reprinted both stories. Franklin's anecdotes had transcended their original intent and were being used for a variety of purposes. Conduct manuals and schoolbooks continued to reprint the anecdotes through the eighteenth century. In both Great Britain and America, these two anecdotes became an important part of the elementary school curriculum.

THE STAMP ACT WRITINGS

Chosen as agent to represent the Pennsylvania Assembly in 1757 and again in 1764, Franklin returned to London under much different circumstances than he had during his teenage years. Then he had hoped to meet some of the major intellectual figures in the city; now he himself was one of the leading intellectual figures in the world. News of his electrical experiments had spread throughout Europe, and he was widely acclaimed for his scientific accomplishments. Returning to the London coffeehouse scene, he joined a circle of friends that included some of the leading literary and scientific figures in London: James Boswell, Andrew Kippis, Richard Price, and Joseph Priestley. These men gathered informally at St. Paul's Coffeehouse in a group Franklin called the Club of Honest Whigs (Crane 1966).

His conversation with these like-minded souls was generally amicable, but he overheard much criticism of the colonies voiced by other Londoners who patronized the same coffeehouses he did. During the mid-1760s, Franklin found himself vigorously defending his country on a regular basis, both officially and unofficially. Taken together, his various comments about the Stamp Act form a diverse body of literature crossing many literary genres and modes of discourse. Overall, his literary treatment of the Stamp Act controversy demonstrates the inextricable relationship between oral, manuscript, and print culture.

Many of the anecdotes Franklin told orally became literature once others wrote them down. Samuel Johnson had James Boswell to record his wit and wisdom: Franklin made every man a Boswell. He regaled others with his anecdotes, which many felt compelled to record for posterity. Stephen Sayre, a British merchant who supported the colonial cause, retold one anecdote that captured Franklin's attitude toward the Stamp Act:

> Dr. Franklin, a gentleman of great abilities, and [who] commands a great share of inoffensive wit, and true humour, was desired by a particular person to point out the particularly grievous parts, and clauses in this act; and after reading the same over very carefully, returned it to his lordship, with the alteration of only one word, as the only alteration which could possibly be admitted, or to any purpose be advised; and this was, that instead of one thousand seven hundred and sixty-five, it should take place in two thousand seven hundred and sixty-five. (Sayre 1768, 19)

In terms of literary history, the second half of the eighteenth century was the era of the ana. Though none of Franklin's contemporaries compiled his various anecdotes, those that survive individually or in small clusters in the writings of his friends, taken together, constitute a major contribution to the history of American humor (Zall 1980).

Franklin's own published writings from the time of the Stamp Act reinforce the interrelationship between oral and written culture. In "Reply to Coffee-House Orators," an article that appeared anonymously in the *London Chronicle*, Franklin, identifying himself solely as "A Friend to Both Countries," refuted the arguments he was hearing in the coffeehouses during the mid-1760s. After beginning with a sardonic comparison between ancient Athenian orators and modern coffeehouse talkers, the essay critiques some loudmouthed Londoners who had been clamoring for war against the American colonies. "It is remarkable," Franklin wrote, "that soldiers by profession, men truly and unquestionably brave, seldom advise war but in cases of extream necessity. While mere rhetoricians, tongue-pads and scribes, timid by nature, or from their little bodily exercise deficient in those spirits that give real courage, are ever bawling for war on the most trifling occasions, and seem the most blood-thirsty of mankind" (Franklin 1987, 590–591). It is easy for those who have never seen combat to clamor for war. It is another thing entirely for those with blood on their hands and death in their memories to yearn for more of the same. As he does in so many of his other essays, Franklin explodes the rhetoric of his opponents, revealing the absurdity of their arguments by exposing their ultimate implications.

Upon its publication in 1766, *The Examination of Doctor Benjamin Franklin* established Franklin as America's foremost spokesman. The *Examination* presented the questions Franklin was asked in Parliament and his answers to them. His balanced, thoughtful answers impressed many British legislators who were present to hear what he had to say. His responses retained their power and authority in their printed form. As one contemporary reader observed, he "answered with such deep and familiar knowledge of the subject, such precision and perspicuity, such temper and yet such spirit, as do the greatest honour to Dr. *Franklin*, and justify the general opinion of his character and abilities." Franklin's *Examination*, this observer noted, offered more "than from all that has been written upon the subject in news papers and pamphlets, under the titles of essays, letters, speeches, and considerations, from the first moment of its becoming the object of public attention till now" (Anon. 1767, 368). More than any other single work, the *Examination* led to the repeal of the Stamp Act.

As he prepared his critique of the Stamp Act and his defense of colonial rights, Franklin spent much time answering the arguments of London's political pamphleteers. Before the mid-1760s, he seldom inscribed his books, but numerous pamphlets from the 1760s and 1770s that survive from Franklin's library contain considerable marginalia in his hand. Some of his marginal comments can be read as first drafts of the political essays he wrote in the years leading up to the American Revolution (Crane 1957). Inscribing the margins of a book, he was recording his thoughts and, in so doing, capturing the mood and the moment of first reading. The margin of a printed page is the place where author and reader meet. Once a book has been annotated, it stops being a one-sided authorial discourse and instead becomes a dialogue (Hayes 2006, 15). Reading Benjamin Franklin's marginalia, you can almost hear him speaking.

Many of his annotated pamphlets have been lost or stolen. Those that survive have often been mangled by overfastidious, edge-trimming bookbinders. The editors of Franklin's papers have transcribed what manuscript material survives in the margins of Franklin's books and presented his marginalia with corresponding passages from the printed pamphlets (Franklin 1959–). The marginalia of one pamphlet that disappeared before the editors of the Franklin papers could get to it can be reconstructed on the basis of partial transcriptions made in the nineteenth century (Sparks 1833, 225–226; Sabin 1875, 151). Franklin's personal copy of *Second Protest, with a List of Voters against the Bill to Repeal the American Stamp Act* (1766) contained marginalia in his hand on almost every page (Wolf and Hayes 2006, no. 1452).

Responding to different passages of text, he frequently echoed the pamphlet's diction. On page 12, for example, the author of *Second Protest* explains that several men have been obliged to vote against the repeal of the Stamp Act on the basis of "our Duty to the King, and Justice to our Country." Inscribing his response onto this page, Franklin remarked: "My Duty to the King and Justice to my Country, will, I hope, justify me if I likewise protest, which I do with all Humility, in behalf of myself and of Every American, and of our Posterity, against your Declaratory Bill, that the Parliament of Great Britain, hath not, never had, and or Right never can have, without our Consent given either before or after, Power to make Laws of sufficient Force to bind the Subjects in America in any Case whatever, and particularly in Taxation." Onto the last leaf of this pamphlet Franklin inscribed a personal comment concerning how he might react if unable to obtain the rights that he, as an American, deserves: "I have some little Property in America. I will freely spend nineteen Shillings in the Pound to defend my Right of giving or refusing the other

Shilling, and after all, if I cannot defend that Right, I can retire chearfully with my little Family into the Boundless Woods of America which are sure to afford Freedom and Subsistance to any man who can bait a Hook or pull a Trigger."

A handful of words impulsively scribbled onto the last page of a political pamphlet: Franklin's comments nonetheless articulate fundamental American impulses. In addition to expressing his willingness to defend his rights, he also articulates his willingness to ignore authority and simply do whatever he wishes. Franklin's remarks convey the profound influence of the wilderness on American political thought. In terms of its imaginative possibilities, the wilderness offered Americans a place where they could exercise their individuality, where they could be free.

THE AUTOBIOGRAPHY

Franklin's autobiography, which he began in England amid the Revolutionary turmoil that was erupting between the time of the Stamp Act and the Declaration of Independence, must be read in relation to both the personal anecdotes he was telling to London friends and the marginalia he was inscribing in his books. Franklin drafted his autobiography on sheets of paper he folded in half lengthwise. The first draft he entered in the left-hand column, and many of his revisions and expansions he added in the right-hand column (Franklin 1981). In other words, the revisions Franklin made to his autobiography during its composition can be seen as comments inscribed in the margins of the work.

Since Franklin continued writing his autobiography off and on until his death in 1790, it has traditionally been seen as one of his last writings, but it really belongs within the context of his literary, social, and political activities of the late 1760s and early 1770s. Listening to his almost endless stock of personal anecdotes, his friends in British scientific and literary circles encouraged him to write up the story of his life. But the primary motivation underlying the autobiography is much the same as the one underlying his other political writings of the early 1770s. Franklin's autobiography constitutes an impassioned defense of the American way of life. In the face of British encroachments on American freedom, Franklin upheld his own life as an example of what a person can accomplish in America given the opportunities it offers. He is a new kind of man known only since the discovery and settling of America, the man whose characteristic behavior transcends the class boundaries that had traditionally differentiated one from another. Franklin is equally at home at his workbench or in his study.

Recalling an episode from his childhood, he explained how he became fascinated with the way workmen handle their tools, something that had continued to intrigue him. By carefully observing workmen, he learned enough to let him "do little jobs my self in my House when a Workman could not readily be got" (Franklin 1987, 1317). Franklin personally embodied the handyman spirit that has become such an important aspect of mainstream American culture. In addition, his practical knowledge allowed him to build basic machines allowing him to conduct his electrical experiments. Directly linking his affinity with the working man and his scientific pursuits, Franklin revealed their continuity. In his day, the pursuit of science was an amateur activity, an endeavor undertaken by the gentleman-virtuoso. Showing how his knowledge of the workman's tools facilitated his gentlemanly pursuit of science, Franklin effectually abolished class distinctions between the two.

A good education traditionally served to separate the classes, but in his autobiography Franklin revealed how he was able to educate himself and thus transcend class barriers. In the paragraph following the one about workman's tools, Franklin explained that he became fond of reading as a young boy and spent what little money he had on books. Elsewhere in the autobiography he said more about how the books he read allowed him to educate himself. His description of his reading, complete with the names of numerous authors and titles, gave his readers a program of study they could follow themselves. They, too, could be like Franklin and get ahead in the world.

Upon drafting the first part of the *Autobiography* in 1771, Franklin set it aside. He did not return to it for more than a dozen years. He was too busy working to establish a new nation to take the time to continue his life story. He returned home from England in 1775 and served as a delegate to the Continental Congress. The next year he played an integral part in the Declaration of Independence. He returned to Europe once the Continental Congress elected him commissioner to negotiate a treaty with France. Franklin succeeded brilliantly as both a diplomat and a socialite. He endeared himself to the kingdom of France. In short, he became the most famous American in the world.

LETTERS AND BAGATELLES

Franklin devoted much of his literary life in France to letter writing, a task for which he was well suited. He has been called "the best of all the letter-writers of the time" (Tyler 1897, 1: 13). Like any good letter writer, he carefully shaped what he wrote to suit his correspondents (Lemay 1972, 217–218). Among the hundreds of letters he wrote from France, three may serve to illustrate his letter-writing abilities.

In a 1779 letter to his daughter Sarah Bache he discussed the proliferation of medallions engraved with his image. They were available in different sizes, "some to be set in the lids of snuffboxes, and some so small as to be worn in rings." This description shows Franklin's fascination with material culture, a fascination his daughter shared. After providing the physical description of the medallions, he pondered their ultimate ramifications. Combined with engraved prints and other likenesses, these medallions, he told her, "have made your father's face as well known as that of the moon, so that he durst not do any thing that would oblige him to run away, as his phiz would discover him wherever he should venture to show it" (Franklin 1987, 1008).

Of course the hypothetical situation is absurd: Franklin was not about to turn into a nefarious criminal. Still, his words foreshadow the technologies of personal identification that would emerge in the next century. Franklin anticipated the disappearance of privacy, a time in the not too distant future when everyone could be identified, tracked, and located. This letter does not dwell on these implications. By the time his hand got this idea down on paper, his mind had already moved on to a new idea. In the very next sentence, Franklin offered Sarah a pseudo-etymology that evolves into a humorous play on words. Speaking of himself in the third person, he observed, "It is said by learned etymologists that the name *doll,* for the images children play with, is derived from the word Idol. From the number of *dolls* now made of him, he may be truly said, *in that sense,* to be *i-doll-ized* in this country" (Franklin 1987, 1008–1009). Despite the humor, Franklin's words embody a wistful melancholy. The dolls that were sent annually from Paris to Philadelphia were dressed to display the latest fashions. Fashions changed every year, and so did the dolls. Someone else would be idolized the next year, he implied, and his face would be forgotten.

Writing to George Washington in 1780, Franklin demonstrated his prescience as he imagined what America would be like after the Revolutionary War. His words seem designed to comfort and encourage Washington in the midst of a trying war. Instead of speaking literally, Franklin used a figure of speech—but not just any figure of speech. He used a Homeric simile, a simile to suit the grandeur of the war and the greatness of the cause. Describing how the United States would flourish after the war, Franklin compared it to a characteristically American motif: "Like a Field of young Indian Corn, which long Fair weather and Sunshine had enfeebled and discoloured, and which in that weak State, by a Thunder Gust, of violent Wind, Hail and Rain seem'd to be threaten'd with absolute Destruction; yet the Storm being past, it recovers fresh Verdure, shoots up with double Vigour, and delights the Eye, not of its Owner only, but of every observing Traveller" (Franklin 1987, 1019–1020).

It has been asked whether Franklin was a pessimist or an optimist (Lemay 1990). The image of America after the war that he projects in this letter to Washington reflects an extraordinary optimism. But the American optimist was a persona Franklin assumed to suit his rhetorical purposes, to encourage Washington's steadfastness in this case. To a different correspondent, he spoke in darkly pessimistic terms. In a 1782 letter to fellow scientist Joseph Priestley that also takes war as its subject, Franklin reflected a grim view of war and a bleak view of mankind:

Men I find to be a Sort of Beings very badly constructed, as they are generally more easily provok'd than reconcil'd, more dispos'd to do Mischief to each other than to make Reparation, much more easily deceiv'd than undeceiv'd, and having more Pride and even Pleasure in killing than in begetting one another; for without a Blush they assemble in great armies at NoonDay to destroy, and when they have kill'd as many as they can, they exaggerate the Number to augment the fancied Glory; but they creep into Corners, or cover themselves with the Darkness of night, when they mean to beget, as being asham'd of a virtuous Action. A virtuous Action it would be, and a vicious one the killing of them, if the Species were really worth producing or preserving; but of this I begin to doubt. (Franklin 1987, 1047–1048)

Is this what Franklin really believed? Or is this yet another persona—the misanthrope—that Franklin assumed specially for this letter to Priestley and abandoned once the letter was through? Where does the persona end and Franklin begin?

Franklin's belletristic writing in Paris also took the form of bagatelles. Each one is a little gem, and all deserve critical analysis. Take "On Wine," for example. Written in the form of an address to his friend the Abbé Morellet, Franklin assumed the persona of an abbé. Speaking as a French ecclesiastic, he claimed the right to pontificate on religious matters. "On Wine" situates wine drinking within the biblical tradition. In his opening paragraph, Abbé Franklin takes the moral high ground, offering "some Christian, moral, and philosophical reflections" in response to Morellet's drinking songs. Identifying what follows as a series of reflections, he paralleled it with Boyle's *Occasional Reflections* and thus identified it as a spoof. The second paragraph begins, "*In vino veritas,* says the wise man." The syntax—proverb followed by tag clause—reiterates a common sentence structure from *The Way to Wealth* and thus establishes the work's authority by paralleling it with Franklin's most famous work and showing that the explanation about to follow will explicate the proverbial text. Franklin thus parodies a biblical explication. Structured as a progress piece, "On Wine" begins in the time of the Old Testament, proceeds through the beginning of the Christian era, and takes its explication into the enlightened eighteenth century. Yet even the most enlightened form of religious worship—scientific Deism—does not escape Franklin's razor-sharp wit. In a postscript to "On Wine," he facetiously offers a rational explanation to show that man was destined to drink wine: his elbow is placed at precisely the correct position to be able to lift a wine glass to his lips conveniently and safely (Franklin 1987, 939–940).

LATE WRITINGS

Home from France, Franklin accepted numerous honors, renewed old friendships, added a new wing to his home to hold his massive library, played with his grandchildren, and continued to write. He worked on his autobiography almost until the day he died, but he also wrote much else. He even contributed to the local magazines. "Letter Relative to the Present State of China" is one of his most important writings from his final years in Philadelphia. It has been called "the most important literary work about China to originate in America in the eighteenth century" and one of Franklin's "most important creations" (Aldridge 1993, 75–84).

Like so many of his writings, "Letter Relative to the Present State of China" embodies a complex narrative stance. It is purportedly written by a Portuguese gentleman, who is relating the experiences of an English sailor who supposedly sailed with Captain Cook aboard the *Resolution* but who jumped ship at Macao to sail to America with a Portuguese captain in order to obtain furs to sell to the Chinese. As the story goes, the two were captured by Korean pirates. Franklin's pirates thus form the earliest reference to Korea in American literature (Aldridge 1993, 83). The Koreans, along with their prisoners, in turn, are captured by the Chinese. The Koreans are beheaded while the English sailor is permitted to live. He escapes from captivity and spends time roaming the countryside and living among Chinese peasants.

"Letter Relative to the Present State of China," while reflecting Franklin's fascination with the Orient, also let him return to some favorite themes, namely, the value of hard work and the folly of false worship:

> That in every house there is a little idol, to which they give thanks, make presents, and shew respect in harvest time, but very little at other times. And enquiring of his master, why he did not go to church to pray as we do in Europe? he was answered, they pay the priests to pray for them, that they might stay at home to mind their business, and that it would be a folly to pay others for praying, and then go and do the praying themselves; and that the more work they did while the priests prayed, the better able they were to pay them well for praying. (Franklin 1786, 20)

Relating another episode from a different part of the world, Franklin created "Sidi Mehemet Ibrahim on the Slave Trade," the last work he published in his lifetime. Written as a letter to the editor of the *Federal Gazette* from the perspective of a fictional persona who calls himself "Historicus," this article is also structured as a frame tale. Historicus provides the explanatory frame, and the speech of Sidi Mehemet Ibrahim fills the bulk of the article. In his opening frame, Historicus explains how a recent speech in which a congressman had admonished his fellow legislators against meddling in the affairs of slaveholders reminded him of a speech made by Sidi Mehemet Ibrahim a hundred years earlier, a speech critiquing "the petition of the Sect called *Erika* or Purists, who prayed for the abolition of piracy and slavery," which he then quotes (Franklin 1790). The speech, of course, is Franklin's invention. It is written from a Muslim perspective and justifies the practice of kidnapping and enslaving Christians. The speech can be taken both figuratively and literally. Figuratively speaking, it functions as an allegory of American slavery, the Muslims representing slaveholding Americans and the Christians representing the enslaved

blacks. Though set a century earlier, this speech also presents a situation pertinent to Franklin's time, when American merchant sailors were being kidnapped
and enslaved by the Muslim pirates of the Barbary Coast. Presenting a work with
two possible interpretations, Franklin offered a message rife with ambiguity. Many
Americans complacently accepted what slaveholders were doing to blacks in the
United States. But when Muslims did much the same thing to American citizens
along the Barbary Coast, their fellow Americans were naturally outraged. Franklin
sustained his subtlety throughout this article, never moralizing or making his parallel explicit. Abolitionists clearly recognized what Franklin was doing, and this essay
was reprinted multiple times in the nineteenth century (Anon. 1831, 1836a, 1836b).

CONCLUSION

Echoing English literary forms from the essays of Addison and Steele to the satires of
Jonathan Swift, Franklin made them his own, oftentimes improving his models and
enhancing their literary complexity. From the early Silence Dogood essays, which
poke fun at the faults and foibles of colonial Boston society, to Americanus, the
stalwart patriotic persona who represented his nation in the face of tyranny and
injustice, to his late writings, in which Franklin speaks to the world at large, the general trajectory of his work moves from the local to the national to the international.
Ultimately, Benjamin Franklin took the whole world as his stage.

REFERENCES

Aldridge, A. Owen. 1949. Franklin as Demographer. *Journal of Economic History* 9: 25–44.
————. 1951. Benjamin Franklin and Philosophical Necessity. *Modern Language Quarterly*
    12: 292–309.
————. 1993. *The Dragon and the Eagle: The Presence of China in the American Enlighten-
    ment.* Detroit, MI: Wayne State University Press.
Anon. 1767. Review of *The Examination of Doctor Benjamin Franklin.Gentleman's Magazine*
    37: 368–373.
Anon. 1831. A Mirror for Apologists, Gradualists, Colonizationists, and Defenders of
    Slavery. *Liberator,* December 17.
Anon. 1836a. An Illustration. *Christian Register and Boston Observer* 15: 12.
Anon. 1836b. An Illustration. *New Hampshire Sentinel,* February 4.
Arner, Robert D. 1993. Politics and Temperance in Boston and Philadelphia: Benjamin
    Franklin's Journalistic Writings on Drinking and Drunkenness. In *Reappraising*

Benjamin Franklin: A Bicentennial Perspective, edited by J. A. Leo Lemay, 52–77. Newark: University of Delaware Press.

Butlin, Robin A. 2004. Maundrell, Henry. In *The Oxford Dictionary of National Biography,* edited by H. C. G. Matthew and Brian Harrison, vol. 37, pp. 442–443. New York: Oxford University Press.

Crane, Verner W. 1957. Franklin's Marginalia, and the Lost "Treatise" on Empire. *Papers of the Michigan Academy of Science, Arts, and Letters* 42: 163–176.

———. 1966. The Club of Honest Whigs: Friends of Science and Liberty. *William and Mary Quarterly,* 3rd ser., 23: 210–233.

[Franklin, Benjamin.] 1786. Letter Relative to the Present State of China. *Columbian Magazine* 1: 18–22.

[———.] 1790. To the Editor of the *Federal Gazette.Federal Gazette,* March 25.

———.1959–. *The Papers of Benjamin Franklin,* edited by Leonard W. Labaree et al. 37 vols. to date. New Haven, CT: Yale University Press.

———. 1981. *The Autobiography of Benjamin Franklin: A Genetic Text,* edited by J. A. Leo Lemay and P. M. Zall. Knoxville: University of Tennessee Press.

———. 1987. *Writings,* edited by J. A. Leo Lemay. New York: Library of America.

Frasca, Ralph. 2006. *Benjamin Franklin's Printing Network: Disseminating Virtue in Early America.* Columbia: University of Missouri Press.

Hayes, Kevin J. 1993. The Board of Trade's "*cruel* Sarcasm": A Neglected Franklin Source. *Early American Literature* 28: 171–176.

———. 1997. *Folklore and Book Culture.* Knoxville: University of Tennessee Press.

———. 1999. Mecom, Benjamin. In *American National Biography,* edited by John A. Garraty and Mark C. Carnes, vol. 15, pp. 232–233. New York: Oxford University Press.

———. 2006. Introduction. In *The Library of Benjamin Franklin,* edited by Edwin Wolf 2nd and Kevin J. Hayes, 3–56. Philadelphia: American Philosophical Society and the Library Company of Philadelphia.

Lemay, J. A. Leo. 1972. Benjamin Franklin. In *Major Writers of Early American Literature,* edited by Everett Emerson, 205–243. Madison: University of Wisconsin Press.

———. 1976. The Text, Rhetorical Strategies, and Themes of "The Speech of Miss Polly Baker." In *The Oldest Revolutionary: Essays on Benjamin Franklin,* edited by J. A. Leo Lemay, 91–120. Philadelphia: University of Pennsylvania Press.

———. 1990. *Benjamin Franklin: Optimist or Pessimist?* Newark: University of Delaware.

———. 2006. *The Life of Benjamin Franklin.* 2 vols. Philadelphia: University of Pennsylvania Press.

Maundrell, Henry. 1703. *A Journey from Aleppo to Jerusalem, at Easter, A.D. 1697.* Oxford.

Nickels, Cameron C. 1976. Franklin's Poor Richard's Almanacs: "The Humblest of His Labors." In *The Oldest Revolutionary: Essays on Benjamin Franklin,* edited by J. A. Leo Lemay, 77–89. Philadelphia: University of Pennsylvania Press.

Royot, Daniel. 2001. Long Live *La Différence:* Humor and Sex in Franklin's Writings. In *Finding Colonial Americas: Essays Honoring J. A. Leo Lemay,* edited by Carla Mulford and David S. Shields, 307–315. Newark: University of Delaware Press.

Sabin, Joseph. 1875. *Catalogue of the Books, Manuscripts, and Engravings Belonging to William Menzies of New York.* New York.

Sayre, Stephen. 1768. *The Englishman Deceived: A Political Piece: Wherein Some Very Important Secrets of State Are Briefly Recited, and Offered to the Consideration of the Public.* London: G. Kearsly.

Sweet, Jesse M. 1952. Benjamin Franklin's Purse. *Notes and Records of the Royal Society of London* 9: 308–309.

Swift, Jonathan. 1973. *The Writings of Jonathan Swift,* edited by Robert A. Greenberg and William Bowman Piper. New York: Norton.

Tyler, Moses Coit. 1897. *The Literary History of the American Revolution, 1763–1783.* New York: G. P. Putnam.

Wilcox, John. 1730. *Bibliotheca Burnetiana: Being a Catalogue of the Intire Library of His Excellency William Burnet Esq.* [London: John Wilcox.]

Wolf, Edwin, 2nd, and Kevin J. Hayes. 2006. *The Library of Benjamin Franklin.* Philadelphia: American Philosophical Society and the Library Company of Philadelphia.

Wroth, Lawrence C. 1928. The Indian Treaty as Literature. *Yale Review* 17: 749–766.

Zall, Paul M. 1980. *Ben Franklin Laughing: Anecdotes from Original Sources by and about Benjamin Franklin.* Berkeley: University of California Press.

PART VI

THE REVOLUTIONARY ERA

CHAPTER 20

EARLY AMERICAN DRAMA

JASON SHAFFER

The phrase "early American drama" is open to different interpretations. A modern theatergoer could be forgiven for assuming "American drama" began in the second decade of the twentieth century with the emergence of Eugene O'Neill. O'Neill, the only American playwright to win the Nobel Prize for Literature and the first American playwright to be admitted by scholars and critics into the literary canon, wrote self-consciously artistic dramas that helped usher in the world of American experimental drama and that often contrasted sharply with the melodramas and comedies that were popular in nineteenth-century America. Scholars of nineteenth-century American theater could make a case that, since most plays staged in America before the nineteenth century were written by British authors, American drama began with nineteenth-century plays written by American playwrights seeking to develop a new drama based on the conditions of everyday American life. During the nineteenth century, theatrical performances extended all the way from the cities of the East Coast to riverboats on the Mississippi and mining camps in California, thereby making theatergoing a practice that extended from the Atlantic to the Pacific, and therefore a cultural mirror image of the expanding country.

Theatrical performances and the written drama, however, are even older than the settlement of English-speaking people in North America, much less the independence of the United States. Theater and drama as we understand them have been produced in the Americas since the first moments of European contact. Despite this long history, however, the hostility with which the theater and drama were received in some parts of early America has led many historians to treat the American the-ater in its developmental phase as, in the words of Odai Johnson, "an unlawful and unauthorized entity struggling to gain legitimacy in the social landscape of colonial America" (Johnson 2006, 186). When speaking of "early American drama" that was actually produced during the early American period, we must expand our under-standing of what "American" means, and must also understand that the story of the drama's development has been colored by a common understanding of the drama as the neglected stepchild of American literature (Richards 2005, 17–33; Wilmer 2002, 16–52). We must also expand our notion of what constitutes a play. The plays per-formed in English between the establishment of English colonies in North America and the early nineteenth century were overwhelmingly British; plays written in the American colonies were rarely staged, and in many cases were not written with staging in mind; even in the wake of independence, the American stage was slow to accommodate plays written by Americans about life in the United States.

This chapter focuses on dramatic texts written in North America between the era of colonial settlement and the 1787 premiere of Royall Tyler's *The Contrast*, a play written by an American author with a setting in the United States and a cast of exclusively American characters, whose prologue declares that it is a study of "native themes" (Tyler 1997, 7). The definition of "dramatic text" will encompass three distinct sorts of texts: plays with plots and individuated characters written for the stage; "closet" dramas written for reading rather than staging or dramatic dialogues that present religious or political arguments instead of plots; and cer-emonial "paratheatrical" texts, such as ritual celebrations of military victories and the dramatic dialogues popular at colonial collegiate commencement ceremonies, which follow scripts but lack the elements of plotting and characterization typically associated with a play. Also worth consideration are texts not written in English; the British plays that were overwhelmingly more numerous in the early American the-ater than plays written in America; and the history of the theater's reception in the political culture of the American colonies. The diverse forms of literature and performance that constitute early American drama bridge the gaps between the page and the stage, between entertainment and political and intellectual debate, and between the colonial and early republican eras of American history.

EARLY COLONIAL DEVELOPMENT

The conventions of European theater were part of the cargo brought by the first European ships to land in the Americas. The idea of a culture where public perfor-mances were used to commemorate significant events, however, seems to be as old as the peopling of the Americas. Many of the indigenous cultures of the Americas already had refined approaches to public performance prior to their initial period of contact with Europeans (Londré and Watermeier 2000, 15–38). In addition to creating theatrical events for religious or entertainment purposes, many of these nations, including the six North American nations that united within the confederation known as the Iroquois League, had developed elaborate forms of public performance for practicing diplomacy and "theatrical" styles of speaking for carrying out the public affairs of their people. So many Anglo-Americans were struck by the eloquence of the public speeches made by members of the indigenous populations that the "eloquent Indian" became a heroic (although often tragic) figure in the early American popular imagination that still exudes a powerful pull in our own day (DeLoria 1998; Gustafson 2000; Sayre 2005).

Cultural interchange with Native Americans both involved theatrical performances and inspired new uses for theatrical conventions. One of the earliest pieces of dramatic writing associated with the Americas is a dialogue by a Portuguese Jesuit named Manuel da Nóbrega, *Dialogue for the Conversion of the Indians* (1548), which considers what the best methods for missionaries in the "New World" might be, including the use of native languages. As Susan Castillo notes, the interplay of multiple voices and points of view available in the dramatic form, even in a dialogue not necessarily intended for performance, aided European attempts to grasp the "radically different and . . . eerily similar" world of the Americas (Castillo 2002, 28, 40). Nearly 200 years later, Benjamin Franklin would use the conventions of theatrical narrative in an effort to capture for his reading audience the intensely dramatic atmosphere generated by the 1744 treaty negotiations carried out between the Anglo-American governments of three provinces and the Iroquois (Gustafson 2000, 119–139). These interactions between prose and drama are not surprising in context. As Jeffrey H. Richards has detailed, the early American period was dominated by the worldview of the *theatrum mundi*, or "world stage," which saw the New World as a new "theater" of human action, a place that generated new kinds of drama in human events almost as fast as it generated wealth (Richards 1991).

Not all the theater created in the Americas was so metaphorical, however. Records exist for performances of religious plays written in Nahuatl (the language of the Aztec empire) and staged by Spanish missionaries in Mexico as early as 1530 or 1531 as part of the effort to Christianize the Aztecs. Similar dramas were acted in Spanish by combined casts of missionaries and soldiers in Florida as early as 1567, and the first play written in Spanish in the Americas dates to the 1598 Spanish campaign to conquer the territory (now the American state) of New Mexico. This lost comedy was performed just north of the Rio Grande. The first play written and performed in the territory of the contemporary United States, then, was in Spanish (Londré and Watermeier 1998, 41; Davis 1998, 217).

Nor were the Spanish alone in the early performance of plays. In 1606 a group of French colonists performed a short play written by settler Marc Lescarbot at the struggling temporary settlement of Port Royal, in Nova Scotia. *The Theatre of Neptune in New France,* which was really "more pageant than drama," featured French actors in hastily constructed costumes as the Greek god Neptune, a chorus of minor sea gods, and several Indians (Meserve 1977, 13–15). In addition to the importance of plays presented in indigenous languages to the Spanish colonization effort, the genres selected by authors and performers working in European languages—religious drama, comedy, pageant—suggest the importance of early American drama and theatrical performance to the first Europeans in the Americas. Plays and performances served as important means not only for coming to terms with the harsh realities of settlement in this new environment but also for maintaining a sense of cultural connection to Europe.

British American drama, like the settlement of Britain's colonies in the Americas, lagged somewhat behind the efforts of the Spanish and the French. The first known American drama written in English was not performed until 1665, when three men staged a play (now lost) called *The Bear and the Cubb* in a tavern on the sparsely settled eastern shore of Virginia. The three men—Cornelius Watkinson, Phillip Howard, and William Darby—performed this play, which was apparently written by Darby, during August 1665 in a tavern in the village of Pungoteague, Virginia. Nothing is known of the play's content, but another local resident, Edward Martin, seems to have taken offense at the performance. The three actors were arrested on his complaint in November 1665 and commanded to appear in court wearing their costumes to perform part of the play before a judge. The three men were acquitted of any offense, however, and Martin was ordered to pay their court costs. The source of Martin's complaint remains unclear, but his attempt to prosecute Darby and his fellow actors established a strong connection between early American drama and the realm of legal and political controversy (Johnson and Burling 2001, 93–94; Davis 1998, 219–220).

Although there is no reason to believe that the Virginia trial directly impeded the growth of drama in the American colonies, the drama did encounter opposition there in the seventeenth and early eighteenth centuries. In Virginia no further dramatic performances were recorded after *The Bear and the Cubb* until 1702, when students at the College of William and Mary staged a recitation of two pastoral dialogues. The first officially sanctioned theater was not established in Virginia until 1716. While in 1690 some students at Harvard College reportedly staged a play titled *Gustavus Vasa,* written by a student named Benjamin Colman, the people of Massachusetts often found themselves trapped between their implicit tolerance of such performances and the antitheatrical doctrine of the colony's Calvinist faith. In 1714 Samuel Sewall, the colony's chief justice, noted with disapproval a rumor that some citizens wished to act out a play in the colony's council chamber. In 1750 the colony finally banned theatrical performances. In Philadelphia, which eventually became one of the leading theatrical cities of the early American republic, the Quaker-dominated Pennsylvania Assembly endorsed the antitheatrical opinions of the colony's founder, William Penn, by repeatedly banning the theater between 1682 and 1711, although these laws were invariably overturned by the Board of Trade, the British body that governed colonial policy (Johnson and Burling 2001, 73–79, 92–102).

While theatrical presentation of plays did not become common in British North America until the mid–eighteenth century, the stage play's cousin, the printed dialogue, began to flourish in the colonies during the mid–seventeenth century. Between 1644 and 1800, more than 200 prose and poetic dialogues were printed in early America. The form gave authors an attention-grabbing way to present multiple viewpoints on important political and religious issues. Those skilled at crafting dramatic dialogue could tailor the presentation of competing arguments so that their own side clearly emerged as the victor, much as a playwright manipulates audience reaction. In some cases, such as William Bradford's "A Dialogue or the Sume of a Conference Between Som Younge Men Borne in New England and Sundrey Ancient Men that Came out of Holland and Old England" (1648) and John Eliot's "Indian Dialogues" (1671), the subject matter of these dramatic dialogues was related directly to the European-American settlement experience. Many of these dialogues, however, focus on religious topics that range beyond the bounds of the colonies. Cotton Mather, for instance, in 1704 wrote a dialogue titled "The Discourse of the Minister with James Morgan, on the Way to His Execution," in which Mather's clergyman brings the condemned man to confession and repentance on his way to the gallows, thus pointing the way to redemption for the dialogue's reading "audience." Other dialogues displayed more partisan approaches to religious issues, such as those written by the Presbyterian minister Jonathan Dickinson, which frequently argue for Calvinist-influenced positions on such topics as infant baptism and predestination. (Castillo 2002, 29; Davis 1998, 222–224; Meserve 1977, 21–23). Nor were clergymen associated with the Church of England immune from the dramatic itch. In 1741 John Checkley, a Boston merchant and Anglican minister, published "Dialogues, Between a Minister and an Honest Country-Man," which argues expressly against the doctrine of predestination (and repeatedly attacked Jonathan Edwards); around midcentury, Thomas Cradock, an Anglican minister in Maryland, composed a series of poems, the *Maryland Eclogues,* many of which were in dialogic form, that sharply criticized colonial life for vice and hypocrisy. (Cradock also penned an unfinished tragedy, *The Death of Socrates,* which treated the Greek philosopher as a barely disguised Christian believer.) Printed dialogues, then, formed an important part of the canon of early American drama well before the establishment of a conventional professional theater in the colonies.

THE EMERGENCE OF SATIRE

The predominance of the dramatic dialogue continued to influence the composition of early American dramatic texts that were more recognizable as plays during the eighteenth century. The plays written prior to the Revolution were, like the dialogues, not always intended for stage performance, even when they showed considerable familiarity with the conventions of the stage. The first plays written in eighteenth-century America, however, differed markedly from the dialogues in their satirical comic outlook. The first printed play in America was a comedy: *Androboros*, a satire written in 1714 by Governor Robert Hunter of New York with help from his political ally Lewis Morris (Davis 1988). Hunter, a Scottish politician who took over the colonial government in 1710, inherited a deeply divided legislature that controlled the governor's funding, a source of major political disputes. Hunter clashed not only with legislative leaders in New York but also with William Vesey, the rector of New York City's Trinity Church, over such troubling issues as the handling of public lands and the financial maintenance of a group of German war refugees that had been sent to New York by the Crown. In 1714, Hunter's political enemies began to close ranks in anticipation of the arrival in New York of General Francis Nicholson, a soldier and former colonial governor appointed as an overseer of the northern colonies' governors. Hunter, a friend of the British satirists Jonathan Swift and Alexander Pope, addressed his political problems by writing a comedy that makes his opponents look ridiculous (Leder 1964).

Androboros (the name means "Man-eater") takes place in an insane asylum, which is managed by a "Keeper," who clearly represents Hunter himself. The various inmates of the asylum represent Hunter's political allies (Lewis Morris is an apparently sane character named "Solemn") and enemies (Vesey is represented by a lunatic named Fizle). The inmates have formed a legislative body with the express intent of having the Keeper removed, although the business carried out in their assembly rarely amounts to much more than speaking loudly over one another. Among their ploys is a clever scene in which Fizle besmears his vestments with excrement and attempts to blame the Keeper for soiling the garment. When this trick fails, however, the inmates pin their hopes on the arrival in the asylum of Androboros (Nicholson), whose own sanity is debatable, and who seeks their support for an expedition (which ultimately fails) against a nation known as the Mulo Machians (the French) that mirrors Nicholson's own failed military exploits against the French in Canada. After Androboros arrives, the inmates determine to depose the Keeper and install Androboros in his place. As part of this plot Fizle and his accomplice Flip set up a throne for the Keeper on a trap door, intending to dispose of him. Meanwhile, the Keeper and his ally Solemn convince Androboros that he is actually dead, and visible only to Solemn (whose reaction to seeing the "ghost" of Androboros brilliantly echoes Hamlet seeing the ghost of his father). After Solemn "reveals" to Androboros that he is alive, but apparently invisible, Solemn temporarily blinds his victim. Androboros runs amok and crashes into the rigged throne, ensnaring Fizle and Flip in their own trap and allowing the Keeper to resume unchallenged control of the asylum. Hunter, likewise, appears to have gained the upper hand in New York politics after the publication of his play, which appears to have turned the political tide in his favor until he returned to Great Britain in 1719 (Meserve 1977, 40; Leder 1964, 157).

Governor Hunter's play, which appears not to have been performed in its own time, followed the first approval issued in New York for a theatrical season around 1700 (Johnson and Burling 2001, 96). There are no records for a full theatrical season in New York, however, until 1732, the year that the next American drama was circulated in Boston (Johnson and Burling 2001, 96, 107–108). The year 1732 seems to have been an active dramatic one in New England: George Lillo's successful tragedy *George Barnwell* (1731), which tells the story of a London apprentice brought down by such offenses as embezzlement and consorting with prostitutes, was published this year in the *New England Weekly Journal* (Meserve 1977, 25). Meanwhile, political opponents of Massachusetts governor Jonathan Belcher privately circulated a satirical comedy usually referred to as *Belcher Apostate*. Belcher, a native of Massachusetts, had formerly been the colony's chief lobbyist in England, and upon the death of his predecessor was elevated to the governorship in 1730. Receiving his new office, Belcher changed his views on an issue about which he was first sent to England to lobby the government. In Massachusetts, like New York, the assembly controlled the governor's purse strings; Governor Belcher quickly came to favor the official Crown policy of a set annual salary, which would free the executive from his dependence on the legislature, thereby removing one of the assembly's main tools for bargaining with their governors (Moody 1980; Shields 1990, 103–107). Carrying on a tradition of circulating satirical manuscripts that dated back at least to the Renaissance, Belcher's opponents took him to task in print.

Belcher Apostate lacks the scatological (and often hilarious) humor of *Androboros*. Its satire is biting, but not generally very funny, and it lacks the sure sense of stagecraft that Hunter's play displays. Much of the exposition of the plot comes from political speeches made by the characters or the reading aloud of letters. Nonetheless, it sharply tells a story of a man's decline from patriotic virtue into political hypocrisy, a popular contemporary plot that mirrors the fall from grace experienced by Lillo's George Barnwell. In the first act, Governor Burnet arrives in Massachusetts and presents the assembly with his instructions from the king, including the demand that the assembly provide him with a fixed annual salary. The opposition to this measure is led by Belcher, who is then nominated by the general populace to be the colonial agent for Massachusetts. In the second act, after Belcher and his son have sailed to England, his letters to his wife suggest that in England he is declining into a state of ambition and luxuriance: He rapidly spends the extra commission he received from the colony of Connecticut to be its agent, and professes a desire for political promotion. When Belcher returns from England in the third act as the new governor, he presents the colonists with the same royal demand for a fixed gubernatorial salary. The play ends with a visit to Belcher from a group of assemblymen who reject this demand, reminding their former ally of the arguments he once made in favor of the legislature's power of the purse, and a brief soliloquy in which

Belcher vows to enslave his countrymen in order to promote his self-interest, which confirms his political corruption.

This close attention to local politics is a common feature of many early American dramas. The first play written in Pennsylvania, *The Paxton Boys,* emerged not out of legislative battles, however, but out of an episode marked by massacre and rebellion. In 1763–1764, a group of Pennsylvania frontier settlers from Paxton and Donegal, angry about the colonial legislature's disinterest in funding their defense against Native Americans during the 1763 uprising known as Pontiac's Rebellion and afterward, assaulted and massacred a group of peaceful Conestoga Indians in Lancaster County. The "Paxton Boys" were acquitted for this act, which inspired a larger mob of some 600 settlers and sympathizers to march on Philadelphia to present their demands and perhaps also to massacre more Indians who had taken refuge in the capital city. The colonial militia was mobilized, and the colony faced the prospect of a civil war between the settlers, who were largely Scotch-Irish Presbyterians, and the combination of Quaker and Anglican interests that dominated Philadelphia politics, although Benjamin Franklin negotiated a peaceful settlement to the crisis (Davis 1988, 233).

This episode resulted in the publication of three dialogues during 1764: *The Paxton Boys,* "A Dialogue Between Andrew Trueman, and Thomas Zealot; About the Killing the Indians of Cannestegoe and Lancaster," and "A Dialogue Containing Some Reflections on the Late Declaration and Remonstrance, on the Back-Inhabitants of Pennsylvania. With a Serious and Short Address, to Those Presbyterians Who (To Their Dishonor) Have Too Much Abetted, and Conniv'd at the Late Insurrection." The latter two dialogues both condemn the Paxton uprising, though the more interesting is perhaps the one purportedly written by a local Presbyterian, in which the conspiratorial planning of two Presbyterians, Positive and Zealot, is interrupted by their fellow conspirator Lovell; Lovell condemns Positive and Zealot for sympathizing with the Paxtons, who he says have committed murder and are about to commit outright rebellion.

The Paxton Boys has more theatrical flair than the other two dialogues. It opens with a panicked messenger arriving in Philadelphia to notify the governor that the Paxtons are marching toward the city from the suburbs. Over the course of the first four scenes, the word spreads rapidly, the militia are called out, and weapons are loaded and aimed before the mob of Paxtons turns out to be a company of Dutch butchers entering the city, presumably to sell their goods. In the concluding three scenes, the play anatomizes the political balance of power in colonial Philadelphia. In the fifth scene, two Presbyterians confer over how best to support the Paxtons, and one of them admits that he has been distributing ammunition to Presbyterians in the suburbs. In scene 6 the Presbyterians are interrupted and interrogated by a Quaker, whom they subtly threaten to hang whenever the opportunity presents itself, and in scene seven the Quaker confers with a member of the Church of England, who joins him in rebuking the Presbyterians. The play ends with another cry that the Paxtons have come, and all the characters rush off to take up arms, including the Quaker, who plans to defend himself against the Presbyterians. In the eighteenth-century theater, the evening entertainment usually featured a full-length play with a shorter comedy known as the "farce." Professional theater began in Philadelphia during 1749, and it appears that by the mid-1760s the author of *The Paxton Boys* had learned enough from the theater to write a competent farce on current events, one that could easily have been staged, although no evidence exists that it was (Johnson and Burling 2001, 130–132). By the mid–eighteenth century, moreover, early American drama had moved beyond the dialogue to not only the farce but also the full-length play.

THE EMERGENCE OF THE DRAMA IN THE 1760S

While it appears that neither Governor Robert Hunter nor the author of *The Paxton Boys* had the opportunity to see his stage-worthy play in performance, by the mid–eighteenth century early American theater and drama were flourishing. Existing records indicate experiments with amateur and professional theatrical performance took place in many major colonial cities, including New York, Williamsburg, and Charleston, during the early eighteenth century. Beginning in 1749, professional theater became a more noteworthy presence in the colonies from New York to Charleston as touring companies began to arrive from England and new companies arose in the colonies as performers broke away from these English troupes. The most successful of these theater companies was the London Company of Comedians managed first by Lewis Hallam Sr., and later by David Douglass, who renamed it the American Company. The London Company arrived at Williamsburg in 1754 and toured through North America and the Caribbean until 1774, when they relocated to Jamaica for the duration of the American Revolution. During the middle decades of the century the professional theater afforded American colonials the luxury of watching plays made popular on the London stage, often performed by actors from Great Britain. The most popular plays in the colonies show the diversity (as well as the conventional "Englishness") of colonial tastes. The most popular play was *Romeo and Juliet,* but colonial audiences also proved to be fond of melodramatic tragedies such as *George Barnwell,* political tragedies such as Joseph Addison's *Cato* (George Washington's favorite play), romantic comedies like George Farquhar's *The Beaux Stratagem,* and musical comedies such as John Gay's *The Beggar's Opera* (Johnson and Burling 2001, 21–29, 64–65). Once introduced to the theater, the colonial consumer quickly developed a sophisticated palate.

New dramatic forms also took root in the colonies outside of the theater. Perhaps no bigger proponent of drama could be found in the colonies during the 1750s and 1760s than the Reverend William Smith of Philadelphia, a Scottish-born Anglican clergyman who served as the first provost of the College of Philadelphia (later, University of Pennsylvania). Smith was a champion of drama's power to mold both actors and audience members into better public speakers and better citizens. In 1757, for instance, Smith's students staged a performance of James Thomson and David Mallett's heroic play *Alfred,* which chronicles the triumph of the Anglo-Saxon king Alfred the Great over a Danish tyrant named Ivar. Smith rewrote the play to suit his youthful, all-male cast by editing out Alfred's wife, and he published an extended account of the production in the *Pennsylvania Gazette* as proof of the theater's potential to create patriotic leaders for the colonies. Smith also introduced the custom of the commencement dialogue to the college in 1761. Smith and his students frequently drew on the older form of the dramatic dialogue to create ceremonial orations in dramatic form that were performed throughout the 1760s and 1770s. Generally involving two or three speakers, the dialogues usually take as their subject the historical importance of current events. The students at the College of Philadelphia commemorated both the death of King George II and the coronation of George III during the 1760s, along with other such notable events as the conclusion of the Seven Years' War in 1763 and the repeal of the Stamp Act in 1766.

Students at the College of New Jersey in nearby Princeton engaged in similar experiments. In 1762 the graduating class there staged a dialogue celebrating "the Military Glory of Great Britain," and in 1772 Philip Freneau and Hugh Henry Brackenridge composed and delivered *A Poem on the Rising Glory of America,* which envisioned the American colonies as the great "stage" where human virtue and freedom would be perfected. In addition to being performed, the dialogues were also reprinted in newspapers and then issued as pamphlets, which allowed them to reach a wide audience. The young tradition of American drama suddenly had a form it could call its own (Shaffer 2007).

The 1760s also saw the rise of another important form of American drama: the "Indian" play. This genre, in which Native Americans play central roles, frequently depicts them as naturally dignified and aristocratic people doomed to extinction because they cannot compromise with the relentlessly advancing modern world. The role of the tragic Indian chief in these plays is simultaneously an anachronism out of place in the bustling world of European Americans, and a hero who represents qualities, such as honor and independence, that were idealized by audience members of the time as essential to the American character. While Indian plays did not gain widespread popularity until the nineteenth century, one of the most important plays in the genre was published in 1766: *Ponteach, or the Savages of America,* a tragedy attributed to the colonial soldier Major Robert Rogers (Sayre 2005).

Rogers, who was born in western Massachusetts, had commanded a company of colonial Rangers during the Seven Years' War and also participated in the British suppression of Pontiac's Rebellion. His chief "Ponteach" is the very image of an outdated but noble tragic warrior determined to reclaim the honor of his people from the insults that they suffer at the hands of the British, who at the beginning of the play have conquered the French territories of North America and begun to mistreat the tribes with whom the French maintained peaceful relationships (Sayre 2005, 126–161). In Rogers's first act, Indians are cheated by British traders as well as murdered and robbed by British hunters, and Ponteach himself must withstand insults from British officers and civilian diplomats who dismiss him as a mere savage. Aided by his sons Philip and Chekitan, Ponteach attempts to unite the nations of the North American interior in a war to remove the British from their territories.

Although Ponteach's forces are initially successful, Rogers's tragic hero is doomed. Ponteach is betrayed to the British by a French priest, and the inability of his sons to manage their honor and their passions dooms his revolt. In an effort to convince the powerful Mohawk king Hendrick to join the war, Philip kills Hendrick's daughter, Monelia, and son, Torax, and then blames this atrocity on the British. Chekitan, however, loved Monelia; when the truth about their murder comes to light, Chekitan slays Philip and then commits suicide to purge his guilt. Doomed to outlive his sons and thus to have no heir to his empire, Rogers's Ponteach retains nothing but his innate nobility at the close of the play, during which he rushes offstage to rally his shattered forces for another doomed attempt to beat back the resurgent forces of the British.

Rogers's tragedy, which may largely have been ghostwritten, helped to earn him a measure of notoriety in England, but the play appears never to have been staged. At Philadelphia in 1767, however, just a year after the publication of *Ponteach*, David Douglass and the American Company staged the first professional production in the American colonies of a play written by a colonial citizen. The play that Douglass had originally scheduled, a comedy titled *The Disappointment*, was written under the pseudonym Andrew Barton and is usually attributed to a local man named Thomas Forrest. Like *The Beggar's Opera*, this play is a ballad opera, a musical satire in which characters often sing new songs arranged to popular tunes. *The Disappointment* pokes fun at the local fad of treasure hunting: four clever young men trick four local dupes (an Irishman, a Scotsman, a Dutchman, and a greedy British American) into going on an expedition for Blackbeard's treasure. Through the use of such clever devices as a fake ghost and a buried chest full of rocks, the four pranksters expose their victims as greedy fools and dash their dreams of easy riches (Seilhamer 1968, 1: 176–184). Douglass had originally scheduled this play for April 20, 1767, but after discovering that some of the characters in *The Disappointment* could be identified as local businessmen he chose a different play for this honor: a tragedy called *The Prince of Parthia*, by Thomas Godfrey, which premiered on April 24 (Johnson and Burling 2001, 271).

The Prince of Parthia can lay no claim to the originality or the contemporary relevance of *The Disappointment*, but the play did have an important connection to Philadelphia: its author had been a student of William Smith's at the College of Philadelphia before obtaining a military commission and withdrawing from the school. Godfrey, who died young of a fever in 1763, completed the tragedy and sent it to Douglass in 1759, but it remained unstaged until 1767 (Moses 1946, 1: 21–24). Godfrey's tragedy treats the theme of unrestrained passions. It centers on King Artabanus of Parthia and his three sons: the virtuous soldier Arsaces, the scheming politician Vonones, and the innocent young Gotarzes. Artabanus, Arsaces, and Vonones are all in love with Evanthe, a captive Arabian princess. Vonones convinces Artabanus that Arsaces wishes to usurp both his love and his throne, and Artabanus jails Arsaces. Shortly thereafter, a courtier associated with Vonones assassinates Artabanus, and Vonones declares himself king. Arsaces is freed by some of his soldiers and defeats his brother on the field of battle. Evanthe, however, thinking that Arsaces is dead, poisons herself, and the distraught Arsaces commits suicide. After this Romeo-and-Juliet-style ending, the young Gotarzes must assume the Parthian throne and restore order to his country. Godfrey's play was not performed again during the early American period, indicating that it was not judged to be an artistic or a commercial success. It is a conventional eighteenth-century tragedy, notable mainly for its occasional gothic excesses, such as Artabanus's queen committing suicide by dashing her brains out against a wall. Nonetheless, the complexity of its plot and Godfrey's competent, if not inspiring, use of the blank verse still commonly used for tragedies in the eighteenth century proved that an American author could write in what contemporary audiences considered to be the most exalted of dramatic genres.

PLAYWRIGHT WITH A CAUSE: MERCY OTIS WARREN

Thomas Godfrey's tragedy may not rank among the major achievements in early American literature, but a more productive early American playwright who occupies a more prominent place in the canon of the period, Mercy Otis Warren, also conducted experiments with the form (Warren 1980). Warren stands out as the leading colonial woman of letters during the Revolutionary era and a major literary presence in the drive for American independence. Born into a politically active family in Plymouth, Massachusetts, Warren was the sister of James Otis Jr., an early opponent of British colonial policies, and her husband, James, was a prominent politician on the patriot side (Richards 1995). In addition to penning a number of satirical poems, carrying on correspondences with John and Abigail Adams and the British republican historian Catherine Macaulay, and completing a three-volume history of the American Revolution, Warren penned at least five and perhaps as many as eight plays.

Warren's dramatic career began with a pair of political tragedies in the early years of the 1770s. She did not publish her first play, *The Adulateur*, a tragedy set in the fictional country of "Servia," as a complete text, but as a series of excerpts in two issues of the patriot newspaper the *Massachusetts Spy* during 1772. A complete version of the play was published the following year as a pamphlet, but a second author had added material to the play. Warren's second play, *The Defeat*, exists only in fragments published during 1773 in the *Boston Gazette*, another patriot newspaper. These works address the conflict of liberty and tyranny, a popular theme in British tragedies of the eighteenth century, and they abound with characters whose Roman names echo the fondness of British Whigs for the Roman republic: Brutus, Cassius, Marcus, and Portius all appear among the heroes, and Warren used a speech excerpted from Joseph Addison's tragedy of *Cato*, which deals with Julius Caesar's conquest of the Roman republic, as her epigraph. *The Adulateur* is not, however, just a neoclassical tale of virtue and vice. It is also an allegorical depiction of contemporary events. Its chief villains are stand-ins for prominent Massachusetts officials. The main villain, the tyrannical governor of Servia, is an obvious stand-in for Governor Thomas Hutchinson, who in addition to being the royal governor of the colony was a political rival of the Otis family. Hutchinson's powerfully connected family members such as his brother Foster Hutchinson (Limpit) and his brother-in-law Chief Justice Peter Oliver (Hazlerod) also feature prominently as villains in Rapatio's conspiracy to rob Servia of its liberty. (Hazlerod, who makes a fulsome speech praising Rapatio in the Servian legislature, is the flattering "adulateur" of the title.) To this tale of local politics, Warren's collaborator added a second plot that parallels the events of the Boston Massacre and its aftermath. In the fragmentary scenes of *The Defeat*, Warren reasserts control over her story line, and the Servians rise up against Rapatio, whose last speech is given on a scaffold, where as he awaits execution he envisions himself descending into eternal damnation.

Warren's third play, *The Group*, which was published in 1775, both in newspaper excerpts and as a completed pamphlet, takes a different turn. In the aftermath of Rapatio's destruction in *The Defeat*, and with Massachusetts hemmed in by a British blockade and governed by the British general Thomas Gage, Warren wrote a scathing satire on loyalist politicians, one that concludes with a powerful warning of the violent days facing both Britain and America. Warren's "group" is a motley crew of aspiring politicians meant to mirror a collection of loyalists who were selected to serve as members of the Governor's Council in Massachusetts, although most of them refused this honor. Assessing their own perilous situation and the united front presented by the patriots of Servia, some members of the group regret having sold their political souls to Rapatio for advancement, while others, such as the bloodthirsty Brigadier Hateall (Timothy Ruggles, a Plymouth resident and another old Otis rival), eagerly anticipate the apparently inevitable conflict between the British and the patriots. Hateall, indeed, eagerly presses the governor, Sylla (Gage), to attack, although Sylla demurs and even expresses some sympathy for the Servian/American cause. This bitterly ironic play concludes with the discovery behind a curtain of the solitary figure of a woman, who predicts imminent tragedy, with blood flowing freely until Britain is humbled by American troops.

Warren's gifts as a satirist cannot be questioned, and chiefly for this reason she is also often credited with penning three other satires that appeared in Boston during or after the American Revolution—*The Blockheads* (1776), *The Motley Assembly* (1779), and *Sans Souci* (1785)—though her authorship of these works has been disputed (Richards 1995, 102–108). These three satires, however, employ a social realism that contrasts sharply with the allegorical program of *The Group,* applying a biting wit to the dilemmas of Boston life during wartime. *The Blockheads* treats the predicament of British troops and Massachusetts loyalists during the American siege of Boston, which eventually led to the British evacuation of the city for Canada. The play mocks both the British generals (giving them names like Puff and Lord Dapper) and the struggles of a loyalist family, the Simples. As the officers watch their men grow thin during a food shortage and Simple laments having left his farm for the security of Boston, Mrs. Simple dallies in what remains of fashionable life in Boston and the Simples' daughter, Tabitha, elopes with Lord Dapper. The play ends aboard a ship bound for Canada, with Simple chastising his wife and warning her to prepare for a long, seasick voyage and British soldiers scoffing at the miseries of their loyalist passengers. *The Motley Assembly* satirizes Bostonians, including those loyalists who did not evacuate with the British, who continue to hold "society" events such as balls and card parties during the war, and also offers a sharp critique to American officers who socialize with such people. *Sans Souci* takes up a similar theme. Set mostly at a card party, it harshly criticizes the decline of the Boston public's dedication to the war effort during the latter stages of the Revolution, when the fighting had shifted far to the south. Mercy Warren features as a character in this last play, which she denied authoring: "Mrs. W——n" visits the card party, in the company of a character named "Republican Heroine" (a stand-in for Catherine Macaulay) and roundly condemns those present for the decline in public virtue evidenced by public gambling (Richards 1995, 106).

During the 1780s Warren returned twice to the genre of tragedy, producing two full-length plays that dealt once again with liberty and tyranny, this time in distant historical settings. *The Ladies of Castille* takes as its subject an uprising against the Spanish king among the nobles of the Spanish province of Castile during the sixteenth century, while *The Sack of Rome* treats the fall of the Roman Empire to Germanic invaders. Warren became an Anti-Federalist during the 1780s, and the moralistic republican ideals that her characters express in these plays, as well as her subject matter, reveal a great deal about her opinion of post-Revolutionary American society. *The Ladies of Castille* is most notable for Warren's introduction of a heroine named Donna Maria, a champion of republican ideals who, like Warren herself, is both the sister of one of the play's patriotic characters and the wife of another one. In *The Sack of Rome,* the empire falls because its political culture has become too decadent to fend off the threat on its doorstep. While almost all of Warren's plays appear to have been written for the page rather than the stage, she did send *The Sack of Rome* to her friend John Adams while he was in London on official business in 1787. Adams wrote back that the play would never succeed because "nothing American sells here" (quoted in Richards 1995, 108). American drama would not reach the British stage until the nineteenth century, despite Mercy Otis Warren's achievements as a playwright.

Virginia's Satirist: Robert Munford

One of the ironies of early American dramatic history is that Virginia, the colony where the form began in 1665 and where attending the theater became a favorite pastime for many famous Virginians such as George Washington and Thomas Jefferson, did not produce many playwrights. However, Robert Munford, the heir to William Darby of *The Bear and the Cubb* fame, did write two of the most polished American comedies of the eighteenth century. Munford was born into the Virginian aristocracy and educated by a wealthy uncle in England; but lacking hereditary wealth, he had to make both a name and a fortune for himself in the colony as a politician and a planter. Fond of the theater himself, he authored two comedies that are both polished and rich in use of local details, both of which display the Virginian upper class's professed devotion to the ideal of public service and a skepticism of the lower orders who increasingly began to demand a share of political power in Virginia during the eighteenth century (Moody 1966, 11–12).

Munford's first play, *The Candidates,* was written in 1770. Munford, who served in both the Virginia General Assembly and the House of Burgesses, uses this play gently to poke fun at the fine art of electioneering. Wou'dbe, a member the General Assembly, is preparing to stand again for office, but his fellow assemblyman Worthy has declined to run for office again. Worthy's absence draws Sir John Toddy, a local planter with social standing and a good heart but a serious drinking problem, into the campaign. Sir John proposes to Wou'dbe that they run a joint campaign, but Wou'dbe refuses on the grounds that Sir John is not suited to hold public office. Meanwhile, two other upstart candidates, Strutabout and Smallhopes, enter the election. Most of the play's funniest moments happen in the second act as the candidates meet the local voters and campaign for votes, plying the local farmers with alcohol and food. Strutabout and Smallhopes at one point strip to the waist and challenge Wou'dbe to a fistfight. Sir John passes out drunk in public, and Guzzle, his main champion, places his own equally inebriated wife next to Sir John as a prank. Meanwhile, Worthy decides to run again, which prompts Sir John to withdraw in favor of the more qualified Worthy, and in the third act the voters return Wou'dbe and Worthy to office.

Sir John's withdrawal and endorsement of Worthy illustrate a disinterested devotion to the public good that was considered to be a hallmark of an eighteenth-century gentleman. Munford's second play, *The Patriots* (probably written in 1777), however, demonstrates the difficulties that such principled people can encounter during periods of political upheaval (Philbrick 1972, 258). In this play, Munford—whose work owes clear debts to the romantic comedies of George Farquhar such as *The Beaux Stratagem* and *The Recruiting Officer*—combines three interlinked romantic plots with the struggles of two Virginia gentlemen who become ensnared by a local committee of safety, a tribunal of patriot sympathizers charged with investigating politically suspicious behavior during the Revolution (Richards 2005, 105–123). The two men, Trueman and Meanwell, find themselves accused of being loyalists for associating with Scottish merchants and not declaring themselves loudly enough as patriot sympathizers. Trueman, as a result, has had a suit for the hand of the lovely Mira Brazen refused by her father, an ardent Whig who plans to marry Mira to a cowardly American recruiting officer named Captain Flash. Meanwhile, Trueman must deal with the local committee, which Munford depicts as a crew of ambitious but ignorant amateur politicians. The committee members, with buffoonish names like "Colonel Strut," are led by one Tackabout, who loudly proclaims his Revolutionary allegiance in public but privately tells Trueman and Meanwell that he is a loyalist. Meanwhile, Mira's friend Isabella, a young woman full of Revolutionary fervor, is courted by Strut, whom she eventually discovers to be a coward; and Meanwell's servant Pickle, in addition to carrying love letters between Trueman and Mira, also arranges a fake marriage to a young country girl named Melinda, using Meanwell's name. When Trueman and Meanwell finally face the committee in the fourth act, they acquit themselves as principled, if not very vocal, patriots and expose Tackabout as a hypocrite and a loyalist. Brazen relents and agrees to let Mira marry Trueman, and Meanwell breaks up Pickle's fake marriage, only to discover that Pickle is in fact the disguised son of his deceased loyalist friend Worthy, and Melinda is in fact his niece. The play ends with the prospect of a double wedding among the Virginia gentry and political peace restored by the expulsion of cowards such as Flash and hypocrites like Tackabout from the play.

Propaganda Plays of the Revolution

The qualities that Robert Munford ridiculed in his comedies—cowardice, drunkenness, and ambitious political maneuvering—often featured in the dominant

American dramatic form of the 1770s: the propaganda play. A 1774 edict from the Continental Congress had banned theatrical performances, along with other "luxuries" such as horse racing, as wasteful, but the written drama served on both sides during the Revolution (Johnson and Burling 2001, 474). Both Mercy Otis Warren and Munford are usually placed in the group of propaganda playwrights. During the Revolutionary era many other authors from both the pro-American and pro-British camps tried their hand at writing plays that mocked the opposing side and turned contemporary political events, such as military victories, into satirical comedy or high tragedy. Some of these plays are merely revivals of the dialogue tradition in prose or verse, but a surprising number of them, especially the pro-independence ones, are sufficiently developed for the stage. Contemporary evidence suggests that students at Harvard College staged several of these plays during the Revolution (Brown 1995, 79, 83). In each text, the political commitments of the author are on full display, and argument rather than entertainment is the order of the day.

Loyalist propaganda plays lean toward comedy. They depict colonial patriots as overheated orators and mere tyrants in waiting, men fueled by self-regard and, on occasion, alcohol. In *A Dialogue, Between A Southern Delegate, and His Spouse, on His Return from the Grand Continental Congress* (1774), for instance, the delegate's spouse mocks him for believing himself knowledgeable enough to act as a statesman when he can barely manage his farm. She also strongly implies that the Congress passed the Suffolk Resolves—a precursor to the Declaration of Independence—under the influence of too much wine. *Debates at the Robin-Hood Society in the City of New-York, On Monday Night 19th of July, 1774* (1744) takes a similar tone. In this dialogue, which parodies a local assembly's passage of the Suffolk Resolves, the debate among the overzealous delegates is managed by a character called Mister Silver Tongue, "a Machiavellian Patriot who manipulates mass opinion" to serve his own political advancement (Wilmer 2002, 35). Against such bombast, loyalist characters offer cool reasoning. The prominent Boston loyalist Jonathan Sewall, for instance, penned a dialogue titled *The Americans Roused in a Cure for the Spleen; or, Amusement for a Winter's Evening,* in which a parson (Sharp), a justice of the peace (Bumper), and a Quaker (Brim) calmly convert two blustering would-be patriots (Puff and Graveairs) into loyalists. The play's most effective patriot speaker, indeed, is a barber (Trim), who freely admits that he only talks about politics so that his customers will not mind a long wait for their shave.

Not all loyalist plays are dialogues, however. The ballad opera *The Blockheads; or, the Fortunate Contractor* (1782) intermingles allegorical scenes featuring figures such as "Americana" and "Liberta" with some very funny scenes involving an American barber trying to sell wigs (or "Whigs," as patriot sympathizers were often known) and a comic Dutchman named Mynheer van Braken Peace (an allegorical representation of New York State, formerly a Dutch colony). The two-act farce *The Battle of Brooklyn* (1776), moreover, skillfully mocks the American commanders after the disastrous loss of New York City to the British. The American generals resemble Robert Munford's committee of safety: William Alexander, Lord Stirling is a coward and a drunkard; Israel Putnam is a bumpkin and a religious bigot who speaks in New England dialect and deals in stolen livestock; Washington questions his own foolish ambition and carries on affairs with chambermaids. The only competent American general, John Sullivan, flees as the British overrun the American entrenchments. The play ends with Putnam's and Sullivan's servants preparing to change sides and apply for amnesty from the Crown, while their masters must flee for their lives.

The Battle of Brooklyn is notably the only loyalist propaganda play to deal with the military, rather than the political, aspects of Revolutionary history. On the pro-American side, however, battlefield events and the history of Anglo-American military operations in the Americas strongly influence the propaganda plays. Unlike the loyalist efforts at comedy, most patriot propaganda worked in the vein of tragedy, much like Mercy Otis Warren's first dramatic efforts. Images of exalted martyrdom were important recruiting tools for the American patriot movement, and later for the Continental Army. Patriot propaganda plays, indeed, are dominated by images of heroic self-sacrifice, mostly in connection with military action (Shaffer 2006).

As in the case of loyalist propaganda plays, the patriot movement's dramas included both dialogues and stage-worthy plays. The most notable author of patriot propaganda dialogues is Thomas Paine, who wrote two of them. In *Dialogue Between General Wolfe and General Gage in a Wood Near Boston* (1775), Paine uses the ghost of General Richard Wolfe, who died in 1760 during the British assault on Quebec, to argue the American case against British imperial policies against Gage, the commander of the British forces stationed in America. In 1776, Paine returned to this supernatural motif by resurrecting General Richard Montgomery, the American general who fell during the ill-fated American attempt to take Quebec on January 1, 1776. In *A Dialogue Between the Ghost of General Montgomery, Just Arrived from the Elysian Fields, and an American Delegate, in a Wood Near Philadelphia,* Montgomery channels Paine's own pro-independence arguments in a dialogue debate with a fictional congressman. Meanwhile, two other authors, Hugh Henry Brackenridge and John Leacock, produced a total of three propaganda plays during the Revolution that show a strong grasp of theatrical convention, and which appear to have been staged at Harvard.

Brackenridge produced two patriotic tragedies: *The Battle of Bunkers-Hill* (1776) and *The Death of General Montgomery, In Storming the City of Quebec* (1777). In both plays, the plot turns on the sacrificial death of a general, Joseph Warren in *Bunkers-Hill* and Montgomery in the latter play. The two plays, however, demonstrate entirely different attitudes toward the British enemy. The British officers of *Bunkers-Hill* respect the valor of their American counterparts and largely lament the weakness of their own troops, and the rhetoric employed to describe battlefield violence suggests something almost holy in the bloodshed, with regiments of the enemy being offered up as sacrifices to either liberty or the glory of royal authority. General Warren, who in reality was shot in the face and died immediately during the battle, is given a lengthy death speech in which he envisions himself joining a pantheon of Roman and British heroes who died for their countries, and General Howe orders that Warren be buried with full military honors as a mark of respect, when in fact the British had been far less respectful of Warren's remains.

In *The Death of General Montgomery,* by contrast, Brackenridge's British officers become dishonorable, demonic villains. General Guy Carleton, the British commander at Quebec, takes the blame from Brackenridge for disrespectfully hanging the corpse of General Montgomery from the city's walls, for breaking his oath in offering terms of surrender to the Americans, and for handing over captive Americans to be tortured and eaten by the Indians allied with the British. Brackenridge also opts not to give Montgomery a showstopping death speech like the one he penned for Warren; indeed, Montgomery's death goes almost unnoticed. The play features two moving eulogies for Montgomery, however. The first is delivered by Montgomery's aide-de-camp, Burr, over the general's corpse: the traumatized Burr promises to display his own uniform, stained with Montgomery's blood, to the American forces in order to rally their sagging spirits. In the second speech, the ghost of General Wolfe appears onstage to welcome Montgomery into the afterlife and to curse the British for their savage oppression of American liberty. In the case of both Warren and Montgomery, Brackenridge helped to elevate a symbolic hero into the new pantheon of American Revolutionary martyrs. As propagandistic drama, his tragedies are impressive achievements.

Another patriot propaganda play, John Leacock's *The Fall of British Tyranny: or, American Liberty Triumphant* (1776), is also an impressive achievement as propaganda. The mood of this five-act play is not as uniformly tragic as that of Brackenridge's plays. Leacock embraces both tragedy and comedy and also includes scenes in locations ranging from London to Canada to Boston to Virginia. The first two acts feature discussions among prominent British politicians who are referred to by symbolic nicknames. The first act features a council of villains surrounding Lord Paramount, a stand-in for the Earl of Bute, a Scottish nobleman and George III's former chief minister. During this first act, Paramount reveals a plan to enslave the American colonies and restore a Roman Catholic member of the royal house of Stuart to the throne, a political nightmare shared by both American revolutionaries and their sympathizers in Great Britain. The second act stages councils between two groups of politicians seen as sympathetic to the American cause, all of whom are determined foes of Paramount. The first group consists of Lord Wisdom (William Pitt the Elder), Lord Religion (the bishop of St. Asaph), and Lord Justice (the Earl of Camden); the second council includes Lord Patriot (John Wilkes), the Bold Irishman (Edmund Burke), and Colonel (Isaac Barré, who had actually fought in North America during the Seven Years' War). These scenes, like Paramount's conspiracy in the first act, move rather slowly, but they are packed with stirring rhetoric of the "liberty or death" variety made popular in America by Revolutionary orators like Patrick Henry.

The third act of Leacock's play moves beyond allegory, however, and switches the setting to the colonies. In the first two scenes, a citizen of Boston, a local politician, and a minister discuss the various crimes committed against the city by the imperial authorities and swear allegiance to the Revolutionary effort. In the third scene, a Bostonian patriot (Whig) "outs" a loyalist (Tory) in a restaging of what must have been a fairly typical debate over royal authority and the right of revolution, at the end of which the loyalist beats a hasty retreat. In the fourth and fifth scenes, the British Lord Boston (General Gage) receives news of the eruption of the Revolution at Lexington and Concord, reacting not with martial determination but with sheer terror. In the sixth scene, Leacock returns to allegory in a long discussion between two American shepherds about British "wolves" that also features a song glorifying Tammany, an Indian chief adopted by the patriot movement as a saint. The co-opting of Native American identity as an alternative to Englishness in this scene ("America" had been figured as an Indian princess in British cartoons for decades), as surely as the gunfire exchanged earlier in the act, indicates a cultural break with Britain. The third act concludes with a tragic shift in tone, however: during a melodramatic moment, a woman named Clarissa is informed that her husband, son, and brother have all fallen as "martyrs to liberty" at Bunker Hill (Leacock 1972, 105).

The play's fourth and fifth acts return to the conflict of tyrants and patriots. The fourth act features a series of scenes starring Lord Kidnapper, a stand-in for Lord Dunmore, the former royal governor of Virginia. After fleeing Williamsburg, Dunmore took refuge on a warship and conducted a brief war against Virginia's patriots using a force that mixed loyalists with escaped slaves who were offered emancipation if they agreed to fight their former masters. The fourth act takes place aboard Dunmore's flagship and feature his interactions with a group of runaway slaves who speak a debased form of "black" English. (Bryan 2000). While the satire's barbs against Dunmore hit the mark, these scenes offer a bitter reminder to the contemporary reader that the libertarian rhetoric of American revolutionaries did not guarantee universal freedom. In the fifth act, the action shifts northward. In the first two scenes, Colonel Ethan Allen, captured in an American attempt to conquer Montreal, boldly defies his British captors, indeed so boldly that he appears ready to die for his country before being asked to do so by the British. In the play's final scenes at Washington's headquarters in Cambridge, Washington and two of his adjutant generals, Charles Lee and Israel Putnam, receive a series of messages that bear the news of General Montgomery's death at Quebec and Allen's capture at Montreal. Despite these setbacks, the three generals draw their swords and swear allegiance to the Revolution, hopefully securing the allegiance of Leacock's reader as well. Leacock's play lacks the formal unity of Brackenridge's tragedies, but, perhaps more than any other text from the early years of the Revolution, it offers the reader a sense of the immense geographic scope of those events, and of the enormous chorus of voices involved in this historical drama.

THE CONTRAST AND EARLY NATIONAL DRAMA

Professional theater returned to the former American colonies in 1781, before the Revolution was officially over, with performances by acting companies in Baltimore and New York (Brown 1995, 147–165). By 1785 performers from the Hallam-Douglass American Company had returned to North America as "The Old American Company" (Nathans 2003: 45–46). Although these players spent much of the first post-Revolutionary decade struggling to reestablish the professional theater and its predominantly British repertoire, early American drama continued to evolve. During the Revolution, for instance, college students had repeatedly engaged in amateur performances, sometimes staging new texts. At Dartmouth College during the Revolution, students acted two dialogues written by Professor John Smith (Moody 1966, 3–4). In 1784 Yale student Barnabas Bidwell wrote a domestic tragedy, *The Mercenary Match,* which was acted on campus and published (Quinn 1943, 62). Dramas not tied to college campuses also appeared. In 1783 John Trumbull published *The Double Conspiracy,* a satire in which New England loyalists scheme to undermine the United States during the Revolution, and in 1784 Peter Markoe published *The Patriot Chief,* a lumbering tragedy on the order of Godfrey's *The Prince of Parthia.* Paratheatrical spectacles, often in praise of Washington, became popular: Francis Hopkinson composed a musical entertainment, *The Temple of Minerva,* in 1781 to honor Washington and the French ambassador. Later, John Parke Custis penned an allegorical spectacle celebrating Washington's birthday, *Virginia: A Pastoral Drama on the Birth-day of an Illustrious Personage and the Return of Peace, February 11, 1784* (Meserve 1977, 130). Yet aside from rare exceptions like the foreign-born actor John Henry's *A School for Soldiers* (1783)—a translation of a French melodrama—few of these early national American plays reached the stage.

In 1787 the United States saw its first professional production of a play by a native-born citizen: Royall Tyler's *The Contrast.* Tyler, a young lawyer and Harvard graduate, had been sent to New York to seek that state's help in rounding up fugitives from Shays' Rebellion in Massachusetts. During his stay in the city, the Old American Company produced two of Tyler's plays at the John Street Theatre: *The Contrast* and a lost ballad-opera farce called *May Day in Town.The Contrast* stayed with the company and was performed later in 1787 at Philadelphia and Baltimore; after its 1790 publication it was performed as far away as Jamaica (Richards 1997,

1–4). The play is famous in part just for being the first American play produced on the stage of the independent new nation, but it is no mere novelty. *The Contrast* owes much to its predecessors in British comedy, especially Richard Brinsley Sheridan's *The School for Scandal,* but its fusion of comic wit with contemporary details about life in post-Revolutionary New York, its inclusion of a variety of social types from the early Republic, and its overt cultural nationalism render it a unique achievement in early American drama.

The "contrast" referred to in the title is the sharp distinction between two of its male characters: Billy Dimple, a foppish, Anglophile New Yorker; and Colonel Henry Manly, a patriotic Revolutionary veteran from New England. Dimple is engaged to the play's sentimental heroine, Maria Van Rough, the daughter of a prosperous merchant, but the romance between the two has cooled. Dimple, indeed, carries on dalliances with two coquettish young women: Manly's sister Charlotte, and her wealthy friend Letitia. When Manly arrives in New York on official business, he and Maria quickly fall in love, although Maria's engagement and her determination to obey her father by marrying Dimple temporarily thwart their romance. As the play builds to its climax, Tyler repeatedly contrasts the hypocritical sophisticate Dimple with Manly, the champion of republican politics and clean living. At the play's conclusion, after Van Rough discovers that Dimple is a reckless spendthrift and Manly prevents Dimple's attempt to assault Charlotte, Manly and Maria become engaged, and the chastened Charlotte vows to be less of a coquette in the future. With the impending union of Maria and Manly, the national "family" is united, and virtue triumphs.

Tyler also provides a comic "low" plot that parallels Manly's progress in New York society as Manly's valet, a feisty New England farm boy named Jonathan, discovers for himself the pleasures and perils of urban life. Like a number of characters from the colonial era, Jonathan speaks in dialect, and the regional slang and the malapropisms that he utters, along with his energy and naïveté, enliven the play considerably. Jonathan is quickly taken under the wing of Dimple's foppish servant, Jessamy, but he does not adapt well to the city. Attempting to court a New York girl, Jonathan can only sing her a few verses of "Yankee Doodle" to pass the time, and when he unintentionally buys a ticket to see *The School for Scandal* at the John Street Theatre, he is unaware that he has entered the place he calls "the devil's drawing-room" (Tyler 1997, 13).

Tyler's joke at the expense of the naive Jonathan—who rejects New York to go home to his country sweetheart—is one of the first examples of metatheatrical self-reference in the history of American drama, but the joke extends beyond the playhouse. The entire world that Jonathan, Colonel Manly, and Tyler's other characters inhabit seems to be a theater, a rapidly changing world that requires constant improvisation. Jonathan, indeed, spawned a new kind of theatrical role that extended its influence well into the nineteenth century and can still be detected in the work of Eugene O'Neill: the stage Yankee. Perhaps the ultimate lesson of Tyler's comedy, and of the entire body of early American drama, is that at its core the idea of "American-ness" is about performance. A country born out of the self-inventive processes of colonial settlement and political revolution must perhaps invariably see itself mirrored in the equally self-inventive world of the theater. Even the simplest character in the drama, a self-proclaimed "true born Yankee American son of liberty" like Jonathan, must invent himself as he goes along.

REFERENCES

Brown, Jared. 1995. *The Theatre in America during the Revolution.* New York: Cambridge University Press.

Bryan, Mark Evans. 2000. The Rhetoric of Race and Slavery in an American Patriot Drama: John Leacock's *The Fall of British Tyranny. Journal of American Drama and Theatre* 12, no. 3: 41–54.

Castillo, Susan. 2002. Imperial Pasts and Dark Futurities: Freneau and Brackenridge's "The Rising Glory of America." *Symbiosis* 6: 27–43.

Davis, Peter A. 1988. Evidence of Collaboration in the Writing of Robert Hunter's *Androboros. Restoration and Eighteenth-Century Theatre Research* 3: 20–29.

———. 1998. Plays and Playwrights to 1800. In *The Cambridge History of American Theatre. Vol. 1, Beginnings to 1870,* edited by Don B. Wilmeth and Christopher Bigsby, 216–249. New York: Cambridge University Press.

DeLoria, Philip. 1998. *Playing Indian.* New Haven, CT: Yale University Press.

Gustafson, Sandra M. 2000. *Eloquence Is Power: Oratory and Performance in Early America.* Chapel Hill: University of North Carolina Press.

Johnson, Odai. 2005. Working up from Postholes: Immaterial Witnesses, Evidence, and Narrativity in the Colonial American Theatre. *Theatre Survey* 46: 183–198.

———. 2006. *Absence and Memory in the Colonial American Theatre: Fiorelli's Plaster.* New York: Palgrave Macmillan.

Johnson, Odai, and William J. Burling. 2001. *The Colonial American Stage, 1665–1774: A Documentary Calendar.* Madison, NJ: Fairleigh Dickinson University Press.

Leacock, J. 1972. *The Fall of British Tyranny: or, American Liberty Triumphant.* In *Trumpets Sounding: Propaganda Plays of the American Revolution,* edited by Norman Philbrick, 39–134. New York: Benjamin Blom.

Leder, Lawrence H. 1964. Robert Hunter's *Androboros. Bulletin of the New York Public Library* 68: 153–160.

Londré, Felicia Hardison, and Daniel J. Watermeier. 1998. *The History of North American Theater: The United States, Canada, and Mexico: From Pre-Columbian Times to the Present.* New York: Continuum.

Meserve, Walter J. 1977. *An Emerging Entertainment: The Drama of the American People to 1828.* Bloomington: Indiana University Press.

Moody, Richard, ed. 1966. *Dramas from the American Theatre, 1762–1909.* Cleveland, OH: World.

———. 1980. Boston's First Play. *Proceedings of the Massachusetts Historical Society* 92: 117–139.

Moses, Montrose Jonas, ed. 1946. *Representative Plays by American Dramatists.* 3 vols. New York: Benjamin Blom.

Nathans, Heather S. 2003. *Early American Theatre from the Revolution to Thomas Jefferson: Into the Hands of the People.* New York: Cambridge University Press.

Philbrick, Norman, ed. 1972. *Trumpets Sounding: Propaganda Plays of the American Revolution.* New York: Benjamin Blom.

Quinn, Arthur Hobson. 1943. *A History of the American Drama from the Beginning to the Civil War.* New York: Appleton-Century-Crofts.

Richards, Jeffrey H. 1991. *Theater Enough: American Culture and the Metaphor of the World Stage, 1607–1789.* Durham, NC: Duke University Press.

———. 1995. *Mercy Otis Warren.* Boston: Twayne.

———, ed. 1997. *Early American Drama.* New York: Penguin.

———. 2005. *Drama, Theatre, and Identity in the American New Republic.* New York: Cambridge University Press.

Sayre, Gordon M. 2005. *The Indian Chief as Tragic Hero: Native Resistance and the Literatures of America, from Moctezuma to Tecumseh.* Chapel Hill: University of North Carolina Press.

Seilhamer, George Oberkirsh. 1968. *History of the American Theatre.* 3 vols. New York: Greenwood.

Shaffer, Jason. 2006. Making "an Excellent Die": Death, Mourning, and Patriotism in the Propaganda Plays of the American Revolution. *Early American Literature* 41, no. 2: 1–27.

———. 2007. *Performing Patriotism: National Identity in the Colonial and Revolutionary American Theatre.* Philadelphia: University of Pennsylvania Press.

Shields, David S. 1990. *Oracles of Empire: Poetry, Politics, and Commerce in British America, 1690–1750.* Chicago: University of Chicago Press.

Tyler, Royall. 1997. *The Contrast.* In *Early American Drama,* edited by Jeffrey H. Richards, 1–57. New York: Penguin.

Warren, Mercy Otis. 1980. *The Plays of Mercy Otis Warren,* edited by Benjamin Franklin V. Delmar, New York: Scholars' Facsimiles and Reprints.

Wilmer, S. E. 2002. *Theatre, Society, and the Nation: Staging American Identities.* New York: Cambridge University Press.

CHAPTER 21

....

THE LITERATURE OF
POLITICS

....

FRANK SHUFFELTON

Writing to Hezekiah Niles in 1818, John Adams remarked on the power of the American Revolution, stating that it "was not a common event. Its effects and consequences have already been awful over a great part of the globe. And when and where are they to cease?" He went on to ask a more difficult question: "But what do we mean by the American Revolution? Do we mean the American war? The Revolution was effected before the war commenced. The Revolution was in the minds and hearts of the people; a change in their religious sentiments of their duties and obligations" (Adams 1819, 233). Putting the Revolution into the past tense, Adams located it in memory, thus restraining its power and its threat to present-day order. His internalization of it into the relatively secret realm of minds and hearts suggested its potential to reemerge in some indeterminate future moment.

Benjamin Rush, reflecting upon his own role in the Revolution, preferred to think forward, calling the American Revolution "big with important consequences to the world." Yet simultaneously he recognized that "the seeds of all the great changes for the better in the condition of mankind, have been sowed years and centuries before they came to pass" (Rush 1970, 161). Rush's "years and centuries" look to a historical continuity many Whig polemicists before the Revolution had long maintained: the grounds for the assertions of the republican rights of the citizenry were originally established in the laws of England as explained by Sir Edward Coke, other legal commentators, the Magna Carta, and ultimately the founding traditions of

Anglo-Saxon liberty before William the Conqueror imposed the so-called Norman yoke. If Rush's version of revolutionary origins—one that Adams subscribed to as well—has the advantage of pointing to its beginnings in an accumulation of political texts and beliefs, it also privileges external circumstances and detracts from the secret, private world of "heart" and "religious sentiments" evoked by Adams. The revolution Adams described was ultimately a revolution of the imagination. Much of it was worked out in a remarkable body of political literature that appeared in the second half of the eighteenth century.

REVOLUTIONARY DISCOURSE AND IDENTITY

The first premonitions of the American Revolution, understood as the political separation of the former North American colonies from the British Empire, can be discerned in a century of conflicts over charter rights in colonies like Massachusetts or over relations with proprietors in a colony like Pennsylvania, as well as squabbles about taxes and prerogatives between legislatures and royal governors in others. Religious protests arguing for the rights of local congregations to rule themselves, or against the imposition of the clerical order of the Anglican Church, or for freedom of conscience (and against taxation to support someone else's denomination) added another dimension to political struggles to assert the rights of individual Americans to control their own affairs. John Wise argued the first point in two forceful pamphlets in the early 1700s, including his *The Churches Quarrel Espoused* (1713), which was reprinted in 1772 in light of a subsequent struggle of local governments to assert their right to self-government.

Jonathan Mayhew in Massachusetts protested a threatened imposition of Anglican order in his widely read sermon of 1750, and Landon Carter and Richard Bland carried on pamphlet warfare with John Camm and other Anglican clergy of Virginia over what they saw as arrogant attempts to supervene the authority of the House of Burgesses, the elected legislative body. Isaac Backus and other Baptist leaders wrote pamphlets arguing for freedom of conscience to worship in their own manner and not to be forced to pay taxes in support of established church orders, be they Congregationalist in Massachusetts or Anglican in Virginia and elsewhere. One could add to this the efforts of John Woolman and other Quakers like Anthony Benezet to persuade their fellow denominationalists of the immorality of slave owning and the essential freedom of all persons.

Protests against authority, whether undertaken by colonists against an imperial center or by marginalized colonists against their local elites, took different forms in every colony, but common themes emerged in all these protests. They all involved the creation of a paper trail in the form of pamphlets and newspaper pieces—the latter often reappearing as the former. On the one hand, this extensive literature of protest was a record of emotional disturbance, of anger, resentment, and injured self-esteem on the part of individuals who felt themselves wronged by figures of authority or regarded as personally or politically inferior. On the other hand, it was a potent force for creating a new political and social order that emerged out of the Revolution. The ideas in this literature go back to British and European political thinkers and polemicists. In some instances, the American writers seem often to be merely quoting their Whig predecessors and models. However, quotations uttered in a new context suggest new meanings, and the political literature of the American patriots led to radical outcomes.

Unlike the other protests noted here, John Woolman's campaign against slavery did not involve an explicitly political argument, but it points more clearly to the underlying reality of much of the political literature. Grounded in Woolman's dreams and his feelings about the inhumanity of slaveholding as he witnessed it, Woolman's message both depended on and called for a change of heart, a new identity that could respond to the world in a new way. Identity was very much the issue in the decades before the Revolution, though its expression took various forms in political, religious, and social terms. Bernard Bailyn attributed the political resistance that ultimately defeated Governor Thomas Hutchinson to "an upsurge of political passion," pointing to its emotional, mysteriously interior origins, and he described a pattern of conspiracy theorizing that he located as a kind of American paranoia. Gordon Wood countered Bailyn's arguments about paranoid tendencies among the Revolutionary generation by arguing that their thinking was grounded in a long tradition of Whig theory and constituted a reasonable attempt to explain and make coherent the actions of the British government. Jack P. Greene has argued that eighteenth-century Americans shaped identities out of overlapping and conflicting sources, idealized memories of their own seventeenth-century origins, and the material circumstances and opportunities opening to them in the aggressive, acquisitive culture of their own time (Bailyn 1974, 75; Bailyn 1968; Wood 1982; Greene 1970; Greene 1993).

These explanations of Revolutionary origins, appealing variously to irrational passion, conscious intellection, or memory and desire, typically fail to take into consideration that the concept of identity is itself available in different versions, identity as a sign of individual uniqueness, for example, or identity as a sign of membership in a group. Furthermore, identity in the modern understanding of a sense of a unique self seems to be a fairly recent construction, one that was in fact taking place in the eighteenth century. Following Charles W. Taylor's masterly demonstration of the historicity of the self, Dror Wahrman has more recently argued that a crucial transformation of the understanding of the self occurred in this period and is specifically marked by the occasion of the American Revolution (Taylor 1989; Wahrman 2004).

In larger terms Wahrman's argument reflects the growing sense of personal interiority in the eighteenth century, a sense that the key site of identity is in mind rather than in social or political definition. We are what we think and feel above all other markers of identity. One curious phenomenon that Wahrman identifies shows external markers such as gender and race becoming harder, more fixed, by the end of the eighteenth century even as a modern, interior sense of self becomes central to the understanding of individual identity. Wahrman's sources are primarily British rather than American, but the shifts in understanding about identity that he traces are clearly evident in the larger Anglo-American world, particularly so in the course of the political literature that emerged in the decades before the Revolution. In its earliest phases, colonials were demanding the "rights of Englishmen" or the rights guaranteed by their charters or by royal acquiescence to historical practices; by 1776 they are demanding rights based on the laws of nature and nature's God, rights not embodied in grants, charters, concessions, or laws but engraved on the human heart itself. The assertion of these natural rights, experienced internally as sentiments of truth and right, in turn supported an assertion of a larger national identity of Americanness as the older self-identification of the colonists as "Englishmen" became increasingly problematic.

The resolution of conflicted identities, both individual and national, was acted out in and enabled by a remarkable body of political literature that emerged in the North American colonies in the third quarter of the eighteenth century. The Seven Years' War of 1756–1763 was an occasion for the emergence of transatlantic misgivings, but even before the war British authorities were becoming convinced of a need to exert greater control over its colonies. Provoked on one side by fears of colonial independence and on the other by fears of a concerted plan to restrict trade and withdraw traditional rights, a vigorous and extensive political literature emerged, particularly on the colonial side of the Atlantic. In its initial stages this polemical discourse focused on economic and constitutional issues about the relationship between the metropole and the colonies, but it quickly revealed deeper anxieties felt by participants on both sides of the Atlantic. By 1776 the language of the political debate between mother country and colonies had moved from discussions of economics and constitutionality to claims about equality and universality, from the rights of political subjects to the rights of subjects as individual moral, political, and psychological agents.

John Adams in his famous *Novanglus* papers of 1774 located the origins of this changed relationship, and the origins of the Revolution itself, in 1754, when Governor Shirley "communicated to [Benjamin Franklin] the profound secret,—the great design of taxing the colonies by act of parliament" (Adams 1819, 15; Franklin 1950, 60–63). Fears of British conspiracies to impose an imperial will on the colonies were ostensibly over political issues, but they were also driven by anxieties about uncertain, unstable colonial identities haunted by suspicion of British motives and resentment over perceived arrogance toward colonial subjects. The political debates of the 1760s and 1770s were certainly about political and legal relations, but they came out of "the discursive ambivalence that makes 'the political' possible" (Bhabha 1994, 24).

THE STAMP ACT

In 1750 Jonathan Mayhew, minister of Boston's West Church, seized the occasion of the anniversary of the execution of King Charles I to preach a sermon, subsequently published under the title *A Discourse Concerning Unlimited Submission.* Mayhew attacked the "mysterious Doctrine of the Prince's Saintship and Martyrdom" that was being promulgated from the center of the Anglican establishment in King's Chapel, where the royally appointed governor and his friends worshiped. Mayhew argued that the "oppression and violence of [Charles's] reign . . . brought him to his untimely and violent end" and that "bigoted clergymen and friends to church power paint this man as a saint" in order to represent present-day religious dissenters as "traitors and rebels and all that is bad." The real meaning of this anniversary, claimed Mayhew, was "that it will prove a standing *memento* that *Britons* will not be *slaves,* and a warning to all corrupt *counselors* and *ministers* not to go too far in advising to arbitrary despotic measures." If the real purpose of the "bigoted clergymen and friends of church power" was "to appear considerable" to colonists who were imputed to be little better than criminals, the answer was an assertion of a truer Britishness entertained by the descendants of Charles's judges (Bailyn 1965, 244–247). Bernard Bailyn has called Mayhew's work "the most famous sermon preached in pre-Revolutionary America," and by introducing language that would be central to subsequent debates about the relationship between Britain and its North American colonies—slavery, corruption, arbitrary despotic measures—as well as by expressing American resentment at metropolitan insinuations of colonial inferiority, it is a benchmark of the drift toward revolution that culminated in 1776 (Bailyn 1965, 204).

Mayhew's sermon attracted attention in London, and at the same time voices were beginning to speak out in the 1750s arguing that the colonial legislative bodies were in fact little parliaments, holding something other than a merely subservient relationship to the British parliament. It is not entirely surprising, then, that James Abercromby, a Scottish vice-admiralty officer with fourteen years experience in the American colonies, voiced in 1752 a commonly held concern among British authorities when he urged the necessity to "render the said Colonies without Distinction Subservient to the Welfare and Interest of their Mother Country" (quoted in Shannon 2000, 64). If such concerns were shared at the ministerial level before

Governor Shirley let out the secret to Benjamin Franklin in 1754 about plans to tax the American colonies, it was after the conclusion of the Seven Years' War, known in America as the French and Indian War, that the first serious attempts were made to bring the colonies under tighter control and simultaneously to use them as a source of income to pay down the immense debt accumulated to sustain the war. Adding to the debt was the continuing cost of maintaining British troops in the North American colonies on a permanent basis, a policy that aroused colonial whiggish anxieties about a standing army and resentment about being expected to pay for a military force they felt they did not need.

The first preparatory steps toward raising a revenue in the colonies in fact began before the Treaty of Paris in 1763 ended the war. They involved reinforcing the numbers and the powers of the customs officers, who were typically British appointees, giving them the power to demand from colonial magistrates writs of assistance that entitled them to search anywhere they pleased and to seize not only contraband but also the ships in which the supposedly illegal imports were carried. Previous enforcement of customs regulations had been lax, but the vigilance of the customs officers was encouraged by awarding them a percentage of the value of all seized goods. This was followed by the Sugar Act and the Currency Act of 1764, which prohibited the colonies from issuing paper money, a practice that had been important to sustain economies that saw little hard money in circulation. The Sugar Act actually lowered the tax imposed on imported sugar and molasses that was used in the New England rum industry, but while the previous tax was usually evaded or compounded, the new tax was more rigorously enforced. There were grumblings and petitions about these laws, but the Stamp Act imposed the following year was a novel tax in the colonies, clearly imposed to raise a revenue, and intrusive into every level of colonial life. The Stamp Act required all paper to bear a tax stamp, including that used for almanacs, newspapers, playing cards, wills, mortgages, and other legal documents; it aroused the first concerted resistance to British policy and the first great cycle of pre-Revolutionary political literature (Morgan and Morgan 1963).

The act was little more than two months old when the Virginia House of Burgesses passed resolves asserting that by practice and by charter right Virginians possessed all "the Liberties, Privileges, and Immunities, that have at any Time been held, enjoyed, and possessed, by the people of *Great Britain.*" Furthermore, "the distinguishing Characteristick of *British* Freedom, without which the ancient Constitution cannot exist," was the people's right to be taxed only by themselves or their representatives by their own consent (Morgan 1959, 47–48). In the course of the debate over the resolutions, Patrick Henry delivered the speech that defined his position as the radical voice of young, potentially disaffected Virginians, proclaiming that "in former times Tarquin and Caesar had their Brutus, Charles had his Cromwell, and he did not doubt but some good American would stand up in favour of his Country." When challenged by the Speaker of the House for speaking treason, Henry protested his willingness to "shew his loyalty to his majesty King

G[eorge] the third, at the Expence of the last drop of his blood" (Morgan 1959, 46). Henry's daring language vacillated between a hinted desire to be the American agent of violence and the expressed willingness to be the passive sufferer for his British loyalty; it was echoed in the resolutions themselves that proclaimed the liberties of the people of Virginia at the same time as they sought the protection of the "ancient Constitution" of Britain. Such conflicted responses were a regular feature of the early protests against the Stamp Act and the later Townshend Acts that replaced the former with a new set of taxes imposed by Parliament.

James Otis's *The Rights of the British Colonies Asserted and Proved* (1764) actually predated the passage of the Stamp Act itself, having been written in response to early news about the ministry's proposal for a stamp tax. Otis's pamphlet was perhaps one of the most systematic attempts by pre-Revolutionary political thinkers to explain the fundamental grounds of the relationship between the government and the colonies, yet at the same time it concluded with what seems to be a thoroughly self-contradictory position (Webking 1988, 20). The pamphlet opens with a gesture that seems in hindsight to be radically prophetic of the position taken by the Declaration of Independence in 1776. Otis in effect moved beyond the traditional Hobbesean and Lockean arguments for the origins of government, denying that it was founded on property alone, or on force, or compact, but "in the *unchangeable* will of GOD, the author of nature, whose laws never vary." Otis in turn claimed to see this unchangeable will in "*the necessities of our nature. It is by no means an arbitrary thing depending merely on compact or human will* for its existence" (Bailyn 1965, 423). Otis agreed with Locke that "in a constituted commonwealth" like Britain "there can be but one supreme power which is the legislative, to which all the rest are and must be subordinate," but he argued from this point both that the people have the power "to remove or alter the legislative power when they find that it acts contrary to the trust reposed in it" and that at the same time "the power of Parliament is uncontrollable but by themselves, and we must obey." Otis in effect argued himself into a corner, hemmed in on the one side by his American indignation at arbitrary measures imposed from abroad and on the other by his dutiful sense of being a British subject in whom it "would therefore be the highest degree of impudence and disloyalty to imagine that the King, at the head of his Parliament, could have any but the most pure and perfect intentions of justice, goodness, and truth that human nature is capable of" (Bailyn 1965, 434, 448). For Benjamin Franklin such a remark would be inflected with a self-critical irony, but Otis seems totally sincere, totally committed to a somewhat fantastic view of the government over the water.

Because Otis later suffered a serious mental collapse, his self-contradictory stance here has sometimes been adduced as a sign of mental confusion, if not a harbinger of insanity itself. He was not alone, however, in trying to maintain simultaneously a position of defiance and one of subordination to the British imperial system. Mayhew had taken a similar position, and most of Otis's American contemporaries held versions of his position, even the fiery Patrick Henry.

Otis tried to resolve his logical and political difficulties by a bit of magical thinking that came right out of the New England Puritan tradition of millennialist thinking. He reminded readers that even the king was "under God, the father of mankind," and that "the cards are shuffling fast through all Europe. Who will win the prize is with God." Otis's ultimate faith was that "the next universal monarchy will be favorable to the human race, for it must be founded on the principles of equity, moderation, and justice. No country has been more distinguished for these principles than Great Britain." Otis earlier let show his provincial resentment at metropolitan disdain toward the colonies evidenced when "even now some of their great men and writers, by their discourse of and conduct towards them, consider them all rather as a parcel of *little insignificant conquered islands* than as a very extensive settlement on the continent." Otis balanced his fears of being thought insignificant with a fleeting vision that the world's last great "universal monarchy" will be an idealized British empire of "equity, moderation, and justice." In so retreating to the visionary and ideal, he deflected his argument from constitutional or economic issues to the darker territory of the imagined self, the unstable world of conflicted identity.

The arguments generated during the Stamp Act crisis on both sides of the Atlantic similarly resorted to various fictions, legal and constitutional, as ways to overcome the crisis of American identity and British political subjectivity. Because these conflicting identities, although grounded in the material facts of daily life, were constructed, fictive realities, the conflicts could be resolved only by working through to new, more self-affirming fictions. In the early phases of the debates about parliamentary taxation of the colonies, many American pamphleteers and even various colonial legislative assemblies claimed to see a difference between "internal" and "external" taxation. The latter were assumed to be a necessary and proper means to regulate trade among the colonies and the home country, the former designed to raise revenue for the purposes of the imperial government. These purposes included creating a permanent salary for governors and other royal officials, thus distancing them from the control of the elected assemblies that had previously paid their salaries on a yearly basis.

Daniel Dulany, a Maryland lawyer and politician, conceded, "A right to impose an internal tax on the colonies without their consent *for the single purpose of revenue,* is denied, a right to regulate their trade without their consent is admitted," and Benjamin Franklin as the agent for Pennsylvania told the House of Commons that the colonists objected only to direct, internal taxes (Knollenberg 2003, 12; Bailyn 1965, 638). This distinction was not long maintained by the colonists, although the British ministry would seize upon it for the next attempt at taxing the colonies. The distinction between an internal and an external tax was hazy at best, at worst no distinction at all, but it was another attempt to explain away internal contradictions between local and imperial identities. Franklin's suggestion that the colonists would refuse an "internal tax," whatever its constitutional logic, might be seen as an attempt to preserve both a political and a personal interior, to preserve the site of an American identity. If the distinction was unsustainable, the debate around it clarified notions about the proper relationship between colonies and the central government. In Britain this led to assertions of parliamentary supremacy; in America it reemerged in somewhat different terms in debates after 1776 about the relationship between individual states and the national government.

Richard Bland of Virginia brushed off the distinction in 1766, asserting that the British ministry's imposition of taxes on the colonies was not in pursuit of "a wise and salutary Plan of Government" but a case of "pernicious and destructive acts of power." Bland's characterization of ministerial behavior was set out as a constitutional argument about the historical and legal relationship between the colonies and the home country, but it was motivated as well by an obvious resentment of British characterizations of "the Inhabitants of North America" as the descendants of "a few unhappy Fugitives, who had wandered thither to enjoy their civil and religious Liberties, which they were deprived of at Home" (Jensen 2003, 17). Daniel Dulany grounded his distinction between forms of taxation by appealing to the charter rights of the colonies, but he also insisted on the necessity of actual representation in any legitimate taxing body. The colonial assemblies had this; the British Parliament did not, and colonial pamphleteers like Dulany called for American representatives in the British Parliament before it could assume the right to tax the colonies. Given the ocean between America and Britain, this was impractical. Ministerial writers such as ex-governor Thomas Pownall and Lord Grenville's private secretary Thomas Whately argued that the colonies were in fact virtually represented in Parliament in the same way that Manchester and Birmingham were represented as part of the whole English people, even though they did not elect their own representatives (Pownall 1765; Whately 1765).

Dulany, Bland, and other colonial writers were quick to refute the notion of virtual representation, but arguments for actual colonial representation in Parliament were not taken seriously on either side of the Atlantic. Rhode Island Tory Martin Howard Jr. dismissed the whole issue of representation, calling it a "Utopian privilege" and "but a phantom, and if possessed in its full extent would be of no real advantage to the colonies; they would, like Ixion, embrace a cloud in the shape of Juno" (Bailyn 1965, 538). But if Howard could sneer at such phantoms and utopian claims as insubstantial fictions, to the colonists they provided solid ground upon which to theorize a revolution. In the meantime, fears of "phantoms" were also a sign of inner uncertainties and conflicts; Thomas Jefferson long after the Revolution said of Bland: "He would set out with a set of sound principles, pursue them logically till he found them leading to the precipice which he had to leap, start back alarmed, then resume his ground, go over it in another direction, be led by the correctness of his reasoning to the same place . . . but finally left his reader and himself bewildered between the steady index of the compass in their hand, and the phantasm to which it seemed to point" (Jefferson 1903–1905, 13: 338).

The Stamp Act was repealed in 1766, less because of the pamphlets of writers like Dulany, Bland, Otis, and Rhode Island's Stephen Hopkins than because of an effective nonimportation movement supported by colonial merchants, a flood of protests and resolutions from colonial assemblies and from the Stamp Act Congress that met in New York in October 1765, and, perhaps most important, vigorous and often violent protests by patriotic mobs. A crowd of laborers and artisans in Boston tore down the house of Andrew Oliver, the stamp distributor, and the office building he had erected for issuing the stamps; to finish off their work, they regathered in the streets twelve days later, marched on Lieutenant Governor Thomas Hutchinson's house, and tore that down, too. Such actions hardened the lines on both sides, emboldening American protesters and convincing British writers like "Anti-Sejanus" to assert in the *London Chronicle*, "The Americans imbibe notions of independence and liberty with their very milk, and will some time or other shake off subjection. . . . In short, the spirit of rebellion is now gone forth, and it is of too fierce and savage a nature to be subdued by kindness and indulgence: It animates the scum and refuse of the people, whose breasts are too callous to be touched by gentle and generous treatment" (Morgan 1959, 134; Nash 2005, 44–59). This attitude in Parliament resulted in the passing of the Declaratory Act the same day it repealed the Stamp Act. The Declaratory Act reaffirmed its insistence on an absolute subordination of the American colonies by claiming its "full power and authority to make laws and statutes of sufficient force and validity to bind the colonies and people of *America,* subjects of the crown of *Great Britain,* in all cases whatsoever" (Morgan 1959, 155). British politicians and writers were creating their own counternarrative to American claims of loyalty to Crown and empire by fostering visions of anarchic mobs spinning off into dangerous independence.

The language of writers like Anti-Sejanus increased colonial resentment toward British arrogance and condescension, suggesting that the colonies had been settled by criminals and debtors and that Britain's Americans were indistinguishable from the savage first inhabitants. Such terms were bound to rankle a population of mixed ethnicities and races that was coming to create a sense of community around shared white racial identification. Benjamin Franklin concluded his "Observations Concerning the Increase of Mankind" by seeing immigration as an opportunity of "excluding all Blacks and Tawneys, of increasing the lovely White and Red" (Shannon 2000, 60–61; Wahrman 2004; Franklin 1987, 374). At the same time, assertions such as those in the Declaratory Act of unlimited parliamentary power over American colonies and individuals strengthened fears that had been in the colonial literature of political protest from the beginning. Jonathan Mayhew had announced in 1750 that "*Britons* will not be slaves," and the fear of enslavement was heard like a drumbeat in pamphlets and periodicals right up to the critical moments of 1775 and 1776. If colonial anarchy and independence were the fears on one side of the Atlantic, the threat of slavery and corruption creeping out from the metropole haunted the other. Each side had its own phantoms to deal with, but the Whig polemicists in

America had what were ultimately more powerful visions, spun out of language that resonated with intellectual elites such as themselves and with the people in the street as well.

Stephen Hopkins began *The Rights of Colonies Examined* (1765) by observing, "Liberty is the greatest blessing that men enjoy, and slavery the heaviest curse that human nature is capable of" (Bailyn 1965, 507). This set the terms for the next dozen years. The frequent expressions of anxiety about being reduced to slavery are complex because they occur in the context, particularly in the context of more southerly colonies, of large enslaved populations that were racially different and were becoming increasingly a matter of concern for white ruling classes. At the same time there was an emerging recognition of the moral wrong of slavery and an increasing animus against it that would lead to the first American abolition movement. The rhetoric about liberty and human rights amplified the abolitionist arguments of John Woolman and Anthony Benezet by compounding their appeals to religious morality with appeals to natural law. While slavery was becoming simultaneously abhorrent in itself, the prospect of being reduced to slavery, to the condition of the black other, was fraught with anxiety because of the threat of being identified with that other. Slavery and liberty thus came to define each other for the colonists in ambivalent and conflicted ways that Britons were not totally capable of appreciating. British commentators tended to dismiss this language as either empty rhetoric or mere hypocrisy; Samuel Johnson's scornful remarks about the loudest yelps for liberty coming from the drivers of slaves was typical. The keyword "slavery" that kept reappearing in the Whig protests against the British ministry and Parliament was, however, not merely an exaggerated expression of anxiety about measures perceived as arbitrary and unconstitutional, it reflected fears about loss of identity, loss of the dignity of a constructed whiteness, but also feelings of guilt and of sympathy for others suffering from the denial of human rights.

John Dickinson's *Letters from a Farmer in Pennsylvania*

The writerly resistance to the Stamp Act was only the first phase of the evolving campaign in newspapers and pamphlets that led up to the revolutionary Declaration of Independence, but it laid down fundamental terms and revealed underlying anxieties about identity that drove subsequent protest and debate. When the British ministry, following the recommendation of Charles Townshend, the Chancellor of the Exchequer, and trusting in the notion that the colonists would accept external taxes on trade, put through Parliament the Townshend Acts of 1767 that imposed taxes on tea, paper, glass, and paint, it provoked a new round of protests. These protests were given more edge because of the New York Suspending Act, which prohibited the New York legislature from passing any other laws until it agreed to abide by the Quartering Act of 1765 and provide for the maintenance of British troops stationed there. The most important pieces of writing to come out of this phase of the transatlantic debate were Franklin's occasional pieces in London newspapers that were reprinted in Philadelphia and elsewhere and John Dickinson's *Letters from a Farmer in Pennsylvania* (1768), the most widely reprinted American political piece before Thomas Paine's *Common Sense.*

The first of Dickinson's twelve letters appeared in the *Pennsylvania Chronicle* on December 2, 1767, and ran through the end of the following month. They were quickly reprinted by nearly every newspaper in the North American colonies and were soon available in pamphlet form in America, London, and Dublin. Dickinson, who had served as a member of the Stamp Act Congress, had trained as a lawyer at the Middle Temple in London, and his tract was in effect a legal brief for the patriot cause, fortified with learned notes and written in a straightforward, readily accessible style.

Letters built upon the arguments that had already been put forth by other writers against the contention that Parliament had the right to levy taxes on the colonists, but Dickinson went farther by pointing to the implications of the Declaratory Act, which had not drawn much notice from colonial writers, who were more inclined to celebrate the repeal of the Stamp Act. The early letters observed that for earlier writers "the single question is, whether the parliament can legally impose duties to be paid *by the people of these colonies only,* FOR THE SOLE PURPOSE OF RAISING A REVENUE, *on commodities which she obliges us to take from her alone,* or in other words whether the parliament can legally take money out of our pockets without our consent." This question was not merely about safeguarding property, however, for as Dickinson pointed out, "All artful rulers, who strive to extend their power beyond its just limits, endeavor to give to their attempts as much semblance of legality as possible. Those who succeed them may venture to go a little further; for each new encroachment will be strengthened by a former" (McDonald 1962, 15, 35).

Pretending that the Townshend duties were meant to regulate trade was merely an artful illusion to disguise the fact that they were an attempt to impose taxes without the consent of the taxed. They were further dishonest because they were to support British interests, to maintain armed forces in Canada and Florida, and to enforce limits on colonial development in the West rather than to serve colonial interests. They would support a horde of patronage appointees, governors, judges, and customs officers, who would be free from any effective control from the colonists once their salaries were paid from London and not by the colonial legislative bodies. This scheme would extend metropolitan corruption to the colonies: "Before such judges, the supple wretches, who cheerfully join in avowing sentiments inconsistent with freedom, will always meet with smiles; while the honest and brave men, who disdain to sacrifice their native land to their own advantage . . . will constantly be regarded with frowns." The deceptive language and maneuvers of the British ministry would lead in the end "unless the most watchful attention be exerted, [to] a new servitude." Dickinson was able in the Farmer's *Letters* to draw upon the pervasive language of phantoms and phantasms to project them on to "powerful and artful" men in London with their "SECRET measures" and their willing accomplices in the colonies. Urging a strategy of suspicion—"Liberty, perhaps, is never exposed to so much danger, as when the people believe there is the least; for it may be subverted, and yet they not think so"—he aggravated colonial anxieties while simultaneously offering explanations in terms of ideas about corruption and conspiracy (McDonald 1962, 53, 35, 41, 74).

The importance of Dickinson's Farmer's *Letters* extends beyond their legal arguments and political analyses. Most authors of political pieces adopted classical pseudonyms such as Cato or Brutus or Publius, but by identifying himself as a "Pennsylvania Farmer," Dickinson was able to locate his identity with a specifically American place and to offer a myth of identity suitable to "a country of planters, farmers, and fishermen." He describes himself in the first letter in terms of the pastoral ideal of the happy man, the recipient of a liberal education who has "been engaged in the busy scenes of life; but [is] now convinced that a man may be as happy without bustle, as with it." His few wants are gratified, his affairs easy, and "undisturbed by worldly hopes or fears," he spends a good deal of time in his library, but his "Benevolence toward mankind, excites wishes for their welfare," which "can be found in liberty only" (McDonald 1962, 3). Dickinson's pose here is borrowed from a literary tradition leading back through John Pomfret and other poets to Horace, every bit as much borrowed as his political ideas were from Locke, Montesquieu, Hume, Beccaria, Burlamaqui, and many others. Yet his self-presentation evoked its responses from New Hampshire to Georgia because many readers thought that it either described the person they thought they were, at once American in simplicity but with the tastes of an English gentleman, or the person they hoped to become. The image of the political Farmer was imitated by the Tory Samuel Seabury's *Letters from a Westchester Farmer* (1774–1775), Crèvecoeur's *Letters from an American Farmer* (1782), and Richard Henry Lee's Anti-Federalist *Letters from a Federal Farmer* (1787–1788).

The pastoral myth with a local habitation was reinforced by the serial form of the letters. There had been a few earlier serial writings about politics, notably the *Independent Reflector* (1752–1753) of William Livingston and his friends in New York, but the seriality of Dickinson's *Letters from a Farmer in Pennsylvania* underlined the importance of systematic and continuing forms of critique and resistance. Previous writings against the Stamp Act and the Townshend Acts had been one-off affairs, and the Stamp Act Congress, like the Albany Congress of 1754, had no successors. Continuous critique from identifiable voices was a precondition for continuing political organization, and the seriality of the *Letters* was a forerunner of Boston's institution of annual orations on the anniversary of the Boston Massacre, of John Adams's *Novanglus* papers, and of Thomas Paine's *Crisis* essays among others.

By situating ultimate powers of judgment in the people about their liberty and linking their liberty to their happiness, Dickinson's *Letters* moved to internalize and personalize arguments about rights. "Ought not the people therefore to watch? To observe facts? To search into causes? To investigate designs? And have they not a right of JUDGING from the evidence before them, on no slighter points than their *liberty* and *happiness?*" Dickinson followed Locke's *Second Treatise* in linking liberty with property, but as the *Letters* unfolded, concern for the people's happiness emerged to refocus a concern for property as such to inner needs, to the desire and emotional security that sought property as a fetish for freedom. Dickinson understood David Hume's assertion that "government is founded on opinion" because "The first principles of government are always to be looked for in human nature" (McDonald 1962, 37, 70). Dickinson's most effective rhetorical move was to ground the legal and philosophical notion of natural rights in the hearts of individual Americans, laying the way for the sentimental strategy of the Declaration of Independence.

BENJAMIN FRANKLIN

The Townshend Acts provoked numerous other writers, but the other most significant writer in this phase of the controversy, although in a series of occasional pieces, was Benjamin Franklin. Franklin had taken up residence in England in 1757 as an agent for the Pennsylvania Assembly and remained there until 1775 when his position became untenable. Ironically, his initial engagement with the British political world was in order to further the Assembly's efforts to revoke the Penn family's proprietary privileges; Franklin's strategy was to urge the transformation of Pennsylvania into a royal colony, putting it under direct control of the Crown and the ministry. By 1775 he came to think rather differently about the desirability of such an arrangement as he became progressively more alienated from successive British ministries. From the beginning of his stay in England, Franklin carried on an active correspondence in the London press, commenting on British misunderstandings of America and on official policies meant to regulate and control the North American colonies. Franklin's writings were overwhelmingly reactive rather than original articulations of political or constitutional arguments; they answered other items in the newspapers or speeches in Parliament that urged hostile policies toward the colonies or belittled the nature of the colonists. They frequently mirrored British critiques of America by discerning the same problems in Britain itself. Franklin responded to criticism of American slaveholding by pointing to the effective enslavement of many British workers, and he countered condemnations of American street violence by noting the mobbing, housebreaking, and attacks on customs officers that happened perhaps more frequently on the other side of the Atlantic.

Many of these occasional pieces were reprinted in America, frequently in the *Pennsylvania Chronicle* but in other newspapers as well, and their repeated accusations of British contemptuousness and arrogance at the highest levels of government fanned provincial insecurities in the colonies. At the same time, his charges of the "Luxury and Effeminacy" into which the British nation had sunk and which necessitated the exploitation of the colonies bolstered colonists' sense of their own virtue and manliness. Franklin's immersion into the give-and-take of the public sphere also was an implicit endorsement of the value of dialogue and conversation as against arbitrary measures of Parliament and ministry. He explicitly urged again and again mutual understanding and better communication of ideas and principles. Lacking a British foil, he was capable of replying and commenting on himself, using a different pseudonym. He wrote as Pacificus and Pacificus Secundus, and after undersigning Q.E.D. to one of his most important contributions, "Rules by Which a Great Empire May Be Reduced to a Small One," he commented in the next issue of the *Public Advertiser* as "A sincere Well-wisher to Great Britain and her Colonies": "If the Ministry have any Sense of Shame remaining, they must blush to see their Conduct with respect to America placed in such a striking Point of Ridicule" (Franklin 1987, 688, 696).

The irony that marked so many of Franklin's London pieces, especially those written after British troops were stationed in Boston and New York to maintain order and put pressure on the assemblies, suggested a strategy to create an American identity for conflicted British Americans. Satire and parody—satire's double-voiced sibling—had earlier been features of American protests against arbitrary measures. Richard Bland's first important essay, *The Colonel Dismounted* (1764), apparently took the side of the Anglican minister John Camm, who had appealed to England to set aside a law passed in the Virginia assembly regarding the terms of compensation for ministers of the established church. Bland pretended to take Camm's side against his antagonist Colonel Landon Carter, but his sarcasm and exaggerated praise for Camm as a "Wonderful genius! Who with infinite wit and humor can transform the most arrant trash into delicious fruit," subverted the latter's arguments and authority (Bailyn 1965, 301).

Franklin was a master of the Swiftian mode of outrageous proposals that exposed the incoherence or immorality of ministerial or parliamentary actions and principles. He could suggest in one essay that the way "of humbling our rebellious Vassals of North America" would be to send over five battalions of British troops, "which our experienced Generals . . . think sufficient to subdue America," and castrate all the males in the colonies. His "Edict by the King of Prussia" parodied British claims of absolute sovereignty over the colonies by purporting to be a Prussian claim to the same sovereignty over England, since "it is well known to all the World, that the first German Settlements made in the Island of *Britain* were by Colonies of People, Subjects to our renowned Ducal Ancestors" (Franklin 1987, 717, 699). This sort of satire worked by parodical repetition of a text or discourse, thus giving it a measure of respectful attention, but at the same time by exposing its inherent instability or impossibility.

American independence depended ultimately on the possibility of a parodic instinct that could reject the claims of British authority even while demonstrating a deeper allegiance to British values reimagined as reason. American Whig polemicists had all along been engaging their British antagonists from a parodic position, albeit one more sophisticated and complex than Franklin's. James Otis had set the precedent for claiming to be a more thoroughly British citizen than the men in Parliament or in the service of the ministry because of an allegiance to supposedly older values of law and to standards of virtue that had fallen into disregard in the home country. As the American patriot writers quoted from the treasury of British Whig thought, they were creating for themselves in an act of colonial mimicry an intellectual tradition that simultaneously embraced Britain even as it repudiated the British government (Bhabha 1994, 85–93).

SAMUEL ADAMS AND THE BOSTON MASSACRE

American protests both in print and in the streets and an effective movement not to import British goods led Parliament to repeal the Townshend Acts in 1769, except for the tax on tea, but in the preceding year British troops had been permanently stationed in Boston. This very quickly moved the debates between the colonies and the mother country into new, more dangerous territory. There was continuing friction between the occupation forces and the locals, leading up to the so-called Boston Massacre of March 1770. In England there were calls for more repressive actions, including arresting the ringleaders of the mobs and bringing them to England for trial. Political writers like Samuel Adams adopted a more extreme tone, more pointedly antagonistic to local representatives of British government, more charged with overt or implied threats concerning violence and rebellion, albeit continuing to protest loyalty to the Crown. Franklin had blamed misleading and sometimes malicious information from a few sources in the colonies for faulty or hostile British policy, but Samuel Adams's *Appeal to the World, or A Vindication of the Town of Boston* (1769) put a name to the general description by accusing Governor Francis Bernard, General Thomas Gage, and Commodore Samuel Hood of "malicious Intrigues to traduce not this Town and Province, alone, but the whole British American Continent" (Adams 1904, 1: 398).

Writing under a variety of pseudonyms such as "Vindex" and "Candidus," Adams kept up a steady barrage of attacks on Bernard and, with even more fervor, on his successor, Thomas Hutchinson. At the same time Adams was the shrewd political manager in the Massachusetts legislature and a director of popular protest in the streets that made Boston a focus of British hostility after 1770. By focusing his critiques upon Bernard and Hutchinson, however, Adams's writings clarified an internal distinction between "true" Americans, that is, those who supported the patriot or Whig side of the transatlantic disputes, as opposed to those whom John Dickinson had named "supple wretches," the Tory supporters of parliamentary sovereignty over the colonies. Adams's personal attacks were also setting the scene for the Declaration of Independence's decisive laying of blame for the dissolution of political bonds not on a faceless ministry or political system but on the king himself.

Adams and other polemicists of the 1770s increasingly recognized that their arguments were likely to have little effect in London. They embraced the insight of the Pennsylvania Farmer that because government was based upon public opinion their real task was to reach the minds and hearts of American readers. The language of many of the most effective political writings of this period became increasingly sentimental and even sensationalist. When a British patrol fired on a crowd of hecklers in Boston on March 5, 1770, killing eleven of them, the patriots lost no time in getting out *A Short Narrative of the Horrid Massacre in Boston,* written by James Bowdoin, Joseph Warren, and Samuel Pemberton, that fixed the label of "massacre" upon the event for all time and implicitly argued that the potential for violence lay with a British military presence enforcing the ministerial agenda rather than with the citizens of Boston themselves.

The massacre became the occasion for annual orations in remembrance that were held until the conclusion of peace in 1783. James Lovell, delivering the first oration in 1771, set the tone for subsequent performances by calling to mind "the horrid bloody scene we here commemorate" and by reminding his audience that "the true strength and safety of every commonwealth or limited monarchy, is the bravery of its freeholders, its militia. By brave militia they rise to grandeur, and they come to ruin by a mercenary army." Lovell announced, "The beam is carried off from our eyes by the flowing blood of our fellow citizens, and now we may be allowed to attempt to remove the mote from the eyes of our exalted patrons. That mote, we think, is nothing but our obligation to *England* first, and afterwards, *Great Britain,* for constant kind protection of our lives and birthrights against foreign danger." Lovell quoted "the patriotic farmer" to counsel against violent response and professed to trust in a gracious king, "the most powerful prince on earth, yet a subject under a divine constitution of law," who would overrule "the declarative vote of the British parliament [that] is the death warrant of our birthrights." Lovell concluded his oration, however, with an appeal not to the king but to "the wise and beneficent ruler of the universe [to] preserve our lives and health, and prosper all our lawful endeavours in the glorious cause of freedom" (Anon. 1807, 3–11). Despite

Lovell's professions of loyalty to the Crown and nonviolence, his depiction of all freeholders as a militia effectively redefined the conflict as one that might be decided not by petitions but by arms. If his sensational evocation of scenes of bloodshed was intended to impress upon the imaginations of his listeners the consequences of ministerial policy, his appeal to a beneficent God reminded them of the power of a spirit felt within themselves.

THE EVE OF INDEPENDENCE

Lovell's oration also functioned as a rehearsal of an evolving American understanding of history by reminding them that they were the descendants of men and women who had established themselves in America by means of their own labor, "assisted by no earthly power." Even as Benjamin Franklin was beginning to portray himself in his *Autobiography* as a self-made man, Lovell was reminding Americans that they were all self-made. Writers as early as Richard Bland in his Stamp Act protest had made a similar point in opposition to British claims of sovereignty over the colonies by arguing that they had been settled without the aid of British money or other resources but by "Englishmen, who becoming private Adventurers, established themselves without any expense to the Nation" (Anon. 1807, 8; Bailyn 1965, 117). The historical argument was rehearsed by other writers, but in the 1770s a number of the most important political writers came back to it extensively as a means to imagine a new understanding of imperial relations.

Thomas Jefferson's *Summary View of the Rights of British America* (1774) compared the original emigrants to Virginia to "their Saxon ancestors [who] had ... left their native wilds and woods in the north of Europe [and] possessed themselves of the island of Britain." The Virginia emigrants in Jefferson's version of colonial history were individuals acting at their own expense who, once in Virginia, freely chose "to adopt that system of laws under which they had hitherto lived in the mother country," thus portraying them as acting under a new civil compact, one in which they retained rights passed down as part of the ancient constitution of England (Jefferson 1984, 106–107). Jefferson argued that American loyalty was only owed to the king himself, not to Parliament or to the fiction of the "king in Parliament." Virginia and the other colonies were not subordinate to Parliament but in effect were independent sister realms owing fealty to the same monarch; this structure was very much like what the second British empire came to when it recognized colonies like Canada as separate dominions.

James Wilson, the Pennsylvania lawyer, described the American colonies as examples of "the dominions of the British crown that are not represented in the

British Parliament" in *Considerations on the Nature and Extent of the Legislative Authority of the British Parliament* (1774). Wilson characterized the connection between the inhabitants of Great Britain and those of America: "They are fellow subjects; they are under allegiance to the same prince; and this union of allegiance naturally produces a union of hearts" (Wilson 1967, 2: 737–745). When the Tory Daniel Leonard, publishing under the name of Massachusettensis, offered a historical narrative of the current troubles in 1775, John Adams's *Novanglus* essays replied with a strongly argued legal argument that agreed with Jefferson and Wilson on what amounted to the inherent independence of the American colonies, restrained only by allegiance to the king, yet in subtle ways he offered a more radical message. "The authority of parliament was never generally acknowledged in America," he contended, pointing to a century of resistance to attempts to infringe on the rights of the colonial legislature and of individuals. Adams later asserted, "We derive our laws and government solely from our own compacts with Britain and her kings and from the great Legislator of the universe" (Adams 1819, 38, 125).

Jefferson concluded his *Summary View* with a sort of rhetorical *lese majesté*, addressing himself directly to the king and reminding him that "kings are the servants, not the proprietors of the people," yet his final words expressed the "fervent prayer of all British America" for "fraternal love and harmony through the whole empire" (Jefferson 1984, 121–122). The imperial federalism Wilson and Jefferson proposed stood little chance in 1774. It was built on arguments that had been developed in the political literature and legislative petitions of the last fifteen years and as consistently dismissed or ignored by successive ministries. "Fraternal harmony" and a "union of hearts" were too weak to hold together British and American identities strained by mutual suspicion and contempt. In the year that elapsed between Jefferson's and Adams's writings, John Adams no longer spoke of a sentimental British American friendship but of one that drew a sharp distinction between "we" in America and "Britain."

Events leading up to the conclusive split unfolded rapidly in the first half of the 1770s. The Boston Massacre was followed by a misguided attempt by the ministry to bail the East India Company out of financial difficulties by giving it monopoly rights to sell tea in the American colonies and at the same time rigorously enforce the last of the remaining Townshend Act taxes, that on tea. The Boston Tea Party in December 1773, destroyed tea before it could be landed, and a series of parliamentary acts closed the port of Boston and amended the charter and laws of Massachusetts. By the end of 1774 the first Continental Congress had met in Philadelphia. Jefferson's and Wilson's treatises were only two of a number of pamphlets written to advise the Congress, not all of them as radical as theirs were. Writers like Thomas Bradbury Chandler, Joseph Galloway, and Daniel Leonard were pointing to the danger of anarchy and violence as reasons to preserve the imperial connection at all costs, but by the close of the Congress Patrick Henry was able to make one more of his dramatic oratorical gestures that signaled a shift in self-identification and political purpose in many of the members. "The distinctions between Virginians, Pennsylvanians, New Yorkers, and New Englanders are no more. I am not a Virginian but an American" (quoted in Nash 2005, 90–91). Before the Second Congress could meet, British troops had fired on colonial militias in Lexington and Concord, and the terms of the political debate had shifted once again. No longer was the central question about clarifying the constitutional relationship between Britain and its North American colonies; it was about the question of independence itself.

In July 1775, Congress passed a "Declaration . . . Setting Forth the Causes and Necessity of Their Taking up Arms" that once again rehearsed the events leading up to the present conflict, but after declaring, "Our cause is just. Our union is perfect," it made a final conciliatory gesture: "Lest this Declaration should disquiet the Minds of our Friends and Fellow-Subjects in any part of the Empire, we assure them that we mean not to dissolve that Union which has so long and so happily subsisted between us" (Jefferson 1950, 1: 217). Thomas Jefferson's original draft of the Declaration had been softened in response to the fears of men like John Dickinson that Americans were not yet ready to face British troops in battle or to the desires of men like Joseph Galloway to preserve the imperial connection. Six months later American forces were demonstrating their success in maintaining a siege of the British forces in Boston and had held their own at Bunker Hill when the most important pamphlet of the Revolutionary era appeared.

Thomas Paine's *Common Sense* was immediately circulated through the North American colonies after its publication in January 1776, with its announcement that "By referring the matter from argument to arms, a new era for politics is struck; a new method of thinking hath arisen." *Common Sense* appeared at the right moment and energized its readers by restating many of the old arguments for colonial rights as arguments for independence and by restating them in language that was at once forceful and transparent. John Adams's *Novanglus* and to a lesser extent James Wilson's *Considerations* were texts that perhaps only a lawyer could really love; Paine's argument for independence rested not so much on the constitutional arguments that had been tested over the previous decade and a half as on an analysis of the geopolitical reality of 1776 and an appeal to a people outraged by the behavior of "the hardened, sullen tempered Pharaoh of England." "There is something very absurd," said Paine, on the one hand, "in supposing a continent to be perpetually governed by an island." On the other, he pointed to a long history of "tyranny which drove the first emigrants from home, [and] pursues their descendants still" in "this new world . . . the asylum for the persecuted lovers of civil and religious liberty from *every part* of Europe." Paine defined the moment not as a constitutional crisis but as a turning point for a sense of individual and national identity best understood as internal change, evidenced by new feelings and new reasoning based in "nature and common sense." "Now is the seed time of continental union, faith, and honor," he wrote, defining the moment less in terms of the long history of British rights and laws than in terms of the future. "Posterity are virtually involved in the contest, and will be more or less affected to the end of time by the proceedings now." *Common Sense* redirected the American argument from attempts to recover an imagined past of Saxon liberties under the ancient English constitution to a vision of a popular government in which "perfect equality" would become the keynote of a new order (Paine 1995, 21, 29, 23, 32).

THE DECLARATION OF INDEPENDENCE

Not everyone shared Paine's readiness for independence, nor did they necessarily accept his suggestions for setting up new governments in the former colonies. John Adams welcomed the call for independence, but he responded to Paine's egalitarianism and radical democracy by drawing up his *Thoughts on Government Applicable to the Present State of the American Colonies* as suggestions for a new Massachusetts constitution that would control democratic energies that Paine encouraged. His call for separation of powers, an executive with strong veto powers, and an independent judiciary provided the checks and balances, a favorite principle of his, that would keep government from wandering into tyranny or populist anarchy. Adams's more cautious plan of government provided a constitutional blueprint for several of the new states, but Paine's call for independence could not be contained. In June 1776, Richard Henry Lee of Virginia proposed in Congress that the colonies should become free and independent states, and a committee consisting of Thomas Jefferson, John Adams, Benjamin Franklin, Roger Sherman, and Robert Livingston was appointed to draft an appropriate declaration to that effect.

The actual work of writing the document fell to Jefferson, although the version eventually accepted by Congress was variously emended by suggestions from Adams, from Franklin, and in debate on the floor by Congress itself. Afterward Jefferson was hailed as the author of the Declaration of Independence, but it can be considered a work of communal authorship, both of a community of peers in Congress and of a historical community of political writers that Jefferson drew on. Jefferson later told a correspondent: "When forced to . . . resort to arms for redress, an appeal to the tribunal of the world was deemed proper for our justification. This was the object of the Declaration of Independence. Not to find out new principles, or new arguments never before thought of, not merely to say things which had never been said before; but to place before mankind the common sense of the subject, in terms so plain and firm as to command their assent, and to justify ourselves in the independent stand we are compelled to take" (Jefferson 1984, 1501).

Nineteenth-century readers paid most attention to the sentences in the second paragraph laying down the ground that all men are created equal and that they are endowed with inalienable rights of life, liberty, and the pursuit of happiness, but this is only a small part of the Declaration. The main part of it is given over to listing "for a candid world" the crimes of George III, the "long train of abuses," that justified revolution. The Declaration's opening echoes the argumentative structure of many of the earlier Whig statements of the American position; they too opened with appeals to either charter or natural rights, and Jefferson had no real need to make more than a token gesture toward the issue of rights and the Lockean dictum that a people had the right to change government when it failed to protect them. The real issue for the Declaration was to demonstrate that the situation had arisen when such a dissolution of political bonds was necessary to protect the lives and liberty of the people. The Declaration did not enact independence—that had been done in a separate action by approving Lee's resolution—but merely announced it to "a candid world" as a prelude to assuming "a separate and equal station among the powers of the earth." The Declaration should be understood in the context of international law and diplomacy more than as a philosophy of human rights. The Declaration emerged out of discussions in Congress about obtaining foreign aid in the war against Britain and was intended in part to assure potential allies that there would be no reconciliation with Britain (Armitage 2007; Rakove 1979, 99).

Yet if Jefferson denied any intention to state new principles, the fact remains that the language of the second paragraph did introduce new terms into the political argument, not so much by invention as by a creative reading of the political discursive tradition he relied on. John Dickinson and many later writers had insisted on the people's happiness as the goal of government, but more often the Whig political writers followed Locke's *Second Treatise* by arguing for the right to own and enjoy property as the key value. Jefferson's "life, liberty, and the pursuit of happiness" derived from Locke's *Treatise Concerning Human Understanding* and spoke directly to the inner concerns of all Americans at an anxious moment, relevant alike to people of property and those without. The Declaration's importance as a statement about human rights emerged in subsequent readings and celebrations after the war, but even in July 1776 it marked a transformation in American political discourse by shifting the grounds from abstract political rights to the scene of anguished feelings and a concluding pledge by members of the Congress of "our sacred Honor."

A NATIONAL IDENTITY

Earlier writing had struggled to find an acceptable resolution to the contradictions of English and American identities, but the next phase of political writing would seek to define and enact American identity as part of the imaginative capital required to create a nation. In its most directly political and organizational manifestations it took the form of the new state constitutions, the Articles of Confederation, and ultimately in the Constitution of 1787. Less overt forms of political discourse appeared in a variety of texts that sought to answer the question put by Crèvecoeur, "What is an American?" Thomas Paine followed *Common Sense* in late 1776 with the first of his "American Crisis" papers that appeared during the course of the Revolutionary War as a means to encourage Americans when things seemed to be going badly for them. "These are the times that try men's souls," began the first "Crisis" paper, but because of that trial, Paine assured his readers, "Not a place upon earth might be so happy as America." Creating this happiness would be the business of a democratic government, but it would also require a profound act of imagination as Paine realized in "The Crisis Extraordinary" of October 1780. "It is impossible to sit down and think seriously on the affairs of America, but the original principles on which she resisted, and the glow and ardor they inspired, will occur like the undefaced remembrance of a lovely scene. To trace over in imagination the purity of the cause, the voluntary sacrifices made to support it, and all the various turnings of the war in its defence, is at once both paying and receiving respect" (Paine 1995, 91, 95, 231). The respect so long denied from England would become a reflexive self-creation in the American heart.

American writers responded by portraying the "lovely scene" of America with histories of the Revolution such as those by William Gordon, David Ramsay, and Mercy Otis Warren and with accounts as various as Crèvecoeur's *Letters from an American Farmer* and Tench Coxe's *View of the United States of America*. Crèvecoeur offered a picture of a pastoral America, best exemplified by the democratic mixture of class and race that gathered at John Bartram's dinner table but haunted by specters of capitalist desire in Nantucket and violent racism in South Carolina. Coxe, on the other hand, described the success to date of the new nation's ability to maintain "with sincerity and vigilance *the freedom of its citizens,* and with energy and firmness, *the rights of property*" (Coxe 1794, 4). The most important of these accounts, at least the most widely reprinted and circulated, was Thomas Jefferson's *Notes on the State of Virginia* (1785), which provided a thorough account of the natural and political situation of Virginia. It importantly refuted a prevailing theory of European natural historians that all life-forms, including the human, degenerated in the New World. Jefferson celebrated the sublimity of the American landscape, the size and variety of its native wildlife, and the nobility of its indigenous peoples while praising its farmers as "the chosen people of God, . . . whose breasts he has made his peculiar deposit for substantial and genuine virtue" (Jefferson 1984, 290). Jefferson presented his native state of Virginia as a synecdoche for the larger United States, and by appending a draft of a proposed constitution for Virginia and the enacted law for religious freedom provided practical models for American political happiness. More powerfully, Jefferson's arguments against slavery, for religious freedom, and for government by ordinary citizens opened space for thinking outside of the constraints of political arenas about the meaning of an American identity not defined by a government but critical and creative about it.

The happy American place prophesied by Paine was to be particularly so for men and, as Jefferson's *Notes* made clear, particularly for white men. Jefferson decried slavery but believed that emancipated blacks would need to be relocated apart from whites; the earlier fears of slavery imposed from without had become fears of the slaves within the nation. The gendering of political discourse had been under way since the late 1770s; Paine's "Forester's Letters," published in early 1776, highlighted this privileging of masculinity when they began by declaring, "To be *nobly wrong* is more manly than to be *meanly right.*" James Lovell's Boston Massacre oration, with its praise for citizen militias, and subsequent calls like Joseph Warren's to be "warlike sons" of "our American forefathers" interpellated citizenship as manly, defined by virtues traditionally coded as masculine (Anon. 1807, 65). Similar calls for "manly" behavior and virtue became more frequent in the political discourse as the colonies moved toward armed resistance, and after the war began, they were ubiquitous. As American identity emerged in various distinctive descriptions that celebrated openness and change, it also became more distinctly gendered in the political discourse.

Manly virtues were a key feature of the republican discourse that the founding generation drew on so greatly, but they were also called forth by the necessity of maintaining a military resistance. In the years after the war, as political debates turned to the problems of establishing an effective national government, a sentimentalized manliness became political coin of the realm in the struggle to create federal authority. This tendency is clearly evident in the *Federalist Papers* and in the extensive debates about the ratification of the new constitution. Seeking to establish the authority of the drafters, John Jay referred to them as "a band of brethren, united to each other by the strongest ties," and went on to describe them as the heroic successors to the soldiers of the Revolution: "The Convention, composed of men . . . many of whom had become highly distinguished by their patriotism, virtue, and wisdom, in times which tried the minds and hearts of men, undertook the arduous task." Their work itself he described as an example of masculine self-control, standing up to power in the tradition established by the last forty years of political discourse. "They passed many months in cool uninterrupted and daily consultations: and finally without having been awed by power or influenced by any passions except love for their Country, they presented and recommended to the people the plan produced by their joint and very unanimous counsels" (Cooke 1961, 9–11).

At the beginning of the political struggle with Great Britain, Parliament insisted upon its holding of absolute power over the colonies in all cases, but the Constitution of 1787 distributed power between a national center and the individual states while providing a set of internal checks and balances for the former. The imperial federalism urged in 1774 by Jefferson and Wilson became in the Constitution a national federalism that, as James Madison explained in *Federalist* number 10, allowed for differences of opinion among the citizens in which majorities would not trample on the rights of minorities. Madison argued that greater national security would be "afforded by a greater variety of parties, in the event of any one party being able to outnumber and oppress the rest." If the language of rights in the Declaration of Independence, in Jefferson's *Notes*, and in Paine's writing opened a space for thinking outside the political arena, the Constitution defined the political arena itself, and *The Federalist*, originally intended to persuade New Yorkers to ratify the Constitution, became its earliest authoritative interpretation.

CONCLUSION

The four decades of political writing that began with charges and fears about phantoms and phantasms ended with an embrace of indeterminacy, now seen as a necessary ground for political discourse rooted in the nature of language itself. Madison defended the Constitution from charges that it was not specific enough about the distribution of power by pointing out the inherent difficulty of all constitutions: "Beside the obscurity arising from the complexity of objects, and the imperfection of the human faculties, the medium through which the conceptions of men are conveyed to each other, adds a fresh embarrassment. . . . But no language is so copious as to supply words and phrases for every complex idea, or so correct as not to include many equivocally denoting different ideas. . . . When the Almighty himself condescends to address mankind in their own language, his meaning, luminous as it must be, is rendered dim and doubtful" (Cooke 1961, 64, 236–237). Madison's admission of the uncertainty of all language became acceptable because of his confidence in an established American identity in which the "band of brethren" at the Constitutional Convention could confidently speak for the people and "the Country." The Constitution, considered as a work of political architecture, justifies Benjamin Rush's understanding of the American Revolution as the result of centuries of legal and political struggle, but in Madison's appeal to the indistinctness of language, an appeal ultimately to the hearts and minds of virtuous citizens, John Adams's explanation of the Revolution as enacted in the possibilities of imagination reaches its fruition.

REFERENCES

Adams, John. 1819. *Novanglus, and Massachusettensis; or, Political Essays, Published in the Years 1774 and 1775, on the Principal Points of Controversy, between Great Britain and her Colonies.* Boston: Hews and Goss.

Adams, Samuel. 1904. *The Writings of Samuel Adams,* ed. Harry Alonzo Cushing. 4 vols. New York: Putnam's.

Anon., ed. 1807. *Orations Delivered at the Request of the Inhabitants of the Town of Boston, to Commemorate the Evening of the Fifth of March, 1770.* Boston: Wm. T. Clap.

Armitage, David. 2007. *The Declaration of Independence: A Global History.* Cambridge, MA: Harvard University Press.

Bailyn, Bernard, ed. 1965. *Pamphlets of the American Revolution, 1750–1776.* Cambridge, MA: Belknap Press of Harvard University Press.

———. 1968. *The Origins of American Politics.* New York: Knopf.

———. 1974. *The Ordeal of Thomas Hutchinson.* Cambridge, MA: Belknap Press of Harvard University Press.

Bhabha, Homi. 1994. *The Location of Culture.* London: Routledge.

Cooke, Jacob E., ed. 1961. *The Federalist.* Middletown, CT: Wesleyan University Press.

Coxe, Tench. 1794. *A View of the United States of America, in a Series of Papers, Written at Various Times, between the Years 1787 and 1794.* Philadelphia: for William Hall.

Franklin, Benjamin. 1950. *Benjamin Franklin's Letters to the Press, 1758–1775,* edited by Verner W. Crane. Chapel Hill: University of North Carolina Press.

———. 1987. *Writings,* edited by J. A. Leo Lemay. New York: Library of America.

Greene, Jack. 1970. Search for Identity: An Interpretation of the Meaning of Selected Patterns of Social Response in Eighteenth-Century America. *Journal of Social History* 3: 189–220.

———. 1993. *The Intellectual Construction of America: Exceptionalism and Identity, 1492 to 1800.* Chapel Hill: University of North Carolina Press.

Jefferson, Thomas. 1903–1905. *The Writings of Thomas Jefferson,* edited by Andrew A. Lipscomb and Albert E. Berg. 20 vols. Washington: Thomas Jefferson Memorial Association of the United States.

———. 1950. *The Papers of Thomas Jefferson,* edited by Julian Boyd, et al. 32 vols. to date. Princeton: Princeton University Press.

———. 1984. *Writings,* edited by Merrill D. Peterson. New York: Library of America.

Jensen, Merrill, ed. 2003. *Tracts of the American Revolution, 1763–1776.* Indianapolis: Hackett.

Knollenberg, Bernhard. 2003. *The Growth of the American Revolution, 1766–1775.* Indianapolis: Liberty Fund.

McDonald, Forrest, ed. 1962. *Empire and Nation.* Englewood Cliff, NJ: Prentice-Hall.

Morgan, Edmund S. 1959. *Prologue to Revolution.* Chapel Hill: University of North Carolina Press.

Morgan, Edmund S., and Helen M. Morgan. 1963. *The Stamp Act Crisis: Prologue to Revolution.* Revised ed. New York: Collier.

Nash, Gary B. 2005. *The Unknown American Revolution.* New York: Viking.

Paine, Thomas. 1995. *Collected Writings,* edited by Eric Foner. New York: Library of America.

Pownall, Thomas. 1765. *The Administration of the Colonies.* 2nd ed. London: for J. Dodsley, and J. Walter.

Rakove, Jack. 1979. *The Beginnings of National Politics: An Interpretative History of the Continental Congress.* New York: Knopf.

Rush, Benjamin. [1948] 1970. *The Autobiography of Benjamin Rush,* ed. George Washington Corner. Reprint. Westport, CT: Greenwood.

Shannon, Timothy. 2000. *Indians and Colonists at the Crossroads of Empire: The Albany Congress of 1754.* Ithaca, NY: Cornell University Press.

Taylor, Charles. 1989. *Sources of the Self: The Making of the Modern Identity.* Cambridge, MA: Harvard University Press.

Wahrman, Dror. 2004. *The Making of the Modern Self: Identity and Culture in Eighteenth-Century England.* New Haven, CT: Yale University Press.

Webking, Robert H. 1988. *The American Revolution and the Politics of Liberty.* Baton Rouge: Louisiana State University Press.

Whately, Thomas. 1765. *The Regulations Lately Made Concerning the Colonies, and the Taxes Imposed upon Them, Considered.* London: for J. Wilkie.

Wilson, James. 1967. *The Works of James Wilson,* edited by Robert Green McCloskey. 2 vols. Cambridge, MA: Harvard University Press.

Wood, Gordon S. 1982. Conspiracy and the Paranoid Style: Causality and Deceit in the Eighteenth Century. *William and Mary Quarterly,* 3rd ser., 39: 401–441.

CHAPTER 22

....

REVOLUTIONARY VERSE

....

COLIN WELLS

Between 1765 and 1800, Americans lived through a series of momentous political transformations; what began as resistance by British Americans against the Stamp Act soon developed into a war for American independence and, in its aftermath, into a series of partisan struggles that culminated in the triumph of Jeffersonian Republicanism in 1800. Not surprisingly, American culture during this period—and, more particularly, American poetry—reflects this broad emphasis upon politics and national affairs. Political poems and songs were a ubiquitous part of Revolutionary and early Republican culture, appearing as pamphlets and broadsides and in the pages of newspapers and magazines. Dozens of individual poets, including many of the most gifted and best-known writers of the time, engaged in satiric warfare against political figures, journalists, and each other. They responded to the most important and the most trivial of political controversies, and they celebrated and demonized figures such as Adams, Hamilton, and Jefferson. Most important, they used poems to exert their influence on the series of public debates waged at the time over the meaning of the American Revolution and the future course the new Republic should follow.

The eighteenth century as a whole has long been renowned for its public and topical verse, and the poets of the American Revolution were schooled in the satiric warfare waged earlier in the century by English precursors like Pope and Swift. This was, moreover, a time of enormous ideological upheaval, as long-held opinions about society were being discredited and displaced by new ones, and the people at large invited to take sides in the struggle. American poets of the latter half of the eighteenth century lent their voices to this contentious atmosphere using a variety of poetic forms, from epics and odes that called into question some of America's most enduring myths to verse satires and parodies that sought to unmask, as illusory or dangerous to the public interest, the sentiments of rival poems.

LITERARY WARFARE IN THE AMERICAN REVOLUTION

Even before the first shots were fired at Lexington, patriot and loyalist poets alike were engaged in verse wars over the Stamp Act and the Townshend Act, the Boston Massacre, and the Boston Port Bill. The poetic warfare only intensified after the outbreak of armed rebellion, as Patriot versifiers answered the need for a poetry that would boost morale by ridiculing the British generals and their army of regulars and mercenaries, while Loyalists mocked the colonial militias through the comic figure of "Yankee Doodle." In time, of course, patriots would themselves lay claim to Yankee Doodle and transform him into a symbol of national pride—a move symbolic of the way literary warfare in the Revolution mirrored and responded to the dynamic of the actual war, as poets attacked and counterattacked in an ongoing struggle to control the discourse of the Revolution.

Two poets in particular stand out from the Revolutionary period: John Trumbull, whose mock-heroic *M'Fingal* would become the most successful major poem not only of the Revolution but for a half century following, and Philip Freneau, who would later be known as the "Poet of the American Revolution." Yet to focus on prominent individuals is in a crucial sense to miss the point of Revolutionary verse, which was public and immediate rather than individual or enduring. Even the most ambitious poets contributed their talents not toward establishing their personal fame—their poems appeared, almost without exception, as anonymous broadsides or pamphlets—but to intervene in the political debate. Chiefly they wrote to ridicule public figures and unmask their hidden motives and to translate narrow political disputes into a broader symbolic, even cosmic, struggle for the survival and future of America.

The most common verse forms during the Revolution, not surprisingly, were satire and parody. No less surprising, given the fact that American poets of the 1760s and 1770s honed their craft while immersing themselves in the works of Pope, Swift, and other English Augustans, is that Revolutionary satire is noticeably Augustan in style, often self-consciously so. Poets like Trumbull, Timothy Dwight, and Joel Barlow not only imitated the style and tone of literary Augustanism but packed their works with allusions to Augustan masterpieces like Pope's *Dunciad* and

Samuel Butler's *Hudibras*. This characteristic was once considered chiefly a matter of style or taste, leading some older critics to dismiss much Revolutionary and early Republican poetry as "unoriginal." More recently, however, such characteristics have been interpreted as a political statement in its own right—an announcement that the literary warfare waged in the 1720s and 1730s against the corrupt Parliament of Sir Robert Walpole has now been revived against a new assemblage of corrupt politicians now conspiring to usurp American liberties (Dowling 1990, ix–xvii).

That Patriot poets saw their work as part of an ongoing, transatlantic literary opposition to a corrupt government is evident not only in Revolutionary but in pre-Revolutionary verse—the body of poems written in protest against the Stamp Act and the Townshend Act. Two early examples are Benjamin Church's *The Times* (1765) and the anonymous *Oppression,* both of which interpret the imposition of excise taxes as one part of a broader attempt by Parliament to erode the long-held rights of British Americans. Both poems, moreover, present themselves as American contributions to a tradition of Opposition satire going back to the 1720s and continuing in the 1760s in the post-Augustan satire of Charles Churchill. Indeed, *The Times* borrows its title and much of its argument from a 1763 poem by Churchill, while *Oppression* opens with an extended allusion to Edward Young's satire *Love of Fame, the Universal Passion* (1728) as it calls on "SATIRE" to "bite with all its rage" not merely against "savage Ex—se" but against the corrupt age in which they now live, ruled by "tyrants" and "traitors" (Anon. 1765, 1–2).

This notion of "poetry against tyranny" would remain in vogue throughout the lead-up to the Revolution, with each new tension or event inspiring additional poems and songs. At the same time, the appearance of a poem or song would often lead to the publication of a rival poem, giving rise to the defining dynamic of attack and counterattack that would characterize Revolutionary War poetry on the whole. One of the earliest examples of this phenomenon is the exchange of rival songs inspired by John Dickinson's popular "Liberty Song" (1768) after the passage of the Townshend Acts. The song, which follows the conventions of Stamp Act protests by associating the payment of duties with the loss of liberty—"Not as slaves, but as freemen our money we'll give," reads one line—was promptly answered by a loyalist wit in "A Parody upon a Well-known Liberty Song" (Anon 1768b) who recasts the Patriot protesters as disreputable smugglers who have turned to "mobbing" only because their habit of stealing from the rich has been curtailed. This song was, in turn, answered by "Parody Parodized" (Anon 1768a) a work that is significant less for how it turns the criminal charge of the "Parody" back upon the loyalists than for how it typifies the emergence of a new Revolutionary poetics, one in which individual poems communicated meaning not as discrete, self-contained works but as distinct discursive "moves" in an ongoing struggle to define the truth of the rebellion.

Such cases as this, of "dueling" songs and ballads, usually sung to well-known British tunes, would continue for the remainder of the war, producing some of the most memorable examples of Revolutionary verse. Often written to commemorate actual events or battles, such songs lampooned the opposing army as cowards or bunglers. In Francis Hopkinson's "The Battle of the Kegs" (1778), for instance, the British are tricked into believing they are under attack after American soldiers float exploding powder kegs down the Delaware River. From the British side, on the other hand, Major John Andre's "The Cow Chace" tells the story of an American assault that is foiled, in part, by a herd of stampeding cows. Nor can a discussion of Revolutionary songs and ballads omit the many versions of the Yankee Doodle motif by balladeers from both sides, including Edward Bangs's *The Farmer and His Son's Return from a Visit to the Camp* (1775)—the most famous version of "Yankee Doodle"—and the loyalist "Yankee Doodle's Expedition to Rhode Island."

The same dynamic of using poetry to negate the ideological content of an opposing text, in fact, would spawn a new subgenre of early American verse—what today would simply be called political verse parody, but what was at the time dubbed "versification." Between the summer of 1774 and the fall of 1775, a series of "versifications"—transpositions of a work of prose into poetry—began appearing simultaneously as broadsides and in newspapers in several colonies, nearly all inspired by the proclamations issued by General Thomas Gage, the newly appointed royal governor of Massachusetts. It was not unusual, to be sure, for a colonial governor to issue his orders via proclamations, but something about Gage's proclamations seems to have struck a nerve among American wits. Whether it was a reaction to the royal proclamations' implicit claim to absolute authority or to Gage's heavy-handed tone in particular, the power of such parodies to undermine Gage's authority soon became evident. Whereas Gage's proclamations were steeped in the language of decorum and royal authority, even in their very headings—. *By His Excellency the Honorable Thomas Gage, Esq; Commander in Chief in and over his Majesty's Province of Massachusetts-Bay, and Vice Admiral of the Same: A Proclamation* (June 12, 1775)— verse parodies of such proclamations recast such language as a vain exaggeration of Gage's real power:

> By Thomas Gage, whom British frenzy,
> Stil'd honourable and Excellency,
> O'er Massachusett's sent to stand her
> Vice Admiral and Chief Commander;
> Whose power Gubernatorial still
> Extends as far as Bunker's-Hill,
> Whose Admiralty reaches clever,
> Full half a mile up Mistic river,
> Let ev'ry clime and ev'ry nation
> Attend once more—
> A Proclamation. (Trumbull, 1775b)

Beyond the point of unmasking Gage as a weak pretender to power (alluding to a similar proclamation issued by the Lilliputian emperor in *Gulliver's Travels*), the anti-Gage versifications embodied popular resistance through the very form in which they appeared. In the form of a broadside, they would probably have been posted publicly in the same location as the original proclamation, thus symbolically displacing it. Though at times the work of a known poet, moreover, they appeared anonymously, and in some cases the same proclamation was parodied independently by more than one poet. This emphasis on a collective, anonymous response (as opposed to an individual performance) cannot be overemphasized in terms of creating a sense of the people at large answering Gage—and, by extension, the king himself—from a position of equality or even superiority, rejecting his demands while creating a community of shared laughter at his expense.

In all, nearly a dozen anti-Gage versifications appeared before General Gage was recalled as governor in October 1775. Yet the vogue continued well after Gage's departure: the first proclamation issued by his replacement, General Howe, was promptly parodied in a broadside, *Howe's Proclamation, Versified* (Anon. 1775). Perhaps the most brilliant example of the genre would come some two years later with a parody by William Livingston of John Burgoyne's famously pompous warning to the people of New York prior to his defeat at Saratoga, "Burgoyne's Proclamation" (Livingston 1777). Nor was versification only a vogue among patriot wits, for shortly after the Continental Congress of 1774 issued its Articles of Association, the pseudonymous "Bob Jingle" produced a lengthy versification of the document, *The Association, &c. of the Delegates of the Colonies*. Yet the significance of the anti-Gage parodies for later Revolutionary War poetry extends further still: for it is in the parodic campaign against Gage that Philip Freneau and John Trumbull began their careers as political satirists.

Soon after Gage issued his proclamation of July 12, 1775, which declared martial law in Massachusetts, two separate verse parodies appeared, the first by Freneau, the second by Trumbull. *Thomas Gage's Proclamation Versified*, formerly attributed to Trumbull, is now recognized as Freneau's work (Trumbull 1868; Paltsits 1903). Unremarkable in itself, *Thomas Gage's Proclamation Versified*, marked the beginning of a string of satiric poems from 1775, all directed against Gage. The common theme in all of Freneau's Gage poems—which include *General Gage's Soliloquy*, *General Gage's Confession*, and *A Voyage to Boston*—is one of exposure, countering the public, authoritative Gage with the "true" Gage as he appears only to himself or his most trusted counselors. The most fascinating of the three exposés is *A Voyage to Boston*, a poetic fantasy in which the poet, alone in the woods, encounters the "Genius of North America," who bestows on him a "magic vest" capable of rendering him invisible. Charged by the spirit to use the vest to serve his country, the speaker travels to Boston and sneaks into the "dome of State" to witness the secret consultations among Gage and his cabal of generals.

The meeting of this "dire assembly" takes place at midnight, as "Infernal darkness reign'd," an obvious allusion to another infernal deliberation, that of Satan and his fellow devils in book 2 of *Paradise Lost* (Freneau 1775b, 10). Indeed, this is one of the first examples of a larger Miltonic motif that would run throughout Revolutionary War poetry, from both the patriot and the Tory side. Such allusions allowed not simply a branding of political enemies as "demonic" or evil. Rather, because *Paradise Lost* was unique as an "inverted" epic (wherein its hero, Satan, and his minions are actually villains), it provided a narrative frame by which to represent one's opponents as openly acknowledging their part in a malevolent conspiracy, usually against American liberty. In this sense, poems like *A Voyage to Boston* served as literary counterparts to the broader discourse of conspiracy that historians of the Revolution (following Bernard Bailyn) have long identified as one of the crucial ideological underpinnings of the move toward independence.

This discourse of conspiracy is seen, for instance, in Freneau's "The Loyalists" (1779), a poem intended to expose "those monsters, whom our soil maintain'd, / Who first drew breath in this devoted land," and who, "Like famish'd wolves ... on their country prey, / Assist its foes, and wrest our lives away" (Freneau 1986, 54). In much the same way, "King George the Third's Soliloquy" (1779) unmasks the king as a cold-blooded tyrant, willing to contemplate committing various atrocities if it will mean winning the war, including freeing Newgate murderers and unleashing them in America:

> Is there a robber close in New gate hem'd?
> Is there a cut-throat fetter'd and condemn'd? ...
> Far to the west I plan your desp'rate way,
> There 'tis no sin to ravage, burn, and slay;
> There without fear your bloody trade pursue,
> And shew mankind what British rage can do.
> (Freneau 1986, 47)

In contrast to Freneau, John Trumbull was already an established verse satirist by 1775, having published three installments of *The Progress of Dulness*, a poem that had taken aim at New Haven's educational and religious establishment. Yet it was the anti-Gage versification *A New Proclamation!* that served as the starting point for the composition of his own most successful poem, *M'Fingal, A Modern Epic Poem* (Trumbull 1775a). Indeed, when Trumbull began composing *M'Fingal* at the urging of some members of the Continental Congress, he incorporated some fifty lines from his earlier Gage versification, in effect, taking General Gage's words and putting them into the mouth of Trumbull's new hero, "Squire M'Fingal." Insofar as both poems involved satiric portraits of Tory apologists—with M'Fingal's justification of British policy resembling that of the parodied Gage in most respects—Trumbull's borrowing can be seen as an attempt to broaden the scope of Revolutionary satire by transforming the figure of Gage into a fictional character who could represent the loyalist side as a whole.

The other important modification involved placing the satirized figure of M'Fingal inside a story that allowed him ample opportunity to demonstrate his folly. While this was fully achieved in the four-canto 1782 edition of the poem, in the single-canto version of 1775 (*M'Fingal: A Modern Epic Poem. Canto First, or the Town Meeting*) the story is limited chiefly to the events of a New England town meeting, which Squire M'Fingal attends to debate the legitimacy of the fledgling rebellion. The deliberation pits M'Fingal against the Patriot "Honorius," who defends the uprising as a necessary protest against a corrupt British government that has long ignored the pleas of its American colonists. In the course of the argument, Honorius condemns not only Gage and Parliament but the "dastard race" of lawyers, judges, and clergymen "who long have sold / Their souls and consciences for gold" (Trumbull 1962, 113).

In response, M'Fingal repeatedly damns himself and his party from his own mouth, as, for instance, in his defense of the loyalist clergy:

> Have not our High-Church Clergy made it
> Appear from scriptures which ye credit,
> That right divine from heav'n was lent
> To kings, that is the Parliament,
> Their subjects to oppress and teaze,
> And serve the Devil when they please?

This passage is typical of Squire M'Fingal's position throughout, which seeks not to deny Honorius's claims of British treachery and deceit but to justify them according to an ethic in which, as he later states, "The self is still, in either faction, / The only principle of action." For Trumbull, the loyalists' great sin is that they are ruled by self-interest rather than virtue or courage, a charge echoed by Honorius near the end of the poem when he calls on the crowd to join the rebellion and leave the rest to their "more heroic wives" (Trumbull 1962, 116, 129, 150).

In addition to drawing on his own anti-Gage parody, Trumbull packed *M'Fingal* with allusions to works by Swift, Churchill, Dryden, and especially Samuel Butler, whose Restoration-era burlesque, *Hudibras,* is the clear model for *M'Fingal* in both form and content. Indeed, this is announced at the outset:

> When Yankies, skill'd in martial rule,
> First put the British troops to school;
> Instructed them in warlike trade,
> And new manoeuvres of parade; . . .
> Taught Percy fashionable races,
> And modern modes of Chevy-chaces:
> From Boston, in his best array,
> Great 'Squire M'Fingal took his way,
> And graced with ensigns of renown,
> Steer'd homeward to his native town.
> (Trumbull 1962, 103)

This passage directly echoes Butler's opening lines in its introduction of a diminished hero who rides out in the midst of a civil war: "When civil Fury first grew high, / And men fell out they knew not why; . . . Then did Sir *Knight* abandon dwelling, / And out he rode a Colonelling." Though Trumbull's subtitle refers to the poem as a mock epic or high burlesque, moreover, M'Fingal more closely follows the low-burlesque conventions of *Hudibras* in its use of octosyllabic couplets, frequent double rhymes for comic effect ("crown'd head / confounded"), and a tone that straightforwardly belittles, rather than ironically elevates, its hero. Even M'Fingal's Scottish extraction, besides associating him with the "Scots faction" in Parliament led by Lords Bute and Mansfield, is meant to recall Sir Hudibras's identity as Scottish "*Presbyterian* true blue" (Butler 1967, 1, 7). In this way, Trumbull paints the so-called loyal party in America as actually the latest embodiment of a long line of Scottish rebels, and the putative American rebellion as a defense of "true English" liberty against a British empire now ruled by Hudibras's symbolic descendants.

As its narrative and thematic emphasis on public debate suggests, the *M'Fingal* of 1775 is a satiric reflection of the entire atmosphere of ideological warfare out of which the poem originated. Insofar as the clear advantage in the debate goes to Honorius and the rebels, the poem stands as the premier example of Revolutionary verse propaganda. Yet between 1775 and the publication of the four-canto version in 1782, *M'Fingal* underwent another crucial transformation into a work that is at once more self-consciously "literary" and more nuanced in terms of satire. The two additional episodes, "The Liberty Pole" and "The Vision," are less Hudibrastic than mock-heroic, with frequent allusions to Virgil, Ovid, and Milton. More important, the story itself—in which M'Fingal is tarred, feathered, and imprisoned by the crowd of rebels—shifts its satiric focus to the new threat of mob violence in post-Revolutionary America. Even the character of M'Fingal is transformed from Tory buffoon to prescient social critic as he warns the crowd to beware of factious demagogues who "Break heads and windows and the peace, / For [their] own int'rest and increase; / Dispute and pray and fight and groan, / For public good, and mean [their] own" (Trumbull 1962, 156). As we shall see, in its evolution from the beginning to the end of the war, M'Fingal would become the common literary ancestor to the two major strains of political poetry in the early Republic: the 1775 version would anticipate the verse of Democratic-Republican poets whose works would seek to unmask the treachery of the so-called aristocratic party of Adams and Hamilton, while parts of the 1782 version would anticipate the verse of precisely those Federalists who would lampoon the supporters of Jefferson as the party of demagoguery and mob rule.

Ironically, among the literary precursors that opened the way for Trumbull's introduction of these themes into the 1782 *M'Fingal* were the dozens of loyalist poems published regularly throughout the war in the British stronghold of New York. Whereas, as we have seen, a great deal of pro-Revolutionary satiric verse sought to unmask a conspiracy by the few to deny liberty to the many, such poetry found its mirror image in a body of poems that satirized the American patriot leaders as factious demagogues. These so-called patriots, wrote Myles Cooper in *The Patriots of*

North America, are actually "Men deprav'd, who quit their sphere, . . . And boldly rush, they know not where; / Seduc'd, alas! by fond Applause, / Of gaping Mobs, and loud Huzzas" (Cooper 1775, 3). In apparent answer to Freneau's Miltonic image of the Tory cabal, moreover, loyalist verse depicted the members of Congress as American "Satans"—as, for instance, in Jonathan Odell's *The American Times,* which symbolically casts the "traitor," George Washington, out of heaven: "Go, wretched author of thy country's grief, / Patron of villainy, or villains chief; / Seek with thy cursed crew the central gloom, / Ere Truth's avenging sword begin thy doom" (Odell 1780, 12). In the end, of course, the "demonic" Washington and his army would prevail, and with the conclusion of the war, the literary counterwarfare offensive waged by loyalist poets would itself come to an end. The most prominent loyalist poets, Odell and Joseph Stansbury, would themselves set sail for Nova Scotia, leaving behind an assemblage of poets now simply called "American," whose thoughts, like those of their fellow citizens, would soon turn to the preservation of national unity.

Post-Revolutionary Verse: National Unity and Partisan Warfare

The Peace of 1783 brought a respite as well from the verse wars of the Revolution, as American poets turned their attention to celebrating independence, memorializing fallen war heroes, and imagining what kind of nation America might become. The emancipated slave poet Phillis Wheatley commemorated the occasion with *Liberty and Peace: A Poem,* which envisions America as a beacon of liberty for other nations (Wheatley 1784). David Humphreys's *A Poem on the Happiness of America* strikes a similar theme of celebration—"Oh happy people, ye to whom is giv'n / A land enrich'd with sweetest dews of heav'n"—while simultaneously advising Americans to shun the luxuries of European society (Humphreys 1786, 27). Yet perhaps the clearest manifestation of a new literary emphasis on national unity was the appearance in postwar America of two long epic poems proclaiming America's rising glory: Timothy Dwight's *The Conquest of Canaan* (1785) and Joel Barlow's *The Vision of Columbus* (1787).

Strictly speaking, *The Conquest of Canaan,* based on the biblical story of Joshua, is not an "American" epic, though a certain kind of literary nationalism is evident in Dwight's youthful ambition to become America's Milton. Still, the story of a virtuous and powerful military hero who leads the chosen people to victory resonated with the emerging mythology of George Washington and the popular conception of America as the "New Israel." Dwight makes this analogy explicit in several places, with references to Revolutionary War heroes and an extended passage in which Joshua is shown a millennial vision of "a new Canaan" rising up in the Western Hemisphere: "Here union'd Choice shall form a rule divine; / Here countless lands in one great system join; / The sway of Law unbroken, unrivall'd grow, / And bid her blessings every land o'erflow" (Dwight 1969, 254–255). A clearer example of a national epic is Barlow's *Vision of Columbus* (later revised and republished in 1807 as *The Columbiad*), which centers around what might be called a secular counterpart to Joshua's millennial vision. At the outset of the poem, as Columbus sits locked away in a Spanish prison, regretting his life as an explorer, he is visited by an angel who comforts him with a vision of the future glory of the continent he found. In the final book of the poem, Barlow takes this optimistic vision even further, placing the story of the new American republic inside a larger narrative of the triumph of enlightenment over superstition, and imagining the United States as heralding a new utopian age of peace, commerce, and technological advancement.

Both *The Conquest of Canaan* and *The Vision of Columbus* would be judged by later generations of readers as long, ponderous experiments in American epic, representative of all that post-Romantic readers would find deficient in neoclassical verse. Yet in the mid-1780s, when one of the most pressing questions was whether America constituted a loose confederation of states or a united republic, such poems were highly appreciated for what they seemed to promise about a cohesive American culture. This is particularly evident in the commercial success of *The Vision of Columbus*—the list of advance subscribers to the poem reads like a "who's who" of Revolutionary heroes and founders, including Washington, Franklin, Hamilton, Adams, and Lafayette. If the epic accomplishments of Dwight and Barlow proved unequal to their ambitions, their works nonetheless served to imagine in poetry an ideal America against which to measure the real one.

At the same time, it had become increasingly clear by the mid-1780s that the real America was in trouble. The postwar economy was in crisis, which had led to armed rebellion in 1786 when a group of indebted Massachusetts farmers, led by Daniel Shays, shut down court proceedings to prevent foreclosures on their farms. States found themselves on the brink of armed conflict over currency and trade disputes and conflicting territorial claims. Against this background of impending catastrophe and the ensuing dispute over whether to replace the Articles of Confederation with a stronger federal government, John Trumbull responded by returning to the satiric strain that had occupied him during the Revolution. Dwight and Barlow, moreover, turned almost immediately from their epics of rising glory to mock epics that envisioned a very different possibility: the moral and political demise of the Republic.

The most memorable example of political verse satire from the 1780s is "The Anarchiad," a series published in the *New Haven Gazette* in 1786–1787 by a collaboration of several of the Connecticut Wits, including Trumbull, Barlow, and

Humphreys. Each number of the series purported to be a fragment from an ancient epic recounting the war waged by "Anarch" to restore "Chaos and substantial night" to his native country. The real subject matter of "The Anarchiad," of course—for which the struggle between Anarch and his antagonist, "Hesper," serves as a symbolic drama—arose from the various threats to the fledgling Republic, including popular rebellion, the printing of unfunded paper money, and the opposition to the proposed Constitution. Thus, for instance, the poem portrays Shays' Rebellion not simply as a threat to law and order but, in the words of Anarch, as the harbinger of the restoration of Chaos: "Thy Constitution, Chaos, is restor'd; / Law sinks before thy uncreating word; / Thy hand unbars th' unfathom'd gulf of fate, / And deep in darkness 'whelms the new-born state" (Riggs 1861, 6–7).

The reference here to the "restoration of Chaos"—a phrase that closely echoes the concluding lines of *The Dunciad*—reminds us once again that the use of Augustan poetic models and allusions continued to pervade verse satire of the early Republic. As in earlier examples such as *M'Fingal*, moreover, the significance of such allusiveness is more than simply stylistic: rather, the "Anarchiad" poets meant to remind their readers that Pope had intended *The Dunciad* as a powerful moral denunciation of a society propelling itself downward through folly and corruption and self-interest. In the same way, "The Anarchiad" insists that the political and economic threats to the republic are themselves symptoms of a similar failure to place the common good before individual self-interest: America is in danger of political collapse, Hesper states, because "Of bankrupt faith, annihilated laws—/ Of selfish systems, jealous, local schemes." By calling to mind the "chaos" and "universal darkness" from *The Dunciad*, the "Anarchiad" poets thus announced themselves as the Augustan poets of their time, determined to "save the sinking state" (Riggs 1861, 58, 54) by means of satiric intervention. That such intervention was being done in the name of the new Constitution, moreover—recasting the debate as a cosmic drama between order and chaos—made "The Anarchiad" a powerful and popular literary counterpart to *The Federalist* and other essays, which were arguing the same case through more measured means.

Resembling "The Anarchiad" in several particulars was Timothy Dwight's mock epic of 1788, *The Triumph of Infidelity*. Like "The Anarchiad," *The Triumph of Infidelity* is filled with allusions to *The Dunciad* and other Augustan works, and it emerged out of the same uneasy political and economic context. Yet rather than highlight the political threat to the Republic, Dwight (the grandson of Jonathan Edwards and a Calvinist minister himself) focused his satire on religious and moral dangers—in particular, the rise of Enlightenment rationalism, deism, and Latitudinarian theology in postwar America. Narrated chiefly by a Satan, the poem lampoons a host of "infidel philosophers," from Europeans like Voltaire and David Hume to American Deist Ethan Allen, but its principle target is the heterodox Christian clergyman Charles Chauncy, who had recently published a treatise denying the doctrine of eternal punishment in hell. To Dwight, the common danger posed by Deism and Chauncy's more optimistic version of Christianity was that of moral complacency, and he plays out this possibility in *The Triumph of Infidelity* in symbolic terms, imagining all the types and characters who are drawn to Chauncy's pleasing doctrine: a corrupt member of Congress whose office serves merely to support a life of profligacy at his constituents' expense; a wealthy creditor who charges excessive interest to the widows and orphans of Revolutionary soldiers; a paid perjurer who "sold his friend, and country, for a song" (Dwight 1969, 365).

For Federalists like Trumbull and Dwight, the ratification of the Constitution and the election of George Washington as president were hopeful prospects, indicating at the very least a temporary victory of public virtue over narrow self-interest. Yet despite a general sense of optimism over the formation of a national government, a few poems from the late 1780s hinted at the impending ideological differences and mutual suspicions that would soon divide the nation into opposing parties. One early example is *The Dangerous Vice* (1789), an anonymous poem sometimes attributed to Edward Church. The poem begins by recalling both *The Anarchiad* and *The Triumph of Infidelity* in its defense of American simplicity against the "dangerous vice" of pride, which has led some in America to become attracted to the pomp and luxury of aristocratic Europe. Gradually, however, the poem reveals also that the "dangerous vice" from the title is also a pun on "vice president," and that its main target is John Adams, who is presented in the poem as "a stickler for a crown, / Tainted with foreign vices, and his own, / Already plotting dark, insidious schemes, / Already dubb'd a King, in royal dreams" (Church 1789, 14). Here again, the language of conspiracy is prominent, recalling the earlier exposés of "demonic" conspiracies in Revolutionary War satire. The crucial difference is that the accused perpetrator of "dark, insidious schemes" against the new nation is none other than the sitting vice president in his first year of office.

Poems such as *The Dangerous Vice* opened the way for a string of antiadministration satires that ran throughout the presidencies of Washington and Adams. Amid the rise of the opposition "Republican" party, complete with partisan newspapers such as the *New York Journal* and the *Aurora* of Philadelphia, poets critical of the Federalist administration published satires against Adams, Hamilton, and other party leaders, usually depicting them as actively plotting to restore monarchy, aristocracy, and an economic system that encouraged bankers and speculators to defraud the common people. The central figure in this literary campaign, once again, was Philip Freneau, who returned to the political fray in the early 1790s as a poet and editor (Freneau 1902; Hayes 2004). Among Freneau's contributions to the body of antiadministration satire is "Pomposo and His Printer," which reinforces the caricature of John Adams (Pomposo) as contemptuous of all but the well-born. Equally important to the Republican cause was Freneau's editorship of such newspapers as the *National Gazette*, where, in addition to printing his own verse, he also published the works of other poets like St. George Tucker of Virginia, whose series of "Probationary Odes" under the pseudonym "Jonathan Pindar" would constitute the largest single collection of Republican political verse.

Readers of eighteenth-century British satire will no doubt recall that Tucker's persona, Jonathan Pindar, is a sustained allusion to Peter Pindar (John Wolcot), the pseudonymous poet who had risen to fame in London in the 1780s with his own satiric odes lampooning King George III and others. Tucker's own genius lay in recognizing the satiric potential of the Pindar character—a cheerfully obsequious hack who offers to write panegyrics in exchange for money or preferment—for the political context of 1790s America. Jonathan's pose of mock awe for the subjects of his verse served perfectly to highlight the perceived "aristocratic" tendencies of the Federalists, as when he addresses John Adams: "O Thou! Whatever be thy Title loved, / King of the Romans, Caesar, Czarowitz, / Dauphin, or Prince of Wales, if more approv'd, . . . Deign from my hands t'accept this sav'ry sprig." More important, as a willing propagandist, Jonathan promises not to expose his subjects' true ambitions and transgressions to the public. "I'll swear to all the world—you never dip'd / In speculator's kennel your pure hands," he writes to Hamilton, and categorically denies having ever even hinted at a conspiracy of Federalists in the Senate: "I never said, in secret you debate, / Like Turkish Divan, or Venetian Peers; / Hatching infernal plots against the State— / Nay my good Lords! I pray you spare my ears!" (Tucker 1796, 9, 15, 20).

In a later ode "To Liberty," Jonathan Pindar remarks that scarcely a decade after the end of the Revolution, Liberty has become a "Cast-off Mistress" in Federalist America, adding that at least she is still held dear in revolutionary France. In making this comparison, Tucker references the other major theme of Republican poetry from the 1790s: the enthusiastic celebration of the French Revolution as the latest sign of the worldwide progress of liberty and reason over the forces of tyranny and superstition. Countless poems and songs emphasizing the unity between the American and French Revolutions appeared in the Republican press, from an English translation of "La Marseillaise" to Freneau's own rewriting of "God Save the Queen" as "God Save the Rights of Man." The emphasis here on the importance of the French Revolution for humanity at large is equally evident in Joel Barlow's *The Conspiracy of Kings* (1792), written in the aftermath of his emigration from Connecticut to revolutionary France and political conversion to Citizen of the French Republic. Though addressed to a European audience, *The Conspiracy of Kings* spoke to American politics by universalizing the ideological differences between the Federalists and Republicans, effectively dividing the entire world between those willing to fight for liberty and equality and those seeking to prop up despotic systems:

> Show me your kings, the sceptered horde parade,—
> See their pomp vanish! see your visions fade!
> Indignant Man resumes the shaft he gave,
> Disarms the tyrant, and unbinds the slave,

> Displays the unclad skeletons of kings,
> Scepters of power, and serpents without stings.
> (Barlow 1970, 2: 72)

Barlow's argument in this passage—that the remaining monarchs of the world are merely fortunate souls who have for too long benefited from a system based on lies and superstition—is standard Enlightenment rhetoric. Yet the emotional power of *The Conspiracy of Kings* and similar poems (such as Freneau's "On Mr. Paine's *Rights of Man*") arises less from the argument per se than from its accompanying tone of extreme moral outrage that such a self-evident truth as the universal rights of man could have been repressed for so long. The same indignation allows Barlow, later in the poem, to compare "Courts and kings" to "vampires" who feed on the labor of peasants and are all too willing to "bid wild slaughter spread the gory plains" when their demands are not met (Barlow 1970, 2: 80–81). Such images of violence and bloodshed at the hands of tyrants are especially common in Republican verse of the early 1790s, and they may well have contributed to the view of many of the Revolution's supporters that even the extreme brutality of the Reign of Terror was fitting retribution against the enemies of the people.

In direct contrast to the satiric or critical register that dominates *The Conspiracy of Kings* is the positive image of the French Revolution as heralding a new age of human dignity and progress. This is the vision one encounters, for instance, in the poem *Decree of the Sun: Or France Regenerated* (1793). Here the Revolution is portrayed not as the result of human agency merely but as something ordained, as it were, by "the Sun," which is, in turn, personified throughout as a kind of guardian of human affairs:

> The Heav'ns were still—the SEAS were calm,
> And Nature shed her healing balm,
> Upon the world of Man;
> Yet still the Sun's unwearied course,
> TO Nature's laws, adds Wisdom's force,
> And teach him how to scan . . .
> Thus was he rambling thro' the sphere,
> And watching (what he held most dear)
> The "*rights of man*" below;
> He saw the chains, with which they're bound,
> He heaves the groans, the heav'ns resound,
> "No more shall it be so."
> (Anon. 1793, 5–6)

Like *The Conspiracy of Kings*, this poem would ultimately argue that the Revolution was an unavoidable response to the despotic rule of the Bourbons and their supporters. Yet what is significant about *Decree of the Sun* is its allegorical rendering of the Revolution's inevitability—decreed by the Sun, the universal symbol of enlightenment—along with the elevated, hymnlike tone in which the images are expressed. Such tone and imagery evoked the powerful mythology of the French Revolution as a providential, rather than merely human, event. This is certainly the point of the poem's final canto, a supplication to God to aid the spread of liberty throughout the world: "Attune thy voice, let burning incense rise! / Let prayers ascend, up to the Holy Throne! . . . Thou, who bequeath'd her Liberty's wide band, / Which will, ere long, encircle all the earth!" (Anon. 1793, 20).

Undoubtedly, such passages served as inspiration for those who saw in the French Revolution a confirmation of their faith in human social progress. Yet for those who were wary of radical republicanism, the same elevated language seemed to confirm their suspicion that enthusiasm toward the Revolution had become not only excessive but dangerously so. It is fitting, in light of this controversy, that the first major Federalist rejoinder against the poetry of the Republican opposition—"The Echo" series, which ran in Hartford's *American Mercury* from 1791 to 1798—directed its satire specifically at the language of radical Republicanism. And it did so, importantly, by reviving the "versification" genre that had been so popular during the Revolution.

Unlike the verse parody of the 1770s, which had presented itself as a form of popular resistance against government proclamations, "The Echo"—a collaboration of the so-called minor Connecticut Wits, Richard Alsop, Lemuel Hopkins, Theodore Dwight, and Elihu Hubbard Smith—tended chiefly to parody articles from the popular press. Indeed, as Alsop would later explain, the series was not originally intended as political satire but rather to "check the progress of false taste" by lampooning examples of "pedantry, affectation, and bombast" in local newspapers (Franklin 1970, iii). Yet as if in tacit recognition that a new era of literary warfare was about to commence, the "Echo" writers soon turned their parody toward the particular affectation and bombast they found in the various paeans to the progress of liberty, as, for instance, in this passage from the Boston publication the *Argus:* "Liberty, that goddess, which is destined to render happy our word, was born yesterday; she now lies smiling in her cradle. The angels of benignity attend her infancy, and the face of nature is changed into joy and festivity" (Franklin 1970, 5). As versified in "The Echo, No. IV," the same passage would read as follows:

> The other day there chanc'd a dreadful rout,
> For lo! Old mother Spunky had "sent out."
> The gossips and the granny had a frolic,
> And ate and drank themselves into the cholic;
> When, to our joy supreme, on yester morn,
> A full twelve-pounder—Liberty was born.
> In swaddling clothes they pinn'd the baby up,
> And laid her smiling in a chicken-coop;
> While mother Mob, that steady wet-nurse, press'd
> The sturdy infant to her milky breast.

> Around benignant angels joyous flock'd,
> Some air'd her clouts and some her cradle rock'd,
> While granddame Nature shook her grisly chin,
> And ey'd the urchin with transporting grin.
> (Franklin 1970, 6–7)

This is classic parodic bathos, transforming the lofty metaphor of the birth of the goddess Liberty into a vulgar rendering of a baby's delivery, complete with a motley gathering of attendants and a dose of backcountry diction ("sent out," "clouts"). Yet beyond this, the author takes special aim at the tendency in Republican discourse to employ vague abstractions such as "the birth of liberty" to refer to real political situations. In direct contrast, the imagery of "The Echo"—particularly the reference to "mother Mob" as Liberty's "wet nurse," reminding readers that democratic revolutions always risked deteriorating into "mobocracy"—is witheringly concrete about what the new age of liberty might actually be like.

A crucial, implicit claim of "The Echo" (and of verse parody in general) is that it is merely an "echo"—that despite its transposing prose into verse, the truth exposed by parody is no less true or discernible in the original, parodied text. In the context of the political struggles of the 1790s, this was a crucial claim, for it allowed "The Echo" to present itself always as a form of poetic "unmasking"—holding a mirror to the Republicans by repeating their very words against them. It was especially effective in verse parodies of speeches and letters that defended the French Jacobins, particularly after the commencement of the Terror. "Are [the Jacobins] not the authors of the greatest and most glorious revolution of which the annals of history can boast?" asked a letter published in the *Virginia Gazette*. "Have they not dethroned tyranny, monarchy, aristocracy, priestcraft, and all their satellites?" Mimicking this rhetoric while filling in precisely the details the original author would wish to leave out, "The Echo" responds:

> Are not the Jacobins the first of men?
> Most certainly they are, I do protest . . . .
> With much politeness and with equal skill,
> Do they not torture whom they mean to kill?
> And fir'd with zeal to render man humane,
> Bear high on pikes the heads of children slain?
> (Franklin 1970, 61, 69)

The poets who made up this second generation of Connecticut Wits were by far the most prolific verse satirists of the 1790s, producing nineteen numbers of "The Echo," as well as perhaps a dozen satiric "New Years" retrospectives (most notably, Lemuel Hopkins's annual "Guillotina" series in the *Connecticut Courant*). In addition, the later Wits can be credited for their contributions to the other popular Federalist verse form of the period: the mock-epic portrayal of the so-called

Democratic-Republican societies. Inspired by the political clubs of revolutionary France (the Jacobins being the most famous), American Democratic clubs formed in the early 1790s in most major cities, often boasting among their members some of the most prominent political names of the period (Sam Adams in Boston, the Livingston family in New York). Their increasingly vocal reaction to the Federalist administration prompted a series of mock-epic responses in 1794 and 1795, including Lemuel Hopkins's *The Democratiad,* Boston poet John Sylvester John Gardiner's *Remarks on the Jacobiniad,* and *Democracy: An Epic Poem* (Franklin 1970, vi). In each case, the object of satire is not merely the political views of the Democrats but their preferred mode of discourse, the open "town-meeting"-style forum. Recasting such debates as travesties of the grand debates found in serious epics like *The Iliad* and *Paradise Lost,* the Federalist Wits portrayed their Democratic opponents as disorderly buffoons, wholly incapable of governing even their own meetings, much less the nation as a whole.

The mock-epic vogue of the mid-1790s was apparently so compelling that one Federalist wit used it as the basis for an even more complex burlesque. At the height of the poetry wars of 1794–1795, as poets on both sides were actively retaliating against each other, an anonymous poem was published under the title *Aristocracy: An Epic Poem.* Purporting to tell the story of a plot to restore aristocratic privilege in America, the poem appeared to be a direct Democratic rejoinder to the similarly titled *Democracy: An Epic Poem.* What readers discovered, however, on closer examination, was not only that the poem was actually the work of Federalist but that its object of satire was none other than Republican senator Aaron Burr. What is remarkable about *Aristocracy* is that it is written in such a way as to obscure its true satiric intent until relatively late in the narrative, revealing itself in the end as a literary game of bait-and-switch. Whether or not the literary hoax surrounding the poem was successful—whether any actual Democrats bought the poem expecting an anti-Federalist satire, only to discover they had been duped—*Aristocracy* stands out for its sheer ingenuity, revealing the comic and imaginative lengths political poets of the 1790s were willing to go in order to ridicule their enemies and amuse their friends.

Between 1794 and 1800, virtually every important political event was memorialized in competing poems appearing regularly in the pages of partisan newspapers. Amid threats of war with Britain in the months leading up to the Jay Treaty, Democratic-Republicans warned against capitulation to foreign powers, while Federalists published antiwar odes. A few years later, amid a new threat of war against France, the reverse was true: Republicans urged restraint while Federalist poet Robert Treat Paine rose to fame as the author of several popular songs of martial glory, such as "Adams and Liberty" and "To Arms, Columbia" (Paine 1812). Every strike from one side, it seemed, inspired a counterstrike from the other. Jonathan Pindar's odes were answered by a new group of Federalists equally indebted to Peter Pindar, calling themselves "Peter Quince" (Isaac Story) and "Simon Spunkey"

(Thomas Green Fessenden). (Poems by the two appeared regularly in the *Farmer's Weekly Museum*, the New Hampshire magazine edited by satirical essayist Joseph Dennie.) At the same time, Paine's "Adams and Liberty" spawned "Jefferson and Liberty" (Anon. 1799) during the election of 1800. And when political enmity led to an unprecedented brawl between rival members of Congress in 1798—the so-called Lyon-Griswold affair—poets on both sides commemorated the event and claimed that their representative had the better of the fight. See, for example, James Carey's *The House of Wisdom in a Bustle: A Poem, Descriptive of the Noted Battle, Lately fought in C——ng——ss*, and John Woodworth's *Spunkiad: or Heroism Improved* and *The Battle of the Wooden Sword: or, The Modern Pugilists.* (Anon. 1798).

The election of 1800—what Jefferson called the "revolution of 1800"—marked the beginning of the end of literary and satiric warfare in the early Republic. Republican poets like Barlow and Freneau, perhaps sensing that Federalism would continue to decline over the following two decades, all but ceased writing political verse. Both poets, moreover, would be remembered in the following generation for their nonpolitical poems such as Freneau's "Indian Burial Ground" (1787) and Barlow's *The Hasty Pudding* (1793), which commemorated America's unique landscapes and culture. A few Federalists, to be sure, would persist in the older strategy of satirizing Jeffersonian democracy as an ideological sham, chiefly beneficial to demagogues and southern slave owners—Thomas Green Fessenden's *Democracy Unveiled* (1805) is a prominent example. Yet, in general, the Federalist wits who had clung, throughout the 1790s, to an ideal of poetry as political intervention now tended to embrace a contrasting notion of literature as a refuge from the world of politics. If the "boist'rous din" of political discourse "delight us not," advised Thomas Sergeant in the poem "Reflections in the City," we can seek our happiness among "the group / Of literary minds, congenial / To our own taste: receiving and imparting / New pleasures from our former studious toil" (Sergeant 1805). Literary Federalists seem to have followed Sergeant's advice, for while political verse satire would not completely disappear from American literature, it would never again equal the cultural importance it had held during the last quarter of the eighteenth century.

REFERENCES

[André, John]. 1780. *Cow-Chace, in Three Cantos, Published on Occasion of the Rebel General Wayne's Attack of the Refugees Block-House on Hudson's River, on Friday the 21st of July, 1780.* New York: James Rivington.

Anon. 1765. *Oppression: A Poem.* Boston.

Anon. 1768a. The Parody Parodized. *St. James Chronicle,* November 8.

Anon. 1768b. A Parody upon a Well-Known Liberty Song. *Boston Gazette,* September 26.

Anon. 1775. *Howe's Proclamation, Versified.* Boston.

Anon. 1780. Yankee Doodle's Expedition to Rhode Island. In *Cow-Chace, in Three Cantos,* by John André, 19–21. New York: James Rivington.

Anon. 1793. *Decree of the Sun: or, France Regenerated. A Poem, in Three Cantos.* Boston: [Belknap and Hall].

[Anon.] 1794. *Democracy: An Epic Poem.* New York.

Anon. 1798. *The Battle of the Wooden Sword: or, The Modern Pugilists, A New Song.* [Philadelphia?].

Anon. 1799. Jefferson and Liberty. *Centinel of Freedom* (Newark, New Jersey), April 23.

[Bangs, Edward]. 1775. *The Farmer and His Son's Return from a Visit to the Camp.* [Boston].

Barlow, Joel. 1970. *The Works of Joel Barlow,* edited by William K. Bottorff and Arthur L. Ford. 2 vols. Gainesville, FL: Scholars' Facsimiles and Reprints.

Butler, Samuel. 1967. *Hudibras,* edited by John Wilders. Oxford: Clarendon.

[Carey, James]. 1798. *The House of Wisdom in a Bustle: A Poem, Descriptive of the Noted Battle, Lately Fought in C——ng——ss.* Philadelphia.

[Church, Benjamin]. 1765. *The Times: A Poem.* Boston: Thomas and John Fleet.

[Church, Edward]. 1789. *The Dangerous Vice: A Fragment.* Columbia [Boston: Thomas and Andrews].

[Cooper, Myles]. 1775. *The Patriots of North America: A Sketch, with Explanatory Notes.* New York.

Dickinson, John. 1768. Liberty Song. *Boston Gazette,* July 18.

Dowling, William. 1990. *Poetry and Ideology in Revolutionary Connecticut.* Athens: University of Georgia Press.

Dwight, Timothy. 1969. *The Major Poems of Timothy Dwight,* edited by William J. McTaggert and William K. Bottorff. Gainesville, FL: Scholars' Facsimiles and Reprints.

[Fessenden, Thomas Green]. 1805. *Democracy Unveiled; or, Tyranny Stripped of the Garb of Patriotism.* Boston: David Carlisle.

Franklin, Benjamin, V, ed. 1970. *The Poetry of the Minor Connecticut Wits.* Gainesville, FL: Scholars' Facsimiles and Reprints.

Freneau, Philip. 1775a. *Thomas Gage's Proclamation Versified.* New York.

———. 1775b. *A Voyage to Boston: A Poem.* Philadelphia: W. Woodhouse.

———. 1902. *The Poems of Philip Freneau: Poet of the American Revolution,* edited by Fred Lewis Patee. 3 vols. Princeton, NJ: Princeton University Press.

———. 1986. *The Newspaper Verse of Philip Freneau: An Edition and Bibliographical Survey,* edited by Judith R. Hiltner. Troy, NY: Whitston.

Gage, Thomas. 1775. *By His Excellency the Honorable Thomas Gage, Esq; Commander in Chief in and over his Majesty's Province of Massachusetts-Bay, and Vice Admiral of the Same: A Proclamation.* Boston.

Gardiner, John Sylvester. 1795. *Remarks on the Jacobiniad.* Boston: E. W. Weld and W. Greenough.

Hayes, Kevin J. 2004. Freneau, Philip Morin. In *The Oxford Dictionary of National Biography,* edited by H. C. G. Matthew and Brian Harrison, vol. 20, pp. 976–977. New York: Oxford University Press.

[Hopkins, Lemuel]. 1795. *The Democratiad: A Poem, in Retaliation, for the "Philadelphia Jockey Club."* Philadelphia: Thomas Bradford.

Hopkinson, Francis. 1778. The Battle of the Kegs. *Pennsylvania Packet.* March 4.

Humphreys, David. 1786. *A Poem on the Happiness of America, Addressed to the Citizens of the United States.* Hartford, CT: Hudson and Goodwin.

Jingle, Bob, pseud. 1774. *The Association, &c. of the Delegates of the Colonies, at the Grand Congress, Held at Philadelphia, Sept. 1, 1774, Versified, and Adapted to Music, Calculated for Grave and Gay Dispositions; with a Short Introduction.* New York.

Livingston, William. 1777. Burgoyne's Proclamation. *New York Journal,* September 5.

Odell, Jonathan. 1780. The American Times: A Satire in Three Parts. In *Cow-Chace, in Three Cantos,* by John André, 27–69. New York: James Rivington.

Paine, Robert Treat. 1812. *The Works, in Verse and Prose.* Boston: J. Belcher.

Paltsits, Victor Hugo. 1903. *A Bibliography of the Separate and Collected Works of Philip Freneau: Together with an Account of His Newspapers.* New York: Dodd, Mead.

Riggs, Luther G., ed. 1861. *The Anarchiad: A New England Poem, Written in Concert by David Humphreys, Joel Barlow, John Trumbull, and Dr. Lemuel Hopkins.* New Haven, CT: T. H. Pease.

[Sergeant, Thomas]. 1805. Reflections in the City. *Port Folio,* June 8.

Trumbull, J. Hammond. 1868. *The Origin of M'Fingal.* Morrisania, NY.

Trumbull, John. 1775a. *M'Fingal, A Modern Epic Poem: Canto First, or the Town Meeting.* Philadelphia: William and Thomas Bradford.

———. 1775b. *A New Proclamation!* Hartford, CT: Ebenezer Watson.

———. 1962. *The Satiric Poems of John Trumbull,* edited by Edwin T. Bowden. Austin: University of Texas Press.

[Tucker, St. George]. 1796. *The Probationary Odes of Jonathan Pindar.* Philadelphia: B. F. Bache.

Wheatley, Phillis. 1784. *Liberty and Peace: A Poem.* Boston: Warden and Russell.

[Woodworth, John], 1798. *The Spunkiad: or Heroism Improved.* Newburgh, NY: D. Denniston.

PART VII

LATE EIGHTEENTH-CENTURY PROSE

CHAPTER 23

....

THE BEGINNINGS OF
THE AMERICAN NOVEL

....

MELISSA J. HOMESTEAD

In September 1742, Edward Kimber left England for North America, arriving in
New York City in November. During a sojourn of nearly two years, he traveled
widely, south from New York to Maryland, Virginia, Georgia, and St. Augustine,
Florida, and then northward from Florida to Charleston, South Carolina, whence
he returned to England, arriving in July 1744. His *Itinerant Observations in America*
appeared serially in the magazine his father edited, the *London Magazine,* from
August 1745 through December 1746 (Kimber 1998, 11–15). As becomes clear in his
Itinerant Observations, earlier encounters with representations of North American
landscapes and people in English print culture framed his perceptions and motivated his desire to travel America to experience it firsthand. For instance, when
describing the beauties of the landscape along a road to the dividing line between
the Maryland and Virginia colonies, he interjects: "And here I can't help quoting
Mr. *Lewis,* when speaking of another Road in this Colony" (Kimber 1998, 52). He
quotes several lines from the poem "A Journey from Patapsco to Annapolis, April 4,
1730," by American poet Richard Lewis, and then, returning to narrating the "present" of his ongoing American journey, he remarks, "Indeed, I can't help, every now
and then, taking him out of my Pocket in this Country; for his descriptive Part is
just and fine, and such a Warmth of Sentiment, such a delicate Vein of Poetry, such
an unaffected Piety runs thro' the Whole, that I esteem it one of the best Pieces
extant" (Kimber 1998, 52).

How did an American poem about a Maryland scenic prospect end up in Edward Kimber's pocket, and what does his reading of it *in Maryland* have to do with the beginnings of the American novel? Lewis's poem first appeared in print in the North American colonies, but Kimber likely carried a clipping of the poem as it had appeared in his father's *London Magazine* in 1733, his father having reprinted it from the *Weekly Register* of London (Kimber 1998, 11). This anecdote thus gestures to the complex transatlantic circulation of persons, texts, and stories. Even more telling, however, for the history of the American novel is an adjacent anecdote in Kimber's *Itinerant Observations* about the life of "Capt. ——, Master of ——," who had been kidnapped off the streets of London sixty years earlier. The ship's captain, who kidnapped him as a boy, subjected him to sexual abuse on the voyage across the Atlantic and then sold him to a Maryland planter "for 14 years for 12 Guineas." Kimber commits to writing Captain ——'s story "as I had it from the very Person himself, who is the chief in the Story" (Kimber 1998, 50). The planter treats the boy as his own son and places advertisements in London newspapers in hopes of locating his parents. These efforts fail, but the boy marries his master's daughter and prospers as a planter. By chance, he buys his kidnapper at a convict auction. Unfortunately, the kidnapper can provide no information about his parents, and the kidnapper commits suicide rather than labor for the man he wronged. A decade after Kimber recorded Captain ——'s life story for magazine publication, he transformed some of these incidents into a novel published in London, *The History of the Life and Adventures of Mr. Anderson. Containing His Strange Varieties of Fortune in Europe and America. Compiled from His Own Papers.*

More than two decades after Edward Kimber crossed the Atlantic from England to the colonies, young Susanna Haswell (later Rowson) made her first transatlantic crossing in 1766, four years after her birth in Portsmouth, England, to join her father and his second wife in America. Susanna spent her childhood and early adolescence in Massachusetts in the runup to the American Revolution. During the war, her father's Royal Navy affiliation drew the suspicions of local patriots, who relocated the family inland and kept them as quasi prisoners from 1775 through 1778, finally exchanging the Haswell family for American prisoners of war (Parker 1986, 1–8). As an adult, Rowson, like Kimber, made American people and places the subject of a novel first published in London, *Charlotte, A Tale of Truth* (1791). Her novel, like Kimber's, also features a central character who crosses the Atlantic at a young age under duress. A student at an English boarding school, Charlotte receives illicit romantic attentions from a British army officer, Montraville, who maneuvers her into an elopement to America when his army duties take him to New York City during the Revolution. Charlotte dies, seduced and abandoned, before she can return to England and her parents. However, her father crosses the Atlantic and finds her on her American deathbed, agreeing to take her illegitimate infant daughter back to England.

In a fitting reversal of Charlotte's trajectory, Susanna Rowson carried her literary offspring—a copy of the British edition of *Charlotte*—to the new United States of America in 1793. *Charlotte* was practically stillborn on the British market—the 1791 London edition seems to have sold relatively poorly, with only one copy of it known to exist today (Davidson 1989, 167–168, 175). Imported copies of the novel preceded Rowson to the United States, with *Charlotte* appearing in booksellers' and libraries' catalogs in New York, Philadelphia, and Boston in 1792 and 1793, including Mathew Carey's Philadelphia bookstore in 1792 (Vail 1932, 77). However, Carey did not publish an American edition until Rowson herself appeared in Philadelphia, having been recruited in London to join a Philadelphia theater company as an actress. Published under Carey's imprint in 1794, the novel became, by some accounts, "the first American best-seller" and Rowson "the first American to succeed in the literary marketplace" (Parker 1986, i). Retitled *Charlotte Temple* in 1797, the novel appeared in many American editions and remained widely available through the nineteenth century (Rowson 1986).

Charlotte Temple and *Mr. Anderson* do not, however, appear together in most accounts of the history of the American novel. For most of the twentieth century, such histories began in 1789, with the publication of William Hill Brown's tale of seduction, *The Power of Sympathy*, which, as Alexander Cowie describes it, is "a comparatively long fictional work laid in Boston, published in Boston, written by an American, and grounded in purely local interests" (Cowie 1948, 10). Analyses of the American novel covering the 1790s most often focus on Hugh Henry Brackenridge's satiric picaresque of early national politics, *Modern Chivalry* (published in sporadic installments beginning in 1792); Hannah Webster Foster's fact-based seduction novel, *The Coquette* (1798); the early novels of Charles Brockden Brown, whose career as a novelist began in 1798; and *Charlotte*, with foreign-born Charlotte taking the place of "an adopted child in a family of biological siblings" all born in America (Stern 1997, 34). Literary history has also, however, often characterized these early novels and others published during the same years as botched or confused. Critics attribute the failure of the early nation to produce novels worth reading and valuing to many factors, such as the moral and religious censure of novel reading, the dispersal of the population across a broad geographic area, the absence of some cohesive American identity capable of expression in literature, and a continuing colonial dependence in cultural matters even after the Revolution (Loshe 1907; Cowie 1948; Fiedler 1960).

Critical judgments shifted in the late twentieth century. Instead of explaining why these stories of seduction, incest, picaresque wandering, and gothic intrigue are pale, belated imitations of British antecedents, critics have analyzed these novels in light of the pressing political questions facing the new nation in the wake of the enactment of the U.S. Constitution in 1789 (Davidson 1986; Stern 1997; Barnes 1997). Other critics have reassessed the chronological and geographic boundaries of the American novel, looking at novels produced as early as the late seventeenth century and representing life in North America, South America, and the West Indies. This chapter strikes a geographic and chronological middle course, focusing on novels published from the 1750s into the 1790s that represent life in the British colonies that became the United States of America, even though most of these novels were first published in London, not the colonies or the United States. Indeed, this chapter argues that the American novel as traditionally defined (set in America, treating American subject matter, written by an American person) necessarily had its beginning from within a transatlantic context. These early novels feature significant American content involving major characters, but they were also written by authors who resided for some period in what would eventually become the eastern United States—or were written by persons who *represented* themselves in print as having resided there. In addition to *Mr. Anderson* and *Charlotte,* this chapter considers Charlotte Lennox's *The Life and Adventures of Harriot Stuart, Written by Herself* (1750); *Emmera, or, The Fair American* (published anonymously in 1767, but by Arthur Young); *The Female American* (also published anonymously in 1767, represented as the edited papers of Unca Eliza Winkfield, a seventeenth-century American woman); and two other Rowson novels of the 1790s.

Julie Ellison has identified a plot trajectory in a number of late eighteenth-century novels she calls "there and back": the central characters of these transatlantic fictions begin in England but leave for the British North American colonies (there), where they recover their fortunes by engaging in colonial enterprise and then return "back" home. Ellison also finds this trajectory in the careers of authors of such novels, including Lennox. Tracing plot trajectories and authorial careers, and adding publishing history and readership, this chapter maps multiple patterns of transatlantic circulation, some of which end with a return to the metropole, but others of which end in the colonies or the American nation. Plots, careers, and publishing history sometimes synchronize, but often these patterns of circulation conflict and compete, and in this conflict and competition, the American novel begins.

Many other novels potentially fall into the category of what might be called the proto-American novel. Daniel Defoe's *Moll Flanders,* for instance, published in 1721, takes the title character to Virginia. Defoe based his depiction of Virginia entirely on secondary sources rather than personal experiences, but the original readers of his anonymously published novel (presented as the first-person memoirs of Moll herself) would not have been able to draw such a distinction. Furthermore, countless other eighteenth-century English novels include American materials, from subplots to mere verbal references (Heilman 1937; Bissell 1925). Still, a slightly narrower focus allows us to ask a pertinent question: before the American Revolution, why weren't novels based on the American experiences of their authors published in New York, Boston, or Charleston rather than in London?

Edward Kimber was firmly planted in England at the time he wrote and published *Mr. Anderson,* and his trip to America seems to have been a gambit for acquiring and importing literary material from America to England, with no intention of Kimber himself acculturating; his career trajectory was unambiguously "there and back." In a broader sense, however, the London publication of such "American" novels speaks to the economic and material constraints on printing and publishing in the colonies. Literary historians often cite the fact that the first novel *printed* in America was Benjamin Franklin's edition of Samuel Richardson's *Pamela*, published in London from 1740 to 1741 and issued in installments in Philadelphia from 1742 to 1743. What they fail to mention, however, is that Franklin's *Pamela* was a financial failure and was thus the *only* novel printed in unabridged form in the American colonies until the late 1760s (Hall 1996, 268–269, 288; Wolf 1988, 188). Because of the high cost of type, paper, and labor in the colonies, printing most books was simply too expensive—printers rarely risked the substantial investment required to print books when they could be imported from London (or from piratical publishers in Dublin) much more cheaply. When colonists read novels, they thus purchased ones imported from London (or Dublin) or, especially later in the century, borrowed such imported copies from circulating libraries (Winans 1975). As Robert Winans has demonstrated, even when American printers other than Franklin began to reprint English novels in the last third of the eighteenth century, "The longer the novel the less likely it was to have been printed in America in even one unabridged edition" (Winans 1983, 181). Indeed, even after the Revolution and peace with England, importing novels remained cheaper, in most cases, than printing them in America until into the very early nineteenth century (Hall 1996, 195–196). Colonial Americans who aspired to write something that might be called an American novel would have had to seek out publishers across the Atlantic in order to address their American neighbors from between the covers of a book-length fiction.

Even before the 1750s, we can catch a glimpse of an imagined transatlantic author-reader address in 1723, when Arthur Blackamore's *Luck at Last; or, The Happy Unfortunate* was published in London. An Oxford graduate, Blackamore emigrated to the Virginia colony in 1707 and served for a decade as master of the Grammar School of the College of William and Mary. The board of governors of the school repeatedly censured him for his drinking, and he finally returned to England, apparently with the hope of taking orders in the Church of England and returning to Virginia as a clergyman (Hayes 1998). *Luck at Last* features no American scenes or characters and is, in fact, derived from Aphra Behn's short prose romance *The Wandering Beauty*, published after her death in 1698. However, in his preface, Blackamore addresses the novel to "the ingenious Mr. David Bray, Merchant of Virginia," Bray being an actual person whose age suggests that he had been one of Blackamore's grammar school students. "You have formerly known me better than to imagine I would write this out of flattery, after the common method of most modern dedicators," he writes. "For had my talent lain that way [in the way of flattery], I had probably fared more successfully in some particular affairs when I was in America." He suggests a resemblance between one particularly admirable character and Bray's deceased mother, and he asks leave "to commit *The Happy Unfortunate* into your hands. And if you shall be pleased to give it a perusal at your leisure hours and a candid admission into your study" (Davis 1967, 22–26, 33; McBurney 1963, xvi, 3–4). Although Blackamore's attempts to return to Virginia in the flesh had not succeeded, he imagines the London publication of his novel as effecting his return to Virginia *in print.*

The 1750s marked the appearance of Kimber's *Mr. Anderson* and Charlotte Lennox's *Harriot Stuart,* both of which draw on the authors' experiences of the American colonies in the previous decade (Kimber also drew on his American experiences to a lesser extent in his novel *The Life and Adventures of Joe Thompson* (1750), while Lennox returned to her American experiences in her epistolary novel *Euphemia* [1790]). The plots of *Mr. Anderson* and *Harriot Stuart* both follow the "there and back" trajectory, as do their authors' careers, and both novels draw on personal experience as well as a variety of sources circulating in transatlantic print culture, including piracy and Indian captivity narratives (Howard 1993; Ebersole 1995, 98–128). The story of Captain —— reported in Kimber's *Itinerant Observations* is certainly not the only source for Kimber's novelistic account of Thomas Anderson's life (Mason and Mason 2007). But the manner in which Kimber grafts the "there and back" trajectory onto the basic outlines of Captain ——'s life reveals Kimber's investment in a version of a colonial narrative that ultimately returns the fruits of colonial enterprise to England. Captain —— never discovered the identity of his parents and was firmly ensconced on his plantation in Maryland, but Kimber engineers a reunion between his title character and his family in England, the Andersons. The man who discovers his identity as Thomas Anderson dissolves his colonial holdings and transports his wife and adoptive family "back" to England.

Nevertheless, the complete geographic trajectory of Tom's life is far more complex than "there and back" implies. After being kidnapped and transported to Maryland as a child, Tom matures to young adulthood in the Barlow family under a cruel master and his kind wife and daughter, Fanny, who treat him as an adopted son and brother. Expelled by Barlow to prevent his marrying Fanny, Tom becomes the adopted son of the man who buys him from Barlow, Matthewson, an Indian trader. With Matthewson and then after Matthewson's death (which leaves Tom a wealthy man), he participates in armed conflict with the French and their Indian allies. Throughout the American episodes, Kimber specifies dates and places with precision, placing Tom in the midst of actual historical events. Kimber even adds footnotes about unusual American flora and fauna (although this information is not always accurate with respect to parts of America Kimber had not studied closely at firsthand [Milne 1947, 248–249]). Tom marches twice from Virginia to Quebec, the first time in a military maneuver and the second time as a captive. The French governor sends captive Tom from Quebec to France, by way of the West Indies, where Tom assists in the capture of an English pirate ship, on which his childhood kidnapper, John Williamson, is a member of the crew. As with Captain —— of Kimber's *Itinerant Observations,* his kidnapper can provide no information about Tom's parents. Set free in France, Tom spends months there before moving on to England, where coincidence leads him to a reunion with his biological parents, the Andersons, a discovery that makes him future heir to yet another large estate. However, he resolves to return to America, to find "His dear *Fanny,* absence from whom was now the only care or concern he had, at length again resum'd empire in his heart, and he found he must see her or dye" (Kimber 1754, 185). On his newly discovered father's ship, he returns to America, where he marries Fanny and takes her and her mother back to England, where they live happily ever after.

This brief summary only begins to trace the multiple transatlantic crossings that litter the pages of the text, including the interpolated life stories of the people Tom meets in his adventures. Additionally, the novel pays close attention to the transatlantic circulation of texts, in both manuscript and print, and to other arcane details of the networks of exchange that connect (or fail to connect) persons separated by the Atlantic Ocean. Kimber introduces the "good" Marylanders by their libraries of fine imported books. Mrs. Barlow's unusually fine education (superior to that of her husband) is evidenced by her "pretty female collections of the politest authors, in whom Fanny and Tom amused themselves so much, that their ideas of men and things began to open surprisingly." Their benevolent neighbor Mr. Gordon, a Scotch clergyman, "had brought a tolerable library into the country, and had since much enlarged it by orders from England, and promised to let them have one by one his whole riches, as their increasing years fitted them for their perusal." When Mr. Barlow sends Tom into exile to be an overseer at one of his distant plantations, another kind neighbor, Mr. Ferguson, brings, as he tells Tom, "a quire of paper, some pens, and some ink, in my bag, and in my pocket Horace . . . to alleviate and brighten some of your solitary hours" (Kimber 1754, 22–23, 74–75).

Although Tom successfully communicates with Mrs. Barlow and Fanny by means of these supplies, his adventures and the adventures of others turn on failed transatlantic communications. Mr. Ferguson, for instance, sends a letter to Paris informing Tom of what has happened to the Barlows in his years away from Maryland, but the ship carrying the letter burns before it reaches France, leaving him unsure of whether Fanny's father succeeded in forcing her into marrying another. The mechanisms through which Thomas transports his accumulating wealth from America, to France, and on to England succeed, however. Although Ferguson's letter does not arrive in Paris, Tom does receive a letter and funds from his agent back in Virginia per his instructions sent from Canada. The coincidence that leads him to his parents involves another such transaction—he unknowingly employs his own father as his financial agent in London. In a fitting gesture mirroring Tom's access to two imported libraries during his years in service in Maryland, his final gesture in Maryland involves a gift of imported books: "Mr. *Anderson* presented to Mr. *Gordon* and Mr. *Ferguson* the library he had purchased for them [in France and England], as a joint possession between them, which cost him near £150." "Mr. *Anderson*" goes "back" to England, but not the new owners of the library, who reject Tom's offer to be "sharers in all his fortune" because "they were now quite wedded to the country and the climate . . . and did not choose to remove to Europe" (Kimber 1754, 143, 150).

Of course, Mr. *Kimber* did go back to England after his American sojourn, as did Charlotte Ramsay, and both used resources form their colonial ventures as literary material for their fiction. As a young adolescent in a marginally genteel American family, Charlotte Ramsay had experiences that did not range as widely as Kimber's. Scholars disagree about the precise details of her early life and the degree to which her life and the life of the eponymous heroine of *Harriot Stuart* intersect. Charlotte Ramsay was likely born in Gibraltar in the late 1720s when her army officer father was stationed there. After some years in England, her father's military responsibilities took his family to the New York colony, where her father was assigned to the fort at Albany. She spent at least three, possibly more, years there in the late 1730s and early 1740s, returning to England as a young woman and marrying Alexander Lennox in 1747. Although Lennox later in life claimed a birth date of 1720, recent research has made it clear that when she wrote *Harriot Stuart* in 1750, she was the age of her young heroine at the close of the novel, about twenty years old (Carlile 2004).

Harriot Stuart, presented in the form of a long letter-memoir to "Amanda," a friend of the heroine, commences when Harriot is eleven years old. A preternatural coquette, Harriot looks forward to her father's post in America and "his design of settling there . . . with a childish pleasure" (Lennox 1995, 67). The space of the Atlantic between New York and England figures significantly in the tangled romantic intrigues in which Harriot becomes implicated. On the ship that takes Harriot and her family to New York, she first meets Dumont, the man she will marry several years later, but whose life is ensnared in a transatlantic romantic double bind. Dumont was born in New York, but his family destined him at birth for marriage with a female cousin back in England. Dumont has been carrying on a notorious public affair in New York with Mrs. B——, a married woman living there although her husband lives in Jamaica, where he is a wealthy planter. During her years in New York, Harriot circulates between New York City, A—— (Albany), and S—— (Schenectady). Her geographic circulation overlaps with her romantic circulation as she turns away a man approved by her family, attempts to elope with a man of whom they disapprove, and is kidnapped by another, who effects the kidnapping disguised as an Indian and assisted by Indians. When her father dies leaving his wife and two daughters in financial straits, Mrs. Stuart sends her young daughter alone to England, where Harriot's aunt, widow of a baronet, promises to take her in and treat her as her own daughter. On her return passage to England, a Spanish privateer captures the ship, but it is the captain of the British ship that takes the privateer, not the Spanish pirates, who threatens Harriot's still-preserved chastity. The nearly deadly stab wound she inflicts upon the captain foils his attempted rape, but when Harriot arrives in England, she discovers that her aunt has gone mad, thus frustrating her hopes of a new and genteel home.

Harriot never returns to America in the course of the novel (although Dumont's English Catholic relatives do have her trepanned and held captive in a French convent, among other extraordinary adventures), and the novel culminates with everyone settled (and wealthy) in England. And despite the fact that she wrote this novel within a few years of her own American experiences, critics have found her representations of the New York colony disappointingly thin. Julie Ellison, for instance, all but dismisses *Harriot Stuart* as a transatlantic fiction because "the social world it portrays is indistinguishable from London" (Ellison 1995, 307). Like other critics, Ellison finds Lennox's fictional representation of New York in *Euphemia*, published long after her personal experience of the place, much richer and more substantive than her novel written with New York fresh in her mind (Howard 2005, 273; Berg 1996; Séjourné 1967, 118, 155). However, the seeming thinness of local color also reflects Lennox's accurate diagnosis of the lives of the class of colonial functionaries central to her novel. As Eve Tavor Bannet observes, Lennox unmasks "the profound economic and social insecurities at home and abroad which led liminally aristocratic Britons to fall back on gentility and polite manners both to signify a governing personal and national superiority, and to gain the edge in competition with other nations for colonial resources" (Bannet 1999, 74). That is, the social world in which Harriot Stuart circulates in New York is "indistinguishable from London" precisely because the colonials are anxiously replicating London manners on American soil.

Lennox, based both on her life experiences and on her novels representing colonial New York, deserves the title Philippe Séjourné bestows on her, "First Novelist of Colonial America." Despite bestowing this title, he wonders whether Harriot Stuart's extraordinary character was possible, "only because she lived in a very different world from that of her readers?" (Séjourné 1967, 99). Looking at the other side of the coin and confronting the apparent lack of success the novel found with readers in England, he hypothesizes, "*Harriot Stuart* would have been more of a success with the much freer society of New York, had the book ever been published there" (Séjourné 1967, 157). Lennox's representations of New York did not, however, circulate only in the metropole, as Séjourné assumes based on his mistaken conflation of place of publication with circulation and readership. In the 1750s and 1760s, *Harriot Stuart* was available in a Boston circulating library, was advertised for sale in South Carolina, and may have been included in William Byrd's private library in Virginia as light reading for his daughters (Hayes 1996, 115, 174). Indeed, as an adolescent who surely read novels voraciously while residing in New York in the late 1730s and early 1740s, Lennox might have anticipated an American colonial audience for her colonial American novel.

Two strikingly fanciful novels of the 1760s, *The Adventures of Emmera* and *The Female American,* deserve consideration alongside Kimber's and Lennox's transatlantic novels even though they likely did not originate in their authors' direct experiences of the American colonies. *Emmera* consists entirely of letters between several groups of correspondents, with the majority of these letters traveling in the transatlantic mails between England and America. The novel bears two subtitles: the first, *The Fair American,* restates the notable characteristics of the beautiful young title character, Emmera; the second, *Exemplifying The Peculiar Advantages of Society and Retirement,* lays out the schematic oppositions of the novel. "Society" (also denominated "the world") signifies England, and "retirement" signifies America. Despite this supposedly clear opposition and separation between England and America, people and texts circulate between the two in dizzyingly intricate ways. The most prolific letter writer, young Sir Philip Chetwyn, in America because his father is considering relocating his family from England to northern New York, wiles away his time exploring the sublime wilds of the Ohio territory. By chance, he stumbles upon an English father and daughter who have constructed an elaborate pastoral retreat far beyond the habitations of white settlers. The dying father entrusts Emmera to Sir Philip's care, even though he lives in the world his father has forsaken. Before seeing Sir Philip, Emmera has seen no white man other than her father. Her father taught her to read, however, from the books he transported from England to the wilds, and he tells her many stories of the bustle of life in England (Young 1974, 29, 39–40). Among the pastoral delights Sir Philip experiences during his time with Emmera are reading Plutarch, *Paradise Lost,* and the *Spectator* aloud to her. Sir Philip sends many long letters singing Emmera's praises to Colonel Forrester in England, a man he believes to be his friend. However, Forrester actually considers Sir Phillip his enemy because Sir Phillip's sister Harriet refused a marriage proposal from him. Forrester thus uses Sir Philip's letters to plot a revenge trip to America. Meanwhile, Harriet carries on her own transatlantic correspondence with her friend Kitty Hervey, a young society woman who embodies the best of society and who counterplots against Forrester and his evil compatriot Edgerton.

A significant portion of the novel consists of a manuscript document that Sir Philip and Emmera find in the chest containing Emmera's small library, a lengthy account of her father's life, including his reasons for removing to America with his infant daughter. This document, which Sir Philip (implausibly) copies into a letter to Forrester, proves to be the key to every plot and subplot in the novel. The manuscript not only reveals Emmera's true identity but also reveals that Harriet's correspondent Kitty Hervey is Emmera's cousin and that the Hervey family is in illegitimate possession of Emmera's father's English estate. The villains decode the mystery first, and they attempt to use this information to their own advantage. By the close of the novel, most of the significant characters have sailed back and forth across the Atlantic at least once. The entire Chetwyn family, of course, has just crossed at the opening of the novel. Colonel Forrester crosses from England to America to humiliate Harriet and to wound Sir Philip by kidnapping Emmera (both plots fail, and he returns to England, where he aids a plot to claim Emmera's estate). After the failed kidnapping attempt, Sir Philip persuades Emmera to leave their seclusion, first to visit his father and sister and then even to cross the Atlantic, hoping to show her that it is possible to live in seclusion in the English countryside. His attempt at persuasion fails, but he succeeds in marrying her (the great obstacle to their marriage in their rural seclusion was the lack of an ordained Christian minister—Emmera regards nearby Indians as her "neighbors" and protectors, but, apparently, she still finds the ecclesiastical authority found only in society necessary to transform their platonic friendship into a conjugal union). Sir Philip and Emmera return to live in their American pastoral hermitage, but the novel ends with a letter to his friend Mr. Sinclair in England (now married to Harriet's correspondent Kitty Hervey) and with a clear future of transatlantic correspondence between these men who have chosen the opposing paths of society (England) and retirement (America).

In some ways, this epistolary novel of the 1760s appears more "American" than *Harriot Stuart*—if one takes the quantity of local color and descriptions of peculiarly American landscapes to constitute Americanness. Sir Philip's letters to Forrester feature a wealth of detail about American landscapes, as well as about the Indians living in the vicinity of Emmera's hermitage. However, much of this detail is extravagantly fanciful (Indians fight with broadswords, for example). Furthermore, the man who was almost certainly author of this novel, Arthur Young, never traveled to America and thus necessarily derived all this detail from secondary sources and from his fertile imagination. The novel (like *Mr. Anderson* and *Harriot Stuart*) appeared anonymously, and in the eighteenth century, no readers or critics had any reason to connect the novel to Young, who, in any event, had not yet made his reputation as an agricultural writer and reformer at the time of the publication of *Emmera* in 1767. Ruth Perry, who makes a strong case for attribution of the novel to Young, reads the American setting of the novel as a sort of nostalgic projection by Young: in the face of the disappearance of small farms in late eighteenth-century England, Young imagines the perfection of small-scale agriculture on American soil (Perry 2004, 290–291, 334). Emmera is not a hunter-gatherer—she tends a bountiful small farm, using the same agricultural techniques Young would later advocate in his reform writings. Although twenty-first-century scholarship has established that *Emmera* is part derivative fantasy, part nostalgic projection, concocted by a man who never stepped foot in the American colonies, eighteenth-century readers could have imagined otherwise. Furthermore, the novel had eighteenth-century readers in the colonies as well as in England—on the eve of the American Revolution, this novel celebrating America as an idealized space still open to the kind of small, independent farmers who were fast disappearing in England circulated in the American colonies (in English-produced copies) shortly after its publication in England. When Lewis Nicola opened the first commercial lending library in Philadelphia on September 10, 1767, for example, he advertised the work as newly arrived from London and available for borrowing (Wolf 1988, 193). The conclusion of *Emmera*, like Kimber's *Mr. Anderson*, imagines that some colonials might choose America in preference to a return to England.

Lewis Nicola also advertised the availability of *The Female American* in September 1767. The novel, like *Emmera,* first appeared in London in 1767, but the identity of the author remains a mystery. Like so many eighteenth-century novels (including *Harriot Stuart*), the novel takes the form of a first-person narrative presented as an authentic document. As the subtitles indicate, the novel consists of *The Adventures of Unca Eliza Winkfield, Compiled by Herself.* In this respect, *The Female American* also resembles the very famous eighteenth-century novel it imitates, Daniel Defoe's *Robinson Crusoe,* with a "female American" of mixed English and Native American ancestry stranded on an island in the Atlantic substituted for Defoe's Englishman. Unlike *Robinson Crusoe* (or *Harriot Stuart*), however, the novel does not frame the "authentic" memoir as having been written at a time roughly contemporaneous with its publication. In the brief "Advertisement" preceding the novel, "The Editor" presents the "following extraordinary History" as a printed version of a memoir "I found . . . among the papers of my late father" (Winkfield 2001, 33). The advertisement thus presents the text as a historical curiosity authored by a person (Unca Eliza Winkfield) long dead. As Laura Stevens points out, the novel thus complexly balances three distinct historical moments: it is "set in the seventeenth century" and presented as having been written at the conclusion of the seventeenth-century events described; it "imitates an early-eighteenth-century novel" (*Robinson Crusoe*); and it was published in the late eighteenth century, "in the decades of tension preceding the American Revolution" (Stevens 2005, 142).

The bulk of the novel takes place on an island in the Atlantic Ocean vaguely situated off the coast of the Americas. However, the Virginia Colony in continental North America serves as an important fulcrum in Unca Eliza's life. Unca Eliza is born in Virginia to a white English settler father, William Winkfield (son of the governor of the colony, Edward Maria Winkfield), and an Indian mother (Unca, daughter of the unnamed "king" of the local tribe). As Michelle Burnham notes, this genealogy makes Unca Eliza "the fictional granddaughter of an actual historical figure"; Edwin Maria Wingfield (Winkfield being an alternate spelling) was the historical first governor of Virginia. William and Unca first meet when she saves him from beheading by men of her tribe, an incident that clearly echoes Captain John Smith's account of his rescue by Pocahontas, thus doubling Unca Eliza's mytho-historical ancestry. The novel passes very quickly over the six years of Unca Eliza's childhood in Virginia, and after an internal power struggle in her tribe results in the assassination of her mother, William Winkfield takes his daughter to England to live in the family of her uncle. William returns to Virginia after a year, leaving Unca Eliza in England until she is eighteen. In England, she adopts a "mixed habit" combining European and Indian traditions, becomes a pious Christian under the tutelage of her clergyman uncle, and acquires an education (including training in classical languages) unusual for an eighteenth-century woman. She is eighteen by the time she returns to her "native country" and to her father, who dies as he prepares to sell his estates and return to England with his daughter. Her third Atlantic

crossing proves the charm—or the curse—that lands her on an "uninhabited island," where the ship's captain deposits her "to be prey to wild beasts" because she
refuses to marry his son (Winkfield 2001, 24, 49, 51, 54).

The mixed cultural training of her first eighteen years ideally prepares her to
survive and even thrive on this island as a chosen home. The captain allows her
her trunk, which contains clothes and several books, and a bow and quiver of arrows. The books prove crucial. She derives spiritual sustenance from her Greek New
Testament and uses an almanac to calculate the passage of time. The island turns
out to have a single, year-round human resident, an English hermit, who dies soon
after Unca Eliza arrives but leaves a lengthy manuscript guide to the island. In her
account, Unca Eliza writes, "As I have this manuscript still in my possession, I shall
do no more than give a very short view of its contents, though the whole of it would
very well deserve to be made public." The novel itself serves as a sort of double of
this hermit's manuscript. The hermit left England (for reasons unstated) and records his life with the intention of leaving this record on the island: "If this book
should ever fall into the hands of any person, it is to inform him that I lived on this
uninhabited island for forty years." By the end of the novel, Unca Eliza has used the
information contained in the manuscript to effect the conversion of the Indians
who periodically visit the island to perform religious ceremonies. After two years,
her English clergyman cousin finds her, and they marry and stay on the island to
minister to Unca Eliza's converts (or, rather, she steps down from the ministry she
has been carrying out as a woman, a ministry that includes translating the Book of
Common Prayer and the Bible into the language of her converts). First, however,
her new husband returns to England to take leave of his family and to buy "a large
library of books." When the ship leaves the island, it carries "these adventures" in the
form of Unca Eliza's manuscript. That is, the "History" of Unca Eliza's adventures
"The Editor" found "among the papers of my late father" were written on the island
and transported to England (Winkfield 2001, 72, 58, 154–155, 33).

In 1767 the *Critical Review* expressed a wish that "Mrs. Unca Eliza Winkfield"
had published "her" book in the wilds of America for the audience of "wild Indians
to whom she is so closely allied" (Winkfield 2001, 192). The reviewer thus depicts
Unca Eliza as an actual eighteenth-century person who sought print publication of
her memoir. Furthermore, for this eighteenth-century critic, "America" seemingly
signified broadly, encompassing both Unca Eliza's Virginia and her Atlantic island.
More recently, Betty Joseph has persuasively argued the island on which most of
the novel transpires should not be read as "America" in a more limited, modern
sense. Instead, she claims, it is "a third space . . . where the founding father has been
displaced by the not-quite-white mother, and where Christianity becomes a female
fantasy of total being that rescues the native population from the history of Anglo
founding and Anglo (male) missionary projects" (Joseph 2000).

Readers in the American colonies and then the American nation, however,
appropriated *The Female American* and made it into an "American" novel. Cathy

Davidson has suggested that *Charlotte Temple* became "American" in the same way Rowson herself did, through a process of naturalization—both the novel and the author emigrated from England to America and were taken up by American readers as their own (Davidson 1989, 166–175). Like *Emmera,The Female American* was imported by American booksellers in 1767 (Wolf 1988, 193). The mid-1760s also marked the escalation of colonial resistance to the authority of Parliament in the wake of the Stamp Act, a resistance leading to the falloff of importation of British-printed books, including novels. Up until and through the American Revolution, American printers devoted their presses to politics and newspapers, not to printing novels (Hall 1996, 291–295). After peace with England, American printers reprinted British novels infrequently, returning instead to importation. Reprinting began to take off at the turn of the century, and in 1800, a printer in Newburyport, Massachusetts, issued an edition of *The Female American.* In 1814, the novel appeared in a second American edition printed in Vergennes, Vermont (Winkfield 2001, 29). Certainly, *The Female American* did not circulate as widely among American readers as did *Charlotte,* but readers (and printers) still appropriated Unca Eliza as their own, claiming both the person and her island as "American."

In light of this history of transatlantic fictions, Susanna Rowson's novels and career look more typical than exceptional. In particular, her two novels in addition to *Charlotte* featuring transatlantic content, *The Fille de Chambre* (also titled *Rebecca, or, The Fille de Chambre*) and *Reuben and Rachel; or, Tales of Old Times,* look back to this earlier literary genealogy. The latter, however, also looks forward to a new, self-consciously national American literary tradition. *The Fille de Chambre* was first published in 1792 for William Lane at the Minerva Press in London (one year after Lane published the first edition of *Charlotte*). Also like *Charlotte,* the original 1792 edition of *Fille de Chambre* survives in only a single copy (and an incomplete one at that) and found more success with American readers than British. Rowson herself likely arranged the first American edition, which appeared in Philadelphia in 1794, and the novel appeared in several later American editions, both authorized and unauthorized (Weil 1976, 186; Vail 1932, 135–137, 142–143).

Unlike the heroine of *Charlotte,* Rebecca, the chambermaid of the title, does not succumb to seduction. Forced to go into service because of her family's straitened finances, Rebecca fights off and evades multiple attempts at seduction and outright rape by titled gentleman. She falls in love with Sir George, son of her first employer, Lady Mary Wroth, but Lady Mary extracts a promise from her never to hear professions of love from her son. After several years of service in various households (most of which she must leave because she becomes an object of seduction), she finally is reunited with Sir George and marries him, being conveniently absolved of her promise to Lady Mary on the grounds that Sir George is really not Sir George—the real Sir George was swiped from his cradle by Gypsies, and his nurse substituted the infant son of a poor widowed sailor. Mr. George Littleton, unlike Sir George, is a man of precisely her own class; he is even of her own family—he is her cousin, son of her father's brother, who left his infant in the care of a wet nurse when his wife died in childbirth.

Although most of the novel is set in England, several central chapters take place in a bucolic, idyllic town on the Massachusetts coast, where Rebecca lives contentedly with English émigrés the Abthorpes, who treat her as a friend and member of the family. Merging Rebecca's story with incidents derived from her own life, Rowson sets up this American idyll only to decry its destruction in the wake of the Revolution: "the unhappy breach between Great Britain and her colonies arose to such a height, that it never could be healed, and war, in her most frightful shape, began to stalk over this once happy land. . . . The son raised his hallowed arm against his parent, brothers drenched their weapons in each other's blood, and all was horror and confusion" (Rowson 1794, 119–120). Rowson did little or nothing to temper her language to suit post-Revolutionary American readers even in the first American edition of the novel (although she did add an apologetic preface to a "revised and corrected" edition [Rowson 1814]). She heaps anathema upon anathema on the patriotic cause, while occasionally praising the kindness of individuals she portrays as good people who were deluded into supporting a bad cause. Like Rowson's father, Mr. Abthorpe refuses to join the cause of the "enemies of his sovereign," and patriots divest the family of its property at gunpoint and march the family members inland "on pretence of his having held correspondence with the enemy." The narrator later commends young men who aid the family: "May the arrows of affliction with which an unnatural war has since wounded you, be drawn forth by the hand of sympathizing friendship, and the anguish of them obliterated by the recollection of your own good deeds." Indeed, supplying actual names of families from Hingham, Massachusetts, in the text and providing additional names in a footnote, Rowson uses the trials of Rebecca and the fictional Abthorpes to offer praise and thanks to those who aided the *Rowson* family. The American episode is relatively brief, however, with Rebecca returning to England and showing no intention at the end of the novel of ever leaving England. Perhaps, despite Rowson's harsh words for the Revolutionary cause, American readers found the reconstituted Littleton family attractive to their sensibilities. Offered a lucrative military post and potential for social advancement, the untitled George Littleton declines, explaining, "For my own part, though in the early part of life accustomed to all the indulgencies of an affluent fortune, I have been long convinced, that abundance of riches cannot secure happiness." Instead, with Rebecca and emulating her "humble spirit," he chooses to live in rural retirement (Rowson 1794, 126, 134–135, 205).

One might have expected Rowson's first novel both written and published in the new United States to feature American subject matter, but instead, *Trials of the Human Heart* (1795) subjects its heroine to suffering entirely on European soil. It was not until her next novel, *Reuben and Rachel,* published in Boston in 1798, that Rowson turned again to American scenes and characters. However, the novel is also her most insistently transatlantic, a sprawling, multigenerational saga the action of which spans in time and place from Christopher Columbus's famous Atlantic crossing in 1492 to mid-eighteenth-century Philadelphia. In the more than three centuries in between, Spaniards, Englishmen, South and North American Indians, Catholics, and several varieties of Protestants meet, intermarry, and migrate back and forth across the Atlantic. The title characters, twin brother and sister whose lives occupy most of the second volume, appear at the end of a tangled family tree that includes Christopher Columbus, the Incan king of Peru, an Algonquian chief, members of the Penn and Dudley families, and various other British nobles and aristocrats.

In her preface, Rowson explicitly states the patriotic motives behind her venture into historical fiction: "When I first started the idea of writing *Tales of Old Times*, it was with a fervent wish to awaken in the minds of my young readers a curiosity that might lead them to the attentive perusal of history in general, but more especially the history of their native country" (Rowson 1798, iii). By featuring Columbus so prominently in the family tree of Reuben and Rachel, Rowson participated with other post-Revolutionary American writers in a crucial shift in English representations of Columbus. Englishmen writing about the history of the exploration and settlement of British North America had claimed the Italian-Spanish explorer as their own as early as the sixteenth century. Before the Revolution, "Columbus" signified in English-language texts "the history of British America." After the Revolution, however, he signified "the early or prehistory of the new nation, transforming *Columbus* from the founder of an empire into the first citizen of an independent republic" (Spengemann 1994, 160).

What kind of republic does Rowson's Columbus found? Most notably, at the close of the novel, all the virtuous characters plant themselves firmly on the American side of the Atlantic Ocean—this novel ends "there," and only the corrupt go "back." "Where heaven-born Freedom holds her court / Let me erect my humble shed" directs the poetic quotation heading the final chapter, and Reuben, Rachel, their spouses, and sundry others do erect their (somewhat) modest homes in America, the land of freedom. Reuben and Rachel take possession of the Pennsylvania estate that their father acquired through his American business ventures, but they decline to accept the hereditary English estates long denied them during their period of greatest need: "As to titles," Reuben tells an English agent, we "renounce them; they are distinctions nothing worth, and should by no means be introduced into a young country, where the only distinction between man and man should be made by virtue, genius and education. Our sons are true-born Americans, and while they strive to make that title respectable, we wish them to possess no other" (Rowson 1798, 363).

The status of the aboriginal inhabitants of this "young country" at the close of the novel is debatable, however. The first volume's founding act is the marriage between the fictionalized son of Columbus and the daughter of a fictional Incan king, a marriage that produces Isabelle, a character who thus shares a status exactly analogous to that of Unca Eliza Winkfield of *The Female American*—she is the fictional mixed-race European-Indian granddaughter of an actual historical figure. Furthermore, in the first volume, many of the mixed-race descendants of this marriage self-consciously claim their dual racial and cultural heritage. In the second volume, however, both Rowson and her characters seem to forget this elaborately created mixed-race genealogy, firmly fixing the identity of Reuben and Rachel as white and English. By so doing, is Rowson accurately mirroring and implicitly mourning the failure of America to live up to its Revolutionary ideals? Or is she reinscribing and claiming the racism of the nation's founding? (Baym 1995, 162; Castiglia 1995, 39; Smith-Rosenberg 1993, 503).

The novel leaves itself open to both readings. Indeed, despite Rowson's invocation of American patriotism and the Revolutionary legacy in her preface, the status of the novel as a nationalistic project is equally ambiguous. As Nina Baym points out, Rowson "ends her story before the American Revolution begins, which means that her characters are still fully English" (Baym 1995, 162). Again, despite Rowson's preface, the novel's conclusion suggests that Rowson hoped to address readers back in England as well as American readers. The appearance of a Minerva Press London edition of the novel a year after the Boston edition supports this inference. Tellingly, this London edition omits the patriotic preface and its address to young readers "native" to America (Rowson 1799).

In the 1790s, then, Rowson's novels and their circulation were decidedly transatlantic, although the nature of her positioning shifted through and in response to changes in her own national status. While a subject of the English Crown, she wrote novels featuring events that transpired during the American Revolution based in part on her own years residing in America; she then ensured that American publishers reprinted those novels after she emigrated. After becoming an American resident, Rowson wrote a historical novel similarly spanning English and colonial American content. She was not quite yet a citizen in 1798, however—the citizenship status of women depended on that of their husbands, so Rowson became a citizen upon her husband's naturalization in 1804 (Davidson 1989, 167). She first published that historical novel in the United States, a young nation that had directed in its Constitution that "The Congress shall have the power: To promote the progress of science and useful arts, by securing, for limited times, to authors and inventors, the exclusive right to their respective writings and discoveries." In 1790, Congress enacted the first U.S. copyright statute, a law that extended protection only to works written by authors who were citizens or residents of the United States (Solberg 1906, 31–32). Because of Rowson's U.S. residence in 1798, her publisher was able to register a copyright for *Reuben and Rachel*, protecting his and Rowson's proprietary interest in the novel or, more accurately, Rowson's *husband's* proprietary interest (Gilreath 1987, 92). However, even a designedly "national" American novel like *Reuben and Rachel*, written and published after the founding of the Republic, celebrating its history, and protected under its laws, could cross the Atlantic. And, increasingly, in the nineteenth century, American printers and publishers devoted their resources to reprinting and distributing novels by British authors first published in London, something that U.S. copyright law allowed and even encouraged them to do without seeking permission from or making payments to those British authors (Barnes 1974; McGill 2003). As a result, more early nineteenth-century American readers read Sir Walter Scott's historical novels about England and Scotland than ever read *Reuben and Rachel*.

REFERENCES

Bannet, Eve Tavor. 1999. The Theater of Politeness in Charlotte Lennox's British-American Novels. *Novel* 33: 73–92.

Barnes, Elizabeth. 1997. *States of Sympathy: Seduction and Democracy in the American Novel.* New York: Columbia University Press.

Barnes, James J. 1974. *Authors, Publishers, and Politicians: The Quest for an Anglo-American Copyright Agreement 1815–1854.* Columbus: Ohio State University Press.

Baym, Nina. 1995. *American Women Writers and the Work of History, 1790–1860.* New Brunswick, NJ: Rutgers University Press.

Berg, Temma F. 1996. Getting the Mother's Story Right: Charlotte Lennox and the New World. *Papers on Language and Literature* 32: 369–398.

Bissell, Benjamin. 1925. *The American Indian in English Literature of the Eighteenth Century.* New Haven, CT: Yale University Press.

Carlile, Susan. 2004. Expanding the Feminine: Reconsidering Charlotte Lennox's Age and *The Life of Harriot Stuart.* Eighteenth-Century Novel 4: 103–137.

Castiglia, Christopher. 1995. Susanna Rowson's *Reuben and Rachel*: Captivity, Colonization, and the Domestication of Columbus. In *Redefining the Political Novel: American Women Writers, 1797–1901,* edited by Sharon M. Harris, 23–42. Knoxville: University of Tennessee Press.

Cowie, Alexander. 1948. *The Rise of the American Novel.* New York: American Book Company.

Davidson, Cathy N. 1986. *Revolution and the Word: The Rise of the Novel in American.* New York: Oxford University Press.

———. 1989. The Life and Times of Charlotte Temple: The Biography of a Book. In *Reading in America: Literature and Social History,* edited by Cathy N. Davidson, 157–179. Baltimore: Johns Hopkins University Press.

Davis, Richard Beale. 1967. Arthur Blackamore: The Virginia Colony and the Early English Novel. *Virginia Magazine of History and Biography* 75: 22–34.

Ebersole, Gary L. 1995. *Captured by Texts: Puritan to Postmodern Images of Indian Captivity.* Charlottesville: University Press of Virginia.

Ellison, Julie. 1995. There and Back: Transatlantic Novels and Anglo-American Careers. In *The Past as Prologue: Essays to Celebrate the Twenty-fifth Anniversary of ASECS,* edited by Carla H. Hay and Syndy M. Conger, 303–324. New York: AMS.

Fiedler, Leslie A. 1960. *Love and Death in the American Novel.* New York: Criterion.

Gilreath, James, ed. 1987. *Federal Copyright Records, 1790–1800*. Washington, DC: Library of Congress.

Hall, David D. 1996. *Cultures of Print: Essays in the History of the Book*. Amherst: University of Massachusetts Press.

Hayes, Kevin J. 1996. *A Colonial Woman's Bookshelf*. Knoxville: University of Tennessee Press.

———. 1998. Blackamore, Arthur. *Dictionary of Virginia Biography*, edited by John T. Kneebone, J. Jefferson Looney, Brent Tarter, and Sandra Gioia Treadway, vol. 1, pp. 516–517. Richmond: Library of Virginia.

Heilman, Robert Bechthold. 1937. *America in English Fiction, 1760–1800*. Baton Rouge: Louisiana State University Press.

Howard, Susan K. 1993. Identifying the Criminal in Charlotte Lennox's *The Life of Harriot Stuart*. *Eighteenth-Century Fiction* 5: 137–152.

———. 2005. Seeing Colonial America and Writing Home about It: Charlotte Lennox's *Euphemia*, Epistolarity, and the Feminine Picturesque. *Studies in the Novel* 37: 273–291.

Joseph, Betty. 2000. Replaying Crusoe/Pocahontas: Circum-Atlantic Stagings in *The Female American*. *Criticism* 42: 317–335.

[Kimber, Edward]. 1754. *The History of the Life and Adventures of Mr. Anderson. Containing His Strange Varieties of Fortune in Europe and America*. Dublin: Richard James.

———. 1998. *Itinerant Observations in America*, edited by Kevin J. Hayes. Newark: University of Delaware Press.

Lennox, Charlotte. 1995. *The Life of Harriot Stuart, Written by Herself*, edited by Susan Kubica Howard. Madison, NJ: Farleigh Dickinson University Press.

Loshe, Lillie Deming. 1907. *The Early American Novel*. New York: Columbia University Press.

Mason, Matthew, and Nicholas Mason. 2007. Introduction. In *History of the Life and Adventures of Mr. Anderson*, by Edward Kimber. Toronto: Broadview.

McBurney, William H. 1963. *Four before Richardson: Selected English Novels, 1720–1727*. Lincoln: University of Nebraska Press.

McGill, Meredith L. 2003. *American Literature and the Culture of Reprinting, 1834–1853*. Philadelphia: University of Pennsylvania Press.

Milne, W. Gordon. 1947. A Glimpse of Colonial America as Seen in an English Novel of 1754. *Maryland Historical Magazine* 42: 239–252.

Parker, Patricia L. 1986. *Susanna Rowson*. Boston: Twayne.

Perry, Ruth. 2004. *Novel Relations: The Transformation of Kinship in English Literature and Culture, 1748–1818*. New York: Cambridge University Press.

Rowson, Susanna. 1794. *The Fille de Chambre: A Novel*. Philadelphia: H. & P. Rice.

———. 1798. *Reuben and Rachel; or, Tales of Old Times*. Boston: Manning and Loring.

———. 1799. *Reuben and Rachel; or, Tales of Old Times: A Novel*. London: Minerva Press, for William Lane.

———. 1814. *Rebecca, or, The Fille de Chambre: A Novel*. Boston: R. P. & C. Williams.

———. 1986. *Charlotte Temple*, edited by Cathy N. Davidson. New York: Oxford University Press.

Séjourné, Philippe. 1967. *The Mystery of Charlotte Lennox: First Novelist of Colonial America (1727?–1804)*. Aix-en-Provence: Publications des Annales de la Faculté des Lettres.

Smith-Rosenberg, Carroll. 1993. "Subject Female: Authorizing American Identity." *American Literary History* 5: 481–511.

Solberg, Thorvald, ed. 1906. *Copyright Enactments of the United States, 1783–1906.* Washington, DC: Library of Congress.

Spengemann, William C. 1994. *A New World of Words: Redefining Early American Literature.* New Haven, CT: Yale University Press.

Stern, Julia A. 1997. *The Plight of Feeling: Sympathy and Dissent in the Early American Novel.* Chicago: University of Chicago Press.

Stevens, Laura M. 2005. Reading the Hermit's Manuscript: The Female American and Female Robinsoniades. In *Approaches to Teaching Defoe's Robinson Crusoe,* edited by Carl Fisher, 140–151. New York: Modern Language Association of America.

Vail, R. W. G. 1932. Susanna Haswell Rowson, the Author of Charlotte Temple: A Bibliographical Study. *Proceedings of the American Antiquarian Society* 42: 47–160.

Weil, Dorothy. 1976. *In Defense of Women: Susanna Rowson (1762–1824).* University Park: Pennsylvania State University Press.

Winans, Robert B. 1975. The Growth of a Novel-Reading Public in Late-Eighteenth-Century America. *Early American Literature* 9: 267–275.

———. 1983. Bibliography and the Cultural Historian: Notes on the Eighteenth-Century Novel. In *Printing and Society in Early America,* edited by William L. Joyce et al., 174–185. Worcester, MA: American Antiquarian Society.

Winkfield, Unca Eliza [pseud.]. 2001. *The Female American,* edited by Michelle Burnham. Toronto: Broadview.

Wolf, Edwin, 2nd. 1988. *The Book Culture of a Colonial American City: Philadelphia Books, Bookmen, and Booksellers.* Oxford: Clarendon.

Young, Arthur. *The Adventures of Emmera.* 1974. New York: Garland.

CHAPTER 24

CRÈVECOEUR'S *LETTERS FROM AN AMERICAN FARMER*

DAVID J. CARLSON

First published in London in 1782, J. Hector St. John de Crèvecoeur's *Letters from an American Farmer* represents something of an odd case in the canon of early American writing. A work that appears to straddle the line between fiction and nonfiction, written by a transplanted Frenchman of ambiguous political leanings, *Letters* has been variously ignored, challenged, and embraced as a vital cornerstone of the national literature of the United States. Initial response to the work in the two decades following its publication was generally favorable in England, France, and America. By the early nineteenth century, though, American readers and critics had virtually forgotten it. It was not until 1923 that D. H. Lawrence would draw attention back to James, Crèvecoeur's eponymous Farmer, designating him as the "emotional prototype" of the American, the complement to Benjamin Franklin, the "practical prototype." Lawrence's archetypal reading of Farmer James is perhaps best appreciated for its canny anticipation of the political considerations that would drive the renaissance of Crèvecoeur's literary reputation during the middle decades of the century. The emergence of American studies as a field during the 1940s and 1950s provided the vital context in which *Letters* was finally established as both a core scripture of American exceptionalism and a classic formulation of the ideal of the ethnic melting pot. The work of Marius Bewley (1959) and Roy Harvey Pearce (1953) made important contributions, but the canonization process probably culminated in Albert Stone's essay "Crèvecoeur's *Letters* and the Beginnings of American Literature" (1962). Indeed, by the time his popular edition of *Letters* appeared two decades later, Stone felt confident in laying down as settled doctrine the idea that "American literature, as the voice of our natural consciousness, begins in 1782 with the publication of *Letters from an American Farmer*" (Crèvecouer 1981, 7).

While recognizing the contributions of these earlier interpreters, recent scholars have tended to acknowledge that the ideological pressures of the cold war period (with its focus on defining and celebrating a singular American experience) influenced the reception of Crèvecoeur's work in potentially misleading ways. Critics from the 1950s through the 1970s often ignored a number of the richest complexities in *Letters from an American Farmer*: its conflicted pronouncements on slavery, its blend of celebratory provincialism and Eurocentric elitism, its contradictory assessments of Anglo-American constitutionalism, and its abrupt tonal shifts from georgic idealism to despondency over the effects of the American Revolution. Such complications did not fit with the picture that was being developed at the time of Crèvecoeur as one of the literary founding fathers of the United States. In contrast, attempts to recover and explain some of these complexities (and to challenge the nationalist paradigms that obscured them) have been more characteristic of recent scholarship on *Letters.* To those who seek to view Crèvecoeur as an unambiguous apologist for the colonial revolutionaries (as one nineteenth-century descendant would have us do), *Letters from an American Farmer* has been revealed to be an equivocal source of evidence (Crèvecoeur 1883). Indeed, it is instructive that one critic has found it possible to maintain (with considerable textual support) that Farmer James actually espouses a "commitment to the superiority of the Englishman in all respects," thus voicing, on Crèvecoeur's behalf, "a characteristic bias of the eighteenth-century French intelligentsia" (Aubery 1978, 575). It is equally instructive that another, more recent reader has found in *Letters* suggestive intersections with the discourses of "Anglo-American loyalism and revolutionary espionage" (Traister 2002, 470).

These intersections, of course, are precisely the kinds of textual features that were obscured or ignored by earlier nationalistic criticism. And yet, if the tendency to read *Letters* as an ideologically homogeneous work has become less prevalent in recent years, the temptation to situate the text (and its author) on one side or another of the political divide of the American Revolution persists. Is *Letters* an American work? A British work? A French work? Was Crèvecoeur a Tory or a loyalist? Which side does James, the American Farmer, take? How do our understandings of the contradictions and tensions within *Letters* bear on these issues? Even now, readers seem continually impelled to understand the book in terms of such dichotomies. The discussion of *Letters* that follows suggests that the persistent inconclusiveness of critical debates framed in this manner raises another possibility: that the paradigms of national literature offer an inadequate foundation for assessing Crèvecoeur's work. The recent transatlantic turn in early American studies (which emphasizes the interpenetration of the material and literary cultures of continental Europe, Britain, and the colonies throughout the Atlantic world) encourages a different assessment of *Letters from an American Farmer,* one that apprehends the tensions and contradictions in the text not as problems to be resolved but rather as indices of its immersion in a range of Enlightenment discourses. If we read *Letters* in such a context, as a philosophical work designed to provoke active, critical reflection on the part of an enlightened, cosmopolitan audience, the text reveals itself as a carefully considered contribution to the eighteenth-century republic of letters, not a prototype of nineteenth-century literary nationalism. Within its pages, Crèvecoeur effects a characteristically eighteenth-century fusion of literary fabulation with philosophical reflection, assessing in the process the limits of theories of political liberalism and moral sentiment. *Letters* raises enduring questions about the relationship and potential conflicts between individualism, property, sociability, and sympathy—questions that continue to have particular resonance in the United States. It is in this respect that Crèvecoeur's text might best be considered an American classic, one that still has much to say to contemporary readers in the United States and elsewhere.

Biographical and Literary Contexts

Michael-Guillaume-Jean de Crèvecoeur was born in 1735 in Caen, Normandy, into an old but relatively poor branch of the Norman gentry. Educated at the Jesuit Collège du Mont, he was sent at age nineteen to live with English relations in Salisbury, where he stayed for a year learning English. In 1755, the opportunistic young man sailed to Canada, where he joined the colonial militia, serving as a surveyor and cartographer for part of the French and Indian War. He was commissioned a lieutenant in 1758 and wounded at the Battle of Quebec in September 1759. One month later, he resigned his commission and migrated to New York City, where he adopted the name James Hector St. John and commenced a new career as a surveyor, Indian trader, and merchant. For several years, Crèvecoeur traveled extensively along the Atlantic seaboard and also visited the Ohio Valley and the Great Lakes. After becoming a naturalized citizen of New York on December 23, 1765, he married Mehitable Tippet, daughter of a prominent local family, in 1769. He purchased 120 acres of land in Orange County, New York, which he subsequently named Pine Hill. This estate became the inspiration for the Pennsylvania farm of the fictional James. Taking up the life of a gentleman farmer, Crèvecoeur began writing the first of his sketches, twelve of which would later be revised and organized into *Letters*.

Dating from this start in 1769, the inaugural phase of Crèvecoeur's literary career seems to have been defined by his physical and cultural mobility, his desire for public recognition as a man of letters, and his ongoing struggle to evade political turmoil. All these factors influenced the way he would write about his colonial experience, and the initial rhythms of his literary output; the roots of a transatlantic writer can be seen early on. During the early 1770s, as Mehitable gave birth to two sons and a daughter, Crèvecoeur continued his routine of farming, travel (making a trip to the Susquehanna Valley in 1774, for example), and writing. The outbreak of war in 1775, however, brought an end to this genteel, stationary pattern of life. By 1776, as the British occupied New York City, Orange County became a war zone, where threats of Indian raids and patriot reprisals were constant. As a result, in 1778, after a visit to the Wyoming Valley (the site of an infamous Indian massacre he would later describe in a sketch), Crèvecoeur sought permission from the American authorities to enter New York City and depart for France. Arriving in the city in 1779 (with his son Ally and his manuscripts), he was arrested and briefly held by the British under suspicion of espionage. After his release, he made his way to Dublin, where he landed in October 1780. Upon his eventual arrival in London in early 1781, Crèvecoeur sold a series of his sketches and essays to the publisher Davis and Davies. While Orange County was being raided (his wife would die there during his absence), the manuscript of Letters was being prepared for British publication. The book appeared in print in 1782, to generally favorable reviews by English critics, by which point Crèvecoeur had moved back to France, apparently harboring ambitions for a wider European readership. By the time he managed to return to New York as French consul in 1784 (where he was reunited with two of his children), a French translation had been published in Paris. When illness drove Crèvecoeur back to France in 1785, however, he began working on yet another, expanded (and stylistically very different) French version of Letters, which would be published in 1787. This auspicious year (when the U.S. Constitution was ratified), then, seems to represent the height of Crèvecoeur's literary fame and success during his lifetime. He had become a writer of some reputation on both sides of the ocean.

By the 1790s, critical responses to Crèvecoeur's writings seem to have turned increasingly toward their historical and political merits, as opposed to their belletristic qualities. Gradually, Crèvecoeur came to be regarded not as the cosmopolitan literary man he aspired to be but as a reliable eyewitness observer of the society (America) that unleashed the forces of radical political change. In 1787, Crèvecoeur returned to New York to resume his consular post, which he held formally until 1792 (though the outbreak of revolution in France necessitated his return to Normandy in 1789). He did continue for a time to enjoy some notoriety as a man of letters, in both France and America. From the beginning of the French Revolution until his death in 1813, his literary labors were consistently interrupted by war. In this context, what ongoing interest there was in Crèvecoeur's writings in post-Revolutionary France and Europe tended to center on his firsthand understanding of the social and political conditions of American colonies—the nominal model for the subsequent convulsions in France and Europe. Circumstances were defining Crèvecoeur more and more clearly as a historical observer of his age. Simultaneously, those circumstances were interfering with his ability to maintain his public profile as a genteel writer. Crèvecoeur tried to resign from the consular service in early 1792, before actually having his position revoked in December of that year. Loss of income and the need for frequent movement during the Reign of Terror and the Napoleonic Wars (Crèvecoeur lived, variously, in Germany, London, and France between 1795 and 1813) proved a subsequent hardship for the aging gentleman. He continued to write during this period, publishing the three-volume *Voyage dans la Haute Pensyl-vanie et dans l'Etat de New-York* in 1801. The appreciative French critics valued the book primarily for its descriptions of American life, its portrayal of Indians, and its advocacy of the rights of man. *Voyages* drew little attention, either positive or negative, in the United States (perhaps a reflection of the souring political relation-ship with France during the 1790s). By the time of his death, then, even though he had published a significant and varied amount of material based on his travels and experiences in the American colonies before Independence, Crèvecoeur was well on his way to becoming the first forgotten man of American letters. Though William Hazlitt appreciated *Letters,* there were only a few mentions of Crèvecoeur in Ameri-can periodicals before the twentieth century.

A major factor in the waxing and waning of Crèvecoeur's status as a literary figure, as this brief biographical sketch suggests, has been the tendency on the part of many readers to assume that *Letters* represents simply an attempt by a moderately talented, provincial amateur to produce a work of history (or, perhaps, of travel writ-ing). Such a reading, of course, involves the errant assumption that Crèvecoeur, the author, and James, the narrator of *Letters,* are identical. This assumption (which was not actively discouraged by Crèvecoeur during his time in the salons of Paris) has been central to the use of *Letters* as a historical document depicting life in the Ameri-can colonies—a process well under way during the 1790s and persisting well into the twentieth century. (As late as 1971, for example, Pulitzer Prize–winning historian Richard Hofstadter would reference *Letters* as a work of autobiographical nonfic-tion.) Treated as evidence of the realities of colonial life, however, *Letters* could not help but appear lacking, even in its own day. Once the initial phase of mythmak-ing and propagandizing during the American Revolution had run its course, even George Washington would remark critically of Crèvecoeur's work that it was "embel-lished with rather too flattering circumstances" (quoted in Philbrick 1970, 162).

If Crèvecoeur's writings failed to hold up historically, even at this early date, the tendency to identify them as primarily nonfictional texts also shaped the interpretive thinking of later, literary critics looking at the material. In the introduc-tions to their 1925 edition of *Sketches of Eighteenth-Century America* (a collection of manuscripts excluded from the original volume of letters), Henri Bourdin, Ralph Gabriel, and Stanley Williams offer strikingly dismissive assessments of Crèvecoeur the writer, even as they present his newly discovered works to the reading public. Gabriel positions Crèvecoeur as "not primarily a literary man," seeing him instead as a "chronicler of unrelated episodes" and "an observer whose primary interest was not in ideas or causes but in people." Williams is even more blunt, positing that "Crèvecoeur does not regard, with the eyes of the literary man, the life about him as artistic material." In such a context, any literary achievements of the author of *Letters* become almost accidental ones—an assumption that hinders readers from seeing many textual features that *are* present in the book. If Williams does praise Crèvecoeur's powers of "short, vivid narratives or descriptions," those powers derive from the fact that a fervency of feeling can sometimes "overflow his crude sentences" (Crèvecoeur 1925). Neither a literary man nor a trustworthy historian, Crèvecoeur becomes just a frontiersman who happened to write, and whose successes are a result of glimpses of raw genius, unrefined by the conscious application of rhetorical talent.

Looking more closely both at Crèvecoeur's biography and at what he actually wrote (in his published and manuscript materials) yields a different picture of the man as artist, however, a move that is an important step in assessing *Letters* as an eighteenth-century literary performance. In his introduction to *More Letters from the American Farmer,* Dennis Moore offers compelling textual evidence of Crèvecoeur's extensive reading and willingness to employ different narrative personae in his sketches (both published and unpublished). Moore uncovers a range of literary models for various elements in Crèvecoeur's work, ranging from John Dickinson's *Letters from a Farmer in Pennsylvania* (1768) and Voltaire's *Lettres Philosophiques* to Ovid's *Metamorphosis* and Hesiod's *Works and Days.* The suggestive parallels between Crèvecoeur's sketches and this range of generic models, combined with his controlled use of narrative point of view, present a picture of a writer who regarded the world around him as artistic material. And then there are the biographical facts of Crèvecoeur's extensive travels (intended, partly at least, as source collection) and reworkings of his material in three separate volumes during the 1780s. Numerous critics who have reviewed the content of both works draw attention to the considerable differences between these two books—the addition of new anecdotes, a new dedication to Lafayette, and a tendency to "espouse the political opinions of [Crèvecoeur's] Parisian friends" (Rice 1934; Allen and Asselineau 1987, 96). These substantive and stylistic changes suggest certain conclusions about the producer of *Letters* and *Les lettres.* Clearly not the story of a one-dimensional chronicler of unrelated events, Crèvecoeur's career reveals a worldly writer who possessed a strong sense of audience and context. His interest in gathering material for his sketches and willingness to drastically rework that material highlight both artistic flexibility and literary aspiration (a desire to reach a broad European audience with his work). Each of these points further position Crèvecoeur as an aspirant to citizenship in the Enlightenment-era republic of letters rather than as an accidental, partial prototype of Henry David Thoreau.

All these observations bear on the recurrent critical debates dealing with Crèvecoeur's intention regarding the generic form and narrative structure of the 1782 *Letters,* issues of considerable import for readers inclined to approach the text as a coherent whole with a structure that can be analyzed. A. W. Plumstead has cogently summarized the debate about the order of the twelve letters in the 1782 edition as a choice between viewing *Letters* as a product of Crèvecoeur's London editors, as a limited collaboration between those editors and Crèvecoeur, or as a product of the author's deep involvement, approval, and agency. All published eighteenth-century texts, of course, reflect some degree of editorial involvement; spelling and capitalization, at the very least were typically left to the discretion of printers. In the case of *Letters*, the more fundamental question involves whether someone other than Crèvecoeur made key decisions—such as concluding the book with the problematic "Distresses of a Frontier Man." Reinforcing the view of other critics (such as Howard Rice, Albert Stone, Thomas Philbrick, and D. H. Lawrence), Plumstead draws on both internal evidence from the twelve letters that made the cut in the 1782 work and a consideration of the materials excluded from that edition to argue that the book indeed reflects Crèvecoeur's selection, arrangement, and revision of material (including his decision to adopt the persona of James as his narrator). The introduction (Letter 1), which establishes James as a character and sets up the fictional Mr. F. B. as the European correspondent (thus framing *Letters* as a transatlantic epistolary narrative), was clearly an innovation of Crèvecoeur's that postdates his original drafting of the sketches included in the book. Plumstead goes on to note that Crèvecoeur "revised his chosen sketches, adding phrases . . . in places to identify his narrator" (Plumstead 1977, 228). This assessment of authorial intent has become the generally accepted (if not universally held) critical view. While we may never know precisely the ratio of editorial to authorial control in creating *Letters*, it seems clear that the text as published was, at the very least, something Crèvecoeur had reworked and authorized.

If we can accept that the content and sequence of *Letters* is neither arbitrary nor primarily a result of editorial manipulation contrary to Crèvecoeur's intent, then, the next question to consider is what interpretive strategies we can derive from a consideration of the possible generic models for this structured, literary work. Here, indeed, is the point where readers are best served by moving away from those narrow readings of *Letters* as either Tory or Revolutionary propaganda toward an appreciation of the work's aesthetic richness and complexity. The choice to rework his sketches as "letters" situates Crèvecoeur's book in relation to two Enlightenment-era genres—the philosophical novel that grew out of the correspondence networks of the early French Enlightenment and the political journalism and pamphleteering of the eighteenth-century Anglo-American Whigs. Each of these generic models would have been meaningful to English *and* French readers of the time, and both intersect with one another.

As a literary form, the philosophical novel must be understood against the background of the emergence of the ideology of "Enlightenment" in Europe. The appearance of a cosmopolitan republic of letters can be traced to the late seventeenth century, when an ideal of international intellectual cooperation began to take shape both in England and on the Continent. The specific French context of this movement may be particularly helpful in understanding Crèvecoeur's use of an epistolary form for his first book. Two key technologies (the printing press and the postal system) were central to the development of the modern public sphere as a zone in which "private persons learned to use their reason publicly" (Goodman 1994, 15). First, the emergence of printing as a trade not entirely controlled by government censors enabled the print shop to emerge as an intellectual center and place of sociability. In a related development, the creation of the public postal service helped to translate the social exchanges of ideas in the print shops into a broader system of epistolary exchange. Thinkers both inside and outside of national borders began to see the use of letters as a means of expanding the body of knowledge to be a duty. Such a project, driven by a new emphasis on the circulation of empirical observations of nature, was central to the Enlightenment. These networks, in turn, helped drive the development of a range of new public, literary modes. By the early eighteenth century, the philosophes in France (like leading thinkers elsewhere throughout Europe and England) transformed their earlier (semiprivate) epistolary exchanges into public literary texts. Rather than just writing letters to one another, in other words, citizens of the emerging republic of letters "deployed an epistolary genre in the public sphere" (Goodman 1994, 137). Gazettes, newspapers, and pamphlets were one form of this deployment, of course. Another was the emergence of the literary genre now sometimes referred to as the philosophical novel.

Practiced by figures ranging from Montesquieu to Voltaire, the philosophical novel combines some of the existing conventions of travel writing with the spirit of epistolary exchanges of Enlightenment intellectuals. The result is a form of fictionalized narrative replete with possibilities for social commentary and scientific reflection. Writers working in this genre typically developed a fictional correspondent (or correspondents) whose letters could comment on a wide range of social and political issues. In Montesquieu's *Persian Letters,* for example, two travelers from the Ottoman Empire record their impressions of European politics, manners, religion, technology, and fashion in a series of epistles home. Through the invented personae of these two outsiders, of course, Montesquieu is able to offer his own commentary, both appreciative and critical, on European culture (Montesquieu 1721). The technique of fictional epistolarity, then, enables a kind of detached, scientific objectivity sometimes bordering on satiric irony. Epistolary narration, in this respect, also encourages the kind of active, critical reading desired by many Enlightenment thinkers. (As Voltaire would write in the preface to his 1764 *Dictionnaire Philosophique,* "the most useful books are those in which the readers themselves supply the meaning" [quoted in Voltaire 1994, xxiv].) Finally, the fictional progression of these letter writers on their travels creates a kind of narrative energy in the form of an episodic plot. Indeed, this is what encouraged Montesquieu himself to see his work as a kind of novel, a nebulous form just emerging itself at this time.

Centered on the travels of the fictional Farmer James throughout the colonies, the narrative arc of *Letters from an American Farmer* would appear to reflect

Crèvecoeur's familiarity with works such as *Persian Letters*. Another example of the eighteenth-century philosophical novel that seems equally likely to have influenced Crèvecoeur is Voltaire's *Lettres Philosophiques* (1734), first published in English as *Letters Concerning the English Nation* (1733). The popular English edition of this work went through fourteen printings during the eighteenth century. (Voltaire's fame as the embodiment of the spirit of Enlightenment also renders his work as a likely model.) At the textual level, there are numerous suggestive parallels between Voltaire's work and *Letters from an American Farmer*. Voltaire's decision to write many of these letters first in English reflects his experimentation with the persona of an English author and desire to cultivate a British readership (Voltaire 1994, ix). This move may have helped inspire Crèvecoeur in his creation of James as the narrator of *Letters* and in his initial literary foray before the English public. In terms of content, too, Voltaire's *Lettres* parallel Crèvecoeur's in striking ways. Voltaire's choice to open his work with a series of pieces on the Quakers echoes Crèvecoeur's considerable attention to the American Quakers in the letters on Nantucket (Crèvecouer 1995). Most significant, perhaps, may be the political emphasis of Voltaire's work. *Lettres Philosophiques* offers readers an early, highly influential history of the Enlightenment, one locating this movement largely as a product of the intellectual history of English Whigs. The heroes of Voltaire's text are Francis Bacon, John Locke, and Isaac Newton, individuals whose scientific daring would see its literary culmination in the satirical assaults of the political Whigs on the administration of Walpole. (Indeed, Voltaire concludes his work praising the satirical literature of Augustan England.) If the Anglophilia of Voltaire's epistolary work partly reflects his anticlerical bias and respect for the emerging British tradition of secularism and toleration, then it also represents a move to locate the crucial political advancements of the early Enlightenment on English soil. It is difficult to avoid thinking of this earlier text as a model for Crèvecoeur's celebrations of the enlightened justice of the English political system taken root in America (the place that, for many Enlightenment thinkers, represented a great laboratory for experiments in the possibilities of human reason).

The invocation of the Whig hagiography running through *Lettres Philosophiques* here is intended to draw attention to another group of epistolary texts that offer a crucial context for reading Crèvecoeur—the political journalism produced by the Anglo-American Whigs throughout the eighteenth century. The most famous "Letters" written by Englishmen during this time were Trenchard and Gordon's *Cato's Letters* (Hamowy 1995). While the republican rhetoric used in these pieces had its particular, partisan origins in the Exclusion Crisis in England during the 1680s, by the 1720s, when the first letters signed by "Cato" appeared in the *London Journal*, Whig political writing had evolved into a fairly complex synthesis of ideas regarding individual sovereignty, governance by consent, and the importance of civic virtue and sentiment in checking self-interest. John Locke's political theories (developed in his *Second Treatise of Government*) and the moral philosophy and discourse of sociability of Locke's student, Lord Shaftesbury (developed in his *Characteristicks*), provided the foundation for early eighteenth-century Whiggism, which would circulate and evolve in a transatlantic context throughout the period (Locke 1988; Shaftesbury 1999). Both Addison's play *Cato* and *Cato's Letters* were among the most widely read works in the colonies [Ellison 1999]. By the time of the American Revolution, of course, the Catonic model had been picked up by a wide variety of colonial writers on both sides of the political conflict with Parliament.

John Dickinson's *Letters from a Farmer in Pennsylvania*, widely read in the colonies, would likely have been familiar to Crèvecoeur. Dickinson's epistolary essays draw widely on its author's knowledge of Anglo-American law and the liberal political theory of the time, which centered on the idea of inalienable, individual property rights (Dickinson 1768). At the same time, Dickinson develops the idea of the Pennsylvania Farmer as an ideal figure through which he might explore the tensions and ambiguities of the contemporary political situation. Dickinson's Farmer crystallizes the Enlightenment belief that "the proper education and free exercise of the right of property will produce independence and tranquility of mind" (Ferguson 1997, 100). What prevents the realization of this promise in *Letters from a Farmer in Pennsylvania* is the assault on the rights of colonial Englishmen by Parliament and the attendant political confusion.

The transatlantic Whig discourse that has been sketched very briefly here arguably exerted an influence on Crèvecoeur's work at least as strong as that of the philosophical novels of the French philosophes. Like writers such as Trenchard, Gordon, and Dickinson, Crèvecoeur shares an abiding interest in the political theory of liberal subjectivity (centered on the image of possessive individuals and their inalienable rights) and a broadly contractarian view of civil society and government. He also shares, with Dickinson in particular, the tendency to see in the American an ideal image of the liberal subject who can be usefully studied and discussed (in the true enlightenment spirit) as a way of testing and exploring the political ideas and aspirations of the age. All these elements represent strong thematic threads running throughout the text of *Letters from an American Farmer*. Finally, the transformation of epistolary form into a broadly targeted political discourse highlights a final innovation in Crèvecoeur's work. (Trenchard and Gordon were journalists, after all, not philosophers.) While Letter 1 of *Letters from an American Farmer* creates the fiction of a genteel European correspondent for James (Mr. F. B.), Crèvecoeur's Farmer represents a decidedly demotic letter writer. Indeed, James and his wife (in consultation with their minister) have an extended debate in that introductory letter regarding the propriety of an ordinary man like himself engaging in such literary and philosophical pursuits. Clearly, James is a man of the people (a term, admittedly, defined more narrowly in the context of eighteenth-century republicanism than today). And in this respect, we can see Crèvecoeur combining in *Letters* elements of the epistolary discourses of the French Enlightenment and Anglo-American political writing. Like the Anglo-American Whigs, he cultivates a literary voice centered in liberal republicanism and targets an audience much broader than the scientific elite. In his somewhat ironic detachment from the subjects explored in *Letters,* however, Crèvecoeur more closely resembles the French philosophes. If Trenchard and Gordon use Cato as a persona through which to aggressively advocate a republican agenda, celebrate Roman-style virtue, and inveigh against public corruption, Crèvecoeur uses Farmer James as a more detached vehicle for exploring many of these ideas. Unwilling, perhaps, to take a strong stand in many of the debates of his time, Crèvecoeur chooses instead to use the form of epistolary narrative in the manner of a philosophical questioner.

A Reading of *Letters*: Crèvecoeur as Transatlantic Philosopher

Having established at least some of the biographical and literary contexts for *Letters,* we are left to turn to a more developed interpretation of the text. A useful opening question in this inquiry would be the following: What is the problem that Crèvecoeur's politically inflected philosophical novel sets out to explore? There are, admittedly, many potential answers to this, but two particular ones seem persuasive. The manifest central theme of *Letters,* of course, is to define America through the portrayal of the American. In developing this theme, Crèvecoeur draws heavily on two transatlantic discourses and their related models of identity: the legal model of possessive individualism central to eighteenth-century legal and political theory and the idea of the feeling subject, a model of human psychology derived from moral philosophy and aesthetics. The central problem posed by *Letters* seems to be the viability of personal and national self-definition in terms of either of these models of self. The subtle ironies (and not so subtle contradictions) woven throughout Crèvecoeur's text make it difficult to either choose or reject one or the other. Instead, the plot of *Letters* dramatizes the messy complications encountered when the theoretical constructions of the Enlightenment (like the idealized liberal subject or the man of feeling) confront real-world challenges (like factionalism and slavery).

There are significant ironic elements in *Letters from an American Farmer.* This claim is based on the idea that James is an unreliable narrator, a facet of the text central to Crèvecoeur's creation of a tone of philosophical detachment in his work. Evidence for this assessment of James can be found throughout the work, in the consistent pattern of contradictory statements that are made by the American Farmer. A particularly strong series of examples appear in his treatment of Quaker society in Letters iv through viii. We should recall that Quakerism, as a political system, had been effectively discredited in the American colonies by the 1770s. The failure of the Quaker-dominated government of Pennsylvania in the early and midcentury to handle violent conflict between English settlers and Indians on the frontier (and their subsequent abdication of governmental offices during the 1750s) would have rendered Quakerism a highly questionable model of good governance for Crèvecoeur's readers. In such a context, then, James's enthusiastic praise of Quaker Nantucket's commitment to the noncoercive resolution of conflict creates considerable ironic distance between Crèvecoeur's narrator and his readers. Admiring the fact that "friends compose two-thirds of the magistracy of this island," James stresses that "with all this apparatus of law, its coercive powers are seldom wanted or required." This miraculous social harmony in Nantucket seems overstated, however; it can be attributed as much to the fact that the island is typically devoid of inhabitants (with the majority frequently abroad on whaling voyages) as to its citizens' ability to "enjoy a system of rational laws founded on perfect freedom" (Crèvecoeur 1981, 124, 109). Frequently employing this kind of rhetoric, James comes across throughout the Nantucket letters as either hopelessly naive or willfully blind to the contradictory or partial nature of his own observations.

His commentary on the whaling voyages that undergird the island's prosperity particularly highlight the questionable nature of James's philosophizing. Wanting to emphasize the apotheosis of freeholding virtue in Nantucket, he refers to its Quaker inhabitants as the "farmers of the sea" and their settlement as "truly and literally . . . a pastorale one." At the same time, however, he notes the barrenness of the island's soil, the unpleasant smells produced by its chief commercial product (whale oil), the ongoing presence of the poor, and the puzzling disappearance of the original Indian inhabitants (owing to the introduction of whiskey and smallpox). Later, employing the hive metaphor for society made popular by Bernard Mandeville in *Fable of the Bees,* James marvels at the way Nantucket "constantly sends out swarms, as industrious as themselves yet always remains full without having any useless drones," yet in the very next paragraph, he confesses that "many die poor" (Crèvecoeur 1981, 113, 148–149).

These few examples reveal a pattern of inconsistency running throughout *Letters.* The most important, interpretive issue to consider in this context, then, is the rhetorical function of this manner of writing. Arguably, a chief result of these inconsistencies and contradictions (and the ironic effects they produce) is to shift the reader's interpretive focus away from assessments of the actual conditions of this new society that James presents us with and toward, instead, assessments of the discourses through which James constructs his own view of America. James and his American ways of thinking, in other words, become the real focus of the text.

If James and his own modes of discourse emerge as the real subject of *Letters,* then, the first major issue foregrounded in the text involves the theoretical connections between the American system of husbandry and the model of legal subjectivity—possessive individualism—that grounds eighteenth-century social contract theory or the political theory of liberalism. Several critics have located *Letters* within the literary tradition of the georgic, drawing close attention to James's depiction as an idealized farmer. One reading is particularly useful in this respect, for he situates this tradition of colonial writing to which Crèvecoeur belongs against the background of contemporary debates regarding the nature of the American agrarian economy and the ideals of republican virtue (Sweet 2002). And yet, even in light of these connections, we should be careful not to overstate the classical dimensions of Crèvecoeur's representations of farm life. James's explicit observation in Letter III that "men are like plants: the goodness and flavor of the fruit proceeds from the peculiar soil and exposition in which they grow" is probably as unambiguous a statement of faith in the virtue of the land as is available in eighteenth-century letters. It feels like something out of Virgil. Nevertheless, it is striking to note how little *Letters* dwells on actually depicting the bucolic or on the glorious work of farming itself, the way Virgil's *Georgics* do. This fact may lead us to conclude that, even more than the classical literary ideal of *ponos*—or virtuous labor—James embodies what has been called the freehold concept, a political idea with specific relevance for eighteenth-century readers.

Early in Letter II, James offers the following, suggestive comment regarding the relationship between his sense of political identity and his possession of farmland: "The instant I enter on my land the bright idea of property, of exclusive right, of independence, exalts my mind. Precious soil, I say to myself, by what singular custom of law is it that thou wast made to constitute the riches of the freeholder. What should we American farmers be without the distinct possession of the soil" (Crèvecoeur 1981, 54).

Crèvecoeur's choice of language here is quite precise, for it places James firmly in step with some of the core assumptions of Anglo-American liberalism of his day. Connecting the idea of liberty with exclusive property rights is, of course, a hallmark of eighteenth-century social contract theory (articulated most influentially by John Locke) and also of a wide range of literary representations of the freeholder. The influential English jurist William Blackstone provides a useful touchstone for exploring this link. In the first volume of his *Commentaries on the Laws of England*, Blackstone, drawing explicitly on Locke, stresses the absolute, natural rights of Englishmen to life, liberty, and property. Echoing the Whig rhetoric that so influenced the American revolutionaries, Blackstone also stresses that the legitimacy of government is based on its commitment to protecting those rights. This premise (the idea that autonomous individuals in a state of nature come together to constitute a society and government that can protect essential property rights), of course, is the core principle of social contract theory. In the second volume of *Commentaries*, Blackstone further develops the connection between land, liberty, and the liberal ideal of self-possession by noting that an "estate of freehold" (a condition of exclusive title to land, or "real estate") represents "property in its highest degree" (Blackstone 1979, 104–105). This legal maxim reinforced for many colonists the already potent imaginative link between the agrarian ideal of freeholding and liberty. While it would be false to say that, in a legal sense, one is not truly a free man unless one is a freeholder, in the popular imagination and much of the political rhetoric of American Revolutionaries such a connection seemed both powerful and essential.

The bond between Crèvecoeur's farmer, the idea of exclusive property right, and the image of the freeholder is a particularly powerful one. At its root, freeholding can be characterized by three main propositions: every man has a natural right to own land; through individual ownership of land a man achieves self-fulfillment and social status; civil society and government function primarily to ensure the "uninhibited development of the farmer" (Eisinger 1947, 44–47). In the specific context of a pre-dominantly agrarian society (like eighteenth-century colonial America), freeholding thus embodies the fundamental principles of Locke's theory of civil government—the natural right to property; the link between political identity, property, and private interest; and the idea that government is constituted to protect property rights. Crèvecoeur's language clearly and consistently invokes this constellation of ideas. Indeed, later in the same section of Letter II cited earlier, James suggestively employs the free-holding ideal to reflect on the way that private landownership fosters political status: "This formerly rude soil has been converted by my father into a pleasant farm, and in return, it has established our rights; on it is founded our rank, our freedom, our power as citizens, and our importance as inhabitants of such a district" (Crèvecoeur 1981, 54). More than just an articulation of James's commitment to an agrarian ideal, such lines demonstrate the way such a commitment marks him as the prototypical legal subject of liberal contractarianism as articulated by figures such as Blackstone and Locke. It is this particular emphasis on private property as the basis (and end) of the social order in Letters that locates it, not primarily alongside georgic literary models but rather as a manifestation of the modern, political idea of possessive individualism. It is this idea, then, that Crèvecoeur sets out to explore in the text of Letters.

One of the strategies that Crèvecoeur uses to explore colonial engagement with the liberal ideology of possessive individualism is to allow James to give voice to a range of contradictory attitudes regarding the Anglo-American legal system. These contradictions effectively expose some of James's own philosophical blind spots while also drawing attention to some of the potentially disruptive aspects of the enlightened political theory of the Revolutionary era. The explicit references to law we find in Letters fall into two broad categories, represented by the following two quotations:

> Here we have in some measure regained the ancient dignity of our species. Our laws are simple and just. We are a race of cultivators; our cultivation is unrestrained; and therefore everything is prosperous and flourishing. (Letter I)

> Lawyers are so numerous in all our populous towns that I am surprised they never thought before of establishing themselves here; they are plants that will grow in any soil that is cultivated by the hand of others; and once they have taken root, they will extinguish every other vegetable that grows around them. (Letter VII)

Farmer James tends to celebrate law while denigrating lawyers, an apparently simple dichotomy that exposes a range of larger issues. The positive treatments of law in *Letters* are generally tied to James's celebration of his freeholding ideals and liberties as a freeholder.

In contrast to such idealized pictures of the freeholding farmer, however, the lawyer becomes the ultimate villain and foil for James (Carlson 2003). Toward the end of Letter III, in fact, James explicitly compares himself to a generic lawyer, an individual whose legalism impedes the ability of American society to maintain the freeholding ideal: "Is it not better to contemplate under these humble roofs the rudiments of future wealth and population than to behold the accumulated bundles of litigious papers in the office of a lawyer?" Later in the text, in Letter VII ("Manners and Customs at Nantucket"), James provides even more detail of the evils he sees embodied in the legal profession and the law it represents. Lawyers, it would seem, are possessive individuals who acquire their fortunes through the misfortunes of their fellow citizens. That is to say, they "promote litigiousness and amass more wealth without labor than the most opulent farmer with all his toils" (Crèvecoeur 1981, 87, 152).

In offering such critical assessments of lawyers, of course, James is registering real contemporary anxieties regarding the rise to prominence of lawyers as a professional class in colonial America. Yet James's peculiar discussion of a tension between lawyer-centered law and constitutions also reveals issues much more central to Crèvecoeur's examination of the political discourse of the Revolutionary era. The following comment is, perhaps, one of the most suggestive along these lines in the entire text of *Letters:*

> They [lawyers] have so dextrously interwoven their doctrines and quirks with the laws of the land or rather they have become so necessary an evil in our present constitutions that it seems unavoidable and past all remedy. What a pity our forefathers, who happily extinguished so many fatal customs and expunged from their new government so many errors and abuses, both religious and civil, did not also prevent the introduction of a set of men so dangerous! In some provinces where every inhabitant is constantly employed in tilling and cultivating the earth, they are the only members of society who have any knowledge. Let these provinces attest to what iniquitous use they have made of that knowledge. (Crèvecoeur 1981, 152)

James is raising a fundamental question, one with which he wrestles throughout his entire correspondence with Mr. F. B. If lawyers and their knowledge are somehow separate from the constitutional law of the land, how can they be necessarily a part of the present constitutions? ("Constitution" in the context of pre-Revolutionary Anglo-American legal discourse refers to the entirety of the English common-law system—not to written text recording a framework of governance.) How, the reader is urged to wonder, can the Whig discourse of civic virtue counteract the corruption and unrestrained self-interest that is, in fact, structurally (indeed, organically) integral to modern liberal societies? Such a query echoes Mandeville's argument in

Fable of the Bees—that private vice is essential for the public welfare and integral to the creation of wealth in dynamic, modern societies (Mandeville 1997). If the constitutional law of Anglo-American liberalism is seen to undergird a perfected new society, though, how is one to deal with the fact that it produces both the American farmer and the American lawyer? Perhaps that law and that society are less perfect than was first assumed? When viewed in this light, the conflict that Crèvecoeur sets up in *Letters* between the indulgent laws that secure the position of the farmer and the litigiousness of the legal professional exposes a central ideological problem underlying the liberal political discourse of the eighteenth century: how can men advance republican liberties without unleashing destructive, Mandevillian self-interest? Initially, James espouses (in an admittedly idealistic form) the basic political principles of the colonial elites (largely men with legal training) who would lead the break away from England. There is a pronounced irony, of course, in the way that the outbreak of the war driven by these principles would subsequently so befuddle and dismay the American Farmer. (He records this distress at length in Letter XII.) In the end, however, this apparent irony may be precisely the philosophical point of *Letters*. In his presentation of the conflict between farmer and lawyer, Crèvecoeur stages a central political uncertainty troubling the heart of the American Enlightenment (the uncertainty that, more than anything else, would divide the colonists themselves into patriot and Tory camps). Even if the connection is lost on James, the reader may be able to see the divisive American lawyer as the mirror image of the virtuous American farmer. Both are products of the same system and the same set of political ideals. Confronting the implication of that fact requires a serious act of self-reflection, one worthy of an enlightened reader of the time.

If Crèvecoeur uses the persona of Farmer James to explore both the promise and the perils of Whig political discourse (the liberal tradition capable of buttressing both the wondrous liberties of the Anglo-American freeholder and the violence and upheaval of the American Revolution), he also seems intent on leading his readers to assess the potential of eighteenth-century moral philosophy as a source of alternative models of social cohesion and reform. Throughout the text of *Letters*, we should note that James is characterized not simply as a freeholding farmer but also as a farmer of feeling—the type of sentimental protagonist most clearly depicted for British readers in Henry Mackenzie's novel *The Man of Feeling* (1771). The period from the 1740s through the 1770s, we should recall, was the high point of sentimental discourse throughout Europe (with literary figures like Rousseau, Goethe, Richardson, Sterne, Sarah Fielding, and others leading the way). Eighteenth-century sentimental fiction, of course, was closely related to the moral philosophy of the age, which sought to develop a rational, scientific understanding of the human passions and emotions as a way of exploring issues of governance and ethics. The list of relevant philosophical thinkers here is an impressive one. For convenience's sake, let us consider a general overview of one particularly influential theory of moral sentiments, flowing through the work of David Hume and Adam Smith. For the theorization of sympathy and feeling we find in the work of these two men helps establish a broader context for what Crèvecoeur seems to be exploring through his depiction of the emotional makeup of his American farmer.

Adam Smith's delineation of the social and moral function of the passions in *Theory of Moral Sentiments* (1759) provides a sophisticated mechanism for balancing the desires of individuals with the well-being of the social order. Like many eighteenth-century theorists, Smith grounds his moral philosophy in self-interest, accepting the idea that human beings naturally seek to avoid pain and feel pleasure. The key element that transforms this mechanical, egotistic response into a moral force, however, is the human capacity for sympathy—the tendency to place oneself, imaginatively, in the situation of others (Smith 1976). Eighteenth-century philosophers like Smith and Hume, of course, tended to view such workings of sympathy as part of a broader epistemological theory. The widely accepted concept of associationism (the idea that the mind tends to move naturally from idea to idea, where those ideas relate to one another through resemblance, contiguity in time or space, or patterns of cause and effect) could explain the way humans both think *and* feel, in other words. In the realm of feeling, in particular, the mechanisms of associationism clarified why naturally self-centered beings like men needed to form lasting, stable, and morally structured communities. Sympathy, as Hume describes it in *A Treatise of Human Nature*, begins in our mind as an idea—the mental image produced by our perception of the situation of another. Rapidly, however, that idea or image is translated into the corresponding impression, and we begin to feel the experience of the other. The process does not end here, however. In the end, the correspondence between idea and impression (what Hume calls a "double-relation") creates a kind of circuit, encouraging the sympathizer to proceed to conceive of himself or herself as potentially being in the place of the "other" (Hume 1978).

The following may suffice as a simplified illustration of this associative process. Imagine seeing someone cruelly and unjustifiably struck. Our minds perceive this first as an idea, but that idea is rapidly translated into an impression. We flinch, having imaginatively come to share in the feeling experienced by the other. At this point, we conceive a new idea—the idea of ourselves in the situation of the other who has been struck. This idea ties us to the other in a relationship of sociability. We experience a moral drive to prevent that individual from being struck again (as we would seek to protect ourselves). Our selfish desire to avoid pain and seek pleasure has extended into a social passion. It must be granted, of course, that even the most optimistic thinkers of the time did not see this process in idealistic terms; there was broad recognition that these natural processes were tendencies, not iron laws of human nature. The capacity for sympathy was something that needed to be cultivated and encouraged, in other words, and even with such cultivation there would still be wicked souls denying the bonds of sociability in favor of narrowly defined desires. Such individuals, however, were seen to have failed to recognize that the greatest pleasure any individual can feel is the pleasure of "fellow feeling" (Smith 1976).

In general, eighteenth-century sentimental literature set out to explore the mechanisms and sociopolitical implications of this philosophical discourse of sympathy and moral sentiments. In such a context, then, Crèvecoeur's character-ization of James as a sentimental narrator should be seen as another manifestation of his broad engagement with Enlightenment thought. The fact that Letter II is titled "On the Situation, Feelings, and Pleasures of an American Farmer" provides a clear signal that James is positioning himself as a narrator seeking readerly sym-pathy. References both to "the train of . . . ideas" that followed the birth of his son and to "the various emotions of love, of gratitude, of conscious pride, which thrill in my heart and often overflow in involuntary tears" also highlight the fact that James understands the idyllic nature of his American situation quite literally as an outgrowth of the associative mechanisms of human sympathy. (Indeed, this may be where James pins most of his hopes regarding the possibility of restraining the forces of selfish interest embodied in the American lawyer.) In such a context, he eagerly accepts his imaginary reader's (Mr. F. B.) impulse to denominate him "the farmer of feeling" and goes on to write accordingly. In the end, though, what is the sympathetic reader to make of the fact that this paragon of sentimental experi-ence and sociability lives by himself, with little contact with the larger community? What are we to make of his confused, emotionally agitated response to the out-break of hostilities during the Revolution. In Letter XII James tells us quite explic-itly that "sentiment and feeling are the only guides I know," but those guides cannot explain the "convulsions" tearing apart the country (Crèvecoeur 1981, 53, 204). And what, finally, are we to make of James's contradictory and ineffective responses to the institution of slavery?

It is in the treatment of slavery, especially in Letter IX (Description of Charles-town), that we see Crèvecoeur's most sophisticated use of textual irony to interro-gate the assumptions of the Enlightenment-era cult of sentiment and to question its ability to check the failures of the modern liberal state. Careful readers will have noted well before this point in the book James's periodic, and troubling, references to his own possession of slaves on his Pennsylvania farm. Blithe assurances that his "Negroes are tolerably faithful and healthy" ring rather hollow, however, especially when juxtaposed to his enthusiastic praise of the "silken bands of mild government" that unite Americans into the "most perfect society now in the world." James's hy-pocrisy (or moral blindness, if one prefers) is exposed most dramatically, however, upon his visit to the South—a region, interestingly enough, that he describes as one where lawyers "have reached the *ne plus ultra* of worldly felicity" (Crèvecoeur 1981, 53, 167). The limitations of James's reliance on the discourse of moral sentiments is particularly apparent in perhaps the most iconic moment in *Letters*, the point in Letter IX when the American Farmer encounters a dying, gibbeted slave begging for a drink of water. For this encounter becomes both a clear test of James's personal capacity for sympathy and also, by extension, a political fable exposing the limita-tions of a politics of feeling to address injustice in the American republic.

James's discovery of the slave takes place at the end of his tour through Charles Town and its environs, a tour that produces in the feeling farmer a deep sense of "melancholy." Much of the narrative setup of the slave tableau is composed of a critical commentary on the luxury, aristocratic pretension, and corruption of the American South, traits from which the somewhat self-righteous James is eager to distance himself. It is no coincidence, of course, that the vices of Charles Town are precisely those designated by the American Whigs as those that led Britain to tyrannical treatment of its American subjects (transforming them from devoted children of the king into slaves of Parliament). In this context, though, James's discussion of northern slavery foregrounds the central hypocrisy of the liberal political discourse of the Revolutionary leaders. James confesses that "we have slaves likewise in our northern provinces," but follows up this admission with a remarkably feeble apologia. "I hope the time draws near when they will all be emancipated," he notes, "but how different their lot, how different their situation, in every possible respect! They enjoy as much liberty as their masters" (Crèvecoeur 1981, 177, 171). It is fairly easy at this point for an attentive reader to pinpoint the source of James's psychological discontent during his southern tour. A gentleman farmer himself, whose leisure depends in part upon the labor of his own slaves, James finds himself confronted with the possibility that the American ideals he embraces and advances in enthusiastic Whig rhetoric throughout his early letters are applied with partiality driven by selfish interest. It is here, of course, that the discourse of sympathy might be expected to intervene to put a check on that self-interest.

James's meeting with the gibbeted slave is set up, not surprisingly, in ambivalent terms; James is "leisurely travelling along" collecting specimens in the southern landscape before encountering a sight that "oppresses" his mind. The sound of "a few inarticulate monosyllables" coming from a cage hung nearby and covered with "large birds of prey" startles the farmer into action. His response ("actuated by an involuntary motion of my hands more than a design of my mind") is to fire a shot at the cage (Crèvecoeur 1981, 177–178). Only an accident prevents him from unwittingly killing a potential object of sympathy, then. James's musket ball drives off the birds, however, revealing a "Negro" covered with wounds and with his eyes pecked out, left to die. Immediately after the birds' departure, as James also notes, a swarm of insects swoops in to cover his body, feeding on his blood and flesh. Such a moment cries out to be read on two levels—both literally and as another political fable. Such images of insect "swarms" recur frequently throughout *Letters,* typically functioning as allusions to the Mandevillian trope for society developed in *The Fable of the Bees.*

The sight of the slave being eaten alive by insects, then, confronts James with both a powerful, visceral example of human cruelty and an allegorical depiction of a human society built on unchecked self-interest and thus willing to consume its own for the sake of gain. If ever there was a moment for the farmer of feeling to respond to the call of sympathy, then, this is it. But what is James's response? He feels something, no doubt, writing that "I found myself suddenly arrested by the power of affright and terror; my nerves were convulsed; I trembled; I stood motionless" (Crèvecoeur 1981, 178). Yet to what does this sublime feeling lead? Any impulse toward sympathetic identification with the slave gives way to paralyzing terror and revulsion. James confesses to wishing that he had a ball in his gun to dispatch the dying man; lacking this, he contents himself only with offering the slave a drink of water. (Why doesn't he simply reload the musket he had just fired?) Most damningly, though, James's subsequent actions evoke further questions for readers. Upon leaving the slave, he tells us, he continued on to the plantation of the slave's owner ("the house at which I intended to dine"), only to sit quietly and listen to the customary justifications of the "doctrine of slavery" and punishment of the man he had met. Especially in light of his earlier confessions regarding his own slave ownership, James's indication of his distaste for these arguments provides little mitigation for his refusal to act upon that distaste. He neither speaks out against southern slavery nor emancipates his own chattel. Perhaps his capacity to translate human sympathy into "social passions" has been undermined by his complicity in the system? Perhaps something is interfering with his ability to project himself into the situation of the "other"? Or perhaps sympathy does not function at all in the way the moral philosophers of the time posit? The reader is left at the end of Letter ix "oppressed" with his or her own disturbing reflections about these questions, and with a sense that the idealized American farmer has come up profoundly lacking at this crucial moment in his moral and political life. It is not so surprising to the reader, now, that James goes on to be unable to choose a side in the Revolution itself.

As in the case of his interrogation of liberal political theory, Crèvecoeur does not provide a clear answer to the problem surrounding slavery—questions that reveal the potential political and social limitations of the Enlightenment discourse of moral sentiments. What we can see in the fable of the gibbeted slave, instead, is a final example of Crèvecoeur's overall rhetorical strategy in *Letters from an American Farmer*, at least as I have presented it here. Throughout the text, by employing the narrative persona of Farmer James, Crèvecoeur forces readers to engage with a range of central philosophical and literary discourses of the Enlightenment. In all these engagements, though, Crèvecoeur's exploration of the problems and contradictions surrounding James do not reach toward larger conclusions. *Letters from an American Farmer* does not solve the problems of the American Enlightenment and the Revolution, in other words. Writing as a cosmopolitan philosophe, a citizen of the republic of letters, Crèvecoeur simply stages those problems. In doing so, Crèvecoeur, the author, invites the careful reader into a larger debate about the meaning and reach of many of the central ideas of his time, filtering those ideas through the carefully drawn figure of James, the narrator. Modern readers coming to *Letters* with this in mind will be astonished by the intellectual richness and artistic ingenuity of the work—complexities that were once concealed by limited assessments of the work as a naive historical document or a testament of American exceptionalism. What Crèvecoeur has accomplished in this most eighteenth-century of literary performances, then, is to provide an entry point into the conflicted ways that the American colonies struggled, within the philosophical framework of the transatlantic Enlightenment, to define themselves. With the exception, perhaps, of Benjamin Franklin's *Autobiography*, there may be no other single work that offers a better comprehensive introduction to the intellectual climate of the American founding. In this respect, even when viewed from the transatlantic perspective, *Letters* remains an American classic, well worthy of continued study for those seeking to understand the history and culture of the United States.

REFERENCES

Allen, Gay Wilson, and Roger Asselineau. 1987. *An American Farmer: The Life of St. John de Crèvecoeur.* New York: Viking Penguin.

Aubery, Pierre. 1978. St. John de Crèvecoeur: A Case in Literary Anglomania. *French Review* 51: 565–576.

Bewley, Marius. 1959. *The Eccentric Design.* New York: Columbia University Press.

Blackstone, William. [1765] 1979. *Commentaries on the Laws of England.* 4 vols. Reprint. Chicago: University of Chicago Press.

Carlson, David J. 2003. Farmer v. Lawyer: Crèvecoeur's *Letters* and the Liberal Subject. *Early American Literature* 38: 257–280.

Crèvecoeur, J. Hector St. John de. 1801. *Voyage dans la Haute Pensylvanie et dans l'État de New-York.* Paris: Maradan.

———. 1925. *Sketches of Eighteenth-Century America: More "Letters from an American Farmer" by St. John de Crèvecoeur,* edited by Henri L. Bourdin, Ralph Gabriel, and Stanley Williams. New Haven, CT: Yale University Press.

———. 1981. *Letters from an American Farmer and Sketches of Eighteenth-Century America,* edited by Albert E. Stone. New York: Penguin.

———. 1995. *More Letters from the American Farmer: An Edition of the Essays in English Left Unpublished by Crèvecoeur,* edited by Dennis Moore. Athens: University of Georgia Press.

Crèvecoeur, Robert de. 1883. *Saint John de Crèvecoeur: Sa Vie et Ses Ouvrages, 1735–1813.* Paris: Librarie des Bibliophiles.

Dickinson, John. 1768. *Letters from a Farmer in Pennsylvania, to the Inhabitants of the British Colonies.* Philadelphia: David Hall and William Sellers.

Eisinger, Chester E. 1947. The Freehold Concept in Eighteenth-Century American Letters. *William and Mary Quarterly,* 3rd ser., 4: 42–59.

Ellison, Julie. 1999. *Cato's Tears and the Making of Anglo-American Emotion.* Chicago: University of Chicago Press.

Ferguson, Robert A. 1997. *The American Enlightenment, 1750–1820.* Cambridge, MA: Harvard University Press.

Goodman, Dena. 1994. *The Letters of the Republic: A Cultural History of the French Enlightenment.* Ithaca, NY: Cornell University Press.

Hamowy, Ronald, ed. 1995. *Cato's Letters: or, Essays on Liberty, Civil and Religious, and Other Important Subjects,* by John Trenchard and Thomas Gordon. 4 vols. Indianapolis: Liberty Fund.

Hofstadter, Richard. 1971. *America at 1750: A Social Portrait.* New York: Vintage.

Hume, David. 1978. *A Treatise of Human Nature,* edited by L. A. Selby-Bigge and P. H. Nidditch. 2nd ed. Oxford: Clarendon.

Lawrence, D. H. 1923. *Studies in Classic American Literature.* New York: Selzer Press.

Locke, John. 1988. *Two Treatises of Government,* edited by Peter Laslett. Cambridge: Cambridge University Press.

Mandeville, Bernard. 1997. *The Fable of the Bees and Other Writings,* edited by E. J. Hundert. Cambridge, UK: Hackett.

Montesquieu, Charles de Secondat, Baron de. 1721. *Lettres Persanes.* 2 vols. [Amsterdam]: chez Pierre Marteau.

Pearce, Roy Harvey. 1953. *The Savages of America: A Study of the Indian and the Idea of Civilization.* Baltimore: Johns Hopkins University Press.

Philbrick, Thomas. 1970. *St. John de Crèvecoeur.* New York: Twayne.

Plumstead, A. W. 1977. Hector St. John de Crèvecoeur. In *American Literature, 1764–1789: The Revolutionary Years,* edited by Everett Emerson, 213–231. Madison: University of Wisconsin Press.

Rice, Howard C. 1934. The American Farmer's Letters, With a Checklist of the Different Editions. *Colophon* 18 (unpaginated).

Shaftesbury, Anthony Ashley Cooper. 1999. *Characteristicks of Men, Manners, Opinions, Times,* edited by Philip Ayres. 2 vols. Oxford: Clarendon.

Smith, Adam. 1976. *The Theory of Moral Sentiments,* edited by D. D. Raphael and A. L. Macfie. Oxford: Clarendon.

Stone, Albert E. 1962. Crèvecoeur's *Letters* and the Beginnings of American Literature. *Emory University Quarterly* 18: 197–213.

Sweet, Timothy. 2002. *American Georgics.* Philadelphia: University of Pennsylvania Press.

Traister, Bryce. 2002. Criminal Correspondence: Loyalism, Espionage and Crèvecoeur. *Early American Literature* 37: 469–496.

Voltaire. 1994. *Letters Concerning the English Nation,* edited by Nicholas Cronk. Oxford: Oxford University Press.

CHAPTER 25

....

HISTORY AS
LITERATURE

....

ED WHITE

What is the significance of early American historical writing, and for whom or what should this body of writing be important? Are these works relevant to the early American literary tradition, and if so how? Why are these works today so little known to readers? Traditionally, early historiography has been the domain of historians rather than a resource for literary critics. The preeminent historian J. Franklin Jameson, in a series of lectures in the 1880s (later published as *The History of Historical Writing in America*), staked the historians' claim in examining "the development of our science from its half-conscious infancy down to the present time." Winnowing the chaff of minor writers in his hunt for those "not . . . mentally annexed to Europe," he focused on those historians with "an original spirit," revealing the historiography in the making of a unique if still nebulous American tradition (Jameson 1961, 160, 162). But this tradition was one of "science," not of writing per se. Jameson confirmed the value of these works as historical documents in the series Original Narratives of Early American History. The progressive advancement of historical science also underlay many of the contributions to the thoughtful collections—*Historians of Nature* and *Man's Nature and Early Nationalist Historians*—edited almost a century later (Leder 1973), which are composed of biographical sketches of prominent practitioners of the craft. The focus on the individual intellectual career not only highlighted the relevance of local context but also provided a measuring tape for evaluating these writers' contributions toward "America's growing maturity" (Leder 1973, 11). Such scholarship, quite typical of the writing on early historiography, should remind us of the profoundly teleological vein of American scholarship, looking to the past to find the anticipated future. But such surveys of "pioneers" also reveal the proscribed value accorded these works. On the one hand, they constitute the archives of facts to which historians must still refer; on the other, they amount to archives of bigotries and factionalism to be carefully assessed for data of a different sort.

EARLY AMERICAN HISTORIOGRAPHY

Early American historiography has conventionally inspired what little interest it has as a troubled information bank for historians. Few studies have ventured assessments of the construction of a uniquely colonial historiographical practice, and rare are the attempts to link these works with more belletristic productions, save at the thematic or referential levels. Indeed, there is surprisingly little sense of what the overall canon is. Few works are easily accessible in modern print editions, and they are rarely anthologized. Scholars with a passing familiarity with Jeremy Belknap, Robert Beverley, and Cadwallader Colden may know only the names and may draw a blank stumbling across Ebenezer Hazard, Robert Proud, or William Stith. Those historians familiar to contemporary scholars are often better known for their more "literary" works; we know Hugh Henry Brackenridge for *Modern Chivalry,* not for *Incidents of the Insurrection in Western Pennsylvania,* and Mercy Otis Warren more for her plays than her history of the American Revolution. Likewise, assessments of eighteenth-century America's historical sensibilities tend to refer to the continental traditions of Machiavellis, Humes, and Gibbons, while paying scant attention to the crude historical productions of the colonies themselves.

This general air of embarrassment and disinterest has been confirmed recently in Jorge Cañizares-Esguerra's *How to Write the History of the New World: Histories, Epistemologies, and Identities in the Eighteenth-Century Atlantic World,* a fascinating survey of the debates of Spanish colonial historiography that passes over the historical writing of British North America, noting that "compared to the vast amounts of scholarship put forth by Spanish American Creoles, British colonial historiography appears negligible and derivative" (Cañizares-Esguerra 2001, 5). Unlike their trifling Anglo-American counterparts, Spanish colonial historians have engaged in far-reaching debates about historiographical epistemology, credibility, and authority, the value and meaning of Native American sources, and intellectual institution-building, eventually crafting historiographical programs more progressive and innovative than their northern European rivals. French and English historians, meanwhile, ignorantly devalued indigenous sources at the moment the intellectual hegemony of the Enlightenment era shifted in their direction. As for *their* New World counterparts, Cañizares-Esguerra has almost nothing to say; they barely deserve consideration as historians, for unlike their Latin American neighbors, they rarely played central roles in imperial scholarly, theological, or political debates.

This verdict about Anglo-American histories is salutary in light of the general drift of American exceptionalism, and is arguably correct in its basic claim for Anglo-America's relatively negligible impact in the Atlantic sphere. The historiography produced in eighteenth-century Anglo-America seems to have circulated narrowly and with little engagement with, or influence upon, international debates about historiography. The best known of these works—Jefferson's *Notes on the State of Virginia*—is perhaps the exception that proves the rule, and has more to do with Jefferson's interlocutors (François Marbois and Buffon) and his own fame than with any well-established intellectual tradition. More representative are William Byrd's two *Histories of the Dividing Line betwixt Virginia and North Carolina*, which remained unpublished, marginal productions from the colonial era (Bauer 2003, 198).

Yet if Cañizares-Esguerra helps us situate these works in their rather modest imperial context, his verdict of their derivative nature rushes too quickly to dismiss them. Marginality need not imply unoriginality, however epistemologically derivative these works may have been. We would do better to examine how these cramped historiographical projects sought to construct a local historical sensibility on the Atlantic periphery. Here a better guide would be J. G. A. Pocock, whose study of the great English historian Edward Gibbon, author of *The Decline and Fall of the Roman Empire*, suggests a method for approaching American historiography. Pocock argues that Enlightenment histories of the eighteenth century—he is speaking of Continental histories—were concerned above all with reconciling disparate modes of writing. Linking an earlier ecclesiastical history with the civil-institutional history of modern Europe, the chief concern was with the "movement through the 'Christian millenium' to 'Enlightened Europe'" or, to put it in different terms, with the "union . . . between the erudite or antiquarian scholarship derived from the Renaissance and the philosophical historiography we think of as Enlightened." Effecting this transition required recourse to "a third component of the historiographic package: that is to say, with narrative, meaning in the first place the classical narrative of the exemplary actions of leading figures, derived from the Greco-Roman model as interpreted by Renaissance humanists." But this integration of narratives through heroic figures unexpectedly metamorphosed into "a narrative . . . of systemic change," for the "foundations of macronarrative" had been "laid by the disputes of Christian and Latin Europe"—church fathers attempting to institute new church systems—which could then be finessed in various ways to connect with histories of civil society. A kind of secular translation of ecclesiastic history was achieved, though "its narrative structure is not very different from that of the historiography it sometimes claimed to replace" (Pocock 1999, 3, 5, 29–30).

While Pocock's analysis of Gibbon's context may seem remote in its particulars from Anglo-America, the contours of his analytic are suggestive. For writers in the colonies and later the United States faced homologous challenges. The colonial writer's earliest historical traditions were sometimes corporate, sometimes ecclesiastic, and sometimes municipal, and from such antiquarian origins they increasingly sought to construct histories of provincial sovereignties. For their American successors, the problem was compounded—constructing a national history from colonial building blocks. Likewise, these historians had inherited a heroic narrative tradition, albeit of exploration, Indian wars, and entrepreneurship. Added to these ingredients were the ostensibly prehistorical traditions of ethnographic and natural writing. One could almost suggest that the crucial literary problem was a formal one—piecing together these disparate elements—although internal and external political conflicts likewise meant that historical writing often had to achieve the balance required of all hegemonic writing, between polemic and integration.

With Pocock's general framework in mind, we can also clarify, at the outset, the well-known cliché that the providential histories of the seventeenth century gradually yielded to the enlightened historiography of the eighteenth. This periodization misleads in basic ways, implying as it does a gradual progression from a more religious *mentalité* to a more secular successor. In fact, providential historiography maintained its influence into the eighteenth century, even if its theological inflections became less pronounced. Our sense that ostensibly secular historiography did not flourish earlier has as much to do with the uneven and variegated history of colonization—Pennsylvania's significant settlement commencing at the end of the seventeenth century, for instance—as with the similarly uneven emergence of colonial printing. Printing was fostered, centralized, and carefully regulated in New England through much of the seventeenth century and found numerous authors among its clerical class; the developing societies and economies to the south were much less favorable to such intellectual activity, with the slight exception of Virginia (Amory and Hall 2000). The apparent transition to secular history is therefore better understood as a marker of nonsynchronicity—in colonization, printing, and historical writing itself.

The disjunction may be illustrated with a few examples from the mid–eighteenth century. In New England, the prolific Reverend Thomas Prince published the first volume of *A Chronological History of New England in the Form of Annals* in 1736, also bringing to public eyes *A Brief History of the Pequot War,* a providential account of the anti-Pequot expedition of 1637 penned by Captain John Mason sometime in the 1670s. Prince's dedicatory foreword praised "the worthy Fathers of these Plantations" for "their *great Concern* that the same Vital and Pure Christianity and Liberty both *Civil* and *Ecclesiastical*" (Prince 1736, sig. A1ᵛ). The same blending of historiographical modes was evident throughout the narration, which simultaneously drew on Bradford and other Puritan authorities to present legal and economic details with the occasional Christian commentary. At about the same time, to the south, James Oglethorpe published his *New and Accurate Account of the Provinces of South-Carolina and Georgia* (1732), a promotional pamphlet surveying rights of settlement, soil and climate, and the plan to settle poor debtors in the colony (Oglethorpe 1994). Is Oglethorpe's a more modern and secular work, as compared with Prince's providential history? One might argue that Oglethorpe's project was more religiously motivated than Prince's. The former's association with Thomas Bray's Society for the Propagation of the Gospel in Foreign Parts played a significant role in his plans for a charity colony, though this impulse was rarely evident in his *Account;* though the latter's work seems more profoundly pious to modern eyes, Prince's aim was the rational coordination of religiously inflected sources, much as his younger brother Nathan pursued in *The Constitution and Government of Harvard College* (1742).

The religious-secular distinction does not take us very far, and barely begins to illuminate the two projects in question. Oglethorpe's work belongs to a tradition of promotional tracts extending back to the early seventeenth century, while Prince's work demonstrates a processing of the archives that rarely occurred before the third or fourth generation of settlement. In sum, providential historiography is less the sign of an era than a mode of writing that found diverse expression under particular social and literary conditions. The religious codification of New England's history did not so much yield to an emerging secular worldview, but rather persisted to be reworked in the documentary record, and in a culture in which clergy and historians were members of the same intellectual class. Secular and pious histories alike faced the problems outlined by Pocock, of coordinating divergent historical sources for the colonial and, later, national contexts. To approach the problem of historical writing and its significance for early American writing, then, we may begin with a clear catalog of what constituted the historiography of the period. Any survey will risk oversimplification and schematism, but the aim of the following pages is to outline four modes of historical writing that predominated in the period.

Provincial Histories

Traditionally the most lauded of the historical works, these histories of particular colonies (and, later, states) appeared with regularity throughout the eighteenth century. Robert Beverley's *The History of the Present State of Virginia* (1705, rev. ed. 1722) was followed by William Stith's *The History of the First Discovery and Settlement of Virginia* (1747) and Thomas Jefferson's *Notes on the State of Virginia* (1785). New England witnessed the publication of Thomas Foxcraft's *Observations, Historical and Practical, on the Rise and Primitive State of New-England* (1730), Thomas Prince's *A Chronological History of New England in the Form of Annals* (1736–1755), John Callender's *An Historical Discourse on the Civil and Religious Affairs of the*

Colony of Rhode-Island and Providence Plantations (1739), Thomas Hutchinson's *The History of the Colony of Massachusetts Bay* (1764), Samuel Peters's *A General History of Connecticut* (1781), Jeremy Belknap's *The History of New Hampshire* (1784), Samuel Williams's *The Natural and Civil History of Vermont* (1794), James Sullivan's *The History of the District of Maine* (1795), Benjamin Trumbull's *A Complete History of Connecticut* (1797), and Hannah Adams's *A Summary History of New England* (1799). Elsewhere saw the appearance of William Smith's *The History of the Province of New York* (1757), Samuel Smith's *The History of the Colony of Nova-Caesaria, or New-Jersey* (1765), Alexander Hewat's *An Historical Account of the Rise and Progress of the Colonies of South Carolina and Georgia* (1779), David Ramsay's *History of the Revolution of South-Carolina* (1785), and Robert Proud's *The History of Pennsylvania* (1797).

It will come as little surprise that all the male authors in this catalog were elites. Most attended (or in some cases led) the top educational institutions, including William and Mary (Jefferson, Stith), Yale (Peters, W. Smith, Trumbull), Harvard (Belknap, Callender, Foxcraft, Hutchinson, Prince, Williams), and the College of New Jersey (Ramsay). Hewat was educated at Edinburgh, while Beverley received an English education, as befitting a son of the plantocracy. (The two Quakers, Proud and S. Smith, were more modestly educated; Irish immigrant Sullivan studied under a lawyer, while Hannah Adams was the self-educated daughter of a failed bookseller.) They predictably came, as well, from the "liberal professions." Many historians, particularly in New England, came from the clergy (Belknap, Callender, Foxcraft, Peters, Prince, Trumbull, and Williams, but also Hewat in the South), confirming not only that profession's central role in providing intellectuals for those colonies' ruling classes, but also a facility with the ecclesiastic mode of history. Several writers were prominent in the contiguous fields of education (Proud, Stith) and medicine (Ramsay), though more devoted themselves to political careers with varying degrees of success; three served as governors (Hutchinson and Sullivan in Massachusetts, Jefferson in Virginia), while two circulated among oppositional factions (Beverley in Virginia, W. Smith in New York). Such careers often gave these authors access to the documentary archive from which histories were composed. A good number of those who lived to see the Revolution were Loyalists (Hewat, Hutchinson, S. Peters, Proud, W. Smith), their histories in most cases confirming their political views. William Smith's history of New York had been written in the 1750s; Hewat's stance forced him to publish anonymously, while Proud waited decades to publish his history of Pennsylvania. Several others served the Revolutionary effort in political positions (Jefferson, Ramsay, and Sullivan serving in the Continental Congress) or in the military, Belknap and Trumbull both serving as chaplains (Garraty and Carnes 1999; Levernier and Wilmes 1983; Matthew and Harrison 2004).

In most instances, provincial historiography was driven by the need to compile the archives, with charters, letters, and laws either reproduced in the text or as appendices; as such these works often read more like annals or chronicles than analytical narratives. But what most unifies these authors is their legalistic orientation, whereby they traced and adjudicated past, present, and potentially future conflicts, whether in individual colonies or within the larger imperial context. It was this orientation that unites the lawyer-politicians of the South with the clergy of the North; from the earliest years, the latter constituted something of a class of *avocats manqués,* and as historians these professionals were clarifying the legal foundations for provincial rule, economic exchange, and imperial management. Hannah Adams's late arrival to this group indicates the challenges for the outsider pursuing the provincial history, as well as an expansion of audience. Her work was only possible once considerable documentation and interpretation were already available, its preface announcing the debt to Belknap, Sullivan, Trumbull, and Williams and others. If the earliest provincial histories had been works for the ruling class, Adams by contrast found her audience in those eager to "peruse a sketch of American affairs, before they have time or ability to acquire more enlarged knowledge" (Adams 1799, 1).

Microhistories

Narrower in scope than the provincial histories, microhistories were nonetheless similarly dependent on archival access. They frequently focused on long-established, religiously affiliated institutions, such as the histories of Harvard (by Nathan Prince, 1742), Dartmouth (by Eleazar Wheelock, 1763), and Yale (by Thomas Clap, 1766), as well as Morgan Edwards's *Material Towards a History of the American Baptists* (1770, 1792) and Isaac Backus's *Church History of New England* (1796), likewise focused on the Baptist movement. One could also include under this heading a series of histories of dissent or outright insurrectionary actions; these were often triggered by conflicts over economic, judicial, or military institutions that authors took pains to explain and historicize. These would include John Peter Zenger's *Brief Narrative of the Case and Tryal of John Peter Zenger* (1736), Daniel Horsmanden's *A Journal of the Proceedings in the Detection of the Conspiracy Formed by Some White People, in Conjunction with Negro and Other Slaves* (1744), and William Smith's *A Brief View of the Conduct of Pennsylvania for the Year 1755* (1756), as well as Benjamin Franklin's "Narrative of the Late Massacres" (1764), Herman Husband's account of the North Carolina Regulation (1770), George Minot's 1788 account of Shays' Rebellion, and longer but still pamphlet-like accounts of the Whiskey Rebellion by Hugh Henry Brackenridge and William Findley (1796). Brackenridge also compiled accounts of soldiers (including several captivity narratives), published as *Narratives of a Late Expedition Against the Indians* (1783). Jonathan Edwards's *A Faithful Narrative of the Surprising Work of God* (1737), a survey of the Great Awakening in the Connecticut Valley, perhaps belongs in this group as well: a situational history determined to critique popular forms of dissent and reassert a unifying authority. One might include, too, works like Mathew Carey's *A Short Account of the Malignant Fever* (1793), which famously prompted one of the first African American historical pamphlets, Richard Allen and Absalom Jones's *A Narrative of the Proceedings of the Black People, During the Late Awful Calamity in Philadelphia* (1794). One may fairly consider such micro-histories as auxiliaries to the provincial histories; indeed, they may be viewed as historiographical luxuries of a sort rarely produced outside of the more populated provinces. The exception among these titles is Husband's "An Impartial Relation of the First Rise and Cause of the Recent Differences in Publick Affairs," taking the neglected North Carolina context as its subject; it is worth noting, however, that this pamphlet's publication location remains unknown, and that Husband hailed from a slaveholding family in Cecil County, Maryland, having migrated into the region from the North (Jones 1982; Levernier and Wilmes 1983).

Typically authoritative in their condemnations or corrections of popular action or, conversely, in their celebration of established institutions, the authors of these works often came from a similar class background as the provincial historians. Indeed, many of the provincial historians engaged in this kind of microhistoriography. William Smith was typical in writing several "annual" pamphlets recounting the events of the preceding year, not to mention occasional pieces linked to charitable organizations and colleges; Belknap and other abolitionists wrote shorter pieces on the institution of slavery in their respective areas; and Trumbull wrote a defense of Connecticut's settlements in the Wyoming Valley during the Yankee-Pennamite controversy. Yet the microhistorians were a broader class of writers, more committed to situational analyses and journalistic or clerical interventions than to projects of scholarly syntheses; the inclusion here of such prominent writers as Edwards and Franklin attests to this different mode of writing. Given the relative absence of populist writers—Husband's defense of the Regulators, and Allen and Jones's defense of Philadelphia's African American population, stand almost alone—readers are justified in asking to whom these microhistories were responding. They are best viewed as published attempts to provide counternarratives to word-of-mouth or less-polished newspaper accounts, often consolidating a hegemonic interpretation of a troubling popular phenomenon; this is true from Edwards and Horsmanden to Franklin and Minot. Again, the legalistic orientation is telling: if the provincial historians were preparing works akin to common-law commentaries—local Blackstones, as it were—the microhistorians were in some sense trying (or literally describing, as with Zenger and Horsmanden) individual cases. Once again, Husband's pamphlet offers diagnostic insights into the genre: its rambling, reactive structure, alternating between official documents and decrees and a running polemical commentary and critique (complete with popular sermons), reads like a plebeian attempt to counter legal discourse, and speaks to the difficulties faced in popular appropriations of this genre. Even at the level of the pamphlet, it is clear that the

Regulators were reacting to a hegemonic interpretation of events, pitting a "natural law" against executive decrees.

Natural and "Indian" Histories

Among this group we may include John Lawson's *A New Voyage to Carolina* (1709), Mark Catesby's *The Natural History of Carolina, Florida and the Bahama Islands* (1731–1747), John Bartram's *Observations . . . Made in Travels from Pensilvania to Onondago, Oswego, and the Lake Ontario in Canada* (1751), John Filson's *The Discovery, Settlement, and Present State of Kentucke* (1784), Thomas Hutchins's *An Historical Narrative and Topographical Description of Louisiana, and West-Florida* (1784), William Bartram's *Travels* (1791), and Gilbert Imlay's *A Topographical Description of the Western Territory of North America* (1793), as well as the various geographic texts published by Jedidiah Morse and his associates. One might also add Le Page du Pratz's *Histoire de la Louisiane,* published in France in 1758; the work was abridged, altered, and translated for an English edition in 1763 and was to become influential in the post-Revolutionary period of westward expansion. As Filson's work makes evident, such writing perpetuated modes established in the earliest years of colonization; his account of Kentucky included surveys of rivers, soil, "quadrupeds," inhabitants, and curiosities, before turning to "Rights of Land," "Trade," and other practical matters surrounding attraction and settlement. Filson's work also included several appendices, including a heroic narrative of Daniel Boone and "An Account of the Indian Nations," reminding us of the ideological linkage between flora and fauna and indigenous peoples for Anglo-American writers (Filson 1784). Thus we might include here James Adair's admittedly exceptional *History of the American Indians* (1775) and a number of northeastern works slightly more remote from the conventions of natural history, including Samuel Penhallow's vitriolic *History of the Wars of New-England with the Eastern Indians* (1726), Cadwallader Colden's more diplomatically oriented *A History of the Five Indian Nations* (1727, rev. ed. 1747), and Daniel Gookin's *Historical Collections of the Indians in New England* (1792).

With the exception of the New England surveys of Indians—frequently military in their orientation—these works typically focused on less populated regions of the greater southwest (Adair, Catesby, Filson, Hutchins, Lawson) or the northern interior (J. Bartram, Colden, Imlay). Perhaps not surprisingly, several of these authors (Adair, Catesby, Lawson) were English-born and thus relatively removed from the intricacies of colonial politics; the Bartrams' Quaker background may have had a similar distancing effect, as did Adair's and Hutchins's frontier service to Great Britain during the Revolutionary era. Hutchins, a New Jersey native, was to become "Geographer of the United States" but had apparently drafted his history while loyally serving Britain during the Revolution. Filson and Imlay devoted their energies to land speculation. The Indian histories often carried on the ethnographic traditions of earlier colonization with little conceptual innovation, plugging new details into an established framework. The exceptions are perhaps the works of Colden and Adair. The former presented, with lasting influence, the Iroquois "Five Nations" as significant historical agents maneuvering among Dutch, French, English, and Jesuit forces. The latter, perhaps the most sustained attempt to link the American Indian with the Lost Tribes of Israel, was laced with references to the ancient European and Near Eastern worlds and concluded with Adair's fascinating attempt to recount Christian history to Chickasaws in "indigenous" terms. After describing the resurrection of "A-Do-Ne-Yo, Minggo Ishtohoollo, 'the divine chief,'" he proceeded to explain the rise of the pope, ruling over his "black scholars" and living "in costly great houses, after the superb manner of our great civil chieftain"; a "holy spirit of fire," concentrated in "two great beloved men in particular"—Calvin and Luther—brought some of the Europeans back to the egalitarian lifestyle of their indigenous American counterparts (Adair 1930, 472–478). Thus Adair may come the closest to the epistemological innovations and debates about Native American sources described by Cañizares-Esguerra.

Does this mean, then, that the natural and indigenous histories do not belong to the tradition of historiography proper? Not exactly. For the "natural histories" would give a strongly geographic inflection to many of the other histories of this period. More important, the tradition of the ethnography would provide a model of social systematicity that would prove influential for later historians, particularly in discussions of race. This tradition had been notably activated by the slave codes. The influential Barbados code of 1661 essentially transposed Indian ethnography into a law against conspiracy among Africans, thereby theorizing slave unrest through an ethnographic lens. This code would become the most influential model for slave codes in the mainland colonies, confirming the tradition of analyzing the conspiracies of nonwhite peoples within an ethnographic framework, while more fundamentally revealing the historiographical potential of a seemingly ahistorical analytic (Engerman, Drescher, and Paquette 2001, 105–112; Hoffer 2003, 17–22).

Macronationalist or Protonationalist Histories

If the foregoing historical genres were resolutely local in orientation, attuned to the specificities of colonies, events, or geography, this historiographical mode undertook the synthesizing work of piecing together colonial components, creating what would eventually become a "national" framework. This is not to suggest an inevitable tendency toward unification; rather, these syntheses were typically impelled by transprovincial conflicts in the imperial framework. Thus we find a large number of

Whiggish historical pamphlets articulating political claims and rationales in three periods: the early 1750s, the middle 1760s, and the early 1770s—the opening years of the Seven Years' War; the years of the Royal Proclamation and the Stamp Act and Townshend Acts controversies; and the American Revolution, respectively. While most obviously "political" pamphlets, often with a strongly legalistic orientation, these works, in responding to global war and the restructuring of the British Empire, often challenged imperial policies with the details of colonial institutions and actions, making historiography an essential weapon in the arsenal of political debate. The project was a difficult one, and in a work like the senior Aaron Burr's "A Discourse Delivered at New-Ark in New-Jersey" (1755), which ventures a synoptic history of a rapacious France, the imagined unification of "America" is enacted more in fantasies of predatory Indians—a unified *Native* America of sorts—and of praying colonists than in any substantive institutional history. Even in the next generation, in work like Richard Bland's *An Inquiry into the Rights of the British Colonies* (1766), the synthesis remained elusive. Bland reconstructed the ancient history of the British constitution before citing the legal foundations for the rights of the "Colonies"; yet Bland, a lawyer and member of the House of Burgesses for more than three decades, was only able to discuss the documentary record of his native Virginia. Even John Dickinson's *Essay on the Constitutional Power of Great-Britain over the Colonies in America* (1774) was more focused on British history than particular colonial histories. As these examples illustrate, macrohistories of Anglo-America were frequently extrapolated from provincial histories or displaced onto narratives of other unified entities (Britain, France, the Indians) against whom "Americans" rallied or trembled.

Yet more substantive macrohistories appeared nonetheless. Among the earliest was William Douglass's *A Summary, Historical and Political, of the First Planting, Progressive Impressments, and Present State of the British Settlements in North-America* (1749), seemingly motivated by the Anglo-French conflicts of the 1740s and ranging across not only the New England colonies but the Caribbean and Canadian islands as well; other segments dealt with sectarian histories; Spanish, French, Portuguese, and Dutch colonization; and Native American societies and wars. Generally silent on the Atlantic and southern mainland colonies, Douglass's *Summary* imagines a triangular, anti-French America of commercial New England, its island exporters to the south, and its island defenses to the north. This anomalous history is partially explained by Douglass's unusual background. Scottish born, educated in Edinburgh, Leyden, and Paris, and for a time a resident of the West Indies, Douglass settled in Boston in 1718. By the early 1720s, this self-styled man of science had alienated himself from local elites over the inoculation controversy. He was thus able to draw on the New England tradition of confederated histories without its insular flavor, and his Continental background and travel enabled him to imagine a unique Atlantic sphere for his writing (Levernier and Wilmes 1983). The other major figure of the midcentury was Thomas Pownall, whose *Administration of the Colonies*

(1764) and *Topographical Description* (1776), drawing on Lewis Evans's mapping project, also began the work of synthesizing local histories from an imperial perspective. Bland's pamphlet, mentioned earlier, had criticized Pownall as "another Writer, fond of his new System of placing Great Britain as the Centre of Attraction to the Colonies," yet it was Pownall, in his synthesis of maps, Indian ethnographies, provincial records, and sectarian microhistories, who was creating the conceptual map in which America would be the center of attraction (White 2005, 122–124).

Though nationalism, contrary to conventional wisdom, was slow to emerge even in the aftermath of the Revolution—Jefferson, writing about Virginia in 1784, still referred to the lone colony as a "nation"—Revolutionary organization facilitated the process of nationalist historiography, inspiring a number of histories of the conflict by South Carolinian David Ramsay (1789), New England's Mercy Otis Warren (1805), and William Gordon, a pro-independence immigrant of 1770 who returned to England in 1786, where he published the three-volume *History of the Rise of the United States* in 1789. Also significant during this period were the commercially successful primers prepared by Jedidiah Morse and his various associates, including the geographically focused *Geography Made Easy* (1784), which later became *The American Geography* (1789), and *A Compendious History of New England* (1804, with Elijah Parish). The Federalist Morse's knack for historical synthesis was perhaps also evident in his better-known sermons on the international conspiracy of the Bavarian Illuminati (Livingston 2005).

If protonational macrohistories resulted from the conjunction of imperial administration (and its opposition) and extensions of the provincial historiographical tradition (as with Ramsay, Morse, and Warren), the confluence of these sources is powerfully evident in the career of the most prominent of the macrohistorians, Ebenezer Hazard. In 1792 and 1794, he published the two volumes of *Historical Collections: Consisting of State Papers and Other Authentic Documents*, each volume consisting of more than 630 pages of archival material. A graduate of the College of New Jersey, Hazard had unsuccessfully attempted, in the late 1760s, to publish a collection of his uncle and college president Samuel Finley's sermons. By the early 1770s, as partner in a New York bookshop, he was preparing a collection of naval trade laws from the various mainland and Caribbean colonies. But by the coming of the Revolution, he was preparing proposals for a collection of colonial records and papers, finding supporters in congressional delegates John Adams and Thomas Jefferson, among others: Adams advised him to follow the model of Hakluyt, while Jefferson referenced Hazard's still incomplete project in his 1785 *Notes*. Hazard collected documents while working as postmaster general of New York and later postmaster general of the United States, establishing close connections with a number of fellow historians: Jedidiah Morse acknowledged his aid, as did Jeremy Belknap, New Hampshire's historian and one of the prominent founders of the Massachusetts Historical Society (Shelley 1955). But the limits of Hazard's synthetic project are as clear as its achievements: while compilation of a national archive played a significant role in a national sensibility and preparing the way for later appreciative historians, Hazard never actually composed a history, and his collection of documents, predictably focused on Virginia and New England, never extended into the eighteenth century. Even this work seems more like scaffolding than an actual synthesis.

How the Types of Histories Interrelate

This admittedly schematic summary has arranged eighteenth-century histories in terms of their spatiotemporal orientations: narratives about provinces, with a stress on imperial origins; more focused narratives of local institutions or events; accounts of the natural nature (wildlife and Native Americans) often paradoxically describing the purported prehistory of a region; and forays into larger, synthesizing histories of multiple colonies. One could usefully rearrange the preceding classification in terms of intracolonial rhythms as well, finding a pattern whereby, in the earliest years of colonization, narratives of exploration flourished alongside natural histories and ethnographies, while only the eventual growth of populations, printing, and governmental institutions made possible the archival projects driving provincial histories and the microhistories. Of course, several histories defy these categories, including immigrant Anthony Benezet's *Some Historical Account of Guinea* (1771) and John Ledyard's *A Journal of Captain Cook's Last Voyage* (1783). The cadences of intracolonial historiography were increasingly punctuated by growing imperial controversies involving war policy, trade, taxation, and representation, providing a growing tendency to revisit and synthesize archival materials; such efforts remained concentrated in Virginia and New England, gradually radiating from there with the slow emergence of protonational histories by century's end. Only then would the nonsynchronicity of colonial historiography be somewhat mitigated, though the persistence of novanglocentrism can be linked in part to this phenomenon.

More important, however, we should stress that many of the listed works could fit under multiple headings. Proud's *History of Pennsylvania,* for example, includes long accounts of soil, rivers, and flora, devotes pages to a hagiography of William Penn, continues with an ecclesiastic history of the Quaker movement, includes a polemical account of the Paxton Riots, and compiles an ethnography of local Native Americans. Proud's example reminds us that our question here is not the types of histories that were written in the period, but their intersection and integration. For the different tendencies enumerated here increasingly converged as so many parts of the historian's machine, accomplishing different tasks in the construction of a synthetic history. Thus Proud's history described Pennsylvania's settlement through its soil and its rivers, its government and political culture through the history of the Quakers, its organizing principles through the figure of Penn, its forms of agricultural and sectarian settlement through an account of its native peoples; and this orderly system finds its disruptive conclusion with the micronarrative of the Paxton massacres, through which fanatical Presbyterian frontiersmen begin the disruptive descent into revolution. It is also the case that a work that at first glance seems local in orientation may have participated in the synthesizing projects of the macrohistories. Thus Horsmanden's account of the New York slave conspiracy responds in part to the controversies pertaining to the War of Jenkins's Ear, while the various local accounts of the Great Awakening, like Edwards's, contributed to an intercolonial, even imperial, revival movement (Doolen 2005; Lambert 1999).

Throughout these historiographical projects, one constant remained: a profoundly legalistic orientation, rivaled only by the Baconian analytic of the natural histories that was nonetheless fused with the legal tradition under the rubric of geography. The predominance of professional elites and the demands of colonial governance overwhelmingly favored a historiography oriented toward documentary precedents and an institutional interpretation of events. This was as true for clerics, shaped by the traditions of ecclesiastic history, and for educators, often beholden to the state for funds and students, as for politicians more firmly anchored in the legal tradition. And this integrative impulse, coordinating and linking different historiographical modes, probably owes much to the legal tradition of reconciling different components of a common-law tradition. The exceptions to this tendency cited here—James Adair, Hannah Adams, Richard Allen, Herman Husband, and Absalom Jones—stand out precisely because of their distance from, even adversarial relationship to, the law. Here we may finally return to the question of literary influence, for such texts would have relatively little direct influence on the belletristic tradition that would constitute "literature" by the dawn of the nineteenth century. The extraordinary role of Thomas Paine's *Common Sense* (1776) is illuminating in this respect. As historians have long noted, Paine's pamphlet broke sharply with the legalistic tradition of anti-imperial publications. The immigrant corset maker had little familiarity with, or interest in, the minutiae of taxation disputes, gravitating instead to the more established British literary conventions of low Protestant sentimentality and universalism. In fact, the tremendous popularity of his pamphlet speaks more to his anomalous intervention in the historiographical tradition than to his rhetorical gifts, which seem like oases in a Sahara of legalese. For better or worse, *Common Sense* still remains more accessible as a work of literature, and thus more situatable in the American literary tradition, than, say, *The Federalist Papers*, written squarely in the longer legalistic tradition of colonial histories.

Before what may be called the "Paine Phenomenon," more narrowly defined "literary" productions had largely gone their separate way from historiography. Thus the early eighteenth-century Connecticut governor Roger Wolcott drew on his colony's archives not to pen a prose history but to compose "A Brief Account of the Agency of the Honorable John Winthrop," his 1725 poem of the Anglo-Pequot War and the granting of the Connecticut charter. But Wolcott's epic style reveals the continuing distance of this tradition from a popular audience, the last two stanzas warning the "Multitude" of the dangerous tendency, "taught in Satan's first Erected School," to resist "every Act of Order or Restraint" (Wolcott 1725, 78). Nonetheless, the late eighteenth century witnessed an emerging synergy between fiction and history. To be sure, the United States witnessed a number of literary productions that adopted British literary modes like the sentimental novel. But an increasing number of works displayed a desire to craft a United States literary tradition with reference to New World historiography; in fact, "the dominant prose tradition of late colonial America amounted to a series of locally developed historiographic formulas" (Drexler and White 2004, 148). It is noteworthy, for example, that the closest Washington Irving ever came to writing a novel was with *A History of New-York from the Beginning of the World to the End of the Dutch Dynasty* (1809), a mock-provincial history purportedly penned by Dietrich Knickerbocker, a figure famously used in the frame narratives of "The Legend of Sleepy Hollow" and other short sketches. For Irving, as for many of his predecessors, the historiographical tradition, straitened as it was, counterintuitively provided a local inspiration for literary production. How could this be? A survey of some contact points between historiography and a broader literary tradition can suggest how we might reexamine the historiographical archive just enumerated.

How Charles Brockden Brown Read Early American History

We may begin with the career of Charles Brockden Brown, best known for his so-called gothic novels written in the late 1790s. During the period of his intense novelistic production, Brown reviewed a number of historical works in the *Monthly Magazine, and American Review,* including Trumbull's history of Connecticut, Proud's history of Pennsylvania, and Hannah Adams's history of New England. In general, he lauded the industry of the American archivist while condemning the lack of conceptual ordering of the material. Trumbull was to be praised for "great fidelity in investigating and exhibiting facts," but he had "thrown together important materials in a method scarcely more digested than meagre annals," while his style was "too generally antiquated" (Brown 1799a). Proud has likewise served up the "uncouth narratives of an old man, uninstructed in the arts of selection, arrangement and expression," his materials requiring the genius of the philosopher for any moral profit (Brown 1799b). By contrast, Hannah Adams was by and large praised for a very different approach: making "liberal use of the works of noted and popular writers on American affairs," she had "exercised the privilege of new modelling and abridging their accounts," achieving "a masculine rectitude of judgment" rare in women writers (Brown 1799c). In another prominent sketch of the period, "Walstein's School of History," Brown imagined a German "school" of historiography centered around one Walstein, history professor at Jena and the author of biographies of Cicero and the Portuguese Marquis of Pombal. Walstein's gifts as a historian were centered on his sense of "the uncertainty of history," and a concomitant speculation about motives and circumstances. The implicit argument was taken further in the sketch of "Engel, the eldest of Walstein's pupils," who composed the compelling "Olivo Ronsica," a "fictitious history" but nonetheless one of tremendous "moral benefit" (Brown 1799d). This fictional review about the virtues of fictional history was to find clarification in the slightly later essay "The Difference between History and Romance," which challenged the distinction between the two genres, stressed their usual imbrication, and called for the "romancers" to carry on the work of the historian. "If history relate what is true, its relations must be limited to what is known by the testimony of our senses. Its sphere, therefore, is extremely narrow," he wrote. "Useful narratives"—romances—"must comprise facts linked together by some other circumstance," but consequently "can never give birth to certainty." The essay ends with the question "How wide, then, if romance be the narrative of mere probabilities, is the empire of romance? This empire is absolute and undivided over the motives and tendencies of human actions. Over actions themselves, its dominion, though not unlimited, is yet very extensive." One must read Brown's reflections on history—his sharp verdict on the archivist, and his insistence that fiction must carry on the purported agenda of the historian—as symptomatic of American historiography. British historians like Hume, Gibbon, or William Robertson were not subject to the same condemnations and were generally treated as writers blending the two genres—as was Thomas More (Brown 1800). Assuming that Brown is not simply an anomaly, the crucial point is that the narrowness and limitations of Anglo-American historiography effectively muddied the distinction between history and romance. Far from establishing a clear generic distinction, the meager narrowness of American histories left fiction writers ample space to pick up the slack. Indeed, Brown's novels of this period may be read as "histories" in this sense, with *Wieland,* for example, exploring the dynamics of the Paxton Riots treated by Proud's history, or *Arthur Mervyn* treating a larger context in which the yellow fever epidemic of 1793 is linked to the Whiskey Rebellion of the following year (White 2004).

But Brown's identification as a historian would become clearer in the period after 1801 when he allegedly abandoned the novel. In his editorship of the *Literary Magazine, and American Register* from 1803 to 1807, Brown continued to write about history in relation to romance, increasingly to the disadvantage of the former. In an essay entitled "Historical Characters Are False Representations of Nature," he argued that "ancient historians compiled prodigies, to gratify the credulous curiosity of their readers; but since prodigies have ceased, while the same avidity for the marvellous exists, modern historians have transferred the miraculous to their personages" (Brown 1806a). It was left to *fiction* writers to create true historical characters. Another essay from the period, "Modes of Historical Writing," contemplated the methods with which the historian might connect observations on "laws, manners, and the rest" with "a mere narrative of transactions" (Brown 1806b). Again, the intertwining of the two modes was more ably undertaken by the novelist.

Yet no longer content to comment on historiography as a partisan of romance, Brown's most ambitious monographs of the period were apparently written as histories of a sort. One of these works, the *System of General Geography,* reportedly 1,200 pages posthumously lost, appears to have been written in the mode of Jedidiah Morse's successful geography texts. But we still have more than 100,000 words of Brown's other final project, known to critics today as the *Historical Sketches.* In "Walstein's School of History," in words confirming Pocock's analysis, Brown had asserted, "The Romish religion, and the feudal institutions, are the causes that chiefly influence the modern state of Europe"; as a result, Portugal "was properly selected"—for Walstein's life of Pombal—"as an example of moral and political degeneracy, and as a theatre in which virtue might be shewn with most advantage, contending with the evils of misgovernment and superstition." The *Historical Sketches* seemed to follow this view, focused almost exclusively as they are on Roman Catholic Europe in the late feudal and early modern periods. Brown had also insisted that "next to property, the most extensive source of our relations is sex," and accordingly this history of feudal institutions is increasingly presented through the lens of marriage, adultery, and conflicts over inheritance, with women increasingly taking a central position (Brown 1799d; Barnard 2004). The last of the *Sketches,* a 32,000-word history of a fictitious Mediterranean island called Carsol, was to venture further, depicting the island's historians studying their own mysterious history, theorizing a periodization of eras, and reconstructing a literary tradition; another figure, Alexandra, ventured colonization of the island of Serendib, concerned to not repeat the historical errors of the Spanish and others in the New World. In a significant departure for Brown, the sketch examined a spate of slave rebellions—typically by the Muslim minority population—as well as attempts to suppress cultural difference, as with the notorious local inquisition, the *Convicata,* created by Michael Praya. In the *Sketches,* then, Brown had turned sharply from New World subject matter and had tested his imagination with ecclesiastical history, narratives of the family, metahistorical commentary, and an interest in rebellion and dissent. The result was unprecedented—a counterfactual quasi-utopian history that at one point imagined a reformist English pope, Felix, transforming the sectarian atmosphere of seventeenth-century Europe. What is more, the problem of historiography itself was repeatedly and profoundly thematized in the *Sketches'* accounts of local history-writing projects. There is no telling the impact that Brown's work might have registered had it made it to print, but the work remains a reminder of the possible connections between historiography and attempts to create an innovative literary tradition on the Atlantic periphery. In some very basic sense, literary oddities like Brown's *Sketches* directly answer the constricted nature of North American historiography, though critics have been slow to realize this.

HISTORICAL-LITERARY HYBRIDS

With Charles Brockden Brown's career-long project in mind, we may return to some earlier works that also ventured, if somewhat more modestly, to bridge the gap between historiography and more popular literary traditions. In 1774–1775, John Leacock, a member of the Sons of Liberty with an artisan background, had published *The First Book of the American Chronicles of the Times.* This satire of the pre-Revolutionary conflicts was written in the mode of the Old Testament history of kings, Leacock specifically citing the tendentious commentary-laden Geneva Bible. One episode, for example, depicted the New England "witch" Elizabeth Carey (tried in the 1690s) conjuring Oliver Cromwell, much as the Witch of Endor had conjured Samuel for Saul (1 Samuel 28; Leacock 1987, 60–65). This understudied work stands as one of the most innovative attempts to synthesize ecclesiastical and political history, drawing on the form of the former to present the content of the latter.

Hugh Henry Brackenridge was also commencing his writing career at about this time, though most of his early works were quite conventional in translating historical materials into epic format, as in his commencement poem (coauthored with Philip Freneau) titled "The Rising Glory of America." By 1783, however, he had compiled a series of captivity narratives, which may have helped inspire the first volumes of *Modern Chivalry* (1792–1793), a Shandean narrative comically recounting local events (like elections or the presidential levy) and offering critiques of new American institutions (philosophical societies or the Cincinnati). But by 1794 he found himself not only involved in the Whiskey Rebellion but also accused of supporting the insurrection. In response he wrote *Incidents of the Insurrection in Western Pennsylvania,* a work that fascinatingly anticipates the later historical novels of Walter Scott as its historically neutral protagonist (Brackenridge himself) carefully walks the fine line between a mass revolutionary movement and elite historical forces. Brackenridge's return to *Modern Chivalry,* which saw expansions in 1797, 1804, and 1815, continued the Shandean reflections of the first volumes but accelerated the historical references; at the outset of volume 4, for example, Teague, the comic Irish sidekick of the first volumes is replaced by the buffoonish Duncan, whose musings are full of muddled references to Scottish history. The work defies easy summary, but Brackenridge, perhaps attuned to the tensions between personal narrative and macrohistory as a result of his entanglement with the Whiskey rebels, increasingly used his encyclopedic novel to catalog comical misinterpretations of historical experience; the ironic narration largely refuses to provide straight commentary, leaving readers to construct some kind of framework for historical interpretation in defiance of the triumphalist norms of the new nation. A similar experiment with historical narration was undertaken in "The Anarchiad," a collectively written poem by several of the so-called Connecticut Wits (probably David Humphreys, Joel Barlow, John Trumbull, and Lemuel Hopkins), published serially in 1786 in the *New Haven Gazette and Connecticut Magazine*. The Wits were by and large elite professionals—Hopkins a doctor, Trumbull a lawyer and legislator, and Humphreys and Barlow in the diplomatic service—and their mock epic, written in the Hudibrastic tradition, at first seems a conventional flight from prose fiction to poetry. But much of the conservative satire of "The Anarchiad" comes from its elaborate textual apparatus, purportedly prepared by a club of antiquarians who had stumbled across an ancient epic. Footnotes and critical commentary thus worked in tandem with the comic experimentation with different verse forms, providing as much commentary on historiographical as poetic genres.

Jeremy Belknap, the historian of New Hampshire, also dabbled in fiction in yet a different vein. In 1792 he published *The Foresters, an American Tale*, an allegorical novel in which the Anglo-American colonies constituted a forest. An odd combination of colonial figures (for example, Tobias Wheatear as the New Haven colony, or Robert Lumber as New Hampshire) and historical personages (Walter Pipeweed's grandson George, representing Sir Walter Raleigh's heir George Washington) interact with John Bull (Great Britain) before forming a partnership (the United States) and achieving freedom from their landlord. Belknap's inspiration for the allegory had perhaps been Ebenezer Hazard, with whom he corresponded for years, and from whom he apparently developed his comparative sense of history. Allegory thus amounted to a synthetic approach to historical material. One finds a similar gesture in Tabitha Gilman Tenney's *Female Quixotism* (1801), whose heroine, addled by novel reading, encounters a series of allegorical figures including a Washington-like Virginian, a Connecticut wit, a New Hampshire plebeian, and a South Carolinian radical. One could read the novel's female protagonist as herself an allegory of the rebel farmer John Fries, leading figure of the Fries Rebellion of 1799.

Mercy Otis Warren, during these years, was preparing her *History of the Rise, Progress, and Termination of the American Revolution: Interspersed with*

Biographical, Political, and Moral Observations, finally published in 1805. In the early years of the Revolution she had anonymously published several propaganda plays, including *The Adulateur* and *The Group.* The latter play portrayed a rambunctious series of loyalists and their divergent motives—ambition, greed, conservatism, misguided loyalty—before concluding with a pro-independence soliloquy by an unnamed Lady of virtue; it was as if Warren found it easier to narrate the opposition than the nebulous Revolutionary cause. When she turned at last to the Revolution, she resorted to annals and archives, but as her subtitle indicates, she made her most original contribution in Machiavellian sketches of various political leaders. At one point, for example, she discussed the fame achieved by John Hancock and John Adams as a result of General Gage's decision to single them out. But contrary to British perceptions, Adams and Hancock were two very different characters, Hancock a "young gentleman of fortune, of more external accomplishments than real abilities," and Adams "a gentleman of a good education, a decent family, but no fortune." The fortuitous pairing—the result of Gage's muddled perceptions—gave the two a notoriety not necessarily warranted by circumstances. For "in the effervescence of popular commotions, it is not uncommon to see the favorites of fortune elevated to the pinnacle of rank by trivial circumstances, that appear the result of accident" (Warren 1994, 116–118). If such sketches were fairly common to European historiography, they nonetheless helped inaugurate an American version of this tradition, countering the popular mythology that had emerged from the Revolutionary-era press.

This list of historical-literary hybrids could continue indefinitely, including Gilbert Imlay's *The Emigrants* (1793), which to some extent translated his *Topographical Description of the Western Territory* into an epistolary novel, thus achieving interesting connections between the English and American histories of the novel's correspondents. While these works should not be reduced to the historiographical enterprise, there is little doubt that each of these writers turned to historical events in a very different manner from their better-known successors of the 1820s. During the well-known boomlet of historical novels, most famously marked by James Fenimore Cooper's *The Spy, The Pioneers,* and *The Pilot,* Catherine Maria Sedgwick's *A New-England Tale* and *Hope Leslie,* or Lydia Maria Child's *Hobomok* and *The Rebels,* writers tended to consult earlier synthetic histories for details while adapting them to the conventions of a tradition popularized by Walter Scott and other Europeans. But at the end of the eighteenth century, a great number of writers, seemingly inspired by the relativizing rupture announced by the American Revolution, experimented with a wide range of literary adaptations, modifications, and defamiliarizations of historiographical conventions. Though these works have often been read as antiquarian failures to achieve Continental polish, one could also read them as early national forays into the techniques of what would later be called modernism. Thus alongside the somewhat traditional heroic portraits of Warren, or Belknap and Tenney's allegories, we find

Leacock's secular scripture, Brackenridge's extreme ironic narration, the Connecticut Wits' foregrounding of textual apparatuses, and Brown's alternative universes. Such experimentation would continue into the second century of the nineteenth century, as any examination of Samuel Woodworth's *The Champions of Freedom,* a novel about the War of 1812, demonstrates (Letter 2006). If the eighteenth-century historiographical tradition, with its sharply legal orientation, was remote from the creative works that flourished at century's end, it remained a significant presence not simply as an archive but as something of a formal problem. Our sense of the period's writing is undoubtedly enhanced when we examine the historiographical landscape. For if we struggle for some sense of the historians' ostensibly literary achievements, the writing experiments of the era can give us some sense of what these could have been.

REFERENCES

Adair, James. 1930. *The History of the American Indians,* edited by Samuel Cole. New York: Promontory.

Adams, Hannah 1799. *A Summary History of New-England, from the First Settlement at Plymouth, to the Acceptance of the Federal Constitution.* Dedham, MA: H. Mann and J. H. Adams.

Amory, Hugh, and David D. Hall, eds. 2000. *The Colonial Book in the Atlantic World.* New York: Cambridge University Press.

Barnard, Philip. 2004. Culture and Authority in Brown's *Historical Sketches.* In *Revising Charles Brockden Brown: Culture, Politics and Sexuality in the Early Republic,* edited by Philip Barnard, Mark L. Kamrath, and Stephen Shapiro, 310–331. Knoxville: University of Tennessee Press.

Bauer, Ralph. 2003. *The Cultural Geography of Colonial American Literatures: Empire, Travel, Modernity.* New York: Cambridge University Press.

[Brown, Charles Brockden]. 1799a. American Review: Art. I. *Monthly Magazine, and American Review* 1: 45–46.

[———]. 1799b. American Review: Art. XII. *Monthly Magazine, and American Review* 1: 216–217.

[———]. 1799c. American Review: Art. XXVIII. *Monthly Magazine, and American Review* 1: 445–449.

[———]. 1799d. Walstein's School of History. *Monthly Magazine, and American Review* 1: 335–338, 407–411.

[———]. 1800. The Difference between History and Romance. *Monthly Magazine, and American Review* 2: 251–253.

[———]. 1806a. Historical Characters Are False Representations of Nature. *Literary Magazine, and American Register* 5: 113–117.

[———]. 1806b. Modes of Historical Writing. *Literary Magazine, and American Register* 6: 431–433.

Cañizares-Esguerra, Jorge. 2001. *How to Write the History of the New World: Histories, Epistemologies, and Identities in the Eighteenth-Century Atlantic World*. Stanford, CA: Stanford University Press.

Doolen, Andy. 2005. *Fugitive Empire: Locating Early American Imperialism*. Minneapolis: University of Minnesota Press.

Drexler, Michael J., and Ed White. 2004. Literary Histories. In *A Companion to American Fiction, 1780–1865*, edited by Shirley Samuels, 147–157. New York: Blackwell.

Engerman, Stanley, Seymour Drescher, and Robert Paquette, eds. 2001. *Slavery*. New York: Oxford University Press.

Filson, John. 1784. *The Discovery, Settlement, and Present State of Kentucke*. Wilmington, DE: James Adams.

Garraty, John A., and Mark C. Carnes, eds. 1999. *American National Biography*. 24 vols. New York: Oxford University Press.

Hoffer, Peter Charles. 2003. *The Great New York Conspiracy of 1741: Slavery, Crime, and Colonial Law*. Lawrence: University Press of Kansas.

Jameson, J. Franklin. 1961. *The History of Historical Writing in America*. New York: Antiquarian Press.

Jones, Mark H. 1982. *Herman Husband: Millenarian, Carolina Regulator, and Whiskey Rebel*. DeKalb: Northern Illinois University.

Lambert, Frank. 1999. *Inventing the "Great Awakening."* Princeton, NJ: Princeton University Press.

Leacock, John. 1987. *The First Book of the American Chronicles of the Times, 1774–1775*, edited by Carla Mulford. Newark: University of Delaware Press.

Leder, Lawrence H., ed. 1973. *Historians of Nature and Man's Nature: Early Nationalist Historians*. New York: Harper and Row.

Letter, Joseph. 2006. *Reinscribing the Revolution: Genre and the Problem of National History in Early American Historical Novels*. Baton Rouge: Louisiana State University.

Levernier, James, and Douglas R. Wilmes. 1983. *American Writers before 1800: A Biographical and Critical Dictionary*. 3 vols. Westport, CT: Greenwood.

Livingstone, David N. 2005. Risen into Empire: Moral Geographies of the American Republic. In *Geography and Revolution*, edited by David N. Livingstone and Charles W. J. Withers, 304–335. Chicago: University of Chicago Press.

Matthew, H. C. G., and Brian Harrison, eds. 2004. *Oxford Dictionary of National Biography*. 60 vols. New York: Oxford University Press.

Oglethorpe, James Edward. 1994. *The Publications of James Edward Oglethorpe*, edited by Rodney M. Baine. Athens: University of Georgia Press.

Pocock, J. G. A. 1999. *Barbarism and Religion*. Vol. 2, *Narratives of Civil Government*. New York: Cambridge University Press.

Prince, Thomas. 1736. *A Chronological History of New-England in the Form of Annals*. Boston: Kneeland and Green.

Shelley, Fred. 1955. Ebenezer Hazard: America's First Historical Editor. *William and Mary Quarterly*, 3d ser., 12: 44–73.

Warren, Mercy Otis. 1994. *History of the Rise, Progress, and Termination of the American Revolution: Interspersed with Biographical, Political, and Moral Observations*, edited by Lester H. Cohen. 2 vols. Indianapolis, IN: Liberty Fund.

White, Ed. 2004. Carwin the Peasant Rebel. In *Revising Charles Brockden Brown: Culture, Politics and Sexuality in the Early Republic,* edited by Philip Barnard, Mark L. Kamrath, and Stephen Shapiro, 41–59. Knoxville: University of Tennessee Press.

———. 2005. *The Backcountry and the City: Colonization and Conflict in Early America.* Minneapolis: University of Minnesota Press.

Wolcott, Roger. 1725. *Poetical Meditation, Being the Improvement of Some Vacant Hours.* New London: L. Green.

....

CHAPTER 26

THE PLACE OF NATURAL HISTORY IN EARLY AMERICAN LITERATURE

....

KEVIN J. HAYES

Shortly before the first edition of *Notes on the State of Virginia* appeared in 1785, secretary of the Continental Congress Charles Thomson, who had read the work in manuscript, wrote Thomas Jefferson to encourage him to change the title. Though Jefferson greatly appreciated Thomson's advice when it came to other aspects of the book, he was loath to alter his title. Calling the book *Notes*, Jefferson helped the printed version retain the aura of a manuscript work, giving it a casual feel and thus masking its meticulous composition. Furthermore, his use of the word "state" in the title is a double entendre. It refers to Virginia as being part of the United States, yet it also aligns the book with earlier works belonging to the "History and Present State" genre such as Robert Beverley's *History and Present State of Virginia* (1705) and Hugh Jones's *Present State of Virginia* (1724). Making his plea, Thomson argued, "I submit it to your consideration whether you do not owe it to your reputation to publish your work under a more dignified title. In the state in which I saw it I consider it a most excellent Natural history not merely of Virginia but of No. America and possibly equal if not superior to that of any Country yet published" (Jefferson 1950, 8: 16). Though the book contains much anthropological, geographic, political, and sociological information, from Thomson's perspective *Notes on the State of Virginia* was, first and foremost, a work of natural history.

Numerous other works of early American literature contain significant elements of natural history: promotion literature, captivity narratives, diaries, histories, and travel writings. In fact, natural history occupies a central place in early

American literature. The American land helped to define the style and content of American literature almost as soon as the first English colonists arrived and continued to do so through the colonial period. In addition to *Notes on the State of Virginia,* there is another late work of early American literature in which natural history plays an integral part, William Bartram's *Travels* (1791). Though Jefferson's work belongs to the "History and Present State" genre and Bartram's is a book of travels, the two share many similarities. Both describe a particular region of North America. Both strongly reflect their authors' personalities, philosophies, and principles. Both captured the attention of educated European readers upon publication. And both, though seemingly nonchalant, are highly crafted works. A structural analysis of these two masterworks provides a fitting conclusion to the history of early American literature.

NOTES ON THE STATE OF VIRGINIA

While serving as governor of Virginia in 1780, Thomas Jefferson received a set of queries prepared by François Marbois, secretary of the French Legation at Philadelphia. Given his gubernatorial responsibilities in wartime Virginia, Jefferson had few spare moments for literary pursuits. Remarkably, he did find time to start drafting his answers to Marbois during his final year as governor. After retiring from office, he devoted the summer of 1781 to answering the queries in full. By year's end, he had completed the task and sent Marbois a copy of the work. Jefferson kept a copy for himself, which he began revising almost as soon as he put Marbois's copy in the mail. He made many changes to his manuscript by entering brief passages of text between the lines. Lengthier revisions he wrote on slips of paper, which he pasted atop the canceled passages they replaced. He further expanded his text by composing additional passages on separate slips of paper, which he pasted tablike to the edges of individual pages (Wilson 2004, 109).

Despite the length of the expanded version, *Notes on the State of Virginia* is structured much as the original version was structured, that is, as a set of responses to a set of queries. Each chapter addresses a specific query, though Jefferson's answers often extend far beyond the scope of each query. The structure effectively masks the amount of thought he put into its organization. In the preface to the London edition, he assumed a casual pose by characterizing the work as merely a set of answers to a list of questions: "The following Notes were written in Virginia in the year 1781, and somewhat corrected and enlarged in the winter of 1782, in answer to Queries proposed to the Author, by a Foreigner of Distinction, then residing among us" (Jefferson 1982, 2).

Jefferson's statement reinforces what the book's structure implies, that the queries being answered are the same ones Marbois had asked. It is a lie. The organization of Marbois's original questionnaire differs from the organization of *Notes on the State of Virginia* in important ways. As Jefferson composed his work, he greatly revised Marbois's original questionnaire, collapsing multiple queries into single ones in some cases and expanding single ones into multiple queries in others. The first query in Marbois's list asks about colonial charters, the second about the current state constitution, and the third about state boundaries. Recognizing that the object of the third query made for a better opening, Jefferson combined Marbois's first two queries into one and shifted them to the middle of his book. Removing these two from the top of the list, he let himself start his work with what had been the subject of Marbois's third query: boundaries.

"Virginia is bounded on the East by the Atlantic": so begins Jefferson's answer to the first query in *Notes on the State of Virginia*. Though not one of the most auspicious openings in the history of American literature, this sentence takes on importance by establishing both the physical boundaries that circumscribe the state of Virginia and the parameters that define the book. Jefferson thus parallels the geographic space of Virginia and the textual space of his book. Making the issue of boundaries his first subject, he reveals his personality as well. His desire to establish boundaries before proceeding any further reflects his personal need to exert control over his subject.

By making the Atlantic Ocean his first boundary, Jefferson distinguishes the New World from the Old and, in so doing, emphasizes its uniqueness. After precisely delineating the remaining boundaries, he computes the total area of Virginia. To illustrate its size, he indulges in a little jingoistic breast-beating. By his calculations, Virginia is one-third larger than Great Britain and Ireland put together. Completing his answer to this query, he briefly lists the charters, grants, and other agreements that had created the present boundaries of the state.

Marbois's sixth query asks about Virginia geography. He expected a "notice of the Counties Cities Townships Villages Rivers Rivulets and how far they are navigable. Cascades Caverns Mountains Productions Trees Plants Fruits and other natural Riches" (Jefferson 1950, 4: 166). Jefferson recognized that this single query demanded far more information than could be manageably contained within a single answer, so he split it into five separate queries. Virginia's rivers, for instance, deserved a chapter of their own. Jefferson made it his second.

The names of the first five rivers discussed sound familiar to anyone cognizant of Virginia geography: James, Chickahominy, Rivanna, York, Potomac. The chapter also mentions the Ohio River. Though Virginia had ceded all territory north of the Ohio to the United States, the land that now forms West Virginia and Kentucky still belonged to Virginia, so the inclusion of the Ohio among Virginia's rivers is perfectly justifiable. Besides, few can quibble with Jefferson's description of the Ohio River. Though he had never seen it himself, he synthesized the accounts of those who had seen it into one grand pronouncement: "The *Ohio* is the most beautiful river on earth." (In his *Travels*, William Bartram also referred to the "beautiful Ohio" [Bartram 1996, 278].) Developing the chapter, Jefferson named other rivers farther west. He included a long discussion of the Mississippi, which he called "one of the principal channels of future commerce for the country." Since his answer to the first query had identified the Mississippi as the western boundary of Virginia, the inclusion of it could be justified, too. By no means did Jefferson stop this chapter at the Mississippi. Next, he mentioned the Missouri, a river that could open "channels of extensive communication with the western and north-western country." Before concluding the next paragraph, he was considering waterways that could reach as far as Sante Fe and Mexico City (Jefferson 1982, 5–16).

Over its course, Jefferson's second chapter becomes the antithesis of his first. After establishing boundaries in the initial chapter, he breaks those bounds in the following one to expand the reach of Virginia across North America to the Gulf of Mexico and the Pacific Ocean. Describing Virginia, he was not only recalling its past but also anticipating its future. In the beginning, all of North America was Virginia. Such had been the gist of Virginia histories from Captain John Smith to William Stith. Lamenting territory lost to other colonies was already a commonplace of Virginia historiography. In the historical account that prefaced the *History of the Dividing Line,* for example, William Byrd showed how New York had once been part of Virginia and lamented the loss: "Another Limb lopt off from Virginia was New York, which the Dutch seized very unfairly, on pretence of having Purchased it from Captain Hudson, the first Discoverer" (Byrd 1967, 7).

Notes on the State of Virginia perpetuates this discursive tradition. But Jefferson went further than previous Virginia historians. Instead of lamenting the loss, he sought to remedy it. His second chapter looks to the future as it foresees the exploration and expansion of the American West. Indeed, this chapter anticipates an important aspect of Jefferson's presidential policy. Richard Price, for one, read *Notes on the State of Virginia* as proof of Jefferson's qualifications to lead the country. Thanking him for a presentation copy of *Notes,* Price mused, "How happy would the united States be were all of them under the direction of Such wisdom and liberality as yours?" (Jefferson 1950, 8: 258).

The third chapter consists of a single sentence in answer to what had been the thirteenth query in Marbois's list. Supplying a "notice of the best sea-ports of the state, and how big are the vessels they can receive," Jefferson observed, "Having no ports but our rivers and creeks, this Query has been answered under the preceding one" (Jefferson 1982, 17). Why did he bother to include this one-sentence chapter at all? Since he had combined some of Marbois's other queries, he could have easily subsumed this tiny one with the previous query and omitted this chapter altogether. The chapter represents a literary experiment on Jefferson's part. It may have been inspired by Montesquieu's *Spirit of Laws,* which contained many one-sentence chapters (Ferguson 1980, 393). Alternatively, he could have had a more belletristic source. Laurence Sterne's *Tristram Shandy,* which Jefferson alludes to elsewhere in *Notes on the State of Virginia,* set a precedent for the short chapter. The thirteenth chapter of the second book of *Tristram Shandy,* for example, is only three lines long, and it continues a dialogue that had been taking place in the previous chapter. Jefferson's chapter functions similarly. Taking the prefatory query and its one-sentence answer together, this chapter presents a dialogue that continues topics discussed in the previous chapter.

This one-sentence chapter contributes another literary quality to *Notes on the State of Virginia:* it enhances the work's verisimilitude by suggesting that its author is dutifully answering each of the questions he has been asked one by one, even when he has virtually nothing new to say. The nonchalance Jefferson affects with this third query is a literary pose that masks the deliberate artistry underlying the structure and content of this work. Furthermore, this chapter serves as a fulcrum that balances chapters 1 and 2 on one side and chapters 4 and 5 on the other. Chapters 4 and 5 also stem from Marbois's sixth query. Chapter 4 treats Virginia's mountains, and chapter 5 discusses its cascades and caverns (Jefferson 1982, 22).

The highlight of the fourth chapter is Jefferson's description of the passage of the Potomac through the Blue Ridge Mountains. Indeed, this description constitutes the most highly crafted literary vignette in *Notes on the State of Virginia:*

> The passage of the Patowmac through the Blue ridge is perhaps one of the most stupendous scenes in nature. You stand on a very high point of land. On your right comes up the Shenandoah, having ranged along the foot of the mountain an hundred miles to seek a vent. On your left approaches the Patowmac, in quest of a passage also. In the moment of their junction they rush together against the mountain, rend it asunder, and pass off to the sea. The first glance of this scene hurries our senses into the opinion, that this earth has been created in time, that the mountains were formed first, that the rivers began to flow afterwards, that in this place particularly they have been dammed up by the Blue ridge of mountains, and have formed an ocean which filled the whole valley; that continuing to rise they have at length broken over at this spot, and have torn the mountain down from its summit to its base. The piles of rock on each hand, but particularly on the Shenandoah, the evident marks of their disrupture and avulsion from their beds by the most powerful agents of nature, corroborate the impression. But the distant finishing which nature has given to the picture is of a very different character. It is a true contrast to the fore-ground. It is as placid and delightful, as that is wild and tremendous. For the mountain being cloven asunder, she presents to your eye, through the cleft, a small catch of smooth blue horizon, at an infinite distance in the plain country, inviting you, as it were, from the riot and tumult roaring around, to pass through the breach and participate of the calm below. Here the eye ultimately composes itself; and that way too the road happens actually to lead. You cross the Patowmac above the junction, pass along its side through the base of the mountain for three miles, its terrible precipices hanging in fragments over you, and within about 20 miles reach Frederic town and the fine country around that. This scene is worth a voyage across the Atlantic. Yet here, as in the neighbourhood of the

natural bridge, are people who have passed their lives within half a dozen miles, and have never been to survey these monuments of a war between rivers and mountains, which must have shaken the earth itself to its center. (Jefferson 1982, 19).

Using the second person, Jefferson effectively puts the reader within the scene. In a way, his word-picture prefigures the visual techniques of the painters of the Hudson River school, who would characteristically depict an individual standing in the foreground of their landscape paintings. Overlooking a beautiful vista, the figure is both an observer of the scene and a participant in it. Using the second-person pronoun and describing the scene from a lofty outlook, Jefferson created much the same effect in words.

He enhanced the literary quality of this passage through the use of allusion. Some years earlier, he had commonplaced an epic simile from Ossian that compared the clash of two chieftains on the battlefield with the confluence of two great rivers. Describing two great rivers in *Notes on the State of Virginia*, he used personification to reverse the comparison. In his rendering, the confluence of the Potomac and the Shenandoah resembles a single combat between two great warriors (Jefferson 1989, 143). Furthermore, his words echo a natural description in Herodotus. Annotating his personal copy of *Notes on the State of Virginia*, he cited the precise section of Herodotus he had in mind and revealed his debt to the ancient Greek historian in terms of both diction and ideas expressed. By echoing Herodotus, Jefferson paralleled Virginia with ancient Greece and thus imbued the local landscape with classical splendor.

The subject of the Natural Bridge is not really even pertinent to the subject of the fifth chapter—Virginia's cascades and caverns—but Jefferson provides a detailed description of his favorite geographic landmark in his answer. After carefully delineating its size, providing precise measurements of height, width, and thickness, and describing the Natural Bridge in geometric terms, he conveys what it felt like to crawl atop it and gaze downward: "Though the sides of this bridge are provided in some parts with a parapet of fixed rocks, yet few men have resolution to walk to them and look over into the abyss. You involuntarily fall on your hands and feet, creep to the parapet and peep over it. Looking down from this height about a minute, gave me a violent head ach" (Jefferson 1982, 24–25). Over the course of these three sentences, Jefferson switches from the third person ("few men") to the second ("You") to the first ("me"). He thus creates a sense of immediacy, making it seems as if the reader has gone from reading about the Natural Bridge to experiencing it in Jefferson's shoes.

He balanced the description from atop with a view from beneath:

If the view from the top be painful and intolerable, that from below is delightful in an equal extreme. It is impossible for the emotions arising from the sublime, to be felt beyond what they are here: so beautiful an arch, so light, and springing as it were up to heaven, the rapture of the spectator is really indescribable! The fissure continuing narrow, deep, and streight for a considerable distance above and below the bridge, opens a short but very pleasing view of the North mountain on one side, and Blue ridge on the other, at the distance each of them of about five miles. (Jefferson 1982, 263–264)

An unusual geologic formation, the Natural Bridge derived its beauty not only from itself but also from its surroundings. As Jefferson's description suggests, the Natural Bridge was beautiful partly because it framed the beauty of the Virginia wilderness. To compose this description, he referred to his memorandum books, in which he had described the Natural Bridge upon seeing it for the first time (Jefferson 1997, 1: 38). This early description contains plenty of measurements and observations but little emotion. Going from the memorandum books to *Notes on the State of Virginia,* he abbreviated the physical description but enhanced the aesthetic appeal of the Natural Bridge. The delight, the rapture, the sublime terror: all were added as Jefferson rewrote his description.

Query Six, "Productions Mineral, Vegetable and Animal," is by far the longest chapter in the book. It corresponds to the twentieth query in Marbois's original list, but it also incorporates aspects of Marbois's sixth query. Marbois's twentieth query had asked for "A notice of the Mines and other subterranean riches" (Jefferson 1950, 4: 166). Jefferson considerably broadened the scope of this query to include virtually the entire natural world. He treats mineral resources first, including a discussion of Virginia's natural hot springs. The middle section of the chapter supplies a long list of plant life in Virginia using both the popular names and the Linnean nomenclature. Some of the listed items contain annotations, and a few contain queries where Jefferson knew the genus but did not know the species.

The third and longest section of the sixth chapter is devoted to animal life. The section begins, "Our quadrupeds have been mostly described by Linnaeus and Mons. de Buffon" (Jefferson 1982, 43). This beginning would seem to suggest his indebtedness to Buffon, the foremost naturalist in France, but Jefferson's intentions were quite the opposite. He intended to refute the Frenchman's theories. Buffon had asserted that animal life deteriorated in the New World. European animals, he argued, were greater in size, weight, and power than their American counterparts (Gerbi 1973). Buffon had no empirical proof to back his theory, and Jefferson knew he was mistaken. This section of the sixth chapter, both its text and the accompanying comparative charts, convincingly refutes Buffon's theory.

Another French philosophe, the Abbé Raynal, had applied Buffon's theories to man. Before finishing this chapter, Jefferson takes on Raynal, too. Here is where Jefferson situated Chief Logan's famous speech, which he found fitting proof to show that the Native Americans could rival the ancient Greeks and Romans in terms of their oratorical skill. The Abbé Raynal had asserted that "America has not yet produced one good poet, one able mathematician, one man of genius in a single art or a single science." Refuting Raynal, Jefferson identified three American geniuses: George Washington, Benjamin Franklin, and David Rittenhouse. Regarding Franklin, for example, Jefferson observed, "No one of the present age has made more important discoveries, nor has enriched philosophy with more, or more ingenious solutions of the phaenomena of nature" (Jefferson 1982, 64).

Jefferson's argument in the sixth chapter of *Notes on the State of Virginia* is a virtuoso performance. Over the course of the chapter, his forceful argument builds to a crescendo. It becomes so forceful, in fact, that the rest of the book is anticlimactic. Still, there are many isolated passages through the remainder of the book that brilliantly encapsulate Jefferson's thoughts on education, government, law, and politics. *Notes on the State of Virginia* is very much a compendium of Jefferson's personal philosophy as well as his political philosophy. Though it fits into the "History and Present State" genre and contains much natural history, this book can be read as a philosophical work, too. Not only does it set forth Jefferson's way of thinking, it also offers a model to guide others. The English traveler John Davis called *Notes on the State of Virginia* "the book that taught me how to think" (Davis 1803, 167). Jefferson's book taught Davis and others to think because it gave them license to see the world afresh and make their own conclusions about what they observed without regard to what others said before them.

WILLIAM BARTRAM'S *TRAVELS*

Describing changes in temperature between the Alleghenies and the Mississippi in *Notes on the State of Virginia,* Thomas Jefferson interjected a note of skepticism by qualifying his description with a big "if": "if we may believe travellers" (Jefferson 1982, 75). As Jefferson's comment suggests, contemporary travelers' tales were notoriously unreliable. Among early American writers, perhaps no one articulated this idea better than Robert Beverley. In his preface to *The History and Present State of Virginia,* he explained, "Travellers are of all Men, the most suspected of Insincerity," not only in their private conversation but also in their "Travels, with which they pester the Publick, and break the Bookseller. There are no Books (the Legends of Saints always excepted,) so stuff'd with Poetical Stories, as Voyages" (Beverley 1947, 8). Aware of the long-standing skepticism toward travel writing, William Bartram nevertheless chose to structure his natural history of southeastern North America as a book of travels instead of taking a more subject-oriented approach like Jefferson's.

Bartram's *Travels* or, to use its full title, *Travels through North and South Carolina, Georgia, East and West Florida, the Cherokee Country, the Extensive Territories of the Muscogulges, or Creek Confederacy, and the Country of the Chactaws: Containing an Account of the Soil and Natural Productions of Those Regions; Together with Observations on the Manners of the Indians,* is subdivided into four parts. The first three parts are organized chronologically. Part 1 begins with his departure from

Philadelphia in 1773, and Part 3 ends with his return to Philadelphia four years later. Each part is divided into chapters, which are structured biographically. The chapters generally begin and end at natural turning points during Bartram's personal journey. All three parts contain much information on natural history interspersed throughout the story of his travels. Part 4 is devoted to an extended discussion of the native inhabitants he encountered while in the Southwest. It is titled "An Account of the Persons, Manners, Customs and Government, of the Muscogulges, or Creeks, Cherokees, Chactaws, etc. Aborigines of the Continent of North America." Though organized differently, Bartram's *Travels* does have one major structural similarity to Jefferson's *Notes on the State of Virginia*. Just as Jefferson presented a lengthy discussion of natural history in his sixth chapter, Bartram included a long chapter almost exclusively devoted to natural history in *Travels*, specifically the tenth chapter of Part 2. Structurally, natural history occupies a central place in both literary works.

The two chapters that frame chapter 10 provide a context for understanding it. Chapter 9 begins as a party of Lower Creek Indians arrives at the trading house where Bartram is staying. It ends as the Creek leave. This chapter contains one of the most fully dramatized episodes in Bartram's *Travels*, in which the Creek, whose belief system prevents them from killing rattlesnakes, ask Bartram to slay a pesky rattlesnake for them. With a well-aimed spear, he kills the snake and, in so doing, earns their everlasting gratitude. Chapter 11 picks up the story where chapter 9 had left off, that is, directly after the Creek leave the trading house. Chapter 10 resumes the discussion of rattlesnakes that had begun the previous chapter, but it does not advance the story of Bartram's journey. It is essentially static, though it does contain some biographical episodes, specifically, a few pertinent anecdotes and a flashback to his boyhood.

The flashback concerns William Bartram's first encounter with a rattlesnake, which occurred when he was on a botanizing excursion in the Catskill Mountains with his father, John Bartram. Walking ahead of his father, William accidentally came across a rattlesnake and was almost bit by it before his father rescued him. William learned much from his father, who was the most distinguished American naturalist of his generation. John Bartram took numerous botanical trips through eastern North America. Crèvecoeur, who devoted an entire chapter of *Letters from an American Farmer* to an appreciation of him, called John Bartram "the first man whose name as a botanist hath done honour to America" (Crèvecoeur 1981, 194). A lengthy trip from Pennsylvania into Canada resulted in John Bartram's *Observations on the Inhabitants, Climate, Soil, Rivers, Productions, Animals, and Other Matters Worthy of Notice . . . from Pensilvania to Onondago, Oswego and the Lake Ontario, in Canada* (1751), which in itself forms a minor classic of early American literature. Henry Tuckerman, for one, appreciated the work for its display of its author's "charm of ingenuous zeal, integrity, and kindliness" (Tuckerman 1961). Jefferson found in John Bartram's description of the black bear additional proof that American animals exceeded their European counterparts in size and weight (Jefferson 1982, 53).

John Bartram's *Description of East Florida, with a Journal . . . upon a Journey from St. Augustine up the River St. John's* (1766) chronicles a yearlong collecting trip through Florida and as far west as the Mississippi he took in 1765. William, who turned twenty-six this year, accompanied his father on this journey, which proved a formative experience. The trip convinced William to follow in his father's footsteps and become a naturalist. As John Seelye has described the effect of this experience on him, Florida "held William in powerful thrall, drawing on something deep within his psyche, a hunger for the unknown and the mysterious that transcended an urge to gather and classify 'curiosities' of nature" (Seelye 1991, 141).

William Bartram possessed the essential skills to become an expert naturalist: a keen eye, a contemplative mind, an expert drawing ability, and a fine writing style. Peter Collinson, his father's British patron, brought William's drawings to the attention of John Fothergill, a British physician and naturalist. Fothergill became William's patron and supported him until 1780, the year Fothergill died (Peck 1999). His patronage made William's four-year excursion through southeastern North America financially possible. The greenhorn who was almost bit by a rattlesnake in his youth had matured into the finest American naturalist of his generation. Yet, as his boyhood anecdote suggests, he still liked to walk ahead of others, to be by himself, to enjoy nature in solitude, even if it meant encountering dangerous creatures along the way. Though a seasoned naturalist by the time he explored Florida for himself, William Bartram still had a bit of the boy about him. Good naturalists often do.

After devoting the first several pages of chapter 10 to a discussion of snakes, poisonous and otherwise, William Bartram discusses the frogs of the region, then the lizards, tortoises, mammals, and finally the birds. He was especially interested in avian migratory habits. Prior to a lengthy chart documenting and cross-referencing his observations, he eloquently defends the study of migratory patterns:

> There may perhaps be some persons who consider this enquiry not to be productive of any real benefit to mankind, and pronounce such attention to natural history merely speculative, and only fit to amuse and entertain the idle virtuoso; however the ancients thought otherwise: for with them, the knowledge of the passage of birds was the study of their priests and philosophers, and was considered a matter of real and indispensable use to the state, next to astronomy; as we find their system and practice of agriculture was in a great degree regulated by the arrival and disappearance of birds of passage; and perhaps a calendar under such a regulation at this time, might be useful to the husbandman and gardener. (Bartram 1996, 236)

Bartram's *Travels*, too, was a book that taught its readers how to think.

Despite his eloquent defense of studying natural history, the charm of the flashback to the Catskills, and the utility of the information chapter 10 provides, its static quality prevents it from sustaining the profound thrill of discovery that shows through the rest of the first three parts of his book. As Evert and George Duyckinck said of Bartram's *Travels*, "All his faculties are alive in his book, whether he describes a tree, a fish, a bird, beast, Indian, or hospitable planter. He detects fragrance, vitality, and health everywhere in the animal world" (Duyckinck and Duyckinck 1855, 1: 224). Bartram's decision to situate his discoveries within a story of personal adventure required much thought. Though he returned from this four-year journey in 1777, he did not publish *Travels* until 1791. The published book is based on his journals, but the portions of his manuscript that survive reveal how heavily he revised the work prior to publication (Hoffmann 1996). The form Bartram chose for his book allowed him to showcase his observations of nature, his incisive writing style, and his vivacious personality.

His introduction provides a good indication of his method. The Horatian paradigm—"to delight and instruct"—continued to serve as a measure of literary quality in Bartram's day. Few authors more insistently combined the two. The most instructive parts of his work are often closely juxtaposed with the most delightful. He frequently combines scientific nomenclature with fanciful figures of speech. Consider the following passage from his introduction, which combines Linnean names with literary personification: "The pompous Palms of Florida, and glorious Magnolia, strike us with the sense of dignity and magnificence; the expansive umbrageous Live Oak with awful veneration, the Carica papaya, supercilious with all the harmony of beauty and gracefulness; the Lilium superbum represents pride and vanity; Kalmia latifolia and Azalea coccinea, exhibit a perfect show of mirth and gaiety" (Bartram 1996, 15). Before Bartram's eyes, nature comes alive and seems to speak.

As the opening chapter of part 1 begins, Bartram departs from Philadelphia on his way to Charleston, South Carolina, in April 1773. He actually left on March 20, but seldom is Bartram particular about dates. Immersed in his text, readers may feel as if they, too, have been transported to a timeless realm. From Charleston, he sailed to Georgia. By mid-May, he had reached Augusta, where he witnessed the treaty negotiations taking place with the Creek. Augusta is beautiful this time of year, and Bartram obviously enjoyed botanizing in the surrounding countryside. Still, he grew restless before long and wished to continue his travels. Always his curiosity spurs him further on up the road. He explains: "As I was never long satisfied with present possession, however endowed with every possible charm to attract the sight, or intrinsic value to engage and fix the esteem, I was restless to be searching for more, my curiosity being insatiable" (Bartram 1996, 53). Bartram's curiosity motivated him throughout his travels. It was responsible for his greatest discoveries and his greatest perils. Letting his curiosity take him where it will, he exemplifies a characteristic American trait. The ever-curious American pushes forward, often oblivious of danger but always ahead of others. Curiosity compels Bartram forward through the murkiest swamps and densest undergrowth.

His sojourn in the American Southeast alternates between lengthy excursions to distant locales and botanizing around central locations. His first major trip takes him through northeastern Georgia with a large surveying party, a group reminiscent of the one William Byrd leads in *The History of the Dividing Line.* Bartram's penchant for solitude made traveling with this raucous and rowdy bunch of surveyors difficult. He much preferred contemplating nature by himself maugre the dangers of solo travel. Upon returning from this excursion, he settled in Savannah for the winter, spending his time making brief forays into the Georgia woods. As part 1 ends, Bartram makes a momentous decision: he will follow up his father's researches and return to eastern Florida.

Part 2—the finest of the book's four parts—starts in March 1774 as William Bartram leaves Savannah, Georgia, for Florida. He travels overland at first but eventually takes to the water to explore the islands along the southern coast of Georgia. On St. Simon's Island he visits Frederica, which had changed significantly in the three decades since Edward Kimber had seen it and described it so meticulously in *Itinerant Observations in America.* Bartram offers a before-and-after picture: "The fortress was regular and beautiful, constructed chiefly with brick, and was the largest, most regular, and perhaps most costly, of any in North America, of British construction: it is now in ruins, yet occupied by a small garrison; the ruins also of the town only remain; peach trees, figs, pomegranates, and other shrubs, grow out of the ruinous walls of former spacious and expensive buildings, not only in the town, but at a distance in various parts of the island" (Bartram 1996, 72–73). Bartram's imagery echoes a passage from "Carthon," one of James McPherson's Ossianic prose poems, which ponders the appearance of Balclutha, a once-great walled city that nature had reclaimed. Like *Notes on the State of Virginia,* Bartram's *Travels* occasionally adopts an Ossianic tone to evoke a melancholy mood.

Upon reaching the St. John's River, Bartram sails inland. In terms of its imagery, this river journey anticipates Marlowe's journey in Joseph Conrad's *Heart of Darkness*—with one major difference. Though some of Bartram's experiences seem darkly foreboding, he can always see divine light piercing the darkness. In his search for new specimens, his "chief happiness consisted in tracing and admiring the infinite power, majesty, and perfection of the great Almighty Creator" (Bartram 1996, 81). As one modern observer has commented, "The reader of the gentle Bartram finds himself transported into a luxuriant Earthly Paradise where the grave botanical recognition of each specimen of semi-tropical vegetation is offered up as a sort of Addisonian hymn of piety to the Great Spirit. The lavish growths of these green swamps and savannahs of colonial Georgia and Florida are treated with an exuberant reverence at once scientific and mystical" (Anon. 1928, 75).

Bartram's description of the tiny insects known as ephemera, which he encounters partway up the St. John's River, exemplifies this scientific-mystic duality. After describing their appearance and behavior upon first hatching, he details their life cycle, noting that these insects make delicious food for birds and frogs. He positions himself to get a closer look. What results from his meticulous observations is not a scientific discourse at all but a figurative description in which these winged creatures are more like gamboling fairies, unaware of the amphibious maws and avian beaks that await them. Yet even their near-certain demise does not dampen the spirit of these fairylike creatures:

> Solemnly and slowly move onward, to the river's shore, the rustling clouds of the Ephemera. How awful the procession! innumerable millions of winged beings, voluntarily verging on to destruction, to the brink of the grave, where they behold bands of their enemies with wide open jaws, ready to receive them. But as if insensible of their danger, gay and tranquil each meets his beloved mate in the still air, inimitably bedecked in their new nuptial robes. What eye can trace them, in their varied wanton amorous chaces, bounding and fluttering on the odoriferous air? With what peace, love, and joy, do they end the last moments of their existence? (Bartram 1996, 87)

Bartram may have been leading us through Florida as he started down the St. John's River, but by this point he has transported us to a different realm. We have left the Florida wilderness for the world of Joseph Rodman Drake's *Culprit Fay.*

The encounter with the ephemera takes Bartram through the threshold dividing man from nature. On one side of this threshold lies the ruined fort at Frederica; on the other is an idyllic world, a place where man can be in harmony with nature. After a description of trout fishing that rivals passages from Izaak Walton's *Compleat Angler* (1653), Bartram expresses feelings of profound contentment:

> How supremely blessed were our hours at this time! plenty of delicious and healthful food, our stomachs keen, with contented minds; under no controul, but what reason and ordinate passions dictated, far removed from the seats of strife.
>
> Our situation was like that of the primitive state of man, peaceable, contented, and sociable. The simple and necessary calls of nature, being satisfied, we were altogether as brethren of one family, strangers to envy, malice, and rapine. (Bartram 1996, 108–109)

This passage reveals a delicate literary touch and, in comparison to what he had originally written, shows his meticulous craftsmanship. In an earlier draft, the first paragraph had contained praise for "the Great and bountifull Deity." In revision, Bartram canceled this phrase and changed the third word of the paragraph from "happy" to "blessed" (Hoffmann 1996, 152–153). The result is both softer and more subtle. In the final version, Bartram acknowledges the presence of the deity without an explicit reference.

Continuing up the river, Bartram ultimately leaves his companions behind to navigate a small boat by himself. The idyllic world he had been imagining will soon be threatened with violence. Seemingly unaware of the dangers that await him, he enters a region heavily infested with alligators. After making camp, he sails to a nearby lagoon to catch some fish for dinner. On his way there he sees an alligator. His initial description of it, like his description of the ephemera, possesses an elevated tone. He comes close enough to get a good look, but not so close to put himself in danger. His use of third-person pronouns to refer to the alligator is typical of his personification of nature:

> Behold him rushing forth from the flags and reeds. His enormous body swells. His plaited tail brandished high, floats upon the lake. The waters like a cataract descend from his opening jaws. Clouds of smoke issue from his dilated nostrils. The earth trembles with his thunder. When immediately from the opposite coast of the lagoon, emerges from the deep his rival champion. They suddenly dart upon each other. The boiling surface of the lake marks their rapid course, and a terrific conflict commences. They now sink to the bottom folded together in horrid wreaths. The water becomes thick and discoloured. Again they rise, their jaws clap together, re-echoing through the deep surrounding forests. Again they sink, when the contest ends at the muddy bottom of the lake, and the vanquished makes a hazardous escape, hiding himself in the muddy turbulent waters and sedge on a distant shore. The proud victor exulting returns to the place of action. The shores and forests resound his dreadful roar, together with the triumphing shouts of the plaited tribes around, witnesses of the horrid combat. (Bartram 1996, 114)

Captivated by this alligator fight, Bartram ignores the personal danger. As the sun sets, several alligators approach his boat. With a heavy club, he initially beats them away, but they redouble their force, surround him, and attempt to tip his canoe. He ably captures the sudden danger:

> My situation now became precarious to the last degree: two very large ones attacked me closely, at the same instant, rushing up with their heads and part of their bodies above the water, roaring terribly and belching floods of water over me. They struck their jaws together so close to my ears, as almost to stun me, and I expected every moment to be dragged out of the boat and instantly devoured. But I applied my weapons so effectually about me, though at random, that I was so successful as to beat them off a little; when, finding that they designed to renew the battle, I made for the shore, as the only means left me for my preservation; for, by keeping close to it, I should have my enemies on one side of me only, whereas I was before surrounded by them; and there was a probability, if pushed to the last extremity, of saving myself, by jumping out of the canoe on shore, as it is easy to outwalk them on land, although comparatively as swift as lightning in the water. I found this last expedient alone could fully answer my expectations, for as soon as I gained the shore, they drew off and kept aloof. (Bartram 1996, 115)

He makes it safely to land, but he still faces a dilemma because he must go back downriver to reach camp. Hugging close to shore, he manages to paddle his vessel safely back to camp, but as he prepares his fish for dinner, a large alligator stealthily approaches. Bartram looks up and sees the creature at the last moment: "It was certainly most providential that I looked up at that instant, as the monster would probably, in less than a minute, have seized and dragged me into the river. This incredible boldness of the animal disturbed me greatly, supposing there could now be no reasonable safety for me during the night, but by keeping continually on the watch" (Bartram 1996, 116). His realization is disheartening. Already tired from a hard day's effort, he now realizes that the only sure way to survive is by maintaining an all-night vigil. The next day promises similar dangers and hardships, yet Bartram's curiosity gets the better of his common sense: he decides to continue deeper into alligator territory for the sake of furthering his observations and witnessing the conical hillocks where the alligators nest. Forced to spend another sleepless night watching for alligators, he grows so tired that he accidentally falls asleep only to be startled awake by an owl, whose hoot awakens him just as a large alligator approaches. "After this," he explains, "I roused up my fire, and kept a light during the remaining part of the night, being determined not to be caught napping so again: indeed the musquitoes alone would have been abundantly sufficient to keep any creature awake that possessed their perfect senses; but I was overcome and stupified with incessant watching and labour" (Bartram 1996, 127).

In a way, Bartram's depiction of the alligators can also be seen as a refutation of Buffon's theory. Bartram was familiar with Buffon's work: he owned a nine-volume English translation of Buffon that Benjamin Smith Barton had presented to him, which survives at the Historical Society of Pennsylvania. Whereas Jefferson refutes Buffon's idea that animals deteriorate in the New World with a combination of lawyerly argument and empirical evidence, Bartram immerses readers in a uniquely American world where large and powerful creatures rule. Bartram's exotic descriptions captured the European imagination (Fagin 1933). His alligators could accomplish one thing more forcefully than could Jefferson's comparative charts: to show European readers how strong and powerful American creatures could be.

Ascending a bluff the next day, Bartram is able to reach safety and finally get a good night's sleep. Ultimately, he makes it beyond the region most heavily infested with alligators and nears his friend's plantation. Though he has survived the alligators, a vicious storm soon descends upon him. Obscured by the surrounding woods, the storm has approached quickly without Bartram's cognizance. His description of it anticipates the visual imagery of J. M. W. Turner: "How purple and fiery appeared the tumultuous clouds, swiftly ascending or darting from the horizon upwards! they seemed to oppose and dash against each other; the skies appeared streaked with blood or purple flame overhead, the flaming lightning streaming and darting about in every direction around, seems to fill the world with fire; whilst the heavy thunder keeps the earth in a constant tremor" (Bartram 1996, 131). Bartram cannot simply witness this thunderstorm from safety. Before he realizes it, he has entered a lake. The hurricane-force winds prevent him from reaching shelter, so he must cross the lake at the peak of the storm. Miraculously, he survives the storm and reaches his friend's plantation at the other end of the lake. The mansion house and the outbuildings are significantly damaged, and Bartram's friend is shocked to learn that he had safely crossed the lake during the storm.

The story of Bartram's journey up the St. John's River is one of the great river journeys in American literature. Though a largely factual account of Bartram's experience, as the surviving fragments of his manuscript suggest, the story assumes the quality of a mythic journey. From the ruins of Frederica through the threshold of the ephemera into the hell of alligator land and through the chaos of the storm, Bartram is ultimately delivered to safety.

Though he devoted part 4 of *Travels* to ethnology, the first three parts contain much information about the Indians he encountered in the Southeast. Like John Marrant, he established a good rapport with the native inhabitants. A Seminole leader who learns why he is traveling through the region appreciates Bartram's scientific mission, grants him "unlimited permission to travel over the country for the purpose of collecting flowers, medicinal plants," and even gives him a name, Puc Puggy or Flower Hunter (Bartram 1996, 165).

Bartram's attitude toward the Indians is sensitive and insightful. Instead of seeing them as so many of his contemporaries did, that is, as ruthless savages, Bartram tries to understand what motivates them to violence. He concludes that the Indians turn to violence for much the same reason that so-called civilized man turns to violence:

> The Indians make war against, kill and destroy their own species, and their mo-
> tives spring from the same erroneous source as they do in all other nations of
> mankind; that is, the ambition of exhibiting to their fellows a superior charac-
> ter of personal and national valour, and thereby immortalizing themselves, by
> transmitting their names with honour and lustre to posterity; or revenge of their
> enemy, for public or personal insults; or, lastly, to extend the borders and bound-
> aries of their territories. But I cannot find, upon the strictest inquiry, that their
> bloody contests, at this day are marked with deeper stains of inhumanity or savage
> cruelty, than what may be observed amongst the most civilized nations. (Bartram
> 1996, 186)

Bartram, a lifelong bachelor, also takes a look at the local women. His descrip-
tion of some young Cherokee women forms one of the most sensuous passages in early American literature. Not until Herman Melville reached Typee valley a half century later would American literature possess a scene as erotic as Bartram's portrayal of the Cherokee:

> Companies of young, innocent Cherokee virgins, some busily gathering the rich
> fragrant fruit, others having already filled their baskets, lay reclined under the
> shade of floriferous and fragrant native bowers of Magnolia, Azalea, Philadelphus,
> perfumed Calycanthus, sweet Yellow Jessamine and cerulian Glycine frutescens,
> disclosing their beauties to the fluttering breeze, and bathing their limbs in the
> cool fleeting streams; whilst other parties more gay and libertine, were yet collect-
> ing strawberries or wantonly chasing their companions, tantalising them, staining
> their lips and cheeks with the rich fruit.
>
> This sylvan scene of primitive innocence was enchanting, and perhaps too
> enticing for hearty young men long to continue idle spectators.
>
> In fine, nature prevailing over reason, we wished at least to have a more
> active part in their delicious sports. Thus precipitately resolving, we cautiously
> made our approaches, yet undiscovered, almost to the joyous scene of action.
> Now, although we meant no other than an innocent frolic with this gay assembly

of hamadryades, we shall leave it to the person of feeling and sensibility to form an idea to what lengths our passions might have hurried us, thus warmed and excited, had it not been for the vigilance and care of some envious matrons who lay in ambush, and espying us gave the alarm, time enough for the nymphs to rally and assemble together. We however pursued and gained ground on a group of them, who had incautiously strolled to a greater distance from their guardians, and finding their retreat now like to be cut off, took shelter under cover of a little grove; but on perceiving themselves to be discovered by us, kept their station, peeping through the bushes; when observing our approaches, they confidently discovered themselves and decently advanced to meet us, half unveiling their blooming faces, incarnated with the modest maiden blush, and with native innocence and cheerfulness presented their little baskets, merrily telling us their fruit was ripe and sound. (Bartram 1996, 291–292)

His editor recommended that Bartram omit this entire section, but Bartram refused to take the suggestion (Hoffmann 1996, 284). Overall, Bartram's work records both the rough and the smooth, the aspects of the Native Americans that make them fearful and those that make them alluring.

Being the story of a personal journey, Bartram's *Travels* is necessarily episodic in structure, yet it does reach a climax in part 3, in which he accompanies a group of traders across Georgia and into Alabama. At Mobile he suffers headache, fever, and severe ocular pain, which causes "a most painful defluxion of pellucid, corrosive water." The precise nature of his malady remains unknown, but it may have been a poison ivy infection or even scarlet fever (Bartram 1996, 339, 601). Unable to recuperate, he visits a friendly Frenchman with a reputation as a healer, who cannot help him either. The valiant Puc Puggy, who had run a gauntlet of alligators and braved hurricane-force winds in an open boat, is done in by a mysterious illness. Without his eyesight, Bartram is helpless. What good is a naturalist who cannot see? He explains: "I was incapable of making any observations, for my eyes could not bear the light, as the least ray admitted seemed as the piercing of a sword: and by the time I had arrived at Pearl river, the excruciating pain had rendered me almost frantic and stupified for want of sleep, of which I was totally deprived; and the corroding water, every few minutes, streaming from my eyes, had stripped the skin off my face, in the same manner as scalding water would have done" (Bartram 1996, 340).

Next Bartram is taken to Pearl Island, the home of a Mr. Rumsey, who has the reputation of being the best healer in the region. Bartram's first night on Pearl Island takes him to the brink of despair. The following day he improves slightly. He continues to improve over his next four or five weeks on the island. His sight never completely returned to what it had been before the illness. Bartram's eye injury actually occurred in 1775; within the text of *Travels*, it comes comparatively late in the narrative. He continues his explorations upon recovering, but they are neither as thrilling nor as adventuresome as they had been during the early parts of his travels. The curious explorer who was formerly willing to risk personal safety for the sake of satisfying his curiosity has been chastened. Upon completing his explorations of the Southeast, William Bartram returned to the family farm on the outskirts of Philadelphia, where, for the most part, he remained for the rest of his life cultivating his garden.

CONCLUSION

Though *Notes on the State of Virginia* first appeared a half dozen years before Bartram published *Travels,* Jefferson continued tinkering with his text well into the nineteenth century with the idea of publishing a revised and updated edition. He refined his descriptions in terms of both clarity and literary power, double-checked additional sources, and filled in details previously left blank. As he revised, Jefferson continued to add books to his library that would help him expand *Notes on the State of Virginia.* After Bartram's *Travels* appeared, he acquired a copy. It, too, became one of his sourcebooks for revising his own book. In his list of Virginia plant life, for example, Jefferson had mentioned the willow and provided its genus. Unaware of the species name, he left a note to look it up. A later parenthetical insertion shows that he found the answer in Bartram's *Travels,* which, according to Jefferson's note, supplies the proper Linnean name, *Salix fluvialis,* on page 393. Sure enough, these words do appear on page 393 of the first edition of Bartram's *Travels.*

Brief as it is, Jefferson's reference to Bartram brings his reading experience alive. Modern readers tend to skip those sentences in Bartram's *Travels* that are overladen with Linnean nomenclature, but Jefferson carefully read Bartram's scientific names not just to learn about the American Southeast but also with an eye toward comparing its flora and fauna to Virginia's plant and animal life. When he came across a familiar genus and an unfamiliar species, he took notice.

Jefferson left no record of what he thought about Bartram's more evocative passages, but the page of *Travels* on which Jefferson read the scientific name of the willow forms a synecdoche for the book as a whole. The page begins with an explanation for why Indians go to war, an explanation that elevates the Indians to the realm of noble savage, attributing to them both magnanimity and sense of principle. The page ends with a moving landscape description. In other words, Jefferson could read on this one page examples of the kind of information that makes Bartram's *Travels* such a compelling book. Indeed, Jefferson could read on this page examples of the same kinds of information that make *Notes on the State of Virginia* such a compelling book. Both Jefferson's *Notes* and Bartram's *Travels* show that natural history is central to early American literature, a literature that celebrates the land in which it was written.

REFERENCES

Anon. 1928. Review of *The Travels of William Bartram,* edited by Mark Van Doren. *Dial* 85: 75.

Bartram, William. 1996. *Travels and Other Writings,* edited by Thomas P. Slaughter. New York: Library of America.

Beverley, Robert 1947. *The History and Present State of Virginia.* Chapel Hill: for the Institute of Early American History and Culture at Williamsburg, Va., by the University of North Carolina Press.

Byrd, William. 1967. *William Byrd's Histories of the Dividing Line betwixt Virginia and North Carolina,* edited by William K. Boyd. New York: Dover.

Crèvecoeur, J. Hector St. John de. 1981. *Letters from an American Farmer and Sketches of Eighteenth-Century America,* edited by Albert E. Stone. New York: Penguin.

Davis, John. 1803. *Travels of Four Years and a Half in the United States of America; During 1798, 1799, 1800, 1901, and 1802.* London: for R. Edwards.

Duyckinck, Evert A., and George L. Duyckinck. 1855. *Cyclopaedia of American Literature: Embracing Personal and Critical Notices of Authors, and Selections from Their Writings.* 2 vols. New York: Scribner.

Fagin, Nathan Bryllion. 1933. *William Bartram: Interpreter of the American Landscape.* Baltimore: Johns Hopkins Press.

Ferguson, Robert A. 1980. "Mysterious Obligation": Jefferson's *Notes on the State of Virginia. American Literature* 52: 381–406.

Gerbi, Antonello. 1973. *The Dispute of the New World: The History of a Polemic, 1750–1900,* translated by Jeremy Moyle. Rev. ed. Pittsburgh: University of Pittsburgh Press.

Hoffmann, Nancy Everill. 1996. *The Construction of William Bartram's Narrative Natural History: A Genetic Text of the Draft Manuscript for Travels through North and South Carolina, Georgia, East and West Florida.* Philadelphia: University of Pennsylvania.

Jefferson, Thomas. 1950–. *The Papers of Thomas Jefferson,* edited by Julian P. Boyd et al. 32 vols. to date. Princeton, NJ: Princeton University Press.

———. [1954] 1982. *Notes on the State of Virginia,* edited by William Peden. Reprint. New York: Norton.

———. 1989. *Jefferson's Literary Commonplace Book,* edited by Douglas L. Wilson. Princeton, NJ: Princeton University Press.

———. 1997. *Jefferson's Memorandum Books: Accounts, with Legal Records and Miscellany, 1767–1826,* ed. James A. Bear Jr. and Lucia C. Stanton. 2 vols. Princeton, NJ: Princeton University Press.

Peck, Robert McCracken. 1999. Bartram, William. In *American National Biography,* edited by John A. Garraty and Mark C. Carnes, vol. 2, pp. 297–299. New York: Oxford University Press.

Seelye, John. 1991. *Beautiful Machine: Rivers and the Republican Plan, 1755–1825.* New York: Oxford University Press.

Tuckerman, Henry T. [1864] 1961. *America and Her Commentators: With a Critical Sketch of Travel in the United States.* Reprint. New York: Antiquarian Press.

Wilson, Douglas L. 2004. The Evolution of Jefferson's *Notes on the State of Virginia. Virginia Magazine of History and Biography* 112: 99–133.

INDEX

. . . .